COLCHESTER ROYAL GRAMMAR SCHOOL AND THE GREAT WAR

Laurie Holmes & Paul Ma

Published by Colchester Royal Grammar School
Publishing partner: Paragon Publishing, Rothersthorpe
First published 2014
© Colchester Royal Grammar School 2014

ISBN 978-1-78222-358-0

Book design, layout and production management by Into Print
www.intoprint.net
01604 832149

Printed and bound in UK and USA by Lightning Source

We gratefully acknowledge the support
of the Old Colcestrian Society
in the publishing of this book.

CONTENTS

FOREWORD

I AM A great believer in the importance of the school magazine. It is not only a snapshot of life at a particular point in the school's history but it is also a faithful barometer of the school's ethos over time. It enables the outsider to see the context in which the school has been operating and portrays the bigger picture in which every group in the school has played a part. *The Colcestrian* in the years of the Great War, reproduced here in this book, both revealed the challenges which faced the school of the time and captured the very special quality that still characterises CRGS today. The care for and about the members of the CRGS family was as obvious and heartening then as it is today.

The students and staff of today have thankfully been spared the horrors of a world war and have not been asked to make the ultimate sacrifice. In a very different context today and in a very different way, however, they are still expected to display courage, strength of character and faith. The CRGS boys of 1914 were no different from the CRGS students of today; they were bright, lively, determined and committed. They were forced to respond to a particular challenge in history and did so admirably. The bouleversement caused by war created an extraordinary backdrop to school life, and the insights given into the preoccupations of the time are truly fascinating. The students of today will read with great interest how their school magazine responded to a very different period in the school's history. They will be immensely proud of their predecessors who once wore purple and also represented Parr's, Dugard's, Harsnett's or School House/Shaw Jeffrey's, but who were thrust into a very different world, the world of war.

I am pleased to write this foreword to a very special edition of *The Colcestrian* which looks back at the magazine in the Great War years. The magazine and the school may well have changed somewhat in the hundred years since the outbreak of the Great War, but we should never forget how important this war period was in our history and how courageously our staff and students responded to the challenge. *The Colcestrian* keeps such memories alive, and long may it do so.

Vitae Corona Fides

Ken Jenkinson

Headmaster
Colchester Royal Grammar School

INTRODUCTION

IT WAS A brilliant idea to re-issue *The Colcestrian* magazines of the Great War for the centenary. These pages are of far wider interest than just to those of us connected in one way or another to Colchester Royal Grammar School. As the editorial of the November 1915 magazine tells us, the school is a microcosm of 'an unfamiliar world seething around us... in a state of change and unrest'.

To read the editorials and articles written 100 years ago in these school magazines is to open a unique window not just onto the masters, pupils, family and friends of CRGS but onto the life of the British nation at home and at the front during the First World War.

Here we have something more than mere history. We have current affairs in the words of people young and old who are right in the thick of it. The immediacy of their writing allows us a remarkable insight that cannot be gained elsewhere.

It takes only a few minutes reading to realize that these people are different from us. They have not been conditioned by the television and the internet, as we have, to over-dramatise and sensationalise virtually everything. The March 1915 magazine, with the subtitle 'Under Fire', matter-of-factly reports that 'Colchester has achieved the distinction in company with Yarmouth, Sheringham, King's Lynn, Coggeshall, and Dover of being subjected to aerial bombardment.' As the editor reports: 'The population behaved with sang-froid, if not correctitude, and utterly refused to be even flustered by the demonstration.'

The lightness of touch of the writing and the extraordinary humour that permeates almost every page seems in stark contrast to the gravity of the situation then facing the country and the school, and the heart-breaking sadness found in every edition in reports of old boys, masters, friends and family killed, wounded and missing in action. Again this illuminates the stoical sense of proportion that was maintained by that generation even in their darkest hours.

Page after page rings with a sublime, yet at the time commonplace, sense of honour, duty and patriotism. We read the words of Headmaster Percy Shaw Jeffrey at speech day in December 1914: ' I cannot tell you... with what humble pride and satisfaction we have seen the rush of our old boys to the colours, for we were always being told that school boys nowadays were of a decadent type, and that better manners showed a softer fibre.'

On arrival H. J. Cape, selected from 98 applicants to succeed Shaw Jeffrey as Headmaster in 1916, was struck above all by 'the wonderful list of those young Colcestrians who had given their services and their lives to the country'. The list of distinctions gained amazed him by its length and diversity – the numbers ran into many hundreds. 'There were Old Colcestrians in France, in Flanders, in Egypt, in the Balkans, and in every scene of the war'.

By this time, from a school numbering only 200 at the start of the war, 310 old boys were serving in the forces. Twenty-three had already been decorated for gallantry and exceptional service under fire. You can read about many of them in these pages. Their inspirational exploits are often recounted first hand and in moving detail; many with a pen still reverberating from the shell-fire of the front line.

We read in July 1918 of an Old Colcestrian, second in command of an Australian torpedo boat, ordered in a howling gale in the Mediterranean to the rescue of a sinking allied ship. Pressed on at an impossible 23 knots, the vessel storms through the waves at such speed she begins to break up, sweeping a young crew-member over the side, never to be seen again. With extraordinary heroism and seamanship they rescue the Italian survivors from an oil-covered sea. They go on to pick up 200 men from another ship torpedoed in front of their eyes: 'her bows rose up in the air until quite perpendicular, and then disappeared into the 400 odd fathoms which covered the ocean bed.'

Lieutenant William King of the Royal Air Force was killed in an accident 'when returning from a bombing raid on the German lines'. His commanding officer wrote to his parents, Mr and Mrs King of Inglis Road, Colchester: 'His death is a real loss to the squadron, for everybody had the very highest opinion of his work, and the sincerest admiration of his character'. Seventeen days later his 21-year-old brother died of wounds sustained in France. We read also of two other pairs of Old Colcestrian brothers Killed in Action. One of them, Geoffrey Barnes, serving with the Merchant Navy, was just 16 years old.

Corporal Conrad Mason's mother shared with the school a letter written by one of his fellow soldiers telling how her son was killed by a shell blast when he left his shelter to try to save the life of a wounded comrade. Both were killed: 'They were buried side by side yesterday. Truly it may be said of him that he gave his life for another.'

There are many accounts of old boys meeting at the battle-front, in the trenches of France, the deserts of Palestine and the shores of the Dardanelles. In 1915 Joseph Watson, serving with the Canadians, wrote from the Western Front that he had seen 'Young Cobbold out here several times... the night before last he fed me on mutton chops and other luxuries, and also had a Colchester paper'. Watson sustained a shrapnel wound the following year, recovered well, then a few months after being commissioned from the ranks, was killed in the quagmire of Passchendaele in November 1917. His younger brother, 2nd Lieutenant Gilbert Watson, won the DSO, one of the highest awards for gallant leadership, in 1915.

In 1916 A.T. Daldy, who somehow combined the role of Secretary of the Old Colcestrian Society with fighting at the front, wrote from France how he had seen 'young F.S. Bultitude last night, and got him to join the OCS, so please have his name enrolled... he went up the line this morning'. The editor goes on to say: 'This was almost the last act of Bultitude's career, for within a few days he joined the OCs who have died for their country.' Daldy himself suffered a gunshot wound to the head two years later but survived to continue both military and OCS secretarial duties until after the war.

In 1916 the editor of Skinner's school magazine wrote to *The Colcestrian's* editor telling him that in a trench 'somewhere in France' an old Skinner's boy had begun singing the school song, and was joined by another officer who sang it with slightly different words, and who turned out to be an Old Colcestrian. 'This prompts me to ask you whether the Colchester School song is a variant of ours?' Shaw Jeffrey, formerly a master at Skinner's, had in fact written the songs of both schools.

As in the country at large, every aspect of life back at the school was dominated by the war during these years. Few older boys remained, so many having left to join the colours. There was great turbulence too among the small teaching staff. By the end of 1914 two had joined up. In early 1916 one master, Mr F.D. Barker, who had previously tried 5 times to enlist, finally succeeded in joining the 3rd Essex after eyesight standards were relaxed. By the end of 1915, five masters of a complement of only 9 were serving. By the end of 1916 two former masters, Lieutenant G.H. Bennett and Captain S.A. White, had been Killed in Action.

Reflecting the school's changed priorities, the cadet corps, the scouts and rifle shooting are all given increased prominence in the magazines of the war years. As the master in charge of cadets puts it in 1914: 'Members of the Corps cannot fail to realize that by displaying keenness and by giving proof of smartness and efficiency, they are doing their duty now and soon they will find that they have a long start in things that will matter very much in Great Britain.'

The cadets always seemed to be attacking or defending nearby villages such as Copford, Heckfordbridge and, more often than not, Layer. The inhabitants of Layer must have wondered what they had done to attract the attention of these bedraggled miniature soldiers, some carrying rifles as big as themselves, constantly assaulting their lanes, fields and woods.

The cadets were always short of carbines, bayonets and uniforms – or at least uniforms that fit properly. Despite the boys' tribulations, the magazines show almost universal dedication and enthusiasm among the members of the corps. However, as with commendably many of *The Colcestrians'* articles on all subjects, the Cadet Corps was not above being openly self-critical. According to the master in charge, their early tactical training 'was at first quite a revelation in suicidal warfare, but we are improving'. Later in the war he sardonically notes the weakness in junior NCOs: 'We are not yet ripe for revolutionary army discipline with "each for himself" as the motto.'

Apart from their lack of firearms and a different shade of khaki, there seemed little to distinguish the activities of scouts and cadets. Both trained in signaling, bugling, 'ambulance' and navigation. And like the cadets, the scouts spent much time attacking and defending the local villages, woodlands and barns. Reading between the lines there seemed to be much unspoken, or at least unwritten, rivalry between the two, especially with frequent reports by the scoutmaster of losing his boys to the cadets.

Early in the war we learn that: 'Football has taken second place in preference to Cadet Corps work, and rightly so. In these times there seems something lacking in the spirit of the game, and it is difficult to infuse the same enthusiasm, when the greatest game of all is going on at our very gates'. Sports continue nonetheless, and we can read many accounts of school and house football, cricket and hockey games, for as the editor observes: 'Games must continue if it is wished that the younger generation should grow up the equal in character and physique of the older now fighting the barbarian all over the world'.

The pages of these magazines show continuing frustration among sports enthusiasts. In 1916: 'We deplore the lack of School Matches, owing to the war, as usual, and the shortage of labour. The field has made an excellent feed for sheep, but as a cricket ground...!' Form 1 reports: 'We have not lost a single match this term (neither have we played any).'

By the last few months of the war 'much of the old enthusiasm for football has returned'. But throughout these years travel has been severely restricted and the school has had to make do with matches against local schools and troops stationed nearby. The latter opponents often seem dauntingly tough – and large – though not necessarily as fleet of foot as our boys. According to the match report from a 1918 game against an Army unit: 'Our opponents were much heavier, but rather slow. The school played up well and finally drew 2-2.'

Throughout these pages we read of acts of sacrifice and self-denial by boys, masters and their parents in order to contribute to the war effort. Almost every non-academic activity of the school, from carol concerts to vegetable cultivation, sought to raise funds to aid and comfort wounded soldiers or the men at the front.

Nowhere was there greater energy than the 'Pre', CRGS's own preparatory department. Throughout the four years of war the small boys worked furiously 'ravelling' pillows for wounded troops. They held frequent collections among parents and friends for chocolate, flowers, cigarettes and magazines to send to the hospitals and the front.

One edition of *The Colcestrian* tells us that the wounded soldiers 'have gone up tremendously in the boys' estimation since they sent a message to the effect that they do appreciate "Rainbow", "Chuckles", and similar literature.' When it was suggested in 1918 that a collection should be made towards a Christmas tree for the wounded, 'several little fellows came straight up with all the money they had in their pockets, and others earned some at carol singing – quite their own idea'.

A comment on these activities in December 1918's Colcestrian applies also to the rest of the school: 'In years to come it will mean a great deal to these boys to be able to say, "I was too young to fight in the Great European War, but I did what I could for those who did fight"'.

Almost invariably the writing in these magazines is superb, and sometimes brilliant. The articles are always fascinating, often entertaining and frequently uplifting. You will find also much that is ineffably sad and deeply moving.

Perhaps most poignant of all is a letter published in the July 1916 Colcestrian. It was written at 8 p.m. on Friday 30th June 1916 by a young Old Colcestrian officer to his parents before going into action the following morning. He arranged for it to be posted should he be killed, and it concludes with these words from Henry Newbolt's 'Ode on a memorial in Clifton College Chapel':

Qui procul hinc, ante diem periit: sed miles, sed pro patria.

(He who died so far from home, died before his time: but he was a soldier, and it was for his country he died.)

The next day, 1st July 1916, was the first day of the Battle of the Somme. The British Army suffered the greatest casualty rate in its history: 20,000 killed and 40,000 missing or wounded on that one day alone. Among the dead was the old boy who wrote that letter, killed at dawn, a few short hours after putting pen to paper. Of the 76 old boys and masters of CRGS who died in the Great War, three others were also killed on the first day of the Battle of the Somme.

The last words go to Percy Shaw Jeffrey, in a speech reflecting on Colchester Royal Grammar School's contribution to the war effort: 'Many schools may have done as well but none have done better'.

Colonel Richard Kemp CBE
President of the Old Colcestrian Society 2014
Old Colcestrian 1970 – 1977

PRE-WAR
THE CADET CORPS
1906 - 1913

Royal Grammar School Cadet Corps.

ø ø ø

The Corps is attached to the local volunteer battalion and wears a neat khaki uniform piped with red.

The cost of this uniform is about 28/-: the cost of accessories (cartridge belt, water bottle, &c.,) is 12/3. The whole outfit, as in block, costs not more than £2/2/-. A boy may sell his uniform when he leaves the Corps or when he grows out of it. There is a terminal subscription of 5/-, to cover the cost of ammunition and management. A temporary Morris tube range is fitted in the Gymnasium pending the completion of the new buildings.

19

JULY 1905

The Colcestrian.

VITÆ CORONA FIDES.

No. 12.]   JULY, 1905.   [New Series.

Editorial.

WE may congratulate ourselves on a glorious summer term, in which many good things have happened to us. With an entry of nineteen we begin to see visions of reaching 150. Education Inspectors have swarmed around us, have beamed upon our good looks, and foretold a brilliant future for our School In the County of Essex. But much depends upon ourselves, and energy and keenness must be displayed by everyone concerned in this ancient and honourable institution. We must aim at an unanimous esprit de corps, which means that every individual must more than ever show a lively interest in all School events, and himself take part in all he can. The keenness of Houses can hardly be improved upon, but we appeal to the whole School to make a greater effort in the future to line up at home matches, and support the XI., with whom the honour of the School football or cricket rests. Our cricket XI. has made some very good fights, and there is plenty of good material, which is gradually and steadily improving. We are glad to see North Town again coming to the fore, and heartily congratulate them on winning the sports shield, for which South were a good second. School House have been shining for the cause of the school in cricket with bat and ball, though they were less successful in their cup match. But School House are always patriotic first.

We may find Fives Courts and a Morris Tube on our return from the holidays, and as for the Cadet Corps, well, there is an energetic Old Boy, who lives over the way, and is only waiting for the chance to give us all the efficient help he possesses to get us well started. Our hearty good wishes for a ripping holiday for everybody, and especially the Head, whose work for the success of the School has this term been colossal.

EDITOR,

APRIL 1906

Cadet Corps.

Rumour says that this will really be started next term. Lord Roberts has promised the Head that he will come down and open our Morris Tube Range when we are ready for him.

THE SCHOOL IN THE FUTURE.

Mr. Orpen made an effective response ; and Mr. Shaw Jeffrey, who also replied, remarked amid applause that the School in the last year had increased in numbers by about 25 per cent.. while in regard to work they had gained their grant in the second instead of the fourth year, and boarders had had to be turned away. Having referred to the progress of the preparatory school, he mentioned also the prospect of the establishment of a cadet corps and Morris tube range, and said he believed there would be no difficulty in getting Lord Roberts to open the range when it was ready. (Applause.) He hoped that in the course of the educational development of the future the School might take a leading part, and might have established a large modern side.

Alderman Marriage, in a genial speech, proposed the toast of " The Old Colcestrian Society," and referring to famous Colcestrians like Gilberd, mentioned the establishment in 1564 of a scholarship at St. John's College, Cambridge, by Robert Lewis. The scholarship was founded for Colchester boys, and he regretted that it had lapsed. (Hear, hear.) He was not without hope that some day they might resume the ancient link between the Grammar School and the Universities, and by means of a more complete educational ladder enable boys of talent to work their way up to distinguished positions. (Hear, hear.) He thought also the creation of a modern side to the School would be of very great service to the town and neighbourhood, and might help Colchester to become again the centre in educational matters for East Essex. In conclusion Alderman Marriage, after brief allusions to the School's past history, spoke of the good done by associations of old scholars interested in their School, and referring to some of the past presidents of the Society, said that they were glad in the Town Council to have Councillor Wallace as one of them, and looked forward to having him, at no very distant date, as their Mayor. (Loud applause.)

Mr. H. L. Griffin, who responded in the absence of the President, expressed the pleasure of all old boys at seeing the School going so strongly, and referred amid applause to the services of Mr. Shaw Jeffrey in connection with its recent development. He alluded also to the need of larger playing fields, and expressed the hope that in years to come they might see the old School blossom out into a much larger and more pretentious establishment than it was at present.

Mr. H. H. Hollaway, one of the hon. secs., also replied, and expressed the hope that on future occasions the function might be honoured by a larger number of the senior " Old Boys " resident in the town. He spoke in warm terms of the assistance rendered to the Society by the present Headmaster, and also acknowledged the services of his colleague, Mr. A. S. Mason. (Applause.)

The toast of " The Visitors " was given by Mr. W. H. King, and acknowledged in brief and able speeches by Mr. H. C. Wanklyn (Town Clerk) and Mr. P. R. Green.

The enjoyment of the dinner was greatly enhanced by the tasteful music of Mr. F. Snelling's orchestra, and the excellent vocal contributions of Messrs. W. Chalk, W. Anthony, A. L. Hall, A. O. Farmer, A. S. Mason, J. H. Nunn, Arthur Nunn, P. Shaw Jeffrey, and the Rev. E. Hartley Parker.

The Colcestrian.

VITÆ CORONA FIDES.

No. 18.]　　　　AUGUST, 1907.　　　　[New Series.

Editorial.

WE have passed through another summer (?) term with more or less success. The weather has really spoilt a promising cricket season, though it has not prevented a solid progress in the art of playing cricket, as will be seen from the report in another column. It is a pleasure to be able to state that all three Houses will supply such a contingent to the Cadet Corps that it will make a strong start early next term. The sports are upon us as we go to press, and the contest for the Cock-House Challenge Shield this year should be a very close one. We shall have the finest prize table we have ever displayed, and the entries for the sports are a record. It only remains for the competitors to establish some records on the track. We take this opportunity of announcing that Mr. St. John Seamer has become a very active co-editor, and of offering him our best thanks for editing the whole of this edition, a most welcome service, seeing that we are much engaged in preparing Speech Day and Sports scrip. for the next edition. Excellent weather and a well-earned recreation to everybody.　　　　EDITOR.

School Notes.

Whit-Monday.

Owing to the fact that Whit-Monday came so near the beginning of the term, we were unfortunately only able to have a half-holiday.

Congratulations.

Congratulations to Hazell on having scored a century against South.

The Cadet Corps.

Thanks to the untiring energy of the Headmaster, there is every prospect of this Corps materialising early next term.

The Colcestrian.

VITÆ CORONA FIDES.

No. 19.]　　　　DECEMBER, 1907.　　　[NEW SERIES.

Editorial.

THE arrival of the Cambridge Locals, and the approach of the end of the Christmas Term, warn us that 1907 is about to give place to 1908. In looking back over all that has happened since last Christmas the most striking feature is again —Progress. The numbers of the School verge on the 170 mark, the staff has been increased to 10—figures probably unprecedented in its history as a school—the Cadet Corps has become a living entity, and for the first time the State Concert will be given without external aid. Everything speaks of growth, of vitality, of progress. And these facts may be mentioned, not in a spirit of boasting, but with a feeling of legitimate pride. We are now, indeed, citizens of no mean city.

But it must be remembered that increase of numbers and importance brings with it increase of responsibility. If the occasion is great, let us see to it that we rise to the occasion and show ourselves worthy of that which has fallen to our share.

For progress does not imply finality. There are heights yet to be won, peaks yet to be scaled. Busy brains are even now planning fit housing for us. The new buildings which have hitherto loomed in the distance are actually imminent, and we hope before another Christmas comes to find them concrete in brick and stone above our heads. *Stet fortuna domus.*

In conclusion we wish all our readers the Happiest of Christmasses and the Brightest of Bright New Years.

THE EDITOR.

The Cadet Corps.

Our newly-established Cadet Corps is now in full swing, and has proved a most popular addition to the corporate life of the School. A serried band of 50 marksmen are now prepared to right-about turn at the presence of the foreign aggressor—or perform any other suitable evolution—while the targets at the Gym. bear eloquent testimony to what the enemy might expect —at 10 yards' range. Inter-House and Form Competitions are being organised for this term and next. The Corpse is giving evidence of surprising vitality.

23

Cadet Corps.

THE Cadet Corps is in being. All boys over 12 are members of the Corps, which we hope soon to see in uniform. All the tedious official preliminaries necessary to its formation, should be over before we meet again next term.

In the meantime much useful work has been done in the way of drill. Since half-term we have had Colour-Sergt. Smith, of the local Volunteer force and late of the K.R.R., to put us through our paces. The Corps has greatly improved both in steadiness and smartness. The Instructor has tested the Corps with some fairly complicated movements, and for mere tyros, a very fair aptitude has been shown. Steadiness in marching and in going through evolutions is a sine-qua-non in a Cadet Corps. Next term the management of the rifle during evolutions will be taught, when the practice in shooting in the Gymnasium with the B.S.A. miniature War Office rifle should prove advantageous. At least members should already know how to handle a gun or rather how not to misuse it.

The amount of keenness shown at the beginning of term has increased—a very satisfactory sign. As the smartness of a body of men depends in a great degree on the knowledge and intelligence of its non-commissioned officers, we commend this remark to the attention of those concerned.

Shooting.

A GREAT feature of this term has been the start of the miniature shooting range in the Gym., and the greatest keenness has been shown on the part of some fifty boys, the crack of whose rifles has been heard every day, and almost every spare moment since half-term. Some were fortunate in having previous experience in the handling of a rifle, and one at least had already won his spurs at the butts, but by far the greater number were quite inexperienced, and many of them are to be heartily congratulated on the quickness with which they have found the bull, and piled up scores some twenty and some thirty. Pointing mi., especially, is to be congratulated on having made the record score of 30 out of a possible 35. This shooting practice has, we are sure, come to stay, and early next term we hope that the Corps will be recognised, when we shall be able to shoot at Middlewick with service rifles, and in the summer term we shall hope to make our first appearance at the Public Schools Shooting Competition of the Eastern Division which is held at Colchester.

The first competition of eight-a-side for the House Shooting Shield was held on Tuesday, the 17th December, and after a keen contest resulted in a win for School House, with 192 points, South Town 164, North Town 161.

intelligence of its non-commissioned officers, we commend this remark to the attention of those concerned.

Since going to press the above-mentioned score has been beaten by Webb ma., with 31.

SHOOTING AVERAGES, XMAS TERM, 1907.

		Total.	Shoots.	Aver.
1	Pointing mi...	264	11	24
2	Rickard	410	18	23·7
3	Blair ma.	255	11	23·2
4	Maile	225	10	22·5
5	Culliston	336	17	19·8
6	Alliston	468	24	19·5
	Cheese	293	15	19·5
	Sennitt	254	13	19·5
	Scott mi.	293	15	19·5
	Webb ma.	566	29	19·5
11	Webb mi.	479	25	19·2
12	Pointing ma...	379	19	19
13	Beard	167	9	18·5
	King	204	11	18·5
15	Everett ma.	181	10	18·1
16	Davies min.	196	11	17·8
	Taylor ma.	285	16	17·8
18	Daldy	173	10	17·3
	Osborne ma...	346	20	17·3
	Osborne mi.	277	16	17·3
21	Watson mi.	376	22	17·1
22	Davies mi.	214	13	16·5
23	Richardson	254	16	15·9
24	Davies ma.	189	12	15·7

		Total.	Shoots.	Aver.
25	Allen	170	11	15·5
	Shepherd ma.	171	11	15·5
27	Hellen	178	13	14·5
28	Tennant	200	14	14·3
29	Blair mi.	170	12	14·2
30	Girling	127	9	14·1
	Shepard mi.	141	10	14·1
32	Prime	136	9	14·0
33	Watson ma.	166	12	13·8
34	Prior	117	9	13·0
35	Bentley	141	11	12·8
	Pulford	115	9	12·8
37	Jones	138	11	12·5
38	Padfield	112	9	12·4
39	Burleigh	160	13	12·3
40	Gibbs	177	15	11·8
41	Cheshire	53	5	10·6
42	Watson min.	84	9	9·2
43	Smith ma.	90	10	9·0
44	Thomas ma.	88	10	8·8
45	Grimwood	108	13	8·3
46	Whitby	51	12	4·2
47	Burbidge	11	3	3·7
48	Smith mi.	8	3	2·7

Shooting.

THIS term 60 boys have taken part in shooting practice. This is a larger number than in any previous term, and the shooting has been of a distinctly high order. The improvement that has been made since we started shooting a year ago is very striking when we compare the averages below with those given in the COLCESTRIAN of December, 1907. It will be seen that in the averages for that term there were only four over 20, the highest being 24. This term we have 32 averages over 20, and 9 over 30. Good wine needs no bush, and these figures speak for themselves. Blair ma. and Watson mi. (twice) are to be congratulated on having made " possibles " on decimal targets, and Cullington, Cheese (twice), and Sennitt on having made the highest scores on Bisley targets, 34 each.

We have had three matches ; against Old Colcestrians, The Masters, and Wellingborough Grammar School. In the first two the School VIII. won easily, and in the last we put 53 on to our score of last April and came within 1 point of the score that Wellingborough then made. They were, however, equal to the occasion, and put 18 on to their previous score, thus beating us by 19 points. We hope to lower their colours in the return match next term.

A new source of interest has been added to our shooting practice in the facilities that will, we hope, soon be afforded of shooting with service rifles at Middlewick. We shall then appreciate the value of our miniature range practice.

3RD NOV.—MASTERS v. BOYS.

(Maximum 100)

Masters.				Boys.				
Mr. A. E. Barker..	..	.. 97	Blair ma. ..	..	..	.. 97
Mr. H. H. Roseveare	..	.. 94	Rickard ..	..	..	.. 96
Mr. E. P. Ward ..	..	.. 91	Barker ..	..	..	.. 94
Mr. M. Townsend	..	.. 84	Cheese ..	...	..	.. 92
Rev. E. H. Parker	..	.. 82	Webb ma...	..	..	.. 91
Mr. E. Reeve ..	..	.. 82	Cullington ..	..	..	.. 91
Mr. G. C. D. Horton	..	.. 80	Webb mi. ..	..	..	.. 89
Mr. H. St. J. Seamer	..	.. 76	Blyth ..	..	..	.. 87
		686				737

10TH NOV.—PAST v. PRESENT.

(Maximum 100.)

Past.				Present.				
Mr. R. Everett ..	..	.. 90	Cullington..	..	..	.. 96
Mr. A. W. Nunn..	..	.. 89	Blair ma. ..	..	..	.. 95
Mr. A. T. Brook ..	..	.- 85	Cheese ..	..	..	.. 93
Mr. H. H. Hollaway	..	.. 85	Webb ma...	..	..	.. 93
Mr. A. O. Farmer	..	.. 80	Webb mi. ..	..	..	.. 93
Mr. F. T. Osborne	..	.. 78	Barker ..	..	..	.. 91
Mr. H. C. Osborne	..	.. 77	Blyth ..	..	..	.. 91
Mr. B. H. Kent ..	..	.. 77	Watson mi.	..	..	.. 91
		661				753
Mr. C. B. Orfeur..	..	.. 76	Rickard ..	..	..	.. 90
Mr. W. H. Stowe..	..	.. 65	Maile ..	..	..	.. 90

26

Nov. 23rd.—v. Wellingborough Grammar School.

C.R.G.S.   (Maximum 100.)   *Wellingborough.*

C.R.G.S.		Wellingborough.	
Barker	97	Beck	100
Rickard	96	Hannay	99
Blair ma.	96	Chalcraft	98
Webb ma.	95	Hammond	98
Blyth	95	Bashforth	97
Cullington	95	Lea	97
Maile	95	Ward	97
Richardson	94	Barnett	96

15th December.—Masters v. Old Colcestrians.

Masters.	200	500	Tl.	Old Colcestrians.	200	500	Tl.
Max.	35	35	70	Max.	35	35	70
H. H. Roseveare	31	33	64	R. Everett	29	29	58
A. E. Barker	29	33	62	A. O. Farmer	26	24	50
E. P. Ward	28	32	60	F. T. Osborne	25	25	50
F. Reeve	27	25	52	A. F. Brook	21	28	49
G. C. D. Horton	27	20	47	B. H. Kent	18	29	47
H. St. J. Seamer	19	27	46	H. H. Hollaway	27	18	45
M. Townsend	18	21	39	A. W. Nunn	24	21	45
P. Shaw Jeffrey	14	12	26	A. J. Clamp	17	15	32
			396				376

Shooting Averages. Xmas Term, 1908.

1	Rickard	32·7	17	Allen	27·5
2	Blair ma.	32	18	Daldy	27·3
3	Webb ma.	31·7	19	Davies mi.	25·9
4	Barker	31·5	20	Scott ma.	25·6
5	Blyth	31·3	21	Lucking	25·3
6	Cullington	30·8	22	Sanger ma.	24·2
7	Cheese	30·7	23	Brown	23·8
8	Richardson	30·6	24	Butcher	23·4
9	Webb mi.	30·4	25	Jones ma.	22·9
10	Watson mi.	29·9	26	Collins ma.	22·8
11	Sennitt	} 29·8	27	Tennant	22·2
	Beard		28	Davies ma.	21·7
13	Alliston	29·5	29	Bain	21·1
14	Maile	28·2	30	Pulford	20·8
15	Davies mi.	} 28·1	31	Peacock	20·1
	Pointing		32	Blair mi.	20

27

Cadet Corps Training.

IT has previously been our pleasant duty to *sing* of the *men* and their deeds, but we hope before long to add a note concerning the *arms* of our Cadet Corps. The Headmaster has once again proved the truth of the old saw that the *pen* is mightier than the *sword* by stirring up the War Office to send the local Adjutant to inspect us. Captain Rose came, saw, and was conquered. He said many complimentary things about the smartness of the drill—close and open order—and examined our shooting arrangements. He hoped we should soon have regular Government rifles.

As we are not eligible for the Officers' Training Corps, we look forward to next year, when the scheme for linking up the best cadet battalions and rifle clubs with the County Associations is expected to come into force. It behoves all to see to it that the reputation for smartness so recently and so deservedly obtained remains ever characteristic of our School Corps.

Colr.-Sergt. Smith has been untiring in his energy and enthusiasm, and great credit is due to him for the good result of the inspection.

The School Marshal has looked after the rifles which we do possess in a most efficient manner.

APRIL 1909

FORMING A RIFLE CLUB.

Mr. A. W. Nunn brought before the meeting the suggestion raised by Mr. Hollaway, as to the formation of a miniature rifle club in connection with the Society, and mentioned that Mr. A. J. Clamp, O.C., had promised to provide a good indoor range. Eventually, after a lengthy discussion, in which the idea was highly commended, a Committee was appointed to consider the suggestion.

The Natural History Society.

On March 31st Mr. Clarke gave us the concluding lecture of the series, taking as his subject " The Boer War." This was illustrated with lantern views made from photos which he had himself taken. One photo of special interest was that of a number of Boer boys, all under 16 years of age, captured with rifles in their hands, and the lecturer pointed out that these were quite as dangerous as the men, for they were all capital shots. Our thoughts immediately turned to the doings of our own Corps. Three hearty cheers were given for the lecturer at the conclusion.

We will conclude by making the request that some of our present boys will endeavour during the coming summer to get something ready for our entertainment before next winter.

Cadet Corps.

TRAINING was started at once on our return, but the Arctic weath r effectually put a stop to all serious work. The Seniors, of whom four have joined the Essex and Suffolk Cyclist Battalion, have at last had a few drills with rifles *and* drill-purpose sticks. These last have been made at the workshop, so we can boast of our own home manufactures as well as the Pageant people. With a few more practices Section I. will be quite handy with their rifles. Section II. have a good deal to learn in the way of smartness and attention. They are very ragged at the diagonal march and at forming section. Drill is an excellent institution for teaching combined action and ought to kill off selfishness and thoughtlessness; but these bad qualities like weeds seem to flourish. When rightly viewed, drill fosters unity and public spirit. One of our ideals is to have squads or half sections formed entirely of boys belonging to the same house. Sections III. and IV. have had most excellent training under Mr. Barker's steadying hand. They should be very smart, like all *real boys* naturally are, when they get big enough to come into Section II.

One last word re *Parades.* When once a cadet has come on to the parade ground and has *fallen in*, all levity must be controlled, and *no talking* in the ranks except by section or squad commanders can be tolerated on any excuse whatever.

Shooting.

THIS term 60 boys have taken part in shooting practice, the same number as last term. Again we may say the general standard of shooting has gone up. This term we have nine with averages over 30, and 38 over 20, as against nine over 30, and 32 over 20 last term. This term, too, it has been a little more difficult to score, as we have not had so many decimal targets. There was at one period quite a " possible " epidemic. Cullington, Barker, Cheese, Watson mi , and Alliston got them on Bisley targets, and Cullington, Webb mi., Pointing, and Davies mi. (twice) on decimal targets. We ought to congratulate Sergt.- Instructor Penn on having made three possibles on Bisley targets, and one on a decimal target. In the House competition,

shot at Bisley targets at 200 and 500 yards range, School House won with a score of 462 out of 560.

We have had two matches against other schools. We beat Woodbridge by 774 to 722, and were beaten by Wellingborough by 785 to 772.

The results of the " Roberts Spoon Competition " for the highest average during the two winter terms were as follow :—

Open	F. D. Barker	Average	31·65
Under 16	C. T. Cheese	,,	31·25
Under 14	G. F. Watson	,,	30·05

We have received the greatest assistance from Sergt.- Instructor Penn, both in the coaching of the shooters and in the care of the rifles.

Shooting colours have been awarded to Webb ma. (capt.), Cullington, Barker, Rickard, Cheese, Webb mi., Watson mi., and Richardson.

26TH MARCH.—HOUSE COMPETITION.

Dugard's.	200 yds.	500 yds.	Possible 70.	Parr's.	200 yds.	500 yds.	Possible 70.
Davies, min.	27	30	57	Pointing ..	31	32	63
Waller ..	28	29	57	Marlar ...	29	21	50
Bain ..	29	28	57	Bond ..	24	25	49
Gregg ..	25	30	55	Town ma. ..	23	24	47
Daldy ..	27	28	55	Sanger ma...	26	21	47
Brown ..	27	21	48	Potter ma...	21	22	43
Shelton ..	25	19	44	Butcher ..	25	15	40
Watson ma.	23	4	27	Brook ..	25	10	35
	211	189	400		204	170	374

Harsnett's.				School House.			
Cheese ..	32	34	66	Webb ma. ..	31	34	65
Davies mi. ..	30	31	61	Richardson	32	31	63
Cullington ..	25	32	57	Blyth ..	28	32	60
Beard ma. ..	27	27	54	Alliston ..	24	35	59
Sennitt ..	26	27	53	Watson mi.	25	30	55
Scott ma. ..	24	26	50	Rickard ..	29	26	55
Prime ..	21	25	45	Webb mi. ..	27	27	54
Pulford ..	20	13	33	Barker ..	22	29	51
	205	215	420		218	244	462

C.R.G.S   *Woodbridge.*

(Maximum. 100.)

Barker	..	98	Lingwood	..	..	99
Rickard	..	98	Wagstaff	..	..	94
Cullington	..	97	Mudd	..	..	93
Cheese	..	97	Keighley	..	..	90
Webb ma.	..	96	Brice	..	..	90
Richardson	..	96	Hunt	..	..	86
Pointing	..	96	Theobald	..	..	86
Watson mi.	..	96	Nicholl	..	..	84
		774				722
Webb mi.	..	95	Fisk	..	..	84
Davies mi.	..	94	Harman	..	..	82

APRIL 2ND.—v. WELLINGBOROUGH GRAMMAR SCHOOL.

C.R.G.S   *Wellingborough.*

(Maximum 100.)

Webb ma.	..	99	Beck	..	..	100
Cullington	..	99	Hammond	..	..	100
Watson mi.	..	98	Barnett	..	..	100
Davies mi.	..	96	Hannay	..	..	99
Barker	..	95	Montgomery	..	..	98
Cheese	..	95	Castle	..	..	98
Webb mi.	..	95	Wand	..	..	95
Rickard	..	94	Mathews	..	..	95
		771				785
Richardson	..	93	Tait	..	..	94
Pointing	..	91	Henry	..	..	94

AVERAGES. LENT TERM, 1909.

1	Barker	31.8	20	Butcher		26.3
	Cullington		21	Scott ma.		25.0
	Cheese..		22	Daldy		24.7
	Davies mi.		23	Gregg		24.5
	Pointing		24	Waller..		24.1
6	Webb ma.	31.3	25	Smith ma.		23.8
7	Richardson	31.1	26	Peacock		23.7
8	Rickard	30.5	27	Paul		23.4
9	Watson mi.	30.2	28	Nicholson		23.2
10	Webb mi.	29.8	29	Potter ma.		23.0
11	Alliston	29.5		Lucking		
12	Beard	28.9	31	Tennant		22.8
13	Blyth	28.7	32	Brook		22.7
14	Sennitt..	28.6	33	Town ma.		22.4
15	Jones	28.5	34	Pepper..		22.0
16	Davies min.	28.3	35	Marlar..		21.4
	Brown..		36	Bolton..		20.8
18	Bain	27.2	37	Watson ma.		20.6
19	Sanger ma.	26.6	38	Plummer		20.0

AUGUST 1909

The New Range.

A new miniature rifle range has been marked out on the site of the old vineries in Gilberd House garden, and it is to be hoped that our marksmen will be able to make use of it in the coming autumn shooting season. The range will be 25 yards—a great improvement on our present distance—and although in the open air, the firing point will be under cover, and the targets electrically lighted. A new bullet-catcher will be in operation to prevent the necessity of continual replacement of sleepers, and the marker will be provided with a bullet-proof mantlet at the side, whence he may supervise the targets and signal the score in safety. With all these advantages we may look for record scores and sensational victories on the part of our VIII.'s.

AUGUST 1910

Rifle Club.

THE new rifle range was in full blast all last term, but the results of the shooting were much below the standard on the old *ten yard* range in the Gym. After many ex eriments it was decided to give more light from the side to counteract the glare from the front skylight. The decided improvement in the averages this term speaks for itsel . Shooting in the Summer Term is an innovation, which has proved itself to be not only a possibility, but a success, notwithstanding the counter attractions o cricket and swimming.

LORD ROBERTS' SILVER SPOONS.

These spoons are given for the highest average score made during the three terms of the year ending at Easter :—

Open..	.. W. G. Cheese ..	..	51'7
Under 16	.. J. Waller ..	..	46'4
Under 15	.. F. M. B. Paul ..	..	44'4

HOUSE COMPETITION IOR WORTHINGTON EVANS CUP.

School House have won it six times, that is to say, from the beginning of the competition two year ago.

Under the new conditions it has to be competed for each te m, and the aggregates for the year decide which House is the winner.

Rifle Club.

Two causes have contributed this term to a considerable improvement in the standard of shooting, on which indeed we thought last term we had reason to congratulate ourselves. At Christmas our Hon. Sec. received a circular from the N.R.A. stating that Colonel Schumacker had very generously made a grant of a thousand converted miniature carbines for the use of schools not having uniformed Cadet Corps. On our making application for some of these we received a grant of three, and they have proved of the greatest service, especially as our old match rifles have taken this favourable opportunity of evincing such signs of wear that we have had to retire them from active service. We have also this term made a change in our ammunition, using Long King's Norton instead of Short U.M.C.

The effect has certainly been most gratifying. The experts now look upon anything under 60 as very moderate, and we have been daily expecting one of the said experts to achieve the distinction of being the first to make a "possible" under present conditions.

Our very hearty thanks are again due to C. S. I. Penn for his nvaluable assistance.

We have had five matches of which we have won four and lost one! We may congratulate ourselves on beating Wellingborough for the second time in succession. Lest we should be too puffed up with pride we were badly beaten at the close of the term by the Colchester Rifle Club.

HOUSE COMPETITION FOR WORTHINGTON EVANS' CUP.—This was left last term in a very interesting state. Dugard's led with an advantage of three points over School House. It was generally expected that Dugard's would increase this lead in the final stage, but owing largely to the unexpected success of Shenton, the latest recruit to School House, this expectation was falsified, and School House won for the third year in succession.

School House.		Dugard's.		Harsnett's.		Parr's.	
Webb..	66	Davies	65	Cheese	63	Johnson	62
Jones ma.	65	Baxter	62	Thomas	62	Orfeur	60
Goldsmith	63	Chapman	62	Prime	56	Lazell	59
Watson	62	Jarrard	58	Bare	56	Bayliss	56
Shenton	62	Shelton	58	Atkin	42	Triscott	48
Malyn	57	Dunningham	57	Gannaway	41	Town	43
Folkard ma.	51	Doubleday ma.	53	Mason	40	Brand	33
Jones mi	49	Nicholson	37	Lawrence	37	Collinge	7
	475		452		397		368
Xmas Term	377		384		301		300
Summer Term	414		410		368		350
Total	1266		1246		1066		1018

MASTERS v. BOYS.—Feb. 3, 1911.

Masters.		(70)	Boys.				(70)
Mr. A. E. Barker		66	Cheese				64
Mr. A. S. Mason		63	Baxter				62
Mr. E. G. Davis		57	Davies ma.				62
Mr. E. Pizzo		57	Webb				56
C. S. I. Penn		56	Orfeur ma.				56
Mr. H. St. J. Seamer		50	Nicholson				53
Mr. C. A. B. Allen		48	Johnson				53
Mr. E. Reeve		39	Dunningham				50
		436					456

The Cadet Corps.

The Cadet Corps has for some time been in its right mind, and now, at last, is also clothèd. There is always something unnatural in a Corps out of uniform. It is a disembodied spirit (if a Corps can be so described), a ghost of a Corps, a mere abstraction. But a tasteful uniform now invests it with reality and reduces it to the concrete. And this, together with the merry bugles (the joy to be derived from blowing a bugle, and legitimately producing ear-splitting sounds, must be intense) ought to ensure for all time a constant supply of eager recruits.

The Cadet Corps.

(Affiliated to the 5th Battalion the Essex Regiment.)

THE Corps has been thoroughly organised this term, and though we are only in the embryo stage at present, the germs of life are passing strong—in fact over sixty strong—and we hope to have by the time the inspection comes round an efficient company of thoroughly keen and smart cadets.

Gen. Heath, commanding the Colchester Garrison, has sent a special letter of congratulation to us.

The Corps has some hard work before it, and after the drills have been mastered war schemes will have to be worked out in conjunction with the 5th Essex Regiment.

The inspection will probably take place in some camp during the summer, by which time we hope that every cadet will know all the ins and outs of the science of war.

There is one rule we wish to emphasize, and that is that when in the ranks and not standing easy, there must be no talking or playing of any kind. The term "sloppy" is generally applied to this kind of soldiering, and we must never lay ourselves open to this epithet.

Promotions will be made from time to time, and it should be the aim of every cadet to earn his stripes by enthusiasm and proficiency.

The following promotions have been made to date:—To be cadet-corporals, Cadets Malyn, Orfeur ma, Lazell, Jarrard, Everett ma., Bowen, Grahame-Brown, Shenton ma.

All announcements will be posted on the order board, and every cadet is responsible for becoming acquainted with them.

We wish to thank Mrs. Clover (Dedham) and Mr. J. A. Jones (Leeds) for presenting bugles to the Corps, and other donors, among whom are H. K. Newton, Esq., M.P., L. Worthington Evans, Esq., M.P., and Mrs. Patrick Crosbie, who, in addition, has promised an annual prize of one guinea for the most efficient cadet.

E. G. DAVIS,
Captain Commanding.

C. R. G. S. Rifle Club.

THERE can be no doubt that the standard of rifle-shooting in the School has this term reached what is up to the present high-water mark. It is probably only a question of time—probably a long time - till all the eight will make possibles.

It is interesting to compare the scores we have made in such a match as Wellingborough on successive occasions. They have been 710, 763, 771, 735, 760, and 766, against their scores of 764, 782, 785, 728, 758, and 762, the first three being at 10 yards and the last three at 25.

The "Worthington Evans" cup is left in a very interesting condition. Dugard's are at present five up with one to play.

The rapid-firing competition took place on Monday, 18th December. Results:—Open, Cheese 70; under 16, Fitch 66; under 15, Chapman 68.

The highest averages for this term are: Open, Cheese 63·4; under 16, Doubleday ma. 60·1; under 15, Chapman 63·2. Chapman's record is worthy of especial mention. We look forward to seeing him do some really good performances at Bisley in the future.

Our very hearty thanks are again due to C.-S.-I. Penn for his invaluable services.

OLD COLCESTRIANS v. SCHOOL.—27th October, 1911.

Maximum 70.

O.C.S.				C.R.G.S.			
F. Sennitt	...	...	61	Cheese	...	...	67
H. C. Osborne	...	...	61	Chapman	...	...	64
F. F. Osborne	...	...	60	Shenton	...	...	61
W. W. Pointing	...	...	60	Doubleday	...	...	60
H. Butcher	...	...	60	Davies	...	...	56
L. H. Johnson	...	...	60	Orfeur	...	...	55
A. O. Farmer	...	...	57	Shelton	...	...	54
A. W. Nunn	...	...	53	Jarrard	...	...	54
			472				471

C.R.G.S. v. ASCHAM COLLEGE (Clacton).—7th November, 1911.

Maximum 70.

Ascham				C.R.G.S.			
Goldecke	...	...	65	Cheese	...	...	66
Haley	...	...	63	Doubleday	...	...	64
May	...	...	62	Orfeur	...	...	62
Farmer	...	...	61	Jarrard	...	...	61
May	...	...	60	Davies	...	...	60
Skipper	...	...	57	Malyn	...	...	60
Young	...	...	57	Shelton	...	...	60
Huggins	...	...	55	Shenton	...	...	59
			480				492

C.R.G.S. v. WOODBRIDGE SCHOOL.—11th November, 1911.

Maximum 100.

Woodbridge.		C.R.G.S.	
Lingwood ma.	91	Cheese	95
Geard	91	Davies	91
Gyde	88	Chapman	89
Wanklyn	87	Malyn	89
Harmer	86	Orfeur	89
Ward	82	Doubleday	87
Taylor	81	Shelton	85
Denoy	79	Shenton	85
	685		710

C.R.G.S. v. WELLINGBOROUGH GRAMMAR SCHOOL.—21st Nov. 1911.

Maximum 100.

Wellingborough.		C.R.G.S.	
Sewell	98	Cheese	97
Ellison	97	Jarrard	97
Caster	97	Goldsmith	96
Bloor	97	Davies	96
Douglas	96	Doubleday	96
Mase	95	Chapman	95
Cubitt	91	Malyn	95
White	91	Orfeur	94
	762		766

OLD COLCESTRIANS v. SCHOOL.—30th November, 1911.

Maximum 70.

O.C.S.				C.R.G.S.			
F. Sennitt	...	...	61	Goldsmith	...	...	66
A. W. Nunn	...	...	60	Cheese	...	...	65
H. C. Osborne	...	...	58	Davies	...	...	64
F. Osborne	...	...	57	Malyn	...	...	64
L. C. Brook	...	...	55	Doubleday	...	...	63
W. R. O. Midgley	...	...	52	Jarrard	...	...	63
C. Bond	...	...	46	Shenton	...	...	61
C. Grimwood	...	...	45	Chapman	...	...	60
			434				506

C.R.G.S. v. COLCHESTER RIFLE CLUB.—4th December, 1911.

Maximum 100.

Rifle Club.				C.R.G.S.			
H. G. Cousins	...	...	99	Goldsmith	...	...	95
W. Hiscox	...	...	98	Chapman	...	...	94
G. Bradbury	...	...	97	Doubleday ma.	...	...	93
G. W. Siggers	...	...	97	Davies	...	...	93
H. O. Cousins	...	...	96	A. E. Barker	...	...	92
C. J. Edwards	...	...	96	Cheese	...	...	92
A. W. Nunn	...	...	93	Orfeur	...	...	92
D. McGregor	...	...	92	Shenton	...	...	91
			768				742

C.R.G.S. 2ND VIII. v. ST. MARY'S CHURCH LADS' BRIGADE.

Maximum 70.

Brigade.		C.R.G.S.	
G. Edwards	67	Bare	62
W. Edwards	66	Lawrence	62
W. Lee	60	Everett	61
Rev. R. E. V. Prichard	59	Goldsmith mi.	61
G. Nunn	55	Doubleday mi.	58
A. Reed	55	Orfeur ma.	58
F. Isom	51	Jones mi.	58
J. Atkins	46	Lazell	51
	459		481

HOUSE COMPETITION.—27th November, 1911.

Maximum 70.

School House.		Dugard's		Harsnett's		Parr's	
Goldsmith ma.	64	Chapman	62	Chesse	66	Orfeur	55
Malyn	64	Doubleday ma.	61	Bare	61	Lazell	53
Jones mi.	60	Jarrard	61	Everett	57	Watsham	53
Shenton	60	Davies	60	Lawrence	55	Town	51
Fitch	59	Doubleday mi.	60	Atkin	47	Bayliss	51
Goldsmith mi.	56	Shelton	58	Osborne	45	Triscott	50
Graham-Brown	55	Eves	47	Page	42	Miller	46
Wenden	52	Bowen	41	Potter	41	Brand	44
	470		450		414		403

SCORES TO DATE FOR "WORTHINGTON EVANS" CUP.

	Summer 1911.	Xmas 1911.	Total.
Dugard's	460	450	910
School House	435	470	905
Harsnett's	390	414	804
Parr's	329	403	732

Debating Society.

President : The Headmaster.

Vice-Presidents : The Assistant Masters.

Committee : C. T. CHEESE, W. E. DAVIES, D. MALYN, E. W. GOLDSMITH.

Secretary : H. LAZELL.

The following subjects have been discussed this term :—

Saturday, October 28th—"That the time has arrived when Woman should be regarded as the equal of Man."
Proposed by H. Lazell.
Seconded by W. E. Davies.
Opposed by C. T. Cheese.
The motion was lost by 16 votes to 10.

The Colcestrian.

VITÆ CORONA FIDES.

No. 31.]   APRIL, 1912.   [NEW SERIES.

Editorial.

THE present Term marks a fresh stage in the upward evolution of the School. In Nature itself uni-cellular life is the lowest form of biological existence, and sub-division is the first step on the path that leads to the multifarious and complex organisms, animal as well as vegetable, of which we are, and in the midst of which we live.

Similarly—and naturally enough—at first a School is organised as a single unit, an arrangement amply suited to its simple needs in the early stages of its growth. But with increase of numbers and complexity this form is soon found to be insufficient. It is bound to sub-divide, lest out of sheer unwieldiness it fall apart or suffer in efficiency. And this stage would seem to have been reached in the present case. Forms I., II. and III. now form a Lower School, organised as a separate entity, under a separate, if subordinate, Head, without losing any of the advantages accruing from its unity with the School, of which it will continue to be an essential part, while the gain both in and out of class-time will be immense. For the purposes of sport, it possesses a Football League of its own, on the model of that which flourishes among the bigger boys, and a troop of Boy Scouts, in three patrols, act as an introduction to the Cadet Corps and Miniature Rifle Club of the School proper.

There is always a certain difficulty in arranging satisfactorily for the work and play of boys whose ages cover a wide range of years, but this division into Upper and Lower School would seem to overcome it in an exceedingly efficient manner. "We are not divided" is an excellent theological proposition, but from a scholastic and biological point of view could only stand for stagnation, weakness, and decay.

THE EDITOR.

The Cadet Corps Matinee.

ON the following afternoon, Thursday, December 21st, a matinée took place in aid of the newly-uniformed Cadet Corps, with a change of programme. The full strength of the Corps paraded in uniform on the platform and sang an opening chorus, "The Young Brigade," words by the H.M. in his usual happy manner, to the "old" tune. Mr. F. D. Barker played "Les Sylvains," a graceful pianoforte solo, while the succeeding song, "The Ringers," gave Mr. Parker's fine and well-trained voice an opportunity of which full advantage was taken. Doubleday mi.'s *vibrato* treble was keenly appreciated in "Ariel's Song," and Mr. Boake Carter gained an encore for a humorous and doggy ballad. Miss Marjorie Bourne delighted the audience with a violin solo, and Miss Julia Larkins again produced a shower of encores for her fresh series of songs at the piano.

The dramatic item, "Wanted, a Companion," formed Part II. in the programme, in which Miss Lockwood in the part of Miss Penuria Nettleship gave a lifelike presentation of an old maid, and Mrs. W. J. Jenks as Miss Dolly Joyce, in search of a place as companion, made an excellent young girl, lively, not to say frivolous.

Part III. consisted of a fresh selection of Carols by the School Choir.

During the interval the Headmaster announced that there were at present 60 members in the corps. The idea had been very kindly received by the neighbourhood. General Heath had written a letter of congratulation ; Mrs. Patrick Crosby, in addition to giving a handsome donation, had promised a yearly prize for the best recruit ; and they had had kind support from Mr. Worthington Evans, M.P., and Mr. Newton, M.P. What they wanted now were funds and a band. They had shot six matches, losing against the Old Colcestrians and the Colchester Rifle Club, but winning against Ascham College, Woodbridge School, Wellington School, and the Old Colcestrians (in the return match). Having referred to the excellent form shown by some of the cadets in rapid firing, the Headmaster remarked that the reason why they could not have a troop of Scouts at the School was because scouting took up too much time. Instead, they had started a Cadet Corps, because it seemed to him that it would provide just the element of discipline which was so much wanted at the present day, not only in schools, but in the nation itself. They might be told that it would encourage an undesirable spirit of militarism, but that was not at all their idea, and they did not expect that any hooliganism would result. Rather they considered they had founded the Corps on four cardinal points—the honour they owed to their King, the duty they owed to their nation, the loyalty they owed to their school, and the discipline they owed to themselves (applause).

scratching at the ball and failing to hit it any distance even when having a clear field in front of them.

Malyn at back played a useful game, hitting hard and clearing well, while Everett in the forward line showed most promise, one of his goals in our last match being quite a good effort. We hope that next season all boys in the Upper School will take to Hockey for the last few weeks of the Lent term.

The Cadet Corps.

(Affiliated to the 5th Battalion the Essex Regiment).

OFFICERS OF THE CORPS—LENT TERM.

E. G. Davis, Captain and O.C.
E. Reeve, Lieutenant.
J. Penn, Col.-Sergt.-Instructor.

D. Malyn, Cadet Sergeant	D. Graham-Brown, Cadet Corporal
H. Lazell ,,	H. H. Bowen ,,
C. H. Jarrard ,,	A. K. Shenton ,,
C. E. F. Everett ,,	R. E. Doubleday ,,
L. B. Fitch, Cadet Lce.-Corpl.	G. Nevard, Cadet Lce.-Corpl. Bugler

THE Company has been doing some hard work this term, and besides the weekly drills the Inspection and one Field Day have been held, while a whole day programme is being arranged in the neighbourhood of Kelvedon in conjunction with the 8th Essex Regiment, by kind permission of Capt. Pearson, the Adjutant, for Easter Monday.

The Inspection, February 29th, 1912.

The Corps was inspected by order of the War Office by Captain Merriman, Adjutant to the 5th Essex Regiment. To be inspected thus early in the year was a severe test, but with a few extra drills for those who had been absent from the regular parades the Corps came out of the ordeal with flying colours.

The inspecting officer saw a certain amount of company drill, the rifle and bayonet exercises, squad drill by the section commanders, and shooting at the range by eight cadets selected at random. He also inspected the armoury and rifle range.

The report, which we are unable to publish in full owing to lack of space, was duly posted in orders. The inspecting officer was full of praise, both in his report and speech, and while making one or two useful suggestions, he was very well satisfied with the work that has been done and the lines on which the Company is working.

The closing remarks in his report on the official form which was sent to Headquarters were :—

"This Corps is extraordinarily good considering the short time it has been formed, and has a great future before it. The rifle shooting has attained a very high standard, and I hope that arrangements can be made for shooting at Middlewick in the summer."

Well, we have already made arrangements for a certain amount of shooting at Middlewick, and although it may not be possible for every cadet to shoot in this the first year, we hope to get the keenest men to fire off their standard test. Before a cadet can be returned as " efficient " in the summer, he must pass the standard test in the miniature range. The standard test at Middlewick is not compulsory, but on passing it a cadet will be permitted to wear the cross guns on his sleeve.

Field Day, March 27th.

A tactical exercise was worked out in the neighbourhood of **SHRUB END** and **LEXDEN**. The special idea was that the Cadet Corps formed the advanced guard of the army which had mobilized at **COLCHESTER**.

Four positions were taken up by the four sections under Cadet-Sergeants Malyn, Lazell, Jarrard and Everett at the cross roads between Lexden Road and the Layer Road. The enemy at first attempted to force a passage into **COLCHESTER** along the Lexden Road. Their attempt was frustrated, however, by No. 1 Section, and they then marched on **SHRUB END** and made a determined attempt to break through No. 3 Section. By a series of messages the whole company concentrated very quickly at **SHRUB END**, and a fierce battle took place. We were wavering and might have been defeated, had not No. 4 Section, which had gone wrong owing to the mis-timing of a message, come up in the nick of time, like Blücher's army at Waterloo, and with this added force a probable defeat was turned into a glorious victory.

The Summer Camp.

No definite arrangements have yet been made for our camp in the summer. We hope that everyone will keep the first week of August open, as we are certain to go into camp at that time.

It has been suggested that several Cadet Corps should camp together at Danbury or Southend, and we have expressed a desire to join in. Some definite announcement will be made in orders during the first month of next term.

Recruits.

There will be a few vacancies for recruits next term. We cannot take more than 60 cadets, and judging from the numbers who have asked to join we shall have to ballot for the few vacancies. We can only hope that the luck of the ballot will give us the smartest and keenest men.

One recruit for next term has already been enrolled, namely, Mr. Reeve, who, we are pleased to announce, is taking up a commission.

Rifle Club.

IT is pleasing to be able to record two increases this term, first in the number of members and secondly in the averages of our best shots. A larger number of the smaller boys have been shooting and of these a good percentage have shown promise of becoming quite good shots in the future. Under the present arrangements the range has been over-crowded at times during the dinner-hour and immediately after school, and it has been proposed that next term the old plan of giving each member a regular time for shooting be re-adopted.

Mr. Barker has presented the Club with his field glasses, which have been used for " spotting " since the present range has been in use. The Committee unanimously passed a vote of thanks to Mr. Barker for this gift.

Next term a little variety will be introduced in the shooting, as " landscape targets " will be used and practice at " rapid shooting " will begin.

The number of boys in the class " under 16 " is very small just now and some re-arrangement of the classes may be necessary at the beginning of the year, which starts next term.

The results of the House Competition are not yet to hand.

We have had 3 matches, all of which have been won.

C.R.G.S. v. OLD COLCESTRIANS.—16th February, 1912.
Maximum 70.

O.C.S.				C.R.G.S.			
W. R. O. Midgley			64	Davies			65
A. O. Farmer			61	Chapman			65
F. Sennitt			58	Shelton			63
D. M. Ely			58	Eves			62
F. Osborne			55	Doubleday ma.			62
H. Daldy			52	Goldsmith ma.			61
A. P. Storrar			51	Malyn			60
A. W. Nunn			51	Cheese			60
			450				498

42

Grammaria.

Losses.

This term the School regrets the departure of two of the Staff. Mr. Davis, who has completed two years in its service, has accepted a post at Berkhampstead School, Hertfordshire. The efficient state of the Cadet Corps is largely due to his untiring efforts, while under his guidance the Games have attained an extremely healthy condition. He took over the House mastership of Parr's when its fortunes were almost at their nadir, and the House will sorely miss his kindly and skilful hand on the reins. He takes with him the good wishes of us all.

Mr. Storrar also, after a too short stay, leaves for fresh fields and pastures new. We wish him every success.

C.R.G.S. Cadet Corps.

(Affiliated to the 5th Battalion the Essex Regiment).

SUMMER TERM.

THE Corps has had a very prosperous term and has got through a large amount of work. Exercises have been held in scouting, skirmishing, etc., the signallers have got into working order, ball firing practice has taken place at Middlewick, and very shortly the buglers and drummers will be blended into one harmonious whole. The great feature of the Term's work has been the excellent shooting of the Cadets at Middlewick. They have shown that miniature shooting goes a long way towards turning out good shots with .303 ball ammunition.

Territorial Sunday, June, 2nd.

The Corps, in company with the Regulars, 5th Essex Regt., Essex Yeomanry, Royal Horse Artillery and the Red Cross Nurses, attended a very inspiring open-air service on the Abbey Field.   After the service General Heath inspected the Corps and expressed himself as being very pleased with their smart appearance.   He mentioned that the Cadets were the soldiers of the future, and for that reason we were given the place of honour behind the band during the march round the town.

Presentation of Prizes and Gifts, July 1st.

After the speeches the Cadet Corps paraded in the front quad, where Mrs. Patrick Crosbie presented her Annual Cup for the best recruit, and Mrs. Jeffrey handed over the two side drums, very kindly given by Mrs. Cresswell Rooke, into the safe keeping of the O.C.   To the above donors and to Mr. Flanagan and Mr. Jeffrey, who have kindly presented serviceable rifles for Middlewick, we offer our best thanks.

After these presentations Captain E. E. Pearson of the Suffolk Regiment, inspected the Corps.   In a short speech he commended the Cadets on their smart appearance, and expressed the hope that they would join His Majesty's Auxiliary Forces after leaving school, which after all is the object of our Corps.

Field Day, July 12th.

The main body of the Corps made an attack on Butcher's Green, advancing by sections in several directions.   The Green was occupied by a skeleton company of soldiers who had real outposts out with blank ammunition.   After much firing, one section forced the outposts back, and captured the Green.   After lunch a scouting scheme with signallers was worked out, the original programme being abandoned owing to the excessive heat.

Camp in Danbury Park.

The end of the first year of our existence will be marked by our first Camp, and by the time this is in print the Corps will have settled down to a soldier's life.   We have been fortunate in securing the services of Lieutenant Coddington and Sergt. Cobb, of the Durham Light Infantry, as Commandant and Quarter-Master-Sergt. of the camp respectively.

The list of the members of the Corps attending the Camp is appended.

In conclusion may I express my thanks to the Corps for its loyalty and devotion to duty during the year. As its first O.C. I think I may say that the Corps is launched on a successful voyage. We have worked, not played, and most of us now are beginning to see what a great subject the science of war is. To Sergt.-Instructor Penn I owe much for his advice and great help ungrudgingly given. I hope my successor will find future years as happy as the past year has been to me.

Best wishes to you all.

E. G. DAVIS, Captain.

MEMBERS OF THE SCHOOL CADET CORPS ATTENDING CAMP AT DANBURY, AUGUST, 1912.

Lieut. Coddington (Durham Light Infantry).	Commandant of Camp.
E. G. Davis - - - -	Captain Commanding.
E. Reeve - - - -	Lieutenant.
Sergt. Dodd (Durham Light Infantry) -	Qr.-Mtr.-Sgt. of Camp.
J. Penn - - - -	Col.-Sergt. Instructor.

Cadet-Sergeants.—D. Malin, H. Lazell, C. H. Jarrard, C. E. F. Everett.
Cadet-Corporals.—H. H. Bowen, G. Brown, A. K. Shenton, Doubleday
Cadet Lance-Corporal Bugler.—G. Nevard.   ma.
Cadet Buglers.—H. T. Cudmore, E. R. Scott, D. T. Wagstaff.

Cadets.

E. V. Andrews	J. M. Clover	H. M. Girling	S. W. Roger
G. Atkin	C. E. Collinge	B. W. T. Hindes	T. G. Smith
W. J. Bare, ma.	F. J. Collinge	R. S. J. Hudson	B. A. Squire
H. G. Bare, min.	B. P. Dicker	E. M. Jones	W. M. Towns
R. B. Bayliss	W. A. Doubleday	E. Lines, min.	V. P. L. Triscott
E. E. Beard	L. C. Flanegan	J. E. Lines, ma.	H. Watsham
H. Burleigh	D. H. French	G. C. Rayner	C. A. Wenden
D. Chapman	S. C. H. French	J. E. Rickword	F. Brand

Shooting.

THE first part of the term was devoted to practice for the House Competition, postponed from last term. Shooting took place on May 24th, and School House lost possession of the cup, which they have held since the competition was started, the new holders being Dugards, who had a lead of 5 points on the results of the two previous terms, increased to 16 for the three terms.

Considerably less time has been at the disposal of would-be shooters, as the demands of cricket prevented shooting after school and the length of dinner-hour having been shortened, the number of day-boys shooting this term has been much smaller than usual. It is hoped that more boys will shoot again next term, as many of the Juniors are showing much promise and have improved their markmanship very much of late. All Cadets should certainly shoot, as practice on a Miniature Range is undoubtedly good experience for the time when they have to use the Service rifle.

The great event of the term was the shooting in the Imperial Challenge Shield Competition, which took place on June 29th. Colonel Young kindly acted as Range Superintendent, and gave the boys every encouragement. The results will not be made known till September, but we hope to be higher in the lists than last year, as our averages were much better. The Juniors did especially well, Doubleday, mi. scoring 49 out of a possible 50 at the Figure Target. The Juniors shot "deliberate," but the Seniors had to shoot "rapid" (10 shots in 90 seconds) at the Figure Target. Open sights had to be used in this competition and so we have had no matches this term. The Orthoptic Sights have now been re-fitted and House Matches will be shot under the usual conditions.

Our best thanks are due to C.S.I. Penn for his superintendence at the Range.

HOUSE COMPETITION.

(Postponed from Easter Term.)

Max. 70.

DUGARD'S.		SCHOOL HOUSE.		HARSNETT'S.		PARR'S.	
Chapman	66	Wagstaff ma	59	Bare ma	57	Watsham ma	58
Doubleday ma	63	Malyn	58	Chambers	56	Triscott	55
Doubleday mi	61	Fitch	57	Everett ma	55	Lazell	53
Jarrard	58	Goldsmith mi	57	Smith mi	48	Brand	51
Davies	57	Graham-Brown	57	King ma	46	Bayliss	47
Eves	54	Goldsmith ma	54	Osborne	39	Cudmore	42
Bowen	53	Jones	48	Atkin	34	Andrews	38
Beckett	36	Shenton	47	Page	29	Orfeur	33
	448		437		364		377
Summer, 1911	460		435		390		329
Xmas, 1911	450		470		414		403
Total	1358		1342		1168		1109

46

IMPERIAL CHALLENGE SHIELD COMPETITION.
June 29th.

SENIORS.

			Deliberate (Bisley)		Rapid (Figure)		Total
Doubleday ma	..	..	42	..	38	..	80
Graham-Brown	..	..	39	..	39	..	78
Shenton	..	..	44	..	34	..	78
Bowen	..	..	37	..	40	..	77
Malyn	..	..	37	..	36	..	73
Jarrard	..	..	39	..	24	..	63
Lazell	..	..	32	..	27	..	59
Watsham ma	..	..	28	..	27	..	55
							563
						Average	70·4

JUNIORS.

			Bisley		Figure		Total
Doubleday mi	..	..	44	..	49	..	93
Chapman	..	..	44	..	45	..	89
Bare ma	..	..	41	..	43	..	84
Wenden	..	..	38	..	40	..	78
Wagstaff ma	..	..	36	..	34	..	70
Jones	..	..	30	..	36	..	66
Dicker	..	..	30	..	31	..	61
Goldsmith mi	..	..	26	..	32	..	58
							599
						Average	74·6

The Colcestrian.

VITÆ CORONA FIDES.

No. 34.]   DECEMBER, 1912.   [NEW SERIES.

Editorial.

PERHAPS the most striking feature of the year's life of the School has been the camping-out during the summer holidays. In the Upper School a large proportion of the Cadet Corps spent a fortnight in camp at Danbury, one of the highest and most picturesque points in Essex, under Capt. Davis and Lieut. Reeve, while in the Lower School an even larger proportion of Boy Scouts pitched their tents near St. Osyth beach in charge of Scoutmaster E. Pepper.

Judging from the photographic reproductions and the accounts of their experiences to be found in another column, they would seem to have passed a most enjoyable and enviable time of it, despite the weather, which, although not ideal, mercifully postponed its worst tantrums until the campers were safely back in the bosom of their families. Safely, indeed ; for there was no case of sickness, and nothing else that could deserve even the name of misadventure during the whole period in either case. It is hard to imagine anything that could afford a better training for after life than this holiday camping. Plenty of open-air exercise, social pleasures, instruction, almost unconsciously absorbed, under interesting and enjoyable conditions, all unite to make the experience one of the happiest of school life.

But there is another point to bear in mind. If the summer is the zenith of the Cadet's or Scout's year, the winter is its nadir. The weather does not lend itself to other than occasional field exercises. Half the glory is departed. And with the end of the civil year, when the leaving list is large, there is a marked tendency toward a diminution of numbers. This can only be counteracted and outweighed by a corresponding increase in the number of recruits. It may be confidently anticipated that parents and boys alike will see to it that the New Year is made one of unexampled prosperity for both C.R.G.S. Cadet Corps and C.R.G.S. Scouts.

THE EDITOR.

The Cadet Corps Camp.

THE first camp of the Cadet Corps took place from July 31st to August 8th in Danbury Park, Chelmsford, by kind permission of Lieut.-Col. the Hon. A. Greville. The camp was beautifully situated on the top of a good slope, and bathing was indulged in daily in the large lake a short distance away in the park. During the previous week great preparations had been going on, as each cadet had to provide himself with a number of camp utensils as per drawn-out list. One or two of course came provided with earthenware plates, etc., and inflicted the usual penalty in such cases, viz.: they shortened the supply of the wiser ones—who had enamelled goods—their own being broken. Everybody waited impatiently for the Thursday, when the Corps trained to Chelmsford and went on to Danbury by motor-bus, reaching the camp about 4 o'clock.

The Southend Technical School and Palmer's School, Grays, contingents had arrived about 12 o'clock in the day, having marched the whole way, and were found asleep in their tents.

The camp consisted of 18 tents, of which five were officers', two sergeants' and cooks', five Southend and Grays and six for Colchester. A large marquee was also erected, but rarely used, as the cadets preferred messing by tents.

Each cadet was provided with one waterproof sheet and two blankets. After tea the marquee was put up and then games were indulged in until bedtime. Most found that there is about as much resemblance between the cold, hard ground and an ordinary bed as there is between chalk and cheese, and obtained little sleep the first night. By six o'clock next morning the majority had dressed, cleaned their buttons and boots and were ready for the following daily routine:—

6.30 a.m.— Reveillé.
6.30 - 7.0—Wash, dress, clean buttons, etc.
7.0 - 7.45—Squad drill.
7.45-8.15—Clean and tidy-up tents.
8.15-8.45—Breakfast.
8.45 - 9.0— Fold blankets and arrange kit outside tents.
9.0 - Tent inspection.
9.0 - 10.0—Fatigue parties clean and tidy-up camp.
10.0-12.45—Drill.
1.0 - 1.30—Dinner.
1.30 - 2.0—Clean up and forage for wood for cooks' fire.

Usually the rest of the day was spent in playing games— cricket, football, bathing, etc. Tea was served at 5 p.m.

and supper at 8 ; lights out 9.30.

Breakfast was the most varied of the meals, and consisted of eggs, ham (with pickles), kippers and sausages on different days. The ration of bread was 2½ loaves per meal per tent, and butter ¼-lb. Dinner always consisted of stewed beef and potatoes, accompanied by macaroni or rice. For tea jam or cheese was provided, and at supper-time porridge. Early in the morning, just before squad drill, a cup of boiling-hot coffee and a few biscuits were served out. The camp was lucky to have two really good army cooks, and from them much of the art of camp cookery was learnt. Each day three separate fatigue parties were arranged, and every cadet did his fair share of work ; there were no shirkers.

Under Lieut. Codington's excellent instruction, several methods of attack and defence were learnt. They consisted of skirmishing in the open and along roads, advance and rear-guards, attacking an imaginary enemy situated on a hill (in the final charge bayonets were fixed), sentry duty and methods of bivou-acking. Two days were allotted to sham-fights which aroused considerable interest in the neighbourhood. On Sunday there was the usual Church Parade, and most of us were glad there was no sermon.

The greatest interest centred in the sham-fights on the last two days. In the first of these Southend and Grays defended Dan-bury, while Colchester did the attacking. This was very interesting, and to make it more real blank ammunition had been served out. The defenders had an excellent position on the top of the hill, and quite early on discovered what was to be the main line of attack on the right of Danbury Common. After a three hours engagement the umpire (Lieut. Codington) decided that it must be called a draw.

On the last whole day—the best of the eight as regards weather—the second engagement took place. Colchester defended the cross roads near the camp. while Southend and Grays tried to force their way into camp. Owing to some excellent scouting by the outposts, the attackers were spotted a good distance from the cross roads. A sharp, fierce engagement took place in a farmyard, and the attackers were forced to fall back, but on bringing up reinforcements the farm was evacuated. The umpire declared this a bad move on the part of the defenders, as in such a position a few men could easily have held a much larger number at bay. After this the outposts were gradually forced to retire back on the main body. Now a desperate conflict took place, the defenders easily holding their own. The umpire's decision was a victory for the defenders. He commended the Colchester scouting, and specially mentioned Pte. Town. He also commended the form of attack of the Southend and Grays detachment.

In addition to the above, three or four route marches were held, and on these occasions the buglers led the way, rendering a very good account of their powers

Monday, Aug. 5th, was Bank Holiday, and the whole camp was invited to attend a fête being held in another part of the park. Races were arranged for the Cadets and Boy Scouts but the former were rather unresponsive. Two of the Colchester Corps took away prizes.

During the week the popular Commander (Capt. E. G. Davis) was presented with a silver wrist watch by the Corps. The camp Cricket XI. defeated Col. Johnson's XI. by five wickets. Many parents of the Cadets paid visits to the camp, and on the Monday Col. the Hon. A. Greville and party held an informal inspection of the camp.

The worst day came at last—that day of ill omen, Friday— and the camp was to break up.   Tents were struck and packed

away, kit bags repacked, b l a n k e t s and waterproofs returned, the camping ground cleaned, ready to say goodbye to Danbury. First the Grays detachment left by 'bus, then the Southend Corps marched off for their native town, and then the 'bus arrived to carry t h e C o l c h e s t e r Corps to Chelmsford, and the Corps disbanded at Colchester.

A very delightful time was spent at this our first camp, despite the bad weather, and it is certain that those who are still in the Corps next summer will be clamouring for the next camp.

During the present term the Corps has not undertaken any military exercises on scouting, skirmishing, etc., owing to the bad weather, but considerable progress has been made in company drill, and the recruits have been brought up to a standard approaching the high level of the Corps. Section commanders have much improved in drilling their respective sections, and give their orders with greater confidence in the results. The Corps as a whole has much benefitted from its experience of soldiers' life at camp.

The distinction of being the first to receive the annual prize, presented by Mrs. Patrick Crosbie for the most efficient recruit, goes to Sergt. Doubleday, who takes possession of the cup received last speech day.

Owing to Cadet-Sergts. Malyn, Lazell and Jarrard leaving the Corps at the end of the last term, the following promotions have been made :— Cadet-Corporals Doubleday, Brown and Girling to be Sergeants. Other promotions will be posted before the end of term. The Corps is badly in need of funds, and it is proposed to find a means of raising some at an early date.

Scouting Notes.

THE first ten days of the summer holidays were spent by the Scouts under canvas at S. Osyth. For many of us, it was the first experience of camp life, some indeed, had never been away from home before, and it was the more gratifying to find that so many boys gave in their names. The following boys were at camp :—

Wolf Patrol	Peewit Patrol	Woodpigeon Patrol	Otter Patrol
P.L. Blaxill ma.	S. Blaxill mi.	P.L. Poulton ma.	P.L. Collinge
S. Everitt mi.	Wheeler ma.	S. Sands	S. Green
King mi.	Everett mi.	Chambers	Marlar
Blyth	Royce	Thomas	Hordern
Burleigh, mi.	Holt	Page	
Weatherall	Goodway	Nicholl ma.	
Gower		Mason	

In addition to these we had two Scout visitors, H. Graham Brown and R. C. Flux, who were attached to the Troop as hon. members just for the period of camp.

We had a beautifully fine day for the start which was made from the School about 11 o'clock. Taking train from S. Botolphs to Thorington, we marched for the remaining six miles of the journey, calling a halt half-way for lunch.

PITCHING CAMP.

On arriving in camp, everyone set to work to pitch the four bell-tents and build the camp kitchens, etc., with the assistance of Scouts Nevard and Cudmore, of the Great Bentley Troop, who had kindly come over to help us.

Shooting.

DURING the holidays the results of the Imperial Shield Competition came to hand., and it is most pleasing to record the Club's excellent performance therein. The Seniors were placed 28th on the list with an average of 70.3 per cent. and were awarded a prize of £2, while the Juniors occupied the 8th place and gained a prize of £3 with an average of 74.8. Mr. Jeffrey received a special letter of congratulation on the latter's performance from Col. Schumacher, the donor of the prizes, in which he states that he hopes to congratulate them at an early date on winning the shield itself. We also hope his wish may be gratified, for we have some promising shots in the Juniors just now.

We have had one match only this term, viz., against our old rivals, Wellingborough, and this we won easily.

A competition was held during the week ending Nov. 30th, for prizes presented by the S.M.R.C. These go to the following :—Open, Watsham ma. 64. Under 16, Chapman 65. Juniors, Wenden 57.

The second round of the House Competition was shot off during the week ending Dec. 14th, and the results were as follows :—

HOUSE SHOOTING COMPETITION.

Michaelmas Term, 1912.

SCHOOLHOUSE		DUGARDS		HARSNETTS		PARRS	
Goldsmith mi.	61	Chapman	66	Bare ma.	63	Triscott	60
„ ma.	59	Doubleday ma.	63	Gannaway	59	Watsham ma.	60
Wagstaff ma	59	„ mi.	61	Clarke mi.	55	Cudmore	58
Jones	59	Flanegan	59	Everett ma.	55	Andrews	57
Graham-Brown	56	Eves	57	Scott ma.	53	Brand	52
Nevard	56	Hudson	54	Deane	49	Orfeur	42
Wenden	44	Rogers	45	Atkin	48	French ma	41
Clover	42	Horwood	25	Chambers	28	Watsham mi	30
	436		430		410		400

C.R.G.S. v. WELLINGBOROUGH.

Wellingborough			C.R.G.S.		
Chalcraft		95	Watsham ma.		97
Brown		94	Doubleday, mi.		97
Whiting		93	Bare ma		95
Knight		91	Everett ma.		94
Douglas		91	Doubleday ma		94
Grocott		90	Chapman		93
Hazelton		89	Wagstaff ma.		92
Seward		85	Graham-Brown		91
		728			753

Our best thanks are again due to C.S.I. Penn, for the excellent manner in which he takes charge of the Range.

APRIL 1913

Shooting.

THIS term has been quite a busy one at the Range, great keenness being shown, especially by the Juniors, who are a good promising lot of shots and should do well for the Club in the future.

Members have adapted themselves very well to open sights, though the removal of the orthoptics has reduced the averages considerably.

The House Cup Competition, counted on the three terms, was concluded, and Dugard's hold the Cup for another year. Here a great levelling-up has taken place, only 36 points separating the highest from the lowest.

In "post" matches we have won two and lost one, being beaten by our old rivals, Wellingborough. We should like to congratulate Bare ma. on his possible v. Ascham College, as this is the first obtained on this Range at 25 yards. We hope there may be many who will follow his example.

We are shooting against Skinner's School, Tunbridge Wells, O.T.C., on Tuesday, April 1st.

Once more we wish to express our best thanks to C.S.I. Penn for the able manner in which he looks after the Range.

LORD ROBERTS' SILVER SPOONS.

These Spoons are given for the highest average score made during the three terms of the year ending at Easter :—

Open	...	...	Doubleday ma.	... ...	57·8
Under 16	...	...	Chapman	... ...	60·9
Under 15	...	...	Wagstaff ma.	... ...	51·5

HOUSE COMPETITION.

Easter Term, 1913.

DUGARD'S		SCHOOL HOUSE		HARSNETT'S		PARR'S	
Doubleday mi.	65	Graham-Brown	63	Gannaway ...	67	Watsham ma. ...	62
Eves ...	63	Jones	61	Everett ma. ...	64	Watsham mi. ...	58
Chapman	63	Wagstaff ma. ...	61	Bare ma. ...	62	Orfeur ...	57
Doubleday ma.	62	Goldsmith ma.	61	Clarke ma. ...	61	Triscott ...	55
Rogers ...	61	Malyn	51	Scott ...	56	Cudmore	53
Hudson ...	60	Wenden ...	51	King ma. ...	49	Andrews	52
Pullen ...	53	Goldsmith mi.	50	Deane ...	47	Brand ...	48
Flanegan	50	Rayner ...	50	Atkin ...	39	Percy ...	43
Total ...	464		448		445		428
Smr. Term, 1912	443		365		369		335
Xmas ,, ,,	430		436		410		400
Grand Total	1337		1249		1224		1163

55

Cadet Corps.

THERE is little to record as regards this term, work having been confined to weekly parades, where routine drill has been the order of the day. Easter Monday we were to have had a Field Day, but this had to be cancelled owing to the boarders going away for the week-end, and it has not been found possible to arrange another day.

On one or two occasions a little extended order drill was taken, and here a smartening up is necessary. It is essential that every Cadet should understand the signals, so that on their conclusion all may obey the order as quickly as possible, and on no account should anyone move from his position until the signal is completed.

The Buglers have made good progress under Sergt. Toohey (2nd D.L.I.) As soon as they become a little more proficient and have learned to "tongue it" better, the Drummers will be taught their part, and we look forward to the time when their combined efforts will cheer us on our marches.

We extend a hearty welcome to Mr. Deakin and our two recruits, Flux and Scott mi.

Cadet Corps.

OUR numbers are steadily increasing and we extend a hearty welcome to the recruits, Koskinas, Dolamore, Lawry, Watsham and Gilbert. There are still a number of boys in the School who would do us and themselves a good turn by joining the Corps.

The time for the Annual Camp is rapidly approaching and the Officers look to the Corps for the attendance and hearty support of at least 80% of the Cadets at this splendid opportunity of learning a military training in readiness for service to one's Country. The Camp will probably be in Danbury Park. We hope to have efficient signalling and cyclist sections by that time.

The Corps is in urgent need of financial help, and we should be exceedingly grateful to any O.C.'s or present Cadets who would give a small subscription to a general Cadet Corps Fund. These resources would be used to improve the serviceable equipment and provide a more thorough advanced training for the Corps.

On Sunday, June 1st, the Corps attended a Territorial Church Parade. There were present the National Reserve, 5th Essex Territorials, Essex R.H.A., Essex Yeomanry, Church Lads Brigade and members of the St. John's Ambulance Corps. Service was held in the Garrison Church, after which General Heath, G.O.C., Colchester Garrison, inspected the various Units of the Parade.

On all sides remarks were made on the smart movement and appearance of the C.R.G.S. Cadet Corps. This should not only be a source of proper pride, but act as an incentive to the attainment of a higher standard of smartness and efficiency.

CADET CORPS CONCERT.

THE School Cadet Corps Concert for 1913, given on Friday, April 4th, attracted a large and appreciative audience.

The opening item, a lively duet by Messrs. Sanger and Barker, O.C.'s, preceded a part song given by the newly-formed School Musical Club, under the guidance of Mr. J. A. Peart, who also conducted Collinge mi.'s "The Little Drummer," and another united choral effect by the Club.

Among those items in which the boys had no share, Madame Reeve's "Carnival" and "Songs my Mother sang to me," and Rev. Hartley Parker's "Drum Major" and "There's a Land" received an applause which showed the varied and appreciative taste of the audience. Of other items in Part I., special mention must be made of the Essex Ballads, by Wagstaff mi., and Collinge mi.'s rendering of Pellissier's "Echoes," which had achieved great success at the V. and VI. House singing earlier in the term. Mr. Oldham was down on the programme for a musical sketch, but was unfortunately absent through indisposition. Mr. John A. Peart kindly consenting to fill the gap, gave an excellent presentation of "Chapeaugraphy" in addition to the most amusing "Recitation Competition" he was "billed" to perform.

The second part of the programme was filled by an amusing farce by T. J. Williams—"Turn Him Out," in which Hudson appeared to great advantage as "Nicodemus Nobbs," and Doubleday mi.'s rendering of the modern "K'nut" caused much laughter. Dicker as "Mackintosh Moke" and Goldsmith mi., as his wife, showed distinct histrionic ability, while Beckett and Cudmore as "porters" displayed great talent as "chuckers-out."

The performance was a great success, both financially and otherwise, realising over £13 as net profit for the funds of the Corps.

THE FIELD DAY.

ADVANTAGE was taken of Whit Monday to hold a Field Day. The Company presented a smart appearance on "falling-in" at the School at 10.30 a.m. It is to be regretted that not every member of the Corps was present.

After a march of about six miles, Layer Breton Heath was reached and a halt called for lunch. The Company was then divided into two parties, one to attack and the other to defend. with a relative strength of three to one. The defenders, under the command of Colour-Sergeant Everett with the valuable practical assistance of Sergeant-Instructor Penn, held Birch ; the attack was under the command of Lieut. Deakin.

Making a slight *détour* to the west and then a sweep to the north, the attacking party came up with a half-flank movement under well-chosen-cover to within range of a hill which formed the main position of defence. Scouts had been sent forward, but the choice of men for the work was hardly a happy one. Losing touch with the main body, they still advanced, practically heedless of cover, and one, on hearing the enemies' shots, exposed himself entirely, hoping presumably to see where the smoke came from, and must have been absolutely riddled with lead.

The outposts of the defence took up a position in a lane which dipped down to a considerable hollow. The range of vision was small and the position easily approached, so that, as could only be expected, this contingent was taken prisoner. And yet a little higher up and not far on one side, behind the hedge nearer home was good cover, looking down absolutely straight upon an open field across which the attack must have come. Little knowledge was shown of how to retire upon the main body, and this, together with the unfavourable position occupied, made their capture certain.

The final attack was made by short independent rushes, ending up with a combined charge, the defenders giving way only at the point of the bayonet. Little doubt could be entertained as to the umpire's verdict declaring the attacking party the victors.

On the return journey, what might have been an interesting ambuscade, was rendered futile and impossible by an irrepressible desire on the part of one of the ambush to shoot immediately he saw the first solitary scout of the oncoming army, but the situation might have been saved by a rapid change of position by the party in ambush. As it was, the advancing troops, now fully warned, made a determined attack and compelled the surrender of the opposing party.

A. G. W.

Shooting.

OWING to the counter attractions of bathing and cricket, no time can be given to shooting after School this term, and our opportunities have been further curtailed by the shortening of the dinner hour. We have, however, an average number of members for the summer term, and the juniors are turning up well. The bullet catchers have been moved up to twenty yards, at which range all practice will take place until we have shot off in the Imperial Challenge Shield Competition. This year our teams, according to regulations, will consist of nine seniors and eight juniors, and it is hoped that they will add to the successes of previous years. We have no other matches arranged for this term at present, but we may arrange a match in July against Skinners' School (Tunbridge Wells) O.T.C., whom we easily accounted for at the end of last term.

C.R.G.S. v. SKINNERS' SCHOOL O.T.C.—April 1st.

C.R.G.S.		Skinners' School O.T.C.	
Watsham ma.	45	Wilkinson	44
Doubleday ma.	44	Jones	42
Doubleday mi.	44	Greenger	40
Graham-Brown	43	Smith	38
Eves	43	Philpott	35
Goldsmith mi.	42	Strange	32
Bare ma.	42	Armstrong	29
Chapman	41	Baker	22
	344		282

NOVEMBER 1913

Cadet Corps.

WE extend a hearty welcome to Mr. Bellward and the large number of recruits. The latter are under his special care and he is also taking a keen part in the formation of a lusty bugle-band. Congratulations to Pte. Dolamore on winning Mrs. Patrick Crosbie's Recruits' Cup; Pte. Halls was a good second. The Commanding Officer wishes to congratulate the Corps on its splendid behaviour in camp at Danbury. There was such abundance of goodwill allround and duties were performed with keenness and light hearts. The work of the N.C.O.'s, under the capable direction of Col.-Sergt. Everett, was great. The company of various old boys at camp was an infinite pleasure and next year we hope for a still larger number to join us. Sergt. Jarrard won the admiration of all hearts by his merry and sportsmanlike ways both at work and play. There are some absent faces we miss from our ranks—especially the ever-willing and witty "maître-chef," Corpl. Cudmore. The signallers and members of the band must work hard at their instruments outside their ordinary parade hours, if they wish to be thoroughly efficient. I wonder if there is any present or past member of Colchester Royal Grammar School who will be kind enough to present the Corps with a drum or bugle, or help us with a subscription towards the band? I should like to repeat my statement that the Corps is to teach boys smartness, discipline and self-reliance, and not merely to become efficient in the art of warfare.

E.B.D.

CADET CORPS' SECOND ANNUAL CAMP
(July 26th—August 6th, 1913).

BY kind permission of the owner, Col. A. H. F. Greville, the second annual camp of the School Cadet Corps, was, like its predecessor, held in the grounds of Danbury Park. On July 26th, an advance guard of six cadets, under Col.-Sergt. Everett, arrived at Chelmsford about 10 in the morning, proceeding thence to Danbury, to assist an army Sergt. and three men in preparing the camp. They were followed two days later by the main body, who arrived in two detachments, the one training to Chelmsford, and marching to Danbury, while the other cycled the whole distance. The latter party enjoyed the kind hospitality of Mrs. French of Ulting Hall, while their less fortunate comrades experienced the delights of their first dinner in camp.

Upon the arrival of the Southend Technical School Cadet Corps, the blankets, ground-sheets and buckets were served out to the various tents. Beyond this, nothing of importance was done that day.

The next morning, at 7.30, following a practice maintained throughout, the respective corps fell in for early morning drill. After breakfast the orderly officer went through the daily tent inspection, which was followed by the customary parade, previous to the military operations of the day.

The Commandant of the camp (Capt. Traill, East Lancs. Regt.), who usually arranged the day's programme, elected that the officers of each detachment should put their commands through the preliminaries of company drill. The officers of the camp had apparently decided that the cadets should be left to their own resources during the afternoons, and conforming to a practice followed throughout the camp, a voluntary bathing parade, at 4 o'clock, completed the official arrangements of the day.

On Wednesday morning before breakfast, Capt. Traill instructed the N.C.O.'s of both corps in the mysteries of outpost duty. After tent inspection, six cadets (four from Colchester, two from Southend), were sent out as scouts, whilst the main body marched to their allotted positions to form a line of outposts across the park. And the fact that none of the lines were pierced shows that the majority of the N.C.O.'s gained some profit from their early morning instruction.

Before breakfast on Thursday, several N.C.O.'s were taught the rudiments of section drill, the remaining operation of the day consisting of a general instruction in the most usual method of attack in modern warfare, an advance by rushes in sections. Meanwhile, a broiling sun beat down

upon the two corps, and by the time the welcome bugle blast announced the readiness of dinner, every cadet was in a condition which may be very aptly described as "done to a turn."

On Friday morning after breakfast, the camp fell in at 10.15 a.m. to be told by the Commandant that a large band of desperate smugglers, carrying a cargo of gin and lace were in the vicinity of the camp, and that in consequence he had received a message from the police, asking him, if possible, to capture them. In the action which followed, the smugglers—in this case Lieutenant Deakin and a party of the School corps—succeeded in eluding capture, and after a smart engagement, effected a masterly retreat at the expense of the aforementioned cargo.

On the following Tuesday, August 5th, the Commandant again addressed the assembled corps on the subject of smugglers. He informed his listeners that in the last engagement the smugglers had lost two famous ruffians, "Cut-throat" Bill and "Bossy-faced" Jack, and that to avenge their losses they had succeeded in imprisoning a party of police. The police, he continued, had managed to get a messenger through to the camp, imploring reinforcements of men and ammunition, and announcing the impossibility of holding out after 1 o'clock Tuesday. Accordingly the camp horse, Maria, was harnessed to its cart, and the Colchester Corps were entrusted with the duty of piercing the lines of the smugglers—in this case the Southend Corps—and carrying the much-needed ammunition borne by Maria to the assistance of the besieged. Lieutenant Deakin and the Colr.-Sergeant took attacking parties to both wings and by thus drawing the opposing forces away from the centre, Maria was safely carried through by a party under Sergt. Jarrard and Ex-Colr.-Sergt.-Instructor Penn.

In both these engagements, as in every other, the School showed itself fully equal and in many cases superior to the Southend Corps in field work, while in drill, the less important part of military knowledge, the Southend Corps in some cases had the better of us.

On Saturday, August 2nd, the two corps marched to a scout camp near by and formed a line of pickets across a given district, to prevent any scouts from piercing our lines, with the object of getting through with a message. A truce was made at dinner time, when the joint party of scouts and cadets told off to cook the dinner, carried "dixies" full of delicious stew and potatoes to the various pickets who enjoyed their mid-day meal at their allotted posts.

On the Sunday preceeding Bank Holiday Monday, cadets and officers marched through Danbury to a church parade at the village church, their "step" en route to and from the service being specially commended.

On the Monday, the cyclists of the camp were told off for despatch riding, while the remainder were marched off for another engagement with the scouts.

During the afternoon the cadets were allowed entrance to Danbury Fête gratis, and during the fun and races which followed, Sergt. Clarke (Southend) and Colr.-Sergt. Everett succeeded in obtaining a prize each, while Sergt. Jarrard shewed his prowess by winning places in three or four events, including the donkey race.

Several night attacks were experienced during the camp and on those occasions the guard for the night—supplied by

the two corps alternately—quickly roused the sleeping cadets
to beat off the enemy.   The enemy, needless to add, were
always beaten off and upon the "cease fire" from the
orderly bugler, the weirdly clad one—for in night attacks, as
someone has wisely said, the clothing thereof savours
somewhat of a fancy dress ball—were dismissed and allowed
to continue their much deserved rest.

This account would not be complete without a reference to
a sing-song which took place one night during camp.   Mr.
Peart, the School Musical Society's most popular conductor,
visited the camp for a few days, and during that time he
shewed his usual energy by playing a large part in the
arrangement of the above-mentioned sing-song.   A large
room—containing a venerable piano, born B.C. 58—in the
famous "Griffin" inn was engaged, and Captain Traill
presiding, the items supplied by the officers and cadets of
both corps, together with several "Gaudies en masse," made
a most enjoyable, if rather noisy, evening.

On Tuesday evening, the last night of camp, some cadets
were seen—with some alarm—to be stealthily surrounding
the Commandant as he stood outside his tent.   But all was
well; and after giving him a rousing " He's a jolly good
fellow " and three equally rousing cheers the cadets dispersed
to their tents.

On the following morning camp was struck, everybody
agreeing, as they rapidly packed tents and utensils, that glad
as they might be to get back home once more, never had they
enjoyed a jollier a time under canvas.

THE CAMP DAILY ROUTINE.

Réveillé	6.30 a.m.
Coffee and biscuits ...	7.0 ,,
Parade	7.30 ,, till breakfast
Breakfast	8.30 ,,
Tent Inspection ..	9.30 ,,
General Assembly prior to day's manœuvres ...	10.15 ,,
Dinner	1.0 p.m.
Bathing Parade ...	4.0 ,,
Tea	5.0 ,,
Porridge	8.0 ,,
First Post	9.0 ,,
Last Post	9.15 ,,
Lights out	9.30 ,,

Shooting.

THE outstanding feature of our shooting last term was the splendid results obtained by our teams in the Imperial Challenge Shield Competition, open to all Boys' Clubs throughout the Empire.

The seniors came out ninth on the list with the high average of 85.33, whilst the juniors were placed 26th with an average of 72·75. The number of entries for the former was 419 and for the latter 323. In the competition for next year aperture backsights are to be allowed, and for this reason new B.S.A. Orthoptics have been fitted to the three Converted Martinis, purchased with the prize-money gained by the teams in this year's competition.

The first term's competition for the Worthington Evans' House Challenge Cup was shot off in July, and Dugards (the holders) gained a substantial lead It is during the Michaelmas Term that most time can be devoted to the range, but at present the number of members scarcely reaches expectation, and it is hoped that a larger number will take part in this excellent pastime during the next half of term.

We have an average number in the open and under 15 classes, but are poorly represented in the class for those under 16.

Once more we have to express our best thahks to C.-S.-I. Penn for his great interest in developing the shooting.

The results of competitions, etc., are given below.

House Competitition for Worthington Evans' Cup:—Dugards.

S.M.R.C. Silver Medal for Highest Average in House Matches :—Doubleday, mi. and Chapman tied. Doubleday won on re-shoot.

S.M.R.C. Bronze Medal for Highest Average in Cup Matches :—Watsham, ma.

N.R.A. Bronze Medal for Rapid Firing :—Doubleday, ma.

Lord Roberts' Spoons for Highest Average in Practice Shoots :—
Open—Doubleday, ma., 57·8.
Under 16—Chapman, 60·9.
Under 15—Wagstaff, ma., 51·5.

HOUSE COMPETITION.—July, 1913.

DUGARD'S		SCHOOL HOUSE		PARR'S		HARSNETT'S		
Chapman	63	Wagstaff ma.	59	Watsham ma.	59	Deane ...	...	52
Hudson	58	Goldsmith mi.	58	Triscott ...	59	Atkin ...	...	51
Doubleday ma.	56	Coquerel ...	45	Andrews ...	54	Everett ma.	...	49
Eves ...	54	Jones ...	43	Cudmore ...	48	Royce ...	...	40
Doubleday mi.	52	Rayner ...	43	Watsham mi.	40	Clark ma.	...	37
Flanegan	48	Goldsmith ma.	41	Brand ..	37	Smith mi.	...	32
Oates ...	37	French ...	40	Wagstaff mi.	30	Chambers	...	26
Horwood ...	33	Wenden ...	28	French ma. ...	25	King ma.	...	15
	401		357		352			302

I.C.S. COMPETITION.—Seniors.

			Deliberate.		Rapid.		Total.
Doubleday ma.	...	...	48	...	49	...	97
Chapman	...	...	48	...	48	...	96
Watsham ma.	...	...	46	...	46	...	92
Doubleday mi.	...	...	46	...	45	...	91
Hudson	...	...	43	...	47	...	90
Cudmore	...	...	40	...	38	...	78
Everett ma.	...	...	44	...	31	...	75
Eves ...	...	...	38	...	37	...	75
Goldsmith ma.	...	...	34	...	40	...	74
			387		381		768

			JUNIORS.			Average	85.33
			Deliberate.		Figure.		Total.
French max. ...	...	...	42	...	45	...	87
Goldsmith mi.	...	...	45	...	39	...	84
Wagstaff mi. ...	...	...	39	...	43	...	82
Wenden ...	...	...	36	...	41	...	77
Andrews ...	...	...	30	...	43	...	73
Watsham mi. ...	...	...	33	...	34	...	67
Pertwee ...	...	...	36	..	27	...	63
Dicker... ...	...	...	29	...	20	...	49
							582
						Average	72.75

Rifle Club.

SINCE last writing these notes the club has entered the "B" Division of the North Essex Rifle Club League, but it cannot be said that we have done as well as we expected up to the present, for out of four matches we have only won one. Our average to date is 543 per match out of a possible 600, giving an average of 90.5 per man. The remaining four matches are with the weaker members of the League and we hope to be successful in all of these, so that our position in the final table should be somewhere near the middle.

We are sorry to lose Doubleday, ma., as he has been one of our most successful shots, and on his departure had the highest average of our members in the above League.

Nine members have at present been tried for the six places in the team, and others are making such good progress that competition for the last two places will probably be very keen in the future.

The second round of the House Competition was shot off the week before the end of the Michaelmas Term, when Dugards succeeded in increasing their lead. It is pleasing to

Cadet Corps.

OUR notes for this issue are somewhat short but it must not be thought that the work of the Corps has in any way slackened. The second half of the Xmas term and the first half of the Lent term comprise our winter period of training, a period in which very little outdoor and field-day work can be done. We now commence a progressive system of training in preparation for the Annual Camp of July next, and Cadets, especially N.C.O.'s, must do all they can to make themselves thoroughly smart and efficient. Wednesday for parade is a distinct improvement, and we are glad to see our invaluable Col.-Sgt.-Instr. Penn again on parade with us.

Our numbers are steadily increasing; we welcome the Lent Term recruits, but alas! there are a large number of strong healthy boys in the School whom we should like to see in our ranks. What splendid service C.R.G.S. might do if every boy would make up his mind to join either the Scouts or the Cadet Corps.

Mr. Bellward, now gazetted to a commission in the 5th Essex Regt., has very kindly presented the Corps with a new side drum and we are very grateful. Mrs. Patrick Crosbie and Mr. Coats Hutton have sent a guinea each towards our Band Fund, and a beautiful cup has been presented by Miss Lovell. The Corps heartily thanks these donors for their kind interest in our work. The Cup will be given for the best shooting at Middlewick this year.

The Band has suffered a great loss in the person of Sgt. Wagstaff, but with much keenness on the part of its present members, it bids fair to eclipse all previous form.

THE CADET CORPS.

Is affiliated to the 5th Essex Territorials, and is officered by Masters and Prefects. It sends a Shooting Eight to compete at Bisley for the Ashburton Shield.

Young Cadet as pictured in the 1912 CRGS Prospectus

In the Autumn 1914, a Volunteer Force was established for boys and men too young or too old to train as an emergency force in case of an invasion. It eventually became known as the Volunteer Corps and was organised by the War Office. Individual firms organised their own units. Paxman's engineering works borrowed the rifles of the School's Cadet Corps until the firm made its own arrangements.

BAB "Dick" Barton, OC

WAR
THE COLCESTRIAN
1914 - 1918

No. 39.]   JULY, 1914.

NEW SERIES.

The Colcestrian.

EDITED BY PAST AND PRESENT MEMBERS OF COLCHESTER SCHOOL.

PRICE SIXPENCE

Colchester:

PRINTED BY CULLINGFORD & CO.,

156 HIGH STREET.

71

O.C.S. Officers for 1913=14.

President:
C. E. BENHAM, Wellesley Road, Colchester.

Vice-Presidents:

W. GURNEY BENHAM, J.P.
R. FRANKLIN
H. L. GRIFFIN

H. J. HARRIS, B.A.
B. H. KENT
OSMOND G. ORPEN

J. C. SHENSTONE, F.L.S.
R. W. WALLACE
C. E. WHITE

Committee:

I. D. BROOK
J. H. NUNN
A. W. NUNN
F. G. MILLS

C. GRIFFIN
G. T. WRIGHT
H. H. HOLLAWAY
A. T. DALDY

G. C. BENHAM
E. W. DACE
J. C. SALMON
W. H. KING (*Chairman*)

The Ex-Presidents are ex-officio members of Committee.

Hon. Treasurer:
T. S. RENTON, 12 Crouch Street, Colchester.

Hon. Secretaries:
A. O. FARMER, 12 Queen Street, Colchester.
F. D. BARKER. (acting) Royal Grammar School.
Rev. E. HARTLEY PARKER, Thorington Parsonage, Colchester.

Members of the O.C.S.

ACLAND, C. S., Lexden House, West Winch, nr. Kings Lynn. [Park, N.
ADAMS, E. A., 22 Gloucester Road, Finsbury
ALLISTON, A. W., Chipping Hill, Witham.
APPLEBY, W. M.
BAILEY, C.
BARNES, F. M., Howell Hall, Heckington, Lincolnshire.
BARNES, ALAN, 171 Maldon Road, Colchester.
BARKER, F. D., Royal Grammar School (Hon. Sec). [Naze.
BARKER, C. F. J., Marine Hotel, Walton-on-
BARKER, CHARLES, Burtoll Tea Estate, Dewan P.O., Cachar, India.
BAWTREE, E. E., 71 High Street, Colchester.
BAXTER, H. G., Fronks Road, Dovercourt.
BAYLISS, S. F.
BAYLISS, R. V. J., Fleece Hotel, Head Street, Colchester.
BAYLISS, B., Fleece Hotel, Head Street, Colchester.
BEARD, E. C., St. Margaret's, Cambridge Road, Colchester.
BECKETT, H., Balkerne Lane, Colchester.
BELLWARD, G. W. F., O.R.G.S.
BENHAM, C. E., Wellesley Road, Colchester. (President).
BENHAM, G. C., Bank Chambers, High Street, Colchester.
BENHAM, Alderman W. GURNEY, St. Mary's Terrace, Lexden road, Colchester.
BLATCH, F., c/o, S. E. Blau, La Paz, Bolivia, S. America.
BLAXILL, G. A., 50 Parliament Hill, Hampstead, N.W.
BLOMFIELD, S., Raonah House, New Town Road, Colchester.
BLOOMFIELD, H. D., 3 Tyler Street, Parkeston.
BLOMFIELD, T.
BLYTH, COOPER, c.o. Isaac Bunting, 100 Yokahama, Japan.
BOGGIS, FRANK, Station Road, Sudbury.
BROMLEY, J. G., Mill House, Great Clacton.
BROOK, T. D., "St. Runwald's," Maldon Road, Colchester.
BROOK, A. T., "St. Runwald's," Maldon Road, Colchester.
BROOK, L. C., "St. Runwald's," Maldon Road, Colchester.
BROOK, S. V., 22 Sugden Road, Lavender Hill, S. W.
BROWN, D. GRAHAM, "Lownd," Witham.

BULTITUDE, R. G., 32 Hanover Road, Canterbury.
BURRELL, F. B., Abbeygate Street, Colchester
BUNTING, A. E., The Nurseries, North Station Road, Colchester.
BURBIDGE, T.
BURGESS, H. G.
BURLEIGH, A., Kudat, N.L.B.T. Co., British North Borneo.
BURSTON, F. G., 57 High Street, Colchester.
BUTCHER, H., Crouch Street, Colchester.
BUTLER, F. H., Cumberland House, Manning-tree.
CANT, Walter, West House Farm, Lexden, Colchester.
CARTER, F. B., O.R.G.S.
CHAMBERS, C., 22 Wellesley Road, Colchester.
CHAMBERS, S. C., 22 Wellesley Road, Colchester.
CHAPLIN, F. S., 5 Verulam Buildings, Grays Inn, W.C.
CHESHIRE, G., 23 Argyle Street, Oxford Street, W.
CHESHIRE, W., 1 Meyrick Crescent, Colchester
CHEESE, C. T., 39 Pownall Crescent, Colchester and St. Austell, Cornwall.
CLAMP, A. J., 122 Priory Street, Colchester.
CLARKE, S. F., Parr's Bank, Holloway, London, N.
CLOVER, J. M., The Hall, Dedham.
COBBOLD, H. F. S.
CULF, C. L. L., General Post Office (Staff), Cambridge.
COLE, H. S., 25 Wimpole Road, Colchester.
COLLINGS, C. E., Capital & Counties Bank, Baldock, Herts.
COLLISON, A. L., Garrison School, Buena Vista, Gibraltar.
CORK, F. F., 38 Trouville Road, Clapham Park, S.W.
CRAGG, Rev. E. E., St. John's Church, Huntington, Long Island, U.S.A.
CULLINGTON, M. W., 53 Oakhill Road, Putney, S.W.
DACE, A. W., 122 George Street, Edinburgh.
DACE, E. W., 17 Honywood Road, Colchester.
DALDY, A. T., 50 South Street, Colchester.
DAVIES, W. E., 118 Butt Road, Colchester.
DAVIES, E. G.
D'EATH, C. V., The Ferns, Southwood Road, Ramsgate.

Continued on Page 3 of Cover.

The Colcestrian.

VITÆ CORONA FIDES.

No. 39.]　　　　JULY, 1914.　　　　[NEW SERIES.

Editorial.

THE Summer Term is always the most pleasureable in the
School Year. The evenings are light, and afford
opportunity for cricket after school, and long games on half-
holidays; the weather, though perhaps for the first few
weeks incapable of making up its mind, is on the whole
warm, dry and pleasant ; and the shadow cast before by the
Locals that darkens the end of the Term is lightened by the
healthier and more airy surroundings that accompany it;
steam-heated classrooms and artificial light are entirely
dispensed with.

It is the great outdoor term. The Cadet Corps performs
its evolutions, and fights its mimic battles in the open. The
Scouts patrol the neighbourhood. Field days are arranged
for both. The Athletic Sports Meeting is held, perhaps the
most popular event in the year. And by luck—or exceeding
virtue—it has never since its re-incarnation been marred by a
wet day.

And now another bright star is to be added to the already
brilliant constellation of open-air events. On Thursday, July
9th, the Anniversary of the Opening of the new Big School is to
be celebrated by a Café Concert, held in the beautiful garden
adjoining the Headmaster's house, the proceeds of which will
be devoted to the Cadet Corps Fund. Light refreshments
will be served, and, in addition to solos and recitations by
amateur artistes who have already won their laurels at C.R.
G.S., promise is made of Morris Dances, an entirely new
feature, while Mr. Geo. O'Hagan will make humourous contributions to the Programme, and Mr. F. B. Carter will shine
in an Original Sketch, entitled "The De Vere."

There can be no doubt as to the response, and it is much
to be hoped that this will only prove to be the first of a long
series of such entertainments. The Musical and Dramatic
Society has hitherto remained dumb during the best term of
the year. It is exceedingly gratifying to find that this
reproach is at last to be wiped away.

THE EDITOR.

73

Valete.

F. J. EVES, VI. K.P. (Dugard's), 1st and House Cricket, Football,
Shooting, Cadet Sergeant.
J. M. CLOVER, Mod. V., Q.P. (School House), 2nd Football, House
Cricket, Football, Shooting Cadet Lance-Corporal.
W. B. FLETCHER, Mod. V. (Harsnett's).
A. B. WENLOCK, Mod. V. (Dugard's), House Hockey, Cadet Private.
A. BARNES, VB. (School House), House Cricket.
P. DALTON, VB. (Dugard's).
C. E. FRENCH, IVB. (School House), Cadet Private.
H. G. HYDER, IVB. (Dugard's).
A. C. ERROL, IVA. (Parr's).
H. FOLKARD, Mod. IV. (School House).
A. S. HYDER, 2nd (Dugard's).
D. WEATHERALL, 2nd (Parr's).
T. HORDERN, 3rd (Harsnett's).
A. J. V. Ramage, 3rd (School House).
U. C. MASON. 3rd (Harsnett's).

Salvete.

Lecœuvre	..	..	..	IVA. School House
Butler, mi.	..	..	..	IVA. School House
Graham Brown	..	..	..	III. School House
Beckett, ma.	..	..	..	III. Dugard's
Hackett	..	..	..	II. Parr's
Sainty	..	..	..	I. School House
Downing	..	..	..	I. School House
Horwood	..	..	..	II. Dugard's
R. Gell	..	..	..	Pre.
F. Gell	..	..	..	,,
N. Tait	..	..	..	,,
J. White	..	..	..	,,
E. Field	..	..	..	,,
D. Short	..	..	..	,,
C. Heasman	..	..	..	,,

Grammaria.

A Menagerie.

Gilberd House garden is gradually assuming the aspect of
a wild beast show. Dens and cages contain rabbits and
guinea pigs, snakes and mice, who really seem very cheerful
in the circumstances; while others, whose purpose remains
for the present obscure, are in course of construction. It is
rumoured that a special sty has been reserved for Piggy, but
our one and only Coquerel left a term too soon to be included
in the collection.

But a Compensation.

On the other side of the enclosure the Pre has—literally—
blossomed out afresh. The border has been divided into a
series of neat beds for the members of that exceedingly

flourishing institution, where they may be seen toiling early and late at their primæval occupation of gardening. They are planting pansies and geraniums, and various things with names longer than themselves. They water the flowers and seeds, and incidentally one another's legs. They sow seeds and dig them up again to learn how they are growing. They hoe up the weeds, and the choicest specimens of plants. They cover the beds, and likewise their hands and faces and clothes, with fertilizing compost. In fact, they are behaving in just that happy, healthy way that small boys should in such a place. Why, we ourselves recollect—but no! this is no place for confessions. Let the dead follies of childhood bury their dead, and see that they keep decently interred.

Not only Blossom but Shoot.

Perhaps, since shoots normally precede blossoms, this new departure may be due to the fact that last term the Pre inaugurated a Rifle Corps which practises very assiduously with an air gun in the range, and considerable proficiency is displayed. The other afternoon, on the conclusion of the shoot, several of the targets showed signs of perforation by a slug, at a range of no less than ten yards.

Further Evidence.

Another piece of evidence leading to the same conclusion is the fact that in the range itself are found some fine samples of wheats and beans grown in specially treated soils, for the benefit of those who are taking up Agricultural Chemistry. We may look for some startling innovations in the methods of Tendring, and Lexden and Winstree farming in the near future; for, despite all proverbs, the eggs that the new generation contends with are widely different from those which their grandmothers painfully acquired the art of sucking, and the dear old ladies may yet find that under the new conditions something is still lacking in their own theory and practice of suction, a something that their grandchildren are now mastering.

Congratulations.

Another name has been added to the lengthening roll of those who have received appointments as Headmaster while on the staff of the School. The Headmaster of the Lower School, the Rev. E. Hartley Parker, has accepted the Headmastership of the London Orphan School, Watford, a school of 200 boys. He has been connected with C.R.G.S. for now over eleven years, and it would be idle to say that his absence will not be sorely felt and deeply regretted; but all the same he will take our sincerest good wishes with him to his new sphere. May the best of good luck and prosperity be his

Another Misfortune.

Congratulations are also due to Mr. Oldham, who is also leaving at the end of the Term. He has accepted a Senior Mastership at King's College School, Cambridge, and takes up his duties in September. No one can be unaware of all the School owes him as Games Master, but again we must mingle our regrets with good wishes. Good luck to him, too !

An Echo of the Scott Expedition.

It will be remembered that before Captain Scott started on his last ill-fated Expedition to the South Pole, the School contributed an Eskimo dog named Hal, to be kept here as a pet on his return, if still surviving. The tragic events which marked its closing scenes, culminating in the death of the leader himself are still fresh in our minds. It was found impossible to fulfil the orginal promise, but a large photograph of Captain Scott in full Antarctic kit has been presented to the School by the Committee as a memento of the dead hero, and an acknowledgement of the part—albeit a tiny one —played by C.R.G.S. in equipping the expedition. It now hangs in Big School, a reminder, an example, and an incitement to us all.

More Room !

So great has been the strain on the existing accommodation for cycles, that it has been found necessary to erect a new cycle shed in the Junior close, for the benefit of the Lower School. Standing room is provided for 25 mounts, and already shows signs of being shortly inadequate to the growing needs of the "Grammar Bikes."

Misguided and Misguiding.

Our noble ship is still in a petulant mood. After remaining for some months as though glued to the S.W., it swung round one night to the N. and there stays obstinately fixed. These vagaries are exceedingly trying to our budding meteorologists in their endeavours to keep a weather record which may be considered reliable. Of course it may have dropped anchors fore and aft, or perhaps— horrible thought— it may have run aground. Some of our naval experts from the Colne ports ought to diagnose the case and suggest a remedy.

Byways of Knowledge.

" John Churchill, Duke of Marlborough was the second son of Sir Winston Churchill. He had a regiment of dragoons presented to him, and married to Sarah Jennings. She persuaded Anne to promote her husband and help him to cover up his bad places.".

"Lord Nelson, *alias* Arthur Wellesley, was an Admiral of the British Fleet. He distinguished himself at the battle of Quiberon Bay.

"William Rufus was shot by Wat Tyler in mistake for a stag."

Prose or Worse.

The following lines, apparently a fragment of a hitherto unpublished Latin poem by an unknown author may perhaps be of interest to our Cambridge Local Boys.

" *Quid omnibus museum ? sanitas, archipelago
Oxo. Nunc dimittis rhododendron transit,
Nux vomica malaria manifesto hiatus.*"

Italian is not such a common acquirement, but the following couplet may appeal to those so fortunate as to understand it.

" *Cavalleria rusticana spaghetti cinquevalli
Andante ma non troppo i pagliacci.*"

Applied Mechanics.

To appease the envy and jealousy of our Mathematical friends, and that they may not feel left out in the cold, we present them with the following :—

MOTOR PROBLEM.

Let U be the driver of a motor-car and V the velocity of the car.

If a sufficiently high value be given to V it will ultimately reach P.C.

V then will instantly $= 0$

For low values of V, P.C. may be neglected, but, if V be high, it will be usually best to square P.C. after which V will again assume a positive value. For by a well-known theorem

$$P.C. + L.S.D. = (P.C.)^2$$

If the value of L.S.D. be made sufficiently large P C. will vanish and V may be extended indefinitely.

But if the difference between P.C. and V be very great, J.P. may be substituted for P.C., in which case the problem becomes very difficult of solution, for no value of L.S.D. has yet been found to effect the elimination of J.P. $(J.P.)^2$ is, in fact, an impossible quantity.

A Pizz-o-cato Note.

Mr. Enrico Pizzo, whom the seniors will recollect as Foreign Language Master a few years back, has been appointed Lecturer in German to Padua University, Italy.

The Athletic Sports.

IN the presence of the Mayor (Alderman Wilson Marriage) and a large number of parents and friends, our Tenth Annual Athletic Meeting was held on Park Road ground on Thursday afternoon, June 4th. The events were keenly contested, and the majority of the races provided very close finishes. The feature was. the success which attended the efforts of Everett ma., who, in addition to winning outright the Old Colcestrians' Challenge Cup offered in the mile race (he having won this race three years in succession), also won the quarter-mile and the long jump, and finished second in the half-mile and third in the open 100 yards, which was won by Town, who, with Brand and Lord, proved to be a successful competitor. Everett also captained the winning tug-of-war team. The entries were good, and large fields turned out for each · event, with the exception of the hurdles: in the sack race no less than sixty-three boys faced the starter. The band of the 1st Rifle Brigade was in attendance, and under the skilled ·direction of Mr. Charles H. Barry, rendered a programme of pleasing selections, including a very taking Saltarello, the composition of Mr. F. B. Carter, C.R.G.S.

A host of officials included Messrs. Paul Aggio, B. H. Kent, and G. E. Moore, judges; E. Reeve, E. B. Deakin, and G. W. Bellward, timekeepers; and Sergt.-Major.-Instr. J. Penn, starter; backed up by a strong committee, presided over by the Headmaster (Mr. P. Shaw Jeffrey). The Rev. E. Hartley Parker again filled the position of hon. secretary and treasurer, and carried out the arduous duties very efficiently.

The prizes were presented to the winners by Mrs. Patrick Crosbie. In introducing that lady, Mr. Shaw Jeffrey said that the meeting was rather a special one, for two reasons. One was that the Rev. Hartley Parker was leaving them, and the other that it was that gentleman's tenth annual sports. During those ten years Mr. Parker had collected more than £400 from the residents of Colchester in prizes for these sports, and that he thought was a great triumph. (Hear, hear.) What was a greater triumph, however, was the skill and the organisation with which Mr. Parker had carried out the sports year after year. (Applause.) Looking back over the whole of the ten years he could not remember a single hitch having occurred. He was sure all would join with him in congratulating Mr. Parker on the successful result of his efforts. (Applause.) The sports were remarkable for one thing, and that was that every boy in the school had entered into them. He would like to take that opportunity of asking those present to' join with him in wishing Mr. Parker every success in his work at his new school. (Applause.)

: Mrs. Crosbie, who had previously been presented with a beautiful bouquet by Everett, ma., then handed the prizes to the winners, and when presenting the. Old Colcestrians'. Challenge Cup to Everett Mr. C. E. Benham stepped forward and announced that he would make himself responsible for the cup to be presented in connection with the next year's mile race, this remark being greeted with applause.

.The distribution over, Mr. Shaw Jeffrey asked Mrs. Crosbie to hand to the Rev. Hartley Parker a silver tankard.

This ceremony having been performed, the Mayor proposed a hearty vote of thanks to Mrs. Crosbie, and spoke of the interest that lady took in the proceedings at the School. He congratulated the Head Master and all the authorities on the success of the day's sport, and went on to say that there had been a record attendance, record entries and a record value in the prizes. With reference to the latter, he had been having a chat with Captain Smythies, R.N., whom he believed to be the oldest boy of the school present and the oldest boy resident in the town, and he had told him (the Mayor) that there were no such prizes given in his days as those presented that day. When they had a jollification in those days it was on the 5th of November—(laughter)—when they went through the town and collected faggots with which they had a bonfire. (Renewed laughter.) There was a great contrast between those days and the present time, and he was sure they would all congratulate the Head Master and Mrs. Shaw Jeffrey on the success that attended their efforts in improving the education in the borough. This was a great pride to the Governors of the school. The only matter that gave them cause for regret was the leaving of the Rev. Hartley Parker. His going would be a great loss to the school and a great loss to sport. (Applause) —Mr. C. E. Benham seconded the vote, and remarked that as President of the Old Colcestrians' Society he would like to mention that that Society took a great interest and pride in the developements of the school. The members of the Society would greatly miss their good friend Mr. Hartley Parker, and he had sympathy for the man who was to follow.

At the close of the proceedings cheers were given for Mrs. Crosbie, the Mayor, Mr. and Mrs. Hartley Parker, and Mr. and Mrs. Shaw Jeffrey.

Appended are the results, with details : —

100 Yards (open), Assistant Masters' Challenge Cup—1 Town, 2 Hudson, 3 Everett ma.. Time, 11 2-5th secs. Won by inches ; close third.

200 Yards (under 11), Dr. and Mrs. Hickinbotham's Cup—1 Nash, 2 Gower mi., 3 Holloway. Time, 32 2-5th secs.

100 Yards (under 15), Assistant Masters' Challenge Cup and Mr. G. Chamber's Cup—1 Lord, 2 Goldsmith, 3 Brook Time, 11 3-5th secs. Won by five yards ; good third.

200 Yards Handicap (under 11).—1 Tait, 2 Child, 3 Downing. Time, 31 4-5th secs. Won easily.

100 Yards (under 14).—Mr. Hetherington's Challenge Cup and Mr. W. Chamber's Cup—1 Brook, 2 Thomas, 3 Hobrough. Time, 13 2-5th secs. A keenly-contested race, ending in a win by inches only ; good third.

Quarter-Mile (open). Lord Cowdray's Cup—1 Everett ma., 2 Brand, 3 Hudson. Time, 60 secs. Everett led all the way and won by four yards ; three yards between second and third.

100 Yards (under 13), Mr. Heasman's prize.—1 Thomas, 2 Cox, 3 Everett mi. Time, 14 secs. Won by five yards ; close third.

Slow Bicycle Race.—1 Pullen, 2 Atkin, 3 King.

300 Yards (under 14). Challenge Cup. 1 Thomas, 2 Brook, 3 Wilson. Time, 46 1-5th secs. Thomas ran well, and taking the lead throughout, won a good race by eight yards ; good third.

120 Yards Hurdles (open), Rev. Hartley Parker's Challenge Cup and Mr. Dicker's Cup.—1 Town, 2 Brand, 3 Pullen. Time, 19 2-5th secs. There were only three competitors, but they cleared the obstacles well, especially Town, who won by five yards.

Quarter-mile (junior), Mrs. Hetherington's Challenge Cup.—1 Lord, 2 Goldsmith, 3 Alderton. Time, 68 secs. Lord and Goldsmith kept well together until nearing home, when the former drew away and won by two yards ; bad third.

220 Yards Handicap (under 13).—1 Child, 2 Nash, 3 Mirrington. Time, 33 2-5th secs. Child received a good handicap and never lost the lead, winning by two yards ; close third.

One Mile (open), Old Colcestrians' Challenge Cup and the Mayor's Cup.—1 Everett ma., 2 Town, 3 Brand, 4 Hudson. Time, 5 mins. 10 1-5th secs. This event was decided previously to Thursday. The cup is now the property of Everett, who has won it three years in succession.

Scouts' Race.—1 Brooks, 2 Wilson, 3 Everett mi. and, Child (dead heat). Time, 33 3-5th secs. Brooks won easily ; good third.

Preparatory School Race, 200 yards (handicap).—1 Tait, 2 Baker, 3 Knight. The winner ran well, but was nearly overtaken by Baker at the finish.

Sack Race.—1 Baskett, 2 Beckett, 3 Watsham.

Old Boys' Race (handicap), 1st prize presented by Messrs. Williams and Co.—1 H. L. Griffin, 2 C. E. Benham, 3 A. O. Farmer. A close finish, three yards covering the first three.

Half-mile (open), Mr. W. W. Hewitt's Challenge Bowl and the Rev. and Mrs. Hartley Parker's prize.—1 Brand, 2 Everett, 3 Hudson. Time, 2 mins. 19 1-5th secs. Everett led for the greater part of the distance, but within 50 yards of the tape he was passed by Brand, who, running strongly, won by three yards ; good third.

120 Yards Hurdles (juniors), Mrs. Hetherington's Challenge Cup and Miss A. O. Aggio's prize.—1 Lord, 2 Goldsmith, 3 Cotterill mi. Time, 20 secs. This proved to be one of the keenest races of the afternoon, Lord winning on the tape.

Bicycle Musical Chairs.—1 Atkins, 2 Baskett, 3 Pullen.

220 Yards (under 12).—1 Holloway, 2 Barnes m., 3 Cunningham. Time, 32 1-5th secs. Holloway early took the lead, and was never passed. Won by two yards ; good third.

Band Race.—1 Hawker (trombone), 2 Devonport (trombone), 3 Nicholson. The competitors caused much amusement, and their hilarious efforts to produce music from their instruments evoked much laughter.

Tug-of-War (House eights), Mrs. Worthington Evans' Challenge Cup. —Harsnett's beat Parr's by two pulls to nil, and Dugard's beat School House by the same margin. In the final Harsnett's beat Dugard's by two clear pulls. The winning team comprised : Everett ma. (capt.), Deane, Oliver, Nicholson ma., Clark ma., King ma., White and Bare.

600 Yards (handicap), Mr. C. E. Benham's Cup.— 1 Town (scratch), 2 King ma. (12 yards), 3 Gilbert (45 yards). The scratch man ran strongly, and quickly overhauled his numerous opponents.

Handicap Race, for brothers of boys at the School and sons of visitors (under 12).—1 Medcalfe, 2 Wilson, 3 Slater.

Relay Race, House Fours (running, walking, hopping and crawling), Colonel Howlett Young's Challenge Trophy.—1 Harsnett's, 2 Dugard's, 3 Parr's

Consolation Race.—1 Horwood.

High Jump (senior).—1 Pullen, 2 Brand, 3 Deane. Height, 4ft. 6¼in.

High Jump (junior).—1 Lord, 2 Goldsmith, 3 Cotterill mi. Height, 4ft. 7in.

Long Jump (senior), Miss Aggio's prize.—1 Everett mi., 2 Brand, 3 Hudson. Distance, 16ft. 10in.

Long Jump (junior).—1 Lord, 2 Goldsmith, 3 Brook, 4 Wenden. Distance, 17ft. 4½in.

Throwing the Cricket Ball (senior). Colonel Merriman's prize.—1 Town, 2 Brand, 3 Oliver. Distance 74 yards, 2ft. 5in.

Throwing the Cricket Ball (junior).—1 Goldsmith, 2 Lord, 3 Carey, 4 Wenden. Distance, 68 yards, 2ft.

The Victor Ludorum Challenge Medal, presented by Colonel Howlett Young, was won by Everett ma., who scored 27 points. Mr. Worthington Evans' Cup was presented to Victor Ludorum and the " best second " medal, awarded to the second to Victor Ludorum, was won by Brand, who credited himself with 19 points. Lord won the Junior Ludorum Medal, with 40 points to his credit. Goldsmith being second with 32 points. The Cock-House Challenge Shield, presented by Mr. and Mrs. Shaw Jeffrey, was taken by Parr's, whose representatives scored 89 points. Harsnett's was second with 68 points.

Hockey.

The Hockey season was brought to a somewhat uninteresting close at the end of last Term, owing to the enormous amount of rain during the second half of March. As the ground was almost continuously under water, play was impossible, and the matches with Frinton, Chelmsford G.S., and Mr. J. D. Ward's XI. had, perforce, to be abandoned.

The first game, with Mr. Ward's O.C. XI., on March 7th was one of the pleasantest of the season. The School played very well and won by 4 goals to 2, after being 2 goals down in the first-half. The team was:—Horwood; Mr. Reeve and Town; Eves, Mr. Deakin and Everitt, ma.; Malyn, Mr. Barker, Mr. Oldham, Goldsmith, and Hudson. The scorers for the School were: Oldham 2, Malyn 1, Goldsmith 1.

On March 12th, against the East Lancs. Regt., the School suffered a rather heavy defeat by 9 goals to 1, but lacked the services of Mr. Reeve and Malyn.

This was succeeded on March 28th, by an unexpected reverse, at the hands of Harwich, at Park Road ; the margin being 8 goals to 1. And as Ipswich Town 2nd failed to raise a team on April 4th this match formed the somewhat unglorious conclusion of the season.

The final analysis of wins and losses was:—

Played	Won	Lost	Drawn	Abandoned
9	4	5	0	4

On the whole the form of the eleven was rather uneven, and the combination among the forwards left a great deal to be desired. Hudson on the left wing was good, but too individual ; while Malyn on the right often over-ran the ball, and centred too near the goal-mouth. The inside men were a little slow. The halves generally were weak, though Brand and Eves showed good form for a first season. Town at back was the most successful member of the team, he played strongly and consistently, often doing the work of three men. Everett was more successful at half than at full-back, his clearances being weak. Horwood did very well in goal, and cheerfully took many hard knocks.

The following were awarded " colours ":—Malyn, Everett, ma., Town, Goldsmith, Hudson, Horwood, Brand, Eves, Lord, Flanegan, Nicholson, ma.

HOUSE MATCHES.

PARR'S v. SCHOOLHOUSE.

The first meeting at Hockey between the two Houses produced an even and interesting game. The two teams were well matched and the smaller members on each side gave a good account of themselves. Parr's attacked and forced several corners which were, however, repulsed by Clover and Rayner at back and Cottrell, mi., in goal. The

Parr's forwards continued to show good combination, and from a pass by Collinge, mi., Brand scored the first goal. Schoolhouse made several determined rushes on the Parr's goal, led by Malyn and Goldsmith, which gave the defenders plenty of work. Lord was playing an ideal centre-half game, marking his opponent and feeding his forward line with good passes. Half-time was at hand when Town dribbled brilliantly from his own circle to that of Schoolhouse and scored. The second-half produced a ding-dong struggle. but no further goals. For Parr's the Collinges and Cheshire showed good form. Malyn and Goldsmith were the best in the Schoolhouse team but were marked too well to be really dangerous. Cottrell, mi., in goal gave a sound display clearing some difficult shots. Final score :—Parr's 2, Schoolhouse 0.

DUGARD'S v. HARSNETT'S.

One of the first of the Hockey House Matches was played on March 5th, and resulting in a win for Dugard's by 5 goals to nil. For some time play was even and mid-field, Horwood and Wenlock for Dugard's and Everett and Bare for Harsnett's distinguishing themselves by smart clearances.

Free hits for "sticks" were fairly frequent, but, on settling down, Dugard's began to assert their superiority, although Harsnett's were always "game." Several fruitless corners were forced, but mid-way through the half Hudson, receiving a pass from Orrin, scored Dugard's first goal. Harsnett's then made a few rushes, and from one Atkin forced a corner, but nothing resulted. Towards the end of the half, Horwood scored Dugard's second goal.

Immediately on the resumption, Flanegan, who played very well all through the game, ran up the wing and centred for Dugard's to again score.

Harsnett's forwards were very weak in front of goal and throughout the half Dugard's had the best of matters, further goals being added by Eves and Hudson.   F J.E.

DUGARD'S v. PARR'S.

Played on Thursday, March 26th. As Parr's had beaten Schoolhouse and Dugard's had beaten Harsnett's, it was thought that the winners of this match would become Hockey Champions. Right from the start both sides were very determined to win, and keenness got the upper hand of judgment in several cases. Free hits for "sticks" were far too frequent, and altogether there was too much whistle.

The play throughout the first half was very even, and Dugard's were lucky to lead at the interval by a goal scored by Hudson. In the second half most of the play was in midfield, excepting a few rushes by Parr's, Dugard's had the better of the exchanges. About a quarter of an hour after the resumption Hudson "got away" and scored a second goal. Parr's then bucked up a bit, and Dugard's goal had some narrow squeaks, but Horlock cleared splendidly.

About five minutes from the end Hudson got the ball away on the left, and centreing well, Eves scored Dugard's third and last goal.
                                                                F. J. E.

HARSNETT'S v. PARR'S.

Thursday, April 2nd. This was a very interesting match as it decided who should have second place in the House Table. Both teams had won their match against School House and both had lost to Dugard's. The result of the match was very doubtful from the first, and at half-time only one goal had been scored on either side. At the beginning of the second half Parr's again scored and maintained their lead until within a few minutes of time, when Harsnett's forwards attacked strongly and succeeded in gaining three goals in rapid succession; thus winning the match by 4—2. Atkin and Alderton were the pick of Harsnett's forwards, while Oliver was a tower of strength at centre-half, and Everett ma. and Nicholson were invaluable to the defence. Parr's goals were both scored by Lord, while for Harsnett's Atkin scored 3 and Alderton 1.

SCHOOL HOUSE v. HARSNETT'S.

The Second round of the House Matches was, as usual, played in rather doubtful weather, but nevertheless the clerk of the weather was good enough to withhold the usual amount of rain.

In the School House against Harsnett's match, a good strenuous game was maintained by both sides, the School House forwards and defence playing hard and well throughout. In this case, School House were stronger on the forward line, while in the case of their opponents, the defence formed much the stronger feature of the side.

Harsnett's played the only possible winning game in heavily marking Malyn and Goldsmith, the only really formidable forwards, with such effect that Malyn only succeeded in getting " clean away " and scoring once, while Goldsmith added the only other goal of his side from a pass at close quarters.

The score was 3—2 in Harsnett's favour at the close of the match, when it was generally admitted that Harsnett's had had bad luck, in that their forwards while pressing most of the second half, were twice unlucky in being offside when the ball was netted.

DUGARD'S v. SCHOOL HOUSE.

This match, which was fixed for April 2nd, had to be postponed owing to very heavy rain, and was ultimately played on April 6th. The weather, although bright, was exceptionally windy and, on winning the toss, Dugard's elected to play with the wind and the sun behind them.

For some time play was even and in midfield, but after about ½ hour Hudson scored from a mêlée in front of the School House goal. Having " tasted blood " Dugard's ran School House off their feet, and their forwards combining well, five more goals were quickly added, Hudson being the scorer in each case. The interval arrived with Dugard's leading 6—0.

Having re-arranged their side and with the wind at their backs School House started the second half in fine style, but they were soon repulsed by Horwood & Co., and Dugard's made tracks for their goal. Time after time they took the ball up the field but were always defeated at the last hurdle by Goldsmith and Cottrell mi. Play was of a ding-dong nature and following a rush by the right wing School House scored their first goal. Soon after a misunderstanding between Dugard's backs let in Cottrell ma. and he scored a second goal for School House. No more goals were scored and Dugard's ran out winners by 6 goals to 2.

For Dugard's the halves played a fine game and for School House Goldsmith was a tower of strength at right back.

Cricket.

At the time of writing we have arrived at the middle of the season with only moderate success. Five of last year's XI. remain with us :— Brand, who again captains the side, Eves, the new vice-captain, Goldsmith, Town, and Everett, ma.

There is a decided "tail" in the batting this year, but the bowling is about up to the average, though we seem to lack a good fast bowler.

The fielding is only moderate at present, but school teams notoriously make vast strides in every direction during the later weeks of a term.

With regard to the matches already played, we have enjoyed a fair share of success, the best performance being the victory over the Town, at Park Road, on May 23rd. The School did remarkably well to get their opponents out for 84, and this was chiefly due to the good bowling of Goldsmith, who had the excellent analysis of 7 wickets for 30.

Appended are the detailed scores of 1st and 2nd XI. matches played up to date:—

The first match of the season was played on March 14th against an XI. representing the Masters. The School won on the first innings by 99 runs to 54. The scores were as below:—

Masters.		School.	
Mr. E. Reeve, lbw, b Goldsmith	3	F. J. Eves, c Deakin, b Oldham	29
Mr. J. D. Ward, b Eves	9	E. J. Brand, st Ward, b Barker	19
Mr. J. H. Oldham, c Town, b Goldsmith	3	W. M. Town, b Barker	11
Mr. E. B. Deakin, c Lord, b Eves	25	W. G. Goldsmith, st Ward, b Oldham	3
Mr. F. D. Barker, c Town, b Goldsmith	7	C. E. F. Everett, b Barker	0
Mr. G. W. F. Bellward, c Oliver, b Goldsmith	0	E. B. Horwood, b Oldham	5
C. Nicholson, c Goldsmith, b Atkin	5	G. C. Rayner, c Ward, b Oldham	3
L. W. Clark, b Eves	0	G. Atkin, not out	7
R. C. Flux, c and b Town	0	S. W. Lord, c Ward, b Oldham	2
J. Collinge, not out	0	T. G. Smith, c Collinge, b Nicholson	1
J. H. King, c Eves. b Town	2	J. L. Oliver, b Nicholson	17
Extras	2	Extras	2
Total	56	Total	99

Masters, 2nd Innings:—Mr. J. D. Ward, retired, 40 ; Mr. E. B. Deakin, b Eves, 11 ; Mr. F. D. Barker, b Eves, 11 ; R. C. Flux, c Brand, b Atkin, 1 ; J. Collinge, not out, 4 ; J. H. King, c Horwood, b Rayner, 4 ; L. W. Clark, not out, 12 ; Extras, 2. Total (4 wkts.) 85.

Bowling :—Mr. Oldham, 5 for 48 ; Mr. Barker, 3 for 26 ; Goldsmith, 4 for 43 ; Eves, 5 for 57.

Our first School match was played against Harwich School, at Park Road, on May 16th. Scores :—

Colchester.		Harwich.	
F. J. Eves, b Butler	11	D. Gray, b Eves	8
E. J. Brand, c and b Gray..	16	J. H. Butler, c Smith, b	
W. M. Town, c and b Butler	2	Goldsmith	6
W. G. Goldsmith, run out ..	11	L. Hill, b Goldsmith	0
C. E. F. Everett, c Hill, b		A. Waller, b Eves., ...	0
Butler	0	H. Gay, b Goldsmith	1
G. Atkin, c Johnson, b Gray	0	H. Moore, b Goldsmith ..	0
J. L. Oliver, c Waller, b Gray	2	W. Johnstone, b Eves	0
G. C. Rayner, c Moore, b		R. Johnstone, b. Eves.. ..	3
Butler	1	A. Durrant, st Brand, b	
J. H. King, not out	3	Goldsmith	0
T. G. Smith, b Gray	0	S. Newton, b Eves	6
S. W. Lord, b Gray	6	D. Cann, not out	0
Extras	0	Extras	0
Total	52	Total	24

Colchester, 2nd Innings :—F. J. Eves, c Gay, b Butler, 13; E. J. Brand, not out, 23; W. M. Town, b Gray, 0; W. G. Goldsmith, b Gray, 10; Extras, 2; Total (3 wkts.) 48.

Harwich, 2nd Innings :—D. Gray, b Goldsmith, 6; J. H. Butler, b Goldsmith, 8; L. Hill, not out, 11; A. Waller, not out, 7; Extras, 1; Total (2 wkts.) 33.

Bowling :—Butler, 5 for 39; Gray 7 for 58; Goldsmith, 7 for 26; Eves, 5 for 30.

On May 23rd we were visited by Colchester and East Essex, who brought a strong team, under Mr. H. D. Swan. The School had the assistance of several masters and of Mr. J. D. Ward, and it was entirely owing to his batting and to the excellent bowling of Goldsmith, who took 7 wickets for 30 runs, that we succeeded in beating the Town team. Scores :—

Colchester and East Essex.		School.	
Capt. A. St. L. Goldie, c		Mr. E. B. Deakin, b Walker	13
Deakin, b Goldsmith ..	17	Mr. J. H. Oldham, c Wilkin-	
Mr. E. S. Missen, c Brand,		son, b Walker	5
b Oldham	9	E. J. Brand, b Walker ..	2
Mr. J. L. Meadowcroft, b		Mr. J. D. Ward, not out ..	63
Oldham	7	Mr. E. Reeve, b Walker ..	0
Mr. J. W. Wilkinson, b Gold-		Mr. P. S. Jeffrey, c Wilkin-	
smith	4	son, b Walker	2
Mr. E. G. Fenn, c Brand, b		Mr. F. D. Barker, b Missen	1
Goldsmith	14	W. M. Town, b Missen ..	2
Capt. C. B. Walker, b Gold-		W. G. Goldsmith, c Wilkin-	
smith	23	son, b Missen	2
Mr. A. S. Cox, b Goldsmith	0	C. E. F. Everett, c Whitby,	
Mr. V. Jasper, b Goldsmith	0	b Missen	4
Mr. H. D. Swan, c Deakin,		S. W. Lord, did not bat ..	—
b Goldsmith	7		
Mr. C. Fairhead, not out ..	1		
Mr. J. M. F. Whitby, run out	1		
Extras	2	Extras	3
Total	85	Total (9 wkts.)	100

Bowling :—Mr. Oldham, 2 for 36 : Goldsmith, 7 for 30.

On May 28th we'visited Framlingham. The home team batted first and scored rapidly, making 163 runs for 5 wickets. They then declared, leaving us with 90 minutes to beat them or to play out time. Brand was out at 19 to a ball from Joyce, and was quickly followed by Town ; but after this matters improved greatly and, thanks to the batting of Eves and Goldsmith, we were able to give a very good account of ourselves, scoring a total of 118. Scores :—

Framlingham.

P. M. Kitwood, not out ..	75
E. G. Joyce, c Goldsmith, b Eves	10
C. L. Waddell, c Town, b Goldsmith	2
R. F. Fitzherbert, not out..	18
C. H. Becker c Lord, b Brand	29
J. F. W. Hawkins, b Brand	12
E. G. Steel, b Goldsmith ..	4
V. L. Fisher ⎫	
L E. Martin ⎪ did not bat	
E. G. Pullan ⎬	
L. A. Hogg ⎭	
Extras	13
Total (5 wkts.)	163

Colchester.

F. J. Eves, b Joyce	26
E. J. Brand, b Joyce	10
W. M. Town, b Joyce.. ..	0
W. G. Goldsmith, c Waddell, b Steel	31
G. Atkin, b Fitzherbert ..	2
G. C. Rayner, b Joyce ..	0
C. E. F. Everett, run out ..	14
J. L. Oliver, b Joyce	12
K. Nicholson, c Martin, b Joyce	1
S. W. Lord, not out	6
C. Nicholson, c Martin, b Joyce	0
Extras	16
Total	118

Bowling :—Joyce, 7 for 50 ; Brand, 2 for 31 ; Goldsmith, 2 for 39.

On May 30th we were visited by Mistley, and were badly beaten by 116 runs to 30. Scores :—

Mistley.

T. H. Boden, c Nicholson, b Goldsmith	4
L. C. Denniss, c Jeffrey, b Oldham	0
A. Rush, lbw. b Brand ..	3
R. White, b Brand	17
H. T. Elmer, b Brand.. ..	11
F. H. Butler, lbw, b Brand	12
J. Alliston, b Brand	25
H. Keeble, b Brand	10
F. Keeble, c Oldham, b Atkin	18
O. T. Marshall, b Atkin ..	6
W. Davey, not out	0
Extras	10
Total	116

School.

Mr. J. H. Oldham, b Denniss	3
Mr. E. B. Deakin, b Davey	0
E. J. Brand, b Davey	14
Mr. E. Reeve, b Denniss ..	2
Mr. P. S. Jeffrey, b Denniss	2
Mr. F. D. Barker, b Davey	3
W. G. Goldsmith, b Denniss	1
C. E. F. Everett, c and b Denniss	0
G. Atkin, not out	2
K. Nicholson, c Boden, b Davey	0
J. H. King, b Davey	0
Extras	3
Total	30

Bowling.—Brand, 6 for 49; Atkin, 2 for 0.

On June 6th we visited Harwich to play the return match with Harwich School. Scores :—

School.		Harwich.	
W. G. Goldsmith, c Hill, b Butler	1	H. Gay, b Brand	2
E. J. Brand, lbw, b Gray ..	0	A. Waller, c Nicholson, b Goldsmith	1
G. Atkin, b Gray	14	L. Hill, b Goldsmith	5
C. E. F. Everett. b Butler ..	7	J. H. Butler, run out	6
J. L. Oliver, b Gray	0	D. Gray, run out	24
G. C. Rayner, lbw, b Gray	0	H. Moore, b Goldsmith .. .0	0
S. W. Lord, st, b Waller ..	5	W. Johnstone, b Goldsmith	4
K. Nicholson, c and b Gray	2	S. Newton, run out	0
E. B. Horwood, b Gray ..	3	G. Torell, lbw, b Atkin ..	2
J. H. King, b Gray	0	J. Warricker, lbw, b Brand	8
C. Nicholson, not out	1	D. Cann, not out	0
Extras	2	Extras	3
Total	35	Total	55

School, 2nd Innings :—W. G. Goldsmith, not out, 17 : E. J. Brand, lbw, b Gray, 0 ; G. Atkin. c Hill, b Butler, 5 ; C. E. F. Everett, c Waller, b Hill, 5 ; J. L. Oliver, lbw, b Hill, 1 ; G. C. Rayner, not out, 2 ; S. W. Lord, K. Nicholson, E. B. Horwood. J. H. King, and C. Nicholson did not bat. Total (4 wkts.) 30.

Bowling :—Goldsmith, 4 for 37 ; Brand 2 for 15.

SECOND ELEVEN.

C.R.G.S. 2nd XI. v. CLACTON GRAMMAR SCHOOL.

Clacton Grammar School.

1st Innings.		2nd Innings.	
F. H. Farquharson, c and b Nicholson	3	b Nicholson	23
C. H. Ansell, b Nicholson	6	c Bugg, b Orrin	15
T. Eagle, c Oliver, b Rayner ...	8	c Rayner, b Nicholson ..	1
H. M. Storer, b Nicholson..	3	b Orrin	0
S. Picard, c and b Nicholson ..	0	b Orrin	0
A. Mole, b Nicholson	0	b Nicholson	0
A. J. Keen, b Nicholson ..	0	run out	1
J. Monson, c Lord, b Nicholson	6	c Cottrell, b Smith	2
A. Wells, c and b Smith	7	not out	5
S. Pawsey, c Lord, b Smith ..	0	b Orrin	0
D. Pawsey, not out	4	b Orrin	0
Extras	0	Extras.	8
Total ..	37	Total ..	55

BOWLING.

1st Innings.	2nd Innings.
Nicholson mi., 7 wickets or 6 runs	3 wickets for 16 runs
Smith. 2 wickets for 16 runs	1 wicket for 22 runs
Orrin, 0 wickets for 2 runs	5 wickets for 6 runs
Rayner, 1 wicket for 8 runs	Wenden ma., 0 wickets for 1 run
	Wenden mi., 0 wickets for 6 runs

C.R.G.S.

G. C. Rayner, c Keen, b Farquharson	8	b Farquharson	3
L. Oliver	o	b Farquharson	3
S. W. Lord, c Keen, b Picard	2	b Picard	o
T. G. Smith, b Picard	o	b Farquharson	1
E. M. Wenden, b Farquharson	3	not out	5
W. R. Orrin, c Eagle, b Picard	o	c and b Picard	o
C. Nicholson, c Monson, b Picard	1	b Picard	3
J. H. Cottrell, b Farquharson	o	b Farquharson	o
E. P. Bugg, run out	9	c Monson, b Picard	3
C. W. Wenden, not out	4	b Picard	5
R. Alderton, b Picard	o	c Storer, b Picard	8
Extras	3	Extras	7
Total	**30**	**Total**	**39**

C.R.G.S. 2nd XI. v. Ascham College.

Saturday, June 13th, 1914.

Result—C.R.G.S. won by 17 runs.

C.R.G.S.		Ascham College.	
L. Oliver, b Walton	1	Walton, c Smith, b Orrin	13
G. C. Rayner, b May	1	Hall ma , b Nicholson	5
S. W. Lord, b Walton	4	Albenhausen, c Smith, b Orrin	3
J. H. King, b Walton	7	Goldecke, b Nicholson	1
E. B. Horwood, b May	5	Vernon, c Smith, b Nicholson	7
E. M. Wenden, b Walton	11	May, b Orrin	o
T. G. Smith, b May	2	Evans, c Cottrell, b Nicholson	7
J. H. Cottrell, run out	13	Hayward, b Wenden	o
E. P. Bugg, c Evans, b May	1	Mayo, b Nicholson	o
C. Nicholson, not out	o	Gedny, b Wenden	2
W. R. Orrin, b Evans	o	Hall mi., not out	2
Extras	9	Extras	1
Total	**58**	**Total**	**41**

BOWLING.

Nicholson,	5	wkts.	for	16
Orrin	3	,,	,,	21
Wenden	2	,,	,,	2
Smith	o	,,	.,	1

Lawn Tennis.

IT was hoped that it would be possible to arrange an inter-House Tournament this term, but very few members of the School have, so far, taken up the game at all seriously, and with the exception of School House it would be difficult to find a House capable of putting a four on the Courts at all.

The Masters, however, propose to hold an informal House tournament, and Mr. J. D. Ward has promised to get up an O.C.'s six to play C.R.G.S. This should prove an interesting match.

Meanwhile we should like to see the excellent Courts at Park Road better patronised by present members of the School on Wednesday and Friday evenings.

House Singings.

L AST term brought in its train the popular "House House-singings," in which friendly rivalry and a worthy spirit of emulation are always manifest. The resulting Concerts, were, we think, a general improvement on last year's efforts. Comparisons being odious, it will suffice to mention some of the outstanding features. Harsnett's gave us an excellent costume parody of the Russian ballet and an amusing farce; with topical songs to lighten the first part. Dugard's revived the ancient "Jollyboy" and gave a good conjuring turn. Hudson, in the concluding sketch, was exceedingly droll. School House gave a selection from its orchestral repertoire, and had reason to be proud of Dickens' character songs. "Box and Cox." their play, was well tackled, considering its difficulty. The last concert, by Parr's, reached a high level musically, thanks to the brothers Collinge. Members of the staff enjoyed the genial "guying" from the poets of Parr's; several débutants gave cause for great delight—the Futurist violin solo was thrilling indeed. The season was closed by a concert given by the Mountebanks, ably coached by Everett ma. It was gratifying to note the improvement in light and shade, the better appreciation of *piano* passages, and the worthier choice of song; the solo "I want somebody to love me" by Collinge ma. was perhaps the best item presented by a boy during the season. A play, written by Clark ma., was an encouraging sign, though it proved slightly reminiscent. Both in this and in the "Sherlock Holmes" skit, acted by another set of players, there was an evident attempt at characterisation, and a more clear, more easy delivery. The independent, unaided work of the "Mountebanks" is to be commended. It is for the rest of the School, during the long interval between now and the next concert season, to work np some item until it can be worthily presented. Think of the ease with which two hundred good "items" could thus be prepared against the dark days of the Concert Season! Choose your item *now*, and master it; try it on your relations and friends, and then offer it to the school. We shall be prepared to appreciate your work.

Cadet Corps.

T HE Summer Term is a hard but very pleasant one for cadets, and the Commanding Officer is sure that each cadet will do his best at everything, and so take a big share in making the C.R.G.S. Cadet Corps second to none in the County of Essex. A hearty welcome is extended to Mr.

Barker, who has taken a commission in the Corps, and to recruits Cottrell Bros., Cockaday, Butler and Bugg. The services of the late Cadet Sergeants Doubleday, Watsham, Malyn, Eves and Clover will be greatly missed. We were getting very proud of our big-drummer!

The date of the Annual Camp is not yet fixed. An official notification will be made to all "O.C." Cadets immediately the date and place is known.

The Corps will probably attend a Week-end Camp with the 3rd Essex Cadet Battalion at Great Horkesley, on June 27th and 28th next. The first part of the Shooting Competition for the "Lovell" Cup will be held at Middlewick on June 18th.

A Cadet Concert is being arranged for July 9th, in order to raise funds. It is to be hoped that all cadets, both past and present, will do their best to make it a social and financial success.

The Commanding Officer has been complimented on the smartness and general deportment of the C.R.G.S. Cadets at the Church Parade on June 7th, and so wishes to congratulate the boys themselves.

field Day.

Bravo, Cadets! You looked extremely smart and fit as you marched through the town on Tuesday, March 24th, on your way to Great Bromley (Black Boy?). The bugle band was in great form and kept us going at a swinging pace. Weather conditions were perfect, and a very happy and pleasant-faced company of cadets set out at 11 a.m. to accomplish a day's hard exercise. Arrived at Great Bromley, we enjoyed a hearty lunch on haversack rations, and at 2.30 p.m. operations were commenced on the following idea :— "A company of Ulster Volunteers (20 cadets), under the command of Mr. Deakin, were bivouacked at Great Bromley Lodge. A company of the 5th Essex Regiment (40 cadets) commanded by Mr. Bellward, and encamped at Little Bentley, had orders either to capture these Irishmen or to prevent them reaching Manningtree by Wednesday morning." By the kind permission of Mrs. Hirst, Messrs. Wenden and Hayward, a large area of ground was available for these operations. The attack was quickly and skilfully delivered, the scouts having soon found the position of the Ulstermen. But the outposts of the latter were exceptionally smart, especially Cadets Baskett, Lansdowne and Watsham, and by a clever ruse, the attack was strategetically drawn in a "blind" direction, while the greater part of the Irishmen dashed off for Manningtree, having slipped by the attackers before they realised their mistake. The outpost arrangements were carried out by Corporals Ward and Chapman, and the bivouac work by Col.-Sergt. Everett.

A section of the 5th Essex, commanded by Sergt. Girling, accounted for a fair number of the flying volunteers, but was unable to prevent the remainder reaching their destination.

At the close of operations a splendid tea was provided by Mr. Wenden, and the boys did full justice to it. The host was loudly cheered for his kind hospitality, and at 6.30 p.m. the Corps, still full of energy and fun, boarded motor buses for the return journey to Colchester. We had enjoyed an excellent day's outing. The Officers and Col.-Sergt.-Instr. Penn were delighted with the boys' behaviour both at work and play, and during the march out, a section of small cadets by their "perfect" and very "military" style of behaviour won the title of "Penn's Angels," but lost it on reaching the "pop" shop.

Shooting.

AS predicted in our last issue we won the remaining matches in the B. Division of the North Essex Rifle Club League and obtained 4th place in the competition with an average of 91 per man. This was a higher average than we expected to get, but our position in the table was lower than we had estimated, for our rivals seemed to be on top of their form when shooting against us. Eves is our first man with an average of 92·3 and is closely followed by Chapman and Doubleday with 92·2. As is usual in the Summer Term a very small number of boys seem to be shooting regularly, but no doubt this is due to the demands of Cricket and Spoken French, which occupy the time after school and in the dinner hour respectively.

The Competition for the Imperial Challenge Shield takes place on Monday, June 29th, and this year we have to enter teams of 9 in both Junior and Senior Competitions. As we have lost so many of our last year's team we do not expect to do so well as we have done in previous years.

The third round of the House Competition was shot off just before the end of last term, when Dugard's again succeeded in increasing their lead, and so retained the cup for another year. Once more there was an increase in the scores obtained by all the Houses.

DUGARD'S		PARR'S		SCHOOL HOUSE		HARSNETT'S	
Doubleday	69	Watsham	68	Wenden	60	Everett	60
Chapman	66	Brand	6:	Goldsmith	58	Clark	59
Hudson	66	Lord	58	Green	56	Deane	57
Eves	65	Percy	58	Rayner	55	Rickword	54
Flanegan	64	Andrews	58	Clover	50	Bare	54
Horwood	59	Town	53	Malyn	49	Burleigh	48
Halls	56	Wheeler	52	Leeming	41	Atkin	48
Fincham	52	Wagstaff	39	Le Cocure	41	Chambers	32
	497		447		410		412
Previous ro'nds	845		756		761		644
	1342		1203		1171		1056

Shooting Colours are awarded to Andrews and Wenden. Once more we offer our best thanks to C-S-I. Penn for his careful supervision of the range.

Scouting Notes.

THE most important scouting event of the term has of course been the visit of our Chief and Lady Baden Powell to Colchester on May 21st. It was the first time he had been able to inspect us since our troop was formed, and the event had long been looked forward to with much eagerness by all the local scouts. It was perhaps unfortunate that the rally and inspection could not be held out of doors, but the whole affair seems to have been a big success, and the Chief specially complimented Mr. Jeffrey on the smartness of the School troop.

I had a talk with the Chief during the evening about the junior scouts, and he wants us to go on as we have begun. The juniors therefore will not adopt a special uniform, but will only differ from the seniors by having no shoulder knot. Then, as they become efficient, they can be promoted without difficulty, when vacancies occur in the senior patrols.

It is very pleasing to note the effort that individual patrols are making to render themselves efficient, especially in the case of Peewit and Curlew patrols. Last, Hazell, Weeks ma., and Barnes have qualified for their badge as second-class scouts, Chambers has won his marksman's badge, and Collinge that of musician.

Four boys have left the troop since last term—P. L. Barnes, scouts Weatherall, Hordern and Mason. The first has taken up engineering; the other three—town boys—have gone to boarding schools. Best wishes to them all. In their place we welcome H. Graham Brown, Havard and Hackett as seniors, and Wilson mi., Dancer and Bailey as junior scouts.

We are at present busily engaged in preparation for our Annual Camp, and up to the present so many boys have given in their names that it will be necessary for us this year to have a man to take charge of the cooking arrangements and of the commissariat generally. In all probability the camp will again be held at St. Osyth from July 28th to August 6th, and I am confident that every scout will do his best to make this camp a record as regards both numbers and efficiency.

G. E. P.

The Pre.

THE Pre. has almost attained its second birthday, and I cannot help feeling very gratified, as I look round upon our increased numbers.

The new members have settled down splendidly, but we still miss Cox whom we are looking forward to having amongst us again next term, quite strong and well.

The border in the Gilbert House grounds is beginning to look promising, but in spite of all the care and water lavished upon the seeds, they seem, to youthful gardeners a very, very long time showing any sign of bloom.

Competition is always helpful, and nasturtiums, escholtzias, calceolarias, and red and white geraniums, as well as the sweet peas are hastening to vie with Slater's glorious pink geraniums, which are the pride of us all, in making the border gay, and even the pensive pansies are doing their humble best to make a show. Most of the boys take a keen interest in this new occupation, and tools are in great request before and after school hours. It will probably be a very difficult task to decide who is to be the lucky winner of the prize, for which all are working so zealously

Sports Day was an occasion of great excitement, and the handicapping of the Pre Race competitors would have baffled any who were not experts at the work.

Tait, Baker, and Knight won some laurels for us, and although all could not gain prizes, everyone seemed to enjoy the day, and particularly the cheers which brought the proceedings to a close.

Especially dear to the heart of the " Pre. Boy " is his share in applauding those in the Big School. (For cricket scores they clap so heartily that in spite of our anxiety for the welfare of caps and hymn books, which are in constant danger of being tipped into the hall below we can only admire the boys' enthusiasm for what at present concerns them but little).

93

With the summer term our cricket is again in full swing
and our little matches are certainly a great improvement on
last season's. We now boast a 1st and 2nd eleven, and
quite serious games may often be seen in progress. The
2nd eleven is kept in splendid order by their Captain, and
the independent manner in which these small people carry
out their game, when most of my attention is given to the
1st eleven is a pattern for our elder boys. There have been
days of course when the bitterly cold winds have compelled
us to desert our game, and turn thankfully to the football, in
order to get a good run, and feel a glow in benumbed fingers
ann toes, that one only associates with winter in its most
relentless mood.

With characteristic optimism we look forward to warm
summer weather, and a profusion of flowers in our little
gardens.

Le Quart d' Heure de Figgs Minor.

"DASHT," said Figgs minor. His collar had slipped again. I
looked round quickly.

"You seem in a bad way, old man," I said.

"So would you be if you had to tog up in your Sunday things all of a
sudden because the pater and mater take a sudden fit in their heads to
come down. Br-r-r-r-," he growled. "I shall choke myself with this
beastly thing before I'm done."

"How much longer are you two going to be?" asked a voice at the
door.

"Just a minute," we replied in a breath.

We got down to the hall after a time, where Colonel Figgs and his
wife were awaiting us.

"Ah! Algernon," said the colonel, putting up his glass. "Full regi-
mentals, eh? Well they needn't have done that, you know."

"No," retorted Figgs minor, wriggling his neck down into his collar
after stretching it for his mother's kiss. "I said so, but old Martha got
the hump at once."

"Got what?" asked his mother in horrified tones. "Really,
Algernon, your language seems appalling. And where's your tie?
Pull it round to the middle."

"Let the boy alone, Jane. He looks very well. So this is – ah—your
chum, eh?"

"Yes," said Figgs, rejoiced to find some subject other than himself
to talk about. "Jones of the Upper IVth."

"Pleased to meet you, Mr. Jones," said the colonel, while I shook
hands gingerly with Mrs. Figgs. "Now perhaps you will show us
round."

"How quiet it seems," said Mrs. Figgs.

"They're all in at dinner," explained Figgs minor. "We had our
tuck-in—I mean our feed – early."

"Is this the dining-hall?" asked his mother, trying to look through
some frosted glass doors. "I should so like to see them 'at meals.'"

"Here, mater," cried Figgs, terrified, "don't go in!"

"Why not?" asked the colonel. "You see the—ah—culinary department appeals to her."

"They'll want to drag you up to the top table, and we should be left outside," I explained. "You see, we've had ours."

"This is the play ground," said Figgs minor, after his parents had been dragged away from the danger area. "They'll be here in a minute."

"Ah!—they seem to be approaching," said the colonel as the fellows came trooping out. "A fine manly lot they look. Up to all sorts of larks, eh?"

"Oh yes," replied Figgs minor, "tons of 'em. Two climbed over the chapel roof the other night. Got swished for it."

"How very dangerous," exclaimed his mother. "I trust *you* do nothing of that sort, Algernon."

"Don't mollycoddle the child, Jane," snapped the colonel. "Of course he does."

"Wish it had been your pater who copped us, instead of Haughton," I whispered to Figgs.

"Rather!" replied that worthy in the same subdued tone.

"These games seem quite dangerous, John," said his wife, who had been gazing at a scratch hockey side. "Why do they try to hit each other with those sticks? I wonder the masters don't put a stop to it."

"They're not *trying* to hit each other," remarked Figgs minor sarcastically. "They want to hit that ball through the posts."

"Oh!" said his mother, surprised. "Oh! look! there are three of them down. They must have hurt themselves."

"That's all right," growled Figgs. "It's quite safe. Why, even girls play hockey nowadays."

"I am quite sure that I shall *never* allow your sister to take part in such a murderous game," replied Mrs. Figgs in disgust.

"Why, bless my soul!" suddenly exclaimed the colonel. "Surely I know that face. Served with me in Egypt, didn't you?" The sergeant saluted. "Good gracious!" continued the colonel, walking off in close conversation, "And what have you been doing since?"

"What a nice little boy," said Mrs. Figgs looking round, and selecting a victim. "Over there. Bring him to me. I should like to speak to him."

"*That* kid," expostulated Figgs. "Why he's the biggest baby—— Here Stubbs, hurry up, I want you."

"You might be more gentle," remonstrated his mother. Stubbs sheepishly approached. "Do you like school," asked Mrs. Figgs. "I'm sure *you* don't go for dangerous climbs over roofs, and frighten everyone."

"Not he," said Figgs.

"Oh! no," murmured Stubbs. "But Figgs there, and——." He caught the murderous gleam in our eyes. "I mean—no." The ball came bounding towards us. Mrs. Figgs drew out of the way with a little gasp, although it was miles off her. "Chuck it up, Stubbs!" shouted everybody. That got rid of *him*.

"Is that a master?" asked Figgs' mater, as Simpson came up.

"Oh no! That's one of the prefects," answered her son.

"Only a boy!" exclaimed Mrs. Figgs. "But he will soon have a moustache." Simpson glared as he went by. He must have heard. And it *was* a good one. He had to shave, too, once a week to keep clean. Figgs looked at me apprehensively, I returned his gaze. We should have to explain to Simpson afterwards.

We were relieved when the colonel came back with the Head. "Mrs. Wilson has kindly asked you in to tea, my dear," said the former. "I will take the boys for a time and then return to catch our train. Come along, boys," said he, after the Head had gone with Mrs. Figg, " we will go and explore the town."

" Righto," said Figgs minor. " I can show you some ripping places where——."

" Where you can tuck in free of charge, eh, you rascal?" laughed his father. " Well, mind you don't make yourselves too ill to say good-bye to your mother, or she might stop here to look after you."

" Oh lor !" muttered Figgs as we went through the gates. Then, dropping behind for a moment, he whispered to me, " Thank heaven ! that's over for another term."

F.B.C.

OLD COLCESTRIAN SECTION.

Editorial.

Rev. E. Hartley Parker.

O.C.'s will keenly regret the impending departure of Rev. E. Hartley Parker, who has been the keenest officer of the

O.C.S. since its inception. We congratulate him warmly on his selection for the important headship of a well-known school in Watford, but the going of this enterprising and enthusiastic organiser will create a vacancy it will be difficult to fill. The success of the long series of O.C. dinners, to say nothing of school functions, has been due to the energy and generalship of Mr. Parker, and he will carry with him the sincerest good wishes of all O.C.'s, who hope to see him a guest at recurrent annual dinners for many years to come.

The Social Season.

The Summer Term has been noteworthy for many pleasant social functions, beginning with the Annual Sports Meeting, which, in spite of an icy breeze, proved very enjoyable. Some excellent events were contested, and the Old Boys' Race again attracted a large field. The President (Mr. Chas. E. Benham) was among the runners, and he would have brought off a popular victory had not he persuaded Mr. H. L. Griffin to enter the lists. Mr. Griffin, ex-President, still retains much of his sprinting powers, and won a good race, with Mr. Benham second. The Old Colcestrians Challenge Cup was won outright by Everett, and already a new one is on the way. The names of contributing O.C.'s will appear in the next issue of the magazine, and, for economic reasons—as the list is already a long one and is still open at the moment of writing—this will be the only acknowledgment given.

Other social events in the Summer programme are the O.C. cricket match in connection with which the President and Mrs. Benham have invited a number of Guests to an "at home" at the Playing Fields ; and a Café Concert which Mr. J. A. Peart is arranging for the 9th of July in aid of Cadet Funds.

Lawn Tennis Club.

Mr. P. Shaw Jeffrey, our esteemed " head " and founder of the O.C.S., has formed an Old Colcestrian Lawn Tennis Club, which is proving a fine success. About 40 members have been enrolled, and the courts at Park Road have been largely patronised, showing the immense popularity of the venture.

THE EDITOR.

An O.C. Wedding.

BENHAM--LEANING.

WHAT may rightly be described as an O.C. wedding was solemnized on June 17th, between Mr. Gerald Carr Benham, O.C., son of Alderman Gurney Benham, ex-President O.C.S., and Miss Lois Blanche Leaning, daughter of Mrs. Leaning, The Chauntry, Colchester. The bride is sister to Dr. Bob and other respected O.C.'s of the Leaning family, and Mr. Gerald Benham, in addition to being one of the keenest and straightest sportsmen of the town, is also a Committee man of the O.C.S. in which he takes much interest, and among whose members he is very popular. With very few exceptions the invitations to the wedding were limited to members of the two families. Nevertheless there was a large attendance at Culver Street Wesleyan Church to witness the interesting ceremony. The Rev. J. W. Bateson, chief Wesleyan Chaplain to the Forces, and the Rev. John Day, of Colchester, officiated.

The bride looked very charming in a dress of ivory satin charmeuse, trimmed with shadow lace and pearl trimming, and she wore a white tulle veil and orange blossom. Three bridesmaids were in attendance. These were Miss Clara Leaning (sister of the bride), Miss Dorothy Webster (niece), and little Miss Mary Leaning (niece). Master Jack Leaning (nephew) also attended as page. Miss Clara Leaning and Miss Dorothy Webster were attired in dainty dresses of pale Saxe blue silk and flowered ninon tunics with blue satin sashes. Each wore a Dolly Varden hat with pink roses and black tulle Little Miss Mary Leaning was dressed in a Kate Greenaway costume of pretty white satin, and Master Jack Leaning was also dressed in satin. Both bride and bridesmaids carried beautiful shower bouquets, the gift of the bridegroom. Each bridesmaid also wore a lovely gold and acquamarine brooch, the gift of the bridegroom. The bride was given away by her eldest brother, Mr. F. Osborn Leaning, and Mr. A. E. Sparling acted as best man. Mr. Ernest H. Turner, A.R.C.O. (the bridegroom's brother-in-law), presided at the organ.

A large number of people congregated to see the departure from the church of the bride and bridegroom, in whose way rose petals were strewn. A reception was held at " The

Chauntry," and at the close of the afternoon **Mr. and Mrs.** Benham left by motor for London, subsequently travelling by rail to North Devon for the honeymoon. The bride's going away dress was of powder blue chiffon, and she wore a taffeta black Leghorn hat trimmed with black feathers.

Mr. Benham, who is a member of the firm of Benham & Wilson, solicitors, is an officer in the 8th (Cyclist) Battalion of the Essex Regiment and in command of the Colchester Company ; is Secretary of the Colchester Lawn Tennis Club, a Vice-President of the Phœnix Bowling Club, and for many years played football for the Colchester Town Football Club.

Among the presents were the following from O.C.'s and others : Mr. and Mrs. W. Gurney Benham tea service ; Mr. Cecil Benham, O.C. and Mrs. Benham, brass fire screen ; Mrs. C. E. Benham, table cutlery ; Mr. C. E. Benham, oval mirror ; The Committee of the Colchester Lawn Tennis Club, rose bowl ; Mr. and Mrs. Cecil Cant, silver asparagus dish ; Mr. and Mrs. C. W. Denton, silver claret jug ; Mr. and Mrs. A. W. Frost, picture ; Dr. and Mrs. R. Craske, Leaning, silver Queen Anne kettle ; Mr. and Mrs. E. Major Leaning, fish knives and forks ; Mr. and Mrs. G. Leslie Moore, Wedgewood dessert service ; Non-Commissioned Officers and Men of " C " Co. 8th Essex (Cyclist) Battalion, barometer ; Mr. and Mrs. E. H. Turner, table glass ; Mr. Frank Watts, letter weight.

A DISTINGUISHED O.C.

Among the large list of distinguished Old Colcestrians must be included Mr. Alfred Philip Wire, a native of Colchester, and a nephew of a Colcestrian Lord Mayor of London, whose death occurred at Leyton on June 12th.

The late Mr. Wire, who was born in 1839, had all the antiquarian instincts of his father, William Wire, and his knowledge of the antiquities of Essex, and of Colchester in particular was extensive. He had collected, with indefatigable industry, innumerable papers, prints, engravings, and photographs connected with the history of the county, and as an enthusiastic photographer himself he enriched his collection very greatly with the aid of his own camera.

Mr. Wire was educated at Colchester Grammar School and at Battersea Training College. After serving as pupil teacher at St. Mary Magdalen National School, and headmaster at Little Baddow and other Essex Schools, he was appointed in 1877 headmaster of Harrow Green Council School, a post he retained up to the time of his death, holding the distinction of being the oldest schoolmaster in England. He was author

of several brochures, including "Knowledge through the Eye," "Two Colchester Legends," etc., and was a frequent contributor to photographic and archæological journals. He was vice-president of the Church Schoolmasters' Benevolent Society, and a member of the Essex Archæological Society, the Survey Committee of London, and Toynbee Antiquarian Society. He was also one of the original members of the Essex Field Club, and their librarian for some years. Mr. Wire was a popular lecturer on many varied subjects.

STILL HOWLING !

Two efforts by a pupil in one of the L.C.C. schools seem to indicate that the rising generation is living up to tradition. Here are his answers in a Bible examination ; —

A sertain man went down from Jerslam to Jerriker and feld among thawns and the thawns sprang up and choaked him. He give tuppens to the hoast to take care on him. And he past bye on the other side.

Abram was the father ot Lot. He had two wives. One named Hoygur and the other Hismale. He kep one at home and hurried the hother into the dessert, where she became a pillur of salt by days and a pillar of fire at nights.

OUR ILLUSTRATIONS.

The portraits in this issue are published by the courtesy of the proprietors of the "Essex County Standard."

DEAKIN, E. B., C.R.G.S.
DENTON, A., Barclay's Bank, Colchester.
DENTON, C. W., Marylands, Shrub End Road, Colchester.
DOUBLEDAY, R. E., Belle Vue Road, Wyvenhoe
DUNNINGHAM, T. G., Manor Road, Dovercourt.
EBERT, Dr. E., Kiel, Fichtestrasse 2, Germany
EVERETT, H. J., Councillor, 28 New Town Road, Colchester.
EVERETT, W. R., c/o B. F. Burrell, Esq , Abbeygate Street, Colchester.
EWING. J. H., South Hall, Ramsey, Harwich
FAIRHEAD. A. E., Bouchier's Hall, Messing, Kelvedon.
FARMER, A. O., 12 Queen Street, Colchester (HON. SECRETARY).
FARMER, H. W., 15 Greyswood Street, Mitcham Lane, Streatham. S.W.
FAVELL, C. V., 28 Udney Park, Teddington, Middlesex.
FENN, E. G., The Hall, Ardleigh.
FIELDGATE, W. H., "Ty Fry," Regent Road, Brightlingsea.
FINCH, F. D., 25 Salisbury Avenue, Colchester.
FITCH, L. B., Welby House, Butt Road, Colchester.
FLEETWOOD, E. C., Bemabague, Shrub End Road, Colchester.
FLUX, J., Lower Clifden Downs Station, Carnarvon, W. Australia.
FOLKARD, G , Copford. Colchester.
FOLKARD, H , Copford, Colchester.
FRANKLIN, Councillor R., Sutherland House, 95 Baddow Road, Chelmsford.
FRANCIS, E. K., Crouch Street, Colchester.
FROST, A. T., Rackbarton, St. Barnabas Road, Cambridge.
FROST, A. W., 13 Head Street, Colchester.
GIBBS, J. W., 249 Maldon Road, Colchester.
GIRLING, T. A., Park Villa. Dunmow.
GIRLING, HUGH, Payne's Farm, Little Bentley.
GODFRAY, C. F.. "Thirlmere," Queen's Road, Springfield, Chelmsford.
GOING, F. W., 125 Maldon Road, Colchester.
GOODY, S., Chelsworth, New Town Road, Colchester.
GOODY, C., Old Heath Road, Colchester.
GREEN, H., Moat Hall, Fordham, Colchester.
GREEN, A. C., Fingringhoe, Colchester.
GREEN, D. A., The Hall Fingringhoe, Essex.
GREEN, A. E., 13 East Stockwell Street, Colchester.
GREEN, C. S., Fingringhoe, Colchester.
GRIFFIN, C., Stanway Villa, Colchester.
GRIFFIN, H. L., Stockwell House, West Stockwell Street, Colchester.
GRIMWOOD, C. H., c.o. Boots, Ltd., Long Wyre Street, Colchester.
HALL. A. L., Caerleon, New Town Road, Colchester.
HARPER, W. C., 6 Queen Street, Colchester.
HARRIS, H. J., Weircombe, Ardwick Road, W. Hampstead.
HARVEY, J. B., Stanley Lodge, Wellesley Road. Colchester.
HARSUM, G. F., Wood Field, Bourne Road, Colchester.
HAZELL, S. G., Long Wyre Street, Colchester, (and Montreal).
HAZELL, R. L., 23 Lexden Street, Colchester.
HEAD, A., 58 Wimpole Road, Colchester.
HEAD, J., 58 Wimpole Road, Colchester.
HELLEN, S., c.o. 6 Queen Street, Colchester.
HEMPSON, R. J.
HOLLAWAY, H. H., 34 Old Heath Road Colchester.
HORWOOD, R. B., Layer Hall, Layer.
HOWARD, W. K.
HURST. H. J. R., 7 St John Street, Colchester.
HUSSEY, F. W., 15 Audley Road, Colchester.

IVEY, S. F.. 63 Kensington Gardens Square, London, W.
JARRARD, C. H., Thorpe, Colchester.
JARRARD, D. G., Alexandra Road, Sible Hedingham.
JASPER, C. V., Langenhoe Hall, Colchester.
JASPER. L. A., Langenhoe Hall, Colchester.
JEFFERIES, C. R., 62 Winnock Road, Colchester.
JEFFREY, P. SHAW, School House, Colchester.
JOHNSON, L. H., 17 Lion Walk, Colchester.
JONES, P. E., c.o. Jones and Watts, Barrack Street, Colchester.
JUDD, L., South Villa, Ardleigh.
KENT, B. H., 182 Maldon Road, Colchester.
KING, W. H., Inglis Road, Colchester
KING, W. H., junr., Inglis Road, Colchester.
KING, G. K., 53 Friar Street. Sudbury.
LANSDOWNE, L. R., Mersea House. Walton.
LAVER, P., Church Street North, Colchester.
LAY. C. V., 2k Portman Mansions, St. Marylebone, London, W.
LAWRENCE, A. D., c.o. Head & Co., Ltd., 27 Cornhill, London, E.C.
LAZELL, HAROLD, Fitzwalter Road, Lexden Park. Colchester.
LEANING, E. M., Welwyn, Wash Lane, Clacton-on-Sea.
LINES, E., The Bungalow, Great Bentley.
LORD, P., North Hill, Colchester.
LUCKING, A. S., 20 Inglis Road, Colchester.
LUCKING. O. D., 64 High Street, Maidenhead.
MALYN, D. P., Bleak House, Braintree.
MALYN, R., Barclay's Bank, Colchester
MANNING, C., The Elms, Weeley, R.S.O.
MANNING, P. E. J., The Elms, Weeley, R.S.O., Essex. [chester.
MANNING, C. L., 162 Military Road, Colchester.
MARLAR, J., North Hill, Colchester.
MARSH, W. E., 180 Longmarket Street, Natal, South Africa.
MARSH, H. V., 43 Loop Street, Maritzburg, South Africa.
MASON, A. S., Perse School, Cambridge.
MASON, B., 10 Crouch Street, Colchester.
MASON, Q., 10 Crouch Street, Colchester.
McCLOSKY, O. A., c.o. Eles Everett, St. Botolph's, Colchester.
MIDDLETON, G. A. T., "Laleham," Clarence Road, Clapham Park, S.W.
MIDGLEY, C. F., "Gunton," Westminster Drive, Westcliffe-on-Sea. [wood.
MIDGLEY, W. R. O, 163 Ongar Road, Brentmills. F. G., 18 Beverley Road, Colchester.
MOY, C. T., c.o. Messrs. T. Moy & Co., Ltd., Colchester.
NASH. BERNARD, King Coel's Kitchen, Stanway.
NICHOLSON, R., 25 Priory Street, Colchester.
NORFOLK, A. E., 76 Chesson Road, West Kensington.
NUNN, A. W., Crouch Street, Colchester.
NUNN, J. H., Melford Villa, Rawstorn Road, Colchester.
NUNN, W. H., Whatfield. Ipswich.
ORFEUR, H. W., Colne Bank, Station Road, Colchester.
ORFEUR, C. B., Colne Bank, Station Road, Colchester.
ORFEUR, R. F., Colne Bank, Station Road, Colchester.
ORFEUR, F. N., Colne Bank, Station Road, Colchester
ORPEN, O. G., Hillside, West Bergholt, Colchester.
OSBORNE, F. F.
OSBORNE, H. C.
PARKER, Rev. E. H., Parsonage, Thorington, Colchester.
PARMENTER, Rev. C. J., 21 Worley Road, St. Albans.
PEART, J. A., C.R.G.S.

PEGLER, Dr. L. H , 58 Harley Street, London W.

PEPPER, V. J., 19 Harsnett Road, Colchester.

PEPPER, G. E., O.R.G·S.

PERTWEE, F., Morehom's Hall, Frating.

PLUMMER, N. A., Station Road, Lawford, Manningtree.

PLUMMER, F. E. Station Road, Lawford, Manningtree.

POINTING, W. W., 148 Maldon Road, Colchester.

POTTER, C. C., 119 Maldon Road, Colchester.

POTTER. F., Middleborough, Colchester.

PRIME, E. J., 37 Crouch street, Colchester.

PROBSER, J. A. B., Lansdowne, Pierremont Avenue, Broadstairs.

REEVE, E., O.R.G S.

RENTON, T. S., 12 Crouch Street, Colchester (HON. TREASURER).

RICHES, A. E., 80 Tower Street, Brightlingsea

RICHARDS, R. F., Head Street, Colchester.

RICKWORD, E. G., 35 Wellesley Road, Colchester.

RICKWORD, G. O., 38 Wellesley Road, Colchester.

ROSEVEARE, H. H., " Craigmore," Newquay, Cornwall.

RYDER, E. W., 74 Wimpole Road, Colchester.

SADLER, F. B., Box P.O. 219, c.o. The Eastern Bank, Ltd., Bombay.

SANDERS, F. A., 108 North Station Road, Colchester.

SANGER, O. W., "Rookerydene," Abbeygate Street, Colchester.

SANGER, H.. "Rookerydene," Abbeygate Street, Colchester.

SALMON, J. G., Wash Lane, Clacton.

SKAMER, H. St. J., O.R.G.S. (Editor)

SENNITT, F. J.. 28 Mersea Road, Colchester.

SHAW, D. E., Holmleigh, Beaconsfield Avenue, Colchester.

SHENSTONE, J. O., 15c Coverdale Road, Shepherd's Bush, London, W.

SHEPHERD, O. W., 110 Magdalen Street, Colchester.

SIGDERS, J.

SLIGHT, R., c.o. One Barrow Lodge, Coalville, Leicestershire.

SLATER, E. M., 201 Maldon Road, Colchester

SMITH, AUBREY, "Mants," 30 Peak Hill, Sydenham, S.E.

SMITH, G. E., Chapel Street, Colchester.

SMITH, EUSTACE T., Wormingford Grove, Colchester.

SMITH, W. G., 23 Roman Road, Colchester.

SMITH, F. R. 23 Roman Road, Colchester.

SMYTHIES, CAPT. P. KINGSMILL R. N., The Turrets, Lexden Road, Colchester.

SPARLING, A. S. B., 21 Creffield Road, Colchester.

SPARLING, Rev. P. W., Helme Rectory. Downham Market.

STOW, W. H., The Willows Great Horkesley, Colchester.

SURRIDGE, P. T., Coggeshall.

SYER, F. N., 8 Studlands Road, Sydenham.

TAYLOR, A. P., Roseneath, East Street, Hazlemere, Surrey.

TENNANT. E. N., Connaught Avenue, Frinton.

THOMAS, A. O., 130 Maldon Road, Colchester.

THOMPSON, W., 365 Hither Green Lane, Lewisham, S.E.

TOWN. H. G., 10 Wellesley Road, Colchester.

TURNER, Capt. A., Essex Hall, Colchester.

TURNER, Lt. DOUGLAS, Essex Hall, Colchester.

TURNER, S. O., Abbeygate House, Colchester.

WAGSTAFF, D. T., Church Farm, Marks Tey, Colchester.

WALLACE, Councillor R. W., "Moelwyn," Inglis Road, Colchester.

WARING, O. E., Froebel, Priory Road, Spalding, Lincolnshire.

WARD, E. A., 122 Caversham Road, Reading.

WARD, J. D., Jun., Bluegates, Elmstead, Colchester.

WARNER, A. E., 8 Myland, Colchester.

WATSHAM, B., Vine Farm, Wyvenhoe.

WATSON, J. L.

WATSON, S. F., 150 Maldon Road, Colchester.

WATSON, G. F.

WATTS, FRANK, 30 Creffield Road, Colchester.

WEBB, G. S., Dairy House, Wix, Manningtree.

WEBB, A. H., Dairy House, Wix, Manningtree.

WHITE, O. E., 57 North Hill, Colchester.

WHITE, F., East Hill, Colchester.

WHITBY, J. F. M., 144 Maldon Road, Colchester.

WIGLEY, W. H., 146 King's Park Road, Mount Florida, Glasgow.

WILLIAMS, F. O., 14 Lexden Road, Colchester.

WILLIS, E. A., 25 Heron Road, Stapleton Road, Bristol.

WIRK, A. P.

WORTS, S. E., Trinity Street, Colchester.

WRIGHT, Lieut.-Col. Percival, Ashanti, St. James, Mirzenburg, Cape Town.

WRIGHT, C. T., Stacey House, Crouch Street, Colchester.

WRIGHT, G., junr., Stacey House, Crouch Street, Colchester.

WRIGHT, Councillor G. F., 47 Crouch Street, Colchester.

WYATT, D. T., Bank Passage, Colchester.

NOTICE TO OLD COLCESTRIANS.

Old Colcestrians who wish to make known their movements in this paper should communicate with Mr. J. HUTLEY NUNN, "Essex County Telegraph" Offices, Colchester.

Subscriptions should be sent to Mr. T. S. RENTON (Hon. Treas.), 12 Crouch Street, Colchester.

Members of the Society are requested to notify any change of address immediately to either of the Hon. Secretaries :—

Mr. F. D BARKER, Royal Grammar School.

Mr. A. O. FARMER, 6 Queen Street, Colchester.

NOTICE TO CORRESPONDENTS.

Contributions to the O.C. Section, articles on various subjects and humorous anecdotes of school-days, will be gladly welcomed by the O.C. Editor, Mr. J. Hutley Nunn.

All contributions for the next number of " The Colcestrian " to be sent in by Oct. 20th, 1914.

No. 40.]
New Series.

NOVEMBER, 1914.

The Colcestrian.

EDITED BY PAST AND PRESENT MEMBERS OF COLCHESTER SCHOOL.

PRICE SIXPENCE

Colchester:
PRINTED BY CULLINGFORD & CO.,
156 HIGH STREET.

O.C.S. Officers for 1914=15.

President:
O. T. WRIGHT, Crouch Street, Colchester.

Vice-Presidents:

W. GURNEY BENHAM, J.P.
R. FRANKLIN
H. L. GRIFFIN

H. J. HARRIS, B.A.
B. H. KENT
OSMOND G. ORPEN
W. H. KING

J. O. SHENSTONE, F.L.S.
R. W. WALLACE
C. E. WHITE

Committee:

F. D. BROOK
J. H. NUNN
A. W. NUNN
F. G. MILLS

C. GRIFFIN
O. T. WRIGHT
H. H. HOLLAWAY
C. F. BENHAM (*Chairman*)

G. C. BENHAM
E. W. DACE
J. O. SALMON

The Ex-Presidents are ex-officio members of Committee.

Hon. Treasurer (pro. tem.):
A. T. DALDY, 50 South Street, Colchester.

Hon. Secretaries:
A. T. DALDY, 50 South Street, Colchester.
A. O. FARMER, 12 Queen Street, Colchester.

Members of the O.C.S.

ACLAND, C. S., Lexden House. West Winch,
nr. Kings Lynn.   [Park, N.
ADAMS, E. A., 22 Gloucester Road. Finsbury
ALLISTON, A. W., Chipping Hill, Witham.
APPLEBY, W. M.
BAILEY, C.
BARNES, F. M., Howell Hall, Heckington,
Lincolnshire.
BARNES, ALAN, 171 Maldon Road, Colchester.
BARKER, F. D., Royal Grammar School (Hon.
Sec).   [Naze.
BARKER, C. F. J., Marine Hotel. Walton-on-
BARKER, CHARLES, Burtoll Tea Estate,
Dewan P.O., Cachar, India.
BAWTREE, E. E., 71 High Street, Colchester.
BAXTER, H. G., Fronks Road, Dovercourt.
BAYLISS, S. F.
BAYLISS, R. V. J., Fleece Hotel, Head Street,
Colchester.
BAYLISS, B., Fleece Hotel, Head Street,
Colchester.
BEARD, E. O., St. Margaret's, Cambridge
Road, Colchester.
BECKETT, H., Balkerne Lane, Colchester.
BELLWARD, G. W. F., C.R.G.S.
BENHAM, C. E., Wellesley Road, Colchester.
(President).
BENHAM, G. C., Bank Chambers, High Street,
Colchester.
BENHAM, Alderman W. GURNEY, St. Mary's
Terrace, Lexden road, Colchester.
BLATCH, F., c/o, S. E. Blau, La Paz, Bolivia,
S. America.
BLAXILL, G. A., 50 Parliament Hill, Hamp-
stead, N.W.
BLOMFIELD, S., Raonah House, New Town
Road, Colchester.
BLOMFIELD, H. D., 3 Tyler Street, Parkeston.
BLOMFIELD, T.
BLYTH, COOPER, c.o. Isaac Bunting, 100
Yokahama, Japan.
BOGGIS, FRANK, Station Road, Sudbury.
BROMLEY, J. G., Mill House, Great Clacton.
BROOK, T. D., "St. Runwald's," Maldon
Road, Colchester.
BROOK, A. T., "St. Runwald's," Maldon
Road, Colchester.
BROOK, L. O., "St. Runwald's," Maldon
Road, Colchester.
BROOK, S. V., 22 Sugden Road, Lavender
Hill, S. W.
BROWN, D. GRAHAM, "Lownd," Witham.

BULTITUDE, R. G., 32 Hanover Road, Canter-
bury.
BURRELL, F. B., Abbeygate Street, Colchester
BUNTING, A. E., The Nurseries, North Station
Road, Colchester.
BURBIDGE, T.
BURGESS, H. G.
BURLEIGH, A., Kudat, N.L.B.T. Co., British
North Borneo.
BURSTON, F. G., 57 High Street, Colchester.
BUTCHER, H., Crouch Street, Colchester.
BUTLER, F. H., Cumberland House, Manning-
tree.
CANT, Walter, West House Farm, Lexden,
Colchester.
CARTER, F. B., C.R.G.S.
CHAMBERS, O., 22 Wellesley Road, Colchester
CHAMBERS, S. C., 22 Wellesley Road, Col-
chester.
CHAPLIN, F. S., 5 Verulam Buildings, Grays
Inn, W.C.
CHESHIRE, G., 23 Argyle Street, Oxford
Street, W.
CHESHIRE, W., 1 Meyrick Crescent, Colchester
CHEESE, C. T., 39 Pownall Crescent, Colchester
and St. Austell, Cornwall.
CLAMP, A. J., 122 Priory Street, Colchester.
CLARKE, S. F., Parr's Bank, Holloway,
London, N.
CLOVER, J. M., The Hall, Dedham.
COBBOLD, H. F. S.
COLE, C. L. L., General Post Office (Staff),
Cambridge.
COLE, H. S., 25 Wimpole Road, Colchester.
COLLINGW, C. E., Capital & Counties Bank,
Baldock, Herts.
COLLISON, A. L., Garrison School, Buena
Vista. Gibraltar.
CORK, F. F., 38 Trouville Road, Clapham
Park, S.W.
CRAGG, Rev. E. E., St. John's Church, Hunt-
ington, Long Island, U.S.A.
CULLINGTON, M. W., 53 Oakhill Road,
Putney, S.W.
DACE, A. W., 122 George Street, Edinburgh.
DACE, E. W., 17 Honywood Road, Colchester.
DALDY, A. T., 50 South Street, Colchester
(HON. TREASURER).
DAVIES, W. E., 118 Butt Road, Colchester.
DAVIES, E. G.
D'EATH, C. V., The Ferns, Southwood Road,
Ramsgate.

Continued on Page 3 of Cover.

The Colcestrian.

VITÆ CORONA FIDES.

No. 40.]   NOVEMBER, 1914.   [NEW SERIES.

Editorial.

"IT is always the unexpected that happens," says the proverb. When the summer term closed and the School dispersed, with visions of a happy and peaceful holiday, and, in some cases, of Continental travel, before its eyes, not even the most unbridled imagination would have conceived, nor the most daring of prophets would have ventured to foretell, that within the space of a fortnight the whole of Europe would have flashed into a blaze, and that England itself would have been involved in the conflagration. But so it was to be. Armageddon was upon us. "The Day" of the Prussian toast had dawned, and the two great world principles were at grips in the death-struggle.

For this is no isolated contest. Its causes lie deeper than the surface of things. It has been brought about by no mere assassination, no impossible ultimatum, no tearing of "a scrap of paper." These are but symptoms. It is part of the eternal strife between Right and Might, Justice and Privilege, Liberty and Tyranny, Democracy and Oligarchy, Christianity and Paganism, that re-appears in all ages It is due to the same causes that pitted Greece against Persia, Athens against Sparta, Rome against Carthage, and in later times, Holland against Spain, and Europe against Louis XIV. and Napoleon. There can be but one end. The Prussian menace must go and Europe be re-partitioned on the basis of free nationalities. And the nation which has granted autonomy to its Dominions, whose government has brought Boer, and French-Canadian, Hindu and Mussulman, Orangeman and Nationalist, into one line in its defence, will see to it that "peace and happiness, truth and justice, religion and piety, shall be established among us for all generations."

And bravely is our School doing its part in the contest. Our Boy Scouts have been guarding telegraph poles, and taking messages. Of the actual staff, two are at present on active service, while O.C.'s almost without number have

107

joined various Corps in the Army of Liberation, that has sprung into being at their country's call, and will remove once and for all the hideous menace of militarism and savagery set up by the wild ambitions of an unspeakable caste and Kaiser.

THE EDITOR.

Valete.

*C. E. F. EVERETT.—K.P., Senior Prefect. Harsnett's, Form VI. 1st XI. Cricket, Vice-Captain 1st XI. Hockey, School Shooting VIII., 2nd XI. Football ; Captain of House Cricket, Football, Hockey and Shooting; on Committee of Debating Society; School Amateur Dramatic Society.

F. J. EVES —K.P., Dugard's, Form VI. Vice-Captain 1st XI. Cricket, 1st XI. Football and Hockey, School Shooting VIII. ; Captain of House Cricket, Hockey and Shooting, House Football.

R. S. J. HUDSON.—Q.P., Dugard's, Form VI. 1st XI. Football and Hockey, School Shooting VIII. ; House Football, Hockey, Cricket and Shooting.

*A. R. MELROSE.—Parr's, Form VI.

*W. M. TOWN. —Q.P., Parr's, Form VA. 1st XI. Football, Cricket and Hockey ; House Football, Cricket, Hockey and Shooting.

*E. B. HORWOOD.—K.P., Dugard's, Form VA. 1st XI. Football and Hockey, 2nd XI. Cricket.

*L. W. CLARK.—Harsnett's, Form VA. House Cricket, Hockey and Shooting.

T. DEVIENNE.—Dugard's, Form VA.

L. G. CHILD.—Dugard's, Form VA.

A. RICHARDSON.—Parr's, Form VA.

H. C. SAMMONS.—Schoolhouse, Form VA.

*J. A. WILLMOTT.—Parr's, Form VA.

S. W. LORD.—P., Parr's, Mod. V. 1st XI. Football, Cricket and Hockey ; House Football, Cricket, Hockey and Shooting.

J. L. OLIVER.—P., Harsnett's, Mod. V. 1st XI. Cricket ; House Cricket, Football and Hockey.

C. A. WENDEN.—K.P., Schoolhouse, Mod. V. School Shooting VIII. ; House Football, Cricket, Hockey and Shooting ; 2nd XI. Cricket

J. H. KING.—Harsnett's, Mod. V. 2nd XI. Cricket ; House Cricket and Football.

C. H. BARNES.—Schoolhouse, Mod. V.

F. E. WHEELHOUSE.—Dugard's, Mod. V.

R. D. COLLINS.—Dugard's, Mod. V. House Football.

B. P. DICKER.—P., Schoolhouse, Form VB. House Cricket.

K. NICHOLSON.—Harsnett's, Form IVA. 1st IX. Cricket and Hockey, 2nd IX. Football ; House Cricket, Football and Hockey.

*L. C. FLANEGAN.—Dugard's, Form IVA. 1st IX. Hockey, School Shooting VIII. ; House Hockey and Shooting.

R. C. FLUX.—Harsnett's, Form IVA.

A. LECŒUVRE.—Schoolhouse, Form IVA. House Shooting.

A. F. CURTIS.—Schoolhouse, Form IVA. House Cricket.

C. BUTLER.—Schoolhouse, Form IVB.

A. A. BIRD.—Harsnett's, Mod. IV.

L. G. CUNNINGHAM.—Parr's, Form I.

V. BARRY.—Schoolhouse, Form I.

* Boys marked with an asterisk have joined the Colours.

Salvete.

T. A. Hawkins	Va.		Schoolhouse
F. W. Syer	Vb.		Parr's
G. Gibb	Vb.		Schoolhouse
J. F. Crighton	Vb.		,,
A. van der Bergh	Vb.		
G. H. White	IVa.		,,
K. Newman	IVb.		Harsnett's
R. W. Woodward	IVb.		,,
A. Wright	IVb.		,,
R. Harwood	IVb.		Dugard's
J. E. Chase	IVb.		,,
T. F. Clough	IVb.		,,
J. D. Ritchie	IVb.		,,
A. H. Twyman	IVb.		,,
J. J. E. Godeuski	III.		Schoolhouse
A. Curtis	III.		,,
F. W. Felgate	III.		Parr's
C. A. Cole	III.		Harsnett's
H. G. Hazell	III.		Dugard's
R. Bion	II.		Schoolhouse
H. Hawkins	II.		,,
L. Cosser	II.		Dugard's
H. van der Bergh	I.		
E. D. Hunneyball	I.		Parr's
L. C. W. Roberts	I.		,,
A. K. Saye	I.		
R. Rolf	I.		Schoolhouse
R. Gell	I.		,,
W. R. Poyser	I.		Harsnett's
L. Worsp	I.		Dugard's
H. Crowther	Pre.		
A. Hordern	Pre.		
R. Hordern	Pre.		
G. Wilson	Pre.		
J. Clark	Pre.		

Grammaria.

"Amurath an Amurath Succeeds."

We heartily welcome Messrs. Worth, Watts and Clarke to the membership of the staff, in the place of those who are now fighting their country's battles, or performing service elsewhere, or apotheosized into Head-ships.

"Whose Subscription?"

It was stated at the Prize Distribution at the Athletic Sports that Mr. Parker had collected more than £400 during his secretaryship. That estimate is well within the mark.

The actual figures run :—

			£	s.	d.
1904	...	...	35	0	1
1905	...	...	37	12	0
1906	...	...	49	16	3
1907	...	...	60	0	0
1908	...	...	61	19	11
1910	...	...	55	12	2
1911	...	...	59	0	6
1912	...	...	65	0	10
1913	...	...	61	3	1
1914	...	...	68	12	5
			£553	17	3

The omitted year (1909) was that of the Pageant, when, of course, the Sports did not take place. The record is in itself a remarkable one, and not less so the continued increase, which bears excellent testimony to the widening interest taken in the annual event, and its increasing popularity.

A Fit of the Blues.

Among the many minor effects of the war may be numbered the covering of top-lights and upper windows of the buildings with dark blue paper. Presumably it is a measure of protection against any casual Zeppelin. But the colour is most inappropriate. One would imagine that we had a fit of the blues. The exact contrary is the truth. Should anyone want to know if we are downhearted, let him put the question, and there will be one spontaneous and universal shout of " No !"—for, as one of the Junior School writes it, we are all " Reddy, aye, Reddy !"

Doffing the Purple.

It is further to be noticed that the accustomed purple and white flag hitherto flown on our flagstaff, has given place to a sort of composite banner embodying the colours of the four Allies—Britain, Belgium, France, and Russia. The motive and idea is excellent, but apart from the somewhat crazy-quilt appearance, the yellow and black of Belgium shouts (as well it may !) when contrasted with the blue, white and red of the other nations.

110

The Final Horror!

Robinson minor is filled with righteous indignation against the "*Sales Prussiens,*" who have not spared the Belgians the utmost and worst of atrocities. He learns that they have decreed that the schools shall be forthwith opened, and the wretched little Belgian children shall attend, even amid the devastation of their country. Can Prussian bullydom farther go?

Literæ Scriptæ.

In the O.C. section will be found extracts from letters written by Old Boys now on service with the Colours, which will be found most interesting reading, especially as some of the writers must be known to most of our present boys. The Editors would be glad to receive letters from O.C.'s with a view to their publication in future issues, especially from those on foreign service.

Speech Day.

This term, Speech Day will take place on December 17th, when the Lord Bishop of Chelmsford has kindly consented to distribute the prizes.

Carol Concert.

As in former years, a Carol Concert will be given on the last Sunday of the term. It is well for us to be reminded that there are still objects at home, disconnected with the war, that deserve our hearty support; and the Poor Children's Christmas Breakfast Fund is not one of the least deserving. It is strongly to be hoped that our collection may reach a total even in excess of the previous ones. Those who come to the feast may rest assured that the musical menu provided will in no way fall short of its accustomed excellence.

Our Occasional Contributor.

THE ASS.

"The pepole ses the ass was a very stiped animal. Tom Brown was a posman, and he youst to go up and down the villig. Tom was lamed, and he went about with his luggig on the ass he takes hold of the asses tal to peld him a long and one day in a sno storm Tom and his ass stuck in the snow."

C.R.G.S. Cadet Concert.

HELD IN THE HEADMASTER'S GARDEN,

ON THURSDAY, 9TH JULY, 1914.

THE Concert in itself was as good as our School Concerts invariably are, but the cool atmosphere of a delightful summer evening, and the charm of a picturesque open-air theatre, with its dainty stage and natural dress-circle, softly illuminated by fairy lamps, combined to make it one of the most delightful we have had for some time.

There were small boys and big boys, arrayed either in flannels and representative blazers or in the Cadet Corps uniform; there were masters gaily apparelled in military dress of varied hue; there were charming ladies persuaded to ices or coffee by irresistible waiters in the guise of pruned and prismed prefects, all lending to the proceedings a character all its own.

The programme was varied and replete. We had country dances by the C.R.G.S. Six mi., and an original sword dance, which well deserved its enthusiastic reception, by the Six ma.; we had humour and pathos from that inimitable exponent of the art, Mr. Oldham, and Sterndale Bennett's catchy little song, " Miss Brown," from Mr. Bellward; we had the violin and the piccolo, the former manipulated by Barrell, who, in conjunction with Dicker at the piano, opened the Concert in flowery style with " Petals," and the latter by Mr. Fred Jones, whose rendering of " Danse des Satyrs " (*Le Thiere*) secured a well-deserved encore. Mr. Renton, Collinge ma. and Collinge mi. gave us songs in their usual finished style, and combined with Mr. Huntley Nunn to provide two of the best items on the programme, the quartettes: " A Franklyn's Dogge " (*Mackenzie*) and " In this Hour " (*Pinsuti*).

In the whole range of music there is probably nothing so delightful to the ear as an unaccompanied quartette, and the open only serves to augment the delight of it. It can readily be imagined, then, with what rapture we sat and dreamed with the adorable aroma of " My Lady Nicotine " rising to our nostrils, and the sweet strains of " In this Hour " falling on our ears.

In the regrettable absence of Mr. George O'Hagan, whom Mr. Peart was introducing to Colchester, Mr. Charles Conyers came forward and kept his audience in constant laughter, scoring a great success as a raconteur and society entertainer.

The programme concluded with a quite admirable comedietta—a home-product of C.R.G.S.—entitled " The De Vere," and written by Mr. Carter. Miss Doris Maberley was very bewitching as Miss Laurie Dean, the flapper from school, and naturally Everett ma. found little difficulty in acting up to her. It goes without saying that Mr. Carter had provided himself with a glorious old-man study. All who have seen his old-men parts know how he excels in them. In this branch of acting he is without doubt second to none, and in " The De Vere " he enhanced his reputation.

Mr. F. D. Barker acted as accompanist throughout, and Messrs. Reeve and Peart may take credit unto themselves for providing as enjoyable a concert as one could wish to see

Cricket.

TAKEN all-round the School has not had a bad season. The bowling and fielding was quite good, but the batting, on the whole, lacked style. Batting needs more practice perhaps than the other two branches of the game. The Summer Term with its counter attractions of Cambridge locals, sports, tennis, and bathing, makes this practice very difficult to get. Indeed, with the exception of two or three members the batting was poor and broke down badly after a good start, as in the case of the Bentley and Woodbridge matches. W. G. Goldsmith bowled exceedingly well during the first part of the season but lost his length and met with little success during July. His batting, with that of F. J. Eves—who heads the averages—was distinctly good. Of the other bowlers F. J. Eves and G. Atkin both kept a good length and did some good performances. W. M. Town did not have the best of luck as a bat, but in fielding he set an example to the rest of the team.

Everyone will deplore the departure of Mr. Oldham after only two seasons' stay. The best of luck to him in the future, and perhaps he will be able to come down on Old Boys' day. In closing mention must be made of A. O. Ward and C. H. Barnes, who, as scorer and umpire respectively, have capably performed their duties.

The Second Eleven.--Played 7, won 4, lost 2, drawn 1. An exciting match with the O.C.'s 2nd XI. resulted in a narrow win for the School.

Appended are the scores of all matches :—

FIRST ELEVEN.

1st XI. v. Old Colcestrians' 1st XI.—Thursday, June 25th, played at Park Road.

The O.C.'s, who had a strong team, batted first, and were all dismissed for 39. The School then went in and scored 73. In the second innings, however, the Old Boys had regained their form, and made 141 for 6 wickets before declaring. They then dismissed the School for 86 and we were thus beaten by 21.

O.C.'s

1st Innings		2nd Innings	
H W Orfeur, c Nicholson, b J H Oldham	o		
A E Green, c and b J H Oldham ...	1	c P S Jeffrey, b J H Oldham ...	9
C V Jasper, c Town, b Goldsmith	2	lbw, b Goldsmith ...	15
R Malyn, c E B Deakin, b Goldsmith ...	3		
J D Ward, c Town, b Goldsmith ...	16	not out	51
E G Fenn, b Goldsmith ...	o	run out	13
B H Kent, c and b Goldsmith ...	o	c Town, b Goldsmith ...	26
J G Bromley, b J H Oldham ...	7	b Eves	8
V Triscott, c Goldsmith, b J H Oldham	4		
F White, not out	1	c and b J H Oldham ...	9
E W Dace, absent	o		
Extras	5	Extras ...	10
	39	(6 wkts.) ...	141

SCHOOL

1st Innings		2nd Innings	
Mr E B Deakin, b Ward ...	o	b Ward	16
Mr E Reeve, b Jasper ...	4	b Ward	16
Mr J H Oldham, b Green ...	30	c Fenn, b Ward ...	9
E J Brand, b Ward ...	2	c and b Green ...	o
Mr P S Jeffrey, b Jasper ...	o	b Ward	3
F J Eves, c and b Jasper ...	6	not out	29
Mr F D Barker, b Jasper ...	3	b Malyn	o
W G Goldsmith, c Jasper, b Ward	6	b Ward	o
W M Town, c Orfeur, b Green ...	o	c Orfeur, b Jasper ...	8
C E F Everett, b Ward ...	8	b Kent	4
K Nicholson, not out	4	c Orfeur, b Ward ...	o
Extras	10	Extras ...	1
	73		86

BOWLING.—Goldsmith, 7 wkts. for 48 ; Mr J H Oldham, 6 wkts. for 51.

1st XI. v. Great Bentley.—Thursday, July 2nd, played at Great Bentley.

On July 2nd we visited Bentley and an exciting match ended in a victory for the School by 25 runs.

GREAT BENTLEY		SCHOOL	
P Z Clark, b Goldsmith ...	o	Mr J H Oldam, c H Gosling, b Horst	31
J Horst, b J H Oldham ...	7	E J Brand, c Lord, b Lowe ...	42
W Lowe, b Goldsmith ...	o	F J Eves, run out	20
H Barker, b Goldsmith ...	35	Mr F D Barker, c and b Clark ...	o
F Lord, b Brand ...	5	W G Goldsmith, b Barker ...	3
F Cowell, hit wkt, b Brand ...	6	J L. Oliver, b Barker ...	3
S Humm, b Brand ...	32	W M Town, b Lowe ...	o
S Newman, c Oliver, b Atkin ...	15	C E F Everett, c sub, b Lowe ...	o
G Gosling, c J H Oldham, b Goldsmith	1	G Atkin, c Lord, b Barker ...	2
H Gosling, b Brand ...	7	E B Horwood, not out ...	24
B Cordy, not out ...	7	K Nicholson, b Barker ...	7
Extras	3	Extras ...	11
	118		143

BOWLING.—Brand, 4 wkts. for 23.

1st XI. v. Woodbridge School.—Saturday, July 4th, played at Colchester.

This match ended in a victory for Woodbridge, who had much the stronger team.

WOODBRIDGE			SCHOOL		
T R Kemplen, c and b Brand	...	9	F J Eves, c Jordan, b Booth	...	10
W S Rope, c and b Brand	...	2	E J Brand, c Fouracres, b Lingwood		26
N J H Goodchild, b Brand	...	1	W G Goldsmith, c Rope, b Ling-		
H P L Lingwood, c Nicholson, b			wood ...	...	26
Brand ...	...	67	J L Oliver, c and b Lingwood	...	1
E J R Kemplen. b Eves		23	C E F Everett, c Kemplen, b King		2
W G B Jordan, c Eves, b Atkin	...	6	W M Town, c Rope, b Lingwood		4
A J Booth, c Atkin, b Goldsmith	...	25	E B Honwood, b King	...	0
W R F Clover, run out	...	29	G Atkin. not out	...	5
L H Tibbenham, b Eves	...	26	S W Lord, b King	...	2
H F I King, not out	...	0	E M Wenden, b Lingwood	...	0
C E Fouracres, c Brand, b Atkin	...	0	K Nicholson, c Rope, b Lingwood		0
Extras	...	18	Extras	...	13
		206			89

BOWLING.—Brand, 4 wkts. for 45.

1st XI. v. Chelmsford Grammar School.—Saturday, July 11th, played at Colchester.

On July 11th we were visited by Chelmsford School, who brought with them three masters, two of whom proved to be very hard hitters, and completely mastered our bowling. The scores were as follows :

CHELMSFORD			SCHOOL		
Mr S G Wintle, c Oliver, b Atkin	...	55	F J Eves, b Squier	...	3
E W Rowland, c Eves, b J H Old-			E J Brand, run out	...	16
ham ...	...	35	Mr J H Oldham, b Wintle	...	19
Mr T Hay, b Eves	...	0	Mr F D Barker, b Squier	...	5
Mr N Squier, c Eves, b Atkin	...	128	W G Goldsmith, run out	...	4
V C Britton, not out	...	51	G Atkin, c H Bowie, b Wintle	...	4
H Clist, b Atkin	...	0	J L Oliver, run out	...	0
J Bowie. c and b Eves	...	0	W M Town, b Squier	...	6
H Bowie, not out	...	5	C E F Everett, not out	...	6
D C F Couch			E B Horwood, c Lewis, b Squier	...	4
G F Shead } did not bat			K Nicholson, c and b Squier	...	0
H Lewis			Extras	...	6
Extras	...	9			
(6 wkts.)...	...	283			73

1st XI. v. Ipswich Secondary School.—Saturday, July 18th, played at Colchester.

The School batted first, and were enabled by the efforts of Goldsmith and Brand to score 141 runs. Ipswich could not, of course, hope to reach this in time, but they made a plucky effort, and, with the help of Wellard, scored a total of 81, the School thus winning the match by 60 runs.

SCHOOL		IPSWICH	
F J Eves, run out	11	Newby, c Oliver, b Brand ...	0
E J Brand, b Mudd	37	Lawes, c Oliver, b Atkin ...	7
C E F Everett, c Feavearyear, b Young...	0	Feavearyear, c Eves, b Brand ...	9
		Randell, c Brand, b Atkin ...	1
W M Town, b Newby... ...	4	Mudd, b Atkin	4
W G Goldsmith, c Lawes, b Wainwright	57	Orvis, b Atkin	6
		Wellard, b Brand	23
J L Oliver, b Randell	0	Northfield, c Oliver, b Brand ...	0
G Atkin, b Wellard	19	Young, c Goldsmith, b Brand ...	2
E B Horwood, b Wellard ...	3	Wainwright, c and b Eves ...	8
S W Lord, not out	4	Barnett, not out	6
K Nicholson, b Wellard ...	0		
C Nicholson, b Wellard ...	0		
Extras	6	Extras	15
	141		81

BOWLING.—Brand, 5 wkts. for 25; Atkin, 4 wkts. for 30.

1st XI. v. Colchester and East Essex.—Saturday, July 25th, played at Castle Park.

COLCHESTER		SCHOOL	
A W Smith, lbw, b Brand ...	82	F J Eves, b Wilkinson ...	0
E S Missen, c J D Ward, b J H Oldham ...	1	E J Brand, b Smith ...	2
E G Fenn, run out	10	Mr J D Ward, b Smith ...	21
E Shorthouse, c and b J H Oldham	5	Mr J H Oldham, b Smith ...	0
R W Macfarlane, c Lord, b Brand...	7	Mr E B Deakin, b Cox ...	3
Creese, c J H Oldham, b Eves ...	24	W G Goldsmith, st Creese, b Smith	5
V Jasper, b Eves	3	Mr F D Barker, b Smith ...	8
A S Cox, c Brand, b Eves ...	19	E B Horwood, b Smith ...	0
J W Wilkinson, b Eves	14	W M Town, c Missen, b Smith ...	0
R R Stone, b Brand	1	G Atkin, b Cox	0
J H Church, not out	8	J L Oliver, not out	4
C Fairhead, did not bat		S W Lord, run out	0
Extras	4	Extras	6
(10 wkts.) ...	178		49

BOWLING.—Eves, 4 wkts. for 13.

SECOND ELEVEN.

C.R.G.S. v. OLD COLCESTRIANS (XIII. aside).

O.C.'s		C.R.G.S.	
A D Laurence, b Atkin ...	4	J L Oliver, b Lucking...	8
J Marlar, c Rayner, b Nicholson ...	4	G C Rayner, b Lawrence ...	3
C Manning, b Atkin ...	5	G Atkin, b Lawrence	2
G F Harsum, b Atkin ...	5	S W Lord, b Lawrence ...	7
R S Sennett, c Horwood, b Nicholson	4	E B Horwood, c Harsum, b Fitch	5
L B Fitch, run out	21	J H Cottrell, c Sennett, b Lawrence	2
A J Lucking, c Lord, b Nicholson	7	C Nicholson, b Lawrence ...	5
A O Farmer, b Nicholson ...	9	J H King, b Fitch	0
L C Brook, b Nicholson ...	1	T G Smith, b Lawrence ...	12
H A Beckett, run out	0	W R Orrin, run out	1
H Watsham, run out	2	E M Wenden, b Marlar ...	7
T S Renton, not out	5	R B Alderton, c Renton, b Marlar	0
C A McClosky, run out ...	4	C W Wenden, not out... ...	5
Extras	2	Extras	6
	61		63

A D Lawrence, 6 for 17   C Nicholson, 5 for 25

C.R.G.S. v. IPSWICH SECONDARY SCHOOL 2nd XI.

Ipswich			C.R.G.S.		
Wilson, c Wenden, b Rayner	...	3	G C Rayner, b Bennett	...	15
Fisk, c Bugg, b Rayner	...	2	E M Wenden, c Shute, b Bennett...		3
Shute, c Bugg, b Rayner	...	1	J H King, b Bennett ...	...	13
Northfield, c Collinge, b Rayner	...	5	C W Wenden, c Campbell, b Bennett		0
Cooper, ma, c Bugg, b Rayner	...	5	J H Cottrell, b Bennett	...	19
Bennett, b Orrin	...	0	T G Smith, b Wilson ...	...	7
Jenkinson, b Orrin	...	0	W R Orrin, not out ...	...	9
Youngman, b Rayner...	...	4	R B Alderton, not out...	..	13
Cooper, mi, not out ...	...	2	E P Bugg		
Campbell, b Rayner ...	...	0	F J Collinge } did not bat		
Hicks, b Wenden	...	4	R H Cottrell		
Extras	...	1	Extras ...	...	16
		27	(for 6)		95

Rayner, 7 wkt. for 9

C R.G.S. v. Clacton G.S., July 2nd, at home, resulting in a draw. Clacton 69 (Orrin 4 for 32). School 54 for 9 (Rayner 12).

C.R.G.S. v. Ascham College, July 11th, at home. Ascham College 51 and 22. School 44 and 47 for 8. School won by 5 wickets. Wenden, ma 15 and 11, Alderton 10, Wenden, mi 10; Rayner 5 for 20, Nicholson, mi 6 for 9.

FIRST ELEVEN AVERAGES.—SEASON 1914.

BATTING.

Name	Total Runs		Most in Innings		No. of Innings		Times not out	Average
F. J. Eves........	158	..	*29	..	10	..	1	17·56
E. J. Brand	207	..	42	..	14	..	1	15·92
W. G. Goldsmith..	175	..	57	..	14	..	1	13·46
G. Atkin..........	60	..	19	..	10	..	3	8·57
E. B. Horwood ...	39	..	*24	..	7	..	1	6·50
S. W. Lord	25	..	*6	..	7	..	2	5·00

BOWLING.

Name	Runs		Wickets		Overs		Maidens	Average per Wkt.
G. Atkin	125	..	15	..	38·4	..	4	8·33
W. G Goldsmith	393	..	37	..	119	..	22	10 62
E. J. Brand	254	..	23	...	74·4	..	7	11·05
F. J. Eves	271	..	21	..	66	..	9	12·90

CHARACTERS OF THE ELEVEN.

E. J. BRAND (Captain). A batsman with a good defence but lacks scoring strokes. Weak on the off-side. Useful left-hand bowler and good field.

F. J. EVES. Strong forceful batsman with a fine drive. Fast right-hand bowler : is somewhat inconsistent. Bowled very well against the Town. Very good field.

W. G. GOLDSMITH. Stylish bat, possessing many good strokes. Played a good innings of 57 v. Ipswich School. Medium right-hand bowler. He failed to get many wickets in the last month.

W. M. TOWN. A really first-class field. Picks the ball up well and returns hard. Has taken some fine catches in the long field. Batting rather weak.

C. E. EVERETT.—A batsman possessing some natural strokes, but lacks finish. Pretty good field.

J. L. OLIVER. Moderate bat with good defence, but has not enough confidence. Smart field.

G. ATKIN. Though small, is quite a good bat. Has a good idea of the forward stroke. Useful change bowler and took a number of wickets at the beginning of the season.

S. W. LORD. A successful wicket-keeper and good deep field. Batting poor. Must learn to keep the ball down.

K. NICHOLSON. Rather disappointing behind the stumps as he failed to reproduce his early season form. Moderate bat.

E. B. HORWOOD. Good bat when he does not hit out rashly. Very fine ground field on his day.

C. NICHOLSON. Useful medium change bowler with an easy action. Rather slow in the field and has failed as a bat.

HOUSE CRICKET.

Some interesting games were played and for once a definite decision was arrived at. Parr's won the Cock House Cup, the other three Houses tieing for second place. Parr's defeated Harsnett's by 20 runs, School House by an innings and 9 runs, and Dugard's by 93 runs. The winning team comprised Brand (captain), Town, Lord, Wenden, Andrews, Wagstaff, Collinge, ma, Collinge, mi, Folkard, French, mi and Cheshire.

HARSNETT'S v. PARR'S. May 21st, 1914.

Parr's batted first and scored 61. With 8 wickets down for 31, things looked bad for Harsnett's. However, King hit out for a plucky 22. Both sides were level on the first innings. At their second venture Parr's made 65. Harsnett's collapsed badly after a good start and were all out for 46. Atkin and Nicholson, mi, bowled very well for Harsnett's.

HARSNETTS.

G Atkin, c Collinge, b Town	...	5	c sub, b Town	... ...	12
C E Everett, run out ...	...	7	b Brand ...	... ...	11
K Nicholson, b Town ...	...	3	st Lord. b Town	... ...	2
J L Oliver, b Town ...	...	0	b Brand ...	... ...	0
J H King, b Brand ...	...	22	b Brand ...	... ...	4
R B Alderton, b Town	...	2	b Town ...	... ...	4
T G Smith, b Brand ...	...	3	b Town ...	... ...	4
C Nicholson, b Town ...	...	1	run out ...	... ...	0
— Cox, c Town, b Brand	...	5	b Brand ...	... ...	1
G F Deane, not out ...	...	12	not out ...	... ...	2
L W Clark, b Brand ...	...	0	c French, b Brand	... ...	4
Extras ...	...	1	Extras ...	... ...	1
		61			45

PARR'S.

W M Town, b Nicholson	...	3	c Nicholson, b Atkin ...	...	16
E J Brand, c Deane, b Atkin	...	19	c Oliver, b Atkin	...	8
S W Lord, b Nicholson	...	0	b Nicholson	...	14
P R Wagstaff, b Atkin	...	5	c Alderton, b Nicholson	...	1
E A Andrews, c Nicholson, b Atkin		10	c Nicholson, ma, b Nicholson, mi		3
E M Wenden, c and b Nicholson	...	3	c Nicholson, b Atkin ...	...	1
F J Collinge, b Nicholson	...	0	b Atkin ...	...	0
H Folkard, c Clark, b Nicholson	...	1	c Oliver, b Nicholson ...	...	8
H H Collinge, b Nicholson	...	3	b Nicholson	...	7
R E French, not out ...	...	12	run out ..	...	4
— Cheshire, c Nicholson, b Smith		5	not out ...	...	2
Extras	...	0	Extras	...	1
		61			**65**

HARSNETT'S v. SCHOOLHOUSE, June 11th.

The Harsnett captain, having won the toss, decided to put his men in first, and accordingly Schoolhouse took the field. Goldsmith and Rayner, who bowled unchanged throughout the innings, did not experience much difficulty from the batsmen, and the side were all out for 46. Cox, who batted very pluckily, and Smith, were the only batsmen who made any runs at all. Schoolhouse also did not realise much at their first venture, and only made 55, of which Goldsmith and Curtis made respectively 31 and 10. In their second innings, Harsnett's did extremely well Atkin and Everett opened the innings, and runs soon came freely. Several changes were made, but were of no effect until Atkin jumped out to a well-pitched ball from Wenden and was bowled. Everett still continued to score freely all round the wicket, and was not despatched until he had made 51. Eventually the side was out for 119, Smith also batting well for 29. Schoolhouse, who required 129 to win, failed miserably, and only made 42, due chiefly to the good bowling of Everett and Atkin, who took all the wickets between them ; Harsnett's thus winning by 86 runs.

HARSNETT'S.

1st Innings			2nd Innings		
Atkin, b Goldsmith ...	...	2	b Wenden ...	...	18
Everett, ma, b Rayner...	...	0	c Rayner, b Cottrell, ma	...	51
Nicholson, ma, b Rayner	...	4	c Green, b Goldsmith ...	...	7
Oliver, b Goldsmith ...	...	0	c Cottrell, ma, b Goldsmith	...	0
King, ma, b Goldsmith	...	6	c Cottrell, mi, b Cottrell, ma	...	0
Deane, b Goldsmith ...	...	0	b Goldsmith	...	3
Alderton, b Goldsmith	...	5	c and b Goldsmith ...	...	0
Cox, b Goldsmith	...	7	b Goldsmith	...	2
Smith, ma, b Goldsmith	...	8	b Goldsmith	...	29
Nicholson, mi, c Barnes, b Goldsmith	5	not out ...	...	3
Clarke, ma, not out ...	...	1	b Goldsmith	...	4
Extras ...	...	8	Extras ...	...	2
		46			**119**

SCHOOL HOUSE.

Butler, ma, run out ...	...	0	b Everett, ma	...	4
Rayner, b Nicholson ...	...	7	c King, ma, b Atkin ...	...	0
Goldsmith, b Atkin ...	...	31	b Atkin	...	10
Wenden, c Everitt, b Atkin	...	1	b Atkin ...	...	2
Cottrell, ma, c and b Atkin	...	0	c Smith, b Everett, ma	...	2
Curtis, not out ...	...	10	c Deane, b Atkin	...	0
Cottrell, mi, c Smith, b Nicholson	5	c and b Atkin	...	0
Green, c Smith, b Nicholson	...	0	b Everett, ma	...	0
Dicker, b Atkin	...	0	b Atkin	...	0
Pertwee, c and b Atkin	...	0	not out ...	...	1
Barnes, mi, b Nicholson	...	0	c Nicholson, ma, b Everett	...	1
Extras ...	...	1	Extras ...	...	3
		55			**42**

119

DUGARD'S v. HARSNETT'S.

Dugard's met Harsnett's on July 16th. Dugard's batted first, and were soon accounted for, being all out for 23. Eves was the only scorer, with 14, while Atkin, for Harsnett's, took 6 wickets for 7. Harsnett's next went in, and fared even worse, for Eves and Orrin dismissed them all for the paltry total of 19, Eves taking 7 wickets for 10.

It was not to be expected that Dugard's would again be got rid of so cheaply, and there was therefore little surprise when Eves and Pullen settled down together and scored steadily. There were no boundaries, and therefore rapid scoring, Eves opening his innings with a 7. He was bowled by Atkin on reaching 28, and the rest of the team gave little trouble, being all out for 71. Pullen scored 20.

Harsnett's now had to get 76 to win, and for a time it seemed possible that they would do this, but once Atkin and Everett were separated the case was hopeless, and they were all dismissed for 48, Dugard's thus winning the match by 28 runs.

DUGARD'S

1st Innings			2nd Innings		
Eves, b Nicholson mi ...	...	14	b Atkin	...	28
Hudson. b Atkin ...:	...	1	b Atkin	...	5
Pullen, b Nicholson mi	...	0	b Everett ...	...	20
Horwood, c Nicholson mi, b Atkin		2	b Atkin ...	...	2
Orrin, c Clarke ma, b Atkin	....	0	run out ...	...	3
Bugg, b Atkin	...	2	c Atkin, b Nicholson mi	...	0
Devienne, c Oliver, b Nicholson mi		0	b Everett ...	...	2
Barrell, not out	...	0	not out ...	...	5
Rogers, b Nicholson mi	...	0	b Nicholson mi	...	4
Kent, b Atkin ...		1	b Everett ...	...	0
Horlock, b Atkin ...	...	0	b Smith ...	...	0
Extras ...	...	3	Extras ...	...	2
		23			71

BOWLING.—Atkin, 9 wkts. for 29 ; Nicholson mi, 6 wkts. for 40.

HARSNETT'S

1st Innings			2nd Innings		
Nicholson ma, lbw, b Orrin	...	1	c and b Eves	...	0
Everett ma, c and b Eves	...	2	b Orrin ...	...	11
Oliver, b Eves ...	...	1	b Eves ...	...	2
Atkin, run out	...	6	b Orrin ...	...	15
King, ma, c Bugg, b Eves	...	0	b Orrin ...	...	3
Deane, b Eves ...	...	1	c Hudson, b Orrin ...	...	2
Alderton, b Eves, ...	...	4	b Orrin ...	...	4
Cox, b Orrin ...	...	0	run out ...	...	3
Smith, not out ...	...	2	b Horlock ...	...	4
Nicholson mi, b Eves ...	...	0	not out ...	...	0
Clark ma, c and b Eves	...	0	b Orrin ...	...	1
Extras ...	...	2	Extras ...	...	3
		19			48

BOWLING.—Orrin, 7 wkts. for 24 ; Eves, 9 wkts. for 34.

PARR'S v. DUGARD'S, July 16th.

Parr's lost the toss and batted first, but were all out for the low score of 39. On Dugard's going in they fared even worse, only making 36. Town bowled well for Parr's, taking 6 for 13. In the second innings Parr's did better, reaching 111 before they were all dismissed. Town hit a vigorous 28 and was well supported by Lord. Collinge ma. also played a good innings of 20, while other members did their share. It seemed that the Dugard's bowling was hardly judiciously managed. With 114 to win, Dugard's collapsed badly after Eves was out, being all out 21. Thus Parr's won the match and the Cricket Cup.

PARR'S

1st Innings		2nd Innings	
S W Lord, c Devienne, b Orrin ...	2	b Eves	19
E J Brand, lbw, b Orrin ...	1	lbw, b Orrin	4
W M Town, c Kent, b Orrin ...	6	c Horwood, b Orrin	28
E W Andrews, c Horwood, b Eves	2	c Bugg, b Orrin	0
E M Wenden, run out	13	b Orrin	8
H Folkard, c Bugg, b Orrin ...	0	b Orrin	10
R E French, c and b Orrin ...	0	c Rogers, b Horwood	0
F J Collinge, c Bugg, b Horwood...	2	c Hudson, b Eves	20
P R Wagstaff, b Orrin ...	1	run out	6
H H Collinge, b Orrin ...	1	not out	8
Cheshire, not out	0	b Orrin	0
Extras	11	Extras	8
	39		111

DUGARD'S

F J Eves, c and b Town ...	10	b Brand	0
R J Hudson, c French, b Town ...	3	b Brand	1
B I Pullen, b Brand	0	b Town	0
E B Horwood, c and b Town ...	14	lbw, b Town	5
S W Rogers, b Town	0	c and b Brand	1
E P Bugg, b Brand	2	st Lord, b Town	8
G Barrell, c Brand, b Town ...	0	c Collinge, b Town	0
W R Orrin, b Brand	2	lbw, b Brand	0
T D Devionne, run out ...	0	c Lord, b Town	1
J Kent, c Cheshire, b Town ...	1	not out	2
Horlock, not out	3	b Town	3
Extras	1	Extras	0
	36		21

football.

IN common with many other Schools during the present crisis, one half-holiday a week is given up to Cadet Corps work and the other to games. Naturally the football has suffered from lack of practice, which is only obtainable after afternoon school. Even this was soon strictly limited in extent by the failing light of late autumn. The fixture list too, has been greatly affected, and several matches have been scratched.

With only four of last year's colourmen remaining, E. J. Brand, W. G. Goldsmith, B. I. Pullen and T. G. Smith, it has been a matter of some difficulty to complete the team. W. A. Doubleday and G. Atkin, two members of last year's 2nd XI., have shown good form, while J. H. Cottrell with a little more experience should develop into an excellent back.

The other members of the team have hardly lived up to their reputation gained in practice. The real weakness lies in the half-back line and this is all the more noticeable as we had three such fine halves last year. The forwards for want of adequate support from their halves have been greatly handicapped, but with the exception of the Woodbridge match they lacked dash and combination. At present there seems to be a dearth of good left wing men, and if this could be rectified the attack would greatly improve.

On the whole however the School has done well against heavier sides and the experience gained, even in defeat, will go far towards winning matches in the future.

Below are appended the matches to date : —

C.R.G.S. v. Chelmsford G.S.— October 10th, played at home, resulting in a win for our opponents 5—2. At the last moment Pullen was unable to turn out and White was called upon to take his place. The School took the lead through Goldsmith, but Chelmsford soon equalised. A free kick against Chelmsford was well placed and in the ensuing mêlée Atkin scored. However Chelmsford got through twice in rapid succession, thus taking the lead. The School halves were weak and failed to hold their opponents, who got two more goals, one from a penalty awarded for handling. The forwards were erratic and lacked dash, especially the two wing men Rogers and White.

C.R.G.S. v. Ipswich Secondary School.—October 17th, played at home, resulting in a win for Ipswich 5—2. Soon after the start the School were two goals down, but the forwards rallied and drew level through Goldsmith and Rogers. In the second half the forwards missed several opportunities of scoring, the left wing being especially at fault. Although the School did most of the pressing Ipswich scored three goals from breakaways. The halves were weak although Cottrell mi. did well for a first appearance. Atkin and Goldsmith were the best of the forwards, while Doubleday and Cottrell ma. did good work in defence.

C.R.G.S. v. Brentwood School.—October 24th, on School Ground, an even game resulted in Brentwood winning 3—0. The School again lacked the services of Pullen, and in consequence the forward line was disorganised. The opening stages of the game were fairly even both sides attacking in turn. However the School forwards failed to avail themselves of opportunities and Brentwood scored shortly before the interval. On resuming the School experienced bad luck in not scoring, Goldsmith and Atkin making good efforts. Two more goals were put on by Brentwood, one of which was lucky as the ball appeared to go behind before being placed in the net. Cottrell ma. played a sound game at back.

C.R.G.S. v. Essex Cyclist Batt.—Played on October 29th, at Clacton, and resulting in a draw 1—1. Included in the School team were Mr. Watts, R. Malyn, H. A. Beckett and S. W. Lord. The ground after a heavy rain was in a deplorable condition and rendered accurate play impossible. The School early took the lead through Malyn, who scored after cleverly beating several opponents. After this our opponents attacked strongly and only the excellent play of Mr. Watts kept our goal intact. In the second half the School attacked hard but failed to score and in the closing stages our opponents equalised, Smith injuring his thumb in attempting to save. After the match the team were entertained o tea by Capt. E. G. Davis, who had arranged the game.

C.R.G.S. v. Woodbridge School.—Played on October 31st, at Woodbridge, and resulted in a great win for the School by 4—0. Losing the toss the School kicked off with the advantage of a slight slope and soon got together. The inside forwards Goldsmith, Atkin and Gibb, combined well together ably supported as they were by Doubleday at half. After pressing for some time Goldsmith scored with an excellent cross shot. Woodbridge then made efforts to equalise but the defence was sound. Half-time arrived with score School 1, Woodbridge 0. On resuming the School again attacked vigorously and good play by the forwards resulted in three goals being scored in rapid succession, Atkin, Gibb, and Rogers each securing a point. Despite many centres put across by Pullen no further score was made although many shots were sent in. Cottrell ma. tackled strongly and saved several critical situations at back, while Alderton made a promising debut in goal. The team was :—R. B. Alderton ; J. H. Cottrell and E. J. Brand ; W. R. Orrin, W. A. Doubleday, and R. H. Cottrell ; B. I. Pullen, G. Atkin, W. G. Goldsmith, G. Gibb and S. W. Rogers.

C.R.G.S. v. Framlingham College.—November 7th, at Framlingham. The School suffered rather a severe defeat being beaten 7 goals to nothing. In the first half the School kicked up a steep slope and for a time held their own. However Framlingham scored twice before half-time. In the second half the defence went to pieces and five more goals were scored. The halves were very poor indeed and left too much work for the backs. Alderton played an excellent game in goal, and but for him the score would have been greater. The forwards deserved better luck, for they played pluckily against a heavy defence.

SECOND ELEVEN.

Several promising players have been discovered this year. French mi., though small, has a good idea of the full-back game. Wenden and Wagstaff have also done well in defence. Of the forwards, Pertwee and Gilbert have shown the best form. Up to the present two matches have been won and lost.

C.R.G.S. v. Clacton G.S.—October 10th, at home, resulting in a win for the School 3—0. The School forwards got together nicely and were well supported in the defence, where Rickword and French played a sound game. The goals were scored by Spencer and Crighton.

C.R.G.S. v. Maldon G.S.—October 15th, on School Ground. The team was made up of five 1st XI. non-colours and the rest 2nd XI. An even game resulted in a win for Maldon by the odd goal in three. Atkin scored for the School.

C.R.G.S. v. Ipswich Secondary School 2nd XI.—October 17th, played at Ipswich, resulting in a defeat 2—4. The forwards lacked combination and missed several chances. White scored one goal for the School and the other was put through by the Ipswich back. Despite the efforts of Wagstaff and French in the defence Ipswich scored two more goals.

C.R.G.S. v. Woodbridge School 2nd XI.—October 31st, at home, resulting in a win for the School 1—0. Pertwee scored the only goal in the first two minutes with a good cross shot. The forwards showed better form with Gilbert at centre and the defence was very sound.

898 THE COLCESTRIAN

House Singings.

THE Saturday Night Sing-songs were resumed with the new academic year, although the summer months have heard the sweet treble of most of our best singers thicken into a rumbling, uncertain bass, with the advent of moustaches and of high collars. In compensation, we find less tone-deaf ears among the new boys than is usual in Essex.

We welcome Chase, Clough and Weeks ma., in their first appearances. Barnes and Collinge mi. have served their houses well, and Graham Brown shows promise with the violin.

There is still far too much indifference among prefects and their houses towards an important part of our School activities. The average House-singing is nothing for a School of two hundred boys to boast about, and it is a painful reflection on our industry and initiative to find only one item in six House-singings worthy of offering to our friends of the new Army. To the faithful six or seven boys who give up at least one of their evenings a week to the School's party for entertaining the Troops, I must express my gratitude, and I appeal to all of you to add to our repertoire some good items which will augment our programme and give the C.R.G.S. Concert Party more rest.

We welcome cordially the Dramatic Society, inaugurated by the Fifths, under Mr. Carter's capable direction; and wish them a successful career. This spirit of initiative, so strong in the time of the " B's," and of A. E. Hall, and kept alive by Everett ma., should be encouraged in every way.

We hope to improve upon last year's standard in the Carol Service on December 20th, a function which becomes annually more popular. The Mayor and his Committee have invited our co-operation at the Christmas Concert for the Troops on Monday, December 21st. Our acceptance must depend upon the progress made in singing in the next few weeks.

J.A.P.

Cadet Corps.

BEFORE writing of present doings in the Cadet Corps we must hark back to a broiling week-end in June—the 27th and 28th, when we were in camp at Great Horkesley with the 3rd Essex Cadet Battalion. A deal of work was crowded into that short period but all enjoyed themselves immensely, especially on the Sunday, when noon found us all very hot but also very enthusiastic over the field day, which ended in the taking of the camp by storm. We heard, too, that it was not bad fun getting "wounded."

124

The next thing to look forward to was the usual Summer Camp. We were nicely settled in near the 5th Battalion Essex Regiment Camp at Great Clacton. With us were Southend, Ongar and Palmer's School, Grays. We had begun to do excellent work under the direction of Major Mackay of the Hampshire Regt., when on the all-eventful Monday we had perforce to strike camp. Ongar especially were to be sympathised with as they had only come in late on the Saturday.

This term, as was to be expected, we are indeed short of Officers, but we are happy in a record of recruits, who make up two of our four sections and who, under the excellent instruction of C. S. J. Penn, have soon become quite smart. Keenness is coming to the rescue and we are at present wrestling with the new " Platoon " drill. We have had a number of route marches and the Thursday " half " has been given over to drill.

Members of the Corps cannot fail to realise that by displaying keenness and by giving proof of smartness and efficiency, they are doing their duty now: and soon they will find that they have a long start in things that will matter very much in Great Britain.

Shooting.

THE results of the Imperial Challenge Shield Competition were issued this term, and we find both our teams lower than last year, but our Juniors are still among the prize winners gaining a prize of £2 with the position of 39th out of 290 teams entered. The Seniors secured 85th place in an entry of 570. Our averages in this competition are the lowest for the last three years and this is remarkable seeing that orthoptics were allowed for the first time this year.

We have a number of new members this term as was only to be expected under existing circumstances, when everyone should learn to overcome gun-shyness at any rate, and we hope to see a still greater number joining the Club.

We had one match this term against the London Orphan Asylum, who beat us rather badly, scoring 510 to our 468.

The first round in the House Competition was shot-off last term and resulted in School House coming out on top, while the other Houses are all close behind there being only 18 points difference between the leaders and lowest House, so that the competition at the end of this term should be very keen.

The following are the scores at present :—

SCHOOL HOUSE.		PARR'S.		DUGARD'S.		HARSNETT'S.	
Leeming	31	Percy	29	Chapman ..	31	Everett	32
Rayner	30	Watsham ..	29	Hudson	31	Atkin	29
Green	30	Brand	29	Doubleday	30	Clarke	28
Goldsmith ..	30	Andrews ..	28	Horwood ..	30	Deane	27
Wenden	29	Lord	28	Flanegan ..	28	Bare	26
Cottrell ma.	25	Town	26	Fincham ..	24	King	24
Le Cœuvre..	25	Wagstaff ..	22	Halls	22	Ward	23
Koskinas ..	24	Melrose	21	Plummer ..	16	Baskett	17
	224		212		212		206

The following are the scores in the I.C.S. Competition :—

SENIORS.

	Deliberate.		Rapid.		Total.
Chapman	43	..	43	..	86
Doubleday	41	..	41	..	82
Everett ma.	38	..	39	..	77
Watsham ma.	38	..	39	..	77
Flanegan	38	..	34	..	72
Hudson	31	..	40	..	71
Clarke	35	..	35	..	70
Andrews	38	..	30	..	68
Rayner	30	..	12	..	42
					645

Average 71·66

JUNIORS.

	Bisley.		Figure.		Total.
Wenden	43	..	48	..	91
Watsham mi.	40	..	40	..	80
Goldsmith	38	..	48	..	76
Halls	39	..	34	..	73
Bare	34	..	39	..	73
Leeming	34	..	36	..	70
Green	36	..	32	..	68
Lord	34	..	32	..	66
Percy	35	..	29	..	64
					671

Average 74·55

The following is a list of awards for the year ending Easter, 1914 :—

S.M.R.C. Silver Medal for highest average in House Matches, Doubleday mi. and Chapman tie.

S.M.R.C. Bronze Medal for highest average in Club Matches, Eves 92·3

MEDAL COMPETITION :—

Bell Medal	..	..	Doubleday ma.
Express Medal	..	..	Doubleday mi.

LORD ROBERT'S SPOONS, for highest average in Practice Shots :—

Open	..	..	..	Chapman 60·6.
Under 16	..	..	Andrews 52·3.
Under 15	..	..	Watsham mi., 53·5.

N.R.A. Bronze Medal for Rapid Firing, Doubleday ma.

Again we have to tender our best thanks to C. S. I. Penn for his services.   E.R.

Scouting Notes.

THIRD ANNUAL CAMP.

(St. Osyth beach. Tuesday, July 28th—Friday, August 7th).

THE Camp of 1914 will probably be remembered by most of us long after the memories of other camps have faded. Little did we think as we started for St. Osyth on that sunny July morning that ere a week had passed England would be plunged into war. The first sign of the coming storm was the sudden recall to barracks of our cook, Corporal Wadmore of the 1st Hants Regt., very early on the morning of the 30th. His departure was a great loss, as he had already made himself very popular, and was teaching us many of those practical "things every Scout ought to know," and which one learns more quickly at camp than anywhere else. Fortunately for us however, Mr. G. F. Stearn was with us again this year, and so we were able to "carry on" without any difficulty. We had thirty-four scouts at camp including one ex-member and one hon. member of the Troop, Weatherall and N. Graham Brown.

The tents were arranged as follows :—

PEEWIT PATROL.	OTTER PATROL.	WOLF PATROL.	WOOD PIGEON PATROL.	BEAVER PATROL.
P.L. Kent	P.L.Collinge	King		P.L. Taylor
Clark	Marlar	Burleigh	P.L. Sands	Child
Everett ma.	Brook	Gower	Chambers	Hickinbotham
Hazell	Barnes	Weatherall	Thomas	Wheeler mi.
Last	Weeks		Page	Smith
Clarke	Hackett	CURLEW	H. Graham-	Dancer
	Wood	PATROL.	Brown	N. Graham-
		P.L. Watkinson	Havard	Brown
		Nicholl		
		Wilson ma.		
		Harman		

A serious accident to Wheeler ma. a few days before camp prevented him from coming with us this year, but he has now happily quite recovered.

By the kindness of Mr. Wilson Blyth we were able this year to pitch the tents on a much better site, quite as near to the sea as in former years, but more conveniently situated for the village. The weather was delightful for the whole of the ten days except for two stormy nights and occasional showers.

In many ways it was a very exciting time. The patrol of sentries just outside the camp, the constant coming and going of officers, the scarcity of definite news, the conflicting rumours and the incessant boom of cannon on August 5th and 6th (possibly the siege guns at Liege) all tended to create an atmosphere of excitement which will long be remembered. In spite of all, however, we had a most successful and enjoyable camp, and carried through to the end the programme we had arranged.

It is impossible to thank individually the many people who helped to make the camp a success, but we should like to offer our sincere thanks to all the generous people who sent presents to the commissarat, to the Mayor who as Chairman of the Governors of the School came down to inspect the camp on July 31st, and lastly to Mr. Brook who again so kindly carted our baggage and equipment to and from St. Osyth.

Since the holidays the troop has been very largely reconstructed. After nearly three years' training as Scouts, the following have passed on to the Cadet Corps :—Collinge, Sands, Watkinson, Brown, King, Clark, Page, Brook, Thomas, Marlar, Tait, Blyth, Everett mi. and Graham-Brown. While wishing them all success in the Corps, I also hope that they will keep in mind the oft-repeated saying of our Chief "Once a Scout, always a Scout," and always endeavour to be true to the great ideal for which the Scout law stands.

We are glad to welcome as recruits :—Poyser, Gell, Beckett, Hawkins, Roberts, Mustard, Cosser, Cole, Dace, and Mirrington.

For the rest, it must be recorded that the Peewit Patrol now stands at the head of the Troops for general smartness and efficiency, thanks to the keenness of its Patrol Leader John Kent, who, with Hazell of the same patrol, has just been awarded the Path-finder badge.

Burleigh, Chambers, and Barnes have become Patrol Leaders of the Wolves, Wood pigeons and Otters respectively.

It is impossible to conclude these notes without a word of farewell to our Chaplain— Mr. Hartley Parker. His unvarying kindness and help ever since the Troop was founded in 1912, and the generous hospitality we have so often enjoyed at Thorington will not soon be forgotten by any of us. We should like therefore to place on record our deep appreciation of the great kindness we have received from him and Mrs. Parker, and to assure them of a real 'Scout' welcome whenever they are able to visit us at Colchester.

The Pre.

IT is said that the pen is mightier than the sword, but just now the sword is so very much in demand that there seems little time or inclination for the pen. The desire to be up and doing is everywhere. Some can only attend more carefully to every duty that comes along—it is all we can do—and at any rate it is the right spirit.

Who would have imagined when we separated for our summer holiday, that we should re-assemble in times of war? The whole country reeks with war, nobody talks of anything but war, even the schoolroom is affected. The horror of the small boys when they recently discovered that George I. came from Hanover, and that Hanover is in Germany was most amusing to witness. How often too is the terrible threat heard, when lines are crooked, or the right foot used instead of the left "You will never make a soldier." We fall into it naturally—we cannot help it.

Now when there are signs of training on every side of us, and *esprit de corps* is burning amongst the British Army from the smallest unit upwards, the future scouts of the Lower School have been missing to some extent that glorious feeling of being a part however unimportant—of the whole. The fact that they have not looked down from the gallery upon their heroes below, heard of their famous victories on the football field, or most thrilling of all—joined in the general applause—seems to have cut them off from the Big School. But during the second half of the term this is being remedied.

We are all looking forward to Speech Day when the medals, which we have won by our little good deeds are to be presented.

We are told that "before the daffodils take the winds of March with beauty" the war will be over. We sincerely hope it will, but, at any rate, we mean to plant our bulbs so that we have a good show when the Spring comes. In fact most of them are already safely in.

To small gardeners this is rather an uninteresting time, so little to show for the work done, and naturally there is a tendency to let the gardens go. But when the blooms do appear, we hope there will be substantial proof that the Pre. did not grow fainthearted with November's gloom, and when the troops do return we shall have learnt some patriotic songs with which to greet them.

We have welcomed five new members to fill the places of Poyser, Worsp, Gell ma. and Roberts who passed up at Midsummer, and several boys, who were moved into our Form II. are doing remarkably well.

129

When we contrast our schools at the present moment with those of our less fortunate Allies, we can only feel thankful. It is a time to count up our good things, and appreciate those that remain to us.

On Tuesday last we were very fortunate in getting a splendid view of the King near the North Station on his way to inspect the troops at Braiswick. Much credit is due to Sergeant Penn on the way the little boys marched, and we hope soon another opportunity will offer itself, when we can again do a miniature route march.

Many thanks to those who so promptly responded to the appeal for magazines, collars, ties and socks for the wounded soldiers. These have been sent to different hospitals, and greatly appreciated.

Old Colcestrian Section.

Editorial.

The Society.

One scarcely regrets that the annual meeting of the Old Colcestrian Society this year was only sparsely attended. It means that the majority of the members were busy with their country's work, for as was only to be expected the eligible old boys of the Colchester Grammar School are in the ranks of the Services, and the ineligibles are fully occupied with the calls of war time upon a commercial nation.

Under the direction of the excellent President (Mr. C. E. Benham), however the business of the meeting was carried through as far as it could be, and vacancies in the ranks of officers were duly filled. Mr. Chas. T. Wright succeeds Mr. Benham in the Presidential Chair, Mr. A. T. Daldy comes in to help Mr. A. O. Farmer in the secretarial duties, and the Committee has been re-elected. It was found quite impossible to settle on a date for the annual dinner, because while the war with Germany lasts the majority of O.C.'s will be otherwise engaged ; so it was decided to leave the matter open till the new year. Then, if the Kaiseristic Kultur has been overwhelmed we shall be able to make the dinner also a welcome home to the lads of the old school who are so well maintaining its proud traditions.

We cannot say goodbye to Mr. Benham, as President, without a word of thanks to him for the way in which he has fulfilled the office, and the brilliant success of his dinner will live long in the Society's records, because it was one of the best attended in the series, and linked the years by bringing into the fold more famous O.C.'s of Mr. Benham's generation. The speech by Mr. J. T. A. Middleton, one of London's most prominent architects, will not soon be forgotten, and he will ever be welcome in our midst—a fact demonstrated by the warmth of his reception at the annual meeting of the Society, and at his brilliant lecture which followed.

The choice of Mr. Chas. T. Wright as the new President will be very popular. One of the best known business men of Essex, he comes to the office with a wide experience of public life, and may be relied upon to bring dignity and honour to the position, even in this trying year. He will lack the wonderful organising skill of Rev. E. Hartley Parker— our late Hon. Sec., whom we heartily congratulate on his

131

appointment—but it is fortunate in the circumstances that Mr. Wright gives place to no one in powers of organisation, whether social or commercial, and we look to him—should we in his year see the end of this terrible war—to set up a new record in demonstrating "how it should be done."

Our readers will pardon us this term for passing lightly over the ordinary events of life. The war has gripped the country—nay, the whole world—and that must be our apology for devoting so many pages to first-hand experiences of O.C.'s in war time. At least they should inspire us each to do his little bit for old England in her hour of need.

THE EDITOR.

for King and Country.

O.C.'s WITH THE FORCES.

THE call of Britons to the Colours to take their part in crushing for ever the world's canker of Prussian Militarism was early heard by old boys of the old school, and offers of service came from all quarters of the Motherland as well as from far Brisbane and British Columbia. The greater number of eligibles, jealous of the alma mater's proud traditions of loyalty, have "joined up," and some O.C.'s have already received their baptism of fire. In all 127 Old Colcestrians have enlisted, and are training in this country or in France, or are on their way from the Colonies to take their places with the sons of Briton fighting so stoutly on the side of the Allies. The following is a list of O.C.'s who are known to have joined the Colours, and there are others :—

Anthony, Wyn., Lieutenant, D.L.I.
Browne, Graham, Public Schs. Battn.
Bellward, G. E. F., Lieut. 5th Essex.
Benham, Gerald C., Captain and Adjutant, 8th Essex
Beard, E. C., Public Schs. Battn.
Bromley, B., Motor Transport.
Bultitude, R. J., 8th Essex.
Bunting, A. E., 9th Essex.
Baskett, Tom, Royal Naval Brigade.
Butler, G. F., Public Schs. Battn.
Bareham, Essex Yeomanry.
Cork, C., Civil Service Rifles.
Child, A.O.D.
Cullington, M.W., Civil Service Rifles.
Cheshire, G., 9th Essex
Cheshire, W. R., Ceylon Tea Planters.

Chambers, C. W., 9th Essex.
Chambers, A. S., A.O.D.
Clarke, L., 5th Essex
Collins, R. C., 20th Hussars.
Collinson, A. L., Censor Eastern T. C., Gibraltar.
Cudmore, Essex Yeomanry.
Denton, C. W., Lieut., 8th Essex.
Denton, A., Lieut., 5th Essex.
Denton, H. W., Public Schs. Battn.
Deakin, E. B., Lieut. 5th Essex.,
Davis, E. G., Captain and Adjutant, 8th Essex.
Davies, E. B., Australian Contingent.
Everett, W. R., 9th Essex.
Everett, C. E. F., Public Schs. Battn.
Fitch, L., Essex Yeomanry.
Green, A. E., 9th Essex.
Green, Harold, Hants Yeomanry.
Green, C. S., Essex Yeomanry.
Head, A., Motor Transport.
Harwood, Irish Rifles.
Judd, A. E., Essex R.H.A.
Jarrard, C. H., R.H.A.
King, Hugh, A.O.D.
Mason, A. S., Lieut., Devonshire Regt. (in India)
Miller, Public Schs. Battn.
Melrose, A., Public Schs. Battn.
Malyn, D. P., Quartermaster A.S.C.
Mason, C., 9th Essex
Orfeur, J. B., Royal Naval Volunteers.
Orfeur, H. W., 8th Essex.
Peacock, R.H.A.
Peacock, R. N. Volunteers.
Potter, J., Motor Transport.
Potter, C. C., Australian Red Cross.
Pepper, V., Canadian Contingent.
Plant, C., Public Schs. Battn.
Prior, C. D., Motor Transport.
Prime, E. J., Essex Yeomanry.
Phillips, Col.
Renton, T. S., 9th Essex.
Slight, R., Manchester Regt.
Siggers, Kent Yeomanry.
Sawyer, C. W., University Battn.
Sawyer, H., 5th Essex.
Turner, A. J., Major, R.F.A.
Town, W. M., 5th Essex.
Watson, J. F., South Wales Regt.

Watsham, A. E., 5th Essex.
Watson, J. L., Canadian Contingent.
Wilmott, J., Public Schs. Battn.
Whitby, J. M. F., 5th Essex.

This list is incomplete, and the Editors would esteem it a favour if relatives of other O.C.'s serving would kindly forward names and corps to which they have been posted, as it is desired to compile a complete list as a permanent record of the School's response to the Country's call in this critical period in the history of the world.

DAVIES FROM BRISBANE.

E. J. Davies—"Jack" of that ilk—joined the 2nd Australian Light Horse, and left for England with the Expeditionary Force. He should have arrived by the time these lines are read, and O.C.'s wishing to renew an old acquaintanceship should write, No. 9574, Driver E. J. Davies, 2nd Austrialian Light Horse, Queensland Contingent, England. Jack's father writes that if opportunity occurs his son intends to re-visit the old school, and would be glad to meet old schoolfellows again, for the greatest regret of the Davies' boys in leaving the Homeland was leaving the old school. Herbert Davies (Fairy) joins his father in cordial greetings.

IN THE TRENCHES.

Some O.C.'s have "gone foreign" for service, in India or Egypt, but Tom Baskett, "D" Coy., 1st Brigade, Naval Division, was the first to taste smoke, and his experiences are worth recording. In an interview with a *Weekly News* reporter at Chelmsford, Tom says :—

"We left Walmer about 12 o'clock and marched to Dover, a distance of ten miles. Here we embarked on a transport, and next morning arrived at Dunkirk. We were equipped with rifles and ammunition, but had no heavy guns. Here we entrained, but were still in ignorance as to our actual destination. The lights on the train were put out, and we all had our magazines charged. Eventually we learned that we were going to Antwerp, and we reached there after travelling by a very roundabout route, arriving about 4 o'clock in the morning. The Belgians gave us a splendid reception. We marched to Vieux Dieu, a suburb of Antwerp, which was to be our headquarters. Here we were billetted in a school.

Two hours after arrival the men assembled, and the Commodore delivered a manly speech, telling us we were to go into the trenches to relieve the plucky Belgians, who had been fighting day and night against the Germans for over ten days.

"After marching some distance word came that the Germans had broken through the outer line of defences of Antwerp, and we had to retreat for some distance. During the afternoon the Drake Battalion (ours) marched out to reinforce some trenches. Two companies went into the trenches and others lay down by the side of a hedge as reinforcements. After waiting for some time we were told to fall in as quietly as possible and march back to Antwerp. I afterwards learned that we marched between two lines of Germans who were close upon us. Eventually we got back into the last line of defences, where the main trenches were situated. The Germans soon got our range, and shelled us with shrapnel and kept on all day long. At the rear of the trenches we had a bomb-proof shelter, to which we retired when the shrapnel became very hot. As soon as it was dark the enemy began infantry attacks, moving up in close column. At the ends of the trenches were two searchlights which kept sweeping the field. The Germans advanced through a wood about 500 yards away. The trenches were protected in front with barbed wire entanglements, a live electric wire which meant death to anyone touching it, stakes, &c.

"Well, the enemy kept worrying us at night with their infantry attacks, and shelled us by day. The trenches had been admirably constructed by the Belgians, and we erected a barricade of sandbags in front and fired through loopholes. We kept the Germans off until last Thursday night, and they had got right up to the entanglements when we were given the order to retreat. We were led by a very gallant Marine officer, to whom it is due that we got through safely. Our retreat was carried out in good order, and after going by a circuitous route we crossed the river by a pontoon bridge. We had a narrow escape before crossing. The petroleum tanks had been set on fire by the Belgians, who had heard that the Germans were very short of petrol, and the flames came right up to the road over which we passed.

"After marching 32 miles we entrained at St. Gille, and eventually reached Ostend, where we embarked on a transport. During the voyage the ship got on a sandbank in a fog off Dunkirk, but righted herself after 12 hours, and Dover was reached safely on Monday morning. I got back to Chelmsford on Wednesday night quite safe and sound, and am quite ready to go out again if necessary."

THE COLCESTRIAN

O.C.'s IN TRAINING.

The following letters from O.C.'s, training in various parts
of the country, are also of interest :—

From Pte. W. M. TOWN, 4th Essex, "K" Coy., The Cross
Keys, S. Faith's, Norwich.

. . . . Since my first letter many changes have taken
place and incidentally a few misfortunes. My first letter was
from Drayton. About two days after I wrote it, Clarke and
I, among others, were ordered to proceed to St. Faith's, a
village about three miles away. The reason for this was
that we were under the age limit for Foreign Service
Volunteers, which is 19. We were naturally rather annoyed
(perhaps that is only putting it mildly), but we tried to "keep
smiling"—like Mr. Pepper's Scouts—and soon settled down
into our new company. We are attached to "K" Coy. of
the 4th Essex now—that is, temporarily attached—for a
Reserve Battalion of the 5th Essex is being raised. The
other day some Foreign Service Volunteers were called for,
so Clarke and I again signed on, and we are now fairly
confident of remaining so. We shall not be attached to the
Service Battalion of the 5th Essex, but to the Reserve 5th,
and, should the former go abroad, those of us who have
volunteered will be called upon to fill up any gaps caused by
illness or casualities.

Now, about our immediate surroundings. St. Faith's is a
small village of about 500 people. Like most villages it has
its pubs - or should we call them inns ? There are six in all,
two so-called hotels. Our Coy. is billeted at the "Cross
Keys," the second largest. We sleep on the floor of a room
above some stables and a pig-sty, and we get the first smell
of breakfast before it is cooked. You see, the floor is
leaky . . . . We have actually had coffee and bread-and-
butter for breakfast for two days, but I fear we go back
to the eternal bacon to-morrow. Our toilet is made in the
stable ; the only thing to wash in being a bucket of uncertain
age . . . .

From Pte. C. W. SANGER, 749 "D" Coy., U.P.S. Royal
Fusiliers, Epsom.

. . . . I joined the Old Public School and University Men's
Corps. We began by drilling a little every day in Hyde
Park, until 18th September, when we were sent down to
Epsom, under the impression that we were going into camp
at Woodcote Park. The Royal Automobile Club had lent us
their new golf course, and here a camp of wooden huts was
being constructed, but when we got here we found we were
billeted in private houses. . . . .

Of course all sorts of rumours have been flying about—some to the effect that we shall soon be sent out to a garrison in France. The general opinion is that we shall be ready for service by the Spring. We form a complete Brigade with headquarters and four battalions—3,300 men being billeted in Epsom, 1,200 in Leatherhead, and 800 in Ashstead. . . . .

H. M. the King came down and inspected us on the Downs last Monday. It was quite an informal affair—no hysterical waving of flags or anything of that sort. In fact, very few people knew anything about it—we were told we were to be inspected, but by whom, we did not know.

I am enjoying the life of a full private enormously, and am feeling as fit as a fiddle. Of course, we have only seen the rosy side of things as yet ; we haven't had to rough it much, as we probably shall have to do sooner or later.

One day about a fortnight after we had arrived here, when we were assembled in Woodcote Park, I spotted Cyril Beard and " Soapy " Miller standing in the Company just in front of me. I hadn't the faintest idea till then that they were here. We all collapsed simultaneously.

Then again, while paying a flying visit to Brighton yesterday week I ran into Green and Folkard (in rather ghastly looking blue uniforms) who were stationed, with Bunting, Renton, and a crowd more from Colchester, at Shoreham. Everyone seemed pleased with life, and himself. . . . .

From Pte. H. W. ORFEUR, " C " Coy., 8th Essex Cyclists, Kirby Cross.

. . . . I was surprised and delighted to hear what a number of O.C.'s are with the Colours. . . . . We are proud to have Gerald Benham for our Captain. He is exceedingly popular with everyone.

We have not been " having a time," like the Territorials, in towns. We have combined training with coast defence, and outpost duty. Of course there are no club-rooms where we can go when off duty, as in towns, and we have been split up, and moved about in various villages near the coast between Walton and Wivenhoe. This relates to " C " Coy., but our battalion (eight companies) is spread all along the coast of Essex to the Thames estuary—or was until recently.

In August I slept " *à l'hôtel de la belle étoile*," and was very happy in hay-stacks. From September onwards it has been barns, and these are colder for sleeping in, as you cannot be surrounded with straw and warm air, but cold draughts naturally play over the lower part and the warmth rises high in the roof.

We take our meals in the open—nearly always in the field where the " cook-house " happens to be—but if rainy we get under cover.

Each of us by turns has outpost duty on the coast and patrols between the coast towns. It is rather lonely up on the cliffs by night—nothing but the sound of waves breaking below. Searchlights sweep the sea, and with a bright moon on a sentry with loaded rifle and gleaming bayonet, it is quite romantic. But if it is a very gloomy dark night, and you put your foot in a rabbit-hole, it is more romantic still! One fellow did this—but not an O.C.—and was lucky not to fall so very far.

It was horribly wet at an inland outpost I was at. We rode seven miles through rain to get there, and we had only a hut made of three or four hurdles, some straw and a rick-cover, for resting in, and the wind and water found their way in on this night.

Since August we have had a taste of trench-digging, manœuvring—one company against another, and cyclists against cavalry in the neighbourhood—concentrating at various points on coast, taking up positions of retirement on withdrawing from coast, in addition to occasional drill and guard, sentry, or patrol duty, so that we have not been on monotonous or unvaried work, and we are all in good spirits, and there has been little ill-health—probably due to the remarkably fine weather since war broke out. . . . . Most of us have volunteered for the front, but have no idea at all when or where or whether we shall go.

It is remarkable how exceedingly kind and generous the people are in all the places we have been to—both rich and poor. It is also true that manners make a difference to the way you are received. I have seen some amusing incidents to illustrate this. There are funny stories of other kinds too, as of a recruit who at night challenged three times, and getting no answer, fired and—it turned out to be a plough.

Good luck to our glorious *Alma Mater*. . . . .

From Pte. J. L. WATSON, 50th Batt. Gordon Highlanders, Willows Camp, Victoria, B.C.

. . . . . As you see, I am now enlisted and ready for anything that turns up. I came here about six weeks ago, and joined the Gordons, not in time unfortunately to get away with the 1st contingent, and I had a narrow shave of being thrown out of active service in the second, on account of my eyesight. However, I happen to have turned out rather a crack shot, and am already in the VIII., so that by dint of making a nuisance of myself to my Company Officers and the C.O. and everybody else, I managed to get passed for active service.

We are all waiting impatiently now to get away. There is quite a bunch of troops here. At the Willows we have the 50th, the 88th Fusiliers, a battery of artillery, and a squadron of horse. At Work Point are the Royal Canadian and Elliott's Horse, a corps of Irregulars, and at Esquimalt are several cruisers, etc., and the garrison artillery. . . . .

England and the Allies seem to be getting rather the worst of it. [German facts (?) and German points of view are better presented and distributed in the Far West than our own. —Ed.] It seems rather ghastly at present but I don't see how they can fail to come out top in the end.

Mr. Jeffrey must be very much in demand now with his knowledge of Germany. What annoys me are the ridiculous stories of German atrocities, etc., and the way the Germans are ridiculed and insulted in all the papers. [See previous note. — Ed.] Even Owen Seaman in *Punch* descends to the level of vituperative washerwomen in the articles and cartoons. Surely it is possible to give a brave enemy his due, even though he is or seems to be getting decidedly the best of it. [This passage throws a lurid light on the German press campaign. —Ed.] Of course it all sounds pretty horrible, but war is horrible, and stern measures are a necessity. I saw that in what little I saw of fighting in Mexico. [German Kultur is evidently the Kultur of Mexico! — Ed.]

Meanwhile I suppose Colchester is an armed camp now. I simply ache to be back in England, and live in fear and trembling lest I should be disqualified even yet. The only thing is to live in hope. I suppose there are all kinds of O.C.'s volunteering. It would have been jolly to have formed a company of them or something.

I came across an old Berkhamstead chum in the Gordons here. He had just joined. Practically all the Canadian contingent are Britishers. The Canadian born percentage is about nine or ten—if so much. . . . .

I hope that C.R.G.S. flourishes like a green bay tree. . . .

It is noteworthy that all the O.C.'s who joined the 9th Essex Regiment were early "spotted" for stripes, and now everyone has one or more. D. P. Malyn, after serving in every stage from a private of the A.S.C. to Quartermaster-Sergeant, has been offered a commission in the Corps.

HIS LIFE FOR HIS COUNTRY.

The foregoing breathe the. spirit of health and impatience to be up and doing—but there is the other side, and .to-day the list of O.C.'s is the poorer by the death of a brave lad, Cyril Waring, a Spalding boy who on leaving the old School went over to the Bank of Montreal. Like other O.C.'s he was among the first to hear his country's call, and at Montreal tried to enlist in the Horse Artillery. In a letter home to his parents he wrote :—

The doctor turned me down because he said I had a rupture of the muscle in the abdomen

Well, the other boys would not go at all if I did not, so we went to try the Victoria Rifles—lo and behold the same doctor. He was very nice and said it was obvious we were all keen— and we were all about 6 feet high—and that there was no reason in the world from a physical point why I should not join if I had an operation at once.

All the other boys have enlisted on this understanding, so Monday, the 26th October, will see me once more in the hospital, and the 27th on the operating table.

Of course, if by any chance the operation does not turn out so successfully as is to be naturally expected, then the army would know me not at all. Still I am hoping for the best.

The doctor at the hospital said at any rate I should be the first of this contingent to shed my blood for the army's sake. Fancy, I shall have a Union Jack draped round the top of the bed. Some swank, eh !

The accountant at the bank says its a plucky thing, but I'm hanged if I can see that, because its got to be done sometime, so why not now. The examination this time is being made even stiffer than the last, so you see I am in excellent condition otherwise, and in three weeks I ought to be absolutely "it."

The Vics. have refused 67 per cent. of applicants during this contingent, as against 42 per cent. last.

Well, dears, I hope to see you some time in January or February, when I hope to be O.H.M.S.

Alas ! the army knew him not, for the operation went badly, and Cyril passed away to the deep regret of all who knew him and will cherish his memory. In a leader note of Nov. 10th, the *Lincolnshire Free Press* published the following kindly appreciation.which will find an echo in the hearts of all O.C's. who had the privilege of calling him a friend :—

" During the past three months of the war we have had many inspiring examples of courage and patriotism, but few have been calculated to create a deeper impression hereabout than the news which has come to Spalding from across the seas during the week just past. The cablegram which last Wednesday brought the sad intelligence of the death of a young Spaldonian in Canada covered a story of heroism of which we all have reason to be proud.

"Mr. Cyril Waring, the life and soul of the Boy Scout movement in Spalding a year or two ago, and lately holding a banking appointment in Canada, was so imbued with the patriotic spirit, and, with his colleagues, so desirous of joining the Canadian contingent, that he voluntarily underwent a serious operation in order to qualify himself for enlistment. That operation unhappily failed, and though a Spalding home has been sadly bereaved, his relatives and friends have the satisfaction of knowing that the one who has gone has left behind him an example of high courage, and that he has as truly given his life for his country's sake as any who have fallen amidst the shot and shell of the battlefield. His story should act as an inspiration to others to emulate the same courageous spirit—a characteristic so much in need to-day."

141

DEAKIN, E. B., C.R.G.S.
DENTON, A., Barclay's Bank, Colchester.
DENTON, C. W., Marylands, Shrub End Road, Colchester.
DOUBLEDAY, R. E., Belle Vue Road, Wyvenhoe
DUNNINGHAM, T. G., Manor Road, Dover-court.
EBERT, Dr. E., Kiel. Fichtestrasse 2, Germany
EVERETT, H. J., Councillor, 28 New Town Road, Colchester.
EVERETT, W. R., c/o B. F. Burrell, Esq., Abbeygate Street, Colchester.
Ewing, J. H., South Hall, Ramsey, Harwich
FAIRHEAD, A. E., Bouchier's Hall, Messing, Kelvedon.
FARMER, A. O., 12 Queen Street, Colchester (HON. SECRETARY).
FARMER, H. W., 15 Greyswood Street, Mitcham Lane, Streatham, S.W.
FAVIELL, C. V., 23 Udney Park, Teddington, Middlesex.
FENN, E. G., The Hall, Ardleigh.
FIELDGATE, W. H., "Ty Fry," Regent Road, Brightlingsea.
FINCH, F. D., 25 Salisbury Avenue, Colchester.
FITCH, L. B., Welby House, Butt Road, Colchester.
FLEETWOOD, E. C., Bemahague, Shrub End Road, Colchester.
FLUX, J., Lower Clifden Downs Station, Carnarvon, W. Australia.
FOLKARD, C., Copford, Colchester.
FOLKARD, H., Copford, Colchester.
FRANKLIN, Councillor R., Sutherland House, 95 Baddow Road, Chelmsford.
FRANCIS, E. K., Crouch Street, Colchester.
FROST, A. T., Rackbarton, St. Barnabas Road, Cambridge.
FROST, A. W., 13 Head Street, Colchester.
GIBBS, J. W., 249 Maldon Road, Colchester.
GIRLING, T. A., Park Villa, Dunmow.
GIRLING, HUGH, Payne's Farm, Little Bentley.
GODFREY, O. F., "Thirlmere," Queen's Road, Springfield, Chelmsford.
GOING, F. W., 125 Maldon Road, Colchester.
GOODRY, S., Chelsworth, New Town Road, Colchester.
GOODY, C., Old Heath Road, Colchester.
GREEN, H., Moat Hall, Fordham, Colchester.
GREEN, A. C., Fingringhoe, Colchester.
GREEN, D. A., The Hall, Fingringhoe, Essex.
GREEN, A. E., 18 East Stockwell Street, Colchester.
GREEN, C. S., Fingringhoe, Colchester.
GRIFFIN, C., Stanway Villa, Colchester.
GRIFFIN, H. L., Stockwell House, West Stockwell Street, Colchester.
GRIMWOOD, C. H., c.o. Boots, Ltd., Long Wyre Street, Colchester.
HALL, A. L., Caerleon, New Town Road, Colchester.
HARPER, W. C., 6 Queen Street, Colchester.
HARRIS, H. J., Weircombe, Ardwick Road, W. Hampstead.
HARVEY, J. B., Stanley Lodge, Wellesley Road, Colchester.
HARSUM, G. F., Wood Field, Bourne Road, Colchester.
HAZELL, S. G., Long Wyre Street, Colchester, (and Montreal).
HAZELL, R. I., 23 Lexden Street, Colchester.
HEAD, A., 58 Wimpole Road, Colchester.
HEAD, J., 58 Wimpole Road, Colchestrr.
HELLEN, S., c.o. 6 Queen Street, Colchester.
HEMPSON, R. J.
HOLLAWAY, H. H., 34 Old Heath Road Colchester.
HORWOOD, R. B., Layer Hall, Layer.
HOWARD, W. K.
HURST, H. J. R., 7 St John Street, Colchester
HUSSEY, F. W., 15 Audley Road, Colchester.

IVEY, S. F., 63 Kensington Gardens Square, London, W.
JARRARD, C. H., Thorpe, Colchester.
JARRARD, D. G., Alexandra Road, Sible Hedingham.
JASPER, C. V., Langenhoe Hall, Colchester.
JASPER, L. A., Langenhoe Hall, Colchester.
JEFFERIES, C. R., 62 Winnock Road, Colchester.
JEFFREY, P. SHAW, School House, Colchester.
JOHNSON, L. H., 17 Lion Walk, Colchester.
JONES, P. E., c.o. Jones and Watts, Barrack Street, Colchester.
JUDD, L., South Villa, Ardleigh.
KENT, B. H., 182 Maldon Road, Colchester.
KING, W. H., Inglis Road, Colchester
KING, W. H., junr., Inglis Road, Colchester.
KING, G. K., 53 Friar Street, Sudbury.
LANSDOWNE, L. R., Mersea House, Walton.
LAVER, P., Church Street North, Colchester.
LAY, C. V., 2k Portman Mansions, St. Marylebone, London, W.
LAWRENCE, A. D., c.o. Head & Co., Ltd., 27 Cornhill, London, E.C.
LAZELL, HAROLD, Fitzwalter Road, Lexden Park. Colchester.
LEANING, E. M., Welwyn, Wash Lane, Clacton-on-Sea.
LINES, E., The Bungalow, Great Bentley.
LORD, P., North Hill, Colchester.
LUCKING, A. S., 20 Inglis Road, Colchester.
LUCKING, C. D., 61 High Street, Maidenhead.
MALYN, D. P., Bleak House, Braintree.
MALYN, R., Barclay's Bank, Colchester
MANNING, C., The Elms, Weeley, R.S.O.
MANNING, P. E. J., The Elms, Weeley. R.S.O., Essex.   [chester.
MANNING, C. L., 162 Military Road, Col-
MARLAR, J., North Hill, Colchester.
MARSH, W. E., 180 Longmarket Street, Natal, South Africa.
MARSH, H. V., 43 Loop Street, Maritzburg, South Africa.
MASON, A., Perse School, Cambridge.
MASON, B., 10 Crouch Street, Colchester.
MASON, C., 10 Crouch Street, Colchester.
McCLOSKY, C. A., c.o. E es Everett, St. Botolph's, Colchester.
MIDDLETON, G. A. T., "Laleham," Clarence Road, Clapham Park, S.W.
MIDGLEY, C. F., "Gunton," Westminster Drive, Westcliffe-on-Sea.   [wood.
MIDGLEY, W. R. O., 163 Ongar Road, Brent-
MILLS, F. G., 18 Beverley Road, Colchester.
MOY, O. T., c.o. Messrs. T. Moy & Co., Ltd., Colchester.
NASH, BERNARD, King Coel's Kitchen, Stanway.
NICHOLSON, R., 25 Priory Street, Colchester.
NORFOLK, A. E., 76 Chesson Road, West Kensington.
NUNN, A. W., Crouch Street, Colchester.
NUNN, J. H., Melford Villa, Rawstorn Road, Colchester.
NUNN, W. H., Whatfield, Ipswich.
ORFEUR, H. W., Colne Bank, Station Road, Colchester.
ORFEUR, C. B., Colne Bank, Station Road, Colchester.
ORFEUR, R. F., Colne Bank, Station Road, Colchester.
ORFEUR, F. N., Colne Bank, Station Road, Colchester
ORPEN, O. G., Hillside, West Bergholt, Colchester.
OSBORNE, F. F.
OSBORNE, H. C.
PARKER, Rev. E. H., Parsonage, Thorington,
PARMENTER, Rev. C. J., 21 Worley Road, St. Albans.
PEART, J. A., C.R.G.S.

142

PEGLER, Dr. L. H., 58 Harley Street, London W.
PEPPER, V. J., 19 Harsnett Road, Colchester.
PEPPER, G. E., O.R.G.S.
PERTWEE, F., Moreham's Hall, Frating.
PLUMMER, N. A., Station Road, Lawford, Manningtree.
PLUMMER, F. E. Station Road, Lawford, Manningtree.
POINTING, W. W., 148 Maldon Road, Colchester.
POTTER, C. G., 119 Maldon Road, Colchester.
POTTER, F., Middleborough, Colchester.
PRIME, E. J., 37 Crouch Street, Colchester.
PROSSER, J. A. B., Lansdowne, Pierremont Avenue, Broadstairs.
REEVE, E., O.R.G.S.
RENTON, T. S., 12 Crouch Street, Colchester.
RICHES, A. E., 80 Tower Street, Brightlingsea.
RICHARDS, R. F., Head Street, Colchester.
RICKWORD, E. G., 38 Wellesley Road, Colchester.
RICKWORD, G. O., 38 Wellesley Road, Colchester.
ROSEVEARE, H. H., "Craigmore," Newquay, Cornwall.
RYDER, E. W., 74 Wimpole Road, Colchester.
SADLER, F. B., Box P.O. 219, c/o. The Eastern Bank, Ltd., Bombay.
SANDERS, F. A., 108 North Station Road, Colchester.
SANGER, C. W., "Rookerydene," Abbeygate Street, Colchester.
SANGER, H., "Rookerydene," Abbeygate Street, Colchester.
SALMON, J. G., Wash Lane, Clacton.
SKAMER, H. St. J., C.R.G.S. (Editor)
SENNITT, F. J., 28 Mersea Road, Colchester.
SHAW, D. E., Holmleigh, Beaconsfield Avenue, Colchester.
SHENSTONE, J. C., 150 Coverdale Road, Shepherd's Bush, London, W.
SHEPHERD, C. W., 110 Magdalen Street, Colchester.
SIGGERS, J.
SLIGHT, R., c.o. One Barrow Lodge, Coalville, Leicestershire.
SLATER, E. M., 201 Maldon Road, Colchester.
SMITH, AUBREY. "Mantz," 30 Peak Hill, Sydenham, S.E
SMITH, G. E., Chapel Street, Colchester.
SMITH, EUSTACE T., Wormingford Grove, Colchester.
SMITH, W. G., 23 Roman Road, Colchester.
SMITH, F. R., 23 Roman Road, Colchester.
SMYTHIES, CAPT. P. KINGSMILL R.N., The Turrets, Lexden Road, Colchester.

SPARLING, A. S. B., 21 Creffield Road, Colchester.
SPARLING, REV. P. W., Holme Rectory, Downham Market.
STOW, W. H., The Willows, Great Horkesley, Colchester.
SURRIDGE, P. T., Coggeshall.
SYER, F. N., 8 Studlands Road, Sydenham.
TAYLOR, A. P., Roseneath, East Street, Hazlemere, Surrey.
TENNANT E. N., Connaught Avenue, Frinton.
THOMAS, A. O., 150 Maldon Road, Colchester.
THOMPSON, W., 365 Hither Green Lane, Lewisham, S.E.
TOWN, H. G., 10 Wellesley Road, Colchester.
TURNER, Capt. A., Essex Hall, Colchester.
TURNER, Dr. DOUGLAS, Essex Hall, Colchester.
TURNER, S. C., Abbeygate House, Colchester.
WAGSTAFF, D. T., Church Farm, Marks Tey, Colchester.
WALLACE, Councillor R. W., "Moelwyn," Inglis Road, Colchester.
WARING, C. E., Froebel, Priory Road, Spalding, Lincolnshire.
WARD, F. A., 122 Caversham Road, Reading.
WARD, J. D., Jun., Bluegates, Elmstead, Colchester.
WARNER, A. E., 8 Myland, Colchester.
WATSHAM, H., Vine Farm, Wyvenhoe.
WATSON, J. L.
WATSON, S. F., 150 Maldon Road, Colchester.
WATSON, G. F.
WATTS, FRANK, 30 Creffield Road, Colchester.
WEBB, G. S., Dairy House, Wix, Manningtree.
WEBB, A. H., Dairy House, Wix, Manningtree.
WHITE, C. E., 57 North Hill, Colchester.
WHITE, F., East Hill, Colchester.
WHITBY, J. F. M., 144 Maldon Road, Colchester.
WIGLEY, W. H., 146 King's Park Road, Mount Florida, Glasgow.
WILLIAMS, F. O., 14 Lexden Road, Colchester.
WILLIS, E. A., 25 Heron Road, Stapleton Road, Bristol.
WIRE, A. P.
WORTS, S. E., Trinity Street, Colchester.
WRIGHT, Lieut.-Col. Percival, Ashanti, St. James, Mirzenburg, Cape Town.
WRIGHT, C. T., Stacey House, Crouch Street, Colchester.
WRIGHT, G., junr., Stacey House, Crouch Street, Colchester.
WRIGHT, Councillor G. F., 47 Crouch Street, Colchester.
WYATT, D. T., Bank Passage, Colchester.

NOTICE TO OLD COLCESTRIANS.

Old Colcestrians who wish to make known their movements in this paper should communicate with Mr. J. HUTLEY NUNN, "Essex County Telegraph" Offices, Colchester.

Subscriptions should be sent to Mr. A. T. DALDY (Hon. Treas.), Head Street, Colchester.

Members of the Society are requested to notify any change of address immediately to either of the Hon. Secretaries :—

Mr. A. O. FARMER, 6 Queen Street, Colchester.
Mr. A. T. DALDY, 50 South Street, Colchester.

NOTICE TO CORRESPONDENTS.

Contributions to the O.C. Section, articles on various subjects and humorous anecdotes of school-days, will be gladly welcomed by the O.C. Editor, Mr. J. Hutley Nunn.

All contributions for the next number of "The Colcestrian" to be sent in by March 1st, 1915.

143

No. 41.]
New Series.

MARCH, 1915.

The Colcestrian.

EDITED BY PAST AND PRESENT MEMBERS
OF COLCHESTER SCHOOL.

PRICE SIXPENCE

Colchester:
Printed by Cullingford & Co.,
156 High Street.

O.C.S. Officers for 1914=15.

President:
O. T. WRIGHT, Crouch Street, Colchester.

Vice-Presidents:

W. GURNEY BENHAM, J.P.	H. J. HARRIS, B.A.	J. O. SHENSTONE, F.L.S.
R. FRANKLIN	B. H. KENT	R. W. WALLACE
H. L. GRIFFIN	OSMOND G. GREEN	O. E. WHITE
	W. H. KING	

Committee:

F. D. BROOK	O. GRIFFIN	G. C. BENHAM
J. H. NUNN	O. T. WRIGHT	E. W. DACE
A. W. NUNN	H. H. HOLLAWAY	J. C. SALMON
F. G. MILLS	G. E. BENHAM (Chairman)	F. D. BARKER

The Ex-Presidents are ex-officio members of Committee.

Hon. Treasurer (pro. tem.):
A. T. DALDY, Head Street, Colchester.

Hon. Secretaries:
A. T. DALDY, Head Street, Colchester.
A. O. FARMER, 12 Queen Street, Colchester.

Members of the O.C.S.

ACLAND, C. S., Lexden House, West Winch, nr. Kings Lynn. [Hill, N.
ADAMS, E. A., 7 Goodwyn's Vale, Muswell
ALLISTON, A. W., Chipping Hill, Witham.
APPLEBY, W. M.
BARR, W. J., Magdalen Street, Colchester.
BARKER, F. D., Royal Grammar School (Hon. Sec). [Naze.
BARKER, U. F. J., Marine Hotel, Walton-on-
BARKER, CHARLES, Burtoll Tea Estate, Dewan P.O., Cachar, India.
BARNES, O., Howell Hall, Heckington, Lincs.
BARNES, F. M., Howell Hall, Heckington, Lincolnshire.
BAWTREE. E. E., 71 High Street, Colchester.
BAXTER, H. G., Fronks Road, Dovercourt.
BAYLISS, S. F.
BAYLISS, R. V. J., Fleece Hotel, Head Street, Colchester.
BAYLISS, B., Fleece Hotel, Head Street, Colchester.
BEARD, E. C., St. Margaret's, Cambridge Road, Colchester.
BECKETT, H., Balkerne Lane, Colchester.
BELLWARD. G. W. F., C.R.G.S.
BENHAM. C. E., Wellesley Road, Colchester. (President).
BENHAM, G. C., Bank Chambers, High Street, Colchester.
BENHAM, Alderman W. GURNEY, St. Mary's
BIRD, A., Bell House Farm, Stanway.
Terrace, Lexden road, Colchester.
BLATCH, F., c/o, S. E. Blau, La Paz, Bolivia, S. America.
BLAXILL, G. A., 50 Parliament Hill, Hampstead, N.W.
BLOMFIELD, S., Raonah House, New Town Road, Colchester.
BLOOMFIELD, H. D., 3 Tyler Street, Parkeston.
BLYTH, COOPER, c.o. Isaac Bunting, 100 Yokahama, Japan.
BOGGIS, FRANK, Station Road, Sudbury.
BROMLEY, J. G., Mill House, Great Clacton.
BROOK, T. D., "St. Runwald's," Maldon Road, Colchester.
BROOK, A. T., "St. Runwald's," Maldon Road, Colchester.
BROOK, L. C., "St. Runwald's," Maldon Road, Colchester.
BROOK, S. V., 22 Sugden Road, Lavender Hill, S. W.
BROWN, D. GRAHAM, "Lownd," Witham.

BULTITUDE, R. G., 32 Hanover Road, Canterbury.
BURRELL, F. B., Abbeygate Street, Colchester
BUNTING, A. E., The Nurseries, North Station Road, Colchester.
BURLEIGH, A., Kudat, N.L.B.T. Co., British North Borneo.
BURSTON, F. G., 1st National Bank Buildings, San Francisco.
BUTCHER, H., 3 Eden Ave., Liscard, Cheshire.
BUTLER, F. H., Cumberland House, Manningtree.
CANT, Walter, West House Farm, Lexden, Colchester.
CAREY, M. C., 49 Lexden Road, Colchester.
CARTER, F. B., C.R.G.S.
CHAMBERS, O., 22 Wellesley Road, Colchester.
CHAMBERS, S. C., 22 Wellesley Road, Colchester. [Inn, W.C.
CHAPLIN, F. S., 5 Verulam Buildings, Grays
CHEESE, O. T., 39 Pownall Crescent, Colchester and St. Austell, Cornwall.
CHESHIRE, G., 23 Argyle Street, Oxford Street, W.
CHESHIRE, W., 1 Meyrick Crescent, Colchester
CHILD, E. G., 14 Wimpole Road, Colchester.
CLAMP, A. J., 122 Priory Street, Colchester.
CLARK, L. W., 16 East Stockwell Street, Colchester.
CLARKE, S. F., Parr's Bank, Holloway, London, N.
CLOVER, J. M., The Hall, Dedham.
COLE, C. L. L., General Post Office (Staff), Cambridge.
COLE, H. S., 25 Wimpole Road, Colchester.
COLLINGE, C. E., Capital & Counties Bank, Baldock, Herts.
COLLISON, A. L., Garrison School, Buena Vista, Gibraltar.
CORK, F. F., 38 Trouville Road, Clapham Park, S.W.
CRAGG, Rev. E. E., St. John's Church, Huntington, Long Island, U.S.A.
CULLINGTON, M. W., 53 Oakhill Road, Putney, S.W.
CURTIS, A. P., Bromley Road, Colchester.
DACE, A. W., 122 George Street, Edinburgh.
DACE, E. W., 17 Honywood Road, Colchester.
DALDY, A. T., 50 South Street, Colchester (HON. TREASURER).
DAVIES, W. E., 118 Butt Road, Colchester.
DAVIES, E. G.

Continued on Page 3 of Cover.

146

The Colcestrian.

VITÆ CORONA FIDES.

No. 41.]   MARCH, 1914.   [New Series.

Editorial.

GENERAL French in one of his earlier despatches ventured upon the remark that the Germans "had no idea of fair play." Whereupon a German newspaper took him severely and solemnly to task for "using towards such a serious matter as war the language of sport." There was no sense of shame in acknowledging the truth of the accusation. Of course, *all* was fair in war. The only surprising thing was that anyone should be found to disagree with the universality of the maxim, or acknowledge the existence of any law higher than the merest self-interest.

Now this is a striking fact, which brings into prominence the yawning gulf that divides the ideal characters of the two races. Contrast the typical English gentleman—the *gentle man*, be it understood—and the equally typical Prussian Junker, a bully to all his subordinates, cringing and servile to all above him.

Nor is the reason for this divergence far to seek. In the whole of Germany there exists nothing that corresponds to the English Public School, nor the discipline for which it stands. From the very outset the German boy is brought face to face with Authority, backed up by brute force, and the condition besets him through life. It is all that he is trained to respect. He finds himself always between those who shake the finger and roll the eye at him, and those at whom he is privileged to do likewise.

In an English School the boy is led, not driven. Any boy developing bullying, meanness, swagger, or any other German vice is promptly set in his place by public opinion—and probably a prefect. He is trained to use, and not abuse his power. For the rest he learns on the Playing Field self-control, fairness, chivalry, unselfishness, and respect for law, even when opposed to his own immediate interest, and with no brute force behind it. The standard of conduct thus set up influences the whole of our English society, and regulates the actions of every individual in the community. The utility of games is sometimes questioned. Here is the answer plain for all folk to see. Look at the products of the two systems, and say which constitutes the higher and nobler character.

THE EDITOR.

Valete.

VI.   DOUBLEDAY, W. A.—K.P., Dugard's.   1st XI. Football, School Shooting VIII. ; House Football, Cricket, Shooting, and Gym. Cadet Sergeant.

VI.   DEANE, G. F. F.—Harsnett's.   House Football, Cricket and Shooting ; Cadet Private. **Has Enlisted.**

VA.   GOLDSMITH, W. G.—Q.P., Schoolhouse.   1st XI. Football, Cricket and Hockey, School Shooting VIII. ; House Football, Cricket, Shooting, and Gym. ; Cadet Corporal-Drummer ; Member of Committee. Debating Society. **Has Enlisted.**

VB.   CAREY, D. M.—Dugard's.   House Shooting.

IVA.   HORLOCK, M.—Dugard's.   House Football and Cricket.

IVA.   LANSDOWNE, L.—Harsnett's.

IVA.   LEWIS, K. M.--Schoolhouse.

III.   GODEBSKI, J. J. E.—Schoolhouse.

II.   BION, R.—Schoolhouse.

II.   GOWER MA., H. F.—Schoolhouse.

I.   GOWER MI., L.—Schoolhouse.

Salvete.

VB.	LILLEY, H.		S.
VB.	MIDDLETON, K. R.		S.
VB.	DEANE, R. P.		H.
IVA.	CAMPBELL		H.
IVA.	NICHOLLS, W. C. F.		D.
	WILKIN, K. M.		H.
IVB.	BAKER, C. B.		S.
IVB.	HABGOOD, P.		D.
II.	MUNSON, L.		S.
II.	SAYER, G.		S.
II.	OSBORNE MA., H.		P.
I.	OSBORNE MI., S. M.		P.
I.	MACKAY, D. M,		S.
I.	TRICKER, P. K.		P.
I.	MILLER MI., A. E. V.		S.

PRE.   HARRIS, H.

Grammaria.

Au Revoir.

Another effect of the war, is that we have had to bid farewell—we hope only temporarily—to C.-S.-I. Penn, the School Marshal, who has been with us now for many years. During that time he proved himself a man of many parts, an excellent Gym. instructor, a Marshal conscientious and painstaking. Keenly interested in the Rifle and Cadet Corps, he may be said to have taken no small part in placing them on the efficient and satisfactory basis on which they stand to-day. The fact that he was a cricketer added to his usefulness in preparing pitches and made him a sound umpire, and he also had a knowledge of football, which stood him in good stead as referee. Moreover he won the esteem of all who came in contact with him. He is greatly missed, and his place will be hard to fill.

Condemned.

The miscreant who suggests that "J. Penn having been lost, we shall have to find a new nib," has already been consigned to solitary confinement in the stoke-hole.

Another Loss.

And Pratt, the school porter has also departed, though not to take his place in a Service Battalion of the new Army. We shall be sorry to lose him. New friends are never like the old ones.

Hang out the Banner!

Dugard's is the second House to possess a richly embroidered silk banner. It is due to the patriotism and generosity of Mrs. A. M. Clarke, who has presented it to the House to which her son was attached *(en tous les sens)*, and is the work of her daughter Miss D. Clarke. Dugard's must indeed be proud and grateful to receive such a beautiful example of embroidery work, and treasure it among the heirlooms of the House *in secula seculorum*.

An Unenviable Record.

A wave of influenza and minor ills, due no doubt to the shocking weather, has swept over the town and neighbourhood during the last month or so. So numerous have been its victims that on one memorable occasion no fewer than fifty-four boys were absent from School. This must constitute a record for the Foundation—and luckily it will, in all probability, never be challenged in the future.

149

Under Fire.

Colchester has achieved the distinction in company with
Yarmouth, Sheringham, King's Lynn, Coggeshall, and Dover
of being subjected to aerial bombardment—damages, one
perambulator, one shed, and some score of panes of glass.
No doubt the Kaiser resented the slight put upon him by the
local authorities in celebrating his birthday week by putting
the streets into darkness and the tramcars into mourning   If
this is a fair specimen of German "frightfulness," nothing
could be more futile.   The population behaved with sang-
froid, if not correctitude, and utterly refused to be even
fluttered by the demonstration.

Avenging Fate.

However, in spite of their stories to the contrary, it seems
extremely probable that the two aviators picked up in the
North Sea, taken by a fishing vessel to Lowestoft, and at
present interned in the Concentration Camp at Bury, are none
other than our redoubtable assailants.   For the aeroplane,
when last heard passing N.E. over Bradfield in the direction
of Chelmondiston was audibly missing fire with some of its
cylinders.   *Sic pereant omnes hostes tui!*

But what of this?

It is an unfortunate coincidence that the two damaged
houses in Butt Road happen to be the property of our late
Marshal, C.-S.-I. Penn.

Friendly Rivals.

It is pleasing to note the appearance of no less than two
unofficial School publications.   "The Idler" anonymously
produced by Form VI. has already reached its third number,
and displays considerable journalistic talent.   And now "The
Modern" has entered the lists from the Modern Side, and
challenges its rival.   Both contain some clever work.   Good
luck to the pair, and may they long survive!   We have taken
the liberty of quotation in another column.

The Rule.

> "Boards (Education) are vexation,
>   Inspection is as bad;
>   When Inspectors three come us to see,
>   They well-nigh drive us mad!"

The Exception.

This particular visitation was to have taken place at the beginning of the Term, but a concatenation of happy chances reprieved us at the last moment, and we had to be content with our usual solitary Inspector. It was a lovely day when he came, and the breath of Spring was in the air. It even reached the heart of our visitant, and melted the ice with which it is traditionally bound. He even suggested that it was wicked to work in School on such a beautiful day! Needless to say the hint was accepted by our pastors and masters, and a half-holiday (O bliss!) was the result! This is surely a unique experience. But it need not necessarily remain so. The Clerk of the Weather will certainly find himself deafened with importunity to provide another perfect day for our Inspector's next visit.

Ce qui donne furieusement à penser.

It was a Stinks Class. The patient Master was endeavouring to extract evidence of some relics of his teaching from the boys before him. "Now how" he asked, "do you test for nitrites?" After a slight pause, "Why" answers our brightest youth, "You put in some of that furious sulphate from the bottle over there!"

Vice Versa.

A middle-aged Schoolmaster who bravely gave his age as 37 and joined the Army at the present crisis in our country's fortunes wrote home to tell of his experiences. "It is not half a bad sort of life," he summed up, "but there is one thing that is gall and wormwood to me, and that is when a bit of a boy, whom I have taught and served the same, stands at my back and looks to see if I have washed behind my ears!"

Speech Day.

OUR Speech Day attracted to Big School on Thursday, December 18th, a large and distinguished audience, over whom the Mayor (Mr. W. Coats Hutton) Chairman of the Board of Governors, presided, supported by the Bishop of Chelmsford, the Right Hon. James Round, Bishop Harrison, the Deputy-Mayor (Alderman Wilson Marriage), the Town Clerk (Mr. H. C. Wanklyn), Alderman Asher Prior, W. G. Benham, and E. A. Blaxill, Councillors A. G. Aldridge, J. W. Bare, W. W. Bunting, W. Cheshire, H. J. Everett, A. M. Jarmin, W. Littlebury, Mr. F. G. Mills, Mr. George Rickword, Chief Constable Stockwell, Canon G. T. Brunwin-Hales, Rev. F. Wilcox, Rev. T. S. Raffles, Mr. J. L. Godlee, and the Headmaster (Mr. P. Shaw Jeffrey, M.A.) and Staff. As the State procession entered the audience sang the National Anthem, led at the piano by A. O. Ward.

151

Mr. Shaw Jeffrey, who was loudly cheered on rising, remarked that they would sympathise with him when he said he had found some difficulty in presenting a coherent report of the events of the past school year, for the war was an event of such tremendous significance that our little everyday doings seem hardly worth reporting. (Hear, hear.) Never before in the history of civilisation had a great and professedly civilised nation absolutely repudiated the moral code of the New Testament, to wage war in the manner of the Kings of Israel and Judah. (Hear, hear). It is a fight not between nations, but between the powers of good and the powers of evil. (Hear, hear.) But out of evil good has come. British methods of colonisation have been vindicated, the idle rich have fought like Paladins, the British soldier has shown his quality, and in Colchester they might well say they had been living for years among heroes and never knew it. (Laughter and applause).

One thing else has been vindicated. Never has the system of education in our British public schools shown itself in brighter colours than under the stress of our common necessity. (Hear, hear.) They have answered their country's call with a unanimity and self-sacrifice that is beyond rubies. (Applause.) Even in their small way they had good cause for honest pride, for already they had a list of nearly 150 on the Roll of Honour, and many still to be accounted for. They could imagine how it had heartened them all up to find that the old boys in their thoughts linked up their old school and the Empire as one and indivisible. To ride hard, shoot straight, hit from the shoulder, and speak the truth were lessons worth learning at school, and properly directed might lead to deeper lessons in after life. (Hear, hear.) I cannot tell you (he added), and I speak not for myself alone, with what humble pride and satisfaction we have seen the rush of our old boys to the colours, for we were always being told that school boys nowadays were of a decadent type, and that better manners showed a softer fibre. Now, at least, we are not ashamed when we speak with our enemies in the gate. (Applause.)

Of the doings of the year we have cause for satisfaction. Doubleday won the Entente Cordiale Scholarship for us for the third time— (applause) —and as in the last eight years we have won this scholarship three times and been proxime four times we may almost say that we have established a " manifest superiority " in this competition, which is open to the whole country. (Applause). Mr. Barker at Oxford won the University Entente Cordiale Scholarship, the first occasion that the two scholarships have been won by the same school in the same year. (Applause.) The Cambridge Local results are in some respects better than usual. Five of the senior candidates earned exemption from the London Matriculation examination. Of five distinctions given for physical geography Mr. Peart's pupils secured two. Leening won the only distinction awarded for Dutch, and we had an unusually large number of distinctions in spoken French, gaining six as against our previous best of two. At the Universities, Webb, Mr. Hewitt's scholar at Corpus Christi, Cambridge, got a brilliant First in Modern Languages, and is now a master at Clifton College—after an unsuccessful attempt to enlist. Sanger only just missed his First in Mathematics at Oxford, and is now training with the University Battalion at Epsom. Cheese has passed the intermediate Exam. of the Civil Service. (Applause.) We are sending no boys this year to the Universities, as our University candidates are all with the Colours. (Hear, hear). Two of our masters, Mr. Deakin and Mr. Bellward, are drilling the recruits of the 5th Essex, and our School sergeant, C.S.I. Penn, has been called up as musketry instructor of the new battalions of the Suffolks. (Applause.)

Having referred to the usefulness of the Cadet Corps, and to the progress of the preparatory school, Mr. Jeffrey said there were now many old boys in distant parts of the Empire, and many with the Colonial forces. He heard frequently from them, but the most curious coincidence is the following : Burleigh, now in British North Borneo, was anxious to get a tennis racquet, and heard of a man who had one to sell second-hand. He bought it, and discovered on the handle the name Burgess in faint ink, with the letters C.R.G.S. after it. He had never heard the name, but wrote home to ask if there had ever been a Burgess at the Grammar School, and he (Mr. Jeffrey) was able to tell him that Burgess was their first boarder. (Applause.) When last heard of he was in Singapore, but how the racquet ever got to Borneo is a mystery, and it is an extraordinary accident that it should have fallen into the hands of another old Grammar School boy. As to what the school has been doing this term, Mr. Jeffrey mentioned that the boys had given up their prize money, and they had been able to send substantial donations to the Belgian Relief Fund, Princess Mary's Fund, the Y.M.C A. War Emergency Fund, and the Red Cross. They had supplied the Military Hospital with magazines, etc., they had lent the football ground on many occasions to the R.F.A. and the Essex Regiment for matches and to the 10th Fusiliers for hockey. They had had French classes in this building every evening for gentlemen of the New Armies, and their band played 600 of the R.F.A. to church a few weeks ago, and would have done so again last week if the weather had been decent. The Boy Scouts had done duty at Headquarters and at the the Social Club, and the Recruiting office, and their efforts had been highly approved of. Last but not least Mr. Peart's Grammar School Concert Party had given weekly entertainments at most of the Camps, and finally with the proceeds of the Carol Concert next Sunday they hoped to provide turkeys for the Christmas dinners at the Essex County Hospital, and also to send some help to the Local Red Cross. (Loud applause.)

The Mayor, who was received with prolonged cheers, expressed, on behalf of the Governors, the boys and the parents, a very hearty welcome to the Bishop of Chelmsford. (Applause.) His lordship, he said, had already gained the reputation of being the busiest man in the Diocese if not in the whole county of Essex—in fact, he sometimes wondered when he read his newspapers whether his Lordship did not share with the German Emperor that inestimable advantage of being able to be in more than one place at the same time. (Laughter.) The Mayor added that he doubted if his lordship had ever been asked to assist in a straighter prize-giving than this. A prize-giving associated itself with a table groaning under the weight of beautifully bound volumes—to-day the boys would receive paper certificates only, the reason being that they had decided upon a very noble act. They had voluntary elected to give up their prizes this year in order that the money they would cost might go to a fund for helping the suffering Belgians. (Applause.) Everyone receiving those certificates would look back upon them and feel glad that the boys of to-day had shown the people that the younger generation of England had been able to emulate the splendid spirit of self-sacrifice manifesting itself throughout the great Empire. (Applause.) If only the same spirit animated the boys throughout their lives, then all would be thankful that England knew how to rear men. (Loud applause.)

The Bishop of Chelmsford then presented certificates and medals to the following :—

FORM VI.

Lord Rosebery's Challenge Silver Inkstand for Mathematics, A. O. Ward. Latin and Greek, A. O. Ward. French, G. F. Butler.

UPPER SCHOOL.

A. C. Sammons, Mathematics; G. E. Fincham, Practical Chemistry and Spoken French; W. A. Doubleday, Latin, French and Mathematics; E. J. Brand, English Composition; F. M. Koskinas, Spoken French; W. R. Orrin, Practical Chemistry; B. P. Dicker, Scripture, Physical Geography and Heat; S. C. H. French, English Literature, Open Mathematics, Latin and Theoretical Chemistry; G. F. F. Deane, Freehand Drawing; E. U. Andrews, English Composition, Mathematics, and Physical Geography; J. H. J. Leeming, French, German and Dutch; G. Atkin, Memory Drawing.

MIDDLE SCHOOL.

Modern Fifth: Top, F. M. Koskinas; Chemistry, C. A. Wenden; English, F. Cheshire. Modern Fourth: Science, W. P. Watkinson; Mathematics, H. H. T. Hunneyball. Upper Fourth: Top, H. J. Cottrell; Science, A. C. King. Lower Fourth: Science, R. E. Cox Mathematics, T. F. Baskett; French, A. F. C. Churchyard; Drawing, J. D. Ritchie; Modern Side Drawing, A. A. White.

LOWER SCHOOL PRIZES.

Lower School English, E. B. Burleigh; Lower School Drawing, J. J. E. Godebski. Form iii.: Top, G. G. Barnes; Latin, John Kent; Arithmetic, H. J. Last. Form ii.: Top, W. P. Wilson, H. N. Butler; Arithmetic, T. Hickenbotham. Form i.: Top, A. W. Dace; Arithmetic, C. Wagstaff; English, T. A. Beckett.

PREPARATORY SCHOOL.

Form i., W. Knight. Form ii., P. Harman. Form iii., D. Short. Form iii., b., E. Field. Gardening, J. Griffen. Stars, J. Baker.

Medals for Good Deeds were presented to Barnes, Baker, Bullock, Buckle, Gell, Heasman, and Tait.

Certificates to R. Poyser, Attendance; J. Baker, Writing; L. Worsp, Arithmetic; N. Tait, Progress; R. Gell, Arithmetic; L. Roberts, Progress.

In the course of his very interesting address, the Bishop told the boys that their parents all loved them—but the boys did not realise how much worry they were. (Laughter.) Towards the end of vacation their mothers were wondering how long it would be before the school reopened—(laughter)—and parents did not realise how much they were indebted to the teachers. The children were home just for the vacation—what about the teachers, who all day long for weeks at a stretch had dozens of boys to look after? Really every teacher must be a monument of patience. Did not the boys think so? (Ominous silence.) Well, if boys were a worry to parents and to teachers, that was nothing compared with the worry the parents and teachers were to the boys. (Loud applause and laughter.) The boy went home for the holidays and he was told " Don't do that ;" he went to school and was told " Don't do that ;" in fact the boy was completely held in by those terrible people—the fathers, mothers, and teachers—and it was difficult to tell which was the greatest worry. (Laughter.) Yet none would be without the other for worlds, for there was between them all the link of love. (Applause.)

His Lordship proceeded to impress upon the boy the tremendous possibility which lay before him. In the little acorn there lay the possibility of a great forest; and as was said of John Knox when a young man, " There's a power of good in you; see that you use it for God and Scotland," so he might say to every boy in the Colchester School, " There's a power of good in you; see that you use it for God and your country." (Applause.) When Lord Kitchener, Sir John French, and Admiral Jellicoe were boys at school nobody could say that one would be at the War Office, another would command the British Army in France in the biggest war of the world, and another would command the mightiest Navy the world had ever seen, but there was the possibility, and if those men had not made it a certainty, they would not have been what they are to-day. (Loud applause.) Therefore he wanted everyone of the boys to have a big dream, for nobody did anything big without having some kind of dream. This fine hall would never have existed but for the dream of the architect. Columbus had a dream of the New World. Let the boys dream what sort of men they were going to be, remembering that a second-rate standard never produced a first-rate result. (Hear, hear.) He would give them three rules—If they had anything to do.

Do it now,
Do it well,
Do it cheerfully.

Boys sometimes thought it did not matter what they did as boys. But it did. As a boy they could see what the man would be; and they wanted him to get the habit of doing things punctually, doing them well, and, like Ruskin, putting his whole soul into everything he did. (Applause.) He was pleased to see one boy had got a prize for writing; and he hoped that boy would grow up to be a clergyman. He would be such a joy to his Bishop. (Much laughter.) He hoped, too, if they were going to read they would learn to read clearly, then if they became clergymen they would add comfort to their congregations. (Laughter and hear, hear). He took this to be a school that turned out the really all-round boy. (Applause.) He must be strong in body and strong in mind, but he wanted something to control and guide and direct the physical and the mental, and that surely was the spiritual behind it all. (Loud applause.) Therefore let them remember that the greatest men were not ashamed to own their God. Let them not be ashamed of prayer, nor neglect it, and in these ways prepare to take their places in the world that needed them. Thousands and thousands of our men to-day are losing their lives for King and country. (Applause.) We want the next generation of men all the more to be specially strong, noble, and all that counts for true manliness. (Loud applause.) You boys are going to be the next generation. Therefore, we appeal to you not to be content with doing work that will just pass muster, but to put your whole back into the work. (Applause.) From what I have heard of this school I believe this the ideal of the headmaster and his assistants, and I venture to think you will continue it in the days that are to come. (Loud applause.)

The Right Hon. James Round proposed a vote of thanks to the Bishop of the Diocese for his excellent address, and said no one could have had a better experience of men in all parts of the world. It must have been a pleasure to present these certificates, and to hear of the School's good work. (Hear, hear.)

Alderman Wilson Marriage, who seconded, said they had every reason to congratulate the headmaster and the staff of this great School on the position attained. (Applause.)

Bishop Harrison extended the meeting's gratitude to the Mayor for his services in the chair, and congratulated him as chairman of the Governors at the wonderful present efficiency of the School.

The Mayor in replying, remarked that the attendance of the Mayor and Corporation at these functions was one of the ancient customs they were most anxious to preserve in the 19th century. (Applause.)

"JULIUS CÆSAR."

Following the singing of the School Carmen—"Now hands about for Colcestere"—two scenes from "Julius Cæsar" were admirably rendered by the following boys:—E. U. Andrews, W. G. Goldsmith, T. Percy, H. T. Cottrell, M. Green, E. Peacock, L W. Loyd, A. C. King, G. Barrell, W. R. Orrin, C. Brown, T. G. Smith, H. Berry, S. Rogers, F. M. Koskinas, C. H. French, H. Collinge, C. Nicholson, H. Burleigh, and J. H. J. Leeming.

The Carol Service.

ON the last Sunday afternoon before Christmas, we held our Carol Service in Big School. This year they sounded as we had never heard them before, for our minds were preoccupied with inevitable reflections on the Empire, which forced itself on our notice all the more insistently from its absence of connection with Christmas carols.

The service was very simple. Prayers were read by the Headmaster, and short lessons by five of the boys. Collinge mi., accompanied by a chorus, sang the beautiful "Cantique de Noël." "We Three Kings" was sung by Pte. Henstock, Messrs. Nunn and Beckett ma., and "Sleep Holy Babe" by Messrs. Hutley Nunn, Constable and Harwood. Somewhat out of the ordinary was the broad and dignified "Battle Hymn." The first verse was sung as a solo by Collinge mi., followed by the trebles and full chorus. The rendering was very effective. The other carols were well known, as familiar as the sunlight, and as welcome.

Mr. Barnes led a serviceable orchestra, with Mr. F. D. Barker at the piano. The collection amounted to £9, and was devoted to providing Christmas turkeys for the County Hospital and the Red Cross.

Our Hall can scarcely be said to produce that chaste and gracious atmosphere of devotion with which we associate a carol service. Under the circumstances, Mr. Peart and his singers are to be warmly congratulated on the spirit and feeling they infused into the old-world music, which breathed all the wonder and romance of Christmas. We listened, and were refreshed.

J.G.W.

Football.

THE First Eleven brought their season to a close with a decisive victory over Woodbridge School. For once in a way football has taken second place in preference to Cadet Corps work, and rightly so. In these times there seems something lacking in the spirit of the game, and it is difficult to infuse the same enthusiasm, when the greatest game of all is going on at our very gates.   But School games must be kept going, for it cannot be that the rising generation grow up unfitted for the very special demand about to be made on their resources.

If one takes into consideration the adverse weather, paucity of practice, and the number of people new to First Eleven honours, the results have been quite creditable.   Woodbridge were twice defeated, which is a record in itself, while an excellent victory was gained in the return match with Ipswich ·under climatic conditions that defy description.   In most of our matches we had to concede considerable advantage in weight to our opponents, a fact which visibly handicapped our light forward line

W. G. Goldsmith led the attack, and secured most of the goals, while he was ably supported by G. Atkin, who put in a great deal of useful ·work.   At outside right, B. I. Pullen, though inclined to be erratic at times, fed his inside men well. In the defence, J. H. Cottrell and W. A. Doubleday, though fresh to the team, fully justified their inclusion.   By an unfortunate accident to his thumb, T. G. Smith was prevented from keeping goal, but R. B. Alderton took his place with excellent results.

And last, but by no means least, E. J. Brand has proved an able and skilful pilot to the team.   Strong in defence, sound in judgment, cool yet vigorous in action, he lays just claim to no small share of the glory accruing to the School on the football field.

C.R.G.S. v. Chelmsford G.S.—Played on November 14th at Chelmsford.   The School were opposed by a strong team, but for a time more than held their own.   Chelmsford scored twice before the interval, and were awarded a penalty for handling, which, however, resulted in nothing.   The School forwards made several individual efforts, but failed to get going as a connected line, and as a consequence achieved but little success.   In the second half, Atkin and Goldsmith deserved better luck with shots which hit the posts.   Cottrell ma. injured his leg, and this let down the defence, which had greatly improved on their first-half performance   Chelmsford obtained two more goals, one of which Alderton should certainly have kept out.

C.R.G.S. v. Ipswich Secondary School.—November 28th, on the Ipswich ground.   This match, although played in torrents of rain, was hotly contested.   In the first minute a mis-kick by the School left back let in the opposing centre-forward to score an easy goal.   For a time a ding-dong struggle ensued, but eventually Goldsmith scored an equalising point.   Good play was rendered extremely difficult, great pools extending over half the field, but the School forwards combined excellently, and shortly before half-time Wenden broke through and gave us the lead.   On resuming, the defence was sorely tried, but resisted all efforts of the Ipswich attack until three minutes from time, when one of their forwards scored with a fine shot.   It seemed certain now that the game would end in a draw, but in the failing light, the

School forwards made one last effort. The ball was worked down well into the opposing half, when Gibb, who had been doing some clever things with a sodden ball, gave Goldsmith a glorious pass with which to go through and score. In this way the School, who were undoubtedly the better team, won an excellent game 3-2.

C.R.G.S. v. Woodbridge School.—Played at home on December 5th, resulting in a win for the School 7-3. Woodbridge won the toss and elected to play against a strong wind. The School forwards with the wind at their backs adopted "first-time" shooting with excellent results. Within a quarter of an hour of the start Goldsmith and Atkin had each scored a goal, and the superiority of our attack was manifest. Goldsmith then added another with a screw shot, whereupon Woodbridge transferred the ball to the School half, and was allowed a rather doubtful goal. In reply to this, Pullen netted from a mêlée in front of goal, and Goldsmith completed his hat. trick. Half-time score—School 5, Woodbridge 1. It was not to be expected that the School would do so well now they were opposed to the wind, but it was some time before Woodbridge scored, twice in rapid succession. This produced a corresponding rally on our part, which led up to goals from Atkin and Goldsmith. The forwards in this match were better served by their halves, and in consequence showed much better combination.

First Eleven Colours for season 1914 have been awarded the following :—E. J. Brand (Capt.), W. G. Goldsmith, B. I. Pullen, T. G. Smith, G. Atkin, J. H. Cottrell, W. A. Doubleday, R. B. Alderton.

The following also played, and have been awarded Second Eleven Colours : – G. Gibb, R. H. Cottrell, E. M. Wenden, W. R. Orrin, S. W. Rogers.

SECOND ELEVEN.

The Second Eleven experienced a fairly good season. Three matches were won and four lost, while 14 goals were scored as against 13. Pertwee and White formed an effective right wing, and Gilbert, though small, played a good centre-forward game. In the defence, Rickword and Wagstaff at half, and French at back, were the outstanding members.

The team was as follows :—J. E. Rickword (Capt.), P. R. Wagstaff, R. E. French, J. W. Pertwee, A. White, R. S. Gilbert, M. H. Green, M. P. Horlock, T. A. Hawkins.

C.R.G.S. v. Saturday Rangers. Played on November 21st, at home, resulting in a win for the School 5-1. The forwards showed good form and shot well. White (3), Pertwee and Gilbert scored for the School.

C.R.G.S. v. Ipswich S.S. 2nd XI.—November 28th on School ground. Ipswich won an even game by the odd goal in three. Smith scored the goal for the School.

.C.R.G.S. v. Woodbridge School 2nd XI.—Played at Woodbridge on December 5th. Woodbridge won by four goals to one. The School forwards failed to get together, and it was left to Orrin to secure the only point.

HOUSE FOOTBALL.

Dugard's v. School House.—Dugard's having won the toss, kicked off with a slight wind in their favour. Doubleday and Orrin combined well as backs, and saved many a critical situation. In spite of numerous shots at goal, the "Wasps" failed to score till Pullen netted the ball from a well judged centre by Rogers. Shortly afterwards the ball was again put through from a scrum before goal by Rogers, who played a very sound game at outside left. In the second half, Cottrell ma., who had been playing back for School House, came forward, and succeeded in rushing the ball through Dugard's defence and scoring twice in succession. This made the score two all. Desperate efforts on the part of both sides failed to gain the winning goal, and the whistle blew without any further score.

Harsnett's v. Parr's.—The usual House match weather prevailed when Harsnett's took the field against Parr's. A strong wind was blowing across the pitch and accurate shooting was almost impossible. In the first half Parr's made several rushes, but they found Smith at back, and Rickword and Bare at half, difficult to pass. In one of these rushes, Folkard gave Parr's the lead with a shot which Alderton could not reach. The teams were very well matched, for both lines of forwards were weak, and just before half-time Atkin, with a long shot, brought the scores level again. In the second half Parr's made a great effort to gain the lead, but they were well watched by Bare and Rickword. Several good shots by Brand were carried over the bar by the wind, and Harsnett's also had bad luck, Atkin and White putting in some good shots, which just failed to find the net. Neither team was able to score again, and a well contested game ended in a draw, 1-1.

Parr's v. Dugard's.—Both sides were below full strength, which spoilt what otherwise might have been an excellent game. Though Dugard's started with only ten men, no score took place before they had their full side. A good deal of scrappy mid-field play went on in the first half-hour, and nothing definite resulted. Pullen twice broke through the opposition, only to shoot wide, while at the other end Barrell cleverly saved some long shots. At length from a mêlée Pullen scored for Dugard's. This roused the Parr's attack to a series of determined onslaughts on their opponents' goal. Their energy was soon rewarded, for Norfolk brought the scores level with a long shot. Half-time found the sides level. In the second half, both teams made spasmodic efforts to gain the lead, but it was not until close on time that Brand went through the opposing backs and put Parr's ahead. Dugards tried hard to obtain an equaliser, but to no purpose, and the whistle blew, leaving the final score—Parr's 2, Dugard's 1.

School House v. Harsnett's.—This was one of the second round of House matches. Up till now, all the Houses had gained one point. The match was played in fine weather, and both captains had their teams at full strength, so that a good game was expected. The School House forwards soon showed themselves superior to their opponents, and would have scored many times, but for Harsnett's defence, which was very good. The score at half-time was 4-1 in favour of School House, Goldsmith having scored three goals and Gibb one goal for School House, whilst Clarke ma. scored for Harsnett's. Harsnett's played harder during the second half, Atkin going back instead of Smith, who took his place in the forward line. Final score 6-2 for School House. Goldsmith and Gibb both scored again for School House, and Nicholson for Harsnett's.

House Singings.

THE majority of the house-singings of last term may be dismissed in the words of our lively contemporary, *The Idler*, as "not worth mentioning." That magazine, the product of some anonymous seniors, voices the disgust we all feel for the boy who never attempts to help at house-singings, and our deeper disgust for the boy who puts on a badly learned and crude item. Horwood mi.'s debut in a recitation, and Barnes as a violinist deserve a word of praise . . . . . "the rest is silence."

On November 28th the VA. Thespians gave a comedietta entitled "Peter's Proposal." Under Mr. Carter's tuition steady progress had been made, and the result was a nicely rounded and smooth performance. The chief claim to distinction in this piece lay in its smart dialogue and clever characterisation. It contrasted most favourably with the usual "knockabout" farce associated with school shows.

Goldsmith as Graham, the novelist, was most finished. Collinge ma. as a curate was distinctly clever, and never exaggerated his picture. Orrin was at home in the part of Halse, a country gentleman, whose daughter, May, was well played by Bugg. Pertwee gave a really clever presentation of Ella Mayfield, with just the right carriage and gestures. Rogers was a neat footed Hebe.

The feature which delighted most, and best revealed the work put into the play by Mr. Carter was the repose of the actors, and the ease with which they could be heard.

The first house-singing this term revealed the lack of fresh talent that marked the concerts of last term. Collinge mi., Clarke mi., and Sands saved the situation in their usual kindly way. Poyser made a creditable entry as a reciter. A Gaudy sing-song followed on the next Saturday, and was rather refreshing, especially as the piano was *hors de combat* and we had to rely on the human instrument alone.

DUGARD'S.

Although the lot of the first performance fell upon Dugard's, there was no evidence of unpreparedness. They gave a miscellaneous programme in which Clarke mi. was less happy in a song, "The Man who would rhyme," than in the part of the Cockney drudge in "Cupid in the Kitchen." This was one of the best pieces of schoolboy acting we have ever seen. Steady, patient work should make Clarke a most capable player. The "Small Nibs" were very charming in "A Terrible Story," whilst Pullen was remarkably restrained in his speech on Workmen's Rights. By the way, when waiting to give this item to the Troops in the Board Room at the

Union, he was given much sympathy as a genuine tramp by a kindly Tommy. Sands in his conjuring act displayed an increasing deftness of hand and an improved stage presence. Horwood recited Father's Fireworks very effectively and won a deserved encore. The songs, Red Rose of England, The Sea is England's Glory, Three Old Maids of Lee, were given with taste and expression, and showed an appreciation of light and shade.

In "Cupid in the Kitchen," Squire and Bugg did some good work; the latter was more confident of himself in "Ringing the Changes." In this playlet Fincham scored a great success. He took on the part at two days' notice, and in the dual part of the Husband (with a delightful drawl) and the Frenchman (with true Gallic fire) he showed unsuspected power; accent, pose and gesture were to the manner born, and all with only one rehearsal. We look for more, Fincham. Dugard's are to be congratulated on their varied and finished work.

PARR'S.

The second house-singing, given by Parr's, was a marked improvement on last year's show. The first part was full of good things. "Horatius," recited by the very junior Parrites, was quite effective, despite the curious draping of the togas. Munson successfully overcame several difficulties in his song "The Modest Curate." The small boys again did very well in the Bad Boy's Book of Beasts, reciting Belloc's verses to illustrations by Norfolk. In Syer, Parr's discovered a reciter with a good delivery and some dramatic power. We must hear him again. In the Songs from the Jungle Book and the Hunting Song (written by Mr. Worth) a capital chorus of six voices displayed both sentiment and skill. Collinge mi. in "Dreaming," and still more in the Jungle songs, sang with the good taste and modest pose which endears him to his audiences.

Wagstaff ma. proved himself still our most faithful exponent of the Essex dialect. The play, "Lights Out," was a triumph for Collinge ma., whose Algernon Cuffe was a real character study. Andrews has still to learn the value of repose on the stage, but his elocution is improving. Marlar made an excellent footman, and the "girls," French ma., Cheshire and Percy acted quite well although their figures did not help the illusion. In a sketch, "The Interview," Payne ma. gave a very finished performance, and again we asked ourselves, why are ordinary house-singings such drab, dull things? If half as much enthusiasm could be worked up in the cause of School as is displayed for House, our weekly entertainments would be worth preserving.   J.A.P.

HARSNETT'S.

On Saturday, March 6th, Harsnett's House gave their annual house-singing under the leadership of Mr. Peart, who has taken on the position of House-master since Mr. Parker left. Needless to say as soon as it was known who was at the head of affairs the audience rolled up in large numbers, a record attendance resulting. The evening's entertainment consisted of a connected piece, *quasi pantomime*, *quasi revue*, founded on the old story of the Babes in the Wood, but replete with up-to-date allusions. All concerned did their work well and did their best not only to shine individually, but also to help to maintain the general ensemble at a high level. Where so much was good, it would seem invidious to pick out certain persons for praise, but mention must be made of a few. Bearing the brunt of the play Atkin as the Baron spoke his lines clearly and acted with the intelligence that was denoted by his dome-like forehead. Baskett, as his wife, proved a pleasant surprise. Abandoning for the nonce his love of exaggeration, he showed a reserve and reticence in his acting which was very praiseworthy. One of the hits of the evening was the Strong Men (Taylor & Beard). Taylor, despite his size, is a great actor. Never hurrying, knowing just what to do, he made every point without seeming effort and evoked hearty laughter. Among other performers Cameron as the Baron's daughter looked winsome and acted daintily. Peacock, the wandering minstrel was in good voice, and the gnomes, headed by Burleigh ma., gave a touch of colour to the scene. Mention must be made of Ward, who, as the Nurse, acted well and sang a topical song on the Masters with great aplomb and clearness. And so—why bless me I've forgotten the Babes. *The Babes.* Of course it was natural that they should both be Moderns. Bare, as the boy—quite a handsome one by the way—and White as the girl—not bad looking either—were quite the thing and when they were allowed out of sight of the nurse they had quite a pretty little quarrel on their own, causing great amusement. They looked quite pathetic as they lay in the forest, being covered with leaves by the Robins, who, led by Rickword, gyrated gracefully around them. Harsnett's gaudy, lustily sung, finished up one of the best House-singings we have had.   F. B. C.

SCHOOL HOUSE.

The last of the house house-singings opened with a chorus, " When the band begins to play," which revealed a sweetness of tone for which we could forgive the uncertainty of grasp evidenced. This was followed by " Hardup Rivals," a repeat of a former success. We could regret that it was revived (especially the worn tag at the end), except that it gave us occasion to note the general improvement in elocution and stage sense.

Middleton made an excellent first appearance, and Gibb as the waiter was capital. Pertwee was carried away by the speed of his delivery. Barnes, who bore a considerable share of the burden of the evening, is to be highly commended for his violin solo, which was memorized, no mean achievement for a beginner. Two recitations, one by Koskinas and one by Vanderburgh, followed. The clear enunciation of the latter was very pleasing. The cosmopolitanism of School-house was demonstrated by these two, sons of Greece and Belgium. A two-part song, " Life's Lullaby," gave Pertwee and Miller ma. an opportunity of showing what can be done with a well-modified alto tone. Barnes, in the two-part song and in his solo, was rather uneven, and should pay more heed to his production. The band scored an easily won triumph, in which Miller mi. shone as the only instrumentalist who fingered his instrument.

In the concluding play, a Petit Guignol thriller, School-house showed what boys can do under careful and patient training. Green was excellent, both with regard to his restraint, and in his delivery, slow and distinct. His death was in the most approved Irving tradition. Koskinas played with quiet force that really gripped the house ; whilst Pertwee, Cottrell ma., Crighton and Rayner did sound work in minor parts.

As with Parr's the improvement on last year's standard was most gratifying to all concerned.

J.A.P.

STAFF HOUSE-SINGING.

The series of special house-singings was begun by the Staff Concert, which, although quite good, did not surpass our expectations. Mr. Worth's first appearance on the stage was unanimously appreciated. Mr. Peart changed his usual tactics by giving a serious recitation ; he compensated us, however, by singing " Excelsior " with Mr. Clarke, easily the best thing on the programme. Mr. Carter's original numbers and turn, " At the piano," were loudly encored, and Mr. Clarke's funny songs made us laugh loud and long. Mr. Watts and Mr. Barker were quite good mimics. Mr. Watts' recitations in different dialects were especially good, and Mr. Barker looked very much the Apache. Miss Cross's song was quite a change in a comic programme. Her voice was, as usual, highly appreciated and she was loudly encored.

We must not forget the Headmaster, whose reading and display of pictures was very much applauded. In the final quartette Mr. Barker excelled as a Yankee, Mr. Peart was too Napoleonic, Mr. Worth was like a cowboy, and Mr. Clarke as he is generally.

K.

Cadet Corps.

THE second half of the Michaelmas Term was spent in improving our acquaintance with Platoon Drill, while the recruits also languished for the new uniforms. Carbines, belts and bayonets were early at a premium, and we should still like to hear of that consignment which was offered by the County Association and accepted by us, but which has not been forthcoming.

Holiday parades, once a week, were not well attended but those Cadets who came in got through a useful amount of "spade-work."

Just before the beginning of this · term the uniforms, *mirabile dictu*, arrived. The appearance of the Corps since then has been in several ways much more "uniform."

We have been pleased to welcome several Scouts as recruits, and with several other new members, our numbers are fully maintained.

We were unfortunate in losing three keen Cadets in Sergt. Doubleday, Corpl. Goldsmith and Lance-Corpl. Deane, but happily we still have a good leavening of keen N.C.O's who, *sauf leur respect*, are much more efficient and capable of taking command than at one time.

We were extremely sorry to lose Sergt. Penn, though only temporarily. He was always ready and willing to give us the benefit of his advice and support. But we are happy to hear that he is well content with his present work and that promotion in his old regiment came to him early. In his absence Colour-Sergt. Ward has been, as always, very keen and has rendered valuable assistance.

Although field-days are necessarily denied us, we are getting a very fair amount of fun from route marches, varied lately by concentration marches ; and also from extended order drill on Thursday afternoons. The latter was at first quite a revelation in suicidal warfare, but we are improving.

And lastly—the Band ! Bugg has filled Goldsmith's place as drummer very creditably. Both drums and bugles, good last term, have still further improved and with their lately extended répertoire are indeed a joy to us. Much honour accrued to the Band last term from the R.F.A. officers and we continue to be justly proud of their performances. Our best thanks are due to Band-Sergt. Atkin for his unstinted efforts on every occasion.

F.D.B.

Shooting.

CONTRARY to expectations, the number of boys who become members of the Rifle Club remains normal and we have yet to exceed our record of 1913, when we had 60 members. Surely now is the time when we should expect to be crowded out by boys anxious to learn the elements of shooting.

Many of our old members have joined "the colours," and we hear from these, how useful they are finding the knowledge of the rifle learnt on our range. Fitch, who will be remembered for his rapid firing has been chosen as a " Sniper " for his regiment.

During the Xmas Holidays the 8th Essex practically commandeered our re-barrelled rifles, and several times this term have had the use of them for short periods, and it is undoubtedly true that acquaintance with the miniature bore is found most useful in teaching recruits how to use the service rifle.

The average of our shooting is not at present so good as that of a few terms back, owing to the departure of our stalwarts among the senior boys. We have a promising lot of Juniors and it is to them we shall have to look to uphold our reputation in the I.C.S. Competition to be held next June. This is shot off at 20 yards range, so it is proposed to hold the final round of the House Competition at the end of March, when the bullet-catchers will be moved up to this distance to allow us to get in some practice at the Bisley and Figure Targets before the end of the term.

In the second round of the House Competition, shot off at the end of last term, Dugard's came out top and as a result of the first two rounds they lead Parr's by 13 points and School House by 19. The final this term should be keen and interesting. Below are the results for last term.

DUGARD'S.		PARR'S.		SCHOOL HOUSE.		HARSNETT'S.	
Doubleday	63	Watsham	61	Cottrell mi.	58	Bare	57
Chapman	61	Percy	61	Goldsmith	55	Deane	55
Squire	52	Wagstaff	59	Leeming	52	Ward	52
Berry	52	Payne	55	Rayner	50	Atkin	50
Carey	52	Brand	52	Green	49	Burleigh	49
Halls	51	Andrews	48	Cottrell ma.	41	Smith	45
Fincham	47	Rose	40	Pertwee	39	Rickword	43
Hazell	47	Wheeler	36	Koskinas	38	Clark	43
Summer Term	425 424		412 424		382 448		394 412
Total	849		836		830		806

We have usually ended these notes with one of thanks to
C.-S.-I. Penn. On this occasion we can only say how much
we miss him and how glad we shall be to welcome him back
again.

E. R.

Scouting Notes.

THE exceptionally wet winter has made outdoor work
almost impossible, so that there is not much to record.
Several Scouts however have been doing their best to be of
service in this great crisis, and it is interesting to read the
official testimony that has been given to the value and
usefulness of the well-trained Scout in different departments
of public service since the outbreak of war.

On March 2nd, the Mayor presented badges to those
Scouts in the Colchester district who had performed twenty-
eight days' service, and amongst the recipients were P. L.
Kent, Wheeler, ma., Hazell and Clarke, all of the Peewit
Patrol.

Kent also has the distinction of being the first member of
the troop to qualify as a First-Class Scout and I hope that
his promotion will be an incentive to other members of the
Troop to work steadily for this badge and not to be content
to remain Second-Class Scouts.

Gower, ma. has left the School and Chambers and
Wheeler, ma. have passed on to the Cadet Corps, but
Osborne ma., Munson, Osborne mi., Hunnyball, Miller and
Tricker have joined us this term, so that our numbers are
more than maintained.

G. E. P.

C.R.G.S. Debating Society.

THE School Debating Society has held five meetings during the present session, all of which have been very well attended. There have not been any speeches which could be classed as brilliant, but we have had 27 different speakers, and when these lose the habit of writing a speech as they would an essay and then reciting it at the meeting, we shall be able to report faster progress.

The subject of the first debate of the session was the rumour that Russian troops had been brought through England. Many interesting stories were recounted, and, there being nothing certain on either side, the House had to decide which were the least unlikely of the rumours. The voting finally went in favour of the Russians having crossed England on their way to France.

At the next meeting the Colchester Tramway system was discussed, and several highly amusing suggestions were made, one being that we should instal a tube system in the town. It was eventually decided that the trams ought to be abolished. The third meeting was a discussion on what would be a fair partition of Europe after the war, and the Xmas Term concluded with an impromptu debate at which we heard a number of maiden speeches of varying merit. During the present term, owing to House Concerts, we have had only one debate, when the motion for discussion was: that instructions in case of invasion should be issued to householders; it was decided by a small majority that this step was advisable.

The Committee have lately been criticized with regard to their arrangements for debates in an anonymous letter signed "Malcontent" and published in the New School periodical, *The Idler*. There can hardly be many who agree with this letter, as we have had an average attendance at our meetings this session of over forty boys. Again, although the majority of our speakers are naturally in the three top forms of the school, there are still many boys in the Sixth and Fifth who are by no means regular speakers, and who do not seem to find the subjects chosen so much beneath the notice of their intellects as does "Malcontent."

It is, of course, much easier to sit in an arm-chair and write letters criticizing the arrangements made than to come to each meeting and assist in raising the standard of the speeches and through them that of the subjects discussed, by an active participation.

A system of House Point marking has been adopted during the session, and at the present time Harsnett's have a substantial lead.

It is doubtful if we shall be able to hold any further meetings this session, but every endeavour will be made to do so.

Pre-Historic Peeps.

WHAT numerous things have happened since the last school magazine was published ! It is indeed impossible even to touch upon a quarter of them. " What are you doing to help them ? " frequently catches my eye, and I feel that within the school walls much *has* been done to help the soldiers.

The Relief Expedition was just what we needed to stir us afresh to the little bit we *can* do.

Nowhere could the plan have been received more enthusiastically than in " The Pre." All were keen to pack up parcels, and each quickly decided what his should contain. It would have cheered the heart of many a wounded man could he have watched the eager faces, and heard all they had to say just then. There was only one moment's hesitation and that was when one little fellow volunteered the information that there were some German soldiers too in the Military Hospital. If one of them should by chance get a " Pre " boy's cigarette, I fear it will choke him so intensely strong is the feeling against those unfortunate Germans, in spite of all we can say to check it. Saturday was a grand morning, every boy arrived proudly laden, and it was quite a business to make a list of what each parcel contained. The supreme moment came when every one of our boys marched over and deposited his parcel in the workshop. For little fellows the ambulance carrying away their treasures was cruelly undemonstrative, but they soon forgot this momentary disappoinment, and were gaily rushing after the football.

The " Pre " boys are by no means fine weather pupils, and in spite of the unusually rough mornings we have experienced they have turned up splendidly. Snow, rain, hail, nothing prevents their coming (except horrid colds) or damps their spirits, as we occasionally find when " break " comes round.

From some mysterious cause our gardens are not looking as promising as we could wish. We are living on the tip-toe of expectation, awaiting the bulbs to burst into bloom. A dark suspicion creeps into our minds—were some bulbs so thoroughly embedded that they are making this an excuse for keeping hidden away in dread of a chance bomb! or was there really some slight mishap about the planting thereof that has enabled them to bloom in some more genial clime? Who can say? We only know there is very little show for all those we scraped together and carried from afar, and sincerely hope our other addition to the border will prove more encouraging. There is a certain falling off in the Good Deeds Service, not that there are fewer, but as some of the boys have been a considerable time in the school; we feel the need of some more decided and serious step towards scouting. In the near future we hope to adopt some new plan.

It is whispered that the Brownies are looking out their costumes again, and although their owners express much anxiety as to their dimensions after a year and more has slipped away we hope by loaning and re-adjusting these quaint garments that the troupe will shortly appear trimly equipped, when they will certainly ask for the same kindly support that helped to make their last concert a success.

Many thanks to the boys who so often bring me magazines and papers, which I send to different hospitals for our soldiers, and they are greatly appreciated.

C.C.

Open Letter.

To the Editor of " The Idler."

MR. EDITOR,

Sir,

I hasten to congratulate you on the excellence of your criticisms on matters musical and dramatic, couched in style and spirit far removed from the banal reports usually considered adequate for such things.

The taste and sureness of touch displayed by "Con Spirito" are delightful, but may I point out a contradiction and attempt a defence?

In the editorial you state that "The recent concerts attained the customary level of excellence, and if they are any criterion, the remainder of the series should prove most attractive." Further on in the Magazine follows an account of House House-singings, generally commended by your critic; indeed, the Press has never before found so much to praise. Yet "Con Spirito" in his opening paragraph states, "We certainly have made little progress with our House-singings, in fact, though the much-used fallacy of the 'good old days' may have something to do with the feeling, it certainly seems that we have deteriorated greatly in this respect since the days in the old Big School." How can this be, I ask, Sir, when the Houses which make up the School have so materially improved? Can your indictment be true, when the School demonstrates annually the increased sense of the Arts in the Carol Service, the State Concert, the Cadet Concert, and the manifold parochial concerts given?

" Con Spirito " adds, " The gaudies are no longer sung with that enthusiasm with which we used to respond to the invitation to ' lift the roof off ' in the old hall." May I suggest, as Music Master, that if we were to hold a House-singing in the old hall we could now blow out the walls as well as the roof, if that were the aim of the art of music, but at the same time we should blow to smithereens the reputation we are slowly building up as a musical community. In complaining of the lack of support from Upper School, I am with your critic, heart and soul. Only when the Arts are regarded as not entirely beneath the notice of what Kipling calls " The giddy Paladins " shall we progress in their cultivation.

Although the sensibilities of the Deputy-Chairman of Debate, the Sub-Drill Instructor, the Master of Harsnett's, and the writer of the Modern Magazine's foreword are, I understand, quivering under your lash, I am personally grateful for your criticisms. In a school that produces " The Idler " there is no room for despair.

I am, Sir,
Yours faithfully,
MUSICO.

TO BE PUBLISHED SHORTLY.

Colchester Gaudies, Glorias
AND OTHER FUGITIVE PIECES.
By J.

We are anxious to collect the various School Songs and Glorias sung at School Entertainments during the past 15 years. Anyone having copies of old programmes would confer a great favour by lending them to the H. M.

Old Colcestrian Section.

Editorial.

O.C.'s and the War.

The Great War is still the absorbing topic, and the Society's programme of festivities must await the happier days of peace. For the first time in the history of the Society the annual dinner has been abandoned, and the pleasant outdoor gatherings in summer will be in abeyance unless events in Europe portend an early settlement of the conflict of arms. Is this too much to hope for?

A Rally to the Call.

One very satisfactory feature of the moment is the rally of Old Colcestrians to the country's help in her time of need. In Canada, New Zealand, India, Ceylon, and Australia the call has reached old boys of the School, and they have answered nobly, and one at least is serving "with Botha in South Africa." Some O.C.'s have already been lucky enough to be in the fighting. Rev. C. A. B. Allen, on board the "Queen Elizabeth," has seen something of modern naval warfare in the Dardanelles. E. G. Fenn and J. D. Secker are in the trenches in France, and Tom Baskett came unscathed through the fighting that preceded the fall of Antwerp.

The Roll of Honour.

The School's Roll of Honour, which appears on another page, is growing to quite respectable proportions, and now comprises nearly 200 names. In all probability there are many more O.C.'s "doing their little bit," but it is difficult to compile a list that will be absolutely complete. Parents and friends can help us by sending in names and particulars of other O.C.'s serving the nation, so that we may have produced a Roll of Honour worthy the best traditions of our Alma Mater, and worthy a permanent place on the walls of Big School.

The Society.

Since the last Annual Meeting of the Old Colcestrian Society its affairs have been put upon a business-like footing. Sentiment is the most potent factor in the maintenance of an old boys' society, but its members must show, not merely a sentimental, but a *practical* interest in it. For that reason many names have been removed from the list of members which appears periodically on the cover of "The Colcestrian," and at the same time we note the addition of more names— men who really do wish to retain a connecting link with the happy days at school.

An Appeal.

These are the men, who, on application, pay up their subscriptions and so give no unnecessary trouble to the honorary officers, busy men themselves. but willing to undertake official duties for the sake of old times. In our honorary treasurer and secretaries the Society has some excellent workers, but all their efforts, without the *practical* support of the members, are unavailing. A large sum has been collected in back subscriptions; there are others still owing, and that must be our apology for this, perhaps, too direct appeal. *Verb. sap.*	THE EDITOR.

O.C.'s Roll of Ðonour.

Tradition gives us pride of birth,
Brave hearts and gentle manners,
For we are sons of men who marched
Beneath the Tudor banners.

So as we pass the torch along
Aglow with high endeavour,
Our kindly mother we acclaim
That she may stand for ever.

THE following is a list of O.C.'s serving their King and Country, and the Editors will welcome corrections and additions, in order that the Roll of Honour may be complete:

Allen, Rev. C. A. B., Naval Chaplain, H.M.S. "Queen Elizabeth"
Archer, E. R., Royal Navy
Anthony, W. B., Lieut., 14th Northumberland Fusiliers
Allen, T., Essex Yeomanry
Allen, F., Royal Engineers (Australian Expeditionary Force)

Burridge, G. J., 5th Lancers
Burrell, B. F., 10th Essex Regiment
Barnes, Dr. F. M., Lieutenant, R.A.M.C.
Bellward, G. E. F., Lieutenant, 5th Essex
Benham, G. C., Captain and Adjutant, 8th Essex

Benham, W. G., Platoon Commander, Colchester Volunteer Training Corps
Beard, E. C., Public Schools Battalion
Bromley, J. G., Motor Unit, A.S.C.
Bultitude, R. J., 8th Essex Cyclists
Bunting, A. E., Lieutenant, 12th Essex
Baskett, T., Royal Naval Brigade
Butler, G. F., Public Schools Battalion
Bareham, C., Essex Yeomanry
Bond, C. T., Australian Contingent
Barnes, L. W. H.
Barnes, J.
Becker, C. H. (wounded), Royal West Surrey
Bloomfield, A., Essex R.H.A.
Barker, F. D , Lieutenant, C.R.G.S. Cadet Corps
Becker, Colonel, A.D.B.O.
Bawtree, D. E., Grenadier Guards
Bacon, S. F., Royal Navy
Bare, W. J., 8th Essex
Barnes, A., Colchester Volunteer Training Corps

Caines, E. C., Essex Yeomanry
Cork, F. F.. Civil Service Rifles
Cullington, M. W., Civil Service Rifles
Cheshire, G., 10th Essex
Cheshire, W. R., Ceylon Tea Planters
Chambers, C. W., Mechanical Transport
Chambers, A. S., Army Ordnance Department
Clarke, L. 5th Essex
Cole, E. H., Colchester Volunteer Training Corps.
Collins, R. C., 20th Hussars
Collison, A. L., Censor Eastern Tel., Gibraltar
Cudmore, H. T., Essex Yeomanry
Cobbold, H. J. T., Royal Naval Reserve
Cobbold, R. G., Canadian Contingent
Campling, C. D., Public Schools Battalion
Coquerel Rene, 3rd Infanterie, Brest
le Coeuvre, Albert, Infanterie (reserve)
Collins, H., 8th Essex Cyclists
Clamp, A. J., Colchester Volunteer Training Corps
Clamp, G., 5th Essex
Clarke, S. F., Hants Cyclists

Denton, C. W., Lieutenant, 8th Essex
Denton, A., Captain, 5th Essex
Denton, H. W., Public Schools Battalion
Davis, E. G., Captain and Adjutant, 8th Essex

Davies, E. J., Australian Contingent
Deakin, E. B., Lieutenant, 5th Essex

Everett, W. R., 10th Essex
Everett, C. E. F., Public Schools Battalion
Essex, P. C.
Essex, B. E.

Folkard, W. E., Army Ordnance Department
Finch, L., Essex Yeomanry (Egypt)
Fenn, E. G., Essex Yeomanry (France)
Flanegan, L. C., R.M.C. (Sandhurst)
Fleetwood, E. C., Essex Yeomanry
Fairhead, S. C., Essex Yeomanry
Fisher, E., 6th Essex
Finch, P. R. C.
Farmer, A O., Colchester Volunteer Training Corps
French, A. H., R.F.A.
Frost, L. A., Queen's Westminster Rifles

Green, A. E., 9th Essex
Green, Harold, 9th Hants Cyclists, Despatch Rider
Green, C. B., Essex R.H.A., Despatch Rider
Gregg, F. G., 12th City of London
Girling, C. J., 5th South Staffordshire Regiment
Graham-Brown, Lieutenant
Goldsmith, E. J., U.P.S. Corps

Humphreys, H., Rifle Brigade
Hall, — 5th Lancers
Hazell, R. L. K., Colchester Volunteer Training Corps
Horwood, R. V., 6th Royal Irish Rifles
Head, J., Essex R.H.A.
Hempson, British Vice-Consul, Cadiz
Hempson, E.
Harwood, P., 10th Fusiliers
Helps, Frank B., Queen's Westminster Rifles
Harrison, Victor, A.S.C.
Hollaway, H. H., Quartermaster, Colchester Volunteer
   Training Corps
Harper, W. C., Colchester Volunteer Training Corps

Jasper, L. V., Essex Yeomanry
Jeffrey, P. S., National Reserve
Jarmin, R.V., R.A.M.C.
Jarrard, D. G., R.H.A.
Jarrard, C. H., 8th Essex Regiment

Judd, A. E., Essex R.H.A.
Jasper, L. A., Midshipman, H.M.S. "Virginian"
Jefferies, C. R., Essex Yeomanry

King, Hugh, Army Ordnance Department
King, Geoffrey, Motor Section, A.S.C.
Knopp, H. A., 5th Essex
Keeble, F. R., Suffolk Yeomanry

Lansdowne, L. R., 10th Middlesex (India)
Lawrence, A. D., Cheshire Yeomanry
Lord, P. C., Essex R.H.A.
Leaning, A., Capt., A.V.C., 5th Cavalry Brigade, Indian
    Expeditionary Force

Maile, Rowland
Matthew, W. S., Gordon Highlanders
Matthews, W., Cameron Highlanders
Mason, A. S., Captain, Devon Yeomanry (India)
Mason, C., 10th Essex
Manning, L., Essex Yeomanry
Manning, C., Essex R.H.A.
Manning, —
Miller, E. S., Public Schools Battalion
Malyn, D. P., Lieutenant, A.S.C.
Melrose, A., Royal West Kent
Marlar, J., Public Schools Battalion
Minor, R., Public Schools Battalion

Nash, B. A., Colchester Volunteer Training Corps
Norfolk, A., Army Service Corps
Nicholl, A. F., Royal Naval Reserve
Nunn, J. H., Colchester Volunteer Training Corps

Orfeur, C. B., Royal Naval Division (Gibraltar)
Orfeur, H. W., 2nd Lieutenant, 8th Essex

Peacock, N., 1st Class Petty Officer, H.M.S. "Vincent"
Peacock, A., Essex R.H.A.
Prior, C. D., Motor Unit A.S.C.
Pawsey, J. S., Public Schools Battalion
Potter, J., Motor Unit A.S.C.
Potter, C. C., Westminster Rifles
Plummer, F. E.
Pointing, W. W., Kensington Rifles
Plane, L. W., A.O.D. Motor Unit
Pepper, V., Canadian Contingent

Palmer, H. V., Lieutenant, Oxford L.I.
Plant, C., Public Schools Battalion
Prime, E. J., Essex Yeomanry (France)
Phillips, Colonel
Puttick, F. M., Otago Mounted Rifles, New Zealand Contingent
Puttick, S. F., with Botha in South Africa
Pointing, M., Army Service Corps
Padfield, C., 16th Lancers
Parsons, W., Essex Yeomanry
Penny, Ronald E., Eng. Lieut., Commander Armoured Vessel, S.S. " Winifred" on Victoria Nyanza, formerly S.S. " Sybil

Queripel, Major, Guernsey Militia

Renton, T. S., 9th Essex
Ritchie, Major A. S. M., D.S.O., Queen's Bays
Ryder, E., 10th Middlesex
Richardson, J. R., 2nd Lieutenant, 12th Essex
Richardson, A. J., Essex Yeomanry
Rowe, P. G.

Secker, J. D., London Rifle Brigade
Sparling, A. S. B., National Reserve
Slight, R. L., Manchester Regiment
Siggers, J. W., Essex Yeomanry
Siggers, O., Royal Naval Reserve
Sanger, C. W., University Battalion
Sanger, H., 5th Essex
Scott-Cooper, Lieutenant, 4th Middlesex
Scott, J. H., Public Schools Battalion
Scott, — Lieutenant, 12th Essex
Scott, — Lieutenant, Middlesex Regiment
Shelton, C. S., Army Ordnance Department
Salmon, A. V., National Reserve
Sparling, A. E., The late, Lieutenant, 8th Essex
Salisbury, W. H., Royal Navy (artificer)

Tucker, Stanley, 15th Battalion London City Regiment
Tye, G. H., Essex R.H.A.
Taylor, A. P., Royal Naval Brigade (Gronigen)
Turner, A. J., Major, R.F.A.
Turner, Frank, Major, Intelligence Dept.
Turner, H. P., Colchester Volunteer Training Corps
Turner, W. M., Captain, R.F.A.
Town, W. M., 5th Essex

Turner, Arthur, Captain, 5th Essex
Turner, S. C., Motor Scout, Essex Regiment

Watson, G. F., Lieutenant, Welsh Field Co. R.E.
Watson, J. L., Canadian Contingent
Williams, F. O., 11th Essex
Warner, A. E., R.A.M.C.
Watsham, H., 5th Essex
Willmott, J., Public Schools Battalion
Whitby, J. M. F., 5th Essex
Whitby, H., 8th Essex
Wanklyn, D. C., Motor Unit, Essex Cyclists
Ward, J. D., Royal Horse Guards
Waring, C., died of operation, Montreal
Walker, B. E. C.

DEAKIN, E. B., G.R.G.S.
DEANE, G. F. F., Longwood, Nayland.
DENTON, A., Barclay's Bank, Colchester.
DENTON, C. W., Marylands, Shrub End Road, Colchester. [E.C.
DICKER, B. P., Grocers' Hall, Prince's Street,
DOUBLEDAY, R. E., Belle Vue Road, Wivenhoe.
DOUBLEDAY, W. A., Belle Vue Road, Wivenhoe.
DUNNINGHAM, T. C., Manor Road, Dovercourt.
EDERT, Dr. E., Kiel, Fichtestrasse 2, Germany
EVERETT, H. J., Councillor, 28 New Town Road, Colchester.
EVERETT, W. R., c/o B. F. Burrell, Esq., Abbeygate Street, Colchester.
EVERITT, C. B. F., 28 New Town Road, Colchester.
EVES, E. J., 17 Morant Road, Colchester.
EWING, J. H., South Hall, Ramsey, Harwich
FAIRHEAD, A. E., Bouchier's Hall, Messing, Kelvedon.
FARMER, A. O., 12 Queen Street, Colchester (HON. SECRETARY).
FAVIELL, C. V., 28 Udney Park, Teddington, Middlesex.
FENN, E. G., The Hall, Ardleigh.
FIELDGATE, W. H., "Ty Fry," Regent Road, Brightlingsea.
FINCH, F. D., 25 Salisbury Avenue, Colchester.
FITCH, L. B., Louisville, Fambridge Road, Maldon.
FLANAGAN, L. C., Beta House, Clacton-on-Sea.
FLEETWOOD, E. C., Bemahague, Shrub End Road, Colchester.
FLUX, J., Lower Clifden Downs Station, Carnarvon, W. Australia.
FLUX, R. C., 27 Old Heath Road, Colchester.
FOLKARD, C., Copford. Colchester.
FOLKARD, H., Copford, Colchester.
FRANKLIN, Councillor R., Sutherland House, 95 Baddow Road, Chelmsford.
FRANCIS, E. K., Crouch Street, Colchester.
FRENCH, R. E., 58 Roman Road, Colchester.
FROST, A. T., Rackbarton, St. Barnabas Road, Cambridge.
FROST, A. W., 13 Head Street, Colchester.
GIBBS, J. W., 249 Maldon Road, Colchester.
GIRLING, T. A., 18 Park Road, Chelmsford.
GIRLING, HUGH, Park Villa, Dunmow.
GODFREY, C. F., "Thirlmere," Queen's Road, Springfield, Chelmsford.
GOING, F. W., 125 Maldon Road, Colchester.
GOODEY, S., Chelsworth, New Town Road, Colchester.
GOODY, C., Old Heath Road, Colchester.
GREEN, H., Moat Hall, Fordham, Colchester.
GREEN, A. C., Fingringhoe, Colchester.
GREEN, D. A., The Hall, Fingringhoe, Essex.
GREEN, A. E., 18 East Stockwell Street, Colchester.
GREEN, C. S., Fingringhoe, Colchester.
GREEN, C. B., Holmwood, Fingringhoe, Essex.
GREGG, F. GORDON, 58 Dennington Road, W. Hampstead.
GRIFFIN, C., Stanway Villa, Colchester.
GRIFFIN, H. L., Stockwell House, West Stockwell Street, Colchester.
GRIMWOOD, C. H., c/o Boots, Ltd., Long Wyre Street, Colchester.
HALL, A. J., Caerleon, New Town Road, Colchester.
HARPER, W. C., 6 Queen Street, Colchester.
HARRIS, H. J., Weircombe, Ardwick Road, W. Hampstead.
HARVEY, J. B., Stanley Lodge, Wellesley Road, Colchester.
HARSUM, G. F., Wood Field, Bourne Road, Colchester.
HAZELL, S. G., Wellesley Road, Colchester (and Montreal).
HAZELL, R. L., 23 Lexden Street, Colchester.

HEAD, A., 58 Wimpole Road, Colchester.
HEAD, J., 58 Wimpole Road, Colchester.
HEMPSON, R. J.
HOLLAWAY, H. H., 34 Old Heath Road, Colchester.
HORLOCK, M. F., High Street, Mistley.
HORWOOD, R. B., Layer Hall, Layer.
HOWARD, W. K.
HURST, H. J. R., 7 St. John Street, Colchester
HUSSEY, F. W., 15 Audley Road, Colchester.
IVEY, S. F., 63 Kensington Gardens Square, London, W.
JARRARD, C. H., Thorpe, Colchester.
JARRARD, D. G., Alexandra Road, Sible Hedingham.
JASPER, C. V., Langenhoe Hall, Colchester.
JASPER, L. A., Langenhoe Hall, Colchester.
JAMS, GEO. E., 28 Llandaff Road, Canton, Cardiff.
JEFFERIES, C. R., 62 Winnock Road, Colchester.
JEFFREY, E. SHAW, School House, Colchester.
JOHNSON, L. H., 17 Lion Walk, Colchester.
JONES, F. B., c/o Jones and Watts, Barrack Street, Colchester.
JUDD, L., South Villa, Ardleigh.
KENT, B. H., 182 Maldon Road, Colchester.
KING, J., 16 Inglis Road, Colchester.
KING, W. H., Inglis Road, Colchester
KING, W. H., junr., Inglis Road, Colchester.
KING, G. K., 53 Friar Street, Sudbury.
LANSDOWNE, L. R., Mersea House, Walton.
LAYER, P., Church Street North, Colchester.
LAY, C. V., 2k Portman Mansions, St. Marylebone, London, W.
LAWRENCE, A. D., c/o Head & Co., Ltd., 27 Cornhill, London, E.C.
LAZELL, HAROLD, Fitzwalter Road, Lexden Park, Colchester.
LEANING, E. M., Welwyn, Wash Lane, Clacton-on-Sea.
LEWIS, K. M., 173 Maldon Road, Colchester.
LINES, E., The Bungalow, Great Bentley.
LORD, P., North Hill, Colchester.
LORD, S. W., 49 North Hill, Colchester.
LUCKING, A. S., 26 Inglis Road, Colchester.
LUCKING, O. D., 20 Inglis Road, Colchester.
MALYN, D. P., Bleak House, Braintree.
MALYN, R., Barclay's Bank, Colchester
MANNING, C., The Elms, Weeley, R.S.Q.
MANNING, P. E. J., The Elms, Weeley, R.S.O., Essex. [chester.
MANNING, C. L., 162 Military Road, Colchester.
MARLAR, J., North Hill, Colchester.
MARSH, W. E., 180 Longmarket Street, Natal, South Africa.
MARSH, H. V., 43 Loop Street, Maritzburg, South Africa.
MASON, A. S., Berse School, Cambridge.
MASON, B., 10 Crouch Street, Colchester.
MASON, C., 10 Crouch Street, Colchester.
McCLOSKY, C. A., c/o Edes Everett, St. Botolph's, Colchester.
MIDDLETON, G. A. T., "Laleham," Clarence Road, Clapham Park, S.W.
MIDGLEY, C. F., "Gunton," Westminster Drive, Westcliffe-on-Sea. [wood.
MIDGLEY, W. R. D., 163 Ongar Road, Brentwood.
MILLS, F. G., 18 Beverley Road, Colchester.
MOY, O. T., c/o Messrs. T. Moy & Co., Ltd., Colchester.
NORFOLK, A. E., 76 Chesson Road, West Kensington.
NUNN, A. W., Crouch Street, Colchester.
NUNN, J. H., Melford Villa, Rawstorn Road, Colchester.
NUNN, W. H., Whatfield, Ipswich.
OLIVER, J. L., Maldon Road, Colchester.
ORFEUR, H. W., Colne Bank, Station Road, Colchester. [Colchester
ORFEUR, C. B., Colne Bank, Station Road

178

OHFKUR, R. F., Colne Bank, Station Road, Colchester.
ORFEUR, F. N., Colne Bank, Station Road, Colchester
ORPEN, O. G., Hillside, West Bergholt, Colchester.
OSBORNE, F. F.
OSBORNE, H. O.
PARKER, Rev. E. H., L.O.A., Watford.
PEART, J. A., C.R.G.S.
PROLER, Dr. L. H., 58 Harley Street, London, W.
PEPPER, V. J., 19 Harsnett Road, Colchester.
PEPPER, G. E., C.R.G.S.
PERTWEE, F., Moreham's Hall, Frating.
PLUMMER, N. A., Station Road, Lawford, Manningtree.
PLUMMER, F. E., Station Road, Lawford, Manningtree.
POINTING, W. W., 148 Maldon Road, Colchester.
POTTER, C. O., 119 Maldon Road, Colchester.
POTTER, F., Middleborough, Colchester.
PRIME, E. J., 37 Crouch Street, Colchester.
PROSSER, J. A. B., Lansdowne, Pierremont Avenue, Broadstairs.
REEVE, E., C.R.G.S.
RENTON, T. S., 12 Crouch Street, Colchester.
RICHES, A. E., 80 Tower Street, Brightlingsea.
RICHARDS, R. F., Head Street, Colchester.
RICHARDSON, A. J., School House, Great Bentley.
RICKWORD, E. G., 35 Wellesley Road, Colchester.
RICKWORD, G. O., 38 Wellesley Road, Colchester.
ROSEVEARE, H. H., "Craigmore," Newquay, Cornwall.
RYDER, E. W., 74 Wimpole Road, Colchester.
SADLER, F. B., Box P.O. 219, o.o. The Eastern Bank, Ltd., Bombay.
SANDERS, F. A., 103 North Station Road, Colchester.
SANGER, W., "Rookery dene," Abbeygate Street, Colchester.
SANGER, H., "Rookerydene," Abbeygate Street, Colchester.
SALMON, J. G., Wash Lane, Clacton.
SAMMONS, A. C., 49 Grafton Street, Fitzroy Square, W.
SEAMER, H. St. J., C.R.G.S. (Editor)
SENNITT, F. J., 28 Mersea Road, Colchester.
SHAW, D. E., Holmleigh, Beaconsfield Avenue, Colchester.
SHENSTONE, J. C., 15c Coverdale Road, Shepherd's Bush, London, W.
SIGGERS, J.
SLIGHT, R., c.o. One Barrow Lodge, Coalville, Leicestershire.

SLATER, E. M., 201 Maldon Road, Colchester.
SMITH, AUBREY, "Mantz," 30 Peak Hill, Sydenham, S.E.
SMITH, G. E., Chapel Street, Colchester.
SMITH, W. G., 23 Roman Road, Colchester.
SMITH, F. R., 23 Roman Road, Colchester.
SPARLING, A. S. B., 21 Creffield Road, Colchester.
STOW, W. H., The Willows, Great Horkesley, Colchester.
SURRIDGE, P. T., Coggeshall.
SYER, F. N., 8 Studlands Road, Sydenham.
TAYLOR, A. P., Roseneath, East Street, Hazlemere, Surrey.
TENNANT, E. N., Connaught Avenue, Frinton.
THOMAS, A. O., 150 Maldon Road, Colchester.
THOMPSON, W., 365 Hither Green Lane, Lewisham, S.E.
TOWN, H. G., 10 Wellesley Road, Colchester.
TOWN, W. M., 10 Wellesley Road, Colchester.
TURNER, Capt. A., Essex Hall, Colchester.
TURNER, Dr. DOUGLAS, Essex Hall, Colchester.
TURNER, S. C., Abbeygate House, Colchester.
WAGSTAFF, D. T., Church Farm, Marks Tey, Colchester
WALLACE, Councillor R. W., "Moelwyn," Inglis Road. Colchester.
WARD, J. D., Jun., Bluegates, Elmstead, Colchester.
WARNER, A. E., 8 Myland, Colchester.
WATSHAM, H., Vine Farm, Wyvenhoe.
WATSON, J. L.
WATSON, S. F., 154 Maldon Road, Colchester.
WATSON, G. F.
WATTS, FRANK, 30 Creffield Road, Colchester.
WEBB, G. S., Dairy House, Wix, Manningtree.
WEBB, A. H., Dairy House, Wix, Manningtree.
WENDEN, C. A., The Chase, Great Bromley.
WHITE, C. E., 57 North Hill, Colchester.
WHITE, F., East Hill, Colchester.
WHITBY, J. F./M., 144 Maldon Road, Colchester.
WIGLEY, W. H., 146 King's Park Road, Mount Florida, Glasgow.
WILLIAMS, F. O., 14 Lexden Road, Colchester.
WILLIS, E. A., 25 Heron Road, Stapleton Road, Bristol.
WORTS, S. E., Trinity Street, Colchester.
WRIGHT, Lieut.-Col. Percival, Ashanti, St. James, Mirzenburg, Cape Town.
WRIGHT, C. T., Stacey House, Crouch Street, Colchester.
WRIGHT, G., junr., Stacey House, Crouch Street, Colchester.
WRIGHT, Councillor G. F., 47 Crouch Street, Colchester.
WYATT, D. T., Bank Passage, Colchester.

NOTICE TO OLD COLCESTRIANS.

Old Colcestrians who wish to make known their movements in this paper should communicate with Mr. J. HUTLEY NUNN, "Essex County Telegraph" Offices, Colchester.

Subscriptions should be sent to Mr. A. T. DALDY (Hon. Treas.), Head Street, Colchester.

Members of the Society are requested to notify any change of address immediately to either of the Hon. Secretaries:—

Mr. A. O. FARMER, 6 Queen Street, Colchester.
Mr. A. T. DALDY, Head Street, Colchester.

NOTICE TO CORRESPONDENTS.

Contributions to the O.C. Section, articles on various subjects and humorous anecdotes of school-days, will be gladly welcomed by the O.C. Editor, Mr. J. Hutley Nunn.

All contributions for the next number of " The Calcestrian " to be sent in by June 1st, 1915.

No. 42.]
New Series.

JUNE, 1915.

The Colcestrian.

EDITED BY PAST AND PRESENT MEMBERS OF COLCHESTER SCHOOL.

PRICE SIXPENCE

Colchester:
PRINTED BY COLLINGFORD & CO.,
156 HIGH STREET.

O.C.S. Officers for 1914-15.

President:
C. T. WRIGHT, Crouch Street, Colchester.

Vice-Presidents:
W. GURNEY BENHAM, J.P.
R. FRANKLIN
H. L. GRIFFIN

H. J. HARRIS, B.A.
B. H. KENT
Osmond G. ORPEN
W. H. KING

J. C. SHENSTONE, F.L.S.
R. W. WALLACE
C. E. WHITE

Committee:-
T. D. BROOK
J. H. NUNN
A. W. NUNN
F. G. MILLS

C. GRIFFIN
C. T. WRIGHT
H. H. HOLLAWAY
C. E. BENHAM (Chairman)

G. C. BENHAM
E. W. DACE
J. C. SALMON
F. D. BARKER

The Ex-Presidents are ex-officio members of Committee.

Hon. Treasurer (pro. tem.):
A. T. DALDY, Head Street, Colchester.

Hon. Secretaries:
A. T. DALDY, Head Street. Colchester.
A. O. FARMER, 12 Queen Street, Colchester.

Members of the O.C.S.

ACLAND, C. S., Lexden House, West Winch, nr. Kings Lynn. [Hill, N.
ADAMS, E. A., 7 Goodwyn's Vale, Muswell
ALLISTON, A. W., Chipping Hill, Witham.
APPLEBY, W. M.
BARE, W. J., Magdalen Street, Colchester.
BARKER, F. D., Royal Grammar School (Hon. Sec). [Naze.
BARKER, C. F. J., Marine Hotel, Walton-on-
BARKER, CHARLES, Burtoll Tea Estate, Dewan P.O., Cachar, India.
BARNES, O., Howell Hall, Heckington, Lincs.
BARNES, F. M., Howell Hall, Heckington, Lincolnshire.
BAWTREE, E. E., 71 High Street, Colchester.
BAXTER, H. G., Fronks Road, Dovercourt.
BAYLISS, S. F.
BAYLISS, R. V. J., Fleece Hotel, Head Street, Colchester.
BAYLISS, B., Fleece Hotel, Head Street, Colchester.
BEARD, E. C., St. Margaret's, Cambridge Road, Colchester.
BECKETT, H., Balkerne Lane, Colchester.
BELLWARD, G. W. F., C.R.G.S.
BENHAM, C. E., Wellesley Road, Colchester. (President).
BENHAM, G. C., Bank Chambers, High Street, Colchester.
BENHAM, Alderman W. GURNEY, St. Mary's
BIRD, A., Bell House Farm, Stanway. Terrace, Lexden road, Colchester.
BLATCH, F., c/o, S. E. Blau, La Paz, Bolivia, S. America.
BLAXILL, G. A., 50 Parliament Hill, Hampstead, N.W.
BLOMFIELD, S., Raonah House, New Town Road, Colchester.
BLOOMFIELD, H. D., 3 Tyler Street, Parkeston.
BLYTH, COOPER, c/o. Isaac Bunting, 100 Yokahama, Japan.
BOGGIS, FRANK, Station Road, Sudbury.
BROMLEY, J. G., Mill House, Great Clacton.
BROOK, T. D., "St. Runwald's," Maldon Road, Colchester.
BROOK, A. T., "St. Runwald's," Maldon Road, Colchester.
BROOK, L. C., "St. Runwald's," Maldon Road, Colchester.
BROOK, S. V., 22 Sugden Road, Lavender Hill, S.W.
BROWN, D. GRAHAM, "Lownd," Witham.

BULLITUDE, R. G., 32 Hanover Road, Canterbury.
BURRELL, F. B., Abbeygate Street, Colchester
BUNTING, A. E., The Nurseries, North Station Road, Colchester.
BURLEIGH, A., Kudat, N.L.B.T. Co., British North Borneo.
BURSTON, F. G., 1st National Bank Buildings, San Francisco.
BUTCHER, H., 3 Eden Ave., Liscard, Cheshire.
BUTLER, F. H., Cumberland House, Manningtree.
CANT, Walter, West House Farm, Lexden, Colchester.
CAREY, M. C., 49 Lexden Road, Colchester.
CARTER, F. B., C.R.G.S.
CHAMBERS, C., 22 Wellesley Road, Colchester.
CHAMBERS, S. C., 22 Wellesley Road, Colchester. [Inn, W.C.
CHAPLIN, F. S., 5 Verulam Buildings, Grays
CHEESE, C. T., 39 Pownall Crescent, Colchester and St. Austell, Cornwall.
CHESHIRE, G., 23 Argyle Street, Oxford Street, W.
CHESHIRE, W., 1 Meyrick Crescent, Colchester
CHILD, L. G., 14 Wimpole Road, Colchester.
CLAMP, A. J., 122 Priory Street, Colchester.
CLARK, L. W., 16 East Stockwell Street, Colchester.
CLARKE, S. F., Parr's Bank, Holloway, London, N.
CLOVER, J. M., The Hall, Dedham.
COLE, C. L. L., General Post Office (Staff), Cambridge.
COLE, H., 25 Wimpole Road, Colchester.
COLLINGK, C. E., Capital & Counties Bank, Baldock, Herts.
COLLISON, A. L., Garrison School, Buena Vista, Gibraltar.
CORK, F. F., 38 Trouville Road, Clapham Park, S.W.
CRAGG, Rev. E. E., St. John's Church, Huntington, Long Island, U.S.A.
CULLINGTON, M. W., 53 Oakhill Road, Putney, S.W.
CURTIS, A. P., Bromley Road, Colchester.
DACE, A. W., 122 George Street, Edinburgh.
DACE, E. W., 17 Honywood Road, Colchester.
DALDY, A. T., 50 South Street, Colchester (HON. TREASURER).
DAVIES, H. W., 118 Butt Road, Colchester.
DAVIES, E. G.

Continued on Page 3 of Cover.

182

The Colcestrian.

VITÆ CORONA FIDES.

No. 42.]   JUNE, 1915.   [NEW SERIES.

Editorial.

AMONG the most noticeable effects of the state of war in which we are living is the great slump that has taken place in games, and in fact in sport of all kinds. In the Autumn football rapidly waned and died ; in the Spring hockey eked out a poor crippled existence, and now cricket and tennis bid fair to die before they have well been born.

And it is quite natural and right that this should be so, when the flower of the manhood of the nation is playing its part on the fields of Flanders, amid the rocks of Gallipoli, or the sands of Egypt and by the waters of the Euphrates, or else is training to take its place there. There are sterner games toward, and a nobler sport. A splendid response is being made to the call of the Motherland. The racket yields place to the rifle, the bat to the bayonet, the ball to the bullet.

· But with boys and those under military age the case is somewhat different. Now that war is come upon us a glimpse can be obtained of the vast educative value of games, and no apology or excuse is necessary for the fact that the playing-fields are still filled with eager crowds of boys. Apart from the formation of character, the mere physical exercise is essential for the young. Kittens and puppies play ; lambs perform extraordinary gambols, all as training for the serious object of their existence. And it is the same with humanity.

True, outside matches have been reduced to the minimum, while scouting and cadet corps claim a larger share of our time, but House-matches will still go on as usual, and the Annual Sports will this year be celebrated with maimed rites, and confined to settlement of the destination of the various · Challenge Cups for the year. Games must continue if it is wished that the younger generation should grow up the equal in character and physique of the older now fighting the barbarian all over the world.

THE EDITOR.

Valete.

BRAND, E. J.—Form VI., K.P., Parr's.   Senior Prefect ; Captain 1st
    XI. Cricket, Football and Hockey ; Captain House Cricket,
    Football, Hockey, Shooting and Gym. ; Member of Committee,
    Debating Society ; Corporal, Cadet Corps.   HAS ENLISTED.
SQUIRE, B. A.—Form VI., Dugard's.   House Shooting ; Private, Cadet
    Corps.
WENDEN, E. M.—Form VI., Probationer, Parr's.   1st XI. Football and
    Hockey ; House Cricket, Football, Hockey ; Private, Cadet
    Corps.
CHAPMAN, D.—Form VI., Probationer, Dugard's.   Captain House and
    School Shooting VIII. ; House Hockey XI. ; Sergeant, Cadet
    Corps.
COLLINGE, J. H.—Form VA., Parr's.   1st XI. Hockey ; House Cricket,
    Football, Hockey ; Corporal-Bugler, Cadet Corps.
COTTRELL, H. J.—Form VA., K.P., Schoolhouse.   1st XI. Football and
    Hockey ; Captain House Hockey ; House Football, Cricket
    and Shooting ; Corporal-Drummer. Cadet Corps.   HAS
    ENLISTED.
PROCTOR, G. D.—Form VA., Schoolhouse.   Private, Cadet Corps.
LOYD, L. W.—Form VB., Dugard's.   Private, Cadet Corps.
BASKETT, T. F.—Form IVA., Harsnett's.   Private, Cadet Corps.
SANDS, B. A.—Form IVA., Dugard's.   House Hockey ; Private, Cadet
    Corps.
BECKETT, J.—Form IVB., Dugard's.   House Football, Hockey and
    Shooting.
GRAHAM-BROWN, H.—Form IVB., Schoolhouse.
WRIGHT, S.—Form IVB., Harsnett's.
FRENCH, R. E.—Modern Form, Parr's.   2nd XI. Football and Hockey ;
    House Cricket, Football, Hockey.
LAWRY, W. M.—Modern Form, Harsnett's.   House Hockey and
    Shooting.
GELL, R.—Form I., Schoolhouse.
POYSER, R.—Form I., Harsnett's.

Salvete.

FARQUHARSON, F. H. R.	..	..	H.	..	VB.
SALEW ma., L. G.	..	..	H.	..	IVA.
WELLS, D. W. B.	..	..	D.	..	IVA.
BECKETT, E. W.	..	..	D.	..	M.
TRACEY, W. T.	..	..	D.	..	M.
SALEW mi, N. R.	..	..	H.	..	III.
WHITEHOUSE, F. L.	..	..	S.	..	III.
BROWNE, F. G.	..	..	H.	..	II.
JEFFERY, D.	..	..	P.	..	II
OVERTON, H. F.	..	..	H.	..	II.
BAKER, J. B.	..	..	P.	..	I.
KNIGHT, R. W.	..	..	P.	..	I.
PHILLIPS, T. C.	..	..	S.	..	I.
HARPER, G.	..	..		..	Pre.
RICHER, C.	..	..		..	Pre.
SMITH, H.	..	..		..	Pre.

Grammaria.

Goodspeed—

Last term closed with regrets at parting with Mr. Clarke, who is seeking pastures new. He has, it is understood, been foiled by the M.O. in his ambition to serve his country in the field, but he will carry with him our heartiest wishes for prosperity and good luck in whatever fresh field he pitches his tent.

—and Welcome !

His place has been taken this term by Mr. R. D. Bastable, M.Sc., of Birmingham University. He comes to us from Wellingboro,' whence, it may be remembered we received another excellent master, who now occupies a Headship in the West of England. *Adsit omen !*

An Old Friend.

After a very brief interval of retirement, Pratt, the porter, has resumed duties at the School. There are no friends like old friends, and it is pleasing to see a familiar face about the place once more instead of some strange new one.

An A-Ward indeed !

Congratulations to Ward on being given a County Major Scholarship of £60 a year on the results of the last London Matriculation Exam. This is all the more creditable, when it is remembered that he was under age at the time for actual attendance at a University.

Sweets for Soldiers, English—

One of the odd discoveries of the present war is that of the longing for sweets among the soldiery, and the extreme value that they possess as a food. Boys of the School have long been convinced of this value, as the tuck-shop keeper well knows, but only lately has it been generally recognized. They have shown therefore, a true fellow-feeling in contributing no less than 56 lbs. of the best milk chocolate for the benefit of the wounded soldiers in the Essex County Hospital.

—and Belgian.

The worst-off army in this respect is naturally the Belgian. Their country is all but entirely over-run by their foes, and their countrymen are for the most part living in exile. It was therefore an exceedingly kindly thought of the Mayoress to raise a store of comforts for these men, to whose bravery and honour Europe owes so much, by means of a Pound Day. The School has contributed 112 lbs. of chocolate to this cause also, a very gratifying total.

A Short-lived Reprieve.

The sensation of relief that greeted the postponement of the General Inspection at the beginning of last term was not of long duration. The dread ordeal duly took place on April 14, 15, 16, when four Myrmidons of the Board of Education descended upon us and continued for the three days wandering up and down the School and going to and fro in it.

An Odd Selection.

The date selected would appear to be rather an unfortunate one, these days being actually the last three of the term, when boys and masters alike are wearied with three months' strenuous efforts, and when work is being wound up in readiness for the coming holidays, the imminence of which hardly conduces to the exhibition of anybody's best.

All's well, etc.

However, it is gratifying to learn that they have expressed satisfaction with the present condition and progress of the School. This is calculated to create a glow of reciprocal satisfaction in the breast of everyone connected with it. For in the eyes of H.M.I.'s all are "unprofitable servants." When the best possible is done it is only what it is one's duty to do. We may congratulate ourselves on passing through the ordeal with flying colours.

The Weather and the Crops.

After a winter of record wetness came a month-belated spring, but at last summer (at the date of writing) would seem to have come into its own. June is really Flaming June—for the time being,—bringing on in a wonderful way the crops that have been sown in the Agricultural Interest in Gilberd House garden. Carrots and onions are looking particularly well, and beans, which but a month ago bade fair to end in failure, now form serried rows, with scarce a "blank file" to be found anywhere. Potatoes, parsnips and parsley are all perky and promising. Much credit is due to our gardeners and their instructors.

A Suggestion.

As some need is felt of a counterblast to the German asphyxiating gases, it has been suggested that chemistry boys, anxious to "do their bit," might devote themselves to bottling and sending to the front the general atmosphere of the Lab. and its immediate vicinity. This would surely prove an effective form of retaliation on the Huns—if not voted too inhuman.

Authorities, Take Note !

A German schoolboy is reported to have written in answer to the question : " What do you consider the best thing about the war ? " that in his opinion it was the extra holidays granted in celebration of the continually recurring German " victories." Now that (according to Mr. Hilaire Belloc) the turning-point of the war has been reached, it is hoped that British schoolboys will not be left out in the cold, when the news of British victories, less frequent perhaps, but more reliable, comes rolling in.

Another Useful Tip.

"*Fas est ab hoste doceri*" may also be applied to another custom in German schools, a custom astonishingly sensible and humane considering the general character of the race. It is to the effect that when the thermometer rises above boiling-point or thereabouts (details not strictly guaranteed) school automatically ceases. The early June outburst will probably not be the last in the present summer term, and were such a rule established, if only by way of precedent, before the arrival of the next heat-wave, it would only display reasonable foresight, and prove that in no instance can we be behind the Barbarians of Europe in civilization and humanity. Depend upon it, not a single dissentient voice would be raised in the School itself at such a proposal.

The Close.

The constant increase of the School both in area and numbers has long rendered cricket, or even practice nets, on the Close impossible, but the present term finds two extra tennis-courts laid out there and enclosed with stop-netting— an excellent move. They are being well patronized during this spell of splendid tennis weather.

Our Occasional Contributor again.

" Allagaters are very funy amails it lives in the summe with only its nose out of the water and its eye and in the winder it bres it self in mud and takes alot of berth and the goes to seellp."

Herodotus on the same subject is simply not in it.

The Elenpten.

"An elenpten is the bigest amail in the world. An Inai elehpant is smaler than a afreken elepant. The Inai elehpant is eser to tam. In the zoo there is not mang afraken because it is to firs to tam. The Inai elhepnt has a round back."

A New Officer.

Mr. Peart, influenced perhaps by the many complimentary remarks made upon his smart appearance as a Sergeant of Artillery last term, has gone one better, and accepted a commission in the Cadet Corps. It is hard to say whether he, the Corps, or the inhabitants of the vicinity are most to be congratulated.

Live and Learn !

Suttee.—" When a husband died the wife had to be burned alive on a bundle of wood ; it was a great ceremony."

" . . . . In the retreat many of the army died of salvation." Hence no doubt the term " Salvation Army."

" At one time children were employed in factories all day and all night, but an Act has been passed to prevent any child being employed until it is of age." Naturally, for before then they are " infants ", in the eye of the law.

" Gen. Havelock died of dynasty."

Hockey.

THERE were but few fixtures last term, only three matches in all being played. These produced some good hockey, and came as a welcome change from the ordinary routine of practice games. The School team naturally suffered from the many changes that were forced upon us during the term. We were unfortunate in losing Cottrell ma., who left prematurely to enlist, and in our last match we were deprived of the services of Atkin, who unluckily broke his right arm in a motor collision.

Several promising players were discovered to fill the gaps caused by the departure of members of last season's eleven. Smith proved a small hard-hitting back, but must learn to clear more quickly. In the half-line, Bare was a tireless and energetic player, though at times inclined to over-run the ball. With practice he should develop into an excellent centre-half. Of the forwards Atkin, Pullen and Gibb showed the best form, but each was an individualist and must learn to control the ball better and combine with the rest of the line.

Despite the fact that so few outside matches were arranged we had some very interesting internal hockey. The idea of a Form League, comprising the four Forms, VB., IVA., IVB., and the Moderns, was eagerly taken up and enthusiastically carried out. The games played after afternoon school were keenly contested, although, as was perhaps inevitable, a little one-sided. Top place was gained by the Moderns, who, although defeated by Vв. at their first encounter, subsequently won the return match and final replay (necessitated by the two being equal). The final table was as follows :—

	Played.	Won.	Lost.	Goals. For.	Against.	Points.
Moderns	7	6	1			12
Vв.	7	5	2			10
IVа.	6	2	4			4
IVв.	6	0	6			0

It is a fact that these matches realized their object, that of providing healthy exercise and unearthing new players of promise, for the last two rounds of the House Matches showed better all-round hockey.

HOUSE HOCKEY.

DUGARD'S v. SCHOOL.

On Saturday, March 27th, Dugard's met Schoolhouse in the first round of the House-hockey matches. Dugard's started off in fine style and had much the better of the game during the first-half. Gibb and Rayner as centre-forward and centre-half combined well for School-house but the rest of the opposing team were far too slow, and cleared badly. When half-time arrived Dugard's were leading by 3-0.

After the interval School-house showed much more promise and made a determined rush which ended in Rayner scoring a goal with a straight drive into the corner of the net. In reply to this Rogers ended up a brilliant rush with a well-placed cross shot against which the goal-keeper had no chance, and Bacon (a very promising forward for his size) succeeded in cannoning the ball off the goal post into the goal.

The whistle blew with Dugard's leading by six goals—the score being 7-1. Pullen 5, Rogers 1, Bacon 1, Rayner 1.

PARR'S v. HARSNETT'S.—Saturday, March 27th.

The afternoon was bright though cold, and a well-contested sporting game ensued. Both sides played with a healthy vigour remarkable for the dearth of minor fouls usually met with in House matches. Parr's were the first to attack but they encountered a sturdy defence in Bare and Smith. At length, however, they were rewarded, French scoring with a feeble shot that Baskett should have saved. The Harsnett's forwards were ill-served by their halves and so failed to get together although, individually, very strong. They brought the score level by rushing the ball past Syer who ran wildly out of goal. Shortly before the interval Parr's regained the lead from a scrimmage in their opponents circle. On resuming a good deal of mid-field play resulted that led to nothing, but Parr's showed the better combination in attack. Cheshire and French on the extreme wings made many excellent runs often beating the opposing backs, but Parr's failed to avail themselves of many glorious opportunities in front of goal. Only one more point was obtained and that by Brand with a hard drive. Atkin, Nicholson, and Alderton made great efforts to reduce the lead but received little support and the whistle went with the final score : Parr's 3, Harsnett's 1.

DUGARD'S v. PARR'S.—Tuesday, March· 30th.

As this was recognised to be the deciding match for the Cup both sides strove with a vigour that was commendable from a healthy excercise point of view, but which was scarcely Hockey as laid down in the rules of the Amateur Association. Dugard's won the toss and bullied off with the sun at their backs. For some time even play resulted, and then suddenly in some unaccountable manner, Parr's defence went to pieces. Three times in almost as many minutes Dugard's shot the ball through their opponent's goal, Pullen (2) and Rogers being the scorers. It seemed that Syer was a little precipitate in rushing out to meet the attack, at any rate he needs more practice and experience to make a successful goal-keeper. Just when the game seemed lost and won, the Parr's forwards galvanised into sudden life, took up the attack, and made great efforts to score. Employing the long passing game, the wing forwards, French ma. and Cheshire, combined excellently with the centre, Brand, which led to his scoring two goals. Indeed, Parr's actually got a third goal, which was disallowed, as a Dugard defender "sticked" just before the shot.

Half-time score : Dugard's 3, Parr's 2.

On resuming the Parrites attack, ably supported by Collinge and Wagstaff, in the half-line, caused their opponents some trouble but were well stopped by Orrin and Chapman. At length, however, Brand made the scores level with a screw shot which Barrell failed to stop.

With twenty minutes to go it was anybody's game and exciting struggles took place in each circle. From a melee in front of the Parr's goal Spencer, unmarked behind a crowd of players, once more gave Dugard's the lead. Shortly before time someone shot at the Dugard goal and Barrell failing to get the ball away, French rushed up and scored. This was the extent of the scoring and time came with the final result : Dugard's 4, Parr's 4.

SCHOOL HOUSE v. HARSNETT'S.

This was one of the second round of Hockey House matches and was played on March 30th.

Contrary to expectations quite fair weather prevailed. Harsnett's were much handicapped by the absence of their captain, Atkin. White at centre-forward led off with a good rush down to the School House goal, but the attack was repulsed by the sturdy defence of Gibb and Cottrell. Leeming also played a sound game. Several rushes were made by School House, but they could not succeed in breaking through the excellent defence of Harsnett's, Bare playing a good game at left-half and Nicholson at outside-right. At length Rayner succeeded in rushing through and scoring for School House. At half-time the score was 1-0 in favour of School House. After half-time the play was mostly in midfield, neither side gaining the advantage, and when the whistle sounded the score was still 1-0.

SCHOOLHOUSE v. PARR'S.—Thursday, April 15th.

Both Dugard's and Parr's had won their match in the first round, drawn with each other in the second. and expected to win this, the third round, so that a re-play would be necessary to decide who should hold the cup. As events turned out, however, this proved non-essential for of the houses concerned the one lost unexpectedly, and the other only just managed to win. This match played on the second pitch proved fairly interesting, though the condition of the ground was all against good hockey. Parr's seemed slightly below form, but even so were distinctly the better team and Schoolhouse owed their light defeat almost entirely to the play of their backs. Most of the pressing was done by

Parr's but they were up against a tough nut in Gibb who played a really good game. Also their forwards were very weak in front of goal, where chances were simply frittered away. Rayner and Pertwee were the best of the Schoolhouse front line but they received little support and never looked like scoring in the first-half. The teams crossed over goalless at the interval.

Play on resuming proved more exciting, Dolamore in the School-house goal being kept busy by the opposing forwards. Parr's continued to have most of the game but Cottrell caught their defence napping and scored from a sudden breakaway. Schoolhouse strove hard to sit on their lead and played a strong defensive game, but luck turned at last for Parr's for Brand shot a goal just as the ball was going over the line in the corner of the circle. Five minutes before time a struggle on the right wing drew the Schoolhouse defenders from their goal. Someone centred, and French, dashing up, shot a hard clean goal that gave Dolamore no earthly chance. So Parr's won by the odd goal in three. For the losers Leeming played a plucky game at half and Pertwee put in some speedy work on the left wing. Watsham was pretty safe at back for Parr's, and Collinge mi. did well at inside-right. Watkinson showed promise at inside-left but must learn to keep his place.

HARNSNETT'S v. DUGARD'S.—Thursday, April 15th.

In the concluding round of the House matches Harsnett's met Dugard's, who so far had proved invincible. The keenest House feeling was displayed, and Dugard's, though they could not hold their opponents in their own half, made several dashes which placed Harsnett's goal in jeopardy. On the other hand, Harsnett's spent most of their time in front of Dugard's goal but failed to score. By half-time neither side had gained a positive advantage.

Early in the second-half Harsnett's pressed heavily and after many failures to score, a good shot from Nicholson found the net. This roused Dugard's, and aided by Pullen they were several times on the verge of equalising, Bugg in particular putting in some excellent shots. Smith did a lot of good work in Harsnett's defence, and the elder Lawry swept all before him. But Harsnett's, though they failed to score again, thus won a keenly contested game by one goal to nil.

HOUSE COMPETITION TABLE.

	Played	Won	Lost	Drawn	Goals. F.	A.	Points
Parr's	3	2	0	1	9	6	5
Dugard's ..	3	1	1	1	11	6	3
Schoolhouse ..	3	1	2	0	3	9	2
Harsnett's ..	3	1	2	0	2	4	2

Cricket.

NO matches have been played this season. This, in itself, is enough to show that cricket has been far from normal. We have had to confine ourselves to nets, and, on halves, to such games as we have been able to arrange. The latter have been enjoyable and have produced some good finishes, and in the last of these games one or two good individual scores were made.

At times, especially at the first, nets were well attended ; the House Matches which commence on June 17th, may stimulate the interest which has somewhat flagged.

In the Lower School cricket has been very popular, and there are signs of future colour-holders among these youthful wielders of bat and ball.

HOUSE MATCHES.

Thursday, June 17—Dugard's v. Schoolhouse.
Saturday, June 19—Harsnett's v. Parr's.
Thursday, June 24—Parr's v. Schoolhouse.
Saturday, June 26—Dugard's v. Harsnett's.
Thursday, July 1—Harsnett's v. Schoolhouse.
Saturday, July 3—Parr's v. Dugard's.

House Singings.

MR. CARTER'S CONCERT.

MR. Carter's Company provided a real treat on March 27, in the shape of an entertainment, particularly strong on the dramatic side. The "*pièce de resistance*" was Conan Doyle's "Waterloo," with Mr. Carter in the part (created by the late Sir Henry Irving) of Corporal Brewster, who, at enormous risk, had supplied the Guards with the powder they lacked at a critical moment in the famous battle. It was an exceeding well-thought-out and carefully-studied impersonation of the character of the poor feeble half-childish old man, a pathetic and yet humorous figure, ending on a poignant note of tragedy, as the expiring flame of life flickers into brilliance for one brief moment before the end, and he dies with the cry on his lips—"The Guards want powder, and by G—— they shall have it !" The other characters serve merely as a background and foil to the principal one. "Waterloo" is essentially a one-part play. They received able treatment from Miss Doris Maberley, who, as Norah, made a charming niece to the old man, Mr. Peart an exceedingly personable Sergeant Macdonald, and Mr. Clarke an adequate Colonel Midwinter, though perhaps his make-up was a little too young for the part.

In "East Linoleum," a Burlesque of the well-known novel and stock drama, "East Lynne," Mr. Carter displayed his extraordinary versatility by appearing as "Lady Isobel," the chief female part. But the company were evidently hampered by the old-fashioned character of the dialogue, which depended for its humour largely on verbal quips, such as found

favour in the eighties, but now seem strangely to have lost
their savour. The actors struggled bravely and made the
best of the rather inferior material. Sir Francis Levison was
in the capable hands of Mr. Peart, Archibald Carlyle received
justice from Mr. Clarke, and Barbara Hare gave Mr. Barker
the opportunity of showing that he was no stranger to a
feminine rôle. Mr. Watts' get-up as Little Willie was
excruciating, while Parker, P. C., and the Maid were suitably undertaken by Mr. Worth and G. Atkin respectively.

The interval was filled by Mr. Jeffrey, with the comic-
sounding "Malbrouck s'en va" in French dialect, some
beautiful "Japanese songs" by Collinge, and a series of
clever conjuring tricks by Sands. Mr. Worth played the
overture, and Chapman and Ward provided entr'acte music.
A most successful evening.

RED CROSS CONCERT.

On April 6, Miss Christine Cross, with the boys of the Pre,
assisted by several friends, gave a most enjoyable entertainment in aid of the local Red Cross Society, to a full and
appreciative audience. Notable among the items provided
by the grown-ups were Mme. Eva Plouffe-Stopes' two piano
solos, each of which received a well-deserved encore, and
Miss Luard's 'cello solos. Her encore to the second was a
particularly pleasing work. Mrs. Craske contributed a
recruiting song which went with a fine swing, and later,
"Until," while Collinge mi.'s magnificently clear and accurate
notes gave full effect to "Come, sing to me." Mr. Peart,
whose wine needs no bush, showed his versatility in a serious
cantillation, "The Despatch Rider" to an original accompaniment composed and rendered by Mr. Carter, and a
clever burlesque "The Stoker's Story," also cantillated, both
items meeting with unstinted applause.

But the most distinctive features of the programme were
of course those in which the small boys took part. There
were two Morris Dances, a chorus song, "Heave-ho" (in
character), while various recitations by the Pre.-boys were
incorporated, by a brilliant idea, in a most amusing scena
"All British," representing the interior of a toy shop at sale-
time, whither a lady (Mr. Carter, arrayed in a magnificent
suit of furs) and her daughter had come to purchase mechanical dolls (the Pre.-boys), which were displayed by the
salesman (Mr. Peart) and their possibilities sampled to a
running fire of smart and topical dialogue.

At the conclusion Mrs. Wren (the Commandant) made an
excellent speech, detailing the scope and progress of the

movement in Colchester. Red Cross nurses in their attractive uniforms acted as programme sellers. Their charming appearance alone is calculated to restore even the worst cases under their charge to convalescence, and further evidence may be seen in the fact that the collection which they "took up" in the course of the proceedings in aid of the Society exceeded £13, a result as gratifying to them as to the performers, and to the Headmistress and promoters of the entertainment.

THE ATHLETIC FUND CONCERT.

This was the last concert of term, and it was made the occasion of raising contributions for the Motor Ambulance Fund and the Athletic Fund. A good programme was made up of items selected from the entertainments given during the term, with additions. "Dainty Ware," a short play, however, made its first appearance, and was a pleasant change from the usual run of comedies. Ward and Rickword performed quite creditably, though their parts demanded no great dramatic effort. Pertwee improved on his Schoolhouse display, but he still requires to put more vim into his words. Then followed a nigger troupe entertainment by the Black Diamonds, the characters of which were only distinguishable by their voices. Barnes sang two good songs "Marie Louise" and "The Dream Man," and Clark repeated "The Porter" with success. The duet, "Life's Lullaby," by Collinge and Miller ma., was especially well done and quite the best item in this part of the programme. The Bigophone Band was revived and again scored heavily, Miller mi. making a vivacious and sprightly conductor. Before the final play Mr. Carter executed some Lightning Sketches of a novel character that were very well done and proved undoubtedly popular. Pullen delivered his Stump Speech in favour of the downtrodden working-man, and then came "Red-Handed," the Schoolhouse drama. Two changes were made from the original caste, but the play was not greatly improved in consequence. Koskinas, in his character of villain, was not quite up to his Schoolhouse showing, yet at times thrilled the audience by the quiet villainy of his acting. As James Fletcher the murdered man, Middleton was fair but evidently is not used to such parts. Gibb, Pertwee and Crighton all did well in minor parts. A word of praise, moreover, is due to the "stage hands" under Bare for some smart and silent work.

Cadet Corps.

SINCE our last notes on the Corps, several calamities have come upon us. Sergt. Atkin had the misfortune to break his arm, and Corpl. Berry his collar-bone. We offer our lusty drummers our sympathies and wish them speedy recovery.

A calamity to the "matériel" was the borrowing of our rifles and carbines : this makes field-days out of the question.

Thus handicapped we have sought variety in distance-judging, tactics of attack and defence, and we are now proposing to run out into the country around and seek more cover than our field affords.

We extend the heartiest welcome to Mr. Peart, who has taken a commission in the Corps this term.

The Corps can now claim to be familiar with the new Company Drill, but must not be content with that, remembering that execution is everything in drill.

Burleigh has foregone a stripe to become a drummer, and he and Peacock, in the same capacity, both promise well.

Our numbers remain about standard.

Congratulations to Corpl. Cottrell, our indefatigable big-drummer, on his joining the Sportsman's Battalion and to Sergt. Andrews on his excellent work with No. 4 Section.

F.D.B.

Shooting.

THE Summer term has always been the time when we have fewest members shooting, but this term our number is smaller than usual even in the cricket and bathing season. At the same time it is pleasing to see the number of our elder boys who turn up regularly, and our falling off is amongst the juniors, very few of whom have at present turned up.

On June 23rd we are due to shoot in the I.C.S. Competition and we cannot hope to do as well as in previous years, for we have neither the numbers to choose from nor are our "shots" of the same calibre as in the days a short time back, when we had several members who were never flustered no matter under what conditions they had to fire. The seniors should make a fair score, but they will have to be on the top of their form if the team is to maintain its hitherto high position in the list.

The final round for the Worthington-Evans Challenge Cup
the House Competition was completed near the end of
it term and resulted in an easy win for Dugard's.   We
pe, as seems likely to be the case, that some other House
ll succeed in winning this cup in the season 1915-16.
As soon as the I.C.S. Competition is over, the bullet-
tchers will be moved back to 25 yards and practice started
decimal targets once more.
We notice in the "Rifleman" that one of our old members,
:., Barrell, scored a possible shooting with the Colchester
fle Club.
Appended are scores in House Competition :—

DUGARD'S.		PARR'S.		SCHOOLHOUSE.		HARSNETT'S.	
apman	62	French	63	Green	55	Cox	60
rrell ..	60	Andrews	58	Leeming	53	Atkin	47
lls ..	60	Percy	54	Rayner	51	Lawry ma	46
icham	57	Watsham	52	Gibb ..	50	Burleigh	42
ckett	53	Syer ..	49	Pertwee	49	Bare ..	36
gers ..	53	Wagstaff	48	Cottrell	48	Ward..	33
tdwell	52	Brand..	46	Koskinas	42	Thomas	33
gg ..	45	Payne	43	Dolamore	34	Lawry mi	22
	442		413		382		319
MMER	424		424		448		412
AS	425		412		382		394
	1291		1249		1212		1125

Scouting Notes.

'HE fine weather we have enjoyed so far this term has
      given many opportunities for renewed outdoor work.
longst other things I am glad to find so many scouts
rking steadily for their "Naturalist" badge, while some
terprising Peewits are doing some really useful gardening.
In addition to the ordinary weekly parades we have already
d two outings—one to Layer for the whole troop, and the
ier for the seniors to West Bergholt.   On the latter
:asion we had a despatch run, but in spite of their good
guise Wood and Wilson ma. failed to get through the
:my's lines.
Everett, Last, Hollaway, Farmer, Osborne and Weeks
ve now joined the ranks of those scouts who have already
alified for the Public Service badge.   I am sure that I
:d not remind all scouts who have the privilege of wearing
s badge of their obligation to continue to do all they can
merit it.

P. G. Bacon, of the Curlews, has passed on to the Cadet Corps this term, and Wilson ma. has taken his place. Poyser has gone to Boarding School, but we have as recruits Salew, Overton, Downing, Horwood and Phillips. Salew comes to us from India where he qualified as a Second-Class Scout, so he is going to take charge of the Beaver patrol, which has long been without a patrol leader.

Camp—generally the great event of the summer term— seems, alas, to be out of the question this year. It is a disappointment to everyone.

G. E. P.

Pre-Historic.

SINCE the last issue of the Colcestrian the " Pre." has been busy. The time for talking about " doing our little bit " is long since past, and in this tenth month of the war we are glad to feel we have a short list of things really done, small though they be.

First there was our Entertainment given on Easter Tuesday. This—quite the largest and widest-known of our efforts—resulted in the handing over of eleven guineas to the Red Cross. With this sum six new beds and pillows were purchased for the invalid soldiers at Gostwycke. To us who must of necessity be content with small things, six beds with accompanying pillows really seem something to be proud of, and we take this opportunity of again thanking all our friends —and we had many—who helped us to attain to such a triumph.

In one popular item of the programme we were told so emphatically of the untiring efforts of the sisters—Susie and Nettie—that we were quite put on our mettle, and not to be outdone by the sewing and the knitting, "the Pre. are picking pillows for the soldiers now "—the wounded ones at the Military Hospital this time. Very busy the little boys have been—actually picking out thread by thread pieces of woollen material. These threads make splendidly soft stuffing for the pillows, which we hear are very much appreciated. They make such a comfortable resting place for aching limbs. The picking is done in odd moments, and quaint little parcels find their way to the schoolroom morning and afternoon, and are emptied into the cases. At the present time we have six pillows finished, and we shall go on making until either the hospital authorities ask us to desist, or patient mothers put in their plea for their piece boxes—so rapidly growing empty.

In our gardens we miss the flowers, but living up to the spirit of the day, we tried to grow vegetables and they are not altogether a success. If a flower blooms it is left alone by our gardeners, who believe it to be doing its duty, but radishes must be pulled up from time to time to see if they are growing properly, or only cumbering the ground.

The lettuces, because they appeared somewhat dispirited on the second day after being transplanted, were considered a disgrace and ruthlessly thrown out.

Last term we were delighted to take a share in sending parcels of writing materials, tobacco and even cigarettes to the soldiers, for these things do not appeal strongly at present to the Pre. boy. Now we have collected £1 to supply Belgian soldiers with pounds of chocolate—not pennyworths but pounds. We of the Pre. at any rate feel we are practising much greater self-sacrifice this time than before, and for whom else would we do it with such real goodwill as for our gallant Belgian Allies! Vive la Belgique! Gifts of magazines and old linen have been most gratefully received, and we take this opportunity of thanking all those who have contributed.

C. C. & A. J.

Old Colcestrian Section.

Editorial.

On Active Service.

The country is still at war with a ruthless European foe, and the calls of a stern duty are louder and stronger even than the sentiment which links the school days with the present strenuous times. The programme of the O.C.S. must perforce remain in abeyance, and the manhood among us get busy on active service. Our Roll of Honour has grown to over two hundred, and will go on growing. We would therefore appeal to parents and friends of O.C.'s who have joined the colours to keep us informed as to their regiments, and particularly of promotions and appointments, in order that the list may be complete and up to date. A roll of National Reserves, Volunteers and others "doing their bit" in other capacities is also being prepared, and names and particulars should be sent to the Editor without delay. Commissions have been numerously granted to O.C.'s, and a still larger number are applying. At the moment of writing Mr. Shaw Jeffrey has signed and supported fifty-five applications for commissions from old boys of the School.

The Casualty Lists.

The old School figures largely in the casualty lists, and some valuable lives have been given for the country and the cause. Thompson Allen, of Horkesley, was killed in the gallant charge of the Essex Yeomanry at Ypres ; E. J. Prime, of Colchester, and John Barker, of Walton, are missing since the same thrilling event ; and S. C. Fairhead, Essex Yeomanry, is wounded and, missing. Sir John French has spoken in terms of high praise of the gallantry of the regiment, and the county is as proud of its yeomen as the old School is proud of its members. C. H. Becker, Royal West Surreys, has died of wounds ; F. G. Gregg, of the 12th City of London, was killed at Zollenboeke ; S. C. Chignell fell with other brave Canadians at Ypres ; J. D. Secker, London Rifle Brigade, was wounded at Ypres ; Captain Hugh Bowen was wounded at St. Julien ; L. Fitch has been invalided home after an operation in hospital at Rouen ; P. Rickard is lying dangerously wounded at Aldershot, "riddled with shrapnel" ; and R. G. Cobbold is dangerously ill with gas poisoning contracted in the Dardanelles. He had to take refuge in a shell crater, the bottom of which was full of poison gas.

D.S.O. for " A.J."

The fighting of the past few months has provided opportunity for heroism, and the lists of promotions and honours for bravery are heavy. Among them we rejoice to read the name of Major Arthur Jervois Turner, R.A., who has obtained promotion to Lieut.-Col. (temp.) and receives the D.S.O. for conspicuous gallantry in the field. Our own "A.J." was born into the Service, and during the South African war he earned distinction by sticking to his guns at Colenso till an arm had been twice broken by the enemy's fire. He was then promoted to a majority for his services, and was the youngest Major in the Army List. Lieut.-Col. Turner learnt his cricket at the Colchester Grammar School, and later became one of the most prominent cricketers of the day, playing for Essex and the Army. He visited Colchester when our County played Worcestershire at the Castle Park. He was also a great exponent of Rugby. His old School is proud of him.

THE EDITOR.

The Roll of Honour.

The chiefest action for a man of great spirit
Is never to be out of action . . . . . .
Virtue is ever sowing of her seeds :
In the trenches for the soldier ; in the wakeful study
For the scholar ; in the furrows of the sea
· For men of our profession : of all which
Arise and spring up honour.

WE give below a list of O.C.'s on active service—with those whose "time is in"—and though we never for a moment doubted that the old School would do its share in helping the country in her hour of need, yet we venture to think the list will be deemed worthy of the best traditions of our public schools.

Allen, Rev. C. A. B., Naval Chaplain, H.M.S. "Glory."
Archer, E. R., Royal Navy
Anthony, W. B., Capt., Durham Light Infantry.
Allen, Thompson, Essex Yeomanry (killed in action)
Allen, F., Royal Engineers (Australian Expeditionary Force)
Appleby, R. J., Dublin University O.T.C. and Sandhurst Military College

Burridge, G. J., 5th Lancers
Burrell, B. F., 10th Essex Regiment
Barnes, Dr. F. M., Lieutenant, R.A.M.C.
Bellward, G. E. F., Lieutenant, 5th Essex
Benham, G. C., Captain and Adjutant, 8th Essex
Beard, E. C., 2nd Lieut., 5th Essex
Bromley, J. G., Motor Unit, A.S.C.
Bultitude, R. J., 8th Essex
Bunting, A. E., 2nd Lieut., 12th Essex
Baskett, T., Royal Naval Brigade (present at Antwerp)
Butler, G. F., Public Schools Battalion
Bareham, C., Essex Yeomanry
Bond, C. T., Australian Contingent
Barnes, A. W. H., Capt., R.A.M.C.
Barnes, J. C. C., Lieut., Border Regt.
Becker, C. H., Royal West Surrey (died of wounds)
Bloomfield, A., Essex R.H.A.
Barker, F. D, Lieutenant, C.R.G.S. Cadet Corps
Becker, Colonel C. T., temp. Brigadier-General
Bawtree, D. E., 2nd Lieut., 8th Yorks
Bacon, S. F., Royal Navy
Brand, Eric J., London Rifle Brigade
Bowen, Capt. Hugh, Essex Regt. (wounded)
Bare, W. J., 8th Essex
Bailey, — Royal Naval Brigade
Balm, A. H., Hon. Artillery Company
Beckett, H., Public Schools Battalion
Barker, J., Essex Yeomanry (missing)
Barker, H., Royal Engineers
Bailey, H. (at the Dardanelles)

Caines, E. C., Essex Yeomanry
Cork, F. F.. Civil Service Rifles
Cullington, M. W., Civil Service Rifles
Cheshire, G., 10th Essex
Cheshire, W. R., 2nd Lieut., Ceylon Planters Rifles
Chambers, C. W., Mechanical Transport, A.S.C.
Chambers, A. S., A.O.C.
Clarke, L. 5th Essex
Collins, R. C., 20th Hussars
Collison, A. L., Censor Eastern Tel., Gibraltar
Cudmore, H. T., Essex Yeomanry
Cobbold, H. J. T., Royal Naval Reserve (wounded)
Cobbold, R. G., Canadian Contingent (wounded)
Campling, C. D., Public Schools Battalion
Coquerel Rene, 3rd Infanterie, Brest
le Coeuvre, Albert, Infanterie Reserve

Collins, H., 2nd Lieut., 8th Essex
Craske, S. F., Hants Cyclists
Chignell, S. C., 10th Bn. Canadians (killed at Ypres)
Clamp, G., 5th Essex
Cottrell, H. J., Sportsman's Battalion
Cole, L. R. R., Royal Engineers

Denton, C. W., Captain 8th Essex
Denton, A., Captain, 5th Essex
Denton, H. W., Public Schools Battalion
Davis, E. G., Captain and Adjutant, 8th Essex
Davies, E. J., Australian Contingent
Deakin, E. B., Lieutenant, 5th Essex
Deane, G. F. F., Public Schools Battalion
Davies, E. G., H.M.S. " Indomitable "

Everett, W. R., 10th Essex
Everett, C. E. F., Public Schools Battalion
Essex, P. C., Royal Naval Reserve
Essex, B. E., Public Schools Battalion

Folkard, W. E., A.O.C.
Fenn, E. G., Essex Yeomanry
Fitch, L., Essex Yeomanry (Egypt) (invalided)
Flanegan, L. C., R.M.C. (Sandhurst)
Fleetwood, E. C., Essex Yeomanry
Fairhead, S. C., Essex Yeomanry (wounded and missing)
Fisher, E., 6th Essex
Fisher, Clifford, 12th Essex
Finch, P. R. C., London Fusiliers
Flux, J., Australian Contingent
French, A. H., R.F.A.
Francis, C. E., New Zealand Contingent
Frost, L. A., Queen's Westminster Rifles

Gray, A., Royal Flying Corps
Green, A. E., 9th Essex
Green, Harold, 9th Hants Cyclists, Despatch Rider
Green, C. B., Essex R.H.A., Despatch Rider
Gregg, F. G., 12th City of London (killed)
Girling, C. J., 5th South Staffordshires
Graham-Brown, Lieut., 9th Lancashire Fusiliers
Gibb, J. W., 1st Cambridgeshire Territorials
Goldsmith, E. J., Public Schools Battalion
Girling, T. A., Public Schools Battalion

Humphreys, H., Rifle Brigade

Hall, — 5th Lancers
Horwood, R. V., 2nd Lieut., 3rd Essex
Head, J., Essex R.H.A.
Hempson, British Vice-Consul, Cadiz
Hempson, E., 2nd Lieut.
Harrison, V., A.S.C.
Hallum, G. B., Essex Yeomanry
Harwood, P., 10th Fusiliers
Hussey, F. W., R.C.V.S.D., London, 27
Hudson, R. J. N., R.E. Telegraph Staff
Helps, F. B., Westminster Rifles
Hill, O. B., Lieutenant, 10th Suffolks

Jasper, L. A., Midshipman, H.M.S. "Virginian"
Jasper, L. V., Essex Yeomanry
Jarmin, R.V., R.A.M.C.
Jarrard, D. G., R.H.A.
Jarrard, C. H., 8th Essex
Judd, A. E., Essex R.H.A.
Jefferies, C. R., Essex Yeomanry

King, Hugh, 2nd Lieut., 8th Essex
King, Geoffrey, 2nd Lieut., Motor Section, A.S.C.
Knopp, H. A., 5th Essex
Keeble, F. R., Lieut., 12th Essex
Kiddell-Monroe, J. E., Queen's Westminsters

Lansdowne, L. R., 10th Middlesex (India)
Lawrence, A. D., Cheshire Yeomanry
Lord, P. C., Essex R.H.A.
Leaning, A., Capt., A.V.C., 5th Cavalry Brigade, Indian
  Expeditionary Force

Maile, R., London Fusiliers
Matthew, W. S., Gordon Highlanders
Mason, A. S., Captain, Devon Yeomanry (India)
Mason, C., 10th Essex
Manning, L., Essex Yeomanry
Miller, E. S., Public Schools Battalion
Malyn, D. P., Lieutenant, A.S.C.
Malyn, R., Hon. Artillery Company
Melrose, A., Royal West Kent
Marlar, J., 2nd Lieut., 3rd Essex
Minor, R., 2nd Lieut., Public Schools Battalion
Marionnaud, J. A., Sous-off., 41e Battie. de 95, 69e Div.
  de Réserve
Matthews, W., Cameronians

Norfolk, A. E., Army Service Corps (killed)
Nicholl, A. F., Royal Naval Reserve

Orfeur, C. B., Royal Naval Volunteers
Orfeur, H. W., Lieutenant, 8th Essex
Oliver, S. T., London Rifle Brigade

Peacock, N., 1st Class Petty Officer, H.M.S. '' Vincent ''
Peacock, A., Essex R.H.A.
Prior, C. D., Motor Unit A.S.C.
Pawsey, J. S., Public Schools Battalion
Potter, J., Motor Unit A.S.C.
Potter, C. C., Queen's Westminster Rifles
Plummer, F. E., 12th Essex
Pointing, W. W., Kensington Rifles
Plane, L. W., A.O.C. Motor Unit
Pepper, V., Canadian Contingent (wounded)
Palmer, H. V., Lieutenant, Oxford L.I.
Plant, C., 2nd Lieut., Royal Irish Fusiliers
Prime, E. J., Essex Yeomanry (missing)
Phillips, Colonel
Puttick, F. V., Otago Rifles, N.Z.
Puttick, S. F., S.A. Field Force
Penny, R. E., Lieut.-Commander Protected Armoured
   Cruiser, S.S. '' Winifred,'' Lake Victoria Nyanza
Parsons, W., Essex Yeomanry
Penn, Sergt.-Major, Suffolk Regiment
Pointing, M., Army Service Corps
Padfield, C., 16th Lancers
Pulford, A. L., 5th Essex

Queripel, Major, Guernsey Militia

Renton, T. S., 9th Essex
Rickard, H. P., 1st British Columbia Regt. (wounded)
Ritchie, Major A. S. M., D.S.O., Queen's Bays
Ryder, E., 10th Middlesex
Richardson, J. R., 2nd Lieutenant, 12th Essex
Richardson, A. J., Essex Yeomanry
Rowe, P. G., A.O.D.

Secker, J. D., London Rifle Brigade (wounded)
Slight, R. L., Manchester Regiment
Siggers, J. W., Essex Yeomanry
Siggers, O., Royal Naval Reserve
Sanger, C. W., University Battalion
Sanger, H., 5th Essex

Scott, Cooper, Lieutenant, 12th Middlesex
Scott, J. H., Lieut., Essex Regt.
Shelton, C. S., A.O.C.
Sparling, A. E., Lieutenant, 8th Essex (died)
Slater, E. M., R.E.
Salisbury, W. H., A.S.C.

Tucker, Stanley, 15th City of London
Tye, G. H., Essex R.H.A.
Taylor, A. P., Royal Naval Bde. (escaped from Grönigen)
Turner, Lieut.-Col. A. J., D.S.O., R.F.A.
Turner, S. C., 2nd Lieut.
Turner, F., Major, Intelligence Dept.
Turner, Arthur, Major, 5th Essex
Town, W. M., 5th Essex
Thomas, R. J., Inns of Court O.T.C.

Watson, G. F., Lieutenant, Welsh Field Co. R.E.
Watson, J. L., Canadian Contingent
Williams, F. O., 11th Essex
Warner, A. E., R.A.M.C.
Watsham, H., 5th Essex
Willmott, J., Public Schools Battalion
Whitby, J. M. F., 2nd Lieut., 3rd Essex
Whitby, H., 8th Essex
Wanklyn, D. C., Motor Unit, Essex Cyclists
Ward, J. D., 2nd Lieut., 12th Essex
Waring, C., Montreal (died of operation)
Walker, B. E. C.
White, S. A., Capt. and Adjt., 2nd Northumberland
  Fusiliers
Watson, S. F., Inns of Court O.T.C.
Wright, Geo., Corps not selected at time of going to
  press.

Corrections and additions to the above list will be gratefully
received by the Headmaster.

Promotions and Appointments.

Allen, Rev. C. A. B., Naval Chaplain, transferred from
  " Queen Elizabeth " to " Glory."
Anthony. W. B., Lieut., Durham Light Infantry, to be Capt.
Turner, Captain Arthur, 5th Essex, to be Major.
Burrell, B. F., to be Regimental Sergt.-Major.
Bellward, 2nd Lieut. G. C. F., to be 1st Lieut.
Beard, E. C., from Public Schools Battalion, to be 2nd Lieut.,
  5th Essex.

Bunting, A. E., 2nd Lieut., 12th Essex.
Barnes, Lieut. A. W. H., R.A.M.C., to be Capt.
Cork, F. F., Civil Service Rifles, to be Sergt.-Major.
Cullington, M. W., Civil Service Rifles, to be Sergt.-Major.
Cheshire, W. R., Ceylon Planters Rifles, to be 2nd Lieut.
Collins, H., 2nd Lieut.
Horwood, R. V., 2nd Lieut., 3rd Essex.
King, W. H., 2nd Lieut., 8th Essex.
Marlar, J., 2nd Lieut. 3rd Essex.
Whitby, J. M. F , 2nd Lieut., 3rd Essex.
Minor, R., from Public Schools Battalion, 2nd Lieut.
Orfeur, H. W., Lieut., 8th Essex.
Plant, C., 2nd Lieut., Royal Irish Fusiliers
Richardson, J. R., from Grenadier Guards, to be 2nd Lieut.,
    12th Essex.
Turner, S. C., 2nd Lieut.
Bawtree, D. E., from Grenadier Guards, to be 2nd Lieut.,
    8th Yorks.
Ward, J. D., from Royal Horse Guards, to be 2nd Lieut.
Barnes, Dr. F. M., to be Capt., R.A.M.C.
King, Geoffrey, Motor Section, A.S.C., to be 2nd Lieut.
Keeble, F. R., from Suffolk Yeomanry, to be 2nd Lieut.
Turner, Major A. J., awarded D.S.O., and temporary rank
    of Lieut.-Col.
Willmott, J., Public Schools Battalion, to be 2nd Lieut., 3rd
    Essex Reserve Battalion.

The late Gordon Gregg, O.C.

GORDON GREGG, O.C., who sailed at Christmas Eve
for France with the 12th London, was killed in action
during the terrible battles of early May, and another popular
lad has laid down his life for his country. Gregg entered the
Grammar School from Ascham College, and an enthusiast on
the playing fields, he gathered round him a circle of friends
who cherish his memory. At seventeen he began a literary
career at the House of Cassell, and became a book editor.
When war broke out he enlisted as a Polytechnic sportsman
in the Rangers, and of his last few days a wounded comrade
writes of him : "He knew what war was, and was prepared
to make the great sacrifice. Would to God I had more of
his ideals myself. Many a time he kept me out of mischief.
I was afraid to do anything wrong before him." An
impressive service to the memory of Gordon Gregg was held
at Hampstead, where the fine example of his life and death
will live for ever.

The Adventures of A. P. Taylor, O.C.

ARTHUR P. Taylor, O.C., of Colchester, has had some
exciting adventures in the war, and his friends have
rejoiced in his escape from Groningen, where he was interned
with others of the Naval Brigade after the fall of Antwerp.

"A. P." the son of Capt. Taylor, of Hospital Road, Colchester, whose ship, the Delmyra, was torpedoed in the

ARTHUR P. TAYLOR, O.C.

Channel, received his education at the Colchester Royal
Grammar School, and previous to the war was in the London
and County Bank at Rickmansworth (Herts). Although
anxious to avoid giving away secrets, Mr. Taylor, in the
course of a conversation on his life and adventures in Holland, proved an interesting conversationalist. It is interesting

to note that; following upon Mr. Taylor's escape, a paragraph appeared in an English weekly stating that the watch over the interned prisoners in Holland would henceforth be more strict. With all an Englishman's pride in his honour, Mr. Taylor made it perfectly clear that he did not escape on leave. " That," as he said, " would have been a rotten trick." For nearly eight weeks he and his companion—a man named Mecklenburgh—were working out plans for their escape, and Mr. Taylor's fluent knowledge of Dutch was a great aid to the success of the attempt. Starting from Groningen on Monday, he arrived in London on Thursday, his journey beginning with a walk of some 60 miles ; after this came a long train journey, during which he changed several times to put the Dutch authorities off the scent, but as Mr. Taylor said, " There is nothing like money to a Dutchman, so we had to keep on tipping suspicious people." On reaching a port he found a ship, and worked his passage across as a fireman. " But, of course," said Mr. Taylor, " I did not feel safe till I was three miles from the Dutch coast." Considerable expense was entailed in the escape, mostly in bribes. With regard to life in Groningen, Mr. Taylor said " it was not so bad." Leave was granted once a week from 1.30 to 4.30 p.m., and about once a month from 6 to 9 p.m. There were 1,500 prisoners in three huts, each holding 500. Their diet was largely a vegetarian one, porridge for breakfast, peas, soup, etc., for dinner, with half a loaf of black bread, margarine for tea and cheese for supper, "but," remarked Mr. Taylor, "it was better than the Dutch soldiers get ; I did not like it, however." " This is our troop of Follies " (producing a photo in which appeared a dozen or so jovial faces above the usual Follies' costume). " We sometimes gave entertainments in aid of the refugees."

Life in the Trenches.

IN a letter to Mr. and Mrs. Jeffrey, J. L. Watson sends some interesting details of life in the trenches in Flanders, and imparts the cheery information that things are going " pretty fairly."

He adds : " We had a very quiet time when in the trenches this last spell, but the weather was bad and the wet makes things pretty uncomfortable. There was a lot of sapping going on where we were, and we had the joyful task of furnishing fatigue parties for the pumps—air and water. The sappers are a heroic bunch. Underneath the ground right under the German lines they go digging away and laying mines. The Germans were also sapping under our trenches, and yesterday morning they blew up some, getting quite a few men.

"The trenches weren't far apart—only about forty yards in some places—and as our artillery had been blowing their wire to pieces, our chaps had to keep up volley firing all night to keep them from mending it. I think we rather scared them into thinking an attack was coming, as they kept on sending up flares and got the trench mortars and grenades going. These are beastly things that hop over the trench without any warning.

"Our platoon had a pretty good job, as we were guardians of a lot of mines that had to be let off if the Germans broke through, our duty being to wait there till everybody else had got away, and then—when the Germans came along—to blow them up!"

At the Dardanelles.

C. BERNARD ORFEUR, O.C., who is serving with the Royal Naval Division, sends home an interesting account of the landing of British Forces on the Gallipoli Peninsular.

The first three nights (he writes) we spent at the base, sleeping in the open, during which time a steady bombardment was kept up and the lines of trenches gradually pushed up. Every night there is an engagement more or less heavy. The enemy hold a predominating hill about ten miles from the base, and have some concealed batteries which alone hold us up. They occasionally send a few of their 3in. shells down to the base or a little shrapnel, which gently initiated us into the way of being under fire. The first three days we pottered about and got our gear together, etc. The fourth night, however, we were called up to stand by as a reserve, owing to one of the lines being broken through very slightly. We advanced up in readiness but did not have to help, although coming under part of the fire. When morning broke we moved up to the third and second lines and later took part in an attack on the hill, covering the advance of Howe Battalion, and later the retreat, as enemy fire was pretty heavy and we required more men and batteries. Our battalion was complimented on its coolness for its first time under fire, and the Maxims as well. There were twelve killed, including officers, and sixty-four wounded in the battalion, which worked alongside with the Hood. None of the gun section were injured but several of us had narrow escapes.

Bernard sends another letter reporting progress :—The day after I wrote you last our battalion was moved up to the first line of trenches, but nothing much happened, a slight attack being turned back higher up the line at night. My range-finder was rigged up on the trench top and used as an observation post, for which it is well suited. I follow up behind the gun in all cases, and can pick up the enemy quickly if he is about, take his range and lay or direct the gun, after watching the fire effect. The next day we left the trenches and took up positions to cover the advance of Anson and Hood Battalions. Two of our crews (A and D) went into action twice under rather heavy fire and were able to do a bit of good ; several of us, however, had narrow escapes. Our officer, like most of the hands in the crews, remains admirably calm under fire, and we all think very highly of him. Our C.O., Colonel Collins, congratulated us all this morning on our good work and rated us all A.B.'s from May 1st.

Each battalion takes its turn in the trenches for a few days, and then returns to its base for a stand off. We have been out rather over our time just now, and are having three days at our base. We returned last night very dirty and rather tired out after a damp night and morning. Rum was served out before piping down, and I spent a very restful night after. The provisions follow us about whenever we move and the food generally is most satisfactory. The Turks fight apparently in a similar manner to the Boers, i.e., relying very much on snipers. These are a continual nuisance, although causing a bit of amusement now and again. They snipe at us when we get in or leave the trenches, and at anyone who shows his head above. They are bad shots, luckily; and the danger is that we are rather inclined to disregard them. The other afternoon we watched a heavy bombardment in front of a village by a large number of heavy guns—the ground seemed to be blown to pieces.

I am quite well, hungry and jolly—four of us have arranged for a small bridge party at the Helles Point this evening—TURKISH DELIGHT to be served !

Still later he writes :—During our time in the trenches we made one advance, by night, of about 200 yards or so, which was done to straighten out the line as it was a bit bow-shaped. I was made an acting leading hand for our crew on May 8th, as our section leader was badly hit on that day, and has died since. All the five crews bar "A" have had some of their men put out of action, in spite of the fact that we have always been to the fore with the battalion.

Our trenches do not have any overhead works, but we undercut them on the front side for sleeping in at night and for protection from shrapnel, and generally a seat is cut on the other side for use during the day. One man is told off to get provisions and he makes one journey each night back to a base and arrives early in the morning with the day's rations in a bag. This consists of tea, bacon, cheese, jam, rolls of bread or biscuits and bully beef—they never send too much.

Every day there is a certain amount of shelling from both sides, and the fleet still helps at times from both sides of the Peninsula. The Turks seldom shell the first line, as it is too close, but the second line catches it, and they also search for our batteries a good deal. The general movements here are now . . (words censored) . . and it looks like being a long job unless something out of the ordinary happens.

More Recruits.

Benham.—On June 18th, at the residence of her mother, "The Chauntry," Colchester, the wife of Captain Gerald C. Benham, O.C., 8th Battalion The Essex Regiment—a son.

Everett.—On June 18th, at 37, Shrub End Road, Colchester, the wife of A. R. M. Everett, O.C.—a son.

DEAKIN, E. B., C.R.G.S.
DEANE, G. F. F., Longwood, Nayland.
DENTON, A., Barclay's Bank, Colchester.
DENTON, C. W., Marylands, Shrub End Road, Colchester. [E.O.
DICKER, B. P., Grocers' Hall, Prince's Street.
DOUBLEDAY, R. E., Belle Vue Road, Wivenhoe
DOUBLEDAY, W. A., Belle Vue Road, Wivenhoe.
DUNNINGHAM, T. G., Manor Road, Dovercourt.
EBERT, Dr. E., Kiel, Fichtestrasse 2, Germany
EVERETT, H. J., Councillor, 28 New Town Road, Colchester.
EVERETT, W. R., c/o B. F. Burrell, Esq., Abbeygate Street, Colchester.
EVERITT, C. E. F., 28 New Town Road, Colchester.
EVES, F. J., 17 Morant Road, Colchester.
EWING, J. H., South Hall, Ramsey, Harwich
FAIRHEAD, A. E., Bouchier's Hall, Messing, Kelvedon.
FARMER, A. O., 12 Queen Street, Colchester (HON. SECRETARY).
FAVIELL, C. V., 28 Udney Park, Teddington, Middlesex.
FENN, E. G., The Hall, Ardleigh.
FIELDGATE, W. H., "Ty Fry," Regent Road, Brightlingsea.
FINCH, F. D., 25 Salisbury Avenue, Colchester.
FITCH, L. B., Louisville, Fambridge Road, Maldon.
FLANAGAN, L. G., Beta House, Clacton-on-Sea.
FLEETWOOD, E. C., Bernahague, Shrub End Road, Colchester.
FLUX, J., Lower Clifden Downs Station, Carnarvon, W. Australia.
FLUX, R. C., 27 Old Heath Road, Colchester.
FOLKARD, C., Copford, Colchester.
FOLKARD, H., Copford, Colchester.
FRANKLIN, Councillor R., Sutherland House, 95 Baddow Road, Chelmsford.
FRANCIS, E. K., Crouch Street, Colchester.
FRENCH, R. E., 58 Roman Road, Colchester.
FROST, A. T., Rackbarton, St. Barnabas Road, Cambridge.
FROST, A. W., 13 Head Street, Colchester.
GIBBS, J. W., 249 Maldon Road, Colchester.
GIRLING, T. A., 18 Park Road, Chelmsford.
GIRLING, HUGH, Park Villa, Dunmow.
GODFREY, C. F., "Thirlmere," Queen's Road, Springfield, Chelmsford.
GOING, T. W., 125 Maldon Road, Colchester.
GOODEY, S., Chelsworth, New Town Road, Colchester.
GOODY, C., Old Heath Road, Colchester.
GREEN, H., Moat Hall, Fordham, Colchester.
GREEN, A. C., Fingringhoe, Colchester.
GREEN, D. A., The Hall, Fingringhoe, Essex.
GREEN, A. E., 18 East Stockwell Street, Colchester.
GREEN, C. S., Fingringhoe, Colchester.
GREEN, C. B., Holmwood, Fingringhoe, Essex.
GREGG, F. GORDON, 58 Lennington Road, W. Hampstead.
GRIFFIN, C., Stanway Villa, Colchester.
GRIFFIN, H. L., Stockwell House, West Stockwell Street, Colchester.
GRIMWOOD, C. H., c.o. Boots, Ltd., Long Wyre Street, Colchester.
HALL, A. L., Caerleon, New Town Road, Colchester.
HARPER, W. C., 6 Queen Street, Colchester.
HARRIS, H. J., Weircombe, Ardwick Road, W. Hampstead.
HARVEY, J. B., Stanley Lodge, Wellesley Road, Colchester.
HARSUM, G. F., Wood Field, Bourne Road, Colchester.
HAZELL, S. G., Wellesley Road, Colchester (and Montreal).
HAZELL, R. L., 23 Lexden Street, Colchester.

HEAD, A., 58 Wimpole Road, Colchester.
HEAD, J., 58 Wimpole Road, Colchester.
HEMPSON, R. J.
HOLLAWAY, H. H., 34 Old Heath Road, Colchester.
HORLOCK, M. F., High Street, Mistley.
HORWOOD, R. B., Layer Hall, Layer.
HOWARD, W. K.
HURST, H. J. R., 7 St. John Street, Colchester
HUSSEY, F. W., 15 Audley Road, Colchester.
IVEY, S. F., 63 Kensington Gardens Square, London, W.
JARRARD, C. H., Thorpe, Colchester.
JARRARD, D. G., Alexandra Road, Sible Hedingham.
JASPER, C. V., Langenhoe Hall, Colchester.
JASPER, L. A., Langenhoe Hall, Colchester.
JAWS, GEO. F., 28 Llandaff Road, Canton, Cardiff.
JEFFERIES, C. R., 62 Winnock Road, Colchester.
JEFFERY, P. SHAW, School House, Colchester.
JOHNSON, E. H., 17 Lion Walk, Colchester.
JONES, P. E., c.o. Jones and Watts, Barrack Street, Colchester.
JUDD, L., South Villa, Ardleigh.
KENT, B. H., 182 Maldon Road, Colchester.
KING, J., 16 Inglis Road, Colchester.
KING, W. H., Inglis Road, Colchester
KING, W. H., junr., Inglis Road, Colchester.
KING, G. K., 53 Friar Street, Sudbury.
LANSDOWNE, L. R., Mersea House, Walton.
LAVER, P., Church Street North, Colchester.
LAY, C. V., 2k Portman Mansions, St. Marylebone, London, W.
LAWRENCE, A. D., c.o. Head & Co., Ltd., 27 Cornhill, London, E.C.
LAZELL, HAROLD, Fitzwalter Road, Lexden Park, Colchester.
LEANING, E. M., Welwyn, Wash Lane, Clacton-on-Sea.
LEWIS, K. M., 173 Maldon Road, Colchester.
LINES, E., The Bungalow, Great Bentley.
LORD, P., North Hill, Colchester.
LORD, S. W., 49 North Hill, Colchester.
LUCKING, A. S., 20 Inglis Road, Colchester.
LUCKING, C. D., 20 Inglis Road, Colchester.
MALYN, D. P., Bleak House, Braintree.
MALYN, R., Barclay's Bank, Colchester
MANNING, C., The Elms, Weeley, R.S.O.
MANNING, P. E. J., The Elms, Weeley, R.S.O., Essex. [chester.
MANNING, O. L., 162 Military Road, Colchester.
MARLAR, J., North Hill, Colchester.
MARSH, W. E., 180 Longmarket Street, Natal, South Africa.
MARSH, H. V., 43 Loop Street, Maritzburg, South Africa.
MASON, A. S., Perse School, Cambridge.
MASON, B., 10 Crouch Street, Colchester.
MASON, C., 10 Crouch Street, Colchester.
McCLOSKY, C. A., c.o. Eles Everett, St. Botolph's, Colchester.
MIDDLETON, G. A. T., "Laleham," Clarence Road, Clapham Park, S.W.
MIDGLEY, C. F., "Gunton," Westminster Drive, Westcliffe-on-Sea. [wood.
MIDGLEY, W. R. C., 165 Ongar Road, Brent-
MILLS, F. G., 18 Beverley Road, Colchester.
MOY, C. T., c.o. Messrs. T. Moy & Co., Ltd., Colchester.
NORFOLK, A. E., 75 Chesson Road, West Kensington.
NUNN, A. W., Crouch Street, Colchester.
NUNN, J. H., Melford Villa, Rawstorn Road, Colchester.
NUNN, W. H., Whatfield, Ipswich.
OLIVER, J. L., Maldon Road, Colchester.
ORFEUR, H. W., Colne Bank, Station Road, Colchester. [Colchester.
ORFEUR, C. B., Colne Bank, Station Road,

ORPEUR, R. F., Colne Bank, Station Road, Colchester.

ORPEUR, F. N., Colne Bank, Station Road, Colchester

ORPEN, O. G., Hillside, West Bergholt, Colchester.

OSBORNE, F. F.

OSBORNE, H. O.

PARKER, Rev. E. H., L.O.A., Watford.

PAART, J. A., O.R.G.S.

PROLER. Dr. L. H., 58 Harley Street, London W.

PEPPER, V. J., 19 Barnett Road, Colchester.

PEPPER, G. E., O.R.G.S.

PERTWEE, F., Morehum's Hall, Frating.

PLUMMER, N. A., Station Road, Lawford, Manningtree.

PLUMMER, F. E. Station Road, Lawford, Manningtree.

POINTING, W. W., 148 Maldon Road, Colchester.

POTTER, C. C. 119 Maldon Road, Colchester.

POTTER, F., Middleborough, Colchester.

PRIOR, E. J., 37 Crouch Street, Colchester.

PROSSER, J. A. B., Lansdowne, Pierremont Avenue, Broadstairs.

REEVE, E., O.R.G.S.

RENTON, T. S., 12 Crouch Street, Colchester.

RICHES, A. E., 80 Tower Street, Brightlingsea

RICHARDS, R. F., Head Street, Colchester.

RICHARDSON, A. J., School House, Great Bentley.

RICKWORD, E. G., 35 Wellesley Road, Colchester.

RICKWORD, G. O., 38 Wellesley Road, Colchester.

ROSEVEARE, H. H., "Craigmore," Newquay, Cornwall.

RYDER, E. W., 74 Wimpole Road, Colchester.

SADLER, F. B., Box P.O. 219, c.o. The Eastern Bank, Ltd., Bombay.

SANDERS, F. A., 108 North Station Road, Colchester.

SANGER, W., "Rookery dene," Abbeygate Street, Colchester.

SANGER, H., "Rookerydene," Abbeygate Street, Colchester.

SALMON, J. G., Wash Lane, Clacton.

SAMMONS, A. C., 49 Grafton Street, Fitzroy Square, W.

SKAMER, H. St. J., O.R.G.S. (Editor)

SENNITT, F. J., 28 Mersea Road, Colchester.

SHAW, D. E., Holmleigh, Beaconsfield Avenue, Colchester.

SHENSTONE, J. C., 15c Coverdale Road, Shepherd's Bush, London, W.

SIGORRE, J.

SLIGHT, R., c.o. One Barrow Lodge, Coalville, Leicestershire.

SLATER, E. M., 201 Maldon Road, Colchester.

SMITH, AUBREY, "Manta," 30 Peak Hill, Sydenham, S.E.

SMITH, G. E., Chapel Street, Colchester.

SMITH, W. G., 23 Roman Road, Colchester.

SMITH, F. R., 23 Roman Road. Colchester.

SPARLING, A. S. B., 21 Creffield Road, Colchester.

STOW, W. H., The Willows, Great Horkesley, Colchester.

SURRIDGE, P. T., Coggeshall.

SYER, F. N., 8 Studlands Road, Sydenham.

TAYLOR, A. P., Roseneath, East Street, Haslemere, Surrey.

TENNANT. E. N., Connaught Avenue, Frinton.

THOMAS, A. O., 150 Maldon Road, Colchester.

THOMPSON, W., 365 Hither Green Lane, Lewisham, S.E.

TOWN, H. G., 10 Wellesley Road, Colchester.

TOWN, W. M., 10 Wellesley Road, Colchester.

TURNER, Capt. A., Essex Hall, Colchester.

TURNER, Dr. DOUGLAS, Essex Hall, Colchester.

TURNER, S. C., Abbeygate House, Colchester.

WAGSTAFF, D. T. Church Farm, Marks Tey, Colchester

WALLACE, Councillor R. W., "Moelwyn," Inglis Road, Colchester.

WARD, J. D., Jun., Bluegates, Elmstead, Colchester.

WARNER, A. E., 8 Myland, Colchester.

WATSHAM, H., Vine Farm, Wyvenhoe.

WATSON, J. L.

WATSON, S. F., 154 Maldon Road, Colchester.

WATSON, G. F.

WATTS, FRANK, 30 Creffield Road, Colchester.

WEBB, G. S., Dairy House, Wix, Manningtree.

WEBB, A. H., Dairy House, Wix, Manningtree.

WENDEN, C. A., The Chase, Great Bromley.

WHITE, C. E., 57 North Hill, Colchester.

WHITE, F., East Hill, Colchester.

WHITBY, J. F. M., 144 Maldon Road, Colchester.

WIGTRY, W. H., 146 King's Park Road, Mount Florida, Glasgow.

WILLIAMS, F. O., 14 Lexden Road, Colchester.

WILLIS, E. A., 25 Heron Road, Stapleton Road, Bristol.

WORTS, S. E., Trinity Street, Colchester.

WRIGHT, Lieut.-Col. Percival, Ashanti, St. James, Mirzenburg, Cape Town.

WRIGHT, O. T., Stacey House, Crouch Street, Colchester.

WRIGHT, G., junr., Stacey House, Crouch Street, Colchester.

WRIGHT, Councillor G. F., 47 Crouch Street, Colchester.

WYATT, D. T., Bank Passage, Colchester.

NOTICE TO OLD COLCESTRIANS.

Old Colcestrians who wish to make known their movements in this paper should communicate with Mr. J. HUTLEY NUNN, "Essex County Telegraph" Offices, Colchester.

Subscriptions should be sent to Mr. A. T. DALDY (Hon. Treas.), Head Street, Colchester.

Members of the Society are requested to notify any change of address immediately to either of the Hon. Secretaries :—

Mr. A. O. FARMER, 6 Queen Street, Colchester.

Mr. A. T. DALDY, Head Street, Colchester.

NOTICE TO CORRESPONDENTS.

Contributions to the O.C. Section, articles on various subjects and humorous anecdotes of school-days, will be gladly welcomed by the O.C. Editor, Mr. J. Hutley Nunn.

All contributions for the next number of "The Colcestrian" to be sent in by November 1st, 1915.

213

No. 43.]
New Series.

NOVEMBER, 1915.

The Colcestrian.

*EDITED BY PAST AND PRESENT MEMBERS
OF COLCHESTER SCHOOL.*

PRICE SIXPENCE

Colchester:
PRINTED BY CULLINGFORD & CO.,
156 HIGH STREET.

O.C.S. Officers for 1915-16.

President:

O. T. WRIGHT, Crouch Street, Colchester.

Vice-Presidents:

W. GURNEY BENHAM, J.P.
R. FRANKLIN
H. L. GRIFFIN
H. J. HARRIS, B.A.

B. H. KENT
OSMOND G. ORPEN
W. H. KING
Rev. E. H. PARKER

J. C. SHENSTONE, F.L.S.
R. W. WALLACE
C. E. WHITE

Committee:

F. D. BROOK
J. H. NUNN
A. W. NUNN
F. G. MILLS

C. GRIFFIN
O. T. WRIGHT
H. H. HOLLAWAY
C. E. BENHAM (*Chairman*)

G. C. BENHAM
E. W. DACE
J. C. SALMON
F. D. BARKER

The Ex-Presidents are ex-officio members of Committee.

Hon. Treasurer (pro tem.):

A. T. DALDY, Head Street, Colchester.

Hon. Secretaries:

A. T. DALDY, Head Street, Colchester.
A. O. FARMER, 12 Queen Street, Colchester.

Members of the O.C.S.

ADAMS, E. A., 7 Goodwyn's Vale, Muswell Hill, N.
ALLISTON, A. W., Chipping Hill, Witham.
APPLEBY, W. M.
ATKIN, G., Hill Crest, Gt. Oakley.
BARE, W. J., Magdalen Street, Colchester.
BARKER, F. D., Royal Grammar School.
BARKER, U. F. J., Marine Hotel, Walton-on-Naze.
BARNES, C., Howell Hall, Heckington, Lincs.
BARNES, F. M., Howell Hall, Heckington, Lincolnshire.
BAXTER, H. G., Fronks Road, Dovercourt.
BAYLISS, R. V. J., Fleece Hotel, Head Street, Colchester.
BAYLISS, B., Fleece Hotel, Head Street, Colchester.
BEARD, E. C., St. Margaret's, Cambridge Road, Colchester.
BECKETT, H., Balkerne Lane, Colchester.
BELLWARD, G. W. F., O.R.G.S.
BENHAM, C. E., Wellesley Road, Colchester.
BENHAM, G. C., 12 Hospital Road, Colchester.
BENHAM, Alderman W. GURNEY, St. Mary's Terrace, Lexden road, Colchester.
BIRD, A., Bell House Farm, Stanway.
BLATCH, F., c/o, S. E. Blau, La Pas, Bolivia, S. America.
BLAXILL, G. A., 50 Parliament Hill, Hampstead, N.W.
BLOMFIELD, S., Radnah House, New Town Road, Colchester.
BLOOMFIELD, H. D., 3 Tyler Street, Parkeston.
BLYTH, COOPER, c.o. Isaac Bunting, 100 Yokahama, Japan.
BRAND, E. J., High Street.
BOGGIS, FRANK, Station Road, Sudbury.
BROMLEY, J. G., Mill House, Great Clacton.
BROOK, T. D., "St. Runwald's," Maldon Road, Colchester.
BROOK, A. T., "St. Runwald's," Maldon Road, Colchester.
BROOK, L. C., "St. Runwald's," Maldon Road, Colchester.
BROOK, S. V., 22 Sugden Road, Lavender Hill, S. W.
BROWN, D. GRAHAM, "Lownd," Witham.
BULTITUDE, R. G., 32 Hanover Road, Canterbury.
BURRELL, F. B., Abbeygate Street, Colchester.
BUNTING, A. E., The Nurseries, North Station Road, Colchester.

BURLEIGH, A., Kudat, N.L.B.T. Co., British North Borneo.
BURSTON, F. G., 1st National Bank Buildings, San Francisco.
BUTCHER, H., 3 Eden Ave., Liscard, Cheshire.
BUTLER, F. H., Cumberland House, Manningtree.
CAREY, M. C., 49 Lexden Road, Colchester.
CARTER, F. B., O.R.G.S.
CHAMBERS, C., 22 Wellesley Road, Colchester.
CHAMBERS, S. C., 22 Wellesley Road, Colchester.
CHEESE, C. T., 44 Victoria Park Road East, Cardiff.
CHESHIRE, W., 1 Meyrick Crescent, Colchester.
CHILD, L. G., 14 Wimpole Road, Colchester.
CLAMP, A. J., 122 Priory Street, Colchester.
CLARK, L. W., 16 East Stockwell Street, Colchester.
CLARKE, S. F., Parr's Bank, Holloway, London, N.
CLOVER, J. M., The Hall, Dedham.
COLE, C. L. L., General Post Office (Staff), Cambridge.
COLE, H. S., 25 Wimpole Road, Colchester.
COLLING, C. E., Capital & Counties Bank, Baldock, Herts.
COLLINGE, F. J., 146 High Street.
COLLISON, A. L., Garrison School, Buena Vista, Gibraltar.
CORK, F. F., 38 Trouville Road, Clapham Park, S.W.
CRAGG, Rev. E. E., St. John's Church, Huntington, Long Island, U.S.A.
CULLINGTON, M. W., 53 Oakhill Road, Putney, S.W.
CURTIS, A. P., Bromley Road, Colchester.
DACE, A. W., 122 George Street, Edinburgh.
DACE, E. W., 17 Honywood Road, Colchester.
DALDY, A. T., 50 South Street, Colchester (HON. TREASURER).
DAVIES, W. E., 118 Butt Road, Colchester.
DRAKIN, E. B., O.R.G.S.
DEANE, G. F. F., Longwood, Nayland.
DICKER, B. P., Grocers' Hall, Prince's Street, E.C.
DOUBLEDAY, R. E., Belle Vue Road, Wivenhoe.
DOUBLEDAY, W. A., Belle Vue Road, Wivenhoe.
DUNNINGHAM, T. G., Manor Road, Dovercourt.
EVERETT, H. J., Councillor, 28 New Town Road, Colchester.

Continued on Page 3 of Cover.

The Colcestrian.

VITÆ CORONA FIDES.

| No. 43.] | NOVEMBER, 1915. | [NEW SERIES. |

Editorial.

IT is with no light heart that we take up the editorial pen. With an unfamiliar world seething around us, we find our own microcosm—the School—in a state of change and unrest; the frequent readjustment of the personnel .on the staff, and the more marked instability among the higher Forms, tend to shake the foundations of continuity and repose upon which school life must be built, if it is to be real and lasting.

By the resignation of Mr. Seamer the staff loses its oldest member and the School one of its most successful coaches. Many O.C.'s with memories of the Pre. will join us in deep regret at the loss of his genial and interesting personality. As Editor of this magazine he brought talent and experience to bear on an arduous and thankless task, with success that we can only try to maintain. May happy days and good fortune attend him !

The decision of the Headmaster to give up his work here in order to devote himself to a wider sphere came as a bomb- shell in our midst. Our School, as we know it, is the direct creation of Mr. Shaw Jeffrey, and its development from very unpromising beginnings could only be the work of a man of great personality and attainment. We find it difficult to con- ceive Colchester School continuing without him.

It is therefore not alone our feeling of unfitness for the editorial chair that fills us with misgiving ; the forces which are playing with the universe seem to be not too proud to enjoy grim sport with us. But we must remember that even darker days were bravely faced by our *Mater Nutrix* when Spanish don or Dutch sailor or Napoleon's trooper was casting envious eyes on our inheritance. The old School has lived through four centuries of change and strife, and ours is the duty of "carrying on" quietly and courageously, that her traditions may be unbroken, her usefulness unimpaired. May they prosper that love her !

THE EDITOR.

217

Grammaria.

Tribus avulsis.

The end of last term found the staff the poorer by the loss of no less than three of its members—Messrs. Worth, Watts and Bastable. The first is commissioned in the A.S.C., and is stationed at Aldershot, whither he takes our best wishes ; the second has been appointed to the Ministry at no great distance from Colchester (and has undertaken other vows as well), to whom congratulations ; while the third has donned the only wear to-day—khaki, and is well on his way towards wielding a Field Marshal's baton, to whom honour. The staff has thus five of its strength of nine serving in the second line of defence. God speed to each and all of them.

Non deficiunt alii.

Their places are filled by Messrs. Barber, Graham and Widlake. The first was on our staff in former years, and we are glad to have him back ; to Messrs. Graham and Widlake we extend a hearty welcome.

What does it mean?

The following is the production of a phonetic genius amongst us, and was written from dictation :—
" De son ton il se mais a na lui carn puer ra garda oho da ore quan a vere qui mais de na qua pa grongé show car ile a are a muer quest a fast der vi ele on toum son a tout le a toul la care de va coule a il sa de plea din quah car puer se ar va guile larose de la rose de la vise plia lon tu monde care dubbitude."

What language is it?

At first sight it looks Frenchy. But then " puer," " vere," " vi," are certainly Latin ; " der " is Hunnish ; " ore," " are," " show," " quest," " fast," " care," " guile," " plea," are English ; " toum " is Turkish ; " na " occurs in the Siamese National Anthem ; " quah " is pure Choctaw. But all can be forgiven for the discovery of that comforting word " dubbitude." A small prize—a voucher convertible at the Tuckshop—is offered for the best attempt at translating it into the original.

What we are taught?

Camels eat very nearly everything, but they like best mixed biscuits and celery.

Camals are very intring things, because their hups are always full of food, and when they not full it shews that they are hungrey. And when its come to a town and smeel water and it grites. A chamel has three parts.

The snake dose not have forked tounges but one long tooth, which when stuck into you a drop of poison runs in and poisons you.

Monkeys are very funey amail, because they stand upon there hind feet and jump and thorgh thing at you. And folow you. And anuther thing about them is that they can chuch hold of a brorch with their tails.

Definitions.

Tabrets—little bits of stone what you wright on.

Water-shed—a safe place of refuge for ships in stormy weather.

Biography.

Shylock—the name of a famous Detective.

Jesse had no mother or father, but she had a stepmother and father; she had a sister as well; she went out into the fields to work and earnt a livining.

General Knowledge (?)

A Double Entente is when two people or countries become friendly and agree to stick by each other in case of war or trouble and help each other. The Entente Cordiale between England and France is the same thing.

How were David and Goliath armed?—The giant was wearing a helmet and a shield and a breastplate, but David wore nothing but a sling.

In Flagrante Delicto means that something is put into very nice persuasive language. When you want a man to do something and you cannot force him to do it, you try to persuade him by speaking to him nicely, or putting it in Flagrante Delicto.

The Blue Ribbon Army is an army which is very fine and nice to look at, and wears many-coloured uniform, but is not much good when it comes to real hard work and fighting.

S.

At the Sign of the Ship.

FORM I.

One of our boys says he is a military policeman and ties his handkerchief round his wrist, and stands at the door of the tuck-shop to stop the bikes.

A programme of our day : —
Get up.   Have breakfast.   Go to school.   Have dinner. Go to school.   Have tea.   Do homework.   Go to bed. What ?

Boys are most peculiar, especially in the First Form.

*   *   *

FORM II.

" More people die for the want of fresh air than by having too much."
" These windows must be kept shut."   Which voice must we obey ?

We were sorry to lose Vandenberg mi., our Belgian member.

Second Form boys are up to tricks, Play like fun and work like bricks,
Second Form boys their fame maintain, Always tidy and never the cane.

*   *   *   (Poetry)

FORM III.

Has a tame bird ; it was made to stand on its perch till it stood nicely. It moves in long strides, but cannot hop properly ; it is called the Coss-coss bird.

A mysterious incident occurred recently. Suddenly smoke was observed to be rising out from one of the inkpots. At the same time a perfume (not of roses) spread through the room. Each boy put on his respirator until the danger had passed.

The Form has made a good show on the football field this term. In the Junior House matches Parr's beat Schoolhouse 4—1.

*   *   *

FORM IV.b.

English :—The dog had a bone but it was lame.
Are there any absentees here ?

One of our members, when he leans his head against the wall, leaves a beautiful pattern on the coloured cement; will he get the distemper?

Can we have larger desks? Some boys have very long legs, and some have a heavy side.

* * *

FORM IV.a.

One evening the whole Form suddenly disappeared from the room, the fact that the door was locked presenting no difficulty.

History :—Henry the eighth ascended the throne in 1896: his daughter afterwards became Queen Victoria.

This term we have played several football matches, most of which we have won, though none is worthy of special mention.

* * *

FORM V.b.

Would like to know :—Why a certain member has a preference for grey socks; is it because grey does not show the dirt?

Why people who used to inhabit Dartmoor make such a song about it?

If N and C found the field off Lexden Road a welcome resting place mid the turmoil of the term?

What a certain master says when he misses the ball at Elmstead.

V.B. has met the rest of the school four times, and as yet has not been defeated.

* * *

FORM V.a.

Who ever heard of darning a bell? One day the bell was out of order and did not give the customary signal; someone remarked that it ought to be darned. Thanks to this advice, and V.A.'s splendid contribution of wool, the bell is now working again.

We hear on good authority that the smell of burning bootlace is the same as that of Potassium Nitrate.

. Look ! Learn ! Worship ! All ye little boys who require to master the art of dress. In V.a. the latest fashions in socks, in hair, in figures, are all displayed ; no extra charge for the boys of the sixth.

* * *

FORM VI

This term our Senate has grown, but it is noted with satisfaction that the addition has in no way diminished the warmth and goodwill which makes us a unity. Yet we almost suspected traitors in the camp a week or two ago ; but, however, it turned out that two members, of an inquisitive mind, were curious to learn at first hand the nature of high explosives and poisonous gases. Or was their experiment prompted by the desire to display their newly-acquired skill in ambulance ?

It was with sincere regret that we and Old Boys (whose ranks we shall all too quickly join) heard of the forthcoming retirement of the Headmaster.

A great part of the Old Boy's affection for his School is centred round the personalities of the Masters, and we shall all feel that Mr. Jeffrey's departure will be a loss indeed.

Yet there is one who will, despite the vicissitudes of the last ten years, remain to father the family, and we sincerely hope that we shall not miss his genial smile for many years to come.

Pre-Historic Peeps.

WE are all so busy there seems little time left for writing of our deeds !

First, we should like to thank all who so kindly helped us with the Red Cross Concert, and there were many behind the scenes who did a great deal to make the entertainment go smoothly. We have handed over five guineas to each of the hospitals (The Essex County and Gostwycke) to provide indoor games for the wounded. Making pillows is still proceeding steadily in the Pre. ; up to the end of last term we had completed 26. Knitting is not an accomplishment amongst our small boys, and in response to my appeal I only know of one of them who is bravely plodding on with a muffler. Mittens, mufflers and socks are all needed.

Gostwycke patients challenged the Pre. boys to a game of football, and although I can hardly say which side was victorious, much amusement was caused — all thoroughly enjoying it.

We miss our old boys, C. Buckle, P. Harman and J. Slater who have left Colchester. T. Cox, we hope, is continuing his good work in the Lower School. Our numbers have been kept up by the coming of T. Gell, G. Harper, M. Wicks and D. Wheatley, for whom school discipline was perhaps a trifle hard to understand, but a good half-term's work has been done. C.C.

Valete.

ATKIN, G.—Form VI., Q.P. Harsnett's. 1st XI. Football, Cricket and Hockey. Captain, House Football and Shooting; House Cricket, Hockey. Band Sergeant, Cadet Corps. Member of Committee, Debating Society.

PULLEN, B. I. — Form VI., K.P. Dugard's. 1st XI., Football and Hockey. Captain, House Football and Hockey. House Cricket.

FOLKARD, H. F.—Form VA., Parr's House Football and Cricket. Private, Cadet Corps.

GLADWELL, O. E.—Form VA., Dugard's, House Shooting.

KOSKINAS, F.M.—Form VA., Q.P. Schoolhouse. House Cricket, Hockey and Shooting. Sergeant, Cadet Corps.

ORRIN, W. R.—Form VA., Q.P. Dugard's. School Football and Cricket. Captain. House Cricket, House Football and Hockey. Lance-Corporal, Cadet Corps.

PAYNE, E. A.—Form VA., Probationer, Parr's. House Shooting. Lance-Corporal, Cadet Corps.

ROGERS, S. W.— Form VA., Dugard's. 2nd XI. Football, House Cricket. Football, Hockey and Shooting. Lance-Corporal, Cadet Corps.

BROWN, C. W.—Form VB., Dugard's. House Cricket, Football and Shooting. Private, Cadet Corps.

BUTLER, R. G.—Form VB., Schoolhouse.

GIBB, G.—Form VB., Schoolhouse. School Football and Hockey. House Cricket and Football, Hockey and Shooting. Private, Cadet Corps.

LEEMING, J. H. J.—Form VB., Schoolhouse. House Cricket, Hockey and Shooting. Corporal-Bugler, Cadet Corps.

SYER, F. W.—Form VB., Parr's. School Cricket. House Cricket, Football, Hockey and Shooting. Drummer, Cadet Corps.

VAN DEN BERGH, A. H.—Form VB., Schoolhouse.

GODFREY. F.—Form IVA., Dugard's.

HOBROUGH, S. J.—Form IVA., Harsnett's. Private, Cadet Corps.

HABGOOD, P.—Form IVB., Dugard's. House Cricket. Private, Cadet Corps.

WATSHAM, C.—Form IVB., Parr's. House Cricket, Football, Hockey and Shooting.

WOOD. C. J.—Form IVB., Harsnett's. House Shooting.

LAWRY, E.—Modern, Harsnett's. House Hockey and Shooting.

WATKINSON, W.—Modern, Parr's. House Hockey. Private, Cadet
   Corps.
NICHOLL, N.—Form III., Schoolhouse.
HARMAN, M.A., B. G.—Form II., Parr's.
HAWKINS, H. B.—Form II., Schoolhouse.
OVERTON, H. F.—Form II., Harsnett's.
VAN DEN BERGH, H.—Form II., Schoolhouse.
BUCKLE, C., Pre.
HARMAN, P., Pre.
SLATER, J., Pre.

Salvete.

Haly, J.	Form IVA.	Dugard's
Harris, C. L.	Form IVA.	Dugard's
Hayes, F.	Form IVA.	Parr's
Keeble, E. R.	Form IVA.	Schoolhouse
Lufkins, C.	Form IVA.	Schoolhouse
Pleasants, R.	Form IVA.	Harsnett's
Sier, H. C.	Form IVA.	Harsnett's
Smith, T. R.	Form IVA.	Parr's
Carlton	Form IVB.	Schoolhouse
De Wachter, J.	Form III.	Schoolhouse
Nicholls, F. R.	Form III.	Dugard's
TrickeJ, P. J. C.	Form III.	Schoolhouse
Harwood, S.	Form II.	Dugard's
Cox, T.	Form I.	Parr's
Rock, J.	Form I.	Schoolhouse
Gell, T.	Pre.	
Wheatley, R.	Pre.	
Wicks, M.	Pre.	

Red Cross Concert.

IN spite of the inclement weather and many counter-attractions, quite a large number of people gathered in the Big School of the Colchester Royal Grammar School on Thursday afternoon, Oct. 28th, to an entertainment given by the boys of the Preparatory School assisted by talented artistes, local and otherwise. It was an invitation concert, but in aid of the Red Cross programmes were sold at a penny each by a bevy of captivating Red Cross nurses, who also, in an interval, made a collection, which amounted to nearly £12 and will be devoted to the purchase of indoor games for the use of wounded soldiers at the Essex County Hospital and at the Gostwycke Red Cross Hospital.

Chiefly delightful among a number of admirable items were the 'cello solos by Miss H. Luard, the pianoforte pieces played by Madam Eva Plouffe-Stopes, and the wonderfully clever and beautiful hand-bell ringing by Lance-Corporal F. Petchey, who, if he is as able a soldier as he is a musician, will distinguish himself in the field when he has his opportunity. Quite a little girl, Miss K. Walker, recited so charmingly that the audience would have liked an encore, and Lieut. W. Tyson contributed an excellent item of short stories under the title of chestnuts. The boys of the Preparatory School gave the opening chorus and supported H. H. Collinge in "Till the Boys Come Home." Songs by Mrs. Craske and Mr. F. Sidney, recitations by Miss B. Wallace, Miss B. Day and Mr. Peart, and pianoforte selections by Mr. Barker were notable and enjoyable items.

A sketch, "Her Diamonds," in which Miss Maberly, Mr. Barker, and Mr. F. B. Carter appeared, concluded a bright entertainment, which was further made interesting by a capital speech from Mr. P. Shaw Jeffrey, the Headmaster, who always has something good to say, and by a brief and charming little address of thanks to performers and audience by Mrs. Wren, head of the Gostwycke Red Cross Hospital. The Headmaster made a special appeal for a bagatelle board, which it is understood was immediately forthcoming.

On Wednesday night, Oct. 27th, a special performance of the concert was given in the school hall, when the wounded from the County Hospital to the number of about 100 were entertained.

Much credit is due to Miss Cross for the able way in which she organised the entertainment.

House Singings.

ON October 2nd, a most successful House Singing took place in which the trebles quite distinguished themselves. Haly, a new boy, sang pleasingly, and Cameron gave "Longshoreman Billy" in good style. Weeks ma. in his song "The Flag," was distinct, a quality not always apparent in Big School. Barnes and Child contributed, and Messrs. Graham and Widlake made their debut as 'cello soloist and accompanist respectively. Their work was enthusiastically encored, and we are happy in the acquisition of added talent on the staff. The fact that the next fixture (Oct. 16th) had to be cancelled came as a great disappointment after the success of the first concert, and it is to be hoped that each individual boy in the school will get one item prepared for future use.

* * *

On Nov. 24th and 25th (afternoons) an Entertainment will be given in the Hippodrome in aid of a fund which provides comforts for wounded soldiers in Colchester. The School has been asked to provide choral accompaniment for the tableaux, and to produce "The Conspiracy." We hope all will combine to make this a most successful event. J. A. P.

Debating Notes..

UP to the present we have had a fairly successful session. The attendances have been large, and we have listened to a number of new speakers. Most of these have been from the very lowest forms admitted to debates, and although we are anxious to encourage boys to start speaking at an early age, yet we should like to see a larger number of the Fifth Forms among our regular speakers. The speeches also have been in many cases rather too concise. A little preparation of the subject before coming into the room would probably make it much easier for members to address us at slightly greater length, though of course we want no essays read at debates. We are hoping to have more of our debates in Big School. The first meeting of the term was held there, and the experiment was most successful. It is, of course, far better training to speak in Big School than in a classroom, and should do away with the mumbling which is still a glaring fault of our debates.

SUMMARY OF MEETINGS.

Oct. 1st.— Business meeting.— Rickword, Andrews, Pertwee and Fincham elected to Committee. Ward re-elected Secretary.

Oct. 9th.— Debate.— " That, in the opinion of this House, Zeppelin raids are beneficial to the civil population of the raided area."
        Proposed by Rickword. Seconder, Andrews.
        Opposed by Fincham. Seconder, Green.
The motion was negatived by 66 votes to 3.

Oct. 23rd.— Debate.— " That, in the opinion of this House, every man ought to work."
        Proposed by French. Seconder, Middleton.
        Opposed by Pertwee. Seconder, Bugg.
The motion was carried by 36 votes to 20.   WARD.

Cadet Corps.

(ATTACHED 5TH ESSEX.)

AS summer term progressed it was felt that, in spite of the absence of carbines and "blank," something must be done in the way of a field day. With this object Fordham Green and the surrounding country was inspected. A preliminary field day was then arranged and a surprise attack on

a gun position was carried out.. This was successful up to a
point, but the attackers really owed their success to the fact
that the ·bearer of a dispatch, though not captured, arrived
just too late.   *   *   *

With the topographical knowledge thus gained a more advanced operation was planned for the last week of term.
Two attacking parties set out from different points and had
to join up unseen by the defence, as near the starting point of
the attack as possible. The party under Sergeant Rickword
was notably successful in this. Unfortunately the attacking
force was spotted soon after joining up, and the final decision
must be considered to rest with the defence.

*   *   *

For some time past we have been seeking a means of
organising sectional work so that it would not be detrimental
to the company ·work. We have found a solution to the
problem by having an extra parade on Saturdays for those
really keen on signalling, ambulance and map-making. This
parade also provides a regular practice for the band who are
now working well..   *   *   *

Sergeant Andrews has shown great keenness in taking
over the ambulance instruction, and we are much indebted to
Mr. E. H. Andrews for his kind promise to assist by lending
the necessary apparatus.

*   *   *

This term we have fewer recruits than usual and our numbers have consequently fallen considerably. In the present
crisis this fact is much to be deplored. However, we venture
to think that the keenness of the Corps is a distinct compensation.   *   *   *

We have had news of Capt. Deakin and Lieut. Bellward.
The former reports himself fit and well, and the latter is well
on the way to recovery from dysentery.

*   *   *

It is hoped that every member of the Corps will take advantage of the opportunities which the Range offers of
developing what is, after all, the most necessary branch of
Cadet work.   *   *   *

The death of Mrs. Patrick Crosbie has robbed the Corps of
one of its most interested and generous patrons.

F.D.B.

Shooting.

THE results of the Imperial Challenge Shield Competition came to hand at the beginning of term, and though neither of our teams is amongst the prize-winners we find ourselves as high in the list as was expected. The Seniors, with an average of 66.55, are 93rd on the list out of a total of 341 ; while the Juniors, with an average of 66.6, are 48th out of a total of 154. The lowest average of the prize-winners in the latter list was 72, so that only a few more points were necessary to have placed us in the coveted position.

* * *

This term the range is packed with enthusiastic shooters both in the dinner hour and after afternoon school. It is pleasing to note that this increase in members is due to the efforts of some of the senior boys, and Fincham deserves special notice for the number of recruits he has enlisted. The Juniors are a very large section, numbering at present 32 members, but we hear rumours that this number is to be increased after half-term. We hope this may be true, as we shall then beat our previous record number of members.

* * *

With the limited time at our disposal the range is somewhat overcrowded at times, and the standard of our shooting would probably be improved if more time could be devoted to individual members, who are apt to be a little careless as to the sighting of their rifles.

* * *

It has been proposed that, in addition to the score, extra points should be given for grouping, and this suggestion we hope to see adopted in the near future. Owing to the lighting restrictions at present in force it will probably be impossible to use the range after 4 o'clock very soon, so that it may be necessary to open before morning school, an arrangement which we believe would be welcomed by some of our members.

* * *

The first round of the House Competition was shot off in July, and School House established a substantial lead. Below are the results of this and the L.C.S. Competitions.	E. R.

HOUSE COMPETITION.

SCHOOL HOUSE.		PARR'S.		DUGARD'S.		HARSNETT'S.	
Middleton	... 59	Syer	... 59	Halls	... 56	Bare	... 55
Green	.. 58	Watsham	... 59	Bacon	... 55	Rickword	.. 54
Rayner	.. 58	Wagstaff	... 54	Brown	..52	Smith	... 51
Pertwee	... 57	Andrews	... 53	Fincham	... 51	Clark	... 51
Leeming	... 54	Percy	... 49	Berry	... 48	Cox	... 49
Gibb	... 48	Brook	... 46	Gladwell	... 46	Lawry	... 39
Cottrell	... 47	French	... 43	Bugg	... 39	Ward	... 38
Crighton	... 39	Payne	... 43	Rogers	... 36	Farquharson	19
Total	... 420		406		383		356

I.C.S. COMPETITION.

SENIORS.

				Deliberate.		Rapid.		Total.
Percy	..	..	..	40	..	36	..	76
Andrews		..	..	36		35	..	71
Leeming..		..	..	33	..	38	..	71
Halls		..	..	38	..	31	..	69
Rogers ..		..	..	36		33	..	69
Bare	..	..	..	38	..	30	..	68
Green		..	..	36	..	28	..	64
Rayner "..		..	..	35	..	22	..	57
Gladwell		..	..	31	..	26	..	57
								602

JUNIORS.

				Bisley.		Figure.		Total.
Watsham		..	..	38	..	37	..	75
Clark	..	..	..	41	..	33	..	74
Bacon	..	..	..	33	..	39	..	72
Middleton		..	..	29	..	40	..	69
Gibb	..	..	..	35	..	33	..	68
Cox	..	..	..	37	..	28	..	65
Wagstaff		..	..	31	..	33	..	64
Rose	..	..	..	27	..	37	..	64
Barnes	..	..	..	27	..	22	..	49
								600

Scouting Notes.

WE have no pleasant record of camp to give, as is usual in our autumn number. Many of our scouts, however, did what they could during the summer holidays to be of public service, and amongst them the following boys have received a letter from the Mayor acknowledging the help they gave in compiling the National Register :—P. L's. Kent, Salew, Second Hazell, Scouts Last, Taylor, Clarke, Beckett, Osborne ma., Osborne mi. and Hackett.

· On the Tuesday of the last week of term we had a field day at Layer. Mr. Royce kindly gave us the run of his woods and pastures, and as the weather was perfect we had a most enjoyable outing. One thing to be remembered is the large quantity of mushrooms we found—brought out by the abnormal rainfall of the previous fortnight—but though many were eaten, nobody was any the worse.

*   *   *

On the last day of term there, was a rally of all the Scouts of the Local Association in the grounds of East Hill House, and the various troops taking part were afterwards inspected by General Jeffreys—himself a keen scout—who afterwards gave us a short speech of encouragement and sound advice.

*   *   *

I am glad to see there is no lack of keenness this term. Wood has left the school, but we have as recruits Nicholls, Loyd, Jeffrey and Pawsey.

*   *   *

The Chief Scout has recently addressed a letter to the Scouts of the Empire asking them for a new motor ambulance to take the place of the one we gave last year. He writes— "The present car has done grand service, but is getting played out in its engines, and the clearance of its body above the ground has been found to be too low for getting over the roads near the fighting line, where they are broken up with shell fire. . . . I have therefore taken upon myself to wire in reply to a call for help—'Don't worry: the Boy Scouts will send you a new car.'"

*   *   *

In fulfilment of this pledge, all Scouts are asked to earn as much money as they can in their spare time during the fortnight—October 25th to November 6th ; and it is confidently expected that the sum raised will be far larger than that needed for one new ambulance. I am sure that I can rely upon every boy in the School Troop to respond eagerly to this appeal.   · G.E.P.

Swimming.

ALTHOUGH we often had literally to sandwich ourselves —or to use a more watery simile—to pack ourselves like sardines—among the many soldiers who frequented the bathing place, we nevertheless had good sport. The weather in most cases was delightful, and the temperature of the river all that could be desired. Several boys managed to become initiated into the art of keeping themselves afloat even though at the risk of a continual bombardment from some more proficient natators.

One thing, however, *was* impossible. That was to carry out scout tests which, on one or two occasions were suggested. These would have involved, in their zig-zag course, the swimming of a distance equivalent to about five times the ordinary distance in order to get from point to point.

Nevertheless everyone managed to enjoy himself greatly in the water, and although we often had to dress à la belle étoile, the Tommies were in every case most courteous and willing to oblige. F.B.C.

Cricket.

PARR'S v. HARSNETT'S.—Played on June 19th.

Parr's batted first and scored 66, Syer comprising a sound 30. Harsnett's made a good start, but after the fall of the first wicket collapsed. The side eventually were out for 50. Thus Parr's won by 13 runs. Score :—

Harsnett's

1st Innings		2nd Innings	
Farquharson, c Everett, b Folkard	15	c Wagstaff, b Folkard	3
Alderton, b Folkard	19	not out	23
Nicholson, c Folkard, b Wagstaff	2	c Andrews, b Folkard ...	1
Deane, b Folkard	1	c Syer, b Wagstaff	8
Cox, c Wagstaff, b Folkard	0	b Folkard	3
White, c and b Wagstaff	1	b Folkard	3
Rickword, b Folkard	2	run out	1
Clark, b Cheshire	2	run out	0
Burleigh, b Cheshire	0	run out	2
Cameron, not out	5	c Cheshire, b Folkard ...	1
Arnold, b Wagstaff	0	b Folkard	1
Extras	10	Extras	6
	57		50

Parr's

1st Innings		2nd Innings	
Cheshire, b Nicholson	2	b Farquharson	8
Folkard, b Nicholson	0	b Nicholson	0
Collinge, b Nicholson	5	b Farquharson	2
Syer. b Nicholson	30	b Farquharson	9
Andrews, c White, b Nicholson ...	0	b Farquharson	0
Wagstaff, run out	4	c Farquharson, b Nicholson ...	11
Marlar, b Nicholson... ...	0	b Farquharson	7
Everett, c Alderton, b Nicholson ...	8	c Rickword, b Farquharson	0
Watsham, c Cox, b Nicholson ...	0	not out	6
French, c Cox, b Nicholson ...	6	b Cox	0
Felgate, not out	0	st Alderton, b Cox	4
Extras	11	Extras	7
	66		54

PARR'S v. SCHOOL HOUSE.—Played on June 25th,

Parr's won the toss and fielded first. School House first innings was very poor, quite a procession, in fact, until Koskinas and Crighton made a plucky last wicket stand. Parr's innings started badly (2 for 6) when Syer and Folkard made a stand. They both scored about a dozen singles and Folkard left with the score at 45. The tail was very poor and the innings closed for 52. School House second innings was even more disastrous than the first. The boys in red did not stand up to the slow bowling of Folkard and Wagstaff. Parr's were left with two to get to win. Cheshire was bowled by Rayner's second ball, but Wagstaff kicked a beautiful leg-bye, the winning hit of the match! Parr's won by 9 wickets and 2 runs. Scores :—

School House 1st Innings		School House 2nd Innings	
Cottrell, run out	1	c Andrews, b Folkard	7
Gibb, b Wagstaff	5	b Folkard	2
Rayner, lbw, b Wagstaff	0	c Marlar, b Wagstaff	0
Leeming, b Folkard	3	b Folkard	·1
Barnes, c Andrews, b Folkard	1	c Andrews, b Wagstaff	0
Green, b Wagstaff	0	b Folkard	7
Baker, b Folkard	3	c Syer, b Folkard	0
Cockaday, b Wagstaff	1	run out	1
Crighton, c Cheshire, b Wagstaff	6	b Folkard	1
Pertwee, c and b Wagstaff	2	not out	2
Koskinas, not out	3	b Folkard	1
Extras	5	Extras	1
	30		23

Folkard 3 for 13, Wagstaff 6f or 11　　　Folkard 7 for 13, Wagstaff 2 for 9

Parr's 1st Innings		Parr's 2nd Innings	
Cheshire, b Rayner	3	b Rayner	0
Syer, run out	21	not out	2
Wagstaff, c and b Gibb	1	not out	0
Collinge, c Koskinas, b Rayner	0		
Folkard, b Rayner	13		
Andrews, b Rayner	2	did not bat	
Everett, c Koskinas, b Gibb	4		
Marlar, b Gibb	0		
Watsham, b Gibb	0		
French, not out	0		
Felgate, b Gibb	0		
Extras	8	Extras	1
	52	For 1 wicket	*3

Rayner 4 for 25, Gibb 5 for 17　　　Rayner 1 for 2

*Innings declared closed

DUGARD'S v. HARSNETT'S.—Played on June 26th.

Harsnett's winning by an innings and 11 runs. Score :—

Harsnett's 1st Innings		Harsnett's 2nd Innings
Alderton, b Orrin	1	
Deane, b Orrin	0	
Farquharson, b Orrin	61	
White, c Bacon, b Orrin	5	
Smith, b Orrin	5	
Cox, b Gilbert	0	
Clark, b Gilbert	1	
Bare, not out	0	
Burleigh, c Brown, b Orrin	0	
Cameron, b Gilbert	2	
Chambers, c Rogers, b Gilbert	0	
Extras	6	
	81	

Gilbert 4 for 5, Orrin 6 for 24

Dugard's

1st Innings				2nd Innings				
Rogers, b Farquharson	...	2	lbw, b Smith...	...	...	...	0
Bugg, c Deane, b Smith	...	0	run out	...	...	...	6
Orrin, b Farquharson	...	2	b Smith	...	...	...	19
Pullen, b Smith	...	1	c Farquharson, b Smith	...	...	2
Gilbert, b Smith	...	0	run out	...	...	...	2
Habgood. b Farquharson ...	...	0	b Farquharson	...	...	...	2
Harwood, c Smith, b Farquharson		2	b Smith	...	...	...	6
Bacon, b Smith	...	0	not out	...	...	...	1
Brown, c Alderton, b Farquharson		0	c Cox, b Smith	...	...	...	0
Kent, c White, b Smith	...	3	b Farquharson	...	...	...	7
Spencer, not out	...	0	b Farquharson	...	...	...	0
Extras	... ...	6	Extras	...	...	...	9
		16					**54**

Bowling—Farquharson 9 for 11, Smith 9 for 45.

HARSNETT'S v. SCHOOL HOUSE.—Played on July 1st.

Harsnett's batted first and Smith made 39 not out. When School House went in only five scored. Cottrell saved the side from collapse, carrying his bat for a sound 32 out of 42. Harsnett's with 29 to the good again took the wicket, and at the call of time Harsnett's were 80 for 5, Farquharson having made 61 not out. Score :—

Harsnett's

1st Innings				2nd Innings				
Alderton, b Rayner ...	...	...	6	b Rayner	...	...	...	7
Deane, b Gibb	...	...	1	b Gibb	...	...	...	4
White, c and b Gibb	...	...	2	c Gibb, b Rayner	..	...	...	0
Farquharson, run out	...	...	4	not out	...	...	...	61
Cox, run out	...	...	0	b Gibb	...	...	...	0
Smith, not out	...	...	39	c Baker, b Gibb	...	...	...	4
Nicholson, run out ...	...	...	5	not out	..	...	...	1
Clark, b Rayner	...	...	2					
Chambers, c Rayner, b Gibb	...	0					
Lawry, run out	...	...	2					
Cameron, c Crighton, b Rayner ...	0					
Extras	...	...	10					
			71					

School House

1st Innings				2nd Innings
Gibb, b Nicholson ...	...	...	4	
Cottrell, not out	...	...	32	
Leeming, b Nicholson	...	...	2	
Rayner, c Chambers, b Nicholson...	1	
Crighton, b Nicholson	...	...	0	
Green, c Cox. b Nicholson ...	...	1	
Barnes, c. Deane. b Nicholson	...	0	
Baker, c Farquharson, b Nicholson	0	
Cockaday, b Nicholson	...	...	0	
Pertwee, b Farquharson	...	...	0	
Koskinas, b Farquharson ...	...	0	
Extras	...	...	...	2	
			42	

C.R.G.S. v. 108TH PROVINCIAL LONDON IRISH REGIMENT—
Played on July 3rd. Score :—

C.R.G.S.		London Irish Regiment	
R H Cottrell, c Stevens, b Lewis ...	5	Stevens, b Farquharson	9
R B Alderton c and b Kingham ...	8	Shales, b Barker	26
Mr Barker, c Lethieullier, b Lewis	0	Lethieullier, c Rayner, b.Farquharson	0
F H Farquharson, c Stewart, b Stevens	17	Kingham, run out	32
Mr Watts, b Kingham	45	Warbois, b Farquharson ...	0
F W Syer, b Shales	0	Merryfield, c Watts, b Barker	0
G C Rayner, b Lewis	22	Stewart, b Farquharson ...	7
T G Smith, c Field, b Kingham ...	5	Field, c Barker, b Farquharson ...	2
C Nicholson, b Dunn	0	Footitt, not out	0
F Folkard, b Kingham	6	Dunn, b Farquharson	3
G Gibb, not out	9	Lewis, b Farquharson	0
Extras	12	Extras	3
	129		82

HOUSE MATCHES.

SCHOOL HOUSE v. DUGARD'S.

This match was one of the third round of House matches, and was played on a fine sunny day. School House made 73 runs, and Dugard's were got out for 48 runs, thus leaving School House the winners of the first innings. The scores were as follows :—

School House		Dugard's	
Cottrell	35	Rogers	11
Gibb	2	Bugg	9
Rayner	14	Orrin	9
Crighton	0	Pullen	2
Leeming	2	Brown	5
Green	3	Kent	0
Barnes	7	Gilbert	2
Baker	0	Habgood	1
Cockaday	0	Harwood	0
Koskinas	1	Bacon	1
Pertwee	2	King	3
	73		48

Bowlers			Bowlers		
Rayner	3 wkts for 22		Orrin	5 wkts for 30	
Gibb	6 wkts for 18		Harwood	5 wkts for 7	

DUGARD'S v. PARR'S—July 8th.

Dugard's won the match by 20 runs. Score :—

1st Innings		Parr's 2nd Innings	
Cheshire, b Gilbert	3	c Pullen, b Orrin	1
Collinge, b Orrin	4	b Orrin	1
Folkard, b Gilbert	2	b Orrin	1
Syer, b Orrin...	6	c Harwood, b Orrin...	6
Andrews, c and b Gilbert	1	b Gilbert	4
Wagstaff, lbw, b Gilbert	25	b Orrin	0
Marlar, c Bugg, b Gilbert	0	b Gilbert	3
Everett, not out	3	c Brown, b Gilbert	0
Watsham, b Gilbert	0	c Rogers, b Gilbert	1
French, b Gilbert	0	c and b Orrin	0
Felgate, c Harwood, b Gilbert ...	2	not out	0
Extras.	3	Extras...	2
	49		19

Bowling			
Gilbert ...	12 wkts for 22	Orrin ...	8 wkts for 41

Dugard's

1st Innings			2nd Innings		
Rogers, c Andrews, b Folkard	...	3	c Cheshire, b Folkard	... ...	5
Bugg, c Folkard, b Wagstaff	...	2	b Wagstaff ..	... ...	17
Orrin, b Folkard	...	6	run out	... ...	o
Pullen, b Folkard	...	1	c and b Wagstaff ...	... ...	o
Gilbert, b Folkard ...	...	1	c Andrews, b Folkard	... ...	1
Habgood, b Folkard ...	..	o	b Folkard	... ...	1
Harwood, c Andrews, b Folkard ...		2	c French, b Folkard...	... ...	5
Bacon, b Wagstaff . .	...	2	c French, b Wagstaff	... ...	o
Brown, c Syer, b Folkard ...	...	11	run out	... ...	4
Kent, not out	...	12	b Wagstaff	... ...	o
King, b Wagstaff	...	o	not out	... ...	o
Extras...	...,	8	Extras...	...	7
		48			40

Bowling

Folkard   ...   11 wkts for 30   Wagstaff   ...   7 wkts for 47

PARR's v. HARSNETT'S—On July 10th.

Harsnett's won by 8 wickets.   Score :—

Parr's

1st Innings			2nd Innings		
Syer, b Nicholson	...	1	c Chambers, b Nicholson ...	...	4
Andrews, b Farquharson ...	...	1	c Cox, b Nicholson ...	...	2
Collinge, b Farquharson ...	...	2	b Nicholson ...	...	2
Folkard, c Smith, b Farquharson...		o	st Alderton, b Nicholson ...	...	o
Wagstaff, c Nicholson, b Farquharson		o	c and b Farquharson	...	12
Cheshire, b Farquharson ...	...	o	c Farquharson, b Nicholson	...	7
Everett, run out	...	o	b Nicholson	...	o
Marlar, b Nicholson ...	...	o	b Nicholson	...	o
Percy, b Farquharson ...	...	1	b Farquharson ...	...	4
Watsham, b Farquharson ...	...	o	c and b Farquharson	...	1
Felgate, not out	...	o	not out	...	1
Extras...	....	4	Extras...	...	5
		9			38

Harsnett's

1st Innings			2nd Innings			
Deane, b Folkard	...	2				
Nicholson, c Folkard, b Wagstaff...		o	b Felgate	...	..	22
Alderton, lbw, b Folkard ...	...	4	not out	...	...	2
Farquharson, lbw, b Folkard ...		o	b Felgate	...	...	o
Smith, lbw, b Folkard ...	...	19	not out	...	...	20
White, b Folkard	...	4				
Cox, b Wagstaff	...	1				
Clark, b Wagstaff	...	3				
Lawry, run out	...	1				
Chambers, c Wagstaff, b Folkard...		1				
Cameron, not out	...	2				
Extras...	...	4	Extras...	...		9
		41				53

football.

1st XI. o v. 1st Colchester Scout Troop 2.—Played on a wet and slippery pitch on Oct. 9th. The first half was fairly even. From a goal kick, through Alderton dropping the ball, the Scouts scored. In the second half the School missed several opportunities of scoring, and from a break away near the finish, the Scouts again scored. Cottrell at back and Wagstaff at centre half were the pick of the team. The School team was—R. B. Alderton ; T. G. Smith and R. H. Cottrell ; F. H. Farquharson, P. Wagstaff and P. E. Rickword.; A. White, F. Cheshire, R. S. Gilbert, M. Green and J. W. Pertwee.

IVA. and IVB. v. 2nd Colchester Scout Troop. – IVA. and IVB. easily won this match on Oct. 16th, the Scouts being much smaller, by 12—0. Rayner (3), Clarke (3), Bacon (2), Wells (2), Salew and Barnes scored.

C.R.G.S. o v. Chelmsford Grammar School 1—Chelmsford arrived late, so only half-an-hour was played each way on Oct. 30th. In the second half Chelmsford pressed and scored. For the School Wagstaff at centre half and Cottrell at back were again the pick of the team. R. B. Alderton ; R. H. Cottrell and C. Nicholson ; H. Bare, P. Wagstaff and F. H. Farquharson ; A. White, F. Cheshire, T. G. Smith, M. Green and J. W. Pertwee.

Old Colcestrian Section.

Editorial.

THE world is still in the throes of war, and like other institutions the Society is " biding the time," looking forward to the days when peace shall reign, and O.C.'s. meet again to revive the memories of the happy past, and to recount the exciting moments before a desperate foe. As our list of those serving shews, over 240 O.C's. have joined the colours, but we have to lament the loss of more brave men who have given their lives for King and Country.

* * *

Since the last issue of the *Colcestrian*, Captain Arthur Denton, of the 5th Essex, the first Secretary of the Old Colcestrian Society, has been killed in action in the Dardanelles, and Jack Flux came all the way from Australia to lay down his life on the battlefield. Both died gallantly facing the foe, and are numbered among our glorious dead.

* * *

On the other hand there have been deeds by O.C's. which call for rejoicing, and notable among the achievements in the field is the winning of the Military Cross by Lieutenant Edwin Cooper Scott, of the 12th Duke of Cambridge's Own, for conspicuous gallantry near Tambour. He led parties to the rescue of gassed miners, and on another occasion he led a party down a shaft 55 feet deep and saved the lives of six miners who had been gassed. Brought up himself almost overcome, he heard there was still another man down the shaft, and he gallantly endeavoured to return. Lieutenant Scott shewed great coolness and absolute disregard of personal danger. This is exhilarating reading, and it is evident that O.C's. will take a not unworthy place among the heroes of this history-making war.

Something like a shock has come to O.C's. by the news of our popular Headmaster's impending resignation. His letter on another page will be read with interest and sincere regret, for Mr. Shaw Jeffrey has made the School what it is to-day, and will ever be affectionately remembered by his own old boys for his share in making the C.R.G.S. something to be proud of, and by the old boys of the former generation as the founder of the Old Colcestrian Society. In scholarly attainments, in organisation and in enterprise, Mr. Shaw Jeffrey has set in Colchester a noble example, and his place will be hard to fill.

THE EDITOR.

On Active Service.

Who, deemed to go in company with Pain,
And Fear, and Bloodshed, miserable train !
Turns his necessity to glorious gain.
This is the happy warrior ; this is he
Whom every man in arms should wish to be

THE following is a list of O.C.'s who are serving —or who, alas ! have served—with the colours on active service. It will be seen that they come from many quarters of the globe to answer the call of the motherland, to make, if need be, the great sacrifice. The list is revised and brought up to date, but the Headmaster would be glad to hear of additions to the number, and any corrections or transfers necessary to make the roll complete.

Allen, Rev. C. A. B., Naval Chaplain, H.M.S. "Glory.'
Archer, E. R., Royal Navy
Anthony, W. B., Capt., Durham Light Infantry.
Allen, Thompson, Essex Yeomanry (killed in action)
Allen, F., Royal Engineers (Australian Expeditionary
   Force)
Appleby, R. J., Dublin University O.T.C. and Sandhurst
   Military College
Atkin, G., London Irish Rifles
Bastable, R., Inns of Court O.T.C.
Blowers, F. J.
Bentley, W. H., Hon. Artillery Company

Burridge, G. J., 5th Lancers
Burrell, B. F., 10th Essex Regiment
Barnes, Dr. F. M., Lieutenant, R.A.M.C.
Bellward, G. E. F., Lieutenant, 5th Essex
Benham, G. C., Captain (8th Essex), Staff Captain 7th Prov. Brigade.
Beard, E. C., 2nd Lieut., 5th Essex
Bromley, J. G., Motor Unit, A.S.C.
Bultitude, R. J., 8th Essex
Bunting, A. E., 2nd Lieut., 12th Essex
Baskett, T., Royal Naval Brigade (present at Antwerp)
Butler, G. F., Public Schools Battalion
Bareham, C., Essex Yeomanry
Bond, C. T., Australian Contingent
Barnes, A. W. H., Capt., R.A.M.C.
Barnes, J. C. C., Lieut., Border Regt.
Becker, C. H., Royal West Surrey (died of wounds)
Blomfield, A., 2nd Lieutenant R.F.A.
Barker, F. D , Lieutenant, C.R.G.S. Cadet Corps
Becker, Colonel C. T., temp. Brigadier-General
Bawtree, D. E., 2nd Lieut., 8th Yorks
Bacon, S. F., Royal Navy
Brand, Eric J., London Rifle Brigade
Bowen, Capt. Hugh, Essex Regt. (wounded)
Bare, W. J., 8th Essex
Bailey, — Royal Naval Brigade
Balm, A. H., Hon. Artillery Company
Beckett, H., Royal Fusiliers
Barker, C. E., 2nd Lieutenant Goorkha Rifles
Baxter, H. G., Middlesex Regiment
Barker, J., Essex Yeomanry (missing)
Barker, H., Royal Engineers
Bailey, H. (at the Dardanelles)
Bailey, A. G., R.N.D.

Caines, E. C., Essex Yeomanry
Cork, F. F.. Civil Service Rifles
Cullington, M. W., Civil Service Rifles
Cheshire, G., 10th Essex
Cheshire, W. R., 2nd Lieut., Ceylon Planters Rifles
Chambers, C. W., Mechanical Transport, A.S.C.
Chambers, A. S., A.O.C.
Clarke, L. 5th Essex
Collins, R. C., 20th Hussars
Collison, A. L., Censor Eastern Tel., Gibraltar
Cudmore, H. T., Essex Yeomanry
Cobbold, H. J. T., Royal Naval Reserve (wounded)

Cobhold, R. G., Canadian Contingent (wounded)
Campling, C. D., Public Schools Battalion
Coquerel Rene, 3rd Infanterie, Brest
le Coeuvre, Albert, Infanterie Reserve
Collins, H., 2nd Lieut., 8th Essex
Craske, S. F., Hants Cyclists
Chignell, S. C., 10th Bn. Canadians (killed at Ypres)
Clamp, G., 5th Essex
Cottrell, H. J., Sportsman's Battalion
Cole, L. R. R., Royal Engineers

Denton, C. W., Captain. 8th Essex
Denton, A., Captain, 5th Essex (killed in action)
Denton, H. W., Public Schools Battalion
Davis, E. G., Captain and Adjutant, 8th Essex
Davies, E. J., Australian Contingent
Deakin, E. B., Lieutenant, 5th Essex
Deane, G. F. F., Public Schools Battalion
Davies, E. G., H.M.S. " Indomitable "

Everett, W. R., 10th Essex
Everett, C. E. F., Public Schools Battalion
Essex, P. C., Royal Naval Reserve
Essex, B. E., Public Schools Battalion

Folkard, W. E., A.O.C.
Fenn, E. G., Essex Yeomanry
Fitch, L., Essex Yeomanry (Egypt) (invalided)
Flanegan, L. C., 2nd Lieutenant, 3rd Essex
Fleetwood, E. C., Essex Yeomanry
Fairhead, S. C., Essex Yeomanry (wounded and missing)
Fisher, E., 6th Essex
Fisher, Clifford, 12th Essex
Finch, P. R. C., London Fusiliers
Flux, J., Australian Contingent (killed in action)
French, A. H., R.F.A.
Francis, C. E., New Zealand Contingent
Frost, L. A., Queen's Westminster Rifles

Gray, A., Royal Flying Corps
Green, A. E., 9th Essex
Green, Harold, 9th Hants Cyclists, Despatch Rider
Green, C. B., Essex R.H.A., Despatch Rider
Gregg, F. G., 12th City of London (killed)
Girling, C. J., 5th South Staffordshires
Graham-Brown, Lieut., 9th Lancashire Fusiliers
Gibb, J. W., 1st Cambridgeshire Territorials

Goldsmith, E. J., Public Schools Battalion
Girling, T. A., Public Schools Battalion
Girling, Hugh, Hon. Artillery Company

Humphreys, H., Rifle Brigade
Haton, C. H. D., Public Schools Battalion
Heath, H., Public Schools Battalion
Hall, — 5th Lancers
Horwood, R. B., 2nd Lieut., 3rd Essex (wounded)
Head, J., Essex R.H.A.
Hempson, British Vice-Consul, Cadiz
Hempson, E., 2nd Lieut.
Harrison, V., A.S.C.
Hallum, G. B., Essex Yeomanry
Harwood, P., 10th Fusiliers
Hussey, F. W., R.C.V.S.D., London, 27
Hudson, R. J. N., R.E. Telegraph Staff
Helps, F. B., Westminster Rifles
Hill, O. B., Lieutenant, 10th Suffolks
Hughes, L. D., 2nd Lieutenant, R.H.A.

Jasper, L. A., Midshipman, H.M.S. "Virginian"
Jasper, L. V., Essex Yeomanry
Jarmin, R.V., R.A.M.C.
Jarrard, D. G., R.H.A.
Jarrard, C. H., 8th Essex
Judd, A. E., Essex R.H.A.
Jefferies, C. R., 2nd Lieutenant, West Riding R.F.A.

King, Hugh, 2nd Lieut., 8th Essex
King, Geoffrey, 2nd Lieut., Motor Section, A.S.C.
King, J. H., Inns of Court O.T.C.
King, S. K., R.N.D. Engineers
Knopp, H. A., 5th Essex
Keeble, F. R., Lieut., 12th Essex
Kiddell-Monroe, J. E., Queen's Westminsters

Lansdowne, L. R., 10th Middlesex (India)
Lawrence, A. D., Cheshire Yeomanry
Lord, P. C., Essex R.H.A.
Leaning, A., Capt., A.V.C., 5th Cavalry Brigade, Indian
    Expeditionary Force
Lucking, A. J., Inns of Court O.T.C.
Lucking, mi.

Maile, R., London Fusiliers
Matthew, W. S., Gordon Highlanders

Mason, A. S., Captain, Devon Yeomanry (India)
Mason, C., 10th Essex
Manning, L., Essex Yeomanry
Manning, C., Civil Service Rifles
Miller, E. S., Public Schools Battalion
Malyn, D. P., Lieutenant, A.S.C.
Malyn, R., Hon. Artillery Company
Melrose, A., Royal West Kent.
Marlar, J., 2nd Lieut., 3rd Essex
Minor, R., 2nd Lieut., Public Schools Battalion
Marionnaud, J. A., Sous-off., 41e Battie. de 95, 69e Div.
    de Réserve
Matthews, W., Cameronians
Mitchell, G., Public Schools Battalion

Nicholson, K., A.O.D.
Norfolk, A. E., Army Service Corps (killed)
Nicholl, A. F., Royal Naval Reserve

Orfeur, C. B., Royal Naval Volunteers
Orfeur, H. W.. Lieutenant, 8th Essex
Oliver, S. T., London Rifle Brigade

Peacock, N., 1st Class Petty Officer, H.M.S. "Vincent"
Peacock, A., Essex R.H.A.
Prior, C. D., Motor Unit A.S.C.
Pawsey, J. S., Public Schools Battalion
Potter, J., Motor Unit A.S.C.
Potter, C. C., 2nd Lieutenant Suffolk Regiment
Plummer, F. E., 12th Essex
Plummer, N. A., Essex Yeomanry
Pointing, W. W., Kensington Rifles
Plane, L. W., A.O.C. Motor Unit
Pepper, V., Canadian Contingent (wounded)
Palmer, H. V., Lieutenant, Oxford L.I.
Plant, C., 2nd Lieut., Royal Irish Fusiliers
Plummer, N. A., Essex Yeomanry.
Prime, E. J., Essex Yeomanry (missing)
Phillips, Colonel
Puttick, F. V., Otago Rifles, N.Z.
Puttick, S. F., S.A. Field Force
Penny, R. E., Lieut.-Commander Protected Armoured
    Cruiser, S.S. "Winifred," Lake Victoria Nyanza
Parsons, W., Essex Yeomanry
Penn, Sergt.-Major, Suffolk Regiment
Pointing, M., Army Service Corps
Padfield, C., 16th Lancers

Pulford, A. L., 5th Essex

Queripel, Major, Guernsey Militia

Renton, T. S., 9th Essex
Rickard, H. P., 1st British Columbia Regt. (wounded)
Ritchie, Major A. S. M., D.S.O., Queen's Bays
Ryder, E., 10th Middlesex
Richardson, J. R., 2nd Lieutenant, 12th Essex
Richardson, A. J., Essex Yeomanry
Rowe, P. G., A.O.D.
Riches, A. E., Royal Engineers

Secker, J. D., 2nd Lieutenant, London R.B. (wounded)
Slight, R. L., Manchester Regiment
Siggers, J. W., Essex Yeomanry
Siggers, O., Royal Naval Reserve
Sanger, C. W., University Battalion
Sanger, H., 5th Essex
Shepard, W. O., Australian Contingent
Shepard, D. T., Australian Contingent
Scott, E. Cooper, Lieutenant, Duke of Cambridge's Own
Scott, J. H., Lieut., Essex Regt.
Shelton, C. S., A.O.C.
Sparling, A. E., Lieutenant, 8th Essex (died)
Slater, E. M., R.E.
Salisbury, W. H., A.S.C.

Tucker, Stanley, 15th City of London
Tucker, A.,
Tenant, E., R.E. Dispatch Rider
Tye, G. H., Essex R.H.A.
Taylor, A. P., Royal Naval Bde. (escaped from Grönigen)
Turner, Lieut.-Col. A. J., D.S.O., R.F.A.
Turner, S. C., 2nd Lieut.
Turner, F., Major, Intelligence Dept.
Turner, Arthur, Major, 5th Essex
Town, W. M., 5th Essex
Thomas, R. J., Inns of Court O.T.C.
Thomason, Corporal, Queen's Westminsters
Watson, G. F., Lieutenant, Welsh Field Co. R.E.
Watson, J. L., Canadian Contingent
Williams, F. O., 11th Essex
Warner, A. E., R.A.M.C.
Watsham, H., 5th Essex
Willmott, J., Public Schools Battalion
Whitby, J. M. F., 2nd Lieut., 3rd Essex

Whitby, H., 8th Essex
Wanklyn, D. C., Motor Unit, Essex Cyclists
Ward, J. D., 2nd Lieut., 12th Essex
Waring, C., Montreal (died under operation)
Walker, B. E. C.
White, S. A., Capt. and Adjt., 2nd Northumberland Fusiliers
Watson, S. F., Inns of Court O.T.C.
Watson, F. C., Royal Flying Corps
Willsher, S., Sea Scoutmaster
Webb, G. A., Princess Patricia's L.I.
Webb, A. E., 2nd London R.F.
Wagstaff, D. T., Coldstream Guards
Wheeler, G., Inns of Court O.T.C.
Worth, O. G., 2nd Lieutenant, A.S.C.
Wright, Geo., Officers' Training Corps

Cbe Fjeadmaster to O.C's.

MY DEAR OLD BOYS,

Wherever you are I hope these few lines will find you—whether you are in the chalk pits of Hullock or the sands of Sulva Bay.

The news of my retirement next july has produced the usual crop of rumours, and so I may as well say that I am going because, after 35 years of continuous schoolmastering, I am anxious to find some rest in a change of occupation, and not because I have any intention of taking another Headmastership.

You and I have fought together to get the things we wanted, and between us we have done, if not all we hoped, at least more than we expected, and I thank you for your loyalty and devotion to our School traditions, and for the many proofs of your affectionate regard which I receive almost daily.

My wife and I have given the best years of our lives to Colchester, and it will be hard to leave it; but our School is now so firmly established that with your continued support it can hardly fail to maintain the position it has won in face of so many and great dangers.

Floreat Sodalitas!

Affectionately yours,

P. SHAW JEFFREY.

At Work for the King.

A BUDGET of letters has been received from O.C's. in various parts of the world engaged in serious work on the battlefield or in camp. It would be quite impossible to find space for all, but the extracts which follow will indicate the varied experiences of O.C's., and all breathe the right spirit :—

We have lost pretty heavily, and owing to large numbers being sick our Battalion is very small at present. Still it is a very cheerful part that is left.

We went forward into the reserve lines the same night we landed and were well in the fray four days later, when we lost the well-known Capt. " Bar " Denton, of Colchester. A splendid fellow he was—always so cheerful and energetic, and for ever thinking of the comfort of his men. For days we were under rifle and shell fire, and rifle fire most of the night.

Our first advance under fire would have made the people of Colchester and Essex in general feel very very proud of their Territorial men if only they could have seen it. A murderous fire assailed us from front and both flanks, but these brave and cheerful men of Essex advanced with smiles and jokes, just as if they were still at their training manœuvres in England. I even saw one little crowd paying strict attention to their " dressing " by the front and right, although walking over rough ground and in a hail of bullets ! The fighting at present is mostly trench warfare ; and it gets very monotonous at times. It is for a good old advance we all long again—this being cramped up in trenches doesn't suit us a bit. One gets no rest at night—too many bombs being thrown about.

You will be glad to hear Watsham was promoted to full corporal yesterday and is doing excellent work. Town was unfortunately knocked over by dysentery and is away on a hospital ship, I believe. It was a great treat to read the June Colcestrian and see the long list of our Roll of Honour.

Jarrard is out here with the 1st Essex somewhere—a note from him was slipped into my hand a few days ago. H. Sanger is still with us and doing his bit in a hard and cheerful way.

[Sanger has since come home to a Bristol hospital.—Ed. T.C.]

We are with the Australians at present and a splendid lot of fellows they are. Numbers of them are Essex men, and one often hears a cheery greeting between an Essex and an Australian man as columns or parties pass each other during the day.

My very kind regards to you all and God grant I may one day see you all again in Colchester.

E. B. DEAKIN.

*   *   *

Life in the Flying Corps is intensely interesting and, as one would naturally imagine, packed full of thrilling excitement. My particular vocation is a " Gnome " fitter. The " Gnome " is a high-powered, high-speed engine which is only fitted to the fastest 'planes in the service.

I was very interested to note that the Active Service Roll of O.C.'s is approaching the 250 mark, and I firmly believe I but voice the sentiment of every O.C. when I say that every one of us will individually see to it that *Alma Mater Colcestriensis* will have cause to be proud of her sons in this shambles of mortality, which sets ten million bayonets gleaming merely at the *atavishe* snarl of super armed twentieth century cavemen.

S. F. WATSON,

2/Air Mech., R.A.S.

*   *   *

We are getting very little shell-fire here but quite a lot of rifle-fire—especially snipers. One of four of us, who have chummed together all along, got killed this morning as he was getting some water. It leaves one with such a helpless rage.

We are quite a long way from the German trenches here—about 400 to 500 yards. Consequently there is lots of work in the way of going out on listening posts and patrols. Another great game is to sneak out and try to mess up the enemy's wire. As they have parties out trying to do the same thing, you can imagine there are some hair-raising moments. Three of us were out last night to see what we could. I got a most frightful scare, getting hung up in a bunch of barbed wire just as they sent up a lot of starlights—they *did* blaze away, but the fates were kind and they all missed—but a "cold perspiration bespangled my brow" all right.

*   *   *

Life here is much as ever though we hope to see some more fighting soon, which will be welcome, as we are all sick and tired of this inaction—nothing but mud and shells. We all want to get into it if need be and get it over.

At present I am becoming a bomb-thrower and being iniated into the gentle art of slinging bombs. They are diabolical affairs but do great work.

By-the-way, I have seen Young Cobbold out here several times—he tells me he was wounded at Festubert, but looks quite fit again and has a soft job as staff cook in the 2nd Battalion, but I think wants to get back to his Company again. I went over to his place the night before last and he fed me on mutton chops and other luxuries, and also had a Colchester paper there.

Gil has been rather distinguishing himself as he and a corporal made some reconnaissance of the enemy's lines and had a special wire of congratulations from the C.O. in charge.

J. L. WATSON,

(Canadian Contingent).

We have been a bit dull on the Canal lately, but now have the French Rear-Admiral's ship moored opposite to our house, and every night and morning we are regaled with three National Anthems—French, English and Egyptian.

R. PERTWEE,

Egypt.

*   *   *

We soon had our first experience of the trenches, it did not seem so bad, except that shells, &c., make rather an unpleasant noise. A bit of shrapnel hit the ground about 2 inches from my boot—quite near enough for my comfort I can assure you. After this my next billet (!) was a dug-out swarming with rats at night and flies and mosquitos by day.

You may remember how fed up we used to get grinding away at French at school, but I find being able to speak French more than useful. It has all come back to me.

With best wishes from Everett, Cheshire and myself.

. . . .

Since I last wrote to you I ran across (literally) Stanley Chambers. He is armourer sergeant in one of our heavy batteries here.

While in these billets we are resting (?) only about 800 yards from the firing line, and my only pane of glass had a bullet put through it the other night. However, taking all in all, things might be much worse.

BRAMLEY F. BURRELL,

R.Q.M.S , 10th Essex.

*   *   *

We have been in France now nearly a month (17th August) and have already had various experiences. I have found the French I learnt with you very useful, both to myself and others. I never was very bright at spoken French—but I get on somehow out here.

I was in charge of a sap used as a listening post. We could hear the Germans talking and moving about. They spotted a periscope we were using and had some pots at it, but failed to hit it. We find the night work the most trying, watching and waiting all night. At times it is like a firework display, flares going, machine guns rattling and big guns booming. Crystal Palace isn't in it !

Wishing you and *the* School the best of luck. I often wish I was back there. Good old North Town !

W. R. EVERETT,

Corpl., 10th Essex.

I was taken ill with enteric, which is caught from the plague of flies or drinking unboiled water (writes Bernard Orfeur from Malta Hospital). We had rather a jolly time at Imbros. The whole island is volcanic, with numerous peaks, none of which are really very high. I climbed one and got a distant view of the Peninsular.

Our machine gun section one day decided to make an excursion further up inland more, and about eight of us hired some small-sized horses for the day. I remember I had a nice grey donkey which was very surefooted on the narrow paths through the steep passes. We enjoyed a good four miles—the valleys being filled with wild pink flowers and opening up beautiful views—when we were held up by a very peppery Provost Marshal, who had pitched a small patrol camp in a clearing in order to guard a pass leading to one of the villages which are out of bounds. He gave us a good lecture on our disorder and for riding, etc., and would not listen to our being out for a day's ramble. The funny part was when we turned to go back six of the men found that the lads who came in charge of their horses had led them off and were out of sight, so they had the pleasure of walking back. It afterwards transpired that they had paid in advance! My old donkey did a good day's work, however, although he sorely tried my patience, much to the amusement of the others. I found it best to let the beast go just where it liked, and thus finished the journey in a rather more dignified way.

BERNARD ORFEUR.

[Now back in Colchester. Congratulations.—Ed. T.C.]

EVERETT, W. R., c/o B. F. Burrell, Esq., Abbeygate Street, Colchester.

EVERETT, C. E. F., 28 New Town Road, Colchester.

EVISS, F. J., 17 Morant Road, Colchester.

EWING, J. H., South Hall, Ramsey, Harwich

FAIRHEAD, A. E., Bouchier's Hall, Messing, Kelvedon.

FARMER, A. O., 12 Queen Street, Colchester (HON. SECRETARY).

FAVIELL, C. V., 28 Udney Park, Teddington, Middlesex.

FIELDGATE, W. H., "Ty Fry," Regent Road, Brightlingsea.

FINCH, F. D., 25 Salisbury Avenue, Colchester.

FITCH, L. B., Louisville, Fambridge Road, Maldon.

FLANAGAN, L. C., Beta House, Clacton-on-Sea.

FLEETWOOD, E. C., Bemahague, Shrub End Road, Colchester.

FLUX, R. C., 27 Old Heath Road, Colchester.

FOLKARD, C., Copford, Colchester.

FRANKLIN, Councillor R., Sutherland House, 95 Maldow Road, Chelmsford.

FRENCH, R. E., Colchester.

FROST, A. T., Rackbarton, St. Barnabas Road, Cambridge.

FROST, A. W., 13 Head Street, Colchester.

GIBBS, J. W., 249 Maldon Road, Colchester.

GIRLING, T. A., 18 Park Road, Chelmsford.

GIRLING, HUGH, Park Villa, Dunmow.

GODFRAY, C. F., "Thirlmere," Queen's Road, Springfield, Chelmsford.

GOING, F. W., 125 Maldon Road, Colchester.

GOODEY, S., Chelsworth, New Town Road, Colchester.

GOODY, C., Old Heath Road, Colchester.

GREEN, A. C., Fingringhoe, Colchester.

GREEN, A. E., 18 East Stockwell Street, Colchester.

GREEN, C. S., Fingringhoe, Colchester.

GREEN, G. B. Holmwood, Fingringhoe, Essex.

GRIFFIN, C., Stanway Villa, Colchester.

GRIFFIN, H. L., Stockwell House, West Stockwell Street, Colchester.

GRIMWOOD, C. H., c/o Boots, Ltd., Long Wyre Street, Colchester.

HALL, A. I., Caerleon, New Town Road, Colchester.

HARPER, W. C., High Street, Colchester.

HARRIS, H. J., Weircombe, Ardwick Road, W. Hampstead.

HARVEY, J. B., Stanley Lodge, Wellesley Road, Colchester.

HARSUM, G. F., Wood Field, Bourne Road, Colchester.

HAZELL, S. G., Wellesley Road, Colchester (and Moutre 1).

HAZELL, R. L., 23 Lexden Street, Colchester.

HEAD, A., 58 Wimpole Road, Colchester.

HEAD, J., 58 Wimpole Road, Colchester.

HEMPSON, R. J., Galton Lodge, Reigate.

HEBROUGH, S. J., Ernest Cottage, Parsons Heath, Colchester.

HOLLAWAY, H. H., 34 Old Heath Road, Colchester.

HORLOCK, M. F., High Street, Mistley.

HORWOOD, R. B., Layer Hall, Layer.

HURST, H. J. R., 7 St John Street, Colchester

HUSSEY, F. W., 15 Audley Road, Colchester.

IVEY, S. F., 63 Kensington Gardens Square, London, W.

JARRARD, C. H., Thorpe, Colchester.

JARRARD, D. G., Alexandra Road, Sible Hedingham.

JASPER, C. V., Langenhoe Hall, Colchester.

JASPER, L. A., Langenhoe Hall, Colchester.

JAWS, GEO. F., 28 Llandaff Road, Canton, Cardiff.

JEFFERIES, C. R., Second Lieutenant R.F.A.

JEFFREY, F. SHAW, School House, Colchester.

JOHNSON, L. H., 17 Lion Walk, Colchester.

JUDD, L., South Villa, Ardleigh.

KENT, B. H., 182 Maldon Road, Colchester.

KING, J., 18 Inglis Road, Colchester.

KING, W. H., Inglis Road, Colchester.

KING, W. H., junr., Inglis Road, Colchester.

KING, G. K., 58 Friar Street, Sudbury.

KOSKINAS, F. M., 24 Pembridge Gardens, Notting Hill, W.

LANSDOWNE, L. R., Mersea House, Walton.

LAX, C. V., 2k Portman Mansions, St. Marylebone, London, W.

LAWRENCE, A. D., c.o. Head & Co., Ltd., 27 Cornhill, London, E.C.

LAWRY, E., Hoe Farm, Aldham.

LAZELL, HAROLD, Fitzwalter Road, Lexden Park, Colchester.

LEANING, E. M., Welwyn, Wash Lane, Clacton-on-Sea.

LEEMING, J. H. J., 27 Liversidge Road, Higher Tranmere, Birkenhead.

LEWIS, K. M., 173 Maldon Road, Colchester.

LINES, E., The Bungalow, Great Bentley.

LORD, P., North Hill, Colchester.

LORD, S. W., 49 North Hill, Colchester.

LUCKING, A. S., 20 Inglis Road, Colchester.

LUCKING, C. D., 20 Inglis Road, Colchester.

MALYN, D. P., Bleak House, Braintree.

MALYN, R., Barclay's Bank, Colchester.

MANNING, C., The Elms, Weeley, R.S.O.

MANNING, P. E. J., The Elms, Weeley, R.S.O.

MARLAR, J., North Hill, Colchester.

MARSH, W. E., 130 Longmarket Street, Natal, South Africa.

MARSH, H. V., P.O. Box 253, Maritzburg, South Africa.

MASON, A. S., Perse School, Cambridge.

MASON, B., 10 Crouch Street, Colchester.

MASON, C., 10 Crouch Street, Colchester.

McCLOSKY, C. A., c.o. Edes Everett, St. Botolph's, Colchester.

MIDDLETON, G. A. T.

MIDGLEY, O. F., "Gunton," Westminster Drive, Westcliffe-on-Sea.

MIDGLEY, W. R. O., 163 Ongar Road, Brentwood.

MILLS, F. G., 18 Beverley Road, Colchester.

MOY, C. T., c.o. Messrs. T. Moy & Co., Ltd., Colchester.

NORFOLK, A. E., 76 Chesson Road, West Kensington.

NUNN, A. W., Crouch Street, Colchester.

NUNN, J. H., Melford Villa, Rawstorn Road, Colchester.

NUNN, W. H., Whatfield, Ipswich.

ORIVER, J. L., Maldon Road, Colchester.

ORFEUR, H. W., Colne Bank, Station Road, Colchester.

ORFEUR, C. B., Colne Bank, Station Road, Colchester.

ORFEUR, E. F., Colne Bank, Station Road, Colchester.

ORFEUR, F. N., Colne Bank, Station Road, Colchester.

OREEN, O. G., Hillside, West Bergholt, Colchester.

ORRIN, W. R., 37 Campion Road, Colchester.

OSBORNE, F. F.

OSBORNE, H. C.

PARKER, Rev. E. H., London Orphan School, Watford.

PAYNE, E. A., 2 Honywood Road, Colchester.

PRART, J. A., C.R.G.S.

PEPPER, V. J.

PEPPER, G. E., C.R.G.S.

PRETWEE, F., Moreham's Hall, Erating.

PLUMMER, N. A., Station Road, Lawford, Manningtree.

PLUMMER, F. E., Station Road, Lawford, Manningtree.

POINTING, W. W., 148 Maldon Road, Colchester.

POTTER, C. C., 119 Maldon Road, Colchester.
POTTER, F., Middleborough, Colchester.
PRIME, E. J., 37 Crouch Street, Colchester.
RREVE, E., C.R.G.S.
RENTON, T. S., 12 Crouch Street, Colchester.
RICHES, A. E., 80 Tower Street, Brightling-sea.
RICHARDS, R. F., Head Street, Colchester.
RICHARDSON, A. J., School House, Great Bentley.
RICKWORD, E. G., Boughton Lane, Loose, Maidstone.
ROGERS, S. W., 5 Caterham Road, Lewisham, S.E.
ROSEVEARE, H. H., "Craigmore," Newquay, Cornwall.
RYDER, E. W., 74 Wimpole Road, Colchester.
SADLER, F. B., Box P.O. 219, c.o. The Eastern Bank, Ltd., Bombay.
SANGER, O. W., "Rookerydene," Abbeygate Street, Colchester.
SANGER, H., "Rookerydene," Abbeygate Street, Colchester.
SALMON, J. G., Wash Lane, Clacton.
SAMMONS, A. C., 49 Grafton Street, Fitzroy Square, W.
SEAMER, H. St. J., C.R.G.S. (Editor)
SENNITT, F. J., 28 Mersea Road, Colchester.
SHAW, D. E., c/o Miss Mills, Queen Elizabeth Walk, Stoke Newington, N.
SHERSTONE, J. C., 15c Coverdale Road, Shepherd's Bush, London, W.
SLIGHT, R., c.o. One Barrow Lodge, Coalville, Leicestershire.
SLATER, E. M. No address.
SMITH, AUBREY, "Mantz," 30 Peak Hill, Sydenham, S.E.
SMITH, G. E., Chapel Street, Colchester.
SMITH, W. G., 23 Roman Road, Colchester.
SMITH, F. R., 23 Roman Road, Colchester.
SPARLING, A. S. B., 21 Creffield Road, Colchester.
SURRIDGE, P. T., Coggeshall.
SYER, F. N., 8 Studlands Road, Sydenham.

TAYLOR, A. P., Roseneath, East Street, Hazle-mere, Surrey.
TENNANT, E. N., Connaught Avenue, Frinton.
THOMAS, A. O., 150 Maldon Road, Colchester.
TOWN, H. G., 50 Essendine Mansions, Maida Vale, W.
TOWN, W. M., 50 Essendine Mansions, Maida Vale, W.
TURNER, Capt. A., Essex Hall, Colchester.
TURNER, Dr. DOUGLAS, Essex Hall, Colchester.
TURNER, S. O., Abbeygate House, Colchester.
WAGSTAFF, D. T. Church Farm, Marks Tey, Colchester
WALLACE, Councillor R. W., "Moelwyn," Inglis Road, Colchester.
WARD, J. D., Jun., Bluegates, Elmstead, Colchester.
WARNER, A. E., 8 Myland, Colchester.
WATKINSON, W. P., Elmstead, nr. Colchester.
WATSHAM, H., Vine Farm, Wyvenhoe.
WATSON, J. L.
WATSON, S. F., 154 Maldon Road, Colchester.
WATSON, G. F.
WATTS, FRANK, 30 Creffield Road, Colchester.
WEBB, G. S., Dairy House, Wix, Manning-tree.
WEBB, A. H., Dairy House, Wix, Manning-tree.
WENDEN, C. A., The Chase, Great Bromley.
WHEELER, G., 10 High Street.
WHITE, C. E., 57 North Hill, Colchester.
WHITE, F., East Hill, Colchester.
WHITBY, J. F. M., 144 Maldon Road, Colchester.
WILLIAMS, F. O., 14 Lexden Road, Colchester.
WILLIS, E. A., 25 Heron Road, Stapleton Road, Bristol.
WRIGHT, C. T., Stacey House, Crouch Street, Colchester (President).
WRIGHT, G., junr., Stacey House, Crouch Street, Colchester.
WRIGHT, Councillor G. F., 47 Crouch Street, Colchester.
WYATT, D. T., Bank Passage, Colchester.

NOTICE TO OLD COLCESTRIANS.

Old Colcestrians who wish to make known their movements in this paper should communicate with Mr. J. HUTLEY NUNN, "Essex County Telegraph" Offices, Colchester.

Subscriptions should be sent to Mr. A. T. DALDY (Hon. Treas.), Head Street, Colchester.

Members of the Society are requested to notify any change of address immediately to either of the Hon. Secretaries :—

Mr. A. O. FARMER, 6 Queen Street, Colchester.
Mr. A. T. DALDY, Head Street, Colchester.

NOTICE TO CORRESPONDENTS.

Contributions to the O.C. Section, articles on various subjects and humorous anecdotes of school-days, will be gladly welcomed by the O.C. Editor, Mr. J. Hutley Nunn.

All contributions for the next number of "The Colcestrian" to be sent in by November 1st, 1915.

No. 44.]
New Series.

MARCH, 1916.

The Colcestrian.

EDITED BY PAST AND PRESENT MEMBERS OF COLCHESTER SCHOOL.

PRICE SIXPENCE

Colchester:
PRINTED BY CULLINGFORD & CO.,
156 HIGH STREET.

O.C.S. Officers for 1915-16.

President:
C. T. WRIGHT, Crouch Street, Colchester.

Vice-Presidents:

W. GURNEY BENHAM, J.P.
R. FRANKLIN
H. L. GRIFFIN
H. J. HARRIS, B.A.

B. H. KENT
OSMOND G. ORPEN
W. H. KING
Rev. E. H. PARKER

J. C. SHENSTONE, F.L.S.
R. W. WALLACE
O. E. WHITE

Committee:

F. D. BROOK
J. H. NUNN
A. W. NUNN
F. G. MILLS

G. GRIFFIN
H. H. HOLLAWAY
C. E. BENHAM (*Chairman*)
G. C. BENHAM

E. W. DACE
J. C. SALMON
F. D. BARKER
J. A. PEART

The Ex-Presidents are ex-officio members of Committee.

Hon. Treasurer (pro tem.):
A. T. DALDY, Head Street, Colchester.

Hon. Secretaries:
A. T. DALDY, Head Street, Colchester.
A. O. FARMER, 12 Queen Street, Colchester.

Members of the O.C.S.

ADAMS, E. A., 7 Goodwyn's Vale, Muswell Hill, N.
ALLISTON, A. W., Chipping Hill, Witham.
APPLEBY, W. M.
ATKIN, G., Hill Crest, Gt. Oakley.
BARE, W. J., Magdalen Street, Colchester.
BARKER, F. D., Royal Grammar School.
BARKER, U. F. J., Marine Hotel, Walton-on-Naze.
BARNES, C., Howell Hall, Heckington, Lincs.
BARNES, F. M., Howell Hall, Heckington, Lincolnshire.
BAXTER, H. G., Fronks Road, Dovercourt.
BAYLISS, R. V. J., Fleece Hotel, Head Street, Colchester.
BAYLISS, B., Fleece Hotel, Head Street, Colchester.
BEARD, E. C., St. Margaret's, Cambridge Road, Colchester.
BECKETT, H., Balkerne Lane, Colchester.
BELLWARD, G. W. F., C.R.G.S.
BENHAM, C. E., Wellesley Road, Colchester.
BENHAM, G. C., 12 Hospital Road, Colchester.
BENHAM, Alderman W. GURNEY, St. Mary's Terrace, Lexden road, Colchester.
BIRD, A., Bell House Farm, Stanway.
BLATCH, F., c o, S. E. Blau, La Paz, Bolivia, S. America.
BLAXILL, G. A., "West Wellow," Romsey, Hants.
BLOOMFIELD, S., Raonah House, New Town Road, Colchester.
BLOOMFIELD, H. D., 3 Tyler Street, Parkeston.
BLYTH, COOPER, c.o. Isaac Bunting, 100 Yokahama, Japan.
BRAND, E. J., High Street.
BOGGIS, FRANK, Station Road, Sudbury.
BROMLEY, J. G., Mill House, Great Clacton.
BROOK, T. D., "St. Runwald's," Maldon Road, Colchester.
BROOK, A. T., "St. Runwald's," Maldon Road, Colchester.
BROOK, L. C., "St. Runwald's," Maldon Road, Colchester.
BROOK, S. V., 22 Sugden Road, Lavender Hill, S. W.
BROWN, D. GRAHAM, "Lownd," Witham.
BULTITUDE, R. G., 32 Hanover Road, Canterbury
BURRELL, F. B., Abbeygate Street, Colchester
BUNTING, A. E., The Nurseries, North Station Road, Colchester.

BURLEIGH, A., Kudat, N.L.B.T. Co., British North Borneo.
BURSTON, F. G., 1st National Bank Buildings, San Francisco.
BUTCHER, H., 3 Eden Ave., Liscard, Cheshire.
BUTLER, F. H., Cumberland House, Manningtree.
CAREY, M. C.
CARTER, F. B., C.R.G.S.
CHAMBERS, C., 22 Wellesley Road, Colchester.
CHAMBERS, S. C., 22 Wellesley Road, Colchester.
CHEESE, O. T., 44 Victoria Park Road East, Cardiff.
CHESHIRE, W., 1 Meyrick Crescent, Colchester
CHILD, L. G., 14 Wimpole Road, Colchester.
CLAMP, A. J., 122 Priory Street, Colchester.
CLARK, L. W., 16 East Stockwell Street, Colchester.
CLARKE, S. F., Parr's Bank, Holloway, London, N.
CLOVER, J. M., The Hall, Dedham.
COLE, C. L. L., General Post Office (Staff), Cambridge.
COLE, H. S., 25 Wimpole Road, Colchester.
COLLINGE, C. E., Capital & Counties Bank, Baldock, Herts.
COLLINGE, F. J., 116 High Street.
COLLISON, A. L., Garrison School, Buena Vista, Gibraltar.
CORK, F. F., 38 Trouville Road, Clapham Park, S.W.
CRAGG, Rev. E. E., St. John's Church, Huntington, Long Island, U.S.A.
CULLINGTON, M. W., 53 Oakhill Road, Putney, S.W.
CURTIS, A. P., Bromley Road, Colchester.
DACE, A. W., 122 George Street, Edinburgh.
DACE, E. W., 17 Honywood Road, Colchester.
DALDY, A. T., 50 South Street, Colchester (HON. TREASURER).
DAVIES, W. E., 118 Butt Road, Colchester.
DRAKIN, E. B., C.R.G.S.
DEANE, G. F. F., Longwood, Nayland.
DICKER, B. P., Grocers' Hall, Prince's Street, E.C.
DOUBLEDAY, R. E., Belle Vue Road, Wivenhoe
DOUBLEDAY, W. A., Belle Vue Road, Wivenhoe.
DUNNINGHAM, T. G., Manor Road, Dovercourt.
EVERETT, H. J., Councillor, 28 New Town Road, Colchester.

Continued on Page 3 of Cover.

Capt. CHARLES S. BROOKE.

Suffolk Regiment, attached 1st Queen's Own Royal West Surreys. Twice wounded at Givenchy, September 25th, and awarded the D.S.O. for conspicuous gallantry in action.

The Colcestrian.

VITÆ CORONA FIDES.

No. 44].   MARCH, 1916.   [NEW SERIES.

Editorial.

THE season of Spring, we are assured by the poets, is an idyllic time, in which our fancies tune themselves to a light and airy key, in harmony with Nature's symphony. Casting off the gloom and discomfort of a long winter, the world is newly clad, and sings with the joy of a fresh awakening. The annual miracle of resurrection unfolds itself, and brings with it the message of Hope.

> *" Le tems a laissié son manteau*
> *De vent, de froidure, et de pluye."*

But there is another aspect to the coming of Spring, another reading of its message. Only the more hardy plant has survived the winter cold, only the strongest flower is able to forestall the warmth of summer. The new growth, the resumed activity, the fresh life, are the outcome of long and severe struggle, the result of mighty if unseen effort.

This is the message which the Spring of this year of strife brings to us ; we need not press its application. In a school, where human life is always in its Spring, hope and energy are never wanting, new life is always pulsing. But, to-day, if ever, we must recognise the value of strenuous effort, of persistent work, of patient endurance. Part of the price we must pay for living in such great times is the surrender of much that makes the springtime of life so joyous, for relentless circumstances call our children into the heat and dust of a world of work and strife before they have wearied of the days of careless play.

It is for us to see to it that they are not cheated of their days of Spring, while we prepare them for the trying times ahead.

Travelling.

BOYS are boys everywhere, and I am quite sure that many English schoolboys of 14 to 17 years of age dream of travelling, of having adventures, of marching for days, of sleeping under the blue sky. All of them read Robinson Crusoe from cover to cover and would like to be another Crusoe. But many obstacles are in the way of making this dream a reality. Nevertheless something ought to be done to utilise for the best this love of travelling, and it is certain that our lads would be very glad if during their holidays they could go for a trip of ten days or a fortnight. But such an excursion costs a lot of money, and many parents would object to their boys being alone for such a long time. With a little organisation these arguments can be brought to silence, and we can easily give several of our pupils a ten days' ticket. The most important problems to solve are the railway fares and the lodging.

The first disappears if we travel on foot or on bicycle—both ways offer a lot of advantages. Remains the lodging which is really important. In some countries this question has been solved in the following way. In towns and villages there are some inhabitants, generally persons who have boys too, who are willing to lodge pupils for a night or more at a very low price, some even ask nothing. Every headmaster of a grammar school possesses a list with the names of these persons and their addresses ; he has also cards which are given to the boys who deserve them. Such a card, which is a letter of introduction, states the necessary information as surname, christian name, age, school, address, etc. A boy arrives for instance at Colchester, he presents himself before 4 p.m. at the Grammar School or at the house of one of the subscribers and asks to stay for the night. He shows his card and is accepted. The persons with whom he stays have special post cards which they fill in to announce to the boy's parents that their son has arrived and will remain for one or two days. The boy is well looked after, he enters a new family, makes the acquaintance of some friends of his friends, and feels at home.

I don't know if anything of the kind exists in England, if not I am certain that English people with their practical spirit are able to take profit by it. I need not insist on the advantages of travelling for boys of that age. By rambling about in their own Motherland they learn a lot of useful things, but especially see what England and her inhabitants are like. And they learn also to be men and to act as honourable men. Of course it wants some organisation before it works properly, but the advantages are so great that it deserves a trial.   E. T'KINDT.

Grammaria.

Arma Virumque Cano.

The latest member of the Staff to be engulfed into the insatiable maw of the Army is Mr. Barker. Though we part from him—temporarily, it is to be hoped—with unfeigned regret, he bears with him our best wishes for his military career. He should at all events be in a position to give the Huns a lesson, and his experience as O.C. the Cadet Corps should stand him in good stead. He has been lying at Warley—appropriately so named.

In Loco.

His place has been taken by M. Kindt, whom we heartily welcome as an ally in added sense, inasmuch as he is a native of Belgium—that sorely tried country, which shall yet rise Phœnix-like from its ashes—and a " Professeur d'Anvers."

Deakinal Functions.

News has come to hand from Mr. Deakin, who was last heard of as convalescing from dysentery in the pleasant island of Cyprus. We congratulate him on a complete recovery, and learn with pleasure that he has returned to duty, and is now engaged in keeping the Senussi in order on the Western desert of Egypt, in company with Lieut. Cyril Beard, O.C.

A Welcome Visitor.

Mr. Bellward, too, paid the old school the compliment of spending a day of his scanty " leaf " within its walls. He was as breezy as ever and looked better and fitter than he even usually does. We were delighted to see him once again.

Honorem Quibus Honores.

In the Annual Examination of the " Société des Professeurs de Français en Angleterre," Public School section, A.·O. Ward gained a prize for Dictation and Spoken French, and he also won one of the coveted Harrow Reading Prizes. Our felicitations.

Fincham in the recent Customs Exam. took 69th place out of 1024 candidates. Selah.

Suspicions verified?

The late heavy gales have discovered many weak spots in the buildings of Colchester. Trees and chimney pots and slates were at one time whirling about like Autumn leaves. Sundry rude people have been heard to declare that they were not at all surprised to find that at Gilberd House there were several "tiles loose."

'Snow Joke.

Following close on the heels of the gales came a fall of snow of such depth and persistence as has not been experienced in Colchester for eleven years. Traffic from the country was a virtual impossibility—for a time at any rate, and school closed prematurely, owing to the small attendance, for which, perhaps, the heaviness of the snowfall was not wholly responsible.

The Chamber of Horrors.

The horrors of the Detention Room have been largely increased by the fact that the M.O.D. has his tea brought in to him there. It is two mortal hours since the tuck-shop closed, and the spectacle must indeed be a trying one for the average boy, fat or otherwise, whose misfortunes or misdeeds have led to his internment.

Treasures New and Old.

In India a man out of one cask may not marry a woman out of another cask.

An Angle is a triangle with only two sides.

A Horsepower is the distance one horse can carry one pound of water in one hour.

A Neuter (Bee) is one belonging to another hive, when two hives are at war.

Sinecure—from the latin "sine curâ" (without a cure).

Toujours la Politesse.

In a first French lesson the class was at last able to say: "La vache est un animal domestique." The lesson proceeds.

Master : "Qu'est-ce que la vache ?"

Pupil : "La vache est un animal domestique."

Master : "Now be polite, and say 'Monsieur.'"

Pupil : "Monsieur est un animal domestique ! ! !"

257

"At the Sign of the Ship."

FORMS I. & II.

The First and Second Forms have been joined up this term, but they do not go well together. They are so different in names, habits, ways, minds, laughs and works.

A strange effect of the snowstorm a few days ago was that so many boys seem to have met on the road.

Biographical :—" Aother thng that he dose there is a cudod rid at the Black of the classe rom. He rapes up a litle tin and adress it to someone. He dotes his pencel about the desk and I dont no watall he dose."

*   *   *

FORM III.

One member of the 3rd has been doing war work for the Corporation—eating the snow !

History :—" When the South Sea Bubble was drawn up, in the reign of Stephen, the men placed it on the table and, sending for Cromwell, asked him to sign it ; when he saw the document Cromwell put on a stern look and cried 'Roll up that bauble.' "

We were fiercely attacked by a corps of nurses during the snowstorm and we did our best to supply them with ammunition ; " *toujours galants*."

*   *   *

FORM IVB.

We were very sorry to lose our Form Master and we all hope that he may once more come back to us ; meanwhile we heartily welcome his successor, M. Kindt, one of our gallant Allies.

? Where are our library books ?

Who smote big P ?
" I," said small t,
" I punched his nose
With blows on blows,
I smote big P."

*   *   *

FORM IVA.

Why does X wear specs ? In order to see through the clouds that surround his cranium ?

The daily hymn of the IV. Maths. set :—

> " The first term square, the first term square,
> Then take the product of both terms there
> And multiply by two.
> The second term, to make it fair,
> You also square with utmost care,
> It's the nutty thing to do."

*   *   *

FORM VB.

Does anyone want to talk to Clarke ?

Has anyone found a leg on the playing field ? One of our masters was heard to exclaim that his leg had gone.

We regret to note that we have four eligibles in the Form unattested. (C.C.R.G.S.C.C.)

We miss Wagstaff, Bare and Cotterell ; but we wish them every success in their new work.

*   *   *

FORM VA.

Why are certain people so keenly interested in the health of one's Pater?

Great excitement was caused by the appearance of the porter's trolley. Is it propelled by " Pratt's Spirit " ?

Ought not a vote of thanks to be passed in recognition of the services rendered by our Form Master in the shooting range ? It is, we feel, owing to his enthusiasm and willingness that boys of the Upper School are able to continue shooting.

Formulæ : The Deane of Alderton was a burleigh fellow, stately as a king with his long white beard. He started life as a plummer at Middleton and then became the village smith. One day recently he heard a peacock sing, which gave him a payne " *dans sa tait* " ; he layzell and sick and " mun soon seek the Churchyard." Many a lilley will you c right on his doorstep laid . . . . (*Ed.*—Enough !)

*   *   *

FORM VI.

How are the mighty fallen ! At least the victim has been patriotic enough to decline to receive German germs.

The Idler.—In times of such strenuous effort why not re-name it and do away with at least one *Idler* in the School ?

Pre-Historic.

"IT is an ill wind that blows nobody any good," and certainly owing to the recent weather—which no adjective adequately describes—a certain soldier has accepted quite a cosy pillow for his wounded arm. The story of how he has been obliged to have a part of the bone removed, and of the great pain that followed, found its way to the Pre. The little boys worked with a will during their leisure, when they were obliged to forgo the usual game of football, and in less than a week the pillow was finished. This was, of course, a record! We understand several of our pillows are to be sent out to France. We trust our readers will not grow weary of our "ravelling," but as it is almost the only thing such small folks can do for the wounded we make no apology, but feel a certain amount of pride in doggedly keeping up our number of pillows as the terms go by.

In spite of the war, Christmas came round in due course, and we proposed a Christmas card for the Gostwycke patients. The joy of producing our pennies was very keen, and altogether we were able to buy quite a little collection of gifts for the wounded.

It is not generally known that Mr. Jeffrey very kindly lent us the Art Room on the day we broke up. The Gostwycke patients bravely climbed the stairs and took part in a quaint and very informal entertainment, but how could we say we were going to sing carols after what we listened to in the Big Hall on the previous Sunday afternoon? We own now that we tried to; the Tommies helped us splendidly. Mrs. Craske and Miss Hazell, good natured as ever, helped us too, so did the parents and friends who turned out on that terribly wet afternoon. Mrs. Craske added "Laddie in Khaki" and "Be a Man" to our little programme, and Miss Hazell "My China Town" and other well-chosen songs. Harris recited "The Pride of Battery B," and Francis Gell "What are you doing for them?" Geoffrey Wilson again "talked to his cat." We sang songs too, whose charm lay in the hearty way in which the boys did their best to amuse the heroes before them. The last item ended, the little presents (chocolates, crackers and fruits) were given to the men by two of the boys, and Corporal McLean replied with a few well-chosen words and proposed a hearty cheer for the boys. This was the height of glory, to be thanked by the brave men who had so recently been fighting for their country, overseas. So we separated for our holidays.

At the end of last term Gell, Harris, Imrie and Tait said good-bye to the Pre. We are pleased to know that two of

them have joined the Scouts. To our numbers we have
added Walkden mi., Robinson mi., and last but not least
Chatterton, and, although the youngest boy and living at
Fordham Heath, he is never late!

C.C. & A.J.

Valete.

Form VI – FINCHAM, G. E. : Cpl. Cadet Corps ; Capt. House
Shooting ; School Eight ; Dramatic Society.
Dugard's. K.P. (Civil Service.)

Form VA.—BERRY, W. C. : Cpl. Cadet Band ; House Football and Shooting. Dugard's. (H.M.S. Fisguard.)

COCKADAY, L. C. : Pte. Cadet Corps ; House Cricket,
Football and Hockey. Schoolhouse.

GREEN, M. H. C. : Pte. Cadet Corps ; Dramatic
Society ; 1st Eleven and House Football ; House
Hockey, Cricket and Shooting. Schoolhouse. Q.P.

NICHOLSON, C. : Pte. Cadet Corps ; 1st Eleven Football
and Cricket ; Captain House Cricket ; Hockey and
Football. Probationer Harsnett's.

Form VB.—BARE, H. G. : Cadet Corps ; School Hockey ;
House Cricket, Football, Hockey and Shooting.
Harsnett's.

COTTRELL, R. H. : Pte. Cadet Corps ; 1st Eleven Football ; House Cricket, Football (Capt.) and Hockey.
Schoolhouse.

WAGSTAFF, R. : Pte. Cadet Corps ; 1st Eleven Football ;
Captain House Football ; Cricket, Hockey and
Shooting. Parr's.

Form IVA.—CHAMBERS, L. E. : Pte. Cadet Corps ; 1st Eleven
Football ; House Football, Cricket. Harsnett's.

KENT, J. : P.L. Scouts ; House Cricket, Football and
Shooting. Dugard's.

LAST, H. : Scout. Dugard's.

Form IVB.—RAYNER : Band Cadet Corps ; 1st Eleven Football and Cricket ; House Hockey. Schoolhouse.

Form III.—HICKINBOTHAM, T. : Scout. Schoolhouse.

Pre.—D. Wheatley.

P. Callaway.

Temp. 2nd Lieut. EDWIN COOPER SCOTT:

MILITARY CROSS.

Temp. 2nd Lt. EDWIN COOPER SCOTT, 12th Bn. The Duke of Cambridge's Own (Middlesex Regt.), attached 178th Tunnelling Co. R.E., was awarded the Military Cross for conspicuous gallantry and devotion to duty near Tambour du Clos, where on two occasions he organised and led parties to the rescue of gassed miners. On the second occasion, Sept. 6th, 1915, he led a party down a shaft 55 feet deep and saved the lives of six miners who were gassed. He remained down till he thought all were rescued, and was then brought up, himself almost overcome, and laid on a bed ; but, on hearing that all the miners had not been rescued, he endeavoured to return, although still suffering from the effects of gas. He showed great coolness and absolute disregard of personal danger.

Salvete.

Forms I and II.	Low, R. D.	...	... Schoolhouse
	Heath-Robinson, G. H.	...	... Harsnett's
	Roberts, S.	...	... Schoolhouse
	Smith, C. E.	...	... Schoolhouse
	Walden, C. G.	...	... Parr's
	Woollard, W.	...	... Harsnett's
	Wells, L.	...	... Dugard's
	Pratt, J.	... -	... Parr's
Form III.	Tarr, W.	...	... Dugard's
	Powell, B.	: ...	... Dugard's
Form IVB.	Dyer, E.	...	... Harsnett's
	Pattle, H. L.	...	... Schoolhouse
	Procter, H. W. ..		... Harsnett's
Pre.	Walkden, mi.		
	Heath-Robinson, mi.		
	Chatterton.		

Cadet Corps.

(ATTACHED TO 5TH ESSEX).

THE outstanding event of this session is the loss of Mr. F. D. Barker, who is now in the 3rd Essex, on garrison duty at Dovercourt ; the revised regulations as to eyesight tests enabled him to join up after five disappointments earlier in the war. He is the fourth successive O.C. of the School Corps to go on active service. Already we miss his genial personality and his skilful direction, and can only hope to carry on with plodding effort, in the endeavour to improve ourselves on the lines he laid down. The two small gifts with which we marked his going are but a slight expression of our gratitude for all his hard work, and of our great esteem.

*　*　*

Our chief aim during the rest of the term must be to smarten up the more elementary movements, and general bearing on parade ; what was before the war a rather jolly game has now a serious and important significance. We look to our N.C.O.'s to be the principal factors here, and those who take the Corps work seriously will have ample opportunity for practice in command. They must study the given portions of the text-book well, getting the orders and instructions verbatim, and practising giving them aloud, clearly and crisply. Each platoon will have to produce candidates for stripes as the seniors leave us.

A most interesting lecture on the History of Musketry was given by Lieut. Tyson (8th Essex) on Friday, February 25th. With a wealth of example, both historical and humorous, he made plain the meaning of the saying "the object is to secure and to maintain, a superiority of fire over the enemy."

Lieut. Thornton (8th Essex) will leeture on the Hand Grenade on Friday, March 10th.

* * *

The Sectional work carried on on Saturdays reveals great keenness, and with more method and definite purpose should produce good results. Cadets who find section work easier than the school work of the last period will be given the opportunity of resuming that school subject.

* * *

As noted elsewhere, we hope to revive the Recruits' Cup, in the form of a trophy, to be held for one year, for the smartest, keenest recruit. We shall try to present it at the end of the school year, and it will be open to all cadets who joined in September, 1915, or after.

It is hoped that Cadets will remember that the C.O. is able to receive subscriptions, issue stores and discuss corps matters—suggestions will always be welcomed—on Fridays, between 1.30 and 3 p.m. As the new O.C. has several other little duties connected with the school, he hopes that this will be duly noted.

* * *

We are now 60 strong, and have passed nearly 180 Cadets through the Corps.

* * *

We welcome Deane, Cameron, Dyer, Cosser, Procter, Sier, Hayes and Nash as recruits. Wilson ma., Hazell ma. and Smith mi. have also joined up since our last report.

* * *

There are now no vacancies in the Corps ; boys desirous of joining next term should give in their names at once.

J.A.P.

We wish to acknowledge, with thanks, the receipt of :—

"The Stonyhurst Magazine"   "Chigwellian"
"Leopard"   "Chelmsfordian"
"Framlinghamian"   "Pelican"
"L.O.S. Magazine"   "Wyggestonian"
"Ipswichian"

Shooting.

DURING the present term the range has been closed to boys under the age of 15, so that our number of members has considerably decreased and is now reduced to 34, about evenly distributed between the two classes "over" and "under" 16.

The range is only opened on two days a week, and there is generally quite a rush of members during the after school session, while several shooters regard the warm hut as a pleasant place to rest in during the dinner hour.

Scores have not ruled very high up to the present, but on the other hand there are not many really weak shots amongst the members, and we hope to be able to record higher scores when the weather and light improve.

In the averages for last term the best scores were :— Seniors, Percy 54·2 ; under 16, Wagstaff 47·6 ; Juniors, Rose 43·4·

* * *

The final round of the House Competition will be concluded during the third week in March, and it looks like a certain win for School House, who at present hold a lead of 64 points over Dugard's. In last term's competition School House again came out on top, increasing their lead of the previous term by 50 points, while Parr's dropped from second to third place on the list.

Below are the scores up to date :—

SCHOOL HOUSE.		DUGARD'S.		PARR'S.		HARSNETT'S.	
Rayner	... 62	Kent	... 58	Percy	... 55	Cox	... 57
Middleton	... 60	Berry	... 53	Rose	... 51	Burleigh	.. 55
Crighton	... 58	Plummer	... 52	Wheeler	... 51	Bare	... 51
Layzell	... 53	Halls	... 51	Wagstaff	 50	Rickword	... 49
Green	... 52	Bugg	... 50	Andrews	... 47	Clark	... 49
Pertwee	... 51	Wells	... 50	French	... 44	Smith	... 40
Lilley	... 41	Bacon	... 41	Hunneyball ...	25	Thomas	... 40
Cottrell	... 40	Fincham	... 35	Collinge	... 13	Farquharson...	36
	417		390		336		380
Summer	.. 420		383		406		356
Total	... 837		773		742		736

E. R.

Scouting Notes.

THE winter season obviously does not afford many opportunities for outdoor work, but there is much to be done in anticipation of the return of Spring and better weather. One group of boys is persevering with bugle practice, another is working steadily for the Ambulance test, and a third at signalling.

* * *

I am glad to find several scouts helping regularly at the Public Hall Social Club twice a week, but I should like just to remind them that they go there to *help*, and not just to have a good time, and also that it is contrary to the Scout Law to accept any payment whatever for a "good turn."

* * *

Just before Christmas each troop in the Local Association was asked to distribute leaflets appealing for donations towards the Belgian Relief Fund, and the senior boys under Kent's guidance did this in their allotted district in a businesslike manner which did them credit.

* * *

There was also keen competition amongst the patrols as to which could earn the most money for the Scouts' Motor Ambulance, referred to in the last issue of these "Notes," and altogether the troop raised £3 12s. 9d.

* * *

Five boys have left the troop. Kent, Last and Hickinbotham have left the School, and Hazell and Cosser have become Cadets. This term's recruits are Gell, Low, Harris and Tarr. Amongst the boys who have left none will be missed more than John Kent, our senior patrol leader. He had been a member of the troop since its foundation in January, 1912, and was a First Class Scout in every sense of the term. There is no boy who has done more for the good name and welfare of the troop as a whole, and the keenness and good work of the Peewit Patrol are very largely due to his leadership.

* * *

Whilst speaking of these, I should like to remind the patrol leaders how much the smartness of the troop depends upon them. It is in fact quite impossible to run a troop of fifty scouts without the help of half a dozen senior boys who are willing to give up their time, and who have the ability to act as real leaders of their patrols. It is often hard and discouraging work, but it is well worth doing, and it is a fine thing for a patrol leader to know, when the time comes for him to pass on to the Cadet Corps or leave the school, that he has trained up a scout to take his place and carry on. This is the only way to make a good tradition and keep it.

G.E.P.

Speech Day.

DECEMBER 9TH, 1915.

A DISTINGUISHED gathering assembled for the presentation of prizes in Big School, the Mayor and Corporation attending in state. The Mayor (Councillor A. G. Aldridge) in introducing Dr. Caldecott, spoke of the Headmaster's approaching retirement, and congratulated the school on its successes.

In the Head's report which followed, these successes were detailed, and the excellent report of His Majesty's Inspectors. who gave a searching inspection last Lent term, was quoted, " The School has achieved a very honourable place of its own amongst schools of its type," was the verdict of the inspectors. Speaking of the representation of the school on the Field, the Head pointed out that of some 370 eligible men, 257 are already serving—70 per cent. of our " possibles." have become " actuals." He spoke, too, of the evident love for the old School, as evinced by the steady flow of visitors—often on very short leave—renewing acquaintance with their *mater nutrix* of earlier days.

The Headmaster drew attention to the fact that Colchester School, founded in the town in 1539 from monastic revenues connected with the place, and having a proud record behind it, is strangely neglected by the Colchester of to-day, which sends 21 boys a year on an average out of its 42,000 inhabitants.

Dr. Caldecott, in his address, traced the development of the School since the appointment of Mr. Shaw Jeffrey, when Dr. Caldecott was on the Board of Governors. He said that the " power to learn " was what school life offered boys to-day, as it had been given to Shakespeare, who left a Tudor Grammar School at the age of thirteen. He spoke of the perplexities confronting young men in those times of stress, and appealed to the boys to " listen to the highest voice, and when they heard it to follow it along the path to which it called them, without faltering step."

After the votes of thanks, associated with the names of Alderman Wilson Marriage, Councillor Wallace, Bishop Harrison and Sir Kenelm Digby, had been carried with acclamation, the War Certificates were awarded to the prizewinners, and the School Gaudy was sung.

A scene from " Julius Cæsar," produced by Mr. F. B. Carter, was performed by selected boys, whose elocution was clear and distinct.

Carol Service.

DECEMBER 19TH, 1915.

THE *Essex County Standard*, after a glowing description of
the transformed Big School, says :—"The choir consisted of some thirty voices, supported by a string quartette,
led by Miss M. South Adams, with Mr. F. D. Barker at the
piano. The absence of that reedy, almost watery tone, so
often observed in choirs which consist in the main of treble
voices, was noticeable, the general effect being full and
mellow. Elvey's " Come ye lofty " was sung as processional,
while the Headmaster, Mr. Shaw Jeffrey, supported by Bishop
Harrison and members of the staff, entered the room. Each
carol was followed by a lesson read by a member of the
school : Clarke, Horwood, Smith, Andrews, Cameron, Pertwee, Ward, Marlar and Burleigh performed their part of the
service well, reading distinctly and comprehensively. Among
the carols were Ouseley's " Listen Lordings," " What Child
is This ? " " A Virgin Unspotted," " On the birthday of the
Lord," " The Manger Throne," and " The Snow lay deep."
The choir is the fortunate possessor of several extremely
good voices, which were heard to advantage in the sweet
solos which occur in many of the carols. It was under the
direction of Mr. J. A. Peart. Before the conclusion of the
service a short address was given by Bishop Harrison, whose
homely but deeply spiritual words gave added significance to
the Christmas festival, held in such sad circumstance."

With the proceeds a gramophone was purchased for the
wounded soldiers in the Essex County Hospital.

Harsnett's House Singings.

IN the draw for the order of precedence of the House
Singings, Harsnetts came out first. Of course, short
time would not particularly matter to a House which has such
a clever House-master at the head of affairs, but owing to
many charitable shows in the town, it was only with great
difficulty that one could get together the necessary people for
rehearsal. At any rate when the time came a good and varied
programme was presented. Rickword, Bare and Cameron
gave a short sketch " The Bottled Bequest" ; Peacock sang
" Reuben Banjo " ; Cameron, "Lady Moon" ; and a general
choir gave two ragtime ditties ; special items were La Barbe's
violin solo "Tirpitz's Dream " ; the scene from Macbeth in
which each character was quadrupled ; and the Lightning

Sketches by White, ma. We discovered quite a good performer in Farquharson. Of a good presence, he has a most clear enunciation, and with a little more repose should be quite useful in the Thespian activities of the School. He gave a patter song "Modern Languages" with vigour and point.

The evening finished with a representation of "The Conversion of Nat Sturge," in which Ward was quite good as the Bishop, while White ma. took the part of Nat, the burglar. His assistant was Burleigh ma., and Taylor was the lisping daughter of the Bishop. The play was well presented and caused hearty laughter.

F.B.C.

Schoolhouse House Singings.

ON the 11th of December Schoolhouse presented a good and varied programme at their Annual House Singing. It commenced with a spirited pianoforte solo, ably executed by Miller ma. The most noticeable performance in the first part of the programme was the singing of "Does this shop stock shot silk socks with spots," by Baker, who rendered this tongue-twisting lay with perfect clearness of utterance and with clever gestures. Crighton sang "Wee doch and dorris," and our nightingale, Barnes, was in good voice in the song "In an old-fashioned town," responding with the ever fresh "Cockles and Mussels." The band was very much in evidence. The evening finished with a presentation of "War Mates," the recruiting play. The four characters in this were represented by Tait as the Foreman, Middleton as the Leader of the Strikers, Green as the V.C. returned from the trenches, and Pertwee as Mary. In this little drama Green was decidedly good and this was a part of long declamatory speeches—which always are difficult to deliver effectively—and he held us, and even once sent a shiver down our backs, a sure sign of success. Pertwee, as always, looked winsome. The other parts would have been much better for more rehearsal, but the many charitable activities in the town had left us little time to get our performers together. The House Gaudy finished up quite a successful show.

F.B.C.

House Singings.

OUR fortnightly sing-songs have been unusually stale and unprofitable, reflecting upon the energy and resource of the House officers, and causing an obvious shrinkage in our audiences. With the exception of good items by Weeks, Low, Alderton and Tarr there are no new features worthy of note.

This is bound to react on the House House-singings, and to impoverish future attempts ; we must see to it that we be ready to fill the gap when the theatres and cinemas are taxed out of existence.

* * *

Despite the many calls upon their time which the above engagements have necessitated, the Concert Party for the Troops continued their good work last term. Among our happiest memories are the entertainment at Headgate Club, and the run out to Great Horkesley, where Mrs. Lermitte made our visit most enjoyable. We shall hope to include new talent in the troupe, should our activities develop.

* * *

On Saturday, February 19th, some friends gave us an excellent show. The pretty Scotch dance by Miss R. Slaughter, the two delightful songs from Miss Hilda Hazell, the fine recitals by Miss Harley, and the tasteful solos by Miss M. Harley, gave an unwonted note of finish to our House Singing. Two old friends, Mr. Barnes with his violin, and Mr. Farmer with songs, were enthusiastically welcomed. With the Headmaster in two French ditties, Mr. Widlake at the piano, and Mr. Carter in his own inimitable vein, the staff was well represented. Our cordial thanks to all the artistes.

* * *

Surely, with the honeyed words of the Press on the one hand, and the bemoaning of the music master on the other, and with such a record of artistic achievement before them, individual performers and the choir as a whole will take heart of grace, and spur on to greater efforts ?

J.A.P.

Hippodrome, November 24th-25th.

THE School rallied to the help of Mrs. W. B. Slaughter, who gave an enjoyable matinee, in aid of the Basket Fund for the Wounded. Between each curtain in a series of patriotic tableaux, the School choir sang National Anthems, seated the while in the boxes, to the perturbation of the people in the stalls, who saw visions of boys falling bomb-like on their innocent heads.

Pertwee, as Herald, emulated the Town Sergeant (old style), and Clarke, heavily disguised, succeeded in "taking the cake," although pursued by a string of pretty coons.

The matinee was rounded off by "The Conspiracy," played by request by the C.R.G.S.D.S. Farquharson's first appearance as the King was highly successful, and the Nobles were a distinct improvement on their predecessors. Mr. F. D. Barker as Brunfels gave the necessary " Prussian." touch to the play, which was well received by the audience. Mr. F. B. Carter, unseen but all-pervading, was invaluable " behind," although suffering acutely because his speech was cut out.

Mrs. Slaughter has shown her appreciation of Mr. Jeffrey's help and the boys' co-operation by promising another show.

2nd Lieut. GILBERT FRANCE WATSON.

D.S.O.

2nd Lieut. GILBERT FRANCE WATSON, Welsh Field Co., Welsh Div. Engineers, R.E. (T.F.). For conspicuous gallantry near Hooge. On the night of Sept. 24-25, 1915, he made an excellent reconnaissance of the enemy's wire, and on the 25th crawled out with two men and successfully cut it before the assault. During the assault, with a party of twelve sappers and twenty-five infantry, he dug 80 yards of a communication trench in two hours, under very heavy fire, by which nearly three-quarters of his men became casualties. He then reported for instructions, and took the remains of his party into the captured positions in order to consolidate them. When retirement was ordered he got back to our original trenches with one sergeant, who was killed almost at once, and three or four men ; and, finding the trenches unoccupied, he collected about twenty-five men of the 4th Batt. Gordon Highlanders, and held on until relieved by another battalion after dark. Second Lieut. Watson set a fine example of bravery and devotion to duty.

Moot Hall Concert, December 21st.

REPORTING this Concert, the success of which was largely due to the ready help of the School, the Press states : " All who were present greatly enjoyed the excellent programme, and practically all the artistes had to re-appear in response to encores.

"A considerable share in the Concert was taken by the choir of the C.R.G.S., who charmed the audience with their carols. These were rendered with a reverence and beauty of style that spoke of careful training, and the effect was enhanced by the organ accompaniment of Mr. W. Christian Everett, or the orchestral accompaniment of Miss South Adams' string quartette. The concluding carol was 'Gloria Domino,' words by the Headmaster."

The organiser of the Concert wishes to thank the talented performers, who made the Concert, from the artistic point of view, one of the most successful ever associated with the School, and the boys, who made a financial success of it.

J.A.P.

Debating Society.

SINCE the issue of the last magazine we have held two ordinary meetings of the Society and one impromptu debate. Our numbers are keeping up well, and there is a great deal of keenness among the smaller boys, but we are not getting adequate support from the Fifth Forms, and in consequence debates are becoming more and more like our ordinary House Singings—all the work is being left to a select few.

Under the new arrangement we require four prepared speeches for each debate. Two of these need only be quite short—the seconders are allowed only five minutes—and if more boys in the Fifths would become regular speakers and make a point of getting up and saying something at every debate, they would soon gain enough confidence to second either the proposer or opposer of a motion.

During the present session we have had six speakers from VA., and five from VB., and half this number have spoken at only one debate out of four. Surely there could be some improvement in this direction.

We are always pleased to welcome suggestions for subjects from members, especially if the members are themselves willing to support or oppose their subjects.

SUMMARY OF MEETINGS.

Sat., Nov. 13th.—Debate.—" That, in the opinion of this House, man should not eat meat."
        Proposed by Ward.   Seconder, Fincham.
        Opposed by Andrews. Seconder, Rickword.
The motion was lost by 43 votes to 11.

Sat., Dec. 4th.—Impromptu Debate.

Sat., Feb. 5th.—Debate.—"That, in the opinion of this House, detailed accounts (official) of Zeppelin raids should be published within twenty-four hours of the raid."
        Proposed by Andrews. Seconder, Rickword.
        Opposed by French.   Seconder, Middleton.
The motion was carried by 23 votes to 11.

A.O.W.

football.

Nov. 13th.—C.R.G.S. v. SATURDAY RANGERS.

This match resulted in the School's first victory. White, Green, Wagstaff and Smith scored. Result, 4—1.

Dec. 11th.—C.R.G.S. v. COLCHESTER JUNIORS.

The School kicked against a very strong wind in the first half, during which the Juniors scored twice. In the second the School had bad luck, several shots hitting the posts, but Wagstaff scored near the end. Result, lost 1—2.

Dec. 16th.—C.R.G.S. v. THURSDAY ROVERS.

This was a very one-sided game ; the School won 9—0. Cheshire (3), Wagstaff (2), French, Green, White and Farquharson scored.

Dec. 18th.—C.R.G.S. v. 1ST COLCHESTER SCOUT TROOP.

An excellent game was lost by 2—1. Chambers scored for the School. Alderton played well in goal.

HOUSE MATCHES.

Nov. 4th.—HARSNETT'S v. SCHOOL HOUSE.

Harsnett's won the toss and kicked against the wind. Within the first five minutes White scored for Harsnett's from an excellent corner taken by Nicholson. There was no further scoring until near the end, when Smith scored Harsnett's second, Harsnett's thus winning by 2—0.

Nov. 18th.—HARSNETT'S v. PARR'S.

The first half of this match was very evenly and keenly contested, but neither side scored, although several opportunities were missed. In the second half, Parr's defence fell away, although Wagstaff played an excellent game. From a corner White scored for Harsnett's, and a very few minutes after Salew scored again. Parr's retaliated, and from an excellent centre from Wagstaff, Osborne ma. scored. Near the end, from a corner, Andrews deflected the ball into his own goal, Harsnett's thus winning by 3—1.

Dec. 2nd.—HARSNETT'S v. DUGARD'S.

There was not much doubt as to which House the cup would go, for within the first ten minutes White scored for Harsnett's, Smith added another, and before half-time White scored again. In the second half, goals came very quickly ; Salew (3), White (2) and Smith (1) again scored for Harsnett's. Harsnett's thus won 9—0.

Nov. 4th.—DUGARD'S v. PARR'S.

This match resulted in a win for Parr's, with a score of 3—1. Parr's goals were scored by Cheshire, Wagstaff and Osborne ma. Gilbert scored Dugard's goal.

Nov. 18th.—DUGARD'S v. SCHOOL HOUSE.

Dugard's defeated School House 2—1. Spencer and Wells scored for Dugard's, and Rayner scored for School House. The slippery nature of the ground greatly assisted Dugard's.

SCHOOL HOUSE v. PARR'S.

One of the third round of House matches. Played on a fine day. The play was fairly even throughout the game. Result, a win for Parr's 2—1. French and Cheshire scored for Parr's, and Cottrell for School House.

Old Colcestrian Section.

Editorial.

WINTER in the trenches gave many combatant O.C.'s the opportunity of a short visit to their homes, and much we learnt from them which, with the fear of the Censor before our eyes, we hesitate to lay before our readers in cold print, but in two conditions our welcome visitors agreed they were cheerily optimistic, and amazingly fit and well. Hardships and open air in combination are evidently a better prescription for one's bodily health than even Tono-Bungay.

OUR BUDGET.

A belated letter from Mrs. A. S. Mason, at Dalhousie in the Himalayas, gives a pleasant account of life in the high lands. "We have a very delightful bungalow for the winter, and so far Indian house-keeping has not proved so terrible as I expected. Dalhousie is very quiet, but we get some tennis still, and my husband (Capt. A. S. Mason of the Devon Yeomanry—Ed.), gets some good shooting. The sun is always very bright, and one needs a sun helmet even when it is freezing in the shade. About 2000 people from Kashmir have stayed lately in Dalhousie on their way to Chamba for the marriage of the Rajah's daughter, but no Europeans went."

Since this letter was written, Capt. Mason and the Devons have joined up with the Indian troops withdrawn from the western front and have transferred to the Persian relief expedition.

* * *

Lieut. J. F. Watson, D.S.O., writes on Jan. 31st, from the Ypres salient :—" I have only met one O.C. out here, namely, Brand, of the 5th London T.F. A short time back the Huns attacked, using gas, but they never got a footing in our trenches, and our guns gave them an awful time. Last week, however, they blew up one of our trenches and did considerable damage. We retaliated by blowing in one of their sapheads.

Everyone out here is *most* cheerful and optimistic. We have now plenty of artillery and plenty of ammunition, and we are all getting very impatient and anxious to receive our order to march on Berlin. I have been out here eight months now, and am thoroughly fed up with trench warfare. I got promoted full Lieutenant last October. I consider myself jolly lucky, seeing I only joined as a Sapper in September, 1914! Also, I consider myself lucky indeed in other respects as Heaven alone knows why I am still alive"!!

* * *

J. L. Watson, elder brother of G. F., who has been fighting for ten months with the Canadian Scottish, hopes shortly to get a Commission in the Welsh Fusiliers.

Capt. W. B. Anthony, of the Durham L.I., has transferred to the Air Service, and is engaged in the hazardous business of the London air patrol.

G. F. Butler has been dangerously ill in Netley with enteric, but is making a good recovery, and R. V. Jarmin, of the R.A.M.C., who was badly gassed. and brought home to England as a stretcher case, has also we are glad to hear turned the corner.

*   *   *

L. R. R. Cole, of the R.E. telegraph. section, writes that when in his dugout before the battle of Loos he saw several O.C.'s he knew march past along the road below him—T. S. Renton for one, but the noise was so great he could not attract their attention.

*   *   *

Corporal Cullington of the Civil Service Rifles, has a poor opinion of the Loos salient. It is all chalky ooze which nearly pulls the foot slogger's boots off, and it had one tree but that has since been cut down. He wishes for his own personal comfort the Germans would retake the position.

*   *   *

C. W. Chambers has been driving an ambulance back and forth across the market square of Ypres for months together, and considers it a most unhealthy spot. He had the misfortune to crush his knee.

*   *   *

His brother, Armourer Staff-Sergeant A. S. Chambers, is looking after a battery of 16 heavy guns in the Ypres salient, and his cousin, R. Chambers, has joined the R.A.M.C.

*   *   *

Sergt. A. E. Green, of the 9th Essex, has been recommended for a commission. He was in the trenches one Thursday morning near Ypres when the order came along that Sergt. Green was to report himself at once at Headquarters in England for a commission. He had been five days in trenches without a wash, and he had in prospect a 15 miles' walk to railhead at Poperinghe. He had hardly got out of the trenches when the Germans started a furious bombardment and he took shelter behind a ruined wall in Ypres. Here he found an imposing motor car with a chauffeur in attendance. When the owner appeared he proved to be the General Commanding the 4th Army. On hearing Green's story he insisted on driving him into Poperinghe, handed him over to the Chaplain with instructions that he was to be thoroughly well looked after, and parted from him with the most cordial good wishes.

A. E. G. has a greatly-improved opinion of the Higher Command.

*   *   *

Sub.-Lieut. "Curly" Taylor, of the Royal Naval Brigade, told us many good tales of life at Groningen prior to his escape on Whit-Monday last. Many devices were tried by the prisoners. Two men got off by rolling themselves up in the matting used for the cricket pitch, and were convoyed into the town on a lorry by Dutch guards. The prisoners' tennis courts abutted on to a wood, and two of the players made good their escape by hitting tennis balls over into the wood where some of their comrades who had passes for the town were in hiding. These cut open the tennis balls, inserted the passes and threw the balls back. The players used the passes to get past the guard, and after returning them to their original owners made tracks and vanished into the circumambient air.

Taylor's escape involved buying mufti from a fish hawker, hocussing a sentry's beer, and walking 40 miles straight off the reel on the first day of freedom. He and his companion reached the coast in three days, and arrived in Colchester in due course very little the worse for wear. On reporting himself at Headquarters A. G. T. was made a Sub-Lieutenant.

* * *

H. P. Rickard of the 1st British Columbia Regt., grievously wounded by shrapnel nine months ago, has had in all nine operations, but is now happily out of hospital.

* * *

Our new D.S.O., Capt. C. B. Brook, of the 1st Queen's Own Royal West Surrey. was twice wounded at Givenchy, Sept. 25th, 1915; before giving in. He was first shot in the jaw, losing two of his teeth, but went on until he was shot again through the chest. As with a becoming modesty he refuses all details of his exploits, we must wait until the official announcement appears. In the meantime we publish portraits of of our three junior heroes, and we hope in our next issue to give portraits of our two seniors, Lieut.-Colonel A. J. Turner, D.S.O., R.F.A., and Major A. S. M. Richie, D.S.O., of The Queen's Bays, whose tale of medals now runs into double figures.

* * *

R. T. Cudmore, Essex Yeomanry, appears in the list of wounded, but no particulars are to hand.

* * *

Lieut. O. Siggers, R.D., R.N.R., now serving on board H.M.S. " Magnificent," has been awarded the Royal Decoration.

* * *

The funeral took place recently of Mr. Edwin Habgood, late principal of Cary College. who resided at 142 Brightwell Avenue, Westcliff. The deceased, who was 63 years of age, died suddenly. He was born at Colchester, was educated at the Grammar School there, and for some time was headmaster at the Medical College, Kingston, Surrey. At Southend he was well known as "The Poor People's Friend." His benevolence was so marked that he impoverished himself to gratify his wishes. He leaves a widow, two sons and two daughters. Both sons are on active service.

Pioneering

FOR THE Y.M.C.A. IN GERMAN SOUTH WEST AFRICA.

By H. V. Marsh (O.C.)

" WELL, that's Walvis, is it ? " A few tin shanties in a flat desert of sand, and four or five chimneys, belonging to the condensing plant, are all that meet the eye, as the party gaze from the deck of H.M.S. " Erna Woermann." Not an inviting spot by any stretch of imagination.

After our last breakfast on board we pass down the gangway with all our personal luggage and deposit it on a launch. A second tender comes alongside while we wait, and so Mr. Holmes and I change over to it, leaving Mr. Haarhoff and Mr. Stowe to come with the luggage later. As we traverse the half mile or so to shore we see one of our aeroplanes rise, which we are told General Smuts is coming down to-day to inspect. Our little boat is filled with men all keen and anxious to get to work, and amongst them are many we have got to know during the short trip up from the Cape.

We sit patiently on top of our luggage from 12 o'clock and fill in the time making a lunch from the wonderful resources of a large biscuit tin packed by loved ones away Natal-wards, which seems to have no bottom. No one seems to be in charge to give definite information about anything, and so the time passes till 3.30 ; we fill it in studying the aeroplanes flying through the air far above us, watching General Smuts as he rides off on his motor trolley from close to where we sit, or looking at the whale bones with which some tents are adorned. A visit is paid, by each of us in turn, to the S.A.G.I. for a drink of cocoa. In the distance are seen the new sheds for the aeroplanes, and round us are buzzing the motor trolleys belonging to this section of our Army.

Suddenly we see a train in motion some 400 yards away and find it is the one for which we have so patiently been waiting, but instead of coming to Mahomet we find Mahomet has to go to where it is now waiting, and that pretty quickly too, if we wish to catch it. So the heavy luggage has to be humped along again at the double, and thrown upon an open truck of mails, while we two scramble on the top of it, not before we have found time to greet a Maritzburg boy, Lieut. Wilson, O.C. Comforts, whom we are pleased to meet so far from home. With wonderful punctuality the mid-day train steams out at 10 past 4 o'clock, and we are at last upon our way.

Rand Rifle Siding is our first and only stop,—just a few tents on a lonely patch, — a half way house for convoys.

Our route lies through what might be described as a huge cemetery for whales, for scattered thickly upon both sides are the skeletons of these mighty monsters of the deep, some lying 30 or 40 feet above high water mark, some 200 or 300 feet inland. Many of the sandbag blockhouses, past which we fly, with their names inscribed in fancy pebbles, are adorned with hump-back jawbones, ribs and vertebræ. One is reminded of the word Walvis (Whale Fish), and we wonder how many scores of years have passed, perhaps hundreds, since these mighty denizens ploughed their way among the deep waters of the Bay.

The Happy Warrior.

Who, deemed to go in company with Pain,
And Fear, and Bloodshed, miserable train !
Turns his necessity to glorious gain.
This is the happy warrior ; this is he
Whom every man in arms should wish to be

THE following is a list of O.C.'s who are known to be
serving—or who, alas ! have served—with the colours
on active service. It will be seen that they come from many
quarters of the globe to answer their country's call. The list
is revised and brought up to date, but the Headmaster would
be glad to hear of additions to the number, and of any corrections or transfers necessary to make our Roll of Honour
complete.

Andrew, M., Inns of Court O.T.C.
Allen, Rev. C. A. B., Naval Chaplain, H.M.S. "Glory."
Archer, E. R., Royal Navy
Anthony, W. B., Capt., Durham Light Infantry (Air
      Service).
Allen, Thompson, Essex Yeomanry (killed in action)
Allen, F., Royal Engineers (Australian Expeditionary
      Force)
Appleby, R. J., Dublin University O.T.C. and Sandhurst
      Military College
Atkin, G., London Irish Rifles

Bastable, R., Inns of Court O.T.C.
Blowers, F. J., London Regiment
Bentley, W. H., Hon. Artillery Company
Burke, A. G., Inns of Court O.T.C.
Barren, R. T., Essex and Suffolk R.G.A.
Brook, Capt. C. S., D.S.O., 1st Q.O. Royal West Surrey
Burridge, G. J., 5th Lancers
Burrell, B. F., 10th Essex Regiment
Barnes, Dr. F. M., Captain, R.A.M.C.
Bellward, G. E. F., Lieutenant, 5th Essex
Benham, G. C., Captain (8th Essex), Staff Captain 7th
      Prov. Brigade.
Beard, E. C., 2nd Lieut., 5th Essex
Bromley, J. G., Motor Unit, A.S.C.
Bultitude, F. S., 8th Essex Cyclists
Bunting, A. E., 2nd Lieut., 13th Essex

Baskett, T., Royal Naval Brigade (present at Antwerp)
Butler, G. F., Public Schools Battalion (invalided)
Bareham, C., Essex Yeomanry
Bond, C. T., Australian Contingent
Barnes, A. W. H., Capt., R.A.M.C.
Barnes, J. C. C., Lieut., Border Regt.
Becker, C. H., Royal West Surrey (died of wounds)
Blomfield, A., 2nd Lieutenant R.F.A.
Barker, F. D., 3rd Essex
Becker, Colonel C. T., temp. Brigadier-General
Bawtree, D. E., 2nd Lieut., 8th Yorks
Bacon, S. F., Royal Navy
Brand, Eric J., London Rifle Brigade
Bowen, Capt. Hugh, Essex Regt. (wounded), Staff Capt.
Bare, W. J., 8th Essex
Balm, A. H., Hon. Artillery Company
Beckett, H., Royal Fusiliers
Barker, C. E., 2nd Lieutenant Goorkha Rifles
Baxter, H. G., 10th Middlesex Regiment
Barker, J., Essex Yeomanry (missing)
Barker, H., Royal Engineers
Bailey, H., Royal Naval Brigade
Bailey, A. G., R.N.D.
Burgess, H. G., Army Service Corps

Caines, E. C., Essex Yeomanry
Cork, F. F., Civil Service Rifles
Cullington, M. W., Civil Service Rifles
Cheshire, G., 10th Essex
Cheshire, W. R., 2nd Lieut., Ceylon Planters Rifles
Chambers, C. W., Mechanical Transport, A.S.C.
Chambers, A. S., R.G.A., Heavy Gun Section
Clarke, L. 5th Essex
Collins, R. C., 2nd Lieut., 20th Hussars
Collinson, A. L., Censor Eastern Tel., Gibraltar
Cudmore, H. T., Essex Yeomanry (wounded)
Cobbold, H. J. T., Royal Naval Reserve (wounded)
Clover, J. M., Inns of Court O.T.C.
Collinge, C. E., Inns of Court O.T.C.
Chambers, R., R.A.M.C.
Caldecott, R., Royal Engineers (invalided)
Cobbold, R. G., Canadian Contingent (wounded)
Campling, C. D., 2nd Lieut., 12th Essex
Coquerel Rene, 3rd Infanterie, Brest
le Coeuvre, Albert, Infanterie de Reserve
Collins, H., 2nd Lieut., 8th Essex
Craske, S. F., Hants Cyclists

Chignell, S. C., 10th Bn. Canadians (killed at Ypres)
Clamp, G., 5th Essex
Cottrell, H. J., Sportsman's Battalion
Cole, L. R. R., Royal Engineers
Collinge, R. D., Inns of Court O.T.C.

Denton, C. W., Captain. 8th Essex
Denton, A., Captain, 5th Essex (killed in action, Gallipoli)
Denton, H. W., Public Schools Battalion
Davis, E. G., Captain and Adjutant, 8th Essex
Davies, E. J., Australian Contingent
Deakin, E. B., Capt. and Adjutant, 5th Essex
Deane, G. F. F., Public Schools Battalion
Davies, E. G., H.M.S. " Indomitable "
Dunningham, A. E. (killed in action)

Everett, W. R., 10th Essex (invalided)
Everett, C. E. F., 2nd Lieut., Loyal North Lancs.
Essex, P. C., Royal Naval Reserve
Essex, B. E., Public Schools Battalion
Eley, D. M., 1st Lieut., R.F.A.
Eves, F. J., Victoria Rifles

Folkard, W. E., A.O.C.
Fenn, E. G., Essex Yeomanry
Fitch, L., Essex Yeomanry (Egypt) (invalided)
Flanegan, L. C., 2nd Lieutenant, 3rd Essex
Fleetwood, E. C., Essex Yeomanry
Fairhead, S. C., Essex Yeomanry (wounded and missing)
Fisher, E., 6th Essex
Fisher, Clifford, 12th Essex
Finch, P. R. C., London Fusiliers
Finch, F. D., 2nd Lieut., 1st E.A. Cyclists
Flux, J., Australian Contingent (killed in action, Gallipoli)
French, A. H., R.F.A.
Francis, C. E., New Zealand Contingent
Frost, L. A., Queen's Westminster Rifles
Folkard, C., Royal Engineers

Gray, A., Royal Flying Corps
Green, A. E., 2nd Lieut., 10th Suffolk
Green, Harold, 9th Hants Cyclists, Despatch Rider
Green, C. B., Essex R.H.A., Despatch Rider
Gregg, F. G., 12th City of London (killed)
Girling, C. J., 5th South Staffordshires
Graham-Brown, Lieut., 9th Lancashire Fus. (wounded)
Gibb, J. W., 1st Cambridgeshire Territorials

Grimwade, H. C., 2nd Lieut., Worcestershire Regt.
Grimwood, C. H. W., 2nd Lieut., 12th Essex
Gibbs, G., H.M.S. "City of Newcastle"
Goldsmith, E. J., Public Schools Battalion
Girling, Hugh, Hon. Artillery Company
Goodey, S., Mechanical Transport

Humphries, H., Rifle Brigade
Horton, C. H. D., Public Schools Battalion
Heath, H., Public Schools Battalion
Hall. — 5th Lancers
Horwood, R. B., 2nd Lieut., 3rd Essex (wounded)
Head, J., Essex R.H.A.
Hempson, British Vice-Consul, Cadiz
Hempson, E., 2nd Lieut.
Harrison, V., A.S.C.
Hallum, G. B., Essex Yeomanry
Harwood, P., 10th Fusiliers
Hussey, F. W., R.C.V.S.D., London, 27
Hudson, R. J. N., R.E. Telegraph Staff
Helps, F. B., Westminster Rifles (killed in action)
Hill, O. B., Lieutenant, 10th Suffolks
Hughes, L. D., 2nd Lieutenant, R.H.A.

Jasper, L. A., Midshipman, H.M.S. "Virginian"
Jasper, L. V., Essex Yeomanry
Jarmin, R.V., R.A.M.C. (gassed)
Jarrard, D. G., R.H.A.
Jarrard, C. H., 8th Essex
Judd, A. E., Essex R.H.A.
Jefferies, C. R., 2nd Lieutenant, West Riding R.F.A.
Jaws, Geo. F.

King, Hugh, 2nd Lieut., 8th Essex
King, Geoffrey, 2nd Lieut., Motor Section, A.S.C.
King, J. H., Inns of Court O.T.C.
King, G. K., R.N.D. Engineers
Knopp, H. A., 5th Essex
Keeble, F. R., Lieut., 12th Essex
Kiddell-Monroe, J. E., 1st London Rifle Brigade

Lansdowne, L. R., 10th Middlesex (India)
Lawrence, A. D., Cheshire Yeomanry
Lord, P. C., Essex R.H.A.
Leaning, A., Capt., A.V.C., 5th Cavalry Brigade, Indian
  Expeditionary Force

Lucking, A. J., Inns of Court O.T.C.
Lucking, mi., Mechanical Transport

Maile, R., London Fusiliers
Matthew, W. S., Gordon Highlanders
Midgley, C. F., Royal Naval Brigade
Midgley, W. R. O., London Scottish
Mason, A. S., Capt. and Adjt., Devon Yeomanry
Mason, C., 10th Essex
Manning, L., Essex Yeomanry
Manning, C., Civil Service Rifles
Miller, E. S., Public Schools Battalion
Malyn, D. P., Lieutenant, A.S.C.
Malyn, R., Hon. Artillery Company
Melrose, A., Royal West Kent
Marlar, J., 2nd Lieut., 3rd Essex
Minor, R., 2nd Lieut., Public Schools Battalion
Marionnaud, J. A., Sous-off., 41e Battie. de 95, 69e Div.
    de Réserve
Matthews, W., Cameronians
Mitchell, G., Public Schools Battalion

Nicholson, R., 10th Middlesex
Nicholson, K., A.O.D.
Norfolk, A. E., Army Service Corps (killed)
Nicholl, A. F., Royal Naval Reserve
Naters, Rev. C. C. T., Chaplain, 37th Brigade

Orfeur, C. B., Royal Naval Volunteers (invalided)
Orfeur, H. W., Lieutenant, 8th Essex
Oliver, S. T., London Rifle Brigade

Peacock, N., 1st Class Petty Officer, H.M.S. " Vincent "
Peacock, A., Essex R.H.A.
Prior, C. D., Motor Unit A.S.C.
Pawsey, J. S., Public Schools Battalion
Potter, J., Motor Unit A.S.C.
Potter, C. C., 2nd Lieutenant Suffolk Regiment
Plummer, F. E., 2nd Lieut., 10th Bedfords
Plummer, N. A., Essex Yeomanry
Pointing, W. W., Kensington Rifles
Plane, L. W., A.O.C. Motor Unit
Pepper, V., Canadian Contingent (wounded)
Palmer, H. V., Lieutenant, Oxford L.I.
Plant, C., 2nd Lieut., Royal Irish Fusiliers
Prime, E. J., Essex Yeomanry (missing)

Phillips, Colonel
Puttick, F. V., Otago Rifles, N.Z.
Puttick, S. F., S.A. Field Force
Penny, R. E., Lieut.-Commander Protected Armoured
　Cruiser, S.S. "Winifred," Lake Victoria Nyanza
Parsons, W., Essex Yeomanry
Penn, Sergt.-Major, Suffolk Regiment
Pointing, M., Army Service Corps
Padfield, C., 16th Lancers
Pulford, A. L., 5th Essex

Queripel, Major, Guernsey Militia

Rainbird, —, Anti-Aircraft Section, R.A.
Renton, T. S., 9th Essex
Rickard, H. P., 1st British Columbia Regt. (wounded)
Ritchie, Major A. S. M., D.S.O., Queen's Bays
Ryder, E., 12th Middlesex
Richardson, J. R., 2nd Lieutenant, 12th Essex
Richardson, A. J., Essex Yeomanry
Rowe, P. G., A.O.D.
Riches, A. E., Royal Engineers

Smith, A. G., Bankers Batt., Royal Fusiliers
Smith, G. E., Singapore Royal Engineers
Smith, W. G., R.A.M.C.
Stark, D., Gordon Highlanders
Skinner, E., King's Royal Rifles
Secker, J. D., 2nd Lieutenant, London R.B. (wounded)
Slight, R. L., Manchester Regiment
Siggers, J. W., Essex Yeomanry.
Siggers, O., Lieut. R.D., Royal Naval Reserve
Sanger, C. W., University Battalion
Sanger, H., 5th Essex (invalided)
Shepard, W. O., Australian Contingent
Shepard, D. T., Australian Contingent
Scott, E. Cooper (Military Cross), Lieutenant, Duke of
　Cambridge's Own
Scott, J. H., Lieut., Essex Regt.
Shelton, C. S., A.O.C.
Sparling, A. E., Lieutenant, 8th Essex (died)
Slater, E. M., R.E.
Salisbury, W. H., A.S.C.

Town, H. G., London Rifle Brigade
Tucker, Stanley, 15th City of London
Tucker, A.,

Tennant, E., R.E. Dispatch Rider
Tye, G. H., Essex R.H.A.
Taylor, A. P., Sub-Lieut., Royal Naval Brigade (escaped from Grönigen)
Turner, Lieut.-Col. A. J., D.S.O., R.F.A.
Turner, S. C., 2nd Lieut.
Turner, F., Major, Intelligence Dept.
Turner, Arthur, Major, 5th Essex
Town, W. M., 5th Essex (invalided)
Thomas, R. J., 2nd Lieut., 9th Bedfords
Thomason, E. A., 16th London Regiment

Watson, G. F., Lieutenant, D.S.O., Welsh Field Co. R.E.
Watson, J. L., Canadian Contingent
Williams, F. O., 5th Essex
Warner, A. E., R.A.M.C.
Watsham, H., 5th Essex
Willmott, J., Public Schools Battalion
Whitby, J. M. F., 2nd Lieut., 3rd Essex (wounded)
Whitby, H., 8th Essex
Wanklyn, D. C., Motor Unit, Essex Cyclists
Ward, J. D., 2nd Lieut., 3rd Essex
Waring, C., Montreal (died under operation)
Walker, B. E. C.
White, S. A., Capt. and Adjt., 2nd Northumberland Fusiliers
Watson, S. F., Inns of Court O.T.C.
Watson, F. C., Royal Flying Corps
Willsher, H. W., Royal Navy
Webb, G. A., Princess Patricia's L.I.
Webb, A. E., 2nd London R.F.
Wagstaff, D. T., Coldstream Guards
Wheeler, G., 2nd Lieut., 3rd Essex
Worth, J. G., 2nd Lieutenant, A.S.C.
Wright, Geo., Officers' Training Corps
Wallace, A. D., 2nd Lieut., 5th Yorks

Two Appeals.

TO O.C.'s ON ACTIVE SERVICE.

WE are establishing a Recruit's Trophy, to be held for a year by the smartest recruit in the C.R.G.S. Cadet Corps. Thanks to the generosity of the late Mrs. Patrick Crosbie, a cup was given annually, to be the property of the best recruit : her death has caused this to lapse.

We think that of infinitely greater interest than a glittering cup that is never filled, would be some souvenir of the Great War, which would be appropriate to the purpose, and also a memento of an old Colcestrian. I should be very grateful for offers of a trophy, shell case or sword hilt, or something of the kind, which could be suitably mounted, and which would be the pride of the Corps.

It is intended to offer the trophy next term.

J. A. PEART, O.C., Cadet Corps,

Colchester R.G. School.

GRAMOPHONE RECORDS FOR THE WOUNDED.

I HAVE been appealing in the local papers for records, and people have been most kind in responding. We have received the following :—Mr. Walter Clarke 12, Mr. Durrant 14, Dr. Hall 14, Mrs. Gale 15, Mrs. Smith (Shrub End) 13, Mrs. Woollard 3, Mrs. Wells 2, Mrs Alderton 1, Mrs. Shaw-Jeffrey 19, Mr. Richer 1, Mrs. Low 8, Mrs. Smith (Roman Road) 2, Proctor 13, Pawsey 1, Walkden 1, Munson 13.

In all 134 double-sided records. We have sent 80 to the County Hospital, 26 to Gostwycke, and 25 to the Military Hospital.

I am now trying to collect 100 for the Military Hospital and if any Old Boy has a record or two to spare and will send me his address on a post card I shall be most grateful, and I can send for the parcel at any time convenient. These records give an enormous amount of pleasure to those to whom we all of us owe so much.

P. SHAW JEFFREY, H.M.

EVERETT, W. R., c/o B. F. Burrell, Esq., Abbeygate Street, Colchester.
EVERETT, O. E. F., 28 New Town Road, Colchester.
EVES, F. J., 17 Morant Road, Colchester.
EWING, J. H., South Hall, Ramsey, Harwich
FAIRHEAD, A. E., Bouchier's Hall, Messing, Kelvedon.
FARMER, A. O., 12 Queen Street, Colchester (HON. SECRETARY).
FAVIELL, G. V., 28 Udney Park, Teddington, Middlesex.
FIELDGATE, W. H., "Ty Fry," Regent Road, Brightlingsea.
FINCH, F. D., 25 Salisbury Avenue, Colchester.
FITCH, L. B., Louisville, Fambridge Road, Maldon.
FLANAGAN, L. O., Beta House, Clacton-on-Sea.
FLEETWOOD, E. C., Bemahague, Shrub End Road, Colchester.
FLETCHER, L. B., 13 Harsnett Road, Colchester
FLUX, R. O., 27 Old Heath Road, Colchester.
FOLKARD, C, Copford, Colchester.
FRANKLIN, Councillor R., Sutherland House, 95 Baddow Road, Chelmsford.
FRENCH, R. E., 58 Roman Road, Colchester.
FROST, A. T., Woodlands Road, Gt. Shelford, Cambridge.
FROST, A. W., 13 Head Street, Colchester.
GIBBS, J. W., 249 Maldon Road, Colchester.
GIRLING, T. A., 18 Park Road. Chelmsford.
GIRLING, Hugh, Park Villa, Dunmow.
GODFREY, C. F., "Thirlmere," Queen's Road, Springfield, Chelmsford.
GOING, F. W., 125 Maldon Road, Colchester.
GOODEY, S., Chelsworth, New Town Road, Colchester.
GOODY, C., Old Heath Road, Colchester.
GREEN, A. C., Fingringhoe, Colchester.
GREEN, A. E., 18 East Stockwell Street, Colchester.
GREEN, C. S., Fingringhoe, Colchester.
GREEN, C. B., Holmwood, Fingringhoe, Essex.
GRIFFIN, O., Stanway Villa, Colchester.
GRIFFIN, H. L., Stockwell House, West Stockwell Street, Colchester.
GRIMWOOD, O. H., c.o. Boots, Ltd., Long Wyre Street, Colchester.
HALL, A. L., Carrleon, New Town Road, Colchester.
HARPER, W. C., High Street, Colchester.
HARRIS, H. J., Weircombe, Ardwick Road, W. Hampstead.
HARVEY, J. B., Stanley Lodge, Wellesley Road, Colchester.
HARSUM, G. F., Wood Field, Bourne Road, Colchester.
HAZELL, S G., Wellesley Road, Colchester (and Montreal).
HAZELL, R. I., 26 Lexden Street, Colchester.
HEAD, A., 58 Wimpole Road, Colchester.
HEAD, J., 58 Wimpole Road, Colchester.
HEMPSON, R. J., Galton Lodge, Reigate.
HOBROUGH, S. J., Ernest Cottage, Parsons Heath, Colchester.
HOLLAWAY, H. H., 34 Old Heath Road, Colchester.
HORLOCK, M. F., High Street, Mistley.
HORWOOD, R. B., Layer Hall, Layer.
HURST, H. J. R., 7 St John Street, Colchester
HUSSEY, F. W., 15 Audley Road, Colchester.
IVEY, S. F., 63 Kensington Gardens Square, London, W.
JARRARD, C. H., Thorpe, Colchester.
JARRARD, D. G., Alexandra Road, Sible Hedingham.
JASPER, C. V., Langenhoe Hall, Colchester.
JASPER, L. A., Langenhoe Hall, Colchester.
JAWS, Geo. F., 24 Churchill Terrace, Cadoxton, Barry, nr. Cardiff
JEFFERIES, O. R., Second Lieutenant R.F.A.
JEFFREY, P. SHAW, School House, Colchester.
JOHNSON, L. H., 17 Lion Walk, Colchester.

JUDD, L., South Villa, Ardleigh.
KENT, B. H., 182 Maldon Road, Colchester.
KING, J., 16 Inglis Road, Colchester.
KING, W. H., Inglis Road, Colchester
KING, W. H., junr., Inglis Road, Colchester.
KING, G. K., 53 Friar Street, Sudbury.
KOSKINAS, F. M., 24 Pembridge Gardens, Notting Hill, W.
LANSDOWNE, L. R., Mersea House, Walton.
LAY, C. V., 2k Portman Mansions, St. Marylebone, London, W.
LAWRENCE, A. D., c.o. Head & Co., Ltd., 27 Cornhill, London, E.C.
LAWRY, E., Hoe Farm, Aldham.
LAZELL, HAROLD, Fitzwalter Road, Lexden Park, Colchester.
LEANING, E. M., Welwyn, Wash Lane, Clacton-on-Sea.
LEEMING, J. H. J., 27 Liversidge Road, Higher Tranmere, Birkenhead.
LEWIS, K. M., 173 Maldon Road, Colchester.
LINES, E., The Bungalow, Great Bentley.
LORD, P., North Hill, Colchester.
LORD, S. W., 49 North Hill, Colchester.
LUCKING, A. S., 20 Inglis Road, Colchester.
LUCKING, O. D., 20 Inglis Road, Colchester.
MALYN, D. P., Bleak House, Braintree.
MALYN, R., Barclay's Bank, Colchester
MANNING, C., The Elms, Weeley, R.S.O.
MANNING, P. E. J., The Elms, Weeley, R.S.O.
MARLAR, J., North Hill, Colchester.
MARSH, W. E., 180 Longmarket Street, Natal, South Africa.
MARSH, H. V., P.O. Box 253, Maritzburg, South Africa.
MASON, A. S., Perse School, Cambridge.
MASON, B., 10 Crouch Street, Colchester.
MASON, C., 10 Crouch Street, Colchester.
McCLOSKY, O. A., c.o. Eves Everett, St. Botolph's, Colchester.
MIDDLETON, G. A. T.
MIDGLEY, O. F., "Gunton," Westminster Drive, Westcliffe-on-Sea.
MIDOLEY, W. R. O., 163 Ongar Road, Brentwood.
MILLS, F. G., 18 Beverley Road, Colchester.
MOY, O. T., c.o. Messrs. T. Moy & Co., Ltd., Colchester.
NORFOLK, A. E., 76 Chesson Road, West Kensington.
NUNN, A. W., Crouch Street, Colchester.
NUNN, J. H., Melford Villa, Rawstorn Road, Colchester.
NUNN, W. H., Whatfield, Ipswich.
OLIVER, J. L., Maldon Road, Colchester.
ORFEUR, H. W., Colne Bank, Station Road, Colchester.
ORFEUR, C. B., Colne Bank, Station Road, Colchester.
ORFEUR, R. F., Colne Bank, Station Road, Colchester.
ORFEUR, F. N., Colne Bank, Station Road, Colchester
ORPEN, O. G., Hillside, West Bergholt, Colchester.
ORRIN, W. R., 37 Campion Road, Colchester.
OSBORNE, E. F.
OSBORNE, H. C.
PARKER, Rev. E. H., London Orphan School, Watford.
PAYNE, E. A., 2 Honywood Road, Colchester.
PAART, J. A., C.R.G.S.
PEPPER, V. J.
PEPPER, G. E., C.R.G.S.
PERTWEE, F., Morehum's Hall, Frating.
PLUMMER, N. A., Station Road, Lawford, Manningtree.
PLUMMER, F. E. Station Road, Lawford, Manningtree.
POINTING, W. W., 148 Maldon Road, Colchester.

286

POTTER, C. O., 119 Maldon Road, Colchester.
POTTER, F., Middleborough, Colchester.
PRIME, E. J., 37 Crouch Street, Colchester.
REEVE, E., C.R.G.S.
RENTON, T. S., 12 Crouch Street, Colchester.
RICHES, A. E., 80 Tower Street, Brightlingsea.
RICHARDS, R. F., Head Street, Colchester.
RICHARDSON, A. J., School House, Great Bentley.
RICKWORD, E. G., Boughton Lane, Loose, Maidstone.
ROGERS, S. W., 5 Caterham Road, Lewisham, S.E.
ROSEVEARE, H. H., "Craigmore," Newquay, Cornwall.
RYDER, E. W., 74 Wimpole Road, Colchester.
SADLER, F. B., Box P.O. 219, c.o. The Eastern Bank, Ltd., Bombay.
SANGER, O. W., "Rookerydene," Abbeygate Street, Colchester.
SANGER, H., "Rookerydene," Abbeygate Street, Colchester.
SALMON, J. G., Wash Lane, Clacton.
SAMMONS, A. O., 49 Grafton Street, Fitzroy Square, W.
SEAMER, H. St. J., "The Gables," East Bergholt.
SENNITT, F. J., 28 Mersea Road, Colchester.
SHAW, D. E., c/o Miss Mills, Queen Elizabeth Walk, Stoke Newington, N.
SHENSTONE, J. C., 15c Coverdale Road, Shepherd's Bush, London, W.
SLIGHT, R., c.o. One Barrow Lodge, Coalville, Leicestershire.
SLATER, E. M. No address.
SMITH, AUBREY. "Manta," 30 Peak Hill, Sydenham, S.E.
SMITH, G. E., Chapel Street, Colchester.
SMITH, W. G., 23 Roman Road, Colchester.
SMITH, F. R., 23 Roman Road, Colchester.
SPARLING, A. S. B., 21 Creffield Road, Colchester.
SURRIDOR, P. T., Coggeshall.
SYER, F. N., 8 Studlands Road, Sydenham.
TAYLOR, A. P., Roseneath, East Street, Haslemere, Surrey.

TENNANT, E. N., Connaught Avenue, Frinton.
THOMAS, A. O., 150 Maldon Road, Colchester.
TOWN, H. G., 50 Essendine Mansions, Maida Vale, W.
TOWN, W. M., 50 Essendine Mansions, Maida Vale, W.
TURNER, Capt. A., Essex Hall, Colchester.
TURNER, Dr. DOUGLAS, Essex Hall, Colchester.
TURNER, S. C., Abbeygate House, Colchester.
VAN DEN BERGH, A. H.
VAN DEN BERGH, H.
WAGSTAFF, D. T. Church Farm, Marks Tey, Colchester
WALLACE, Councillor R. W., "Moelwyn," Inglis Road, Colchester.
WARD, J. D., Jun., Bluegates, Elmstead, Colchester.
WARNER, A. E., 8 Myland, Colchester.
WATKINSON, W. P., Elmstead, nr. Colchester.
WATSHAM, H., Vine Farm, Wyvenhoe.
WATSON, J. L.
WATSON, S. F., 154 Maldon Road, Colchester.
WATSON, G. F., Abergwili Palace, Carmarthen.
WATTS, FRANK, 30 Creffield Road, Colchester.
WEBB, G. S., Dairy House, Wix, Manningtree.
WEBB, A. H., Dairy House, Wix, Manningtree
WENDEN, C. A., The Chase, Great Bromley.
WHEELER, G., 10 High Street.
WHITE, C. E., 57 North Hill, Colchester.
WHITE, F., "Kennington," Myland, Colchester.
WHITBY, J. F. M., 22 Lexden Road, Colchester.
WILLIAMS, F. O., 14 Lexden Road, Colchester.
WILLIS, E. A., 25 Heron Road, Stapleton Road, Bristol.
WRIGHT, C. T., Stacey House, Crouch Street, Colchester (President).
WRIGHT, G., junr., Stacey House, Crouch Street, Colchester.
WRIGHT, Councillor G. F., 47 Crouch Street, Colchester.
WYATT, D. T., Bank Passage, Colchester.

NOTICE TO OLD COLCESTRIANS.

Old Colcestrians who wish to make known their movements in this paper should communicate with Mr. J. HUTLEY NUNN, "Essex County Telegraph" Offices, Colchester.

Subscriptions should be sent to Mr. A. T. DALDY (Hon. Treas.), Head Street, Colchester.

Members of the Society are requested to notify any change of address immediately to either of the Hon. Secretaries :—

Mr. A. O. FARMER, 6 Queen Street, Colchester.
Mr. A. T. DALDY, Head Street, Colchester.

NOTICE TO CORRESPONDENTS.

Contributions to the O.C. Section, articles on various subjects and humorous anecdotes of school-days, will be gladly welcomed by the O.C. Editor, Mr. J. Hutley Nunn.

All contributions for the next number of "The Colcestrian," to be sent in by June 1st, 1916.

No. 45.]
New Series.

JULY, 1916.

The Colcestrian.

EDITED BY PAST AND PRESENT MEMBERS
OF COLCHESTER SCHOOL.

PRICE SIXPENCE

Colchester:
PRINTED BY CULLINGFORD & CO.,
156 HIGH STREET.

O.C.S. Officers for 1915-16.

President:

C. T. WRIGHT, Crouch Street, Colchester.

Vice-Presidents:

W. GURNEY BENHAM, J.P.	B. H. KENT	J. O. SHENSTONE, F.L.S.
R. FRANKLIN	OSMOND G. ORPEN	R. W. WALLACE
H. L. GRIFFIN	W. H. KING	C. E. WHITE
H. J. HARRIS, B.A.	Rev. E. H. PARKER	

Committee:

T. D. BROOK	O. GRIFFIN	E. W. DACE
J. H. NUNN	H. H. HOLLAWAY	J. C. SALMON
A. W. NUNN	C. E. BENHAM (Chairman)	F. D. BARKER
F. G. MILLS	G. C. BENHAM	J. A. PEART

The Ex-Presidents are ex-officio members of Committee.

Hon. Treasurer (pro tem.):

A. T. DALDY, Head Street, Colchester.

Hon. Secretaries:

A. T. DALDY, Head Street. Colchester.
A. O. FARMER, 12 Queen Street, Colchester.

Members of the O.C.S.

ADAMS, E. A., 7 Goodwyn's Vale, Muswell Hill, N.
ALLISTON, A. W., Chipping Hill, Witham.
APPLEBY, W. M.
ATKIN, G., Hill Crest, Gt. Oakley.
BARE, W. J., Magdalen Street, Colchester.
BARKER, F. D., Royal Grammar School.
BARKER, U. F. J., Marine Hotel, Walton-on-Naze.
BARNES, O., Howell Hall, Heckington, Lincs.
BARNES, F. M., Howell Hall, Heckington, Lincolnshire.
BAXTER, H. G., Fronks Road, Dovercourt.
BAYLISS, R. V. J., Fleece Hotel, Head Street, Colchester.
BAYLISS, B., Fleece Hotel, Head Street, Colchester.
BEARD, E. O., St. Margaret's, Cambridge Road, Colchester.
BECKETT, H., Balkerne Lane, Colchester.
BELLWARD, G. W. F., C.R.G.S.
BENHAM, C. E., Wellesley Road, Colchester.
BENHAM, G. C., 12 Hospital Road, Colchester.
BENHAM, Alderman W. GURNEY, St. Mary's Terrace, Lexden road, Colchester.
BIRD, A., Bell House Farm, Stanway.
BLATCH, F., Mina Santiago, Lucine, Bolivia, S. America.
BLAXILL, G. A., "West Wellow," Romsey, Hants.
BLOMFIELD, S., Raonah House, New Town Road, Colchester.
BLOOMFIELD, H. D., 3 Tyler Street, Parkeston.
BLYTH, COOPER, c.o. Isaac Bunting, 100 Yokahama, Japan.
BRAND, E. J., High Street.
BOGGIS, FRANK, Station Road, Sudbury.
BROMLEY, J. G., Mill House, Great Clacton.
BROOK, T. D., "St. Runwald's," Maldon Road, Colchester.
BROOK, A. T., "St. Runwald's," Maldon Road, Colchester.
BROOK, L. C., "St. Runwald's," Maldon Road, Colchester.
BROOK, S. V., 22 Sugden Road, Lavender Hill, S. W.
BROWN, D. GRAHAM, "Lound," Witham.
BULTITUDE, R. G., 32 Hanover Road, Canterbury
BURRELL, F. B., Abbeygate Street, Colchester
BUNTING, A. E., The Nurseries, North Station Road, Colchester.

BURLEIGH, A., Kudat, N.L.B.T. Co., British North Borneo.
BURSTON, P. G., 1st National Bank Buildings, San Francisco.
BUTCHER, H., 3 Eden Ave., Liscard, Cheshire.
BUTLER, F. H., Cumberland House, Manningtree.
CAREY, M. C.
CARTER, F. B., C.R.G.S.
CHAMBERS, C., 22 Wellesley Road, Colchester.
CHAMBERS, S. C., 22 Wellesley Road, Colchester.
CHAPMAN, D., Alma Street, Wivenhoe.
CHEESE, O. T., Surveyor of Taxes Office, Aberystwith, Cardiff.
CHESHIRE, W., 1 Meyrick Crescent, Colchester
CHILD, L. G., 14 Wimpole Road, Colchester.
CLAMP, A. J., 122 Priory Street, Colchester.
CLARK, L. W., 16 East Stockwell Street, Colchester.
CLARKE, S. F., Parr's Bank, Holloway, London, N.
CLOVER, J. M., The Hall, Dedham.
COLE, C. L. L., General Post Office (Staff), Cambridge.
COLE, H. S., 25 Wimpole Road, Colchester.
COLLINGS, O. E., 3 East Hill.
COLLINGS, F. J., 146 High Street.
COLLISON, A. L., Garrison School, Buena Vista, Gibraltar.
CORK, F. F., 38 Trouville Road, Clapham Park, S.W.
CRAGG, Rev. E. E., St. John's Church, Huntington, Long Island, U.S.A.
CULLINGTON, M. W., 53 Oakhill Road, Putney, S.W.
CURTIS, A. P., Bromley Road, Colchester.
DACE, A. W., 122 George Street, Edinburgh.
DACE, E. W., 17 Honywood Road, Colchester.
DALDY, A. T., 50 South Street, Colchester (HON. TREASURER).
DAVIES, W. E., 118 Butt Road, Colchester.
DRAKIN, E. B., C.R.G.S.
DEANE, G. F. F., Longwood, Nayland.
DICKER, B. P., Grocers' Hall, Prince's Street, E.C.
DOUBLEDAY, R. E., Belle Vue Road, Wivenhoe.
DOUBLEDAY, W. A., Belle Vue Road, Wivenhoe.
EVERETT, H. J., Councillor, 28 New Town Road, Colchester.
EVERETT, W. R., c/o B. F. Burrell, Esq., Abbeygate Street, Colchester.

Continued on Page 3 of Cover.

290

The Colcestrian.

VITÆ CORONA FIDES.

No. 45].   JULY, 1916.   [NEW SERIES.

About Lighting Candles.

I AM told to say farewell to you all on this page. I refuse.
    Years ago I came over from America in company with
Gipsy Smith. We were to leave New York harbour at noon,
but at 7.30 a.m. a crowd of Gipsy Smith's supporters gathered
on the quay and sang—apparently without taking breath,
from 7.30 a.m. till noon—a hymn with the chorus "We'll
never say goodbye," repeated many times over.

They never did say goodbye. We heard them in the
distance shouting defiance when we were half-way to Sandy
Hook, and if my wife and I do any singing at all in the train
which carries us north, it will be certainly this song we shall
choose in spite of the guard and the Company's regulations.

But I want to talk about lighting candles. There is a
passage in Stephen Graham's book, "The way of Martha
and the way of Mary," which seems to apply very aptly to
our life at school :—

    "Man's heart is a temple with many altars, and it is dark
to start with and strange. But it is possible, with every
ordinary impression of life to light a candle in that Church till
it is ablaze with lights like the sky.

    That is the function of ordinary sights, to be candles.

    So the night of ignorance is lit up with countless stars."

    Every fresh thing we learn at school is another candle lit
in the night of our ignorance, so that presently the head of
the industrious apprentice is ablaze with lights like the sky,
and he becomes not only a light to himself but a beacon for
all of us on the road to success. A solitary candle makes a
poor illumination but if every boy in the school keeps his
candle-burning we shall have a brave show.

And then there is that other candle which the Oxford martyrs lit.

So I ask you to keep on lighting candles. No boy is so dull that he cannot light one at least, and each fresh candle lit makes it easier to light another.

As for my wife and I, we shall keep a big candle burning to the memory of Colchester School (the special sort they sell to Schoolmasters made entirely of whacks), and some of you I hope, when you take your bedroom candlesticks, will think at times of us.

J.

P.S.J.—An Appreciation.

AT the present time it is impossible to escape from the shadow of coming events—events now almost at the doors. Already the anchor has been cast, the sails are being furled. Already the ladder has been lowered, and the Captain, under whose skilled guidance the good ship 'C. R. G. S. ' has achieved such a prosperous voyage, even now stands ready to leave the quarter-dock for his own yacht, therein to enjoy a well-merited and halcyon leisure,—and may it be a long and happy one! Bon voyage! God-speed!

It is perhaps a fitting moment to pass in review the man and his work within the limit of a few paragraphs. When, at the beginning of the present century, he was appointed to the Headmastership, he had already established a reputation both as a teacher and a master, but Headship, the great test of character and organizing powers was yet to come. He found the School wellnigh at the nadir of its fortunes. Its numbers, after the golden prime of the Acland régime, had dwindled to a handful of less than thirty scholars. Its standard was far below that of even a Secondary School. Its constitution was antiquated; and it had become the prey and play-thing of evenly matched and bitterly opposed factions in the Borough. To anyone with less faith and less capacity the situation might well have seemed hopeless.

His task therefore involved nothing less than a reconstitution of the entire school on a completely new and modernized basis. For a year or so it was a case of hard work and pertinacious courage. Then the reward began to appear. Numbers rose, slowly at first, but with increasing speed, as the fact and character of the School's new birth became more widely known and recognised. The row of class-rooms, which now house the Junior School became a necessity to cope with the growing multitude, who came to profit by the educational opportunities that had been brought to their doors.

Still there was no check to the current of well earned success. Existing buildings again became inadequate, and after an interval during which the School lived in "tabernacles" its present splendid home was erected and inaugurated. *Finis coronavit opus.*

The rest is recent history. Is it not written in the Chronicles of the Borough of Colchester? Looking back it would be hard to say on whom the Governor's choice could have better fallen than on the man under whose guidance the School has reached its present stature and reputation, and who is about to lay down his office at the present time.

But though his personal direction and control be gone, he can never be wholly lost to us. The spirit he has infused, the tradition he has established, the results of his care, his thought, his labour still remain, and will remain with us. C.R.G.S as we know it, is essentially his own creation— "*monumentum aere perennius, et regali situ Pyramidum.*"

Grammaria.

To Fresh Fields.

Mr. Widlake leaves us at the end of this term, to the great regret of all who have been brought into contact with him. It is understood that he has been offered a post at the Perse School, Cambridge, whither he will take with him our best wishes for his future.

Give Him Beans.

A serious misadventure has befallen our agricultural department. At the back of the rifle-range samples of various crops had been raised, and were displaying considerable promise, in spite of the vagaries of the weather. But some ill-disposed screw of a horse, who chanced to be bringing a load to the School, halted within hail—one might even say "within range." In the momentary absence of his driver he dragged his load nearer, and stretching out his neck, engulfed the better part of a row of beans before he could be stopped.

Chivalry.

To show the growth of charity and chivalry in our midst (no doubt induced by the war) Mr. Reeve is understood to have remarked in the most kindly and forgiving way that, if he could only have come across the ill-conditioned brute and its driver, he would have given them both beans. What a noble example to all of us!

The Weather and the Crops.

Experts inform us that there is an almost record hay crop this year, and this will be borne out by those who have been playing cricket on the Park Road ground. A new Boy was heard to observe that until now he had never had a clear notion of what was meant by "the long field."

Addled ?

Reports come from Kent to the effect that the vibration of the firing on the Flanders front has upset all the incubators in the county, with the result that the eggs therein have been addled. Without expressing any opinion as to the reason, it is a curious fact that our termly collection of "bloomers" has swollen considerably since the Big Push began to manifest itself.

A Tiara of Brilliants.

In sella dormit . . . . he sleeps in the cellar.
Quantum ratione provideri poterat . . . . The quantity of
rations he was able to provide
Quand elle se met en colère . . . . when she puts on colour
Est-il parti ? Tant mieux. . . . Is there a party ? My Aunt !

Definitions.

Tonsure . . . . a tooth drawer.
Mercery . . . . what is used in a barometer.
Windage . . . . the thing you have at the top of a well.

From "The Lyonian."

A Subaltern is one who has position but no magnitude.
A Turkish Communiqué lies equally on any point.
A Trench has length, breadth, and stickiness.
A Soldier equal to a Tommy is equal to anything.
If things are double the price of the same thing obtainable elsewhere, it is a War Office contract.

To a Correspondent.

No, there is no truth in the suggestion that the place where Moses was on the occasion when the lighting restrictions were first promulgated was C—chester, though the difference would be hard to detect.

"At the Sign of the Ship."

FORMS I. & II.

Our cage now includes an eagle and a gosling; two sparrows were recently released by Mr. K.

There have been several "scraps"—not always the fault of the fighters.

> "Now First Form boys delight to fight,
> They seem to think it 'quite alright';
> But when their noses start to bleed
> They think it very wrong indeed."

We hear that Lowe is having a high old time at Trouville.

* * *

FORM III.

. There will be no paper famine in this form—there is a large supply of T.'s notes to use up.

Wright is often wrong, and Last is sometimes first: even Tarr is not always up to pitch.

Is it unpatriotic to read in war time? We suppose it is, as our library is still closed.

We are all sorry to hear of the death of two relatives of our boys—O.C.'s who died for their country; we are glad to know Everett's brother is better.

* * *

FORM IVB.

We have played one form match this season against IVA. and were beaten by three runs. Arnold took seven wickets for us.

The Shorthand Set regret to announce that there will be no more Strawberry Feasts this term, because . . . (censored) and 'Cornish Cream' is running out.

Where *are* those pencils?

* * *

FORM IVA.

We have a big library (thanks to our Form Master), although we have not yet learned Book-keeping.

Rose, Beckett and Brook are sorely missed, but we hope they will meet with success in their new occupations.

Is chalk good for the complexion?

* * *

FORM VB.

Heard in the Lab. : "A non-metal is a gas with no shape."
"Lime is used for making limestone and lime juice."

Is it the picturesque beauty of Stanway Green or its military value that attracts him?

. If the N.C.O.'s said what they thought, would not the new buildings ripen in colour?

* * *

FORM VA.

Certain boys were detained for "cutting dinner." Ought they to eat it whole?

We wonder if the "remainders" of VA who do not go into the Lab. enjoyed themselves on a certain Friday afternoon?

Does one of the masters imagine that the shooting range is a branch of the Joscelin's Café?

It is sad to think that after this week we shall be "in solution"—some to proceed with dignity to the Sixth, some to form cogs in the industrial machine, some to cross the seas —but all to remember kindly "J," and "Daddy," and VA.

* * *

FORM VI.

Employment needed during the vac. for two members of the above Form. Experienced as envelope addressers, tax collectors, policemen, lay readers (once a week), groundsmen, drill sergeants, etc., ete., etc.

"Time is money." But, owing to the absence of both these commodities, the VIth has to apologize for the non-appearance of another number of "The Idler."

* * *

DIFFERENT KINDS OF FORM NOTES.

Form I. & II.	... ...	? (a Note of Interrogation.)
Form III.	...	D Flat (Decidedly).
Form IVB.	... ...	B Natural (Bit. Natural).
Form IVA.	... ...	Middle C.
Form VB.	... ...	! ! !
Form VA.	... ..!	Exam. Notes.
Form VI.	... ...	Treasury Notes.

Finally, may we raise an objection to Form Notes on account of the many "Notes" which have been sent (for "Form's" sake) from U.S.A. to Germany?

Our notes would not be complete without some mention of the regret felt by the whole School at the departure of the H.M. and Mrs. Jeffrey. The benefits that all have received at their hands are so many that we cannot adequately express the measure of our loss.

The Pre..

A T the end of the Summer Term comes the feeling that, truly indeed, " The old order changeth, giving place to new," and it is with a very sincere regret that we of the Pre say good-bye to our Headmaster. His great confidence in, and consideration for the Preparatory School, has been a great help to us, and only we know how much we shall miss him. We are not keen politicians, but we boldly assert (without any compunction) that we are tremendously conservative where old friends are concerned. Our best wishes go with him and Mrs. Jeffrey.

We learnt only a few weeks ago that Gostwycke patients were greatly in need of cigarettes, as their usual supply has not been coming in at all plentifully lately. This is almost the most distressing thing that can happen to mankind, so the Tommies tell us, and each week we have collected a nice little number. The boys have wheedled single cigarettes out of long suffering fathers, and brought them carefully along. If the men saw the anxiety caused by getting them safely to our box without squeezing them, they would surely overlook any damage that may have been done.

The appeal for Serbian children made a fortnight ago, was well received and with the generous donation of ten shillings from Mr. and Mrs. Chatterton to head the list our pennies amounted to 19s.

Our unwearying work of pillow making goes on, and our total number has now amounted to 35.

The gardens are not really a success. It is so trying to produce fine 'lettuces for slugs to feed upon, and now the daylight saving bill is in force, they seem to have things all their own way. One can't sit up till midnight in these days to go slug hunting.

We have added to our number, F. Horwood, G. Roberts. W. Dowsett, G. Harwood, R. Mitchenall, and F. Manning.

When we reassemble in September we are looking forward to welcoming our new Headmaster, Mr. Cape, who found time to take a peep at us on his last visit to the School,

C. C. & A. J.

Valete.

PERTWEE, J. W. Form VI. K.P., School House. 1st XI. Football. Captain, House football, Hockey and Shooting. House Cricket. Member of Committee, Debating Society. Band Sergeant, Cadet Corps.

SMITH, T. G. Form VA. Probationer, Harsnett's. Captain, 1st XI. Football. 1st XI. Cricket. Captain, House Football and Hockey. House Cricket and Shooting. Lance-Corporal, Cadet Corps.

EVERETT, C. Form VB. Parr's. House Football, Hockey and Cricket. Bugler, Cadet Corps.

MARLAR, G. E. Form VB. Parr's. House Football, Hockey and Cricket. Private, Cadet Corps.

MILLER, E. Form VB. School House. House Hockey. Private, Cadet Corps. (H.M.S. Worcester.)

BECKETT, E. Form IVA. Dugard's. House Hockey.

BROOK, F. W. Form IVA. Parr's. House Football. Cricket, Hockey and Shooting. Private, Cadet Corps. (H.M.S. Worcester)

HAZELL, L. E. Form IVA. Dugard's. House Football, Cricket, Hockey and Shooting. Drummer, Cadet Corps.

ROSE, C. P. Form IVA. Parr's. House Shooting. Private, Cadet Corps.

CARLTON. O. Form IVB. School House. Private, Cadet Corps.

LOWE, R. S. Form II. School House. Scout, Wolf Patrol.

GELL. E. Form II. Parr's. Scout, Wolf Patrol. (Died after operation.)

Salvete.

LAST, F. A.	Form III.	Dugard's.
PRATT, L. W.	Form III.	Parr's.
WRIGHT, J. M.	Form III.	Harsnett's.
DOWSETT. A. J.	Form II.	Dugard's.
EAGLE, N. H.	Form II.	Dugard's.
GASCOIGNE. J. F.	Form II.	Dugard's.
GOSLING, A. J.	Form II.	Parr's.
HOWARD, ma., R. E.,	Form II.	Parr's.
HOWARD, mi., J. E...	Form II.	Parr's
DOWSETT, W.	Pre.	
HARWOOD. G.	Pre.	
HORWOOD, F.	Pre.	
MANNING, F.	Pre.	
MITCHENALL, R.	Pre.	
ROBERTS, G.	Pre.	

Cadet Corps.

(ATTACHED 5TH ESSEX).

FRIDAY, APRIL 7th,

On Friday, April 7th, a most enjoyable Field-Day was held at Layer-de-la-Haye. The scheme was an attack on the village of Layer, which was held as a salient by an outpost force of an army situated further south. The attack was under Sergt. Rickword, who showed an excellent grasp of the essential facts of the position. Sergt. Andrews, who commanded the Defence, drew up a comprehensive scheme of defence, and devoted much time and trouble to going over the ground and choosing his defensive positions.

Both sides were ably commanded during the operations themselves, and the Defence must be especially commended for the orderly manner in which they retired. They made, however, a serious mistake in retiring too soon, so that, although they escaped loss themselves, they did not succeed in inflicting any material loss on the enemy. The weak points of the Attack were—that insufficient attention was paid to the necessity of keeping, so far as was possible with such an extensive area, in touch with the other units of the force. The scouts sent out by the Attack did not show enough smartness and keenness in their job, so that some of them would never have got back to their parties, even with the unreliable information which they thought they had obtained.

On the whole, however, good work was done by both sides, and, in spite of a tendency to pay insufficient attention to the near presence of an enemy, which caused one outpost commander to be captured, good promise was shown in several individual cases.

SATURDAY, MAY 13th.

On the afternoon of May 13th, we had a scheme which included map reading and concentration marching. Four parties started out under the Sergeants who had to march to a certain fixed spot, and open " sealed orders " at a given moment. These instructions gave them a further route to a spot near which a tin was to be found. This tin would contain final instructions, which would bring all parties to the same point. Unfortunately, the tins were hidden in very difficult places, and several mistakes were made in map-reading, so that only one party, which had had phenomenally good luck the whole way, succeeded in reaching the rendezvous.

SATURDAY, MAY 27th.

On Saturday, May 27th, we again visited Layer. The signalling section sent messages through a line of Stations, several at excellent speed, while the map-makers made a careful and accurate traverse in the district. The remainder of the Corps did extended order work and attacked and defended woods with fairly good results.

SATURDAY, JUNE 3rd.

On Saturday, June 3rd, we went out on a scheme which combined concentration marching and despatch carrying. The signalling and mapping sections again worked independently, and the remainder of the Corps was divided into three sections under Sergts. Bugg, Rickword, and Andrews (cyclists). Map reading was again at fault in several cases, and, although all three parties eventually reached their positions on the main road from Colchester to Nayland, the despatch was quite an hour late in passing through.

W.

SATURDAY, JUNE 22ND. -

As a concession to the mile-hungry cyclists a circle of some twenty miles was marked out, and, with the help of a party on foot, was patrolled in the hope of preventing some spies from breaking through. All the "flies" got through, which is not remarkable considering the size of the circle ; the fact that the O.C. was allowed to slip through with three men within 100 yards is, however, very disappointing.

A pleasing feature of the afternoon was the way in which the forty cyclists kept their lines, presenting a very creditable appearance. This exercise made a happy change from routine work.

WEDNESDAY, JUNE 27TH.

A most successful Field Day was enjoyed at Fordham, after postponement from Whit Monday. The scheme, given in skeleton form to the Commanders, was for a rearguard action, following a defeat of a White force between Lexden and Fordham, their base. Both Sergt. Bugg and Corpl. French, in charge of attack and defence respectively, carefully elaborated their plans, effectively examining and mapping the terrain.

Two bridges across the Colne proved to be the keys to the problem and both parties showed their appreciation of that fact : much depended on scouting and rapid movement on the flanks. The results, carefully weighed by Co. S. M. Ward and Sergt. Andrews, showed a decisive victory for the attack. In the consequent pow-wow various individuals were apportioned a meed of praise or blame, and lessons were deduced.

The best features, in the opinion of the O.C. were the care and skill displayed by Sergeants Bugg and French, and the good style in which the Corps (led by an ever improving band), returned after a heavy afternoon.

The weakest points were the lack of control, of smartness, of capacity in giving directions and in map reading, on the part of the lance corporals and privates in command of small parties. Much practice in silent, skilful scouting is needed.

SATURDAY, JULY 1ST.

Under ideal marching conditions a route march of some nine miles was enjoyed, via Heckford Bridge to Stanway

Green, where a platoon competion in taking cover was held. The honours went to platoons I and II.

On the march an improvement in steady pace was apparent, and the Band earned commendation.

* * *

Two most interesting and useful lectures on the hand grenade, with an exciting demonstration on the Close were given at the end of last term by Lt. Thornton (8th Essex.)

* * *

The Corps is much indebted to the officers of the 8th, Essex, whom the exigences of the service have, unfortunately, removed from Colchester. Prizes for the best reports of the lectures were won by Corpl. French, Cadets Smith and Crighton.

* * *

We have been fortunate this term in securing the services of Sergt.-Dr. McGorman and a bugler, both of the 2/6 Lancs. Fusiliers, as band instructors. They were sent through the kindly offices of Major-General Blomfield, commanding the garrison, and they have pulled the band together wonderfully.

* * *

Two side drums have been purchased by the Corps this term, and have justified the outlay, by the marked improvement of our drummers. We hope, however, that the strange epidemic of punctures has now died away.

* * *

During the Summer term the Corps has had thirty drills and exercises registered, as well as sundry unmarked parades. This is a record of enthusiasm and hard work upon which we may congratulate ourselves.

* * *

Seven cadets are putting in a fortnight at the Public Schools Camp, at Marlborough, and we wish them a useful and jolly time. The O. C. would like to be accompanying the contingent, but he is attached, as instructor, to the Eastern Command School for N. C. O's., for the vacation.

* * *

L. Corpls. Hill and Middleton are promoted Corporals : Acting L.Cpls. Cheshire, Dolamore, and Crighton are promoted Lance Corporals.

J. A. P.

Scouting Notes.

THIS term has in many ways produced some of the best work ever done by the school troop which now numbers fifty.

To begin with, we have had, in addition to the two weekly parades, half a dozen field afternoons at Layer, West Bergholt and Butcher's Green where we have done various scouting work ; attack and defence. dispatch running, tracking, pathfinding and map making, and we hope to be able to finish the term with a day in the woods and uplands of Mr. Royce's off hand farm, since, sad to say we are again unable to go to camp.

One of the things in which we have most improved, is in marching, and this is due in a large measure to the excellent work done by the buglers. This improvement really dates back to the Easter holidays when Kent (still an hon. member of the troop) and Clarke won their " Bugler " badges, the former thus completing the test for his "cords" as an " all round Scout." Since that time, Everett, Osborne ma., Burleigh and Downing have been steadily qualifying for the same badge, and should be able to obtain it very soon. The troop was able to purchase a new bugle at the end of last term, and a few weeks ago, Scout H. Smith of the Peewit Patrol very generously presented us with a fourth " Hawkes " bugle, so that we now have a complete front line of buglers.

I am also glad to hear a good account of the work done by our scout helpers on Thursdays and Sundays at the Social Club. It is not easy work, especially after the novelty has worn off and some of the scouts have stuck to it very faithfully. Six more boys have now won their " public service " badges. P.L.'s. Burleigh, Barnes, Salew, Child, and Scouts Alderton, Horwood and Weeks mi.

We are very sorry to have to record the death of Francis Gell of the Wolf Patrol, which occurred early in the Easter holidays. He was about to undergo a slight operation, but the anæsthetic had hardly been administered when he suddenly passed away. He was a very keen and loyal Scout, and his sad death was a grief to us all. The Wolf Patrol and some of the other senior boys gave him a scout funeral and Kent and Clarke sounded the " Last Post " at the graveside.

Scout Low of the same patrol left at the end of the term to go to France, but we hope some day to have him back again.

We have often spoken of the importance of the *Patrol* as a unit, and I am glad to see that this is being more and more recognised. Several patrols, as patrols, have done specially good work this term. The Beavers have done some good signalling, the Otters have worked hard at the ambulance

test, .and the Peewit and Wolf Patrols have had several parades and outings entirely on their own initiative. This is excellent, and says much for the keenness and enterprise of the patrol leaders, and the following badges have been awarded this term in addition to those already mentioned :—
" Naturalist " Clarke, Farmer, Weeks. ma.
" Musician " P. L. Child.
" Entertainers " Clarke, Barnes.
" Second Class Scout " Mirrington, Littlebury, Alderton, Loyd and Hollaway.   G.E.P.

Shooting.

THIS term the range has been open before Morning School and in the Dinner Hour, but the attendance at the earlier period has been quite small. Our rifles are showing distinct signs of wear and we should be glad to get some new ones, but prices are almost prohibitive and funds are decidedly low. The cost of munition and all other necessaries has gone up considerably, but up to the present we have been able to carry on at the old price, though it may be found necessary to raise the charge slightly next term.

No. 1 has been the favourite this term, and it is interesting to note how a few good scores obtained by a painstaking shot with one particular rifle immediately secures its popularity. No. 2, the old favourite, is clearly the worse for wear and as soon as possible new barrels should be obtained. Of the B. S. A. Rifles, No. 27, which we remember as " the." rifle in the old days, when the range was in the Gym, has not been used at all this term.

As predicted in our last number, School House came out quite easily as Cock House in the Competition for the Worthington Evans' Cup, increasing their lead over Dugard's by 13 and finishing up with 77 points to the good. Below are the final scores.

SCHOOL HOUSE		DUGARD'S		HARSNETT'S		PARR'S	
Crighton	58	Bugg	56	Cox	55	Wheeler ma	59
Middleton	53	Wells	52	Clark ma.	49	Andrews	53
Tait	52	King ma.	51	Farquharson	49	Percy	50
Layzell	48	Plummer	49	Smith ma.	49	French	45
Lilley	46	Hazell ma.'	46	Arnold	46	Brook	42
Barnes	45	Halls	45	Rickword	44	Rose	42
Pertwee	45	Gilbert	42	Burleigh	40	Cheshire	38
Dolamore	41	Bacon	34	Deane	40	Hunneyball	33
	388		375		372		362
Summer	420		383		356		406
Xmas	417		390		380		336
Totals	1225		1148		1108		1104

This year we entered a Senior Team only for the Imperial Challenge Shield Competition. Shooting took place on Tuesday June 27th and the day was anything but ideal, as rain was falling the whole time and this no doubt acted adversely, but at the same time we scarcely did as well as expected. We must congratulate Middleton on his score, especially as for the second year he was an easy first in the Rapid. Below are the scores :—

				Deliberate.	Rapid.	Total.
Middleton	..	..	..	42	44	86
Percy	..	..	..	37	37	74
Halls	..	..	..	40	34	74
Crighton	..	..	..	30	37	67
Cox	..	..	..	35	31	66
Lilley	..	..	..	34	31	65
Andrews	..	..	..	32	32	64
Clarke	..	..	..	33	25	58
Plummer	..	..	..	24	24	48
						602
					Average	66·88

Shooting Colours are awarded to Middleton, Percy, Halls.

E. R.

House Singings.

PARR'S.

This took place in March, and was quite a creditable show, especially when one remembers that Parr's Master has been taken from their head so recently. Andrews worked hard to attain a successful concert, generously assisted by Mr. Carter. Cheshire's debut as a humourist, Collinge's solo and the excellent topical song, "When the Masters join the ranks," were the best items in the first part: .

The play, "A Message from the Front," was a difficult test, in which Parr's quite sustained their dramatic fame ; Percy did particularly well in a very trying part ; Andrews was happily more free from distracting mannerisms. The interest and "go" were maintained right up to the effective climax.

DUGARD'S.

The audience always expects an excellent entertainment when Messrs. Reeve and Carter "present" a programme, and they are never disappointed. The first part had the saving qualities of originality and clearness ; the smallest Nob and tiniest Lark made himself heard. Tarr, who appeared as a pianist as well, sang in good style, and Harwood ma. gave what we fear is his "Swan Song" with excellent effect. In the "Antiques," an original topical number, Horwood and Harwood mi. were very amusing. Clarke and Beckett were delightful in the skit on "Sensational Novels."

"A Quiet Little Dinner," the clever little comedy which followed, was acted in a confident and finished manner and gave Spencer the opportunity of showing us the best study of a girl part which the School has.

ever seen. Clarke and Ritchie did well, whilst Beckett ma. and Gilbert made the most of their character sketches. Bugg and King were not so happy ; but on the whole it was a very good performance. Congratulations, Dugard's !

We strongly urge that every boy should learn one new recitation or song during the vacation, so that we may have variety and freshness in next term's House Singings. There has been a lamentable falling-off in the ordinary " sing-songs," and we must show Mr. Cape of our best.

J.A.P.

Bockey Bouse Matches.

DUGARD'S v. PARR'S, March 18th.

Though Parr's were handicapped by the loss of their Captain, Andrews, who was ill, this match was a good one, and singularly free from any (visible) signs of ill-feeling. From the start, Bacon and Wells (Dugard's centre-forward and inside-right) played well together, and it was not long before the former scored. After the bully, Dugard's forwards again made a rush, but they were stopped (as they were many times during the match) by the good play of Parr's left-back, Marlar. It was now Parr's turn to spurt, and their outside-right, Brook, seemed likely to score when Gilbert, who played a fine game at back throughout the match, pulled him up. After some ding-dong play in mid-field, Clough, with a lucky shot, scored for Dugard's. At the end of the first half, the score was 2—o in favour of Dugard's.

In the second half, with the advantage of the slope of the field, Dugard's seemed certain of success, but Parr's rallied and led off well. Nothwithstanding this, soon after the start, Bacon again scored. Parr's made a determined effort, and French, at centre-forward, had extremely hard luck on more than one occasion. No goals were scored by Parr's, however, and, towards the finish of the game, Wells scored a goal for Dugard's. The score was then 4—o for Dugard's, and thus it remained until the finish of the match.

The game was a hard one, and though Dugard's deserved their victory, Parr's are to be sympathised with, as they put up an excellent fight.

DUGARD'S v. HARSNETT'S, March 23rd

This match was a fairly even one. At the start, the match seemed as if it would end in a draw, but after a good deal of play, Harsnett's began to bombard Dugard's goal until Thomas scored. Dugard's began to forge ahead slightly after this, and a goal for them seemed certain, but it did not eventuate. Harsnett's again got together, and it was not long before Salew ma..with a good shot scored. For the rest of the first half Dugard's were employed in defending their goal, only making occasional rushes into their opponents' half, but no more goals were scored.

Dugard's appeared to have the better of the game in the second half, but, chiefly owing to Harsnett's left back, Farquharson, they were unable for some time to score. Then Harsnett's had another run up and Salew ma, again scored, but as an appeal for off-side was given, the score still remained 2—o for Harsnett's. This was changed to 3—o in a few minutes by Thomas, who again scored. Dugard's again had a try at Harsnett's goal, but it was some time before Spencer managed to put in a good shot, which brought the score to 3- 1. This was the final score, for though there were rushes on both sides, no more scoring was effected.

PARR'S v. SCHOOL HOUSE, March 23rd.

This match took place on Thursday, 23rd March. The weather at first was fine, although there was a little snow towards the end. From the start there was no doubt as to what the result would be. Schoolhouse were a very small and weak team, while Parr's, although without Andrews and Collinge, were much the better eleven. Pertwee at back was easily the best of Schoolhouse, and it was not his fault that his side lost. Barnes at centre was also good, but was very poorly supported by the other forwards. Parr's were very good at forward, while Felgate at half, and Marlar and Everett at back, defended in good style. Wheeler, Parr's goalkeeper, stopped what shots came his way with a combination of luck and skill. Play was mostly in the Schoolhouse half. Not long after the start, Cheshire succeeded in running through on his own. Many of Parr's shots went wide, while time after time they were pulled up by Pertwee when right in the goalmouth. At length French scored with a hard shot at very close quarters, and not long after Percy scored with a very good shot from a pass from the left. Half-time arrived with no further score. The second half developed more or less into shooting practice for Parr's, who, however, shot very badly, and only obtained one goal more, the time being chiefly taken up by " 25 " bullies.

PARR'S v. HARSNETT'S, March 28th.

On Tuesday, 28th March, we were promised the next afternoon as a half-holiday on which to play house matches; but on Wednesday morning snow lay two to three inches deep. It all cleared off, however, by dinner time, and house matches were arranged at the last minute. This match took place on the first pitch, which was rather slippery. The game was very even most of the while, play being first in one half, then in the other. Parr's were poor in shooting and always missed by a fraction. Harsnett's shot straight, but were for a long time kept out by Parr's goalkeeper, Wheeler. At length they were successful, and followed up about ten minutes later by another goal. There was no further score before half-time. In the second half Parr's forwards made many good individual rushes, but failed to combine well. Harsnett's kept well together, and about ten minutes after re-starting obtained another goal. Marlar at back played very well for Parr's, and many times pulled up the Harsnett forward line, and cleared with hard shots. Parr's now made desperate onslaughts on Harsnett's goal. A shot from French hit White's pads, and Percy, rushing up, scored. Harsnett's then had their turn, but were kept out for a long time by Wheeler, who played well in goal. After some time they succeeded in getting the ball between the post and the goalie, a distance of about six inches. Play was now fast and furious, but Parr's gradually hemmed Harsnett's in their own half, and the last ten minutes were all in their favour. In saving a shot from Percy, White fell in the goalmouth, and French was able to rush the ball through. Parr's, however, could get no more goals, their shots all going wide; and the game ended with the the score 4—2 for Harsnett's.

DUGARD'S v. SCHOOLHOUSE, March 29th.

This match was played on an extra half-holiday, on a Wednesday. Rain had fallen heavily on the preceding night, but the pitch had dried nicely and was not too hard.

Schoolhouse won the toss, and played facing the sun for the first half. Though Dugard's pressed heavily, either their forwards were bad shots or else Schoolhouse defence was very good, for the first goal was not scored until some time after the start, when Bacon managed to score. Soon after this Spencer made a weak shot at goal, and, the School-house goalkeeper mishitting, the ball rolled into the goal. With only occasional spurts from their forwards, Schoolhouse backs were kept busy. Pertwee, especially, seeming to be in every place where he was needed. .

Soon after the start of the second half, Bacon, from a scrimmage in front of goal, again scored. The game now developed into " shots at goal " by Dugard's to a great extent, with rushes now and then by the Schoolhouse forwards. Of these, Tait and Barnes tried hard, and de-served goals. The game ended in a win for Dugard's. 6—o. The other goals were scored by Harwood (1), Spencer (1), and Bacon (1).

Cricket.

We have to deplore the lack of School Matches, owing to the war, as usual, and the shortage of labour. The field has made an excellent feed for sheep, but as a cricket ground. . . . . !

We have had to content ourselves with the inter House and Form Matches only, and although the scoring in all cases has been exceedingly low, we are pleased to see a great improvement in the fielding and bowling generally. This lack of scoring may be due to the fact that the pitches have been in a perpetual state of soddenness.

We still think that with the co-operation of the bigger fel-lows there might be more games than there have been, espe-cially as the monotony to some is varied by the Cadet Corps afternoons.

Our thanks are due to the seniors who have materially assisted some of our overworked staff by umpiring.

Below is a resume of the House Matches :—

PARR'S AND SCHOOL HOUSE. Thursday, June 1st, 1916.

A very close game which looked like a victory for School House until Brook saved the game by some hard hitting and thus gave Parr's the victory by one run.

DUGARD'S AND HARSNETT'S. Saturday, June 10th, 1916.

Delayed for some time but resulted in a win for Dugard's by 7 runs. It was a very evenly contested game and was won by Dugard's superior fielding.

HARSNETT'S AND SCHOOL HOUSE. Thursday, June 15th, 1916.

This match was chiefly notable for somewhat higher indi-vidual scoring. Cox and Farquharson made an excellent stand, the latter scoring 57. Harsnett's won by 74 runs.

307

DUGARD'S AND PARR'S. Thursday, June 29th, 1916.

In this match Parr's seemed to collapse before the bowling of Gilbert and Harwood, whilst King did some hard hitting for Dugard's who won by 86 runs.

HARSNETT'S AND PARR'S. Thursday, July 6th, 1916.

Played in the rain, as usual. The opportunities given on both sides were many, but few were taken. Cox bowled very well throughout. Harsnett's won by an innings and 8 runs.

DUGARD'S AND SCHOOL HOUSE. Saturday, July 8th, 1916.

This was the only match entirely played on a fine day. Dugard's showed an overwhelming superiority over School House, as regards fielding, and won by an innings and 9 runs This match made Dugard's Cock House.

The Houses are placed as follows :—

	Played.	Won.	Lost.	Points.
Dugard's	3	3	—	6
Harsnetts	3	2	1	4
Parr's	3	1	2	2
Schoolhouse	3	—	3	—

Old Colcestrian Section.

Our Founder.

THERE are degrees of Old Colcestrianship. There are those of us who are not merely Old Colcestrians through having spent or mis-spent part of our boyhood in the old Colchester School. We are "O.C.'s" in a variety of other ways. We are lucky enough, some of us, to be Colcestrians by birth, and we have the misfortune to be old by the same token. Also by family associations, by business interests, and by lifelong citizenship we are part of Old Colchester. Those who are thus unmitigated Old Colcestrians, whose Old Colcestrianism is, as it were, the very marrow of their bones, can best value the worth of Percy Shaw Jeffrey's Headmastership of Colchester School.

We remember the School as it was when we attended it. Probably we were proud of it though we may not have shown our pride in a practical way. We recollect how it gradually decayed and dwindled until we began to feel ashamed of it. It became a reproach to Colchester. Then came Mr. Shaw Jeffrey, and chiefly by his genius and personality the School became a credit to Colchester, a valuable asset of the town, and once more a source of pride to those who were Old Colcestrians.

Comparisons are invidious and often unjust, and Mr. Shaw Jeffrey would be the first to admit that he began his Head-mastership with certain advantages denied to all his predecessors. A new Scheme of Management had—after many delays—been drawn up. A modern system of government was provided and gradually more ample funds became available. But these things, useful and necessary, would have been unavailing without a man who knew how to make the right use of them. The reputation of the School was below zero. It was a very difficult task to restore public confidence. To Mr. Shaw Jeffrey belongs the credit of having overcome all difficulties and obstacles—and they were innumerable—and of raising the reputation of the School almost instantaneously. In a few years it had far surpassed

all previous records as to numbers, and had risen to the rank
of an important public school.

This is not the place to trace in detail the progress of the
School under Mr. Jeffrey's Headmastership. How many
years is it since he first came to Colchester? I cannot say
exactly from memory, but I know that although the duration
of that Headmastership may have seemed long to Mr. Jeffrey
and to his popular and invaluable helpmate, Mrs. Jeffrey, it
has been a very short period indeed when considered in re-
lation to the almost magic transformation of the School which
has been accomplished. How it has all been done is best
known to Mr. and Mrs. Jeffrey. We are all aware that from
the first the new Headmaster's energy and enthusiasm were
unbounded. In a hundred different ways he stimulated the
School and infused new and honourable traditions into it,
never, however, forgetting its past glories and its ancient
and interesting foundation.

Of course we Old Colcestrians are all very proud—quite
unreasonably proud—of what Mr. Shaw Jeffrey has done for
the ancient School. We have, for the most part, done comparatively little to help him, but we have not been allowed to
do nothing. Soon after Mr. Jeffrey's arrival, the small
remnant of Old Colcestrians in the Borough found that they
were not to be mere idle onlookers. The new Headmaster
took the old boys in hand. He stirred them up. He set to
work and educated them. Probably he found them even
more stubborn and reluctant than the young Colcestrians. He
must have often wished that he could use the same means of
coercion which are so effective in the School itself. As we
most of us neglected our opportunities whilst at School, so it
is to be feared we did not make the very most of our chances
as Old Colcestrians, when the new Headmaster pointed
out insidiously and pertinaciously that our school duties were
not over.

He formed us into a class, called the Old Colcestrian
Society, and he set us tasks. Gradually we learnt a few
simple lessons, and we had an annual speech day or speech
night in the form of a dinner. Whenever he could he made
us stand in rows and sing some of those admirable chanties
which he composed, which will be a lasting memorial of his
Headmastership. We also had "The Colcestrian" to study
month by month. These things were all devised and started
and kept going by the energy of the Headmaster, and now
that we are about to lose him it behoves us to remember
what he has taught us, and to see that the wholesome discipline is in no way relaxed in the future. The Old Colcestrian
Society has done something, might have done more, and in

310

the future ought to do more, for the good of the ancient
School which we all desire to see flourishing.

The town of Colchester will always be heavily in debt to
Mr. Shaw Jeffrey. He has been one of its greatest benefactors in modern times, and every Old Colcestrian will join
heartily in thanking him, in acknowledging his courage,
forcefulness, and brilliant achievement, and in wishing him
—and Mrs. Jeffrey—all happiness and honour and prosperity
in their new sphere of life.

W. GURNEY BENHAM.

Editorial.

NEWS from the front this term is very scanty as for weeks
prior to the big push no letters were allowed to come
through.

* * *

F. H. Butler is making good progress towards convalescence, and is
soon proceeding to a Cadet School. Martin Slater is in the East
London Hospital, recovering from typhoid.

* * *

J. L. Watson is in hospital at Aberdeen, suffering from the effects of a
bad shrapnel wound in the back. He is the only survivor of his original
platoon of 55 men. Three were left to go into the last action : of these,
two were killed, and J. L. was wounded. His brother, G. F. Watson,
D.S.O., is recruiting at Abergwili Palace, from the effects of a wound
in the foot. Lieut. Berridge, son of the Rev. Jesse Berridge, was
wounded on July 1st.

* * *

"Country Life" for June contains an illustrated article on Howth
Castle in Ireland the seat of the Barons of Howth. It is interesting to
remember that one of the earlier Barons of Howth was a boy at
Colchester School viz :—William Lord Baron of Houth (sic), baptised
Stoke 14th Sept : 1628. Admitted to Colchester School 10th Jan : 1639.
His pedigree is given in Dr. Horace Round's "Colchester School
Admissions" printed by Messrs Wiles for the Essex Archæological
Society.

* * *

Brook and Miller ma. have this term joined the training ship Worcester.
Brook writes they give them the ropes end in their pyjamas "which is
much worse than the cane." Lieut. A. E. Bunting has been "promoted
Capt. while commanding a company." J. C. Miller of the University of
Edinburgh has passed his first professional examinations of the Royal
Veterinary College. J. B. Procter has joined Sandhurst Military
College. Appleby and Flanegan have passed out into the regular army.
The Headmaster has so far signed 98 applications for commissions on
the part of sundry O.C's. He hopes to complete his century before retiring. H. A. Beckett, after passing the cadet school at Cambridge,
has been gazetted to the 11th Devons. He passed out 5th of his
company of 160. Sergt. M. W. Cullington, late Civil Service Rifles, after

many months in the trenches is spending the summer at the Cadet School in Cambridge. Private F. D. Barker has joined the Cadet Training School at Cambridge for a four months' course.

* * *

PROMOTION OF LIEUT. A. S. MASON.

In the "Times" of June 2nd, appeared the announcement that Lieut. A. S. Mason was gazetted to a captaincy from March 8th (the day he was wounded). Since then the Army Headquarters have approved of his taking up the post of Deputy Assistant Quartermaster General on the Staff of the General Commanding the Lahore Division. He writes that he is "feeling and probably looking" as well as he ever did in his life, and has been passed by the Army Medical Board for light duty.

Sed Miles sed pro Patria.

THE following beautiful letter was written by a young (O.C.) officer to his parents the night before going into action. He was killed at dawn.

I am writing this letter to you just before going into action to-morrow at dawn. I am about to take part in the biggest battle that has been fought in France and one which ought to help to end the war very quickly. I never felt more confident or cheerful in my life before and I would not miss the attack for anything on earth. The men are in splendid form and every officer and man is more happy and cheerful than I have ever seen them. I have just been playing a rag game of football in which the officer had a revolver and a whistle.

My idea of writing this letter is in case I am one of the "costs" and get killed. I do not expect to be but such things have happened and are always possible.

It is impossible to fear death out here when one is no longer an individual but a member of a regiment and of an army. What an insignificant thing the loss of, say, forty years of life is compared with them. It seems scarcely worth talking about. Well goodbye, my darlings, try not to worry about it and remember that we shall meet again quite soon.

This letter is going to be posted if I get it in the neck.

* qui procul hinc
aute diem periit
Sed Miles
Sed pro Patria

3 p.m. Friday, June 30th, 1916."

If this is the spirit of the new armies—and we cannot doubt it —we who are left can only thank God and take courage.

* This quotation is from the "Ode on a memorial in Clifton College Chapel" by Henry Newbolt.

We beg to acknowledge the receipt of the following Magazines :—L.O.S., Leopard, Barrovian, Framlinghamian, Wyggestonian, Oxford High School, Dame Owens', Ipswichian, Chelmsfordian, Chigwellian and Pelican.

IN PIAM MEMORIAM.

CAPTAIN C. B. BROOKE, D.S.O., KILLED.

Second-Lieutenant and Temporary Captain C. B. Brooke, D.S.O., aged 21, of the Yorkshire Regiment, killed in action, was the only son of Mr. and Mrs. C. B. Brooke, Junr., Colne House, Brantham, Suffolk. He was for two years a boarder in Schoolhouse, and left us for Bilton Grange Rugby. and Bradfield College. He was gazetted to the Suffolks. (special reserve) on the outbreak of the war, and was sent to France, attached to the Queen's, in December, 1914, and rose to the rank of Captain. He was seriously wounded while leading his men in the attack on September 25, 1915, and was mentioned in despatches and awarded the Distinguished Service Order. In January, 1916, he was chosen for a commission in the Regular Army, and was gazetted to the Yorkshire Regiment. He was killed in action on July 1, while leading his company into action. The award of the D.S.O. to the late Captain Brooke aroused great interest amongst the staff and employees of the British Xylonite Company, Brantham, of which his father is manager, and when the gallant captain was home on short leave in April last a concert in his honour was organised and a presentation made to him.

The following is an extract from a letter from the Colonel Commanding the Yorkshire Regiment :—"May I write to tell you how very deeply, the whole of my Battalion deplore the death of your most gallant son, and how very much our sympathy goes out to you, who must have been so proud of him. We recognised in him, as soon as he joined us, a born leader of men, and I at once put him in command of a company. He was in command of it on Saturday, and was leading it to the assault, when he was shot. He is buried at the south end of the Talus Boisée, close to Carnoy, with three more of our officers and some men. He was a great favourite with all of us, and with the men, and had he been spared I am sure he would have had a great career. I am personally most grieved at his loss ; but he died as I think he would have liked to do."

The circumstances under which he won the D.S.O. on Sept. 25, are described by Major Bunbury, 1st Batt. The Queen's, to which the 3rd Suffolks were attached. Major Bunbury says of the deceased :—

"He was the most gallant and cheerful young officer I have ever met, and remarkably capable in every way. I

always used all my influence with him to prevent him from
taking unnecessary risks.

As regards Sept. 25, his Company (B) and mine (D) formed
the attacking line on that day, and we advanced together in
successive lines of platoons.

Capt. Brooke was over the parapet like a flash and lead his
Company on my left most gallantly, taking three lines of
trenches very quickly. I was wounded in the head, right
arm, and abdomen as soon as we reached the German trenches,
and for some hours lay out unable to move, but able to hear,
and got a fair grasp of what was going on, with intervals of
unconsciousness. Nearly every officer of the two companies
was killed or severely wounded, and Capt. Brooke, though
wounded in the face almost at once, was the only one left on
his legs, and carried on alone in command of the remnants
of B and D Companies, and the fragments of two other Battalions of the Brigade (the H.L.I. and Oxford L.I.), who
had got mixed up with them.

Our casualties were very heavy, and the battalions on our
right and left were driven out of the German trenches very
quickly, so that we were attacked in front and on both flanks,
while communication was severed with our own front line,
owing to heavy barrage artillery fire and enfilade machine
guns. No support could reach us, except one subaltern and
a few men of a platoon of C Company, who tried, but failed,
to bring up supplies of bombs, which were urgently required.
Capt. Brooke carried on the fight with wonderful courage
and endurance. Our men were gradually driven back by
bombing attacks from both flanks, first to the German second
line, and then to the first line, and I could hear Capt.
Brooke directing our bombers and encouraging his men. All
our bombs were soon used up, and they then used all available
German bombs. In about four hours time the situation was
desperate, as no bombs were left, and the enemy were in
overwhelming force, and Capt. Brooke was again wounded
through the chest. He then withdrew the remainder of our
men to our front line, the retirement being carried out under
terrific fire, and with great difficulty. Capt. Brooke was the
last to leave the German trenches, and I managed to crawl
back at about the same time.

I am glad to say I was able to report on his conduct and he
received the D.S.O. for it, though he richly deserved the
V.C. I heard that he personally accounted for several Germans with revolver, rifle, and bayonet, and all our men who
got back could not say enough in praise of his gallantry
throughout the action. His conduct was exactly what I
should have expected of him.

SEC.-LIEUT. WILLIAM ROBERT CHESHIRE.

Sec.-Lieut. Cheshire was the son of Councillor and Mrs. W. Cheshire, of Colchester, and was killed in the recent British advance.

Lieut. Cheshire, who joined the Ceylon Planters' Rifles on the outbreak of war, went through the campaign in Gallipoli, where he contracted jaundice. He was afterwards given a

commission in the Essex Regiment. He was in his 28th year, and was, when at school, a distinguished athlete, representing the School in the Public Schools' Gymnastic Competition at Aldershot in 1906 and again in 1907. He won many events in the School Sports and also in the sports of his Brigade at Felixstowe.

Before proceeding to Gallipoli he spent several months in Egypt training the Australian troops.

SEC.-LIEUT. R. B. HORWOOD.

Second.-Lieut. Ronald Bentall Horwood, who was killed in France on July 1st, was the eldest son of Mr. and Mrs. Henry S. Horwood, of Leighton House, Victoria Road, Colchester. Lieut. Horwood responded to his country's call in the early days of the war. He enlisted in the Royal Irish Rifles in September, 1914, and served six months as a private and corporal, when he was gazetted as a Second-Lieutenant to the Essex Regiment. He served in the Dardanelles, where he was severely wounded, and was sent to Alexandria for recovery, subsequently going to France with his Battalion. He was 22 years of age.

A fellow officer, writing to Mr. Horwood, says that Lieut. Horwood had got within 20 yards of the Germans when he was shot, on getting up from a shell hole in which he and his friend Lieut. Chawner had sheltered. The writer adds, " A nicer fellow in all the world there could not have been. He died a hero."

Another officer, writing to Mr. and Mrs. Horwood, says : I have been soldiering with your boy for nearly a year now, and I know what a good fellow he was. He was always thinking about his men and their comfort—as a matter of fact it was so noticeable that we others used to chip him about it ; he was always thinking of his platoon.   I cannot tell you how he died, but from what I know of him I am sure he was doing his duty up to the last."

Lieut. Horwood was a most capable officer. In the examination which followed the special 'training course of the O.T.C., at Tunbridge Wells, he took first place on the list.

WILLIAM HUNTER SALISBURY.

W. H. Salisbury was lost in the sinking of H.M.S. Hampshire.   When at school he won the first of two Dockyard Studentships offered for competition in the County by the E.C.C., and was so successful at Portsmouth that he passed out top of his year. His first appointment was as Engineroom Artificer to the Hampshire, and he was only 19 when he lost his life.

SEC.-LIEUT. ROLAND MINOR.

Roland Minor was among the killed on July 1st.   He was Sec.-Lieut. in the King's Own Royal Lancasters, and was attached to his C.O. as interpreter of German.   He was leading his platoon in the advanced line with great courage when he fell, and he died as bravely as he lived.

To an O.C. on Active Service.

Our thoughts go out to you, when Prayers are read—
To that dim Purgatory we call " out there."
We wonder how with "laughter and kind face "
You come and go in that abhorred place.
Again we see you here, a boy at prayer,
And we are one with you, when Prayers are read.

DO NOT FORGET TO BUY

A Copy of the

SCHOOL PICTURE BOOK

Alma Mater Colcestriensis

CONTAINING

36 Full-page and 40 Half-page Photographs of School Buildings and Groups, 1900-1916.

Price   -   bound and gilt   -   2/6

"   -   in stiff covers   -   1/6

Postage 4d. in each case.

Edited by 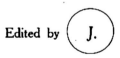 J.

With an Introduction by

Alderman GURNEY BENHAM, J.P.. O.C.,

And published at the office of the "Essex County Standard."

IT WILL INTEREST YOU.

EVERETT, C. E. F., 28 New Town Road, Colchester.
EVES, F. J., 17 Morant Road, Colchester.
EWING, J. H., South Hall, Ramsey, Harwich
FAIRHEAD, A. E., Bouchier's Hall, Messing, Kelvedon.
FARMER, A. O., 12 Queen Street, Colchester (HON. SECRETARY).
FAVIELL, C. V., 28 Udney Park, Teddington, Middlesex.
FIELDGATE, W. H., "Ty Fry," Regent Road, Brightlingsea.
FINCH, F. D., 25 Salisbury Avenue, Colchester.
FINCHAM, G. E., 52 Myland Road, Colchester.
FITCH, L. B., Louisville, Fambridge Road, Maldon.
FLANAGAN, L. C., Beta House, Clacton-on-Sea.
FLEETWOOD, E. C., Bemahague, Shrub End Road, Colchester.
FLETCHER, L. B., 13 Harsnett Road, Colchester
FLUX, R. C., 32 Old Heath Road, Colchester.
FOLKARD, O, Copford, Colchester.
FRANKLIN, Councillor R., Sutherland House, 95 Baddow Road, Chelmsford.
FRENCH, R. E., 58 Roman Road, Colchester.
FROST, A. W., 13 Head Street, Colchester.
GIBBS, J. W., 249 Maldon Road. Colchester.
GIRLING, T. A., 18 Park Road. Chelmsford.
GIRLING, HUGH, Park Villa. Dunmow.
GODFRAY, C. F., "Thirlmere," Queen's Road, Springfield, Chelmsford.
GOING, F. W., 125 Maldon Road, Colchester.
GOODRY, S., Obelsworth, New Town Road, Colchester.
GOODY, C., Old Heath Road, Colchester.
GREEN, A. O., Fingringhoe, Colchester.
GREEN, A. E., 18 East Stockwell Street, Colchester.
GREEN, C. S., Fingringhoe, Colchester.
GREEN, C. B., Holmwood, Fingringhoe, Essex.
GRIFFIN, C., Stanway Villa, Colchester.
GRIFFIN, H. L., Stockwell House, West Stockwell Street, Colchester.
GRIMWOOD, C. H., c.o. Boots, Ltd., Long Wyre Street, Colchester.
HALL, A. L., Caerleon, New Town Road, Colchester.
HARPER, W. C., High Street, Colchester.
HARRIS. H. J., Weircombe, Ardwick Road, W. Hampstead.
HARVEY, J. B., Stanley Lodge, Wellesley Road. Colchester.
HARVEY, W., Central Secretariat, Lagos, Nigeria W. Africa.
HARSUM, G. F., Wood Field, Bourne Road, Colchester.
HAZELL, S G., 39 Wellesley Road, Colchester. (and Moutre l).
HAZELL, R. L., 23 Lexden Street, Colchester.
HEAD. A., 58 Wimpole Road, Colchester.
HEAD, J., 58 Wimpole Road, Colchester.
HEMPSON, R. J., Galton Lodge, Reigate.
HOBROUGH, S. J., Ernest Cottage, Parsons Heath, Colchester.
HOLLAWAY, H. H., 34 Old Heath Road, Colchester.
HORLOCK, M. F., High Street, Mistley.
HORWOOD, R. B., Layer Hall, Layer.
HURST, H. J. R., 7 St. John Street, Colchester
HUSSEY, F. W., 15 Audley Road, Colchester.
IVEY, S. F., 63 Kensington Gardens Square, London, W.
JARRARD, C. H., Thorpe, Colchester.
JARRARD, D. G., Alexandra Road, Sible Hedingham.
JASPER, C. V., Langenhoe Hall, Colchester.
JASPER, L. A., Langenhoe Hall, Colchester.
JAWS, GEO. F., 24 Churchill Terrace, Cadoxton, Barry, nr. Cardiff
JEFFERIES, C. R., Second Lieutenant R.F.A.
JEFFREY, P. SHAW, Bagdale Old Hall, Whitby.
JOHNSON, L. H., 17 Lion Walk, Colchester.

JUDD, L., South Villa, Ardleigh.
KENT, B. H., 182 Maldon Road, Colchester.
KING, J., 16 Inglis Road, Colchester.
KING, W. H., Inglis Road, Colchester
KING, W. H., junr., Inglis Road, Colchester.
KING, G. K., 53 Friar Street, Sudbury.
KOSKINAS, F. M., 24 Pemlridge Gardens, Notting Hill, W.   [Naze.
LANSDOWNE, L. R., Mersea House, Walton-on-
LAY, O. V., 2k Portman Mansions, St. Marylebone, London, W.
LAWRENCE, A. D., c.o. Head & Co., Ltd., 27 Cornhill, London, E.C.
LAWRY, E., Hoe Farm, Aldham.
LAZELL, HAROLD, Fitzwalter Road, Lexden Park. Colchester.
LEANING, E. M., Welwyn, Wash Lane, Clacton-on-Sea.
LEEMING, J. H. J., 27 Liversidge Road, Higher Tranmere, Birkenhead.
LEWIS, K. M., 173 Maldon Road, Colchester.
LINES, E., The Bungalow, Great Bentley.
LORD, P., North Hill. Colchester.
LORD, S W., 49 North Hill. Colchester.
LOWE, STANLEY, Warwick House' East Dereham.
LUCKING, A. S., 20 Inglis Road, Colchester.
LUCKING, C. D., 20 Inglis Road, Colchester.
MALYN, D. P., Bleak House, Braintree.
MALYN, R., Barclay's Bank, Colchester
MANNING, C., The Elms. Weeley, R.S.O.
MANNING, P. E. J., The Elms, Weeley, R.S.O.
MARLAR, J., North Hill, Colchester.
MARSH, W. E., 180 Longmarket Street, Natal, South Africa.
MARSH, H. V., P.O. Box 253, Maritzburg, South Africa.
MASON, A. S., Perse School, Cambridge.
MASON, B., 10 Crouch Street, Colchester.
MASON, C., 10 Crouch Street, Colchester.
McCLOSKY, C. A., c.o. Eles Everett, St. Botolph's, Colchester.
MIDDLETON, G. A. T.
MIDDLEY, C. F., "Gunton," Westminster Drive, Westcliffe-on-Sea.
MIDGLEY, W. R. O., 163 Ongar Road, Brentwood.
MILLS, F. G., 18 Beverley Road, Colchester.
MOY, C. T., Stanway Hall, Colchester.
NORFOLK, A. E., 76 Chesson Road, West Kensington.
NUNN, A. W., Crouch Street, Colchester.
NUNN, J. H., Melford Villa, Rawstorn Road, Colchester.
NUNN, W. H., Whatfield. Ipswich.
OLIVER, J. L., Maldon Road, Colchester.
ORPEUR, H. W., Colne Bank, Station Road, Colchester.
ORPEUR, C. B., Colne Bank, Station Road, Colchester.
ORPEUR, R. F., Colne Bank, Station Road, Colchester.
ORPEUR, F. N., Colne Bank, Station Road, Colchester
ORPEN, O. G., Hillside, West Bergholt, Colchester.
ORRIN, W. R., 37 Campion Road, Colchester.
OSBORNE, E. F.
OSBORNE. H. C.
PARKER, Rev. E. H., London Orphan School, Watford.
PAYNE, E. A., 2 Honywood Road, Colchester.
PHART, J. A., C.R.G.S.
PEPPER, V. J.
PEPPER, G. E., C.R.G.S.
PERTWEE, F., Morehum's Hall, Frating.
PLUMMER, N. A., Station Road, Lawford, Manningtree.
PLUMMER, F. E. Station Road, Lawford, Manningtree.

POINTING, W. W., 148 Maldon Road, Colchester.

POTTER, C. C., 119 Maldon Road, Colchester.

POTTER, F., Middleborough, Colchester.

REEVE, E., O.R.G.S.

RENTON, T. S., 12 Crouch Street, Colchester.

RICHES, A. E., 80 Tower Street, Brightlingsea.

RICHARDS, R. V., Head Street, Colchester.

RICHARDSON, A. J., School House, Great Bentley.

RICKWORD, E. G., Boughton Lane, Loose, Maidstone.

ROGERS, R. W., 5 Caterham Road, Lewisham, S.E.

ROSEVEARE, H. H., "St. Breca," Newquay, Cornwall.

RYDER, E. W., 74 Wimpole Road, Colchester.

SADLER, F. B., Box P.O. 219, c.o. The Eastern Bank, Ltd., Bombay.

SANGER, C. W., "Rookerydene," Abbeygate Street, Colchester.

SANGER, H., "Rookerydene," Abbeygate Street, Colchester.

SALMON, J. G., Wash Lane, Clacton.

SAMMONS, A. C., 49 Grafton Street, Fitzroy Square, W.

SRAMER, H. St. J., "The Gables," East Bergholt.

SENNITT, F. J., 28 Mersea Road, Colchester.

SHAW, D. E., Beaconsfield Avenue, Colchester.

SHENSTONE, J. C., 15c Coverdale Road, Shepherd's Bush, London, W.

SLIGHT, R., c.o. One Barrow Lodge, Coalville, Leicestershire.

SLATER, E. M.

SMITH, AUBREY, "Mantz," 30 Peak Hill, Sydenham, S.E.

SMITH, G. E., Chapel Street, Colchester.

SMITH, W. G., 23 Roman Road, Colchester.

SMITH, F. R., 23 Roman Road, Colchester.

SPARLING, A. S. B., 21 Creffield Road, Colchester.

SURRIDGE, P. T., Coggeshall.

SYER, F. N., 8 Studlands Road, Sydenham.

TAYLOR, A. P., "Cromer," Westgrove, Woodford Green, Surrey.

TENNANT, E. N., Connaught Avenue, Frinton.

THOMAS, A. O., 150 Maldon Road, Colchester.

TOWN, H. G., 50 Essendine Mansions, Maida Vale, W.

TOWN, W. M., 50 Essendine Mansions, Maida Vale, W.

TURNER, Capt. A., Essex Hall, Colchester.

TURNER, Dr. DOUGLAS, Essex Hall, Colchester.

TURNER, S. C., Abbeygate House, Colchester.

VAN DEN BERGH, A. H.

VAN DEN BERGH, H.

WAGSTAFF, D. T., Church Farm, Marks Tey, Colchester

WALLACE, Councillor R. W., "Moelwyn," Inglis Road, Colchester.

WARD, J. D., Jun., Bluegates, Elmstead, Colchester.

WARNER, A. E., 8 Myland, Colchester.

WATKINSON, W. P., Elmstead, nr. Colchester.

WATSHAM, Il., Vine Farm, Wyvenhoe.

WATSON, J. L., Abergwili Palace, Carnarvon.

WATSON, S. F., 154 Maldon Road, Colchester.

WATSON, G. F., Abergwili Palace, Carnarvon.

WATTS, FRANK, 30 Creffield Road, Colchester.

WEBB, G. S., Dairy House, Wix, Manningtree.

WEBB, A. H., Dairy House, Wix, Manningtree.

WENDEN, C. A., The Chase, Great Bromley.

WHEELER, G., 10 High Street.

WHITE, C. E., 57 North Hill, Colchester.

WHITE, F., "Kennington," Myland, Colchester.

WHITBY, J. F. M., 22 Lexden Road, Colchester.

WILLIAMS, F. O., 14 Lexden Road, Colchester.

WILLIS, E. A., 25 Heron Road, Stapleton Road, Bristol.

WRIGHT, C. T., Stacey House, Crouch Street, Colchester (President).

WRIGHT, G., junr., Stacey House, Crouch Street, Colchester.

WRIGHT, Councillor G. F., 47 Crouch Street, Colchester.

WYATT, D. T., Bank Passage, Colchester.

NOTICE TO OLD COLCESTRIANS.

Old Colcestrians who wish to make known their movements in this paper should communicate with Mr. J. HUTLEY NUNN, "Essex County Telegraph" Offices, Colchester.

Subscriptions should be sent to Mr. A. T. DALDY (Hon. Treas.), Head Street, Colchester.

Members of the Society are requested to notify any change of address immediately to either of the Hon. Secretaries :—

Mr. A. O. FARMER, 6 Queen Street, Colchester.

Mr. A. T. DALDY, Head Street, Colchester.

NOTICE TO CORRESPONDENTS.

Contributions to the O.C. Section, articles on various subjects and humorous anecdotes of school-days, will be gladly welcomed by the O.C. Editor, Mr. J. Hutley Nunn.

All contributions for the next number of "The Colcestrian" to be sent in by Dec. 1st, 1916.

No. 46.]
NEW SERIES.

DECEMBER, 1916.

The Colcestrian.

*EDITED BY PAST AND PRESENT MEMBERS
OF COLCHESTER SCHOOL.*

PRICE SIXPENCE

Colchester:
PRINTED BY CULLINGFORD & CO.,
156 HIGH STREET.

O.C.S. Officers for 1915-16.

President:
C. T. WRIGHT, Crouch Street, Colchester.

Vice-Presidents:

W. GURNEY BENHAM, J.P.
R. FRANKLIN
H. L. GRIFFIN
H. J. HARRIS, B.A.

B. H. KENT
OSMOND G. ORPEN
W. H. KING
Rev. E. H. PARKER

J. C. SHENSTONE, F.L.S.
R. W. WALLACE
C. E. WHITE

Committee:

F. D. BROOK
J. H. NUNN
A. W. NUNN
F. G. MILLS

C. GRIFFIN
H. H. HOLLAWAY
C. E. BENHAM (*Chairman*)
G. C. BENHAM

E. W. DACE
J. C. SALMON
F. D. BARKER
J. A. PEART

The Ex-Presidents are ex-officio members of Committee.

Hon. Treasurer (pro tem.):
A. T. DALDY, Head Street, Colchester.

Hon. Secretaries:
A. T. DALDY, Head Street, Colchester.
A. O. FARMER, 12 Queen Street, Colchester.

Members of the O.C.S.

ADAMS, B. A., 7 Goodwyn's Vale, Muswell Hill, N.
ALLISTON, A. W., Chipping Hill, Witham.
APPLEBY, W. M.
ATKIN, G., Hill Crest, Gt. Oakley.
BARE, W. J., Magdalen Street, Colchester.
BARKER, F. D., Royal Grammar School.
BARKER, C. F. J., Marine Hotel, Walton-on-Naze.
BARNES, C., Howell Hall, Heckington, Lincs.
BARNES, F. M., Howell Hall, Heckington, Lincolnshire.
BAXTER, H. G., Fronks Road, Dovercourt.
BAYLISS, R. V. J., Fleece Hotel, Head Street, Colchester.
BAYLISS, B., Fleece Hotel, Head Street, Colchester.
BEARD, E. C., St. Margaret's, Cambridge Road, Colchester.
BECKETT, H., Balkerne Lane, Colchester.
BELLWARD, G. W. F., C.R.G.S.
BENHAM, C. E., Wellesley Road, Colchester.
BENHAM, G. C., 12 Hospital Road, Colchester.
BENHAM, Alderman W. GURNEY, St. Mary's Terrace, Lexden road, Colchester.
BIRD, A., Bell House Farm, Stanway.
BLATCH, F., Mina Santiago, Lucine, Bolivia, S. America.
BLAXILL, G. A., "West Wellow," Romsey, Hants.
BLOMFIELD, S., Raonah House, New Town Road, Colchester.
BLOOMFIELD, H. D., 3 Tyler Street, Parkeston.
BLYTH, COOPER, c.o. Isaac Bunting, 100 Yokahama, Japan.
BRAND, E. J., High Street.
BOGGIS, FRANK, Station Road, Sudbury.
BROMLEY, J. G., Mill House, Great Clacton.
BROOK, T. D., "St. Runwald's," Maldon Road, Colchester.
BROOK, A. T., "St. Runwald's," Maldon Road, Colchester.
BROOK, L. C., "St. Runwald's," Maldon Road, Colchester.
BROOK, S. V., 22 Sugden Road, Lavender Hill, S. W.
BROWN, D. GRAHAM, "Lound," Witham.
BULTITUDE, R. G., 32 Hanover Road, Canterbury
BURRELL, F. B., Abbeygate Street, Colchester
BUNTING, A. E., The Nurseries, North Station Road, Colchester.

BURLEIGH, A., Kudat, N.L.B.T. Co., British North Borneo.
BURSTON, F. G., 1st National Bank Buildings, San Francisco.
BUTCHER, H., 3 Eden Ave., Liscard, Cheshire.
BUTLER, F. H., Cumberland House, Manningtree.
CAREY, M. C.
CARTER, F. B., C.R.G.S.
CHAMBERS, C., 22 Wellesley Road, Colchester.
CHAMBERS, S. C., 22 Wellesley Road, Colchester.
CHAPMAN, D., Alma Street, Wivenhoe.
CHEESE, O. T., Surveyor of Taxes Office, Aberystwith, Cardiff.
CHESHIRE, W., 1 Meyrick Crescent, Colchester
CHILD, L. G., 14 Wimpole Road, Colchester.
CLAMP, A. J., 122 Priory Street, Colchester.
CLARK, L. W., 16 East Stockwell Street, Colchester.
CLARKE, S. F., Parr's Bank, Holloway, London, N.
CLOVER, J. M., The Hall, Dedham.
COLE, C. L. L., General Post Office (Staff), Cambridge.
COLE, H. S., 25 Wimpole Road, Colchester.
COLLINGS, C. E., 3 East Hill.
COLLINGS, F. J., 146 High Street.
COLLISON, A. L., Garrison School, Buena Vista, Gibraltar.
CORK, F. F., 38 Trouville Road, Clapham Park, S.W.
CRAGG, Rev. E. E., St. John's Church, Huntington, Long Island, U.S.A.
CULLINGTON, M. W., 53 Oakhill Road, Putney, S.W.
CURTIS, A. P., Bromley Road, Colchester.
DACE, A. W., 122 George Street, Edinburgh.
DACE, E. W., 17 Honywood Road, Colchester.
DALDY, A. T., 50 South Street, Colchester (HON. TREASURER).
DAVIES, W. E., 118 Butt Road, Colchester.
DRAKIN, E. B., C.R.G.S.
DEANE, G. F. F., Longwood, Nayland.
DICKER, B. P., Grocers' Hall, Prince's Street, E.C.
DOUBLEDAY, R. E., Belle Vue Road, Wivenhoe.
DOUBLEDAY, W. A., Belle Vue Road, Wivenhoe.
EVERETT, H. J., Councillor, 8 New Town Road, Colchester.
EVERETT, W. R., c/o B. F. Burrell, Esq., Abbeygate Street, Colchester.

Continued on Page 3 of Cover.

OUR NEW HEADMASTER.

The Colcestrian.

VITÆ CORONA FIDES.

| No. 46]. | DECEMBER, 1916. | [NEW SERIES. |

Editorial.

"God rest you merry, Gentlemen, let nothing you dismay."

IT is easy, sitting in physical comfort in the editorial chair, to grow gloomy and despondent ; to view this sadly shaken world through the greenest of spectacles. One must turn for a sane and wholesome outlook on life to the wretched conditions of water-logged and shell-swept trenches, or to the pain-wracked wards of the hospitals. There spirit has conquered matter, and peace ensues.

Our part it is to emulate the heroism of the thousands of our brothers "out there" and the silent fortitude of the bereaved at home. Ours it must be to push on with our appointed task " with laughter and kind faces ;" duty done cheerfully is duty well done.

For the sake of the young lives budding into a world gone so awry, it is not enough that we keep the stiff upper lip, they need the boon of blessed laughter to sun them into growth. For your own weal " God keep you brave " : for theirs, " God rest you merry." To you O.C.'s in places perilous on land and sea, we wish as Happy a Christmas and as Glad a New Year as the circumstance of war will permit. To you who can but wait and hope at home we send our greetings. Here, in the happy, careless heart of the schoolboy is the answer to your riddle : here is the promise of continuity, of immortality, of eternity. Sing you then your Carols, lustily, lest they hear the catch in the throat :

"God rest you merry, Gentlemen, let nothing you dismay."

A Message from Our Headmaster.

ONE evening about a year ago I was passing through
Chatham High Street on the top of a tram in the almost
complete darkness to which lighting regulations have con-
demned us. A working man who was, I fear, not very sober,
stumbled up the staircase, lurched along the gangway and
fell into the seat by my side. After a few minutes he became
conversational. He looked at me and said, ".What do you
do ? Work in the Dockyard?" I said "No." He then
said "Cement Labourer?" "No." "Steel Works?" "No."
His ideas were exhausted. He gave the problem up and said
"Well, what are you then ?" "A schoolmaster." He looked
at me with envy and said "Ah ! I should like a nice, soft job,
too." That is one view. The other was that expressed by
the late Dean Farrar, himself one of the greatest schoolmasters
and, I think, one of the noblest men who ever lived. One of
his Marlborough boys came to him and said that he hoped to
become a schoolmaster. Dr. Farrar looked at him sorrow-
fully and said " Better break stones."

I am afraid that I should not altogether agree either with
the Dean or with my neighbour of the Chatham tram. Schoolmastering is in many ways distinctly preferable to stone-
breaking. At the same time it is not exactly a " soft job."
But I know no profession which has more interest or greater
charm. Schoolboys are always interesting, both the big boys
and the little ones, the clever boys and the dull ones, and the
dull, perhaps, in some ways more than the clever. The
schoolmaster feels a thrill of personal joy when Jones Tertius
at last rises one place above the bottom of the form, or when
poor, backward Robinson Quartus after many struggles gets
some faint understanding of the cheerful facts about the
square of the hypotenuse. Schoolboys, moreover, are to my
mind the most reasonable beings in the whole world. They
are always willing to make allowances ; they even tolerate in
their masters that peculiar snappish spirit which we in the
profession call end-of-term-ishness.

We schoolmasters do appreciate this reasonable spirit. We
do value the cheery welcome that is given to us and, if I may
descend now from the general to the personal, I am very
anxious not to let slip this, my best, opportunity of expressing
real and grateful thanks for the very friendly reception given
to me by the masters and boys of the Royal Grammar School
in my own first term here. So genial and hearty a welcome
does much—more, perhaps, than many would realise—to
remove the difficulties which lie before a new headmaster. I
trust most earnestly that this cordial spirit of co-operation

may never grow weaker.

One word more. "The youth of a nation are the trustees of posterity," wrote Disraeli in "Sybil." There was never a truer thought, and its meaning has greater weight now than before. The boys who are now at school will be the men ever before whom lies the task, appalling in its magnitude, of reconstructing what is now being destroyed and of building up again the fabric of civilisation. It is now the sacred duty of every schoolboy to do all that lies in his power to fit himself for the work of life which lies before him and to prepare himself for his share of the general task. It is his duty not only to himself but to his country.

H.J.C.

"Vive Le Roi."

AT the age of nine years Mr. Cape entered the Grocers' Company's School, Hackney Downs, London. While there he brought great credit to the school by coming out first in all England in mathematics at the Cambridge Local Examination in 1891, when he obtained First Class Honours in the First Division, with distinction in no less than five subjects, i.e., English, Latin, French, German and Mathematics. For two years he was Captain of his School. After leaving school Mr. Cape spent three years in the city, devoting his evenings to study with such success that he gained First Class Honours in the Final B.A. of the University of London. The following year he gained two exhibitions at Magdalen College, Oxford, and after four years stay there he left with Honours in Mathematics and Modern History. While at Oxford Mr. Cape was frequently seen on the running track, and perhaps his finest performance was a good second to Mr. C. R. Thomas, the famous Welsh sprinter.

After leaving Oxford Mr. Cape went to the King's School, Canterbury, where he remained ten years. Here his efforts proved to be a great success both in school and out of it. He taught nearly every subject in the school curriculum and proved himself invaluable to the boys in their games. Under his direction all school athletic records were broken. It was while he was at Canterbury that Mr. Cape took his B.Sc. with First Class Honours, and at the same time won the Gladstone Prize for Economics. In 1910 Mr. Cape was appointed Headmaster of Sir Joseph Williamson's Mathematical School, Rochester ; a large day school of 250 boys, but larger still when Mr. Cape left it by another 200. During his time there a new cricket field close to the school was acquired, a magnificent swimming bath, a rifle range, fives courts, and a new wing to the main building. He further introduced the House System, a Cadet Corps, an annual production of Gilbert and Sullivan Operas, and, bless him, Merit Holidays. To show how dearly he was loved and respected by the boys and masters of this school the following is taken from " The Williamsonian." " We all feel we are losing a kind and sympathetic headmaster, a distinguished scholar, a successful teacher, and an enthusiastic sportsman. He will carry with him the best wishes of masters and boys for his future happiness and success."

H.L.T.

Grammaría.

Hail to the Chief!

We extend a hearty welcome to Mr. H. J. Cape, on his accession to the Headship. Assured of the warm support of masters and boys, we hope to see him lead us from success to greater success.

Welcome!

The Staff has been strengthened by the appointment of Mr. Twentyman to fill the vacant place. He comes with the Head from Rochester and he is, we hope, already at home with us. As Dictator of the Tuck shop he deserves all the sweets o' life. Parr's House is especially grateful to him and to Mrs. Twentyman for taking pity on a House that has suffered much vicissitude.

Again.

To Miss Pretty we extend our welcome, on her return to Schoolhouse : we congratulate the boarders on the care and efficiency with which her experienced hand guides and directs.

O.H.M.S.

During the term we have had visits from Capt. Deakin, home on leave after lengthy but business-like interviews with the Senussi : from Mr. Oldham, recovering from wounds in jaw and ankle, sustained in the July offensive : Lt. F. D. Barker, on his way to join his new unit, and our late Headmaster also honoured the new dining hall in Gilberd House. Good news, too, is received of Messrs. Mason and Davis, both of whom hold high office. Capt. S. A. White, Northumberland Fusiliers, is the second of our old masters to pay the Great Price, the first being Lt. G. H. Bennett.

A Phoenix.

On the ashes of the old modern side Agriculture rises a practical scheme for teaching some of the arts of tillage. As Mr. Reeve explains elsewhere part of the playing field is given up to those who dig the virgin soil. The experiment deserves hearty support all round.

"At the Sign of the Ship."

FORM I.

One of our boys curls his hair with a piece of string; now we know the meaning of "his locks entwine."

There is an Author in our form who is writing a book on "The Art of taking in Grub." We are looking forward to its coming out.

Our new form master is Mr. Twentyman: we welcome him here and hope he will be with us a long time.

* * *

FORM III.

Many compasses have been lost lately: someone points out that they have legs.

Four of our members have played for their houses—Osborne mi., Tricker mi., Hackett and Beattie ma.

"Mother, I don't feel well" said Sonny. "Where do you feel worst dear?" "In school" was the prompt reply.

* * *

FORM IVB.

We are all pleased to know that a boy in this form got the greatest number of good tickets during the first month.

The extreme height of misery—a small boy with a new pair of boots and no puddle.

Is jelly a useful food? If so plenty can be obtained from IVB inkwells.

Acting on M. Kindt's hint on how to use spare time, Dace has already made a successful model aeroplane.

We have played one form match—against IVA, and won by 7—5.

* * *

FORM IVA.

A combined team of IV A and B played the C.H.S., and after an exciting game beat them.

Lost—A cap; answers to the name of "Nutty."

When the Zepp. came down near (Ed. *Hush*)—some of the boys who had not already seen it were taken to view the remains, by the kindness of the Head and M. Kindt.

FORM VB.

Overheard : "The opposite sides of a triangle are parallel."
Why is he so anxious to show, by word and deed, that he does not deem himself worthy of his name of '' Reverend ''?

VB Room seems to be made of glass—and valuable glass at that.

Wanted—expert carpenter to mend desks ; also capable seamstress to mend other little things.

* * *

FORM VA.

Has the greatest collection of prefects and probationers of any form, not excepting the " gods." (Is '' collection '' the right word ?)

Sayings overheard : " When the war is over we shall be allowed more daylight."

We are so far unbeaten in form matches.

Sorry to find a member of the Sixth seeking a new explosive in the lab : on parade he doesn't seem to feel its need.

We are grateful to Messrs. Reeve and Pepper for their services in the Range during these icy days.

" There are some folk who call me a gasbag,
Another one calls me a fool.
One rude boy has called me the talkative bloke,
Another the ass of the school.
There are some who have said what I dare not repeat
And some who have said I'm a swank.
But I certainly won't tell the name of the man
Who says to me, just as no other man can,
'' You're an infantile, puerile, cacaphonous tank
A blankety—so on—blank blank.' "

* * *

FORM VI.

Resting.

The Pre.

IT is difficult to write a concise account of the work in the Preparatory School, and there must be a certain amount of repetition from time to time, as the resources of children under nine are naturally limited.

At the present moment the little boys are busy with their usual end of term writing. This they regard as a very serious matter, and the amount of trouble some of them take over it, shows great promise for the future.

They have been very interested to watch the soldiers at drill on the " Close." It is such an encouragement to learn that some of the exercises they do, are actually the same as those used by the " real " soldiers—even by their own fathers.

. " Real wounded " soldiers too have come and given them some jolly games at football, and the boys are, in return very eagerly making a Christmas Card. Collection, with which they hope to give some little gifts to the men now at Gostwyke as they did last year.

This has been a record term for pillows for the wounded. Surely this reveals marked steadfastness of purpose on our part not to have tired of ravelling after two years and more. The boys are now divided into five parties, as competition is very keen. Field and his helpers have already completed three pillows, and head the list. By Christmas we hope to have finished nine this term, and G. Wilson has just brought one which he has entirely filled at home, making a total of 46.

Unfortunately Mrs. Tyler, who has been very kind in giving us ravelling material, now finds some difficulty in keeping us supplied with pieces. If any Mother can help us next term, we shall be very grateful. Any odd fragments will be acceptable.

Every week, the boys bring quite a number of magazines which are sent to the patients in the Military Hospital. The men have gone up tremendously in the boys' estimation since they sent a message to the effect that they *do* appreciate " Rainbow," " Chuckles," and similar literature.

Whatever depression may exist outside in these stern days of war the youngsters keep in marvellously good spirits, and are looking forward to Christmas as much as ever. It is essentially a children's festival, and it is good to know, that they, at least will break up with all the pleasure of anticipation, and we sincerely hope nothing will happen to disappoint them.

In our gardens the wet weather prevented much being done beyond just making the border neat and leaving the ground ready to set useful plants, that do not need too much space, when spring comes along.

We are very pleased to note that Dace and several of our old boys have been moved up. We always watch their progress eagerly. I cannot finish our notes this time without thanking our new Headmaster for the keen interest he takes in the work done by our little ' Pre ' boys.

Last term J. Bullock, H. Crowther, M. Barnes and J. Clark said good-bye to the Pre, and are now doing, we hope, good work in the Lower School.

Our new members, R. Stiff, G. Pawsey, E. Barnes, and S. Agnew are all making a good beginning.

A. J. & C. C

Valete.

Form VI.

ANDREWS, E. U.—Parr's. K.P. Captain, School and House Shooting. Captain, House Footer, Hockey, Cricket. Sergeant, Cadet Corps. Debates Committee. Dramatic Society.

RICKWORD, J. E.—Harsnett's. Q.P. 2nd XI. Cricket. Captain, House Footer. Cricket and Shooting. Sergeant, Cadet Corps. Debates Committee. Joined Artists' Rifles, O.T.C.

BUGG, E. P.—Dugard's. K.P. Captain, House Footer, Hockey and Cricket. Sergeant of Cadet Band. Dramatic Society.

PERCY, T.—Parr's. Probationer. School and House Shooting. House Footer, Cricket and Hockey Elevens. Dramatic Society.

VA.

MIDDLETON, K. R.—Schoolhouse. Probationer. School and House Shooting. House Footer, Hockey, Cricket. Corporal, Cadet Corps.

BEARD, E. E.—Harsnett's. Probationer. House Hockey. Lance-Corporal Cadet Corps.

FARQUHARSON, F. H.—Harsnett's. House Prefect. 1st Eleven Cricket and Footer. Captain, House Cricket. Hockey, Footer. House Shooting. Big drummer, Cadet Corps. Dramatic Society.

TAIT, E. T.—Schoolhouse. House Cricket and Hockey. Cadet.

KING, A. C.—Dugard's. House Cricket and Hockey. Corporal, Cadet Corps.

VB.

SALEW, L.—Harsnett's. House Footer, Cricket, Hockey. Cadet.

IVA.

BACON, W. O. E.—Dugard's. House Footer, Cricket, Hockey, and Shooting. Cadet.

PAGE, G. S.—Harsnett's. House Shooting. Cadet.

IVB.

CLARK, F.—Harsnett's. House Cricket, Footer, Shooting. Cadet.

RAMAGE, J.—Schoolhouse. (Scholarship to Christ's Hospital).

III.

ASCROFT, N. F.—Schoolhouse.

COSSER, L. G—Dugard's. Cadet.

DE WACHTER, G.—Schoolhouse.

WHITEHOUSE, L. F.—Schoolhouse.

II.

PHILLIPS, C. T.—Schoolhouse. Scout.

MILLER, A.—Schoolhouse. Scout.

PRE.

GELL, T.

Salvete.

VI. WILSON (S.) WARDEN (S.)

VA. BLANDFORD (S.)

VB. PRESCOTT (S.) HARVEY (S.) LINFOOT (S.) HENRIQUES (S.)

IVA. JACOBY (D.) HUM (D.)

IVB. INGLE (H.) BROOM (P.) WRIGHT MI. (P.) JONES (D.) WOODWARD MI. (P.) JACKSON (H.) WYNCOLL (P.) MURPHY (S.) PRIOR (P.)

III. APPLETON (H.) BEATTIE MA. (H.) CUNNINGHAM (rejoined P.)

I. ADAMS (D.) BEATTIE MI. (H.) TURNER (S.) MEESON (S.) GIRLING (S.) DAVIES (P.) I. DAVIES (P.) JEFFREY MI. (P.) HOARE (S.) CRAN (D.) WRIGHT MI. (D.)

PRE. STIFF, R. BARNES, E. PAWSEY, G. AGNEW, S.

Cadet Corps.

SATURDAY, SEPTEMBER 30TH.

After an inspection by our new Headmaster, Major Lang's report on the July inspection was read on parade ; followed the welcome announcement of the Head's decision to give us the rest of the morning for Corps work. An hour of section practice, rounded off by a route march, made an interesting morning.

SATURDAY, OCTOBER 7TH.

The afternoon was devoted to a map-reading and concentration scheme, which was marred by the frailty of the human intelligence (even in Corporals) and the inclement weather.

THURSDAY, OCTOBER 19TH.

After a preparatory lecture on Outposts (given on Wednesday) a very successful Field Day at Aldham took place. Good maps were prepared, and the work of the C.S.M. Ward was excellent. The attack, under Sergt. Andrews, made the most of limited opportunities. The picquet positions were on the whole well chosen, but it must be remembered that a position affording good cover is useless unless it also gives a good field of fire.

SATURDAY, OCTOBER 28TH.

A scheme was carried out at Stanway in order to correct errors revealed at Aldham, and great improvement was noted. We have yet to recognise, however, that a position may often be best defended at points quite outside, and probably distant from, the base to be held.

SATURDAY, NOVEMBER 9TH.

This afternoon was given up to Drill on the Playing Fields, a proceeding which we fear must recur unless there is increased smartness and efficiency in the formal work of the term.

THURSDAY, NOVEMBER 22ND.

Convoy scheme at Layer. Some good scouting work was done in very bitter weather.

SATURDAY, DECEMBER 2ND.

Concentration march at Stanway Green. There was a difference of 12 minutes between the arrivals of the first and last parties — time enough for catastrophe in active operations — but the second rendezvous was punctually reached. The unavoidable absence of senior N.C.O.'s gave the juniors a chance of showing that they are capable of sound work.

* * *

During the term Supt. Andrews, of St. John's Ambulance Association, has been instructing the Ambulance section. We are very grateful to the Supt., whose time is very occupied, often in cases of real injury.

* * *

Again we have been fortunate in securing the services of Instructor Owen, 2/5th Manchesters, in teaching bayonet fighting to a senior sixteen. We have to thank Major Fisher for arranging this useful addition to our syllabus.

* * *

We welcome as recruits :—Goodway, Nicholls mi., Pleasants, Arnold, Harvey, Twyman, Clarke, Henriques, Taylor, Jones, Warden, Wilson, Linfoot, Havard, Powell, Last, Wagstaff, Cunningham, King, and Appleton—a record bunch, both as to numbers and keenness. We are bigger than ever before, and we look for recruits next term among new boys who have so far " sat on the fence." At the same time, a judicious combing out of some of our slacker members will probably deplete our ranks next term.

Every third half-holiday has been given to Corps work this term, and in all some 30 drills have been registered.

* * *

This term has brought the war more nearly home to us. In Douglas Wagstaff, whom to know was to love, we have lost the first of our Corps members on active service ; Cottrell ma. is reported wounded and missing ; Crickmore (of Braintree) died, in November, of pneumonia, contracted during the early days of his training. Lieut. C. E. F. Everett, Watsham ma.. Oliver, Bare ma., and Eves are all well on the way to recovery. Town and Watsham are back on duty. Clover, Pertwee, J. Scott, Collinge, Rickword, French are in O.T.C.'s.

We should be grateful for news of Old Cadets for this part of our Mag.

* * *

Hearty congratulations to our late O.C., Mr. Barker, who is commissioned to the 3rd Essex Regt. Also to Deane ma.. 2nd Lieut , Essex Regiment.

Good luck and a safe return !

* * *

Staff-Major Lang, who inspected at the end of last term, expressed himself as highly pleased with what he saw of our work. We hope to profit by his suggestions, and live up to his praises.

* * *

Our crying needs are " More men, more time ; " and we hope, under the sympathetic rule of Mr. Cape, that both needs will be satisfied.

* * *

The new subscription scheme (3/- terminally) puts us on a more solid financial basis, and removes doubts as to the amount each Cadet owes. The dangerous method of " rebates " to discharged members will now die out.

* * *

For the first time recorded in our history we have been allowed the £5 " grant in aid " by the Territorial Association. Part of it will provide slings for the carbines.

* * *

Pte. R. Harwood was awarded the medal for " Best Recruit " of last term.

J.A.P.

AT MARLBOROUGH CAMP.

Seven of us were fortunate enough to spend a fortnight with 1,300 Cadets at the Public Schools Camp on Marlborough Common.

This is a typical day :—Reveille at 6, Parade at 7, and after a short and simple service we moved off to our respective parade grounds and indulged in physical "jerks " until 8. In footer shorts, with no boots and sleeves uprolled—augh ! I shudder still. Breakfast at 8.15, followed at 10 by that glorious institution—the incoming post ; and to think I used to scorn letters ! At 10.30 full Battalion parade—often very trying in the great heat ; but the officers made the work most interesting, and several schemes were carried out. Dinner at 1, followed at 2.30 by a short parade, generally musketry instruction, entailing little physical effort. After this we were free for the rest of the day to explore the countryside or to enjoy the College grounds, and the facilities for cricket and swimming.

After spending a fortnight of healthy and beneficial instruction in the arts of war we returned to the humdrum of civilian life at Colchester.

We must especially thank Capt. Tench, Lieut. Ferris, and Sergt. Crotch for their friendly help. Everyone thoroughly enjoyed the time in camp, and we hope that our numbers may be considerably augmented next summer.

WHITE MA.

Scouting Notes.

AT the end of the Summer term there was a joint inspection of the Cadet Corps and Scout Troop by Staff Major Lang who is also a Scout Commissioner. After the inspection of the whole troop, Major Lang went round to see the various patrols at work, and before he left he gave us a talk which consisted partly of praise and partly of criticism and good advice. Whilst specially mentioning how hard the troop was hit by losing its senior boys so early, he thought there were too many boys who had been members of the troop for some time and yet had won no proficiency badge. He strongly urged every boy to work always with one definite aim, and mentioned several badges for practical and useful things which were within the power of every Scout to win.

Our numbers this term have increased. Scouts Ascroft and Phillips have left the school, and Clarke, Goodway and Taylor have passed on to the Corps. Our recruits are Prescott, Murphy, Turner, Girling, Clarke and Crowther. Of these Prescott and Murphy were Scouts already, both being members of the 2nd Gibraltar Troop, and the former has done excellent work this term with the Woodpigeon Patrol, over which he has charge. Loyd of the same patrol has qualified for his 1st Class badge. Other boys who have won proficiency badges are Everett, Gardener's badge, Clarke, Farmer, Weeks, Naturalist badge.

We have had several interesting field afternoons this term, every third half-holiday in fact being given up to these. We have been to Layer, Abberton and Fordham, but quite the best work of the term was done last Saturday at Stanway. The buglers have added much to our smartness on the march, and Everett, Prescott, Osborne and Downing deserve praise for their regular attendance at the bugle practices.

On Sunday, November 19th, a parade of all the Local Troops was held in Big School. After prayer had been read by Mr. Parry, Chaplain of the 4th Colchester Troop, an address was given by Mr. Harris, Commissioner for North London, who spoke to us of John Cornwell's deed of heroism and the manner in which the Scouts of England propose to perpetuate his memory. All scouts are now working in order to earn money to found Scholarships for which boys who have won the "Cornwell" badge will be eligible. I hope that our own effort will be worthy of the School Troop.

G.E.P.

Shooting.

THE Range has been open this term during the dinner hour and not always then. This seemed to be the best time for all concerned, but many of our older shots find difficulty in coming at this time, as our interval between morning and afternoon school is all too short.

The price of ammunition has advanced more than 50 per cent. since the outbreak of war, and other requisites having advanced in like proportion, it has been found necessary to increase the charge from 3/- to 4/- for the 24 shots of 7 rounds each. In our last notes we referred to the pressing necessity of obtaining new barrels at the earliest opportunity, but the present price for rebarrelling is prohibitive as far as we are concerned. No. 2 was sent to hospital, but the advice received was " leave it until after the war," so this rifle is having a well-earned rest. It would be interesting to know how many thousand rounds have been fired from this trusted weapon.

The first of the new series of rounds in the competition for the House Challenge Cup was shot off in July, when School House, the present holders, once again secured a very substantial lead, being 44 points ahead of Dugard's. A lead of $5\frac{1}{2}$ points per man is a very useful start, and will want a lot of overhauling. Scores were as follows :—

SCHOOL HOUSE		DUGARD'S		HARSNETT'S		PARR'S	
Middleton	... 60	Bacon	... 55	Clark	... 52	Wheeler	... 48
Crighton	... 58	Plummer	... 53	Cox	... 52	French	... 47
Layzell	... 56	Halls	... 51	Page	... 51	Munson	... 46
Tricker	... 56	Bugg	... 51	Arnold	... 48	Percy	... 43
Tait	... 49	King	... 47	Deane ·	... 42	Collinge	... 38
Lilley	... 47	Hazell	... 41	Burleigh	... 40	Cheshire	... 37
Dolamore	... 39	Wells	... 37	Hill	... 39	Hunneyball	... 30
Barnes	... 37	Gilbert	... 23	Salew	... 27	Andrews	... 27
	402		358		351		316

The results of the I.C.S. Competition are to hand, and our team was placed 92nd in order of merit out of 324 entries.

Gardening,

THE odd corner of our playing-field nearest to Cambridge Road is in process of being turned into Garden Plots. The Governors have approved heartily of the idea, and have made a grant of £10 towards the initial expense in the purchase of tools and other necessities. The plots will be 10 in number, each 50 by 20 feet, with three-foot pathways dividing them, and it is hoped to have flower borders on the north and west sides of the ground, though attention is to be given chiefly to the cultivation of the vegetable crop.

The nature of the crops grown will vary from year to year, but each plot will be sown with the same quantity of seed, so that comparison may be made of the effect of different manures, chiefly artificial, on the produce. For this reason the chief crops will be carefully weighed and a record kept in note-books, each plot having its own note-book, to be kept by the boys responsible for that plot.

A piece of each plot will be left to the boys' own discretion, and there they will be allowed to grow any vegetables they wish.

At the present time most of the trenching remains to be done, but it is hoped that much more may be finished before the end of term, for the sooner this part of the work is done the better will be next year's results, the beneficial effects of frosts on newly turned ground being well-known.

Each party has a numbered spade, fork, rake and hoe, whilst other tools required will be provided as occasion arises. To obtain the best results all tools should be kept as clean as possible, and this also secures more ease in working the ground.

Trenching new ground is always hard work, so that there is much need for labour at the present time, but in future years the hardest work will be in the months of March and April.

The produce of the crops will be sold to the boys, and here again complete records of such sales must be made in each plot note-book.

The chief object of this innovation is not to give the boys skill in horticulture, but to increase their powers of observation, giving them a taste and love for nature and making them think for themselves.

Gardening is a useful and healthy outdoor occupation, teaching one of the greatest of economic lessons, "the dignity of labour." Success to the venture.

E.R.

football.

HOUSE MATCHES.

TWO rounds of House Matches have been played, and the third will probably have taken place by the time of publication. In the first round Dugard's tied with Schoolhouse and Harsnett's beat Parr's. In the second round Schoolhouse beat Parr's, and Dugard's beat Harsnett's in a very good game. In the third round, if both Schoolhouse and Dugard's win, a replay will be necessary, but if either loses this will probably not be necessary.

First Round, Saturday, November 25th.

HARSNETT'S v. PARR'S.

As was anticipated Harsnett's won comfortably. Kicking with the wind in the first half, they kept the ball mainly in Parrite territory, and scored four goals without response. In the second half, Parr's forwards made several dashes towards their opponents' goal, but they failed to combine well, and were easily knocked off the ball by Burleigh and Deane. At the other end, after a period of mis-shooting, Harsnett's at last found the mark, and added five more goals in quick succession, and the game ended 9-0 in their favour.

For Parr's, French proved a tower of strength in the defence, and it was mainly due to his efforts that further goals were not registered. The Osborne brothers and Tricker played well in the forward line, though easily knocked about by Harsnett's backs. For Harsnett's, the forwards, whilst individually good, did not combine. White was easily the pick of the defence, and he was ably supported by Beatty, who is a very promising player. Burleigh, Deane and Peacock did what little they had to do, well.

Thomas (4), Salew (3) and Cox (2) scored for Harsnett's.

DUGARD'S v. SCHOOLHOUSE.

This match was played during weather conditions which were ideal for football. It was very evenly and keenly contested, Dugard's proving superior about half-way through the second half, while Schoolhouse retaliated by gaining the mastery of the game during the last quarter-of-an-hour. Dugard's, winning the toss, secured a favourable wind, while the setting sun was disconcerting to the Schoolhouse team, but in spite of this half-time arrived without either side having scored. Schoolhouse drew first blood owing to a nice piece of play by Wilson mi., the outside right. Powell equalised soon after, and the struggle grew sharp and fierce with the result that Jones scored for Dugard's. Although

Schoolhouse had the upper hand in the latter stage of the game it was some little time before a scrimmage round Dugard's goal-mouth resulted in Barnes scoring.

As regards individual play, Prescott and White treated the spectators to some good football, and Gilbert and Nicholls ma. and mi. played in their customary splendid style.

Second Round, Thursday, November 30th.

DUGARD'S v. HARSNETT'S.

From the kick-off this game was very equal. The Dugard's forwards soon came very near scoring, but Peacock, in Harsnett's goal, who played a very good game throughout, was equal to the situation. When nearing half-time the Dugard's forwards made a rush, and Powell, who was unmarked on the left, scored with a low shot. There was no further score before half-time, which thus arrived with the score 1-o for Dugard's. After half-time Harsnett's forwards rallied well but failed to score. The Dugard's forwards then took the ball, but were robbed of it by White, who dribbled through the opposing halves and scored with a long high shot. After the centre the Dugard's forwards tried hard to score but did not succeed until about a qnarter-of-an-hour before time, when Wells scored with a good shot. Harsnett's tried hard to equalise but were pulled up time after time by Gilbert, who played well at back. There was no further score, and the game ended in a win for Dugard's, 2-1.

For Harsnett s, White ma. and Beatty played well at half and Peacock was safe in goal. For Dugard's, Powell and Nicholls were good at forward, while the two backs, Gilbert and Spencer, saved their side in many tight corners.

SCHOOLHOUSE v. PARR'S.

From the start there could be no doubt as to the result, for Schoolhouse were more than twice as heavy as Parr's. It came as a surprise therefore, when Osborne opened the scoring for Parr's. Before half-time Schoolhouse only succeeded in getting one goal, and so the score stood 1-1. In the second half Parr's kept their end up well for some time, but weight eventually told and Schoolhouse succeeded in getting four goals, and in missing as many hundreds. For Schoolhouse, the two outsides Wilson mi., and Barnes were the best of the forwards, and White and Blyth at back and Prescott at half were the pick of the defence. For Parr's, Wagstaff played a good game in goal, Hackett was excellent at back and Collinge at half played a very plucky and useful game. The forwards played well together, and their combination was much superior to that of the Schoolhouse forwards, but unfortunately they suffered from a chronic lack of weight.

Wilson ma., Wilson mi., Barnes, Prescott and White scored for Schoolhouse, and Osborne for Parr's.

Old Colcestrian Section.

Editorial.

WE are as short of news this term as the housewife is of sugar ; the reasons for the shortage of both are not dissimilar—lack of organisation is the chief factor. Before this number is in your hands we hope this will have been remedied, and the honours thrust upon us will adorn another.

*　　*　　*

A. T. Daldy writes :—" I saw young F. S. Bultitude last night, and got him to join the O.C.S., so please have his name enrolled . . . . He went up the line this morning." This was almost the last act of Bultitude's career, for within a few days he joined the O.C.'s who have died for their country.

*　　*　　*

Mrs. Essex says of her two sons :—" They have always kept the motto of the School over their beds, and acted up to it. Percy, reported missing, was lost in ' no man's land,' which was subjected to a continuous barrage of artillery fire, and no wounded except those who got back of their own accord were recovered, so there is just a faint hope that he may be a prisoner." (2/Lt. Lancs. Fus.) His brother Bertram has done 9 months in the firing line, and will soon enter a Cadet School.

*　　*　　*

Maurice Jones is Captain of Shooting and Q.M.S. of Mill Hill O.T.C. ; he is shortly leaving school to join up.

*　　*　　*

" Somewhere in France " an officer started "The Leopard Song " in a trench and was joined by another officer who sang it with slightly different words, and who turned out to be an Old Colcestrian. This prompts me to ask you whether the Colchester School song is a variant of ours ?." Thus the editor of the Skinner's School Mag., who will recall the fact that Mr. Jeffrey (who founded both Old Boys' clubs) also wrote both school ditties to the music by Cronk, whose melody is rivalled only by " Forty Years On." and is beaten by none.

The brothers Brook (A. T. & L. C.) have joined the R.N.V.R.

* * *

We deplore the loss of Mr. H. Lainson Griffin, President O.C.S. 1904-5, who died suddenly, in October last. Our sympathy is extended to the bereaved family, whose loss is shared by the whole borough, of which he was a prominent citizen.

* * *

Geoffrey Cheshire, now home on sick leave, lost an eye in a recent attack. A week previously he had earned the Military Cross. Sympathy and congratulations!

* * *

Tom Cork (C.S.R.) has made a wonderful recovery, after being seriously wounded; we are pleased to hear a similar good report from Rickard.

* * *

Do you find this section of the Mag. disappointing? Certes, my master, it is your own fault; you have not contributed even one full stop! Why not write us—once a term—some personal experience, or episode, or school reminiscence? Or mark passages in your letters, which your friends would dish up for us? Even the War Loaf needs *some* ingredients.

* * *

F. Patey Shuter (24th R.F.) is home for short leave after a year in France. He sends greeting to all O.C. contemporaries.

* * *

Reg. Bultitude, who joined up in 1914, although never of robust health, improved considerably during the early days of his training. The wet spring, however, brought a recurrence of lung trouble, to which he recently succumbed.

* * *

Brand has recovered, and is once more in the trenches. Butler ma. has completed his course at Cambridge, and will soon be joining his unit. Butler mi. is serving in the Auxiliary Navy; Gibb (of Rotterdam) has recovered from his attack of malaria and rejoins his ship shortly.

* * *

We had a visit recently from Bond, one of the few O.C.'s serving with the Australian Forces; his smile is as cheery as ever, despite grim experiences "out there."

* * *

A. H. Webb, who left the staff at Clifton to join up, has completed his training for commission. King ma., we learn, will probably be given a post in which his special knowledge of the life and language of the Boche will be valuable. His younger brother J. H. K. has recently joined up.

PROMOTIONS.

Willmott, J., 2/Lt. 3rd Essex.
Butler, F. H., 2/Cadet Battalion.
Collinge, C. E., 2/Lt.
Deane, G. F., 2/Lt. 3rd Essex.
Barker, F. D., 2/Lt. 3rd Essex.

CASUALTIES.

Thomas, R. J., 2/Lt. 9th Beds., wounded.
Bare, J. W., 8th Essex, wounded.
Eves, F. J., Q.V.R., wounded.
Cheshire, G., wounded.
Marlar, J., 2/Lt. 3rd Essex, wounded.
Essex, P., Lancs. Fus., wounded and missing.
Pulford, A. L., 5th Essex, wounded and missing.

KILLED.

Bultitude, F. S., 8th Essex.
Bultitude, Regd. (died in England).
Wagstaff, D. T., Coldstream Guards.
White, A. S., Capt., Northumberland Fus.
Bennett, G. F., Lt.,
Horwood, R. B., 2/Lt., 3rd Essex.
Cheshire, W. R., 2/Lt., C.P.R.

Roll of Honour.

ADDITIONS.

Bayliss, R. V. J., L.R.B.
Bowen, H. H., 2/Lt., R.G.A. (B.E.F.)
Brook, A. T., R.N.V.R.
Brook, L. C., R.N.V.R.
Chapman, D., 31st Royal Fusiliers.
Harvey, Claude L., 1st Bttn. London Scottish.
Horwood, E. B., Artists Rifles.
King, J., 8th Essex.
Lines, R., Royal Fusiliers.
Ladbrooke, H. M. J., Essex and Suffolk R.H.A.
Rainbird, W. B., 31st Royal Fusiliers.
Rickword, J. E., Artists Rifles
Scott, J. J., Artists Rifles O.T.C.
Stow, W. H., 3/1st Essex Yeomanry (Aldershot).
Waller, James.

Christmas in the Piney Woods.

BY P. SHAW JEFFREY.

BY the greatest piece of luck we had caught a bush turkey ; one of the dog literally fell over it while it was being invited to dinner by a large rattlesnake. A timely shot disposed of the rattler and the turkey, still dazed by the fascination of its prospective host, put up but a feeble flutter and was easily taken.

For weeks we had fed it with assiduous care and for weeks we had watched it growing plumper and juicier and then on Christmas Eve its perch was empty and our cupboard was bare. One of the niggers employed on the orange grove had shared our hopes and expectations and would in due course eat our turkey for his Christmas dinner.

That is why our Christmas Day began at 4 a.m. for as there was no longer a turkey we must shoot duck for the pot.

It was pitch dark except for the stars and our teeth chattered as we drank an early cup of coffee before starting to row up the lagoon to a drinking pool in the Piney Woods where we were pretty sure to find duck if we could get there before dawn.

The lagoon looked like black velvet spangled with stars and the palmettos held their jagged fans up against the skyline while the Spanish moss hanging on the live oaks swayed to and fro like a giant's washing hung out to dry.

And it was very quiet with the strange silence that comes just before daybreak. Sometimes a bull frog cried far away on the marshes or the dull boom of the drummer fish rose under our keel, but for the most part there was no sound but the dip of oars as they splashed into the phosphorescence that hung over our ugly home-made flat-bottomed boat with chains and stars of diamonds.

Half-an-hour's steady pull brought us to our landing place and drawing up our boat on the shell beach we picked our way cautiously through the hammock land to the piney woods beyond. Caution was necessary because we knew that the edges of the bayou, or creek, which we were following were certainly fringed with deadly moccassin snakes though these were happily quite as anxious to avoid us as we were to avoid them

Before long we reached our drinking pool putting up a couple of those curious wood ducks whose plumage looks as if it had been painted by a colour blind futurist artist, and then we started in desperate haste to make our duck blinds by cutting down palmetto fans and building them into a

screen, for there was already a hint of daybreak in the East
and we knew that in these subtropical latitudes the sun would
be fully risen within ten minutes of the first faint streak of
dawn.

The ducks flying inland to their pools are so wary that the
sportsman who is not securely hidden behind his blind before
daylight has but little chance of a shot.

We however were fortunate, and half-an-hour's patient
waiting brought a flight of widgeon wheeling down to the
decoys. we had sent sailing on our pool. Two or three shots
gave us all the birds we wanted and we set off home again
with our Christmas dinner in leash.

Breakfast was quite gay.   The old negro mammy who
cooked for us had gotten (as she said) cherokee roses and
magnolia blooms to take the place of mistletoe and holly and
we ate flap-jacks and maple syrup, scuppernong grapes,
oysters, guava jelly, and johnny-cake with the courage of
men to whom dyspepsia was unknown.

The morning was hot and as a preparation for the evening
festivities we went to have our hair cut at the village store.

The Storekeeper was only by courtesy a barber as indeed
he was by courtesy most other things and we sat on a pork
barrel in the verandah while he hovered round and snipped
us where we stuck out most.

Then we assisted at a marriage ceremony reduced to its
lowest terms.   The happy couple arrived on muleback, the
lady riding pillion.

They were Minorcans, descendants of the colonists who
invaded the Palmetto State in its prosperous days of slavery
when the cotton fields still blossomed and the indigo mills
brought affluence to Southern Florida.

The Storekeeper was a notary public and as such authorised
to tie the marriage knot.

His preliminaries were short—he put on his coat.   Then
the happy couple lined up in front of the counter.

" Will you have this woman to be your wedded wife ? "
he asked the embarassed groom.   " Yessir," was the answer.

" Will you have this man to be your wedded husband ? "
" Yessir," from the bride.

" Righto " said the Storekeeper " sign the book and take
a drink while I write your lines."

The ceremony concluded with the hilarious congratulations
of the crowd of loafers chewing the plug of sweet and bitter
fancy against the verandah uprights.

Over our Christmas dinner I prefer to draw a veil. We
had eaten duck twice a day for many months except on the
days when a northwester blew the waters out of the lagoon

so that we could not reach the mangrove flats where duck are found; and on these days we ate squirrel, so that duck for us had lost the bloom of novelty and it was annoying to remember the fine fat turkey we ought to have enjoyed. True we ate cranberries with our ducks but that seemed only to add insult to injury.

The real Christmas note came only with the evening when we drove out to the schoolhouse in the piney woods for our Christmas Tree.

The village shrew got a tin of lip-salve. The Storekeeper, whose whiskey was scandalously below proof, received a large bottle of water labelled "Danger—dilute before drinking."

But there were plenty of ribbons for the ladies and cigars for the men, and to wind up the proceeding we danced. Yes, we danced in our wood-pegged high sandboots till the dust rose up and choked us and the stamping of the mules and broncos warned us to inspan and be off if we wished to reach home with a whole skin.

And as we jogged home under the splendid stars we could hear the settlers singing "Good Christian men rejoice", as bravely as it was being sung no doubt in many a snow swept village three thousand miles away.

Retirement of Mr. P. Shaw Jeffrey.

(Reprinted from the Essex Telegraph, August. 26, 1916,)

THE close of a memorable 16 years work for Colchester's School was marked on Monday by the presentation of a framed portrait in oils to Mr. Percy Shaw Jeffrey, M.A., who is retiring from the headmastership: The portrait was painted by Mr. Frank Daniell, a distinguished Colchester artist, and was the gift of the Governors of the School and members of the Old Colcestrian Society, the secretaries of the presentation committee being the Clerk to the Governors (Mr. H. C. Wanklyn) and Mr. C. E. Benham. The Mayor and Mayoress (Councillor and Mrs. A. G. Aldridge) kindly entertained the numerous friends who attended to witness the ceremony.

THE PRESENTATION

In handing over the portrait the Mayor said : We are met here to-day to do honour to whom honour is due, and I regard myself as singularly fortunate in having the privilege, as Mayor of this borough, of taking so prominent a part in expressing the town's regard and esteem to one of its most prominent and most valued citizens. It is a matter of the deepest regret that the function should partake also of the nature of a parting gathering. Unfortunately, it is because of that fact that we are here now; and it is Mr. Shaw Jeffrey's approaching departure that has provided the occasion for an expression of heartfelt gratitude for the conspicuous and successful services he has rendered to the cause of education here. The Governors of the Grammar School and members of the Old Colcestrian

Society spontaneously felt they could not allow an occasion like this to pass without an opportunity being provided to all who had come into contact with and under the influence of Mr. Shaw Jeffrey to show their feelings and sentiments towards him. The movement was immediately taken up with eagerness and delight, and the result is the presentation I shall presently have the honour of making. It will only be in a sadly imperfect way that I can refer to the feelings of regret which Mr. Shaw Jeffrey's severance of his connection with the School has caused, and to the profound gratitude felt by those whose lives he has moulded and whose characters he has helped to build up. In Mr. Shaw Jeffrey the Governors have had a faithful servant, and they are convinced that his work at the School has been of a high order, not merely in the imparting of knowledge, but in the higher work still of the development of character—which I put first as essential ground work—and latent faculties and in the cultivation of the power to think and judge.

EDUCATION AND DISCIPLINE.

He has taught discipline, but it has been the right kind of discipline—not the kind we see in the ranks of the enemy in the field to-day, which is that of the automatic figure, whose movements are entirely guided and controlled from without, but the discipline that comes from within—the power to control one's self, the discipline that teaches us to suppress our passions and our desires generally to do wrong. Education that fails in this fails in all that makes for true greatness and that character which makes men and exerts powerful influence in the world. In that grandest and noblest of work Mr. Shaw Jeffrey has achieved the highest success. The affectionate esteem in which he is held by old pupils and those now in the School is a reward for him which I know he will not lightly regard. He will treasure it all his life as a sweet recompense for his labours. His worship proceeded to recall what Mr. Shaw Jeffrey had done for the school in the inauguration of the house system, and mentioned that the school had been raised to be one of the foremost schools in the country in the teaching of modern languages, and was one of the four schools chosen by the Board of Education as models in the matter of modern language teaching. The scholastic successes attained by Mr. Jeffrey's boys were also enumerated, and the Mayor observed that the school had been conducted on the lines of high ideals. Who should say where its influence has extended ? The record which I have indicated (the Mayor went on) is one of which not only the Headmaster but the Governors, may well feel proud. The name and reputation of the School have reached many distant shores ; it has produced good citizens and capable men who have assisted in the general progress of the world, men who have distinguished themselves in many spheres of labour. All honour to their teacher and guide ! No review of the work of the School would be complete without a very special acknowledgment being made of the part played by Mrs. Shaw Jeffrey. Her labours and influence have been invaluable, and have found a fitting complement to those exercised by her husband. She has sacrificed time, leisure and even health itself in order that she might give of her best in the highest interests of the School. She has worked tirelessly for the boys' good, and she has earned the deep gratitude of all who have benefited by her gracious and kindly influence. I speak, I am sure, for the Governors, the members of the Old Colcestrian Society, past and present pupils, and, indeed, for the whole Borough of Colchester when I say that the heartiest and most cordial good wishes of all, go with you, Mr. Shaw Jeffrey, to your new sphere. It is now my pleasure to ask you to accept the portrait of yourself, and I trust it may remind you for many years to come of the host of friends you have left at Colchester, and whose kindest thoughts will accompany you to your new home.

MR. JEFFREY'S REPLY.

Mr. SHAW JEFFREY, in the course of an eloquent reply, said his wife and he had been placed in circumstances which had enabled them to do a good piece of work, but the whole town of Colchester had been their coadjutor, and the whole town should take credit to itself for what it had been able to accomplish.   He added : You may perhaps think it curious that there were exactly 50 per cent. more candidates for the headmastership of your Town School in 1900 than there were recently in 1916. There were 147 applications in 1900 and 98 in 1916.   For this the war is only partly responsible.   A school on its beam ends is always attractive to speculative schoolmasters, and Colchester School had fallen so low in 1900 that unless the bottom fell out altogether it could hardly go lower, and so it happened that the successful candidate for the headmastership in 1900 appeared in the person of Mr. Bingham Turner, 8th Classic and Fellow of Jesus College, Cambridge—a whale among minnows as far as the rest of us were concerned.   Mr. Turner asked for a week to consider the Governors' offer, and I was selected as second string in case of accidents.   A week later I got a wire at Clifton telling me Mr. Turner had withdrawn, so that the Colchester sportsmen brought me down with their second barrel.

THEN AND NOW.

What the School was like when I first saw it it would take too long to describe, but you may be interested to hear that there was no bathroom in school-house either for boys or masters, the dormitory windows were not made to open, the school drains had never been connected up with the main sewer, and the big schoolroom had not been cleaned for over five years.   I am, like most schoolmasters, a very superstitious person, and I held the idea which is fairly common—that if I went to look round the buildings of any school for which I was a candidate before my appointment I should never be its headmaster, so I never actually saw the place until after my appointment—and I can only say that if I had seen it I should not have been here to-day, for the interior offended both the eye and the nose.   Well, at any rate we have changed all that, and for this I and you have many people to thank ; indeed, there is hardly anyone present here this afternoon who has not personally contributed something towards making your School the success which it undoubtedly is, and which it will undoubtedly continue to be under its new headmaster.   Speaking generally, what I have personally to thank the people of Colchester most for is not so much their generosity or their kindness or their sympathy—though these have been both constant and uniform— but most of all for their forbearance.   I came to Colchester with educational ideas—mostly heretical—sprouting all over me.   Some of these I have made good, some have proved unworkable, but in every case both the School Governors and the public of Colchester have treated my vagaries with courtesy and consideration.   I have had from first to last in Colchester a fair chance, and I think the very desperateness of the situation must have appealed to the well-known sporting instincts of the men of Essex.

SOME WORTHY COLCESTRIANS.

I should be ungrateful if I did not acknowledge the great assistance which the school has had from the Old Colcestrian Society.   There was always a danger that with so many changes in your old school the general public might come to look upon it as something entirely new, but when they saw the hoary heads of the older members of the O.C.S. they had to realise that the school must date back some considerable distance into the mists of antiquity.   The younger members of the Society have proved themselves worthy of the best traditions of this School—310 of them are serving their country, five have won the D.S.O.

two the Military Cross, two the Royal Naval Decoration, and 14 have been mentioned in despatches. Many schools may have done as well but none have done better in proportion to their available numbers. There is one mistake about this portrait, and it is rather a serious one. I think you have painted the wrong person. As far as the success of a school like this is concerned the wife is of more importance than the husband. I believe this is always so. I appeal to the married men in this audience, but in no case is it more certain than in the management of a school boarding-house. My wife has devoted all the best of her energies, her leisure, her health, and her powers of organisation to the care of her boarders, and boarders are a very important element in the life of small school. So I think my wife's portrait ought to be in that frame instead of mine.

Many people ask me why I am retiring. I can give you lots of reasons. One is that on January 19th last I completed my 35th year of continuous teaching, and I was afraid that if I went on much longer I should end by becoming a schoolmaster, which is a fate that no one can contemplate without a shudder. I have always considered that no man should continue to " teach school " when he is no longer able to take an active part in the games of his boys. A man who does not share in the games of his boys loses half his chances of influencing them, and as soon as I found that I was getting stiff in the joints I thought it time to look about for other work I could do as well and relinquish work which a younger man might do better. Before sitting down I should like to thank Mr. Frank Daniell for his care and skill and patience in painting my portrait. He has an eye like an accusing conscience, and that I endured it without flinching is due to what Mr. Pepys would call "the diversity and agreeableness of his conversation." We spent many improving hours in his studio at Hammersmith, and I for one am more than satisfied with the result. One of the sad things about a head-master's position is that when he retires he can never settle down among his friends in the town where he has been headmaster, otherwise he becomes sooner or later an embarrassment to all concerned, but though my wife and I are going into exile we shall take with us most grateful memories of our life in Colchester, and shall seize every possible excuse to come back and shake hands with you all again.

It was announced that a replica of the portrait—which was admired by all—will be hung in the School as a memorial to Mr. Jeffrey and the original will adorn the walls of his new home.

Mr. Jeffrey has been the recipient of other presentations, as under :— An aluminium feather-weight Blick typewriter in travelling leather case, from the boys of the School ; a silver salver and solid silver rose bowl, inscribed, from past and present masters of the School ; and a silver flask from the boys of the Preparatory School.

Drake.

Drake of old was a sailor bold,
    And he sailed through distant seas.
From Spanish hold he took the gold
    Old England's Queen to please.
When her mighty foe swept past the Hoe
    He stayed to finish his game,
Then Eastward Ho ! to the Spaniard's woe
    And the glory of England's name.

(Pattle).

Annual Meeting.

THE Annual Meeting of the Old Colcestrian Society was held on December 8th, at Gilberd House, Mr. President C. T. Wright occupying the chair. Among others present were the new Head (Mr. H. J. Cape), Alderman W. G. Benham, Messrs. C. E. Benham, E. P. Bugg, A. O. Farmer (hon. sec.), C. Griffin, H. H. Hollaway, W. H. King, B. Mason, J. H. Nunn, J. A. Peart, E. Reeve and H. L. Twentyman.

Mr. Farmer, in the absence of Mr. A. T. Daldy (on active service), presented a statement of accounts showing an improved condition compared with a few years back. A number of subscriptions are still outstanding, however, and it was stated the early work of the new secretary would include the collection of as many as possible.

On the proposition of Mr. Hollaway, seconded by Mr. Reeve. Mr. Charles Wright was unanimously re-elected President of the Society, and congratulated upon assuming office for the third year—a record unique in the history of the Society.

Mr. Farmer tendered his resignation as secretary owing to lack of time for the work, and he proposed that Mr. Bernard Mason be elected to serve as secretary and treasurer with Mr. Daldy. Mr. Hollaway seconded, and the election was unanimous.

The Committee was re-appointed as under :—Messrs. C. E. Benham (Chairman), J. H. Nunn, F. G. Mills, C. Griffin, H. H. Hollaway, A. W. Nunn, G. C. Benham, E. W. Dace, J. G. Salmon, W. H. King, F. D. Barker and J. A. Peart; with the addition of Mr. Cape and Mr. Reeve.

At the conclusion of the ordinary business, Mr. Cape expressed his great pleasure at meeting members of the Society, and stated that he was in entire sympathy with old boys' associations. He had been a member of his own old boys' club for 24 years, and had attended every dinner till the last two years, when that part of the programme had been in abeyance. Whatever he could do for the O.C.S. would be done with the greatest pleasure, for he regarded an old boys' association as a vital and important adjunct to the School.

Alderman Benham, on behalf of O.C.'s, conveyed to Mr. Cape a hearty welcome, and, speaking as one of the Governors, he said they were most fortunate in having him as Headmaster; he came to Colchester with a record of most important work at Rochester, and they hoped to see the old school at Colchester go on thriving under his direction.

The President added his welcome to the new Head, and said it was hoped to arrange early in the new year a gathering of O.C.'s in order to meet Mr. Cape.

Speaking for the members he knew all would do everything in their power to assist the present Head of their beloved School.

"THE COLCESTRIAN."

The meeting appointed a Sub-Committee (The President, Messrs. Cape, Peart, Benham and Nunn) to discuss the future of the magazine, with powers to re-organise, so that "The Colcestrian" may continue to form the connecting link between the old school and the old scholars, especially those doing the country's work in the trenches, where, we have reason to know, the issue is eagerly anticipated.

Acknowledgments.

We beg to thank the respective Editors of the following for copies received :—Arrow, Wyggestonian, Chigwellian, Chelmsfordian, L.O.S., Leopard, Barrovian, Framlinghamian, O.H.S., Ipswichian and Pelican.

EVERETT, O. E. F., 28 New Town Road, Colchester.
EVES, F. J., 17 Morant Road, Colchester.
EWING, J. H., South Hall, Ramsey, Harwich
FAIRHEAD, A. E., Bouchier's Hall, Messing, Kelvedon.
FARMER, A. O., 12 Queen Street, Colchester (HON. SECRETARY).
FAVIELL, C. V., 28 Udney Park, Teddington, Middlesex.
FIELDGATE, W. H., "Ty Fry," Regent Road, Brightlingsea.
FINCH, F. D., 25 Salisbury Avenue, Colchester.
FINCHAM, G. E., 52 Myland Road, Colchester.
FITCH, L. B., Louisville, Fambridge Road, Maldon.
FLANAGAN, L. C., Beta House, Clacton-on-Sea.
FLEETWOOD, E. C., Bernabague, Shrub End Road, Colchester.
FLETCHER, L. B., 13 Harsnett Road, Colchester
FLUX, R. C., 32 Old Heath Road, Colchester.
FOLKARD, G., Copford, Colchester.
FRANKLIN, Councillor R., Sutherland House, 95 Baddow Road, Chelmsford.
FRENCH, R. E., 58 Roman Road, Colchester.
FROST, A. W., 13 Head Street, Colchester.
GIBBS, J. W., 249 Maldon Road, Colchester.
GIRLING, T. A., 18 Park Road, Chelmsford.
GIRLING, HUGH, Park Villa, Dunmow.
GODFREY, C. F., "Thirlmere," Queen's Road, Springfield, Chelmsford.
GOING, F. W., 125 Maldon Road, Colchester.
GOODEY, S., Chelsworth, New Town Road, Colchester.
GOODY, C., Old Heath Road, Colchester.
GREEN, A. C., Fingringhoe, Colchester.
GREEN, A. E., 18 East Stockwell Street, Colchester.
GREEN, C. S., Fingringhoe, Colchester.
GREEN, C. B., Holmwood, Fingringhoe, Essex.
GRIFFIN, C., Stanway Villa, Colchester.
GRIFFIN, H. L., Stockwell House, West Stockwell Street, Colchester.
GRIMWOOD, O. H., c.o. Boots, Ltd., Long Wyre Street, Colchester.
HALL, A. L., Caerleon, New Town Road, Colchester.
HARPER, W. C., High Street, Colchester.
HARRIS, H. J., Weircombe, Ardwick Road, W. Hampstead.
HARVEY, J. B., Stanley Lodge, Wellesley Road, Colchester.
HARVEY, W., Central Secretariat, Lagos, Nigeria W. Africa.
HARSUM, G. F., Wood Field, Bourne Road, Colchester.
HAZELL, S. G., 39 Wellesley Road, Colchester (and Montreal).
HAZELL, R. L., 23 Lexden Street, Colchester.
HEAD, A., 58 Wimpole Road, Colchester.
HEAD, J., 58 Wimpole Road, Colchester.
HEMPSON, R. J., Galton Lodge, Reigate.
HOBROUGH, S. J., Ernest Cottage, Parsons Heath, Colchester.
HOLLAWAY, H. H., 34 Old Heath Road, Colchester.
HORLOCK, M. F., High Street, Mistley.
HORWOOD, R. B., Layer Hall, Layer.
HURST, H. J. R., 7 St. John Street, Colchester
HUSSEY, F. W., 15 Audley Road, Colchester.
IVEY, S. F., 63 Kensington Gardens Square, London, W.
JARRARD, C. H., Thorpe, Colchester.
JARRARD, D. G., Alexandra Road, Sible Hedingham.
JASPER, C. V., Langenhoe Hall, Colchester.
JASPER, L. A., Langenhoe Hall, Colchester.
JAWS, GEO. F., 24 Churchill Terrace, Cadoxton, Barry, nr. Cardiff
JEFFERIES, C. R., Second Lieutenant R.F.A.
JEFFREY, P. SHAW, Bagdale Old Hall, Whitby.
JOHNSON, L. H., 17 Lion Walk, Colchester.

JUDD, L., South Villa, Ardleigh.
KENT, B. H., 182 Maldon Road, Colchester.
KING, J., 16 Inglis Road, Colchester.
KING, W. H., Inglis Road, Colchester
KING, W. H., junr., Inglis Road, Colchester.
KING, G. K., 53 Friar Street, Sudbury.
KOSKINAS, F. M., 24 Pembridge Gardens, Notting Hill, W. [Naze.
LANSDOWNE. L. R., Mersea House, Walton-on-
LAY, C. V., 2k Portman Mansions, St. Marylebone, London, W.
LAWRENCE, A. D., c.o. Head & Co., Ltd., 27 Cornhill, London, E.C.
LAWRY, E., Hoe Farm, Aldham.
LAZELL, HAROLD, Fitzwalter Road, Lexden Park, Colchester.
LEANING, E. M., Welwyn, Wash Lane, Clacton-on-Sea.
LEEMING, J. H. J., 27 Liversidge Road, Higher Tranmere, Birkenhead.
LEWIS, K. M., 173 Maldon Road, Colchester.
LINES, E., The Bungalow, Great Bentley.
LORD, P., North Hill, Colchester.
LORD, S. W., 49 North Hill, Colchester.
LOWE, STANLEY, Warwick House East Dereham.
LUCKING, A. S., 20 Inglis Road, Colchester.
LUCKING, C. D., 20 Inglis Road, Colchester.
MALYN, D. P., Bleak House, Braintree.
MALYN, R., Barclay's Bank, Colchester
MANNING, C., The Elms, Weeley, R.S.O.
MANNING, P. E. J., The Elms, Weeley, R.S.O.
MARLAR, J., North Hill, Colchester.
MARSH, W. E., 180 Longmarket Street, Natal, South Africa.
MARSH, H. V., P.O. Box 253, Maritzburg, South Africa.
MASON, A. S., Perse School, Cambridge.
MASON, B., 10 Crouch Street, Colchester.
MASON, C., 10 Crouch Street, Colchester.
McCLOSKY, C. A., c.o. Edes Everett, St. Botolph's, Colchester.
MIDDLETON, G. A. T.
MIDGLEY, O. F., "Gunton," Westminster Drive, Westcliffe-on-Sea.
MIDGLEY, W. R. O., 163 Ongar Road, Brentwood.
MILLS, F. G., 18 Beverley Road, Colchester.
MOY, C. T., Stanway Hall, Colchester.
NORFOLK, A. E., 76 Chesson Road, West Kensington.
NUNN, A. W., Crouch Street, Colchester.
NUNN, J. H., Melford Villa, Rawstorn Road, Colchester.
NUNN, W. H., Whatfield, Ipswich.
OLIVER, J. L., Maldon Road, Colchester.
ORFEUR, H. W., Colne Bank, Station Road, Colchester.
ORFEUR, C. B., Colne Bank, Station Road, Colchester.
ORFEUR, R. F., Colne Bank, Station Road, Colchester.
ORFEUR, F. N., Colne Bank, Station Road, Colchester
ORPEN, O. G., Hillside, West Bergholt, Colchester.
ORRIN, W. F., 37 Campion Road, Colchester.
OSBORNE, F. F.
OSBORNE, H. C.
PARKER, Rev. E. H., London Orphan School, Watford.
PAYNE, E. A., 2 Honywood Road, Colchester.
PHART, F. A., C.R.G.S.
PEPPER, V. J.
PEPPER, G. E., C.R.G.S.
PERTWEE, F., Moreham's Hall, Frating.
PLUMMER, N. A., Station Road, Lawford, Manningtree.
PLUMMER, F. E., Station Road, Lawford, Manningtree.

349

POINTING, W. W., 148 Maldon Road, Colchester.

POTTER, C. O., 119 Maldon Road, Colchester.

POTTER, F., Middleborough, Colchester.

REEVE, E., C.R.G.S.

RENTON, T. S., 12 Crouch Street, Colchester.

RICHES, A. E., 80 Tower Street, Brightlingsea.

RICHARDS, R. F., Head Street, Colchester.

RICHARDSON, A. J., School House, Great Bentley.

RICKWORD, E. G., Boughton Lane, Loose, Maidstone.

ROGERS, S. W., 5 Caterham Road, Lewisham, S.E.

ROSEVEARE, H. H., "St. Breca," Newquay, Cornwall.

RYDER, E. W., 74 Wimpole Road, Colchester.

SADLER, F. B., Box P.O. 219, c.o. The Eastern Bank, Ltd., Bombay.

SANGER, O. W., "Rookerydene," Abbeygate Street, Colchester.

SANGER, H., "Rookerydene," Abbeygate Street, Colchester.

SALMON, J. G., Wash Lane, Clacton.

SAMMONS, A. O., 49 Grafton Street, Fitzroy Square, W.

SRAMER, H. St. J., "The Gables," East Bergholt.

SENNITT, F. J., 28 Mersea Road, Colchester.

SHAW, D. E., Beaconsfield Avenue, Colchester.

SHENSTONE, J. C., 15c Coverdale Road, Shepherd's Bush, London, W.

SLIGHT, R., c.o. One Barrow Lodge, Coalville, Leicestershire.

SLATER, E. M.

SMITH, AUBREY, "Mantz," 30 Peak Hill, Sydenham, S.E.

SMITH, G. E., Chapel Street, Colchester.

SMITH, W. G., 23 Roman Road, Colchester.

SMITH, F. R., 23 Roman Road, Colchester.

SPARLING, A. S. B., 21 Creffield Road, Colchester.

SURRIDGE, P. T., Coggeshall.

SYER, F. N., 8 Studlands Road, Sydenham.

TYTLER, A. P., "Cromer," Westgrove, Woodford Green, Surrey.

TENNANT, E. N., Connaught Avenue, Frinton.

THOMAS, A. O., 150 Maldon Road, Colchester.

TOWN, H. G., 50 Essendine Mansions, Maida Vale, W.

TOWN, W. M., 50 Essendine Mansions, Maida Vale, W.

TURNER, Capt. A., Essex Hall, Colchester.

TURNER, Dr. DOUGLAS, Essex Hall, Colchester.

TURNER, S. O., Abbeygate House, Colchester.

VAN DEN BERGH, A. H.

VAN DEN BERGH, H.

WAGSTAFF, D. T. Church Farm, Marks Tey, Colchester.

WALLACE, Councillor R. W., "Moelwyn," Inglis Road, Colchester.

WARD, J. D., Jun., Bluegates, Elmstead, Colchester.

WARNER, A. E., 8 Myland, Colchester.

WATKINSON, W. P., Elmstead, nr. Colchester.

WATSHAM, H., Vine Farm, Wyvenhoe.

WATSON, J. L., Abergwili Palace, Carnarvon.

WATSON, S. F., 154 Maldon Road, Colchester.

WATSON, G. F., Abergwili Palace, Carnarvon.

WATTS, FRANK, 30 Creffield Road, Colchester.

WEBB, G. S., Dairy House, Wix, Manningtree.

WEBB, A. H., Dairy House, Wix, Manningtree.

WENDEN, C. A., The Chase, Great Bromley.

WHEELER, G., 10 High Street.

WHITE, C. E., 57 North Hill, Colchester.

WHITE, F., "Kennington," Myland, Colchester.

WHITEY, J. F. M., 22 Lexden Road, Colchester.

WILLIAMS, F. O., 14 Lexden Road, Colchester.

WILLIS, E. A., 25 Heron Road, Stapleton Road, Bristol.

WRIGHT, O. T., Stacey House, Crouch Street, Colchester (President).

WRIGHT, G., junr., Stacey House, Crouch Street, Colchester.

WRIGHT, Councillor G. F., 47 Crouch Street, Colchester.

WYATT, D. T., Bank Passage, Colchester.

NOTICE TO OLD COLCESTRIANS.

Old Colcestrians who wish to make known their movements in this paper should communicate with Mr. J. HUTLEY NUNN, "Essex County Telegraph" Offices, Colchester.

Subscriptions should be sent to Mr. B. MASON, (Hon. Treas.), Crouch Street, Colchester.

Members of the Society are requested to notify any change of address immediately to either of the Hon. Secretaries:—

Mr. B. MASON, Crouch Street, Colchester.

Mr. A. T. DALDY, Head Street, Colchester.

NOTICE TO CORRESPONDENTS.

Contributions to the O.C. Section, articles on various subjects and humorous anecdotes of school-days, will be gladly welcomed by the O.C. Editor, Mr. J. Hutley Nunn.

All contributions for the next number of "The Colcestrian" to be sent in by Mar. 1st, 1917.

No. 47.]
NEW SERIES.

MARCH, 1917.

The Colcestrian.

EDITED BY PAST AND PRESENT MEMBERS OF COLCHESTER SCHOOL.

PRICE SIXPENCE

Colchester:
PRINTED BY CULLINGFORD, & CO.,
156 HIGH STREET.

O.C.S. Officers for 1915-16.

President:
C. T. Wright, Crouch Street, Colchester.

Vice-Presidents:

W. Gurney Benham, J.P.
R. Franklin
H. L. Griffin
H. J. Harris, B.A.

B. H. Kent
Osmond G. Orpen
W. H. King
Rev. E. H. Parker

J. C. Shenstone, F.L.S.
R. W. Wallace
C. E. White

Committee:

F. D. Brook
J. H. Nunn
A. W. Nunn
F. G. Mills

O. Griffin
H. H. Hollaway
C. E. Benham (*Chairman*)
G. C. Benham

E. W. Dace
J. C. Salmon
F. D. Barker
J. A. Peart
E. Reeve

The Ex-Presidents are ex-officio members of Committee.

Hon. Treasurer (pro tem.):
B. Mason, Crouch Street, Colchester.

Hon. Secretaries:
A. T. Daldy, Head Street, Colchester.
B. Mason, Crouch Street, Colchester.

Members of the O.C.S.

Adams, H. A., 5 Gisburn Rd., Hornsey, N.
Alliston, A. W., Chipping Hill, Witham.
Appleby, W. M.
Atkin, G., Hill Crest, Gt. Oakley.
Bare, W. J., Magdalen Street, Colchester.
Barker, F. D., Royal Grammar School.
Barrell, G., Tower House, High Road, Epping, Essex.
Barnes, F. M., Howell Hall, Heckington, Lincolnshire.
Baxter, H. G., Fronks Road, Dovercourt.
Bayliss, R. V. J., Fleece Hotel, Head Street, Colchester.
Bayliss, B., Fleece Hotel, Head Street, Colchester.
Beard, E. C., St. Margaret's, Cambridge Road, Colchester.
Beckett, H., Balkerne Lane, Colchester.
Bellward, G. W. F., O.R.G.S.
Benham, C. E., Wellesley Road, Colchester.
Benham, G. C., 12 Hospital Road, Colchester.
Benham, Alderman W. Gurney, St. Mary's Terrace, Lexden road, Colchester.
Bird, A., Bell House Farm, Stanway.
Blatch, F., Mina Santiago, Lucine, Bolivia, S. America.
Blaxill, G. A., " West Wellow," Romsey, Hants.
Blomfield, S., Raonah House, New Town Road, Colchester.
Bloomfield, H. D., 3 Tyler Street, Parkeston.
Blyth, Cooper, c.o. Isaac Bunting, 100 Yokahama, Japan.
Brand, E. J., High Street.
Boggis, Frank, Station Road, Sudbury.
Bromley, J. G., Mill House, Great Clacton.
Brook, T. D., " St. Runwald's," Maldon Road, Colchester.
Brook, A. T., " St. Runwald's," Maldon Road, Colchester.
Brook, L. C., " St. Runwald's," Maldon Road, Colchester.
Brook, S. V., 22 Sugden Road, Lavender Hill, S. W.
Brown, D. Graham, " Lound," Witham.
Bugg, E. P., Creffield Road, Colchester.
Burrell, F. B., Abbeygate Street, Colchester
Bunting, A. E., The Nurseries, North Station Road, Colchester.
Burleigh, A., Kudat, N.L.B.T. Co., British North Borneo.

Burston, F. G., 1st National Bank Buildings, San Francisco.
Butcher, H., 3 Eden Ave., Liscard, Cheshire.
Butler, F. H., Cumberland House, Manningtree.
Carey, M. C.
Carter, F. B., O.R.G.S.
Chambers, C., 22 Wellesley Road, Colchester.
Chambers, S. C., 22 Wellesley Road, Colchester.
Chapman, D., Alma Street, Wivenhoe.
Cheese, C. T., 39 Pownall Crescent, Colchester.
Cheshire, W., 1 Meyrick Crescent, Colchester
Child, L. G., 14 Wimpole Road, Colchester.
Clamp, A. J., 122 Priory Street, Colchester.
Clark, L. W., 16 East Stockwell Street, Colchester.
Clarke, S. F., Parr's Bank, Holloway, London, N.
Clover, J. M., The Hall, Dedham.
Cole, C. L. L., General Post Office (Staff), Cambridge.
Cole, H. S., 25 Wimpole Road, Colchester.
Collinge, C. E., 3 East Hill.
Collinge, F. J., 146 High Street.
Collison, A. L., Garrison School, Buena Vista, Gibraltar.
Cork, F. F., 2e New Town Road, Colchester.
Cragg, Rev. E. E., St. John's Church, Huntington, Long Island, U.S.A.
Cullington, M. W., 38 Meyrick Crescent, Colchester.
Curtis, A. P., Bromley Road, Colchester.
Dace, A. W., 122 George Street, Edinburgh.
Dace, E. W., 17 Honywood Road, Colchester.
Daldy, A. T., 50 South Street, Colchester
Davies, W. E., 118 Butt Road, Colchester.
Drakin, E. B., O.R.G.S.
Deane, G. F. F., Longwood, Nayland.
Dicker, B. P., Grocers' Hall, Prince's Street, E.C.
Doubleday, R. E., Belle Vue Road, Wivenhoe.
Doubleday, W. A., Belle Vue Road, Wivenhoe.
Everett, H. J., Councillor, 8 New Town Road, Colchester.
Everett, W. R., c/o B. F. Burrell, Esq., Abbeygate Street, Colchester.
Everett, C. E. F., 28 New Town Road, Colchester.
Eves, F. J., 17 Morant Road, Colchester.
Ewing, J. H., South Hall, Ramsey, Harwich

Continued on Page 3 of Cover.

The Colcestrian.

VITÆ CORONA FIDES.

No. 47].　　　　　　MARCH, 1917.　　　[NEW SERIES.

Economy.

THE watchword of the day, screaming at us from every hoarding and each newspaper is Economy. That there is grievous need for us to husband our resources, in food, in paper, in growing crops, in cash, is very apparent to all, from the Prime Minister to the youngest schoolboy. We are painfully conscious as we walk the street of the shortage of paper, producing an unwonted reticence on the part of newsagents ; on the other hand we have heard joyous hopes expressed by small scholars when they were told that Easter Exams. depended on the supply of the essential paper. A correspondent patriotically demands that the practice of Homework and Detention should be given up, as wasteful and unnecessary.

Seriously, however, there is much that even schoolboys can do to help their country in its need : none is too young to curb his indulgence—in " picture going," in eating sweets, in buying playthings, in taking leisure. Every victory over ourselves gives an added strength, and our temporary denials of self bring permanent enrichment of character.

Several of our boys are proving the reality of their desire to win the war by giving their spare time to digging : others by an increased keenness and devotion to duty as Scouts or Cadets try to make themselves more worthy of their birthright. For each of us there is a way, and it is for us to find it. The way found, we needs must follow.

In two commodities we must use no economy, but spend generously and freely. With WORK we must be unsparing ; though peace be signed long before we reach the end of our schooldays our future and the future of our homeland depend upon our patient, unwearying efforts.

In KINDNESS too, we must not be stinting : the strain of war and want and worry fray out the edges of what we elderly people call " nerves." It is up to you, bright, happy, irresponsible youngsters to let the spring sun of your kindness lighten the darkness and point the way to unselfishness.

o　Grammaria.

The most delightful feature of an otherwise dreary term has been the revival of systematic instruction in Gymnastics, under the keen and able supervision of Mr. Harold Watkin. He has done marvels already, and the enjoyment of the boys is an index of their appreciation of his efforts. We feel sure that everyone will combine to make the Gym display most successful in every way.

The Close.

For a brief while the close is again its peaceful, inviting self; after cruel treatment under the iron heel of the invader the shy grass is once more lifting its head, and the brown is shot with green.

Heuristic methods.

We are able to announce that the recent experiments in the lab. have proved beyond all doubt the truth of certain obiter dicta frequently adumbrated by the Science Master. Meanwhile let us remark on the great increase in the cost of men's clothing.

Another Transformation Scene.

The old Workshop, once a dining hall, formerly a gymnasium, and earlier a cloak-room, has now been partitioned off to make a roomy Club room for the School Scout Troop. The great importance of such a meeting place, solely for troop use, cannot be over estimated : and we congratulate the Troop and their energetic S.M. on this addition to their resources.

Ex ovo.

This term has seen a revival of House Matches for boys under fourteen and the contests have been delightfully keen and strenuous. The Headmaster has very kindly promised a cup for Cock House in these Junior events.

Grave O.C's.

Recently Gilberd House was visited by a very distinguished soldier, whose breast was adorned by a row of medal ribbons, and whose schooldays here were of the remote past. He came to see the old tables, lovingly preserved, on which he and his schoolfellows had carved their names. To witness the delight of this worthy old Son of our Mater Nutrix, and to hear his reminiscences was to feel that the " painful trade " of teaching had its compensations, after all.

Magazine.

We hope that the strong and representative Committee appointed last term to carry on the magazine will be in full working order before the next number goes to press. The regrettable illness of Mr. Charles Benham has delayed the début of the new Committee.

"At the Sign of the Ship."

Form 1 reports ;--We have not lost a single match this term (neither have we played any).

* * *

When are you in the best of health? When you are in *form.* See?

* * *

A new use is advertised for Spearmint, to stick on stamps in these days of gum shortage.

* * *

We are extremely glad that gym. has been started again, thanks to Mr. Cape and Mr. Watkin.

* * *

Our gardeners have begun work very seriously—grave diggers in fact.

* * *

Is Stirling the key to Loch Lomond?

* * *

C.R.G.S.C.C.

Our School is patriotic, no doubt is there of that,
Though some of us are long and lean, and some of us
    are fat.
Our fellows drill like heroes (if not too cold outdoors)
With Prefects for each section, for ever forming fours.
    Its " left incline " and " right incline "
      And " throw your shoulders back,"
    You never saw so smart a corps,
      So absolutely crack.

Our discipline is awful the C.S.M. doth vow,
But Jack Pertwee and Brand and Eves are Tommy Atkins
    now.
What? Yes of course I'm chaffing, it would not be a lie
To say that for their country Cadets and all would die.

> Its " left incline " and " right incline "
> And " halt " and " dress " and " shun,"
> Hurrah for " P " hurrah for " C,"
> Hurrah for everyone.
>
> (CRIGHTON).

*   *   *

In order to encourage enthusiastic gymnasts the gate of the Close is now kept locked.

*   *   *

The Dardanelles.

> Sad spot and dread
> Where the pick of our race
> Fell to the Turkish lead.
> What can we do for our dead?
> Honour their peerless name
> Rev'rence their noble fame,
> For us they bled.
>
> (PROCTER).

Pre-Historic.

DURING the past three weeks " The Pre " have beee. busily engaged in weighing over the pros and the cons of the One Hour Club, and finally twelve of the boys havs decided, with the aid of their respective parents, that the responsibilities in connection with the aforesaid club are not too heavy to take upon themselves. In short they have paid their subscriptions, filled up their forms, promised faithfully to put in one hour each day either at work in the garden or in looking after poultry or rabbits, and are seriously endeavouring to do their bit towards producing food in these days of stress. It all sounds terribly ambitious, but " little drops of water " do " make the mighty ocean," don't they ?

Each of the members has had the delight of seeing his name in print, and is proud possessor of a badge. This is in the form of a large green stud with a brown bee depicted thereon, and round it are the words, " Improve each shining hour." Should any reader find one of these decorations, it would be a truly good deed to send it with all possible speed to the Headmistress, as great distress will reign should one be missing, and since studs are such illusive articles, this will probably happen.

On the first fine day we went out and marked off the border plots afresh. The weather since has not allowed us to sow our seeds, but we hope to do a great deal during the next fortnight, and so leave everything in order, when we break up.

We are indeed grateful to Mr. and Mrs. Chatterton for the very practical interest they are taking in our gardening, and to Mr. Reeve, who has handed over to us a more promising piece of ground near the Shooting Range. Here we hope to grow vegetables—perhaps enough potatoes to supply our Gostwycke friends for several days.

At the present moment we are trying to grow cress in the schoolroom, which we want to send them one afternoon for tea.

At the end of last term the boys were enthusiastic over the Christmas Card Scheme. It was again successful and with the money raised, they sent a nice gift of cigarettes, sweets, oranges and apples to Gostwycke.

Owing to the very severe weather the attendance has not been good this term. This and the loss of Field, who was a very keen raveller, and even now finds time to help us a little, has reduced our number of pillows to half, but thanks to Mr. Horwood we have been well supplied with pieces for ravelling.

At the suggestion of our Headmaster, Pratt has moved the blackboard for us to the other end of the " Pre " building with the result that the light is much better, and the room generally improved.

Miss Bond thanks the boys for magazines and papers sent in week by week for the Wounded in Wards 2, 3 and 4 and the T.B. Hut of the Military Hospital, and she will be glad to receive any others, or books, which are always welcome.

C.C. & A.J.

Valete.

SPENCER, S. G. Form VA. Dugard's. House Football, Cricket, and Hockey. Lance-Corporal (acting), Cadet Corps. Amateur Dramatic Society.

PLUMMER, H. S. Form VA. Dugard's. School Shooting, VIII. House Shooting. Private, Cadet Corps.

SALEW, N. R. Form IVA. Harsnetts'. House Football, Cricket, Hockey and shooting. Patrol Leader, Scouts.

HAZELL, H. G. W. Form IVA. Dugard's, House Shooting. Private, Cadet Corps.

CUNNINGHAM, L. G. Form III. Parr's. Private, Cadet Corps.

ROCK, I. F. Form III. Schoolhouse. Scout.

CRAN, D. L. Form I. Schoolhouse.

Salvete.

GEORGE, A. E.	..	..	H	..	.. VA.
LING, J. S.	..	..	H	..	.. VB.
MORTON, V. A., mi.		..	P	..	.. VB.
WYNCOLL, F. P., ma.	..	..	D	..	.. IVA.

CHARLTON, D. R., ma.	..	H	..	.. IVB.
CHARLTON, H. C., mi.	..	H	..	.. IVB.
CURTIS, R., mi.	..	S	..	.. III.
SMITH, E. H., quartus	..	S	..	.. III.
TAYLOR, L. W., mi.	..	D	..	.. III.
LONGCROFT, E. S.	..	S	..	.. III.
MORTON, C. L., mi.	..	P	..	.. II.
DENNIS, F. E. G.	..	H	..	.. I.
DUNN, A. D.	..	D	..	.. I.
FIELD, E. W.	..	H	..	.. I.
GRIFFIN, J. H. L.	..	H	..	.. I.
WALKDEN, B.	..	P	..	.. I.
WEEKS, D.	..	..	..	.. Pre.
PAWSKY, C.	..	..	..	.. ,,
PERTWEE, C.	..	..	..	.. ,,

"Parragraphs": Collected by P.S.J.

SAMUEL PARR—HEADMASTER C.R.G.S. 1777.

In 1752 Samuel Parr entered at Harrow. He was a free scholar. Parr once told a friend that as a boy he used to rise at 5 o'clock and go into the garden with a Greek Grammar for his companion. Keeping these hours and this kind of company, it is not to be wondered at that before he had completed his fourteenth year he was head of the school and to the last hour of his life he could talk Greek. From his youth up Parr was only happy in an atmosphere of Greek and Latin.

In 1767, Dr. Sumner—the then Headmaster of Harrow offered him the post of "Head assistant," and his offer was accepted. Parr seems to have been a success as a master, and was evidently much liked by the boys. He was supposed to have caught the fancy of a well-to-do widow. One day the following lines were found lying on his desk.

> When Madame Eyre prefers her prayer,
> Safe from the eyes of men,
> Tis this alone her lips make known,
> Parr—donnez moi.—Amen.

This clever quatrain has been attributed to Richard Brinsley Sheridan who was a schoolboy at Harrow at the time.

The untimely death of Dr. Sumner was followed by a school rebellion (1771). The boys supported the election of Dr. Parr as Sumner's successor: the Governors elected Dr. Heath. Parr promptly resigned and started a private school at Stanmore where he was followed by forty scholars "the flower of the school." This enterprise however failed and, following this Dr. Parr came to Colchester school as its Headmaster.

Samuel Parr had a shrewd tongue. Sir Leslie Stephen summed him up as having "Johnson's pomposity without his force of mind, Johnson's love of antithesis without his logical acuteness, and Johnson's roughness without his humour ", but added that his personal remarks were pointed though laboured. Pointed was certainly his reply to a man who had observed that he would not believe anything he could not understand, " Then, young man, your creed will be the shortest of any man's I know." To an antagonist of whom he had a poor opinion, however, he used the bludgeon rather than the rapier " you have read a great deal, you have thought very little, and you know nothing."

Sir James Mackintosh was once taking Parr for a drive when the horse became restive and the scholar became nervous " Gently, Jemmy," said Parr " don't irritate him : always sooth your horse, Jemmy." The horse was stopped enough for the purpose, and no sooner had Parr safely descended than his advice changed, " Now, Jemmy, touch him up. Never let a horse get the better of you. Touch him up, conquer him, don't spare him. And now I'll leave you to manage him— I'll walk home."

One of these boring people who will discuss their health had been enlarging upon various symptoms, and came to a pause after saying that he could not go out without catching a cold in his head " No wonder," commented Parr, " you always go out without anything in it".

In clerical company the conversation having turned upon the then head of the Church, Dr. Parr having listened for some time to the stricture of his companions called in apt alliteration's artful aid and broke in with " Sir, he is a poor paltry prelate proud of petty popularity, and perpetually preaching to petticoats."

Oh, Memory !

When IVA. was a form of sport
  What games we used to play !
But now alas all that is gone
  How time does fly away.

When we were boys not old and staid
  Such were the cries we screamed :
" How's that ? Not out ! No goal ! Well done !"
  Oh ! how the masters beamed.

They smiled and nodded all the time
  Their houses egging on.
But those fine happy days we had
  Alas, they all are gone.

Now on the field each time a match
   Is played the Captain bold
Plays men like pawns in silent chess—
   The war has made us old.

DYER.

Telegrams

Regretting unavoidable absence from the Easter breaking up party have been received from :

Haig—Having a breaking up party here.

Hindenburg—Cannot come. Ancred for the present.

Nicholas—Cannot afford the trip—have not even a crown left.

Willie—Thanks, enough Champagne here for me.

Young Turk—Dare not risk it lest they Bagdad.

Wilson—Too tired. Note follows.

Devonport—Do be rational. You know there are no luncheon trains on G.E.R.

Mrs. Wheeldon—Can't, am in detention.

E. R.—K $\overline{O}$ T. H$_2$S O$_4$.

P. 1—Frightfully sorry, must cultivate my patch.

P.2—Must stop at home and write it up.

C.—Short-handed, cannot get away from business.

W.—Not if VB remove their boots.

K.—Mille regrets ; but the chair of my uncle is good.

T.—Sorry, but sugar shortage threatens closure.

Censor——— ——— (——— ———).

Cadet Corps.

(ATTACHED TO 5TH ESSEX).

WE are delighted to record that our strength is now greater than ever before, our numbers having grown from 56 to 76 during the last year. Several boys have their names down to take the places of any who may leave at Easter. The unusual demand for uniforms has made a tremendous hole in our cash balance, but there can be no better cause for expenditure.

* * *

The persistently bad weather has curtailed our work considerably, two out of the few half-days available having been " washed out : " this must make us pull in our belts the tighter and work harder when opportunity occurs. We hope to get in one complete field day before the end of term.

* * *

On Saturday, March 3rd, there was an interesting afternoon's work in scouting when an area in the West Bergholt district was searched for escaped Hun prisoners. Five cadets, under Corpl. Crighton, were wondrously disguised, and did some clever work in endeavouring to break through; the captives were most humanely treated.

We still do not realise the great importance of silent movement, and the necessity of learning to choose and use good cover. This must be corrected by the constant attention of the N.C.O.'s and privates who lead sections, however small.

* * *

Thursday, March 15th, was unexpectedly fine, and a useful afternoon was spent in the Stanway area. A defensive line was held along the Straight Road, and the signal section quite capably kept the force in touch with the imaginary main body. A simultaneous move forward under cover was ordered, but the timing was very weak. The afternoon was not long enough to allow the second change of front to be made, but several valuable lessons were learnt. More practice is needed by section commanders, whose discipline must be maintained; they must insist on quiet movement and careful approach, and not be content with anything but the best of which their men are capable.

There was good marching on both journeys, due largely to the hard work of the band.

* * *

A recent parade was attended by 2/Lt. C.E.F. Everett, who gave a thorough inspection, afterwards helping with the tests for promotion.

This is the first occasion on which we welcomed an old member of the Corps, as an official visitor; we are pleased to know that his recent operation was successful, and that he is progressing favourably.

* * *

Lieut. Silvester, attached H.Q. Staff in Colchester for a time is an old boy of this school. He has seen service both in Gallipoli and in France, and has earned his important position. He very kindly came to inspect the Corps, and to give a lecture on Communications. Full of useful "tips" and advice, his lecture was of great value; we hope to see him again before long.

361

The prize for the best account of Lt. Silvester's lecture was won by White ma., the lecture on trench fighting by the O.C., was best reported by Haly and Cameron.

* * *

The ordinary work of the term has proceeded without incident, the most satisfactory feature being the improvement in company drill. Our recruits show good progress under Sergt. Hill, and L-Cpl. Burleigh. Our lack of carbines and bayonets is more than ever felt. -

* * *

Recruits this term include :—Ling, Wright ma., Wright mi., Wyncoll ma., Tarr, George, Barnes, Sainty, Hunneyball mi., Charlton ma., Charlton mi., Taylor mi., Tracey, Lilley. Woodward ma., Woodward mi., Wyncoll mi.

* * *

We continue to receive cheery letters from Lt. F. D. Barker, whose facility in the French tongue has earned him the arduous office of Caterer at large for his Mess. His hunt through adjacent villages for a coffee strainer makes quite pathetic reading. We are pleased to hear that he is well and cheery as ever, having suffered no greater casualty than a broken watchglass.

J. A. P.

Scouting Notes.

THE sum earned by the troop towards the Cornwell Memorial Scholarship Fund, details of which were recorded in our last issue, amounted to £3 10 0.

Amongst last term's events, we must also record the Scout Party so generously given to us by the Headmaster. After tea in the School Hall, we adjourned to the Art Room for games which were much enjoyed and the troop wish to express their appreciation of Mr. Cape's kindness.

We have also to thank Mr. Cape for offering us the use of a part of the old gym. as a club-room which is always a great asset to any troop, and of which we have long felt the need. Other acquistions this term include a drum for the band and complete morse telegraphic outfit for sending and receiving messages, which is much appreciated by the signallers.

Another activity of the term is the Ambulance Class taken on Wednesday evening and Saturday morning by A. S. M. Andrews, O.C., of the Hythe troop. The members have been very keen and regular in their attendance and I hope they will all shortly qualify for their ambulance badge.

I am glad to see some of our Scouts working on the field Garden plots, and to hear that others are cultivating land elsewhere. It is a really useful thing to do especially at this time and most of the troop will probably remember that Major Lang, when he inspected us last July, particularly urged us to work for the gardener's badge.

We have now formed a Wolf Cub Pack for boys between the ages of nine and eleven years, so that in future no one will be admitted to the troop until he is eleven years old. We have as recruits this term Walkden, Adams, Griffin and Jeffrey mi., but we have lost Rock who has gone to school at Portsmouth and Hunneyball who has joined the Corps.

G. E. P.

football.

XMAS TERM, 1916.

SCHOOL v. NICHOLSON'S XI., Saturday, December 9th.

This was the only school match of the term. Our opponents were individually stronger, but showed no combination. Their right defence was much weaker than the left, and all three of the school goals were scored on that side. The visitors scored first after much hard pressing, and there was no further scoring before half-time. In the second half the school had the better of the game. They scored three times in rapid succession in the middle of the second half, and finally won 3—1. The school defence played up well, and the outstanding members were White and Burleigh.

HOUSE MATCHES.

3rd Round. Thursday 30th November.

SCHOOLHOUSE v. HARSNETT'S.

Schoolhouse pressed immediately on starting and Prescott and Crighton succeeded in scoring. This aroused Harsnett's, and the game became very fast. Harsnett's defence played up well but their forwards were weak in front of goal. At half-time the score stood 2—0 for Schoolhouse. The second half was very well contested. The defence on both sides was very good but the forwards were weak. Towards the end of the game Harsnett's succeeded in scoring their only goal and in the end Schoolhouse won 2—1.

DUGARD'S v. PARR'S.

This match played on the second pitch was very much onesided. Dugard's were far superior to Parr's and easily won 15—0.

DUGARD'S v. SCHOOLHOUSE.—Replay.

As both Schoolhouse and Dugard's had obtained the same number of points; a replay took place on December 16th. There was a thick fog, but nevertheless a good number of spectators were present. From the kick-off Dugard's had the better of the game and for the greater part of e first half the play was round the Schoolhouse goal; but Blyth and hite mi. played well for Schoolhouse. Half-time arrived with no

score. Soon after the kick-off however, Powell scored a good goal for
Dugard's and soon after Jones added another. The Schoolhouse forwards now rallied but Spencer, who played a very good game throughout,
stopped them again and again. Towards the end of the game however,
Wilson ma. scored a very good goal for Schoolhouse. No more scoring
took place so that Dugard's won a very good game by the small margin
of 2—1.

For Schoolhouse Wilson ma. and Tricker ma. were the pick of the
forwards and White ma. and Blythe of the defence. Nicholls ma., Powell
and Wells played a good game for Dugard's ; and Spencer was very
safe at back.

LENT TERM. 1917.

SCHOOL v. 1st COLCHESTER SCOUTS. Saturday January 20th.

This match was played in vile weather, and it snowed most of the time.
The school were the better team, but failed repeatedly in front of goal.
Many shots went wild, perhaps owing to the slippery ground. The
Scouts were well served by their left back, who repeatedly pulled up the
school forwards, when just on the point of scoring. Finally the school
won 3—0

SCHOOL v. TECHNICAL COLLEGE. Saturday 10th February.

The school were without Blyth, but our opponents, we understand,
were far from full strength. The game was extremely one-sided, and
hardly merits description. In the end the school won 12—0.

SENIOR HOUSE MATCHES.

1st Round, Thursday, February 22nd.

SCHOOLHOUSE v. DUGARD'S.

This match was played on the first pitch. Schoolhouse, winning the
toss, decided to play against the wind. At the start the game was fairly
even. Dugard's opened the scoring with a shot from Powell, and a
little later, they again scored. Schoolhouse now played up better, and
had the better of the game, but at half-time they had not succeeded in
scoring. The second half was very well contested, and both sides had
hard luck in not scoring. At length Schoolhouse suceeded in scoring
from a scrimmage after a corner. Play became still faster, and two
minutes before time, Crighton scored the equaliser with a long shot, and
the game ended in a draw 2—2. Gilbert was the mainstay of Dugard's
defence, and Dolamore deserves praise for many excellent saves in the
Schoolhouse goal.

HARSNETT'S V. PARR'S.

Harsnett's were a much heavier team than Parr's but their forwards
lacked combination. Parr's, on the other hand, while small were quick
and clever, and combined well together. Osborne opened the scoring
for Parr's with a weak shot. Harsnett's were now stung to action, but
they were always foiled when close to goal, and only succeeded in
scoring once before half-time. Harsnett's had the better of the second-
half, but it was some time before they scored a second goal. Just before
time they again scored, Thomas rushing through from a mis-kicked
goal kick; and the game ended 3-1 in Harsnett's favour.

2nd Round, Monday, 26th February.

DUGARD'S v. HARSNETT'S.

At the outset Dugard's had slightly the better of the play, and after
some twenty minutes a free kick was given and Dugard's scored.
Peacock had no chance, the ball being deflected by Sier into his own

net. Ten minutes later Nicholls scored Dugard's second goal. The play was then transferred into Dugard's half, but Harwood mi. could not be beaten.

At half-time the score stood 2-0 for Dugard's. Immediately on re-starting Dugard's pressed, but Harsnett's defence always had the situation well in hand. Ten minutes from time White ma. ran through the opposing defence, and scored Harsnett's only goal. The remainder of the game was fairly even, but no further score was registered, Dugard's therefore winning by the odd goal in three. For Dugard's Gilbert must be especially mentioned. He always had the opposing forwards under control Nicholls ma. was prevented from being dangerous, owing to the close attention paid him by White. For Harsnetts', the praise is wholly to the defence, who all played exceedingly well. The forwards were very dissapointing on either side. Harsnett's especially being very weak.

PARR'S v. SCHOOLHOUSE.

This match, played on Monday February 26th, resulted in a draw of 1 goal each. Parr's are to be congratulated on a very plucky display against a much heavier team and owe much to French and Osborne ma., while Pratt played a really sound game at back. In the first half Parr's started off with a rush and early in the game Osborne ma. scored from a scrimmage in front of goal, but during the rest of the time the game was of a ding-dong nature. In the second half Schoolhouse kept the ball well in Parr's half of the ground for the greater part of the time, and the goal was bombarded for three parts of the time, but it was not until two minutes before time that Schoolhouse managed to obtain the equalising goal. It certainly looked as if Parr's were going to snatch a victory, but this would not have represented the run of the game, for Schoolhouse were clearly the better side and must be regarded as unlucky in only sharing the points.

3rd Round. Saturday 17th March.

HARSNETT'S v. SCHOOLHOUSE.

Schoolhouse were without Blyth at back, and re-organised their team, with beneficial results. Harsnett's, winning the toss, played against the wind in the first half. The game was fairly even at the start. After a quarter of an hour Wilson opened the scoring for Schoolhouse. The game until half-time, was of a ding-dong nature, with no further scoring. Soon after restarting, Harsnett's were awarded a free kick near the Schoolhouse goal, and White scored. A little later Crighton scored for Schoolhouse with a long shot. A little before time Prescott scored with a corner kick, Peacock touching the ball as it went through. There was no further scoring, and Schoolhouse won 3—1. Schoolhouse forwards played the best game they have played this term. Harsnett's defence was excellent, but their forwards did not combine, and repeatedly failed in front of goal.

DUGARD'S v. PARR'S.

Parr's winning the toss played with the wind in the first half. The game was slightly in the favour of Parr's at the start, the wind greatly helping them. Twyman opened the scoring for Dugard's with a feeble shot, which was taken through by the wind. Soon after they again scored. Parr's then pressed strongly, and eventually French scored with a corner kick, the wind baffling the goalie. At half-time the score stood 2-1 for Dugard's. In the second-half Dugard's were aided by the wind, but Parr's played up well, and it was some time before Dugard's scored their third goal. A little before time Dugard's scored four goals in rapid succession, and at the end the score stood 7—1 in their favour, so that once more they are the winners of the Cup.

JUNIOR HOUSE MATCHES.
1st Round. Thursday, 1st March.

DUGARD'S v. SCHOOLHOUSE.

Schoolhouse had much the better of the game, but as is usual with juniors, they could not score goals. The game was too much of a scramble, and no real football was seen. Harwood mi. was the outstanding member of Dugard's team, while Horwood was next best. For Schoolhouse, Munson mi. and Downing were very energetic, but much too mild, and fond of wandering about. The result was 1-0 in favour of Schoolhouse.

PARR'S v. HARSNETT'S.

This game was extremely onesided. Harsnett's had only seven men' while Parr's were at full strength, and have quite a strong team. The one noticeable feature of the game, was the way in which members of both teams kept their places. For Harsnett's, Beatty and Ingle played very well. For Parr's, Osborne ma. at centre half was the outstanding member, but all were quite good. The game ended 12-0 in favour of Parr's.

LEAGUE MATCHES.

Owing to the lack of school matches, league games were started this term.

The 1st round was played on Saturday 17th February. The Jays easily beat the Tits 12-4, and the Chicks won an easy victory, 6-2, over the Wrens. The third game between the Owls and the Snipes was better contested, and the Owls won 3-2. The 2nd round took place on Saturday, 24th February. The Chicks beat the Owls 12-0, but the latter were not at full strength. The Jays beat the Wrens 6-4, and the Tits made up for their heavy defeat in the 1st round, by beating the Snipes 7-2.

The 3rd round was played on Thursday. 8th March. The chief match was that between the Jays and Chicks. The Jays were without their centre forward Prescott, and suffered accordingly. Finally the Chicks won 3-2, but the deciding goal was exceedingly lucky. The Snipes won their first victory over the Wrens 5-2. The Tits beat the Owls 12-1, but the latter were far from full strength.

The League Table at present stands :—

Team	P.	W.	D.	L.	F.	A.	Pts.
Chicks	3	3	0	0	21	4	6
Jays	3	2	0	1	20	11	4
Tits	3	2	0	1	23	15	4
Snipes	3	1	0	2	9	12	2
Owls	3	1	0	2	4	26	2
Wrens	3	0	0	3	8	17	0

Acknowledgments.

Our thanks are due to Editors of the following :--
The Viking, Stortfordian, Framlinghamian, Wyggestoniua, O.H.S., Chelmsfordian, Williamsonian, Ipswich G.S. Mag., Chigwellian.

Old Colcestrian Section.

Editorial.

MILITARY MEDAL AWARDED.

Pte. Cecil H. Jarrard, of the Essex Regiment, who was in Camp at Clacton with the Cadets when war began, has been awarded the Military Medal for gallantry and devotion to duty in France. He has been reported missing since October last.

From the Press of February 17th, 1917, we quote :—

Pte. Cecil H. Jarrard, of the Essex Regiment, son of Saddler Corporal Jarrard, A.S.C., and Mrs. Jarrard, of Thorpe Street, has been awarded the Military Medal for gallantry and devotion to duty in France on January 8. Pte. Jarrard before enlistment was a school teacher and was very popular in the village, and though the news has caused much admiration, it is tempered with regret that the gallant young soldier has been missing since October and the attempts of his anxious parents to trace his whereabouts have up to the present been unsuccessful. He enlisted soon after the outbreak of war. He saw service first in Gallipoli and was invalided to Egypt with enteric fever, and after his period of convalescence he was transferred to France, where he arrived in March, 1916, and saw much fighting and experienced many hardships in various parts of the British line.

Clarence W. Sanger, has been gazetted 2nd Lieut. in the Machine Gun Corps. He served in France through the winter of 1915-16 with the 19th Royal Fusiliers (University Battalion), and was laid up in hospital with pneumonia.

Second Lieut. H. P. Turner, Essex Regiment, has been taking a course of instruction at a Divisional school in France, and has been awarded a Silver Cup, presented by the Colonel for the best Officer in the school.

A. T. Daldy left his regiment in France on December 26th, and is now in training with the 9th (Scottish) Officer Cadet Battalion.

W. R. Everett, who went to France with the 10th Essex Regt. in July, 1915, is now back in England, training with a Cadet Battalion at Oxford.

Second Lieut. P. L. Plant has transferred to the Royal Flying Corps, and is now serving in France.

Claud H. Barnes, Royal Navy, died on February 9th at the Royal Naval Hospital from pneumonia.

Lieut. S. G. Hazell recently visited the school ; he came over with a contingent of the Canadians. When the Cadet Corps was first mooted, he was Captain of the school and keenly supported the movement.

F. J. Collinge is in the Cadet Battalion at Queen's College, Cambridge.

ESSEX COUNTY STANDARD, FEBRUARY 17th, 1917.

Mr. and Mrs. J. H. Thomas, 150 Maldon Road, have received news that their second son, Second-Lieut. Reginald Thomas, 9th Bedford Regiment, is severely wounded. This is the second time he has been wounded. He is 19 years of age. Latest reports state that he is in hospital at Newcastle and is doing well.

ESSEX COUNTY STANDARD, DECEMBER 16th, 1916.

We regret to announce the death, which took place at Hove, Sussex, on December 13th, of Second-Lieut. John Devereux Secker, of the Essex Regiment, eldest son of Mr. and Mrs. J. H. Secker, of 53 North Hill, Colchester. Lieut. Secker was only 22 years of age.

Second-Lieut. H. A. Beckett, (N. Devons) lies wounded at Manchester. He is progressing favourably and is incurably pessimistic—as ever. When he visited Gilberd House a few weeks ago he enjoyed himself mightily in raising our back hair.

Gilberd House has seen many welcome visitors this term. Rifleman Eves, (L. R. B.) fresh from new conquests at the Canadian Hospital, Taplow, loomed large and fit; his diary of experiences in France makes splendid reading.

Pte. Wm. Bare, (attd. Royal Sussex Regiment) after a long convalescence in Scotland, called during his leave, before rejoining his unit. He has made a wonderful recovery.

Pte. Pullen, (Royal Berks) who has spent several weeks in Tankland, came to say good-bye before leaving England.

Leonard Brook, (Signaller) of H.M.S. Crystal Palace, home on leave after a bout of unromantic measles, paid us a visit; he finds his work most interesting and absorbing.

Cadet Daldy, now exiled at Gailes, came to report a considerable increase in avoirdupois, after his experiences in France. He is as keen on his O.C. work as ever.

R.Q.M.S. Burrell, who has done good work, looked very fit and well; he is on his way to a well-earned commission, which he had been offered some time ago, an honour he then declined.

Pte. W. R. Orrin has joined the R.F.C.

Roll of Honour.

ADDITIONS.

Pullen, Basil, A.S.C. (now Royal Berks).
Rickword, Evan G., Army Service Corps.
Rickword, Gerald O., Royal Berks Regt.
Orrin, W. R., Royal Flying Corps.
Appleby, Wm., 3rd Dorset Regiment.
Appleby, R., 2nd Durham L.I.
Midgely, W. R. O., London Scottish.
Midgely, C. F.

FAIRHEAD, A. E., Bouchier's Hall, Messing, Kelvedon.
FARMER, A. O., 12 Queen Street, Colchester.
FAVIELL, C. V., 28 Udney Park, Teddington, Middlesex.
FIRDGATE, W. H., "Ty Fry," Regent Road, Brightlingsea.
FINCH, F. D., 25 Salisbury Avenue, Colchester.
FINCHAM, G. E., 52 Myland Road, Colchester.
FITCH, L. B., Louisville, Fambridge Road, Maldon.
FLANAGAN, L. O., Beta House, Clacton-on-Sea.
FLEETWOOD, E. O., Bemahague, Shrub End Road, Colchester.
FLETCHER, L. B., 13 Harsnett Road, Colchester
FLUX, R. O., 52 Old Heath Road, Colchester.
FOLKARD, C., Copford, Colchester.
FRANKLIN, Councillor R., Sutherland House, 95 Baddow Road, Chelmsford.
FRENCH, R. E., 58 Roman Road, Colchester.
FROST, A. W., 13 Head Street, Colchester.
GIBBS, J. W., 249 Maldon Road, Colchester.
GIRLING, T. A., 18 Park Road, Chelmsford.
GIRLING, Hugh, Park Villa, Dunmow.
GODFREY, C. F., "Thirlmere," Queen's Road, Springfield, Chelmsford.
GOING, F. W., 125 Maldon Road, Colchester.
GOODEY, S., Chelsworth, New Town Road, Colchester.
GOODY, C., Old Heath Road, Colchester.
GREEN, A. C., Fingringhoe, Colchester.
GREEN, A. E., 18 East Stockwell Street, Colchester.
GREEN, M. H. C., Fingringhoe, Colchester.
GREEN, O. B., Holmwood, Fingringhoe, Essex.
GRIFFIN, C., Stanway Villa, Colchester.
HALL, A. L., Caerleon, New Town Road, Colchester.
HARPER, W. C., High Street, Colchester.
HARRIS, H. J., Weircombe, Ardwick Road, W. Hampstead.
HARVEY, J. B., Stanley Lodge, Wellesley Road, Colchester.
HARVEY, W., Central Secretariat, Lagos, Nigeria W. Africa.
HARSUM, G. F., Wood Field, Bourne Road, Colchester.
HAZELL, S. G., 39 Wellesley Road, Colchester (and Montreal).
HAZELL, R. L., 23 Lexden Street, Colchester.
HEAD, A., 58 Wimpole Road, Colchester.
HEAD, J., 58 Wimpole Road, Colchester.
HEMPSON, R. J., Galton Lodge, Reigate.
HOBROUGH, S. J., Ernest Cottage, Parsons Heath, Colchester.
HOLLAWAY, H. H., 34 Old Heath Road, Colchester.
HORLOCK, M. F., High Street, Mistley.
HORWOOD, R. B., Layer Hall, Layer.
HURST, H. J. R., 7 St. John Street, Colchester
HUSSEY, F. W., 15 Audley Road, Colchester.
IVEY, S. F., 63 Kensington Gardens Square, London, W.
JARRARD, O. H., Thorpe, Colchester.
JARRARD, D. G., Alexandra Road, Sible Hedingham.
JASPER, O. V., Langenhoe Hall, Colchester.
JASPER, L. A., Langenhoe Hall, Colchester.
JAWS, GEO. F., 24 Churchill Terrace, Cadoxton, Barry, nr. Cardiff
JEFFERIES, C. R., Second Lieutenant R.F.A.
JEFFREY, P. SHAW, Bagdale Old Hall, Whitby.
JOHNSON, L. H., 17 Lion Walk, Colchester.
JUDD, L., South Villa, Ardleigh.
KENT, B. H., 182 Maldon Road, Colchester.
KING, J., 16 Inglis Road, Colchester.
KING, W. H., Inglis Road, Colchester
KING, W. H., junr., Inglis Road, Colchester.
KING, G. K., 53 Friar Street, Sudbury.
KOSKINAS, F. M., 24 Pembridge Gardens, Notting Hill, W.

LANSDOWNE, L. R., Mersea House, Walton-on-Lay, C. V., 2k Portman Mansions, St. Marylebone, London, W.
LAWRENCE, A. D., c.o. Head & Co., Ltd., 27 Cornhill, London, E.C.
LAWRY, E., Hoe Farm, Aldham.
LAZELL, HAROLD, Fitzwalter Road, Lexden Park, Colchester.
LEANING, E. M., Welwyn, Wash Lane, Clacton-on-Sea.
LEEMING, J. H. J., 27 Liversidge Road, Higher Tranmere, Birkenhead.
LEWIS, K. M., 173 Maldon Road, Colchester.
LINES, E., The Bungalow, Great Bentley.
LORD, P., North Hill, Colchester.
LORD, S. W., 49 North Hill, Colchester.
LOWE, STANLEY, Warwick House' East Dereham.
LUCKING, A. S., 20 Inglis Road, Colchester.
LUCKING, C. D., 20 Inglis Road, Colchester.
MALYN, D. P., Bleak House, Braintree.
MALYN, R., Barclay's Bank, Colchester
MANNING, C., The Elms, Weeley, R.S.O.
MANNING, P. E. J., The Elms, Weeley, R.S.O.
MARLAR, J., North Hill, Colchester.
MARSH, W. E., 180 Longmarket Street, Natal, South Africa.
MARSH, H. V., P.O. Box 253, Maritzburg, South Africa.
MASON, A. S., Perse School, Cambridge.
MASON, B., 10 Crouch Street, Colchester. (HON. TREASURER).
MASON, C., 10 Crouch Street, Colchester.
McCLOSKY, O. A., c.o. Edes Everett, St. Botolph's, Colchester.
MIDDLETON, G. A. T.
MIDGLEY, C. F., "Gunton," Westminster Drive, Westcliffe-on-Sea.
MIDGLEY, W. R. O., 163 Ongar Road, Brentwood.
MILLS, F. G., 18 Beverley Road, Colchester.
MOY, C. T., Stanway Hall, Colchester.
NORFOLK, A. E., 76 Chesson Road, West Kensington.
NUNN, A. W., Crouch Street, Colchester.
NUNN, J. H., Melford Villa, Rawstorn Road, Colchester.
NUNN, W. H., Whatfield, Ipswich.
OLIVER, J. L., Maldon Road, Colchester.
ORFEUR, H. W., Colne Bank, Station Road, Colchester.
ORFEUR, C. B., Colne Bank, Station Road, Colchester.
ORFEUR, R. F., Colne Bank, Station Road, Colchester.
ORFEUR, F. N., Colne Bank, Station Road, Colchester
ORPEN, O. G., Hillside, West Bergholt, Colchester.
ORRIN, W. R., 37 Campion Road, Colchester.
OSBORNE, F. F.
OSBORNE, H. C.
PARKER, Rev. E. H., London Orphan School, Watford.
PAYNE, E. A., 2 Honywood Road, Colchester.
PEART, J. A., C.R.G.S.
PEPPER, V. J.
PEPPER, G. E., C.R.G.S.
PERTWEE, F., Moreham's Hall, Frating.
PLUMMER, N. A., Station Road, Lawford, Manningtree.
PLUMMER, F. E. Station Road, Lawford Manningtree.
POINTING, W. W., 148 Maldon Road, Colchester.
POTTER, C. C., 119 Maldon Road, Colchester.
POTTER, F., Middleborough, Colchester.
REEVE, E., C.R.G.S.
RENTON, T. S., 12 Crouch Street, Colchester.
RICHES, A. E., 80 Tower Street, Brightlingsea.

RICHARDS, R. F., Head Street, Colchester.
RICHARDSON, A. J., School House, Great Bentley.
RICKWORD, E. G., Boughton Lane, Loose, Maidstone.
ROGERS, S. W., 5 Caterham Road, Lewisham, S.E.
ROSEVEARE, H. H., "St. Breca," Newquay, Cornwall.
RYDER, E. W., 74 Wimpole Road, Colchester.
SADLER, F. B., Box P.O. 219, c.o. The Eastern Bank, Ltd., Bombay.
SANGER, O. W., "Rookerydene," Abbeygate Street, Colchester.
SANGER, H., "Rookerydene," Abbeygate Street, Colchester.
SALMON, J. G., Wash Lane, Clacton.
SAMMONS, A. C., 49 Grafton Street, Fitzroy Square, W.
SEAMER, H. St. J., "The Gables," East Bergholt.
SENNITT, F. J., 23 Mersea Road, Colchester.
SHAW, D. E., Beaconsfield Avenue, Colchester.
SHENSTONE, J. C., 15c Coverdale Road, Shepherd's Bush, London, W.
SLIGHT, R., c.o. One Barrow Lodge, Coalville, Leicestershire.
SLATER, E. M.
SMITH, AUBREY, "Mantz," 30 Peak Hill, Sydenham, S.E.
SMITH, G. E., Chapel Street, Colchester.
SMITH, W. G., 23 Roman Road, Colchester.
SMITH, F. R., 23 Roman Road, Colchester.
SPARLING, A. S. B., 21 Creffield Road, Colchester.
SURRIDGE, P. T., Coggeshall.
SYER, F. N., 8 Studlands Road, Sydenham.
SPENCER, S. G., The Mitre Hotel, Cathedral Gates, Manchester.
TAYLOR, A. P., "Cromer," Westgrove, Woodford Green, Surrey.
TENNANT, E. N., Connaught Avenue, Frinton.
THOMAS, A. O., 150 Maldon Road, Colchester.

TOWN, H. G., 50 Essendine Mansions, Maida Vale, W.
TOWN, W. M., 50 Essendine Mansions, Maida Vale, W.
TURNER, Capt. A., Essex Hall, Colchester.
TURNER, Dr. DOUGLAS, Essex Hall, Colchester.
TURNER, S. C., Abbeygate House, Colchester.
VAN DEN BERGH, A. H.
VAN DEN BERGH, H.
WAGSTAFF, D. T. Church Farm, Marks Tey, Colchester.
WALLACE, Councillor R. W., "Moelwyn," Inglis Road, Colchester.
WARD, J. D., Jun., Bluegates, Elmstead, Colchester.
WARNER, A. E., 8 Myland, Colchester.
WATKINSON, W. P., Elmstead, nr. Colchester.
WATSHAM, H., Vine Farm, Wyvenhoe.
WATSON, J. L., Abergwili Palace, Carnarvon.
WATSON, S. F., 154 Maldon Road, Colchester.
WATSON, G. F., Abergwili Palace, Carnarvon.
WATTS, FRANK, 30 Creffield Road, Colchester.
WEBB, G. S., Dairy House, Wix, Manningtree.
WEBB, A. H., Dairy House, Wix, Manningtree.
WENDEN, C. A., The Chase, Great Bromley.
WHEELER, G., 10 High Street.
WHITE, C. E., 57 North Hill, Colchester.
WHITE, F., "Kennington," Myland, Colchester.
WHITBY, J. F. M., 22 Lexden Road, Colchester.
WILLIAMS, F. O., 14 Lexden Road, Colchester.
WILLIS, E. A., 25 Heron Road, Stapleton Road, Bristol.
WRIGHT, C. T., Stacey House, Crouch Street, Colchester (President).
WRIGHT, G., junr., Stacey House, Crouch Street, Colchester.
WRIGHT, Councillor G. F., 47 Crouch Street, Colchester.
WYATT, D. T., Bank Passage, Colchester.

NOTICE TO OLD COLCESTRIANS.

Old Colcestrians who wish to make known their movements in this paper should communicate with Mr. J. HUTLEY NUNN, "Essex County Telegraph" Offices, Colchester.

Subscriptions should be sent to Mr. B. MASON, (Hon. Treas.), Crouch Street, Colchester.

Members of the Society are requested to notify any change of address immediately to either of the Hon. Secretaries :—

Mr. B. MASON, Crouch Street, Colchester.
Mr. A. T. DALDY, Head Street, Colchester.

NOTICE TO CORRESPONDENTS.

Contributions to the O.C. Section, articles on various subjects and humorous anecdotes of school-days, will be gladly welcomed by the O.C. Editor, Mr. J. Hutley Nunn.

All contributions for the next number of "The Colcestrian" to be sent in by July 1st, 1917.

No. 48.]

NEW SERIES.

JULY, 1917.

The
Colcestrian

PRICE SIXPENCE.

BENHAM & COMPANY, LIMITED, COLCHESTER.

The Colcestrian.

VITÆ CORONA FIDES.

No 48].　　　　JULY, 1917.　　　　[NEW SERIES

Dead Leaves.

Oh, the calm glory of the red setting sun,
Tinting the trees with hues like the autumn leaves
Blowing so roughly and carelessly on the ground.
They are dead, they are parched, they are crisp, they are hard and dry,
Yet not in their lifetime looked they so wonderful,
Seemed they so glorious, grand, and magnificent,
As now when they toss on the breast of the dying wind,
Blown through lanes in the bright crimson after-glow
Of the sun that has cast its last beams o'er the countryside.
Had they known death was this, they would have pined for it.
The things we hold dear in life, holiness, bravery,
Cleanness of flesh and soul, faith and devotion,
The beauty and tenderness, sadness and hope of Love,
The joy and the happiness of motherhood, fatherhood,
When the tiny voice blesses the greatness of Love and Life,
Is not the thought of the quiet approaching grave,
When labour has ceased to be and cares are grown silent,
When, all the long years behind, trouble shall be no more,
Is not this among the great things we hold dear in life?
When the calm wind shall blow the tree branches overhead
And all shall be still.

[Included by kind permission of "The New Age," above is the work of Colchester Mason (aged 15), who left us for the Perse Sch. in 1913.]

Grammaria.

Floreat Sodalitas.

Despite the war, with its manifold effects, our numbers increase, and we recently held high holiday to celebrate the record achieved. When we recall that our family numbered less than 20 when the school was reorganised in 1900, we can but feel proud of the results so laboriously attained, and hopeful for the future of the "old show," as our visitors affectionately style it.

Vale.

Departures from the staff have been singularly few since the great exodus of our junior members, for service with the King's armies. This term, however, sees the severance of

Messrs. Carter and Watkin, who are taking up scholastic posts elsewhere. The former has been with us since 1913, and has helped much in building up the great reputation deservedly won by the school in its musical and dramatic efforts. We shall long remember his striking study in "Waterloo," and the Dugard's House singings produced by him.

The latter had in a year instilled a real enthusiasm for "gym," and gave practical testimony of his work at the recent display. To both we extend our very heartiest wishes for the future.

"A Better 'ole.'

We have decided to be "not at home." to uninvited Hun visitors. When the Maid with the Raucous Voice announces their arrival we silently steal down to the stoke hole with two feet of reinforced concrete between us and them. This morning during a long wait the small fry made time hustle, the while they played round games. Their reverend signors discussed high politics ; the matter of fact demeanour and evident enjoyment displayed would have assured and gratified the hearts of their parents.

"Bags."

All who affectionately recall him as pupil or master will be glad to hear that he is making good progress, and explores the wilds of Devizes in a bath-chair. He sends the cheeriest of greetings to Schoolhouse and those who know him. Of our other colleagues, Capt. Deakin, Lieut. Bellward, Lieut. Worth, and Pte. Oldham, we have nothing but good news.

With the O.C.S. the school will mourn the loss of A. H. Webb, one of her most brilliant sons, and B. C. Orfeur, the second of four brothers who came to us. Both died on active service, after long and bitter hardships suffered cheerfully.

Ourselves.

This is the last number for which we shall be personally responsible, and the white cover should dumbly appeal for your indulgence as to the past five numbers, produced under difficulties. It should hold promise for the future, when an art cover with an appropriate and original design shall enfold the contributions you will gladly send : the disappearance of the names on the cover foreshadows the yearly issue of a complete list of Old Colcestrians, whether members of the O.C.S. or not, with addresses and titles. In order that the first may be a successful list you are urgently requested to send a P.C. with these particulars, for yourself, and for any O.C.'s whom you know. The appearance of the advertisements proves the desire of your committee to make the Magazine pay for itself.

J. A. P.

"At the Sign of the Ship."

Form VI.

Not since the Virgin Queen gave her a Charter in 1585, has the School had such an unique compliment as she received one fine morning recently. An old boy, flying an up-to-date plane, looped the loop over the school grounds and dipped in salute. Surely Bluff Hal and Good Queen Bess smiled pleasedly in their sleep!

Form Va.

> Come, sing, ye bards, and wake the strain
> Of Cambridge Locals come again,
> Of masters gloomy, in despair,
> Of masters wildly tearing hair,
> Of masters raging everywhere,
> Of masters hustling might and main,
> Of boys whose hopes now wax, now wane,
> Of local boys in bright array,
> Of flowing ink and " block " by pecks,
> Of mixing tans and cots and secs,
> Preparing for that Awful Day.   O.L.O.R.

Form Vb.

Student of Henry V. to man delivering coals for next term. " Is this a ton of Moys' ? "

     *   *   *   *

Who *is* Godfrey Daniel ?

Form IVa.

An interesting debate was held in form, on " Should we abolish homework and continue school until 5.45 ? " Nicholls, Dyer, Wyncoll, mi. and Taylor ma. opened the debate : the motion was lost by 5 votes.

     *   *   *   *

The form regrets that our Form Master, Mr. Carter, is leaving us this term. He has practically created our library and has done good work for his form. May good luck attend him !

Form IVb.

This form has won two cricket matches against IVa ; the first by two runs, and the second by eight.

     *   *   *   *

We are proud of Osborne ma, who made 59 for Parr's and was presented with a bat.

Form III.

In cricket this term we have defeated the I. and II. in two matches.

     *   *   *   *

Since June 1st we have had gym. on the close. It was so jolly we forgot to wish for the sound of the siren.

Form II. and I.

One master told us we had brains ; we don't thank him but we do believe him.

*   *   *   *

" On fridyday there was a hool holday becors we beet the record " (in spelling ?)

The Pre.

Since our Lent term finished, as it began, with snow falling, we had to lock our seeds away with our books and trust that even such a winter would at last change to spring.

We were not disappointed. With the glorious weather of May and June irregular attendance became a thing of the past, and we all set to work to make up for lost time. One result of this is that our gardens are doing fairly well. On two great days some of the produce has been carried round to Gostwycke Hospital. The beans will soon be fit to go, and we hope the potatoes will follow—that is if anyone proves brave enough to take them up. Our great fault seems trying to grow too much in a small space.

Again Mr. and Mrs. Chatterton have been most kind in helping us. We have to thank Mr. Denman, too, for the cucumber plants, which are reviving with the recent rain.

Thanks to Mr. Horwood ravelling continues. By this our readers will understand the war is not yet ended. When it is our pillows should fetch a good price since feathers and down will be scarce if poultry restrictions continue.

In conclusion we are proud to add that the Pre. has a record number of pupils this term.			A. J.
			C. C.

Valete.

Ward, A. O., Form VI., Harsnett's, School Captain House Shooting, Hon. Sec. Debating Society, C.-S.-M. Cadet Corps, Dramatic Society.

Munson, A. G., Form VI., Parr's, House Shooting, Cadet.

Mead, R. H., Form Va, Schoolhouse, House Shooting, Cadet.

Peacock, F., Form Va., Harsnett's, 1st XI. Football, House Football, Cricket, Shooting, Lce.-Cpl. Cadet Corps.

Collinge, H. H., Form Va., Probationer, Parr's, House Football, Cricket, Hockey, Shooting, Lce.-Cpl. Cadet Corps, Dramatic Society.

Cameron, A. H., Form Va, Harsnett's, Cadet.

Blyth, D. P., Form Vb, Q.P. Schoolhouse, 1st XI. Football, House Football, Cricket, A.-S.-M. School Scouts, Cadet.

Nicholls, W. C., Form Vb, Dugard's, 1st XI. Football, House Football, Cricket, Shooting, Cadets.

Wheeler, J., Form IVa, Parr's, House Football, Cricket, Shooting, Cadet.

Havard, A. G. E., Form IVa, Harsnett's, Cadet.

Tarr, W. L. E., Form IVb, Dugard's, House Football, Cadet.

Littlebury, G. W., Form IVb, Parr's, Scout.

Salvete.

Goslin, R. A. J.	. Vb., Dugard's	Wombwell, L. A. R.	.. Harsnett's
Ebsworth, A. W.	.. IVb., Parr's	Ryder, R. J. ..	.. Harsnett's
Moore, R. W.	.. Dugard's	Forsdike, F. W.	.. Dugard's
Barrett, A. C.	.. Dugard's	Barrett, O. O'C.	.. Dugard's
Ebsworth, E. A.	.. III. Parr's	Weller, M. B.	.. Schoolhouse
Wilby, J. G.	.. Dugard's	Wilson, S. E.	.. Schoolhouse
Moore, J. B. ..	.. Dugard's	Butler, A. R.	.. Schoolhouse
Webber, W. H.	.. Dugard's	Field, D. F. ..	.. Schoolhouse
Cheshire, K. S.	.. I. Parr's	Smith, J.	.. Schoolhouse
Nunn, W. R. ..	.. Parr's	Frost, H. ..	.. Schoolhouse

Oakley B. Pre, Wombwell M. Pre. Mills V. Pre. Wicks R. Pre. Harper L. Pre.

Gym. Display.

An excellent display of school gym. was given by Mr. Harold Watkin at the end of last term. A large number of parents and friends witnessed a varied demonstration of the exercises taught week by week in school, interspersed as they are by fascinating games built on scientific lines, with a definite instructive purpose.

What struck one most, apart from the keen enjoyment of the competitors, was the high average attained, and the fact that the whole school performed, and not merely picked gymnasts. It is with deep regret that we shall part with Mr. Watkin at the end of the term, whilst wishing him success in his new venture.

The second part of the programme was undertaken by the Scouts, who gave displays of ambulance, sick nursing and Morse telegraphy work. Their smartness and the thoroughness of the work done reflected the greatest credit on their Scoutmaster, Mr. Pepper, and P. L. Prescott, who was responsible for the signalling events.

Mr. Hind Smith's Lecture.

On Friday, June 29th, a visit was paid to us by Mr. Hind Smith, who gave a most interesting lecture on the work of Dr. Barnardo's Homes. The lecturer devotes most of the year to this onerous task and he speaks from first hand knowledge and with burning enthusiasm: his arguments with regard to the work from the point of view of national needs were very ably developed. From the smallest to the biggest the school voted him " topping." On the following morning some six guineas were handed to him as a practical testimony of our appreciation of the magnificent work done by these homes.

Cadet Corps.

(Attached to 5th Essex)

An interesting scheme in dispatch running was carried out at Greenstead on May 17th, with competition between the platoons. Glorious weather favoured us, and the afternoon's work was very useful. Results : Plat. I., 14 ; IV. 13 ; III., 12 ; II., 11 points.

*　　*　　*　　*

On Whit Monday a delightful day was spent at Thorpe, in practice on the attack, followed by a route march to Clacton, and culminating in a bathing parade, which gave a welcome holiday touch to the day's programme. This was certainly one of the red letter days of the term.

*　　*　　*　　*

A convoy scheme, under Sergts. French and Halls, was successfully developed at Heckford Bridge on Thursday, June 21st, in spite of rainy weather. The "tank" did not succeed in getting through in the stated time, but the work of the left protecting flank of the convoy was commendable, as was the general disposition of the defence.

*　　*　　*　　*

In all the field work of the year the great weakness lies in the Junior N.C.O.'s and senior privates in command of small parties, who must be trained to recognise the "brief authority" which must be exercised ; we are not yet ripe for revolutionary army discipline with "each for himself" as the motto.

*　　*　　*　　*

Throughout the term the ordinary routine work has gone on steadily, in spite of competing claims. A pleasing feature has been the keenness of the P.C.'s, whose efforts we hope to see rewarded : all good, serious work has a beneficial effect on the Corps, as well as upon the individual. We hope to have a permanent memorial of the best platoons, whilst the Inspection will show the results of the work of all.

*　　*　　*　　*

With deep regret, but yet with pride, we have to chronicle the death of Sec.-Lieut. Deane (Essex R.), killed in action ; of Malyn mi, of Clark ma, and of Jarrard mi. Each was a Cadet not more than four years ago, and each died on active service. We believe we are right in stating that Jarrard, with the Military Medal, was the first cadet to be decorated.

*　　*　　*　　*

Munson ma, White ma, and Ward have left to join His Majesty's Forces ; the latter had been a Cadet since the inception of the Corps, and had always been a keen, hardworking member. He was a most valuable C.S.M., and he takes with him our very best wishes.

Lieut. Barker is slowly recovering from serious wounds, which have left undiminished his cheery spirit : his great ambition is to be allowed to walk alone, and we all hope his convalescence will be hastened. Bare ma is again wounded. this time in the ankle. Chapman also has been wounded.

* * *

We are very grateful to Supt. Andrews for his helpful work with the Ambulance Section ; his time is very fully occupied and his Thursday lecture is a generous sacrifice of well-earned leisure.

* * * *

Our gratitude is due, also, to Mr. and Mrs. Twentyman, whose labours at the Tuckshop resulted in such, profit that the Committee was enabled to make a grant to the Corps of £4 10s. With recruits flocking in and consequent expense in the matter of uniforms, help of this kind is most welcome.

* * * *

We hope to send some 24 cadets to the Public Schools Camp at Marlborough for ten days' training in August. There will be over 1,400 boys there, and we hope not to be the least smart and efficient.

* * * *

At the end of last term a most successful field day was enjoyed at Layer, which was again defended and attacked. The N.C.O.'s in charge drew out thoughtful schemes, and improvement in detail was noted. To the satisfaction of the umpires (who included several old boys) the result was a definite win for the attack.

* * * *

To our amazement favourable notice has at length been taken of our constant appeal for arms. More rifles are to come—some day ! Recruits this term : Layzell, Blandford, Pryor, Woollard, Longcroft, Smith 4, Tricker mi, Dancer, Moore ma, Munson.

* * * *

N.C.O.'s : Acting C.S.M. Hill ; Sergeants : (I.) French, (II.) Halls, (III.) Dolamore, (IV.) Crichton ; Corporals : Burleigh, White, Deane, Chase ; Lance-Corporals : Harwood, Cox, Felgate, Tricker.

J. A. P.

Scouting Motes.

Once more the summer term—with all its opportunities for scouting work—is drawing to a close, without any prospect of a troop camp. But I am glad to know that several boys have already made arrangaments for spending part of their holiday in doing farm work or some other form of national service.

The number of recruits this term is very gratifying, and for the first time in the history of the troop we have over sixty scouts on the roll. The recruits are :—*Scouts :*—Ingle, Knight, Baker, J. B. Moore, G. H. Robinson, J. Wright. *Wolf Cubs :*— Smith, Heasman, Meeson, Wilson, Dunn, Forsdike, and Weller. Scouts who have left the troop are Dancer, Jeffrey ma, Munson, and Tricker mi, who have joined the Cadet Corps.

We have had several good field days·this term, every third half-holiday being given up to these. On Whit Monday we went out for the whole day with the other troops of the Association. The operations took place on land belonging to Bishop Harrison and Mr. Round, both of whom gave us the run of their woods. After work was finished, we cooked our dinners, and the remainder of the day was spent in various scouting games.

At the conclusion of the ambulance course, mentioned in the notes of our last issue, twelve boys offered themselves for examination, and the following eight qualified for the Badge : P.L.'s Burleigh, Everett, Prescott and Osborne ma, Scouts C. Smith, Farmer, Hollaway and Loyd. We are most grateful to Assistant Scoutmaster Andrews for all the work he did to obtain this good result.

By obtaining his ambulance badge, P.L. Prescott also qualifies for his " All round cords," and he has the additional distinction of being the first member of the troop to obtain these.

Other badge winners are :

Swimmers' badge.—P.L. Everett, Scouts Hollaway and W. Wilson.

1st Class Scout badge.—P.L.'s Everett, Prescott and Burleigh.

2nd Class Scout badge.—Butler, W. Wilson, Horwood ¡and Harris. Everett, Burleigh and Loyd also deserve mention for the good work they have done on their garden-plots. Everett has obtained his badge, and the others will shortly qualify for it. I hope next season to see many more of the older scouts doing this useful work.

A few weeks ago, we had a very acceptable present of a cheque for £4 10s. from the treasurer of the School Tuck Shop, this sum representing one-third of the profits of the shop during the Michaelmas and Lent terms. For this we are much indebted to Mr. and Mrs. Twentyman, to whom we offer our sincere thanks.   · G. E. P.

Gardening.

Having been asked to write a few notes about the plots, I took a stroll up to·the field one evening in July, and my first impression was certainly one of disappointment. The long plot on the right as one enters was quite good and clean, but without exception the remaining plots badly needed·the use of the hoe, while the paths should have been kept in better order.

As regards the crops themselves I was most favourably impressed with the potatoes and dwarf beans, both of which should yield well, judging by present appearances. The smaller crops such as onions, carrots, beet, etc., were in many cases almost choked by weeds. It was quite pleasing to see such a large variety of vegetables being grown, and I commend the practice of intercropping the potatoes.

The smallest plot of all presented the neatest appearance, with what might be called an excess of carrots. Given permission, I should like to pay another visit in about a month's time, for I consider quite a useful amount of vegetables should be raised, and my impression on leaving was undoubtedly that this would be the case. AMATEUR GARDENER.

Shooting.

The range has been used more frequently this term than last, but our standard does not increase as we should like.

At the end of last term the final round of the House Shooting Competition was held, and School House once more succeeded in winning the Worthington Evans Challenge Cup. Final scores were as follows :—

SCHOOL HOUSE.		DUGARD'S.	
Crighton	55	Halls	54
Prescott	52	Chase	53
Tricker ma.	52	Loyd	48
Harvey	51	Twyman	47
Dolamore	48	Harwcod ma.	44
Blandford	46	Gilbert	35
Layzell	44	Nicholls ma.	34
Lilley	35	Clough	29
	383		344
Previous Score	777		767
	1160		1111

HARSNETT'S.		PARR'S.	
Arnold	53	French	61
Cox	50	Wheeler ma.	46
Burleigh mi.	46	Wagstaff	42
Burleigh ma.	45	Smith	40
Dean	44	Hunneyball ma.	38
Peacock	44	Felgate	35
Thomas	44	Tricker mi.	35
Hill	35	Munson	10
	361		307
	733		622
	1094		929

Practice this term has been at 20 yards in preparation for the I.C.S. Competition, shot off on Friday, June 29th, when Major Becher kindly acted as range official. Our average in this is a decimal lower than last year, and we hope to find ourselves a little above the half-way line when the results come to hand. Scores were :—

	Deliberate.	Rapid.	Total.
Lilley	37	37	74
Gilbert	38	36	74

Cox	..	..	..	..	..	36	36	.72
Halls	..	..	..	..	..	37	30	·67
Prescott	..	..	..	..	..	33	33	66
Crighton	..	..	..	..	..	37	28	65.
Warden	..	..	..	..	..	37	28	65
Arnold	..	..	..	..	..	36	·20	56.
Layzell	..	..	..	..	..	33	18	51

590

E. R.

Football.

JUNIOR HOUSE MATCHES.

As reported last term, in the 1st round, Parr's easily beat Harsnett's 12—0, while Schoolhouse, after a grim fight, beat Dugard's by 1—0. In the 2nd round Parr's were again victorious, beating Schoolhouse 6—0; while Harsnett's made up for their heavy defeat in the 1st round by beating Dugard's 9—0. The 3rd round was played during a snowstorm. Parr's had an easy victory over Dugard's by 23—1, and Schoolhouse beat Harsnett's by 5—1. Thus Parr's easily won the Cup, with Schoolhouse as runners up.

LEAGUES.

The fifth round was not played, owing to lack of time, and the Chicks were placed top as the result of the first four rounds.

Team :—Gilbert (Capt.), Peacock, Wilson max, Tricker ma, Tracey, Felgate, Thomas, Mirrington, George, Nash and Wheeler ma.

Cricket.

The field at the beginning of the term badly needed cutting. The square and two other pitches were, however, soon prepared for use, and we are much indebted to the military who have cut a good-sized piece round the square. The cricket on the whole has been much better than last season. The Juniors are especially promising, Osborne ma and Beattie ma being the two outstanding stars. The former secured a place in the 1st XI. for general all round excellence, and the School has presented him with a bat for his excellent performances. Beattie has bowled remarkably well in House Matches, securing an extraordinary number of hat tricks. When he has learnt to use his head as well as his hands he should be a remarkably deadly bowler.

SCHOOL MATCHES.

On Thursday, 14th June, a mixed eleven of past and present boys played the D.L.I., but were badly beaten by 106—18.

Our next match was against the 56th Mobile Section A.V.C. The School made 39 and 41, and the soldiers 53, and 36 for 1 wicket; thus winning by 9 wickets. On Saturday, 23rd June, we visited West Bergholt. The home side, batting first, made 33, and the school were dismissed for 77. On resuming after tea, Bergholt made 53; and the School, securing the necessary runs for the loss of 3 wickets, won by 7 wickets and 10 runs.

On Wednesday, 27th June, we again played the D.L.I. The military, batting first, secured 75. The school started extremely badly, 9 wickets falling for 14 runs. An excellent last wicket stand, however, brought the score to 50, of which Osborne made 22, and Lilley 12 not out. On Saturday, 7th June, West Bergholt were our visitors. The school, batting first, did badly, only making a total of 26. West Bergholt batted better, securing 53 before being dismissed. After tea the school again batted, and did much better and made a total of 60. Our visitors easily secured the required runs and won by 9 wickets.

HOUSE MATCHES.

Senior.

In the 1st round, Harsnett's had a hard tussle with Schoolhouse, and finally won by 2 runs. In the other game, Parr's, after winning the 1st innings, finally lost to Dugard's by 8 runs. For Dugard's Harwood batted well, making 30 out of a total of 75.

In the 2nd round, Harsnett's easily beat Parr's by 60 runs, and Schoolhouse succeeded in beating Dugard's by 8 runs.

In the 3rd round Schoolhouse beat Parr's by 47 runs, owing to some good batting, especially by Wilson, who made 30. Harsnett's, beating Dugard's by 7 wickets, won the Cup.

Junior.

In the 1st round Parr's easily beat Dugard's by an innings and 54 runs. Harsnett's, owing to the good bowling of Beattie, beat Schoolhouse by innings and 27 runs.

In the 2nd round Schoolhouse beat Dugard's by 53 runs. Parr's had an easy victory over Harsnett's by an innings and 64 runs. Beattie was not bowling so well as usual, while Osborne ma, for Parr's, made an excellent 59 not out.

Hymn.

Harken, all ye who mourn the days
When, spread before your eager gaze,
Tuck was displayed in tempting show
And prices still were " fairly low."
List ye and comfort him who weeps—
Our tuckshop is not dead, but sleeps.

This is to ye, oh hungry ones,
Who miss the piles of currant buns ;
The pastry, and, alack, the cake ;
The chocolate purchased in the " break " ;
Who dream of sweets in mighty heaps—
Our tuckshop is not dead, but sleeps.

To comfort him who hates the Huns,
And patriotically shuns
All tuck ; who with a drooping jaw
Gazes upon the closéd door
And murmurs as away he creeps—
" Our tuckshop is not dead, but sleeps."

CHASE.

Acknowledgments.

Our thanks are due to Editors of the following :—
The Viking, Stortfordian, Framlinghamian, Wyggestonian, O.H.S., Chelmsfordian, Williamsonian, Ipswich G.S. Mag., Chigwellian.

Old Colcestrian Section.

OFFICERS FOR 1916-17.

President : C. T. WRIGHT, Crouch Street, Colchester.

Hon. Treasurer : B. MASON, Crouch Street, Colchester.

Hon. Secretaries : A. T. DALDY, Head Street, Colchester (O.A.S.) ; B. MASON, Crouch Street, Colchester.

Old Colcestrians are requested to notify any change of address and to forward contributions to the O.C. Section to Mr. B. Mason, Hon. Sec., Crouch Street, Colchester.

MAGAZINE COMMITTEE.

The first meeting of the above was held at Gilberd House, and the following resolutions were passed :

(1.) The financial position was such as to warrant the continuance of the Magazine, limiting the issue to 16 pp.

(2.) Once a year a complete list of Old Boys should be included, starring members of the society and marking Life Members with an " L."

(3.) Mr. Charles Benham was appointed Editor in Chief, Mr. Peart continuing as Editor of the school section, and Mr. Mason as Advertisement Manager.

OUR ILLUSTRATIONS.

Pte. CECIL H. JARRARD, Essex Regiment, reported wounded and missing, October 20th, 1916, now reported killed. He was awarded the Military medal for gallantry and devotion to duty in France on January 8th. A fuller notice appeared in the Colcestrian, March, 1917.

Lieut. F. R. KEEBLE, M.C., was awarded the Military Cross for the part he took in a raid with two other officers and a party of men. The raid took place at 1 o'clock a.m. on the first of July, 1916.

He was the first one into the enemy trench and shot three Germans before one threw a bomb at him. He was wounded in the shoulder, the right leg and in the right arm. The cross was presented to him at Buckingham Palace on the 2nd of May. He and his brother were at Colchester Royal Grammar School in 1905.

A. H. WEBB.

Second-Lieutenant A. H. Webb, of the 4th Buffs, was killed in France at the end of June. He and his brother were among the first of Mr. Jeffrey's boarders, and they grew up with the school. A. H. became Senior Prefect and Captain of the school, crowning his career here with the Hewitt scholarship, which took him to Corpus Coll., Cambridge. Thence he took a first class in the Modern Language Tripos, sharing meanwhile to the full in the athletic and social life of his college, whose cricket came under his captaincy. After graduation he became House tutor and master of languages at Clifton College ; for years he spent his vacations in France and Germany, perfecting his study in languages.

When war broke out he tried several times to enlist, but

Lieut. F. R. KEEBLE, M.C.

Pte. C. H. JARRARD, Essex Regt., M.M.

was rejected. Later, however, he passed from the O.T.C. to Gailes Cadet battalion and was gazetted to the East Kents, proceeding soon after to the front. A. H. Webb will be sorely missed by a large circle of friends : we extend our deepest sympathy to his family.

Sub-Lieut. C. B. ORFEUR.

Observer Sub-Lieut. CHARLES B. ORFEUR, R.N., second son of Mr. C. E. Orfeur, North Station Road, Colchester, has died of wounds in France. Mr. and Mrs. Orfeur have other sons on active service, and great sympathy is felt with them in their sad loss. Orfeur joined the Royal Naval Division in September, 1914, and went to the Dardanelles, being among those who landed on the 4th day, i.e., April 29, 1916, at Cape Hellas. He served with the Machine Gun Section at the Peninsula till early in July, when he was invalided to Malta with enteric, and returned to England, September 15. In the early part of 1916 he received a commission of Sub-Lieut. in Royal Naval Division and later entered the Naval Air Service and was appointed " Observer," and also to the R.N. on May 27, 1916. He left for Dunkirk on May 22. On June 27 he wired (or someone on his behalf) that he was slightly injured, and this was officially confirmed, but on July 1 official information was received that he had died of wounds.

[From the *Essex County Standard*, 7th July, 1917.]

O.C.'s in the Wide World.
WITH THE EGYPTIAN FORCE.

Gunner Leonard W. Judd, of the Essex Artillery, writes :

DEAR MR. JEFFREY,—

Thanks very much for your letter and good wishes. It was very kind of you to take so much trouble over us. I may not tell you where we are, but we are in a desert with numerous small hills or dunes and groves of palm trees. I believe it is the land in which the Israelites wandered when they left Egypt At one place we were at there is an old tree close to a small mosque under which the Holy Family are said to have rested during their flight into Egypt.

I found the place very interesting at first, but the country soon begins to pall, as the word SAND completely describes it. There is very little actual fighting out here now, as you know by the papers, but we were lucky enough to be " there " on the fourth of August. It was quite exciting while it lasted, but then the Turks were in full retreat in thirty-six hours. The Turks had some biggish guns about six-inch, I think, with which they tried to knock us out. They managed to go all round us, but the nearest shell was fifty yards off.

None of us poor gunners at the battery had any chance to distinguish himself. All the decorations went to signallers.

CLAUDE HARVEY WOUNDED.

Claude Harvey, O.C., who has been a private in the London Scottish, was wounded on the Somme on Oct. 7, and eventually reached England. He is strongly recommended for a commission by Major Frank Whinney, one of the partners in the firm where has been employed for the last seven years.

A STAFF OFFICER'S REVISIT.

Lieut. R. S. Silvester, R.F., has revisited the school after many years, and sends the following letter, which will be of interest to his contemporaries :—

DEAR EDITOR,—

I have been reading the "Colcestrian" for June, 1915, after having returned from the front some little time.

Strange things happen in one's army career, for I have been in Colchester this month on a Special Course of Instruction, and while there paid a visit to the old school. It is some 14 years or so since I was there, and consequently was surprised to see the old "quad" taken up with new buildings. I paid my respects to the new Head, who had me shown round the schools.

I received my commission as a Second Lieutenant on December 1st, 1914, and am now a full Lieutenant, hoping soon to be transferred to the General Staff. Should any of the old boys see this letter I should be very pleased to get into communication with them for old time's sake.

With all best wishes to all my old school chums and success to present Colcestrians, believe me, sincerely yours, REGINALD S. SILVESTER, Lieut Royal Fusiliers.

A DISTINGUISHED O.C.

Another visit of interest was that paid in February last, by Lieut. Colonel Ritchie, D.S.O., who came to Colchester to take out a Fusilier Battalion. He looked up a contemporary—our good friend Ben Kent—and naturally the old school had to be visited. Lieut.-Colonel Ritchie was exceedingly interested in what he saw, and we can imagine the welling up of tender memories that occurred in the talk over old times and old friends between these two, who more than 30 years ago sat side by side at school, and probably had not seen each other since. There is something very human in the sentiment which links the school days with the harrying present, and if the O.C.S. does nothing more than foster it, it is well worth the doing.

BUMPS CRASKE, O.C.

Hugh Craske, O.C.—Bumps of the old days—has had some exciting experiences in the war. Leaving school, he went to Australia, and like others of our brave Colonials joined up for the war. He went through the horrors of Gallipoli, then on to Suez, being next sent for duty among the snows of a French winter. Here he was wounded, but he recovered and returned again to the fray.

COUNCILLOR "DICK," O.C.

Mr. Richard Franklin, O.C., formerly a member of the Chelmsford Town Council, is now resident at Gidea Park, and has been elected a member of the Romford Urban Council.

CAPTAIN W. GURNEY BENHAM, O.C.

Captain W. Gurney Benham, Past President, O.C.S., has been appointed to the command of the 2/2nd Battalion Essex Volunteer Regiment, whose headquarters are at Colchester, and in which Messrs. A. O. Farmer, O.C., and H. H. Hollaway, O.C., are among the officers. There are many O.C.'s in the Corps, both among the " over-agers " and the eligibles, who have been exempted because of their indispensability in their civilian occupations.

CLIFFORD MITCHELL, R.F., recently visited the School after exciting experiences at the Front. A shell dropped into his group, killing or wounding all. Mitchell and another soldier carried their wounded officer to a newly captured trench, whence the other soldier went to obtain help. Mitchell and his officer were left alone for four days and nights, keeping themselves alive on shellwater and a biscuit.

* * * *

F. W. HUSSEY, Second-Lieut., 4th Leicesters, was placed among the first six out of six hundred in a recent examination for officers.

* * * *

CECIL F. MIDGLEY writes that after eighteen months on a patrol boat he is taking the course in gunnery at Whale Island. He is Sub-Lieut., R.N.V.R., and his brothers after good service are seeking commissions in the R.N.A.S.

* * * *

ARNOLD PEACOCK, Sergeant in the Essex R.H.A., is applying for a Commission after three years' service. His brother Norman is an engineer on H.M.S. St. Vincent.

* * * *

Mr. P. SHAW JEFFREY is helping as an assistant master at Wellington College this term. He has forwarded nearly 150 applications for commissions from O.C.'s, and successful candidates are requested to communicate with him, or with the Sec., O.C.S.

* * * *

Hearty congratulations to Second-Lieut. D. W. WALLACE (O.C. and son of Councillor Wallace, O.C.) on the award of the Military Cross. Fuller details will follow.

* * * *

J. L. WATSON has been granted a commission in his old regiment, the Canadian Scottish.

* * * *

A. E. BLAXILL, Prob. Flight Lieutenant, R.N.A.S., after several successful solo flights has met with a slight accident, resulting in the breaking of his leg.

A. T. DALDY, Second-Lieutenant, Essex Regiment, our indefatigable joint secretary, having successfully graduated from Gailes Cadet Battalion, has proceeded to the Front. He had already experienced trench life as a private.

* * * *

Our congratulations to Captain F. D. FINCH, A.C.C., on his marriage with Mabel, second daughter of Mr. and Mrs. R. E. Milton, of Colchester. The best man was Lieut. F. E. Plummer, Bedfordshire Regiment.

* * * *

We extend our sympathy to Mr. and Mrs. A. S. MASON, on the premature loss of their infant son. They are stationed at Dalhousie, India, where centres Capt. Mason's work as D.A.Q.M.G.

PROMOTIONS.

W R. Everett, 2/Lt. Essex Regiment.
Hall, A. L., 2/Lt. 2/8th Lancs. Fus.
Clover, M. J., 2/Lt. Essex Regiment.
Burrell, F. B., 2/Lt. Tanks.
Folkard, C., 2/Lt. Tanks.
Daldy, A. T., 2/Lt. Essex Regiment.
Wallace, D. W., 2/Lt. West Yorks, M.C.
Collinge, F. J., 2/Lt. Oxon. & Bucks. L.I.
Collinge, R., 2/Lt. Civil Service Rifles.
Hussey, F. W., 2/Lt. 4th Leicesters.

CASUALTIES.

Beard, E. C., missing.
Bare, W. J., wounded (second time).

KILLED.

Webb, A. H., 2/Lt. 4th Buffs.
Orfeur, B. C., Flight Lieut., R.N.A.S.
Deane, G. F., 2/Lt. Essex Regiment.
Jarrard, C. H., Essex Regiment (previously reported wounded and missing).
Clark, L., Essex Regiment.
Bareham, W., East Yorks.
Malyn, R., Hon. Artillery Company.

ROLL OF HONOUR.

ADDITIONS.

Ward, A. O., Training Reserve.
Blaxill, A., Prob. Flight Lieut. R.N.A.S.
Dicker, B., Cadet Sandhurst.
Fisher, H. H., Civil Service Rifles.
Lines, R., Royal Fusiliers.
Triscott, V. P. L., A.S.C.
Girling, A. T., R.G.A.

No. 49.]
NEW SERIES.

DECEMBER, 1917.

The Colcestrian

PRICE SIXPENCE.

BENHAM & COMPANY, LIMITED, COLCHESTER.

The Colcestrian.

VITÆ CORONA FIDES.

No 49].　　　　DECEMBER, 1917.　　　[NEW SERIES.

Editorial.

THE new Editor, in making his bow, looks round. Behind him is the Past, redolent with memories of the old school days under the headmastership of the reverend Charles Lawford Acland. In front is the impenetrable veil that hides the Future; and before it stands the Present, darkened with the shadows of these fearsome times.

Turning toward that Past, the diminishing number of O.C.'s of our day and generation will realise what are our feelings on visiting the present school with its modern developments and improvements. We miss that fragrant mustiness that ever pervaded the corridors, the school-room and the class rooms of the seventies. The dear old carved desks and benches are there no more; the giant stride and step ladder and the famous " pit " in which we used to " put the shot " have disappeared for ever; the whole place is transformed and transfigured. Yet here and there some corner surviving of the old house and playground, or it may be just the friendly well-remembered face of the superannuated clock that once did duty in the big schoolroom, and always seemed to smile at a quarter past twelve, will bring back flashes of the vision that memory cherishes, somewhat as the remains of an ancient temple stand " hinting the fair completeness " that once was.

For the Present, the times are indeed out of joint—more so than any that ever Hamlet knew. But, as our pages show, quarter by quarter, these terrible years have at least served to show us the stuff that some of our O.C.'s are made of. As for the school itself, with all the advantages now lavished on its lucky scholars, we older O.C.'s can only look on with wonder and pride and a little touch, perhaps, of envy.

As to the Future, though it lies hidden, one thing shines through the veil, the certainty that great things are yet to come and that from within the walls of the Colchester school there will, undoubtedly, emerge, as time goes on, many a trained young warrior in the battle of life, whose influence will be felt by posterity throughout the country and throughout the Empire.

In all that goes on in the old school masters and scholars alike may rest assured that every O.C. will continue to take the deepest and most watchful interest. Our Latin may be getting rusty, but we can at least say without fear of correction FLOREAT SCHOLA COLCESTRIENSIS. C. E. B.

Grammaria.

Numbers.

The outstanding feature of the year has been the great increase in our numbers. The School this term has more new boys, more day-boys, more boarders, more Colchester boys, more little boys in the Preparatory School, and, of course, a larger total than at any previous time in its long history.

Ave !

We welcome on the Staff this term Mr. P. Mathews, late acting Head of Drax School, and long associated with our Headmaster at Rochester. He has speedily won his way to our respect and affection ; we must, therefore, beseech him not to make rash experiments with gas fires—we should deplore his sudden promotion to other spheres !

Mr. Watson comes to us from St. Dunstan's, bringing a record of long experience and scholarly attainment to help us in these times of difficulty ; with him in our welcome we would associate Mr. Bisson, who is taking Gymnastics—in pleasant contrast with his late strenuous work in France. Our old friend, Mr. J. H. Nunn (O.C.), resumes his work as Visiting Master.

Facienda.

Overshadowed by the tremendous happenings in the great world outside, our little Cosmos seems placid and uneventful. But the first Speech Day for two years, with Sir Arthur Duckham as chief speaker, has come and gone. Then follows the Annual Carol Service, reminding us of unchanging fundamentals in the midst of overwhelming, but temporary, catastrophe.

Lares et Penates.

During the summer vacation new desks were obtained to accommodate our growing numbers, and the lower school was re-decorated in bright tones. A still greater improvement is the inauguration of the long-planned School Library ; the generosity of the Governors and parents has made possible a useful and ever increasing collection of good books. We owe very grateful thanks to Mr. Twentyman for his most careful and painstaking work as Librarian.

In the last Imperial Challenge Shield Competition, the
C.R.G.S. team was placed 105th out of 344 entrants. Our
average was 65.1.

It is interesting to note that Australian teams swept the
board this year.

In Mem.

In addition to a large number of her faithful sons, gone in
their prime, the school mourns the loss of a very old and generous
friend—Mr. W. W. Hewitt, who not only founded a School
Exhibition at Corpus Christi, Cambridge, but who showed, in
many kind, quiet ways, his real and personal interest in Colchester School. He numbered among his pupils at Rottingdean
Sir John Jellicoe.

Salvete !

To all O.C.'s, at home and abroad, in the trenches, or in
training, on the sea or in the sky, we send a cordial wish for a
Happy Christmas and a Bright New Year. The old school
waits, like an aged mother with folded hands, to give you welcome home when you lay down your arms. And to those whose
Christmas will be saddened because of the vacant chair, we send
our message of sympathy and hope.

The Wagstaff Memorial.

On Friday, September 28th, the unveiling of the Wagstaff
Memorial (Platoon Trophy) took place. The ceremony was
short, simple, but very impressive. At 3.45, p.m., lessons over,
the cadets and scouts assembled in the Big School, while the
remainder took seats in the gallery. As soon as the Wagstaff
family had entered the hall, the boys sang : " Fight the Good
Fight " ; then the head prefect read the lesson, Ecclesiasticus
xliv., which was followed by the " Lord's Prayer." After
the prayer of memorial and prayer of dedication, Mr. Wagstaff
recalled that his boy had been an active member of the Cadet
Corps, which he appreciated very much. At the outbreak of
the war he went out to France, where he died for his King and
Country. As a memorial of the happy days he spent in the
Royal Grammar School, and in the Cadet Corps, Mr. Wagstaff
asked the Headmaster to accept this Platoon Trophy. Dr.
Rendall answered by thanking Mr. Wagstaff and family for
their kind offer, speaking of the glorious death of their beloved
son. Addressing himself especially to the boys, he showed the
greatness of the sacrifice of our soldiers, who gladly lay down
their lives for their King and Country. Mrs. Wagstaff unveiled
the memorial ; the offering and blessing of the Colours took

place, followed by a memorial prayer. The Last Post was sounded and the ceremony ended with the National Anthem. This is, in short, what happened. What passed through the hearts of those who were present would be rather difficult to say, but certainly every one was greatly touched and deeply moved. For myself hymn, prayer, speeches, all moved me deeply. I felt the sorrow of the parents, especially when Mr. Wagstaff spoke of his son's affection towards the Cadet Corps, and I am quite sure that at that moment he saw his boy again by looking at the young lads standing before him. Helas ! his life was short but glorious. Far away from home, in a foreign land he died. In imagination I see his grave in beautiful Northern France. I honour his memory, for he died not only for his fatherland, but for the liberty of the whole world. I owe him a great debt, for the life he gave so bravely away, will help to liberate my poor stricken Belgium. When the Last Post was sounded it seemed to be a last farewell to him who did so well. At that moment came to my mind the beautiful lines of our great poet, Victor Hugo, where he speaks of those who die for their country, and I repeated after him as a prayer :

> " Ceux qui pieusement sont morts pour la patrie.
> Ont droit qu'à leur cercueil la foule vienne et prie.
> Entre les plus beaux noms leur nom est le plus beau.
> Toute gloire près d'eux passe et tombe éphémère.
> Et, comme ferait une mère,
> La voix d'un peuple entier les berce en leur tombeau !

E. t'K.

The Pre.

It has been said that "nothing great was ever achieved without enthusiasm." Perhaps it is due in a measure to the fact that this quality is certainly not lacking amongst the "under nines " that we do our little deeds term by term. What should we have to write about without them ?

With its increased numbers "The Pre " is very hard at work, and the term is passing away with little to vary the weekly routine, so the boys are looking forward to Speech Day more than usual.

On Saturday, 10th, we brought a goodly number of " pounds " for our friends at " Gostwycke," and various small gifts from our gardens at home, and at school, have been carried round with pride and pleasure that are good to see in the little war workers. Our tomatoes and potatoes did very well. The leeks and turnips are coming on, and we still hope to have greens fit to send in due course, though the caterpillars had it all their own way during the holidays.

As records are all the order of the day, we intended making this a record pillow term, and it was with great consternation that we learnt the War Work Depot was in difficulties. A grand opportunity for us to show in a practical way how much we have appreciated the ravelling supplies thus offered itself, and the boys raised 10s., which was forwarded to Mrs. Hutton with their good wishes for her splendid work. Considering what a number of calls there are to-day, even upon people in the weekly-pocket-money stage, it is gratifying to know that many of the boys brought their share from their own little boxes.

We are glad to take this chance of thanking all who have sent magazines, etc., for the wounded, and pieces of ravelling. Also G. Wilson (one of our old boys), F. Horwood, G. Roberts and S. Chatterton, who have made pillows at home in order to bring our number up to eleven by Christmas.

.A. J. and C. C.

Valete.

Churchyard, A. F. C., Form VI., Schoolhouse, Pte. Cadet Corps.
Deane, R. P., Form VI., Pro. Harsnett's, House Football, Cricket, Hockey, Shooting, Cpl. C. Corps. (R.M.L.I.)
Payne, T. H., Form VI., Harsnett's, House Hockey.
White, A. A., Form VI., Q. P. Harsnett's, 1st XI. Football and Cricket, Captain House Football, Cricket, Hockey, Cpl. C. Corps, Member of Committee Debating Society. (T.R.)
Dolamore, C. W. G., Form Va, Schoolhouse, School Shooting VIII., House, Football, Cricket, Hockey, Shooting, Sgt. C. Corps.
Arnold, E. C., Form Vb, Harsnetts', House Football, Cricket, Shooting, Cadet.
Curtis, A, Form Vb, Schoolhouse, House Cricket.
K ng, P. D, Form IVa, Harsnett's, Cadet.
Hackett, C. H., Form IVa, Parr's, House Football, Cricket.
White, H. C. P., Form II., Schoolhouse.

Salvete.

VA.		IVB.	
Holloway, E.	.. Dugard's	Bloom, D. J.	.. Harsnett's
VB.		Brown II., E. A.	.. Harsnett's
Denman, A. B. C.	.. Harsnett's	Brown III., W. C.	.. Harsnett's
		Coulsell, W. M.	.. Harsnett's
IVA.		Gunton, S.	.. Dugard's
Eaves, H. L.	.. Parr's	Hunt, A. F.	.. Dugard's
Joel, R. T.	.. Schoolhouse	Johnson, L. E. W.	.. Harsnett's
Jones, C. W.	.. Parr's	Meale, F. H.	.. Dugard's
Payne, K. S.	.. Parr's	Temple, G.	.. Harsnett's
Walkden III., F.	.. Parr's	Tyson, L. T. I.	.. Schoolhouse
Wilson VII., G.	.. Dugard's	Underdown, G. W.	.. Harsnett's
Bullough, C. C.	.. Dugard's	Hick, J. D.	.. Parr's

III A.

Wallis, S. H.	..	Dugard's
Wilson. VIII., H.	..	Dugard's
Gosling II., J. N.	..	Schoolhouse
Harrington, S W.	..	Schoolhouse

IIIB.

Church I., A. L.	..	Schoolhouse
Last II., E.	..	Dugard's
Wilson VI., D.	..	Parr's

II. & I.

| Birdsey, T. C. | .. | Schoolhouse |
| Calvaley, C. E. | .. | Parr's |

Church II., O. W.	..	Schoolhouse
Dowsett II., W. F. (from Pre.)		
Hearsum, R. G.	..	Parr's
Manning, F. W. (from Pre).	..	Harsnett's
Muirhead, A. H. V.	...	Harsnett's
Oakley, B. (from Pre.)		Harsnett's
Rolfe, T. C.	..	Schoolhouse
Thurston, C. F.	...	Harsnett's

Moore, D., Pre, Joscelyne, R., Pre.
Richer, A., Pre, Maude, J., Pre.
Mitchell, K., Pre, Hill, C., Pre.
Rogers, D., Pre. Mitchell, R., Pre.

Cadet Corps.

(Attached 5th Essex.)

Two excellent Route Marches have been enjoyed this term, one in the West Bergholt area, the other through Stanway. The good style which the band has now attained is a great aid to march discipline.

*   *   *   *

An interesting afternoon was spent in a scheme of the " iron ring " type, when Sergt. French succeeded in taking the greater part of his force through a weak flank of the defenders. Both French and Sergt. Crighton had given careful attention to working out details of their plans.

*   *   *   *

Staff-Capt. Dunne (H.Q.) inspected the Corps very thoroughly on July 27th. With him was an officer who, before the war, had had considerable experience in the conduct of Cadet Corps. The inspection was therefore both fair and thorough ; and the various sections of our work were carefully examined. Capt. Dunne, who expressed his affection for, and gratitude to, his own old school corps, gave a helpful and heartening talk to the boys, in words they will not soon forget.

*   *   *   *

The report of the Inspecting Officer, given in detail, and touching on all points of essential importance, was very gratifying. I congratulate the corps on such a result of their hard work and loyal co-operation. The blots which the report pointed out, the lack of equipment and the ill-fit of the uniforms, are matters rather beyond our power to remedy.

*   *   *   *

At the beginning of this term the trophy given by Mr. Wagstaff, in memory of our old comrade, Douglas Wagstaff, was formally unveiled. It is a handsome panel in English oak, carved and decorated with gesso work in gilt and colour ;

above the bold torch, typical of effort and continuity, is the school crest, flanked by sprays of oak and laurel. Eighteen copper-gilt shields surround the panel ; on each will be placed the winning platoon, three years on each shield. In addition to the inscription are the words "Pass the torch along," from the school song, and the beautiful line of Rupert Brooke : " He leaves a white, unbroken glory." The trophy was designed and executed by Mrs. D. Allen, of Colchester, and was won, after a contest in seven distinct branches of Cadet work, by Sergt. Crighton's platoon (No. 1).

* * * *

As we go to Press we have received intimation that Watsham ma., a cadet of long service, who proved so sound an N.C.O., is wounded. 2nd Lieut. Flanagan, 3rd Essex, who transferred to the Tanks, is reported killed in action. Capt. Deakin, our former O.C., is also posted as wounded : we hope to hear that he is progressing favourably.

* * * *

A large number of recruits joined this term ; they have in good spirit accepted the grievous necessity of wearing ill-fitting uniforms, in these times of excessively high prices and restricted khaki supplies.

* * * *

We are grateful to the O.C. Colchester Company, Essex Volunteer Regiment, for the loan of carbines ; the increase in our strength from 56 to 85 in two years has made us feel the need of further equipment.

* * * *

A detachment of 21 cadets went to the Public Secondary Schools camp at Marlborough, at the close of last term. Heavy and constant rains curtailed the programme of work, but not the enthusiasm of the cadets. The splendid way in which the N.C.O.'s carried on was very pleasing, and I was very proud of the cheery, unselfish spirit displayed by our boys, and was conscious of shame when called away to do duty in the comparative comfort and shelter of Hertford Barracks. In punishment, my four days of holiday were exceedingly wet. Our thanks are due to Capt. Tench (Norfolk Regiment) for his untiring efforts on our behalf at Camp.

* * * *

Hearty congratulations to J. A. Willmott (2nd Lt. Essex Regiment), on winning the Military Cross. He left the Corps in 1914, and has early earned laurels for himself, his regiment, and his old school.

* * * *

H. G. Bare, Nicholson mi., Ward and Archie White (all of the T.R.), " Bertie " Dicker (from Sandhurst, en route for the

Indian Army), Bugg and Brand (newly commissioned to the Essex R.), "Tubby" Bare (now recovered from his second "Blighty" wound), 2nd. Lieut. Horwood (stationed now at Aldershot), 2nd Lt. F. J. Collinge (fresh from successful courses with the Ox. and Bucks L.I.), Tommy Atkins (great in the ways of Ac-emma and straight from the mud of Flanders), 2nd Lieut. D. L. Oliver (O.C. road-makers in the tracks of the Huns), these old cadets, known to most of you, are among recent welcome visitors to Gilberd House. Freddy Farquharson, now full Lieutenant (B.W.I. Regt.), after many months in France, sends greeting to his House and all who remember him. Can we forget, O Thou of the Big Drum and wily bowling ?

* * * *

We are pleased to hear of Dan Chapman's recovery, after several months in hospital. He was a fine shot as a cadet, and has maintained his high standard ; his experiences have been hard and deep indeed; and some day he will have much to tell us.

* * * *

Ronald Orfeur, also, is making satisfactory progress in recovery from serious wounds.

* * * *

Barrell; Rogers, Squire and Syer are recent cadets who have joined up ; the Flying Corps is attracting many of our late members.

J. A. P.

Acknowledgments.

We beg to thank Editors of the following for sending copies —The Viking, Stortfordian, Framlinghamian, Wyggestonian, O.H.S., The Arrow, Chelmsfordian, Williamsonian, Ipswich G.S.M., Chigwellian.

Scouting Notes.

On July 25th a lecture was given in Big School to the Scouts of Colchester and District by Mr. John Hargraves, on Woodcraft. Later in the evening he presented badges won during the term. The badge winners were all mentioned in last month's magazine, with the following exceptions : *Clerk's badge*, P.L. Prescott ; *Swimmer's badge*, P.L. Burleigh.

Promoted to Patrol Leaders, Scout Hollaway, Sec. Loyd.

The weather this term has been very favourable on the whole for outdoor work, and up to the present we have had three field days. Several half-holidays in the earlier part of the term were devoted to the collection of chestnuts. We have now a very large quantity waiting to be sent off, as soon as the authorities tell us where they are tc be sent.

* * * *

We have to thank Mr. Cape for his kindness in giving us three hundred Scout record cards. Besides giving the complete record of the Scout's progress, the card contains the Scout law and a good scheme for inter-patrol competitions. We are very grateful to the Headmaster for this further token of interest and help.

* * * *

As recruits this term we welcome Wilson 8, Denman, Payne, Walkden, Bullough, Underdown, Church and Harrington. P.L. Prescott has joined the Cadet Corps this term. We miss him very much from parades, but he has taken charge of the Wolf Cub pack this term and has done excellent work, with the assistance of Scouts Farmer and Mirrington. Prescott's report is as follows :—

C.R.G.S. Pack of Wolf Cubs.

The Pack is nineteen strong, and is divided into three Sixes or Patrols, the "Reds," "Greens," and "Browns," the three respective cub-leaders being Barnes, Griffin and Jeffrey.

This term's recruits are Cubs Manning, Wilson 6, Rolfe, Smith 6 and Calveley. Barnes and Peter Robinson were inadvertently omitted from last term's list. Cubs Girling and Walkden have passed on to the Scout Troop on becoming eleven years of age. The following cubs have qualified for their first star :—C.L.'s Barnes, Griffin, and Jeffrey, and Cubs Wombwell, Smith 5 and Heasman The others have not quite finished their tests.

Field Days.—Saturday, Sept. 29, the Pack went out to Blackheath and came back with a creditable load of chestnuts.

Thursday, Nov. 8th, the Pack marched out to Butchers Green and had some scouting games. Patrol competitions were held. The Cubs then made a camp fire and cooked their tea before marching home.

G. E. P.

Gardening.

Looking back on the first year's work on our plots, I think we may safely say the results on the whole are very satisfactory, while in many cases they exceed expectations. Our main crop was of necessity potatoes, and these turned up very well; though we did not go to the trouble of spraying, there was very little sign of disease. We are glad to hear from several sources that the quality when cooked is excellent.

Some of our green crops also did very well, and several plots had a really good show of cauliflowers, but we were sorry to see many of these left too long before being cut. Plot No. 9 has done the best on the whole, and this is undoubtedly due to the extra attention it received at the hands of Loyd and Burleigh mi., both of whom we are pleased to note have succeeded in obtaining their Scout's Badge for Gardening.

Bar the lifting of the crops, not much work has been done this term, but we hope that during the Christmas holidays plot holders will do all they can to make certain that every possible square yard of ground has been turned over, and this should be left rough. By doing this in good time a large amount of labour will be saved in the spring, while next year's crop should show a substantial increase. Now is the time to map out the ground for next year's crop, remembering that the same ground should not have the same crop as last year.

E. R.

Football.

SCHOOL MATCHES.

Seven members of last year's eleven still remain to help the school, and as a consequence the first XI. is an improvement on last year's. Owing to the impossibility of travelling, all school matches have been played at home, and against soldiers. The first two matches were with D. Coy. 252nd Infantry Battalion. The School each time had the best of the game, but owing to bad shooting both matches were lost, the first 7—3, the second 6—3. The third match was against the 56th Mobile Section A.V.C. The school, with only a half-strength team, succeeded in tying 3—3. The fourth was against C. Coy. Berkshire Yeomanry. The school had a strong team, and the game was the best of the term. The final result, 4—4, is a fair estimate of the game. A special word of praise is due to Crighton, who saved some good shots in a very tricky wind.

HOUSE MATCHES.

Senior:

This term has seen a great levelling of the senior House teams. Schoolhouse have the best individual players, but they fail to combine. Dugard's have fallen from last year's strength, but still possess a capable and hard-

working team.. Harsnett's have. lost. mcst. of their sturdy champions,.
while Parrs's till .largely rely .on juniors, and must patiently await the
future. ·

1st Round.

The game Schoolhouse v. Harsnett's was very one-sided, play being
nearly all in Harsnett's half. Their defence, however, played up pluckily,
and the result, 5—o for Schoolhouse, is really a credit to Harsnett's.

Parr's and Dugard's contested their match much more evenly. Dugard's
had the best of the first half, and half-time score was 3—o in their favour.
Parr's played up much better in the. second half, and secured the only
goal, Dugard's thus winning 3—1.

2nd Round. ·

Schoolhouse again had an easy win, beating Parr's 6—1. Parr's played
up well in the first half, but _ell away towards the end ; although one
might say that Schoolhouse won in spite of their talent.

The Dugard's and Harsnett's match was an easy win for Dugard's,.
by 7—2. Harsnett's played pluckily and kept going well throughout
but they were overcome by superior strength, and had to admit defeat.

3rd Round.

The Parr's and Harsnett's match was fairly well contested. Parr's
were rather superior in the first half, but .wasted many golden
chances, and the score at half-time was 4—2 in their favour.
The second half was very even. Parr's again failed to score,
although opportunities were many. Harsnett's, forwards many.
times got away, and succeeded in scoring two goals. Thus the whistle
blew, when the result was 4—4. In an extra twenty minutes, Parr's
gradually fell to pieces, and Harsnett's,scoring two more goals, won 6—4.

The other game, Schoolhouse v. Dugard's, was also very even. Schoolhouse played by no means as well as they should have done, while Dugard's
played their hardest the whole time. Dugard's scored a goal in each
half, and thus ran out winners by 2—o, thereby becoming Cock House for
the term.

JUNIOR HOUSE · MATCHES.

The Junior teams are by no means so well matched as. their seniors..
Parr's still have a great preponderance of talent, but the other Houses
are fairly well matched. .

In the first round Parr's beat Dugard's 10—2, and Schoolhouse had a
comfortable win of 6—o over Harsnett's.

In the second round Parr's again had an easy win, beating Schoolhouse
10—1, but the other game was very well contested, Harsnett's finally
beating Dugard's 3—2.

In the third round Schoolhouse beat Dugard's 3—1, and are again
runners-up. Parr's easily beat Harsnett's 11—1, and so again become
Cock-House.

LEAGUES.

Leagues have again been started this term, and so far have been quite
a success. Only three of five rounds have yet been played, and a fuller
report will be given next term.

The Song of the Waits.

The wind is rude, our coats be thin,
And we be come a carolin',
So you who make good cheer within
Bethink you of our plight.
From house to house we wend our way
To cheer poor souls with lilt and lay,
So we be come a carolin'
To sing for your delight.

There's Ben the smith to take the low,
And Tinker Jan the higher,
And 'times their lines apart do go,
And 'times they draw them nigher.
To keep the twain in proper heart
That all may come together,
Myself do sing the middle part
With lungs so stout as leather.

Old Gaffer Jarge, an ancient hind,
Hath brought his concertina,
And for the tunes he hath in mind
'Twere well his wits were keener,
But sith our songs be stout and free,
Both tunable and chancey,
His wind-box don't a-hinder we
So much as you med fancy.

Then ere we pass upon our way,
The good Saint Benedight we pray
To bless this house till peep o' day
From every wicked wight,
That when you lay your heads to rest
No warlock may your sleep molest
When we be gone a carolin'
Afar into the night.

                                P. Shaw Jeffrey.

406

Captain D. W. WALLACE.

Private HARRY SANGER.

Old Colcestrian Section.

OFFICERS FOR 1916=17.

President : C. T. WRIGHT, Crouch Street, Colchester.
Hon. Treasurer : B. MASON, Crouch Street, Colchester.
Hon. Secretaries.: A. T. DALDY, Head Street. Colchester (O.A.S.) ;
B. MASON, Crouch Street, Colchester.

Old Colcestrians are requested to notify any change of address and to forward contributions to the O.C. Section to Mr. B. Mason, Hon. Sec., Crouch Street, Colchester.

Our Illustrations.

CAPTAIN DUDLEY WHISTLER WALLACE, M.C.

Captain DUDLEY WHISTLER WALLACE, M.C. (son of Alderman and Mrs. R. W. Wallace), who fell on October 9, was awarded the Military Cross for a gallant and successful raid which he conducted a few months before his death, the success of the enterprise, carried out without casualties, being entirely due to his courage and skilful leading. The officer in command of his battalion writes :—

"Captain Wallace was most popular with his brother officers and men, and was always ready to take on any work he was detailed to do, and did it thoroughly well. We all miss him very much, as he was always at his best in a hot corner. Your son was killed leading his Company under a heavy fire and fell doing his duty."

PTE. HARRY SANGER.

Pte. HARRY SANGER, Essex Regt., who died on November 1 as the result of injuries received in action, was a gifted young musician, and when quite a boy was appointed organist at St. Martin's Church. He left the Grammar School in 1913, and became an efficient member of the staff of the Harwich Division Conservative Association. He went through the Gallipoli campaign and did strenuous service in France.

Mr. Osmond G. Orpen.

A highly esteemed O.C. in the person of Mr. Osmond G. Orpen has passed away. He died very suddenly on October 7, at his residence, Hillside, West Bergholt, aged 62. His fame as an amateur horticulturist was great and he was also keenly interested in all matters connected with the welfare of the district in which he lived. If he had a motto, it was the simple word "Thorough," an attribute that may be applied to his career in respect of everything he undertook.

Bravo, Siggers!

Lieut. J. W. Siggers is now M.C., as well as O.C. The award was made to him for coolness and devotion to duty on the nights April 24–25, 1917. Though shot through the thigh, he bravely led his platoon through a heavy barrage right to the top of the hill which was the objective, and held it for three hours till ordered to retire, which he did with his men in good order, all the wounded being also safely brought in.

The Volunteers.

Capt. W. G. Benham, commanding 2/2ND E.V.R., has been promoted Major.

*   *   *   *

Capt. H. H. Hollaway, of the same battalion, has been promoted Assistant Adjutant.

Casualties.

KILLED.

Everett, 2/Lt. W. R., Essex Regiment.
Wallace, Capt. Dudley W., West Yorkshire Regiment.
Mason, Corpl. Conrad, Essex Regiment.
Sanger, Harry, Essex Regiment.
Fieldgate, L.
Keeble, J. R., 2/Lieut. R.F.C.

WOUNDED.

Bond, Cyril T., Australian Force.
Butler, F. H., 2/Lieut.
Chambers, 2/Lt. H. C. W., Lincolnshire Regiment.
Watsham, Sergt. Harold.
Orfeur, R., 2/Lt.

MISSING.

Pulford, A. L.

French, A. H., R.G.A., died of wounds after being gassed in France.

ROLL OF HONOUR.

ADDITIONS

Bare, H. G., Training Reserve.
Barrell, G., Training Reserve.
Davis, W. E., R.N.D.

Fisher, C. E. (discharged).
Koskinas, F. M., Greek Army.
Lord, S. W., Training Reserve.

Munson, A. G., Training Reserve.
Nicholson, C., Training Reserve.
Percy, T., Training Reserve.
Rogers, S. W., Training Reserve.
Squire, B. A., R.N.A.S.

Syer, F. W., R.F.C.
White, H., Training Reserve.
White, A. A., Training Reserve.
Williams, F. O., 2-5th Gloucesters.

PROMOTIONS.

Blythe-Cooper, 2nd Lieut.
Brand, E. J., 2nd Lieut., Essex Regt.
Bugg, E. P., 2nd Lieut., Essex Regt.
Farquharson, F. H., 1st Lieut., B.W. Ind. Regt.
Harvey, C. L., 2nd Lieut., 7th Queen's (W. Surrey) Regt.

Midgley, E. L., Prob. Flt. Lieut.
Lucking, C. D., Capt., Devon R.G.A. (T.).
Rainbird, H. W., 2nd Lt., East Lancs.
Wilmot, J. A., 2nd Lieut., M.C., Essex Regt.

Our curtailed space does not allow of our doing justice to the deeds of our gallant O.C.'s at the front, and we must be content with but brief mention of one or two who have laid down their lives for their country. Fuller accounts have already appeared in the local Press.

LIEUTENANT J. H. KEEBLE.

Lieutenant J. H. Keeble, R.F.C., second son of Mr. and Mrs. J. R. Keeble, of Brantham Hall, has been killed in a flying accident. The funeral at Brantham was attended by a large number of sympathisers and a pathetic figure in the procession was the young officer's favourite dog, which he had hoped to take back to France with him.

G. F. F. DEANE.

George Frederic Field Deane, who left the Grammar School in January, 1915, at the age of 17, went to France in November, and served in the trenches for six months. After six months' training as a Cadet at Oxford, he received his commission in the Essex Regiment in November, 1916, and went out to France, where he was killed at the front near Lens by a shell on April 22 last. Ralph, his only surviving brother, left the school last July, and is now a sub-Lieutenant in the R.M.L.I., stationed at Deal.

CORPL. CONRAD MASON.

Corpl. Conrad Mason, who is among the many O.C.'s who have fallen in action, was the eldest son of Mrs. Ernest Mason, of Crouch Street, Colchester. It was on October 1st, while Conrad was doing his best for a wounded soldier, that he was killed by the bursting of a shell. He was buried side by side with the man whom he was trying to rescue. Corpl. Mason commenced his career at the Grammar School in January, 1907, and joined the Essex Regiment September 5, 1914. He was at home on short leave only a few weeks before his death.

Mrs. Mason has received from one of his comrades a letter, in which the following passage occurs :—" It is a terrible blow to me, and even though I attended Conrad's burial this afternoon,

410

I can hardly realise that he has gone from us. It happened early on the morning of the 1st. A shell dropped in the dug-out occupied by the officers' servanrs. Only two of the servants were in the place at the time. Conrad heard their appeal for help, and ran over to render first aid. One man had several slight wounds ; the other was terribly wounded, and it was whilst Conrad was doing his best for him that he got killed by another shell bursting close by him. By the time that it was possible for someone to get to them the man Conrad tried to rescue was dead. They were buried side by side yesterday. Truly it may be said of him that he gave his life for another."

We learn with regret that Lieut. R. ORFEUR, third son of Mr. C. E. Orfeur, of North Station Road, has been severely wounded in France, resulting in the loss of a leg. We are glad to say, however, that he is now making satisfactory progress.

*   *   *   *

We have reason to believe that Lieut. E. C. BEARD, who was reported missing, is now safe and a prisoner of war in Palestine.

*   *   *   *

Sub-Lieut. C. F. Midgley, R.N., is now at home on leave, after being rescued when his ship was blown up.

*   *   *   *

Another cheerful letter from F. D. Barker comes to hand, this time from Blandford, where he is still undergoing medical treatment. He says he is rather tired of hospital life, though it has compensations.

*   *   *   *

Kenneth R. Middleton has been putting in a good deal of spare time with the Volunteers at West Norwood. He shot in the Company team the other day, and scored 94 out of a possible 100.

*   *   *   *

Dan Chapman has had rough experiences at the front, and in going "over the top" on May 3rd got a bullet wound which knocked him down. He lay all day, and at night started to crawl, but had only strength to struggle 200 yards before day-break. He crept into a shell hole, when a whizz-bang exploded close by and got him in the arm and back. At last he was picked up by a patrol just at night-fall. Within a week he was in Blighty, and is in hospital at Southport. His spine was just touched—another quarter inch and he would have been paralysed. He has undergone two operations in England, and one in France, but his wounds have now healed, and he writes in the best of spirits with thoughts of the old school, and hopes that it lives up to its old traditions.

*   *   *   *

Our best thanks are due to a valued correspondent's suggestion for a War Memorial, which has been sent to the Head and will have the fullest consideration.

413

No. 50.]
NEW SERIES.

APRIL, 1918.

The Colcestrian

PRICE SIXPENCE.

BENHAM & COMPANY, LIMITED, COLCHESTER.

The Colcestrian.

VITÆ CORONA FIDES.

No 50].   APRIL, 1918.   [NEW SERIES.

Grammaria.

Captain Deakin, M.C.

We are all very proud at the thought of another M.C. to our list. Many of us remember Captain Deakin at School, and in charge of the Cadet Corps in its earliest days. We wish him continued good luck, in the strafing of the " Turkey-Man."

Visitors.

Many old friends still roll up to the School and to Gilberd House. They all, officers and men, look very fit. It would seem that although we may not all fly, the ambition of nearly every boy leaving School is to join the R.N.A.S. or the R.F.C.

Gas !

Some of us have heard this cry in earnest, but on the Playing Field, to the accompaniment of a " chime " from an empty shell-case or a hanging piece of rail, it only reminds us that our Pavilion is still a Gas-Chamber. It has a great fascination for some of our small boys, who at times have to be " shoo-ed " out of range of its fetid breath.

S. C. H. French.

At the beginning of this term French achieved a particularly notable success for the School. In gaining an open Mathematical Scholarship of £70, at Peterhouse, Cambridge, he headed the list of his group. He is shortly leaving to join up : all luck to him !

Floreat Sodalitas.

Our numbers are still on the increase. We have a larger number of day-boys, of boarders, and of boys in the Pre. than ever before. Shall we see, midst red tabs, green tabs, and other tabs, a revival of the once famous Tin Tabs ?

Mr. J. H. Oldham,

We are glad to be able to announce the appointment of Mr. Oldham to a tutorship at Cheltenham College. We have good news of him and his recovery.

417

The Pre.

For years past the list of " good deeds " has been faithfully added to week by week in the Pre., and this is all the recognised preparation we gave the Wolf Club Patrol, which is such a success in the Lower School.

Now that of necessity military training has recently become such an important part of every boy's education, it was felt that even the youngest might be encouraged to do work that would stand them in good stead in future training. If it be true that during the first seven years a little child forms the habits of a life time—then the sooner we can teach something of Scout Law the better. At any rate six weeks ago the " Pre Patrol " was duly instituted, and the work is now in full swing. Our first inspection took place on Friday, February 22nd, and was of an entirely private nature. Some badges were presented, and the Folk Dances (particularly those by the new members) showed that time this term has been well used.

A week later a second inspection of a far more imposing character took place. On this occasion Mrs. Cross kindly presented the badges, and watched the Patrol Leaders drill their men. The exercises were quite creditable, and though much remains to be desired in the matter of quiet and exact movement, there is already a marked improvement. It is rumoured that Mr. Cape, with his habitual kindness, has consented to be present at a function fixed for the end of the term, and for which the Pre Scouts are all working in deadly earnest.

The fine weather has enabled us to begin gardening earlier than usual. The border was portioned out afresh, and although eight boys took over the plot near the Shooting Range, there were still six members without a piece of ground, so Mr. Cape has kindly given up a border of his vegetable garden, and we can begin operations. The gardener's badge is among the most coveted.

At Christmas and twice since, goodly collections of vegetables have found their way to Gostwycke.

Our collection this term is again to be in aid of the War Needlework Depot, and has already amounted to ten shillings.

We are still ravelling, and are proud to say we have completed our 75th pillow ! (Space forbids any further details ; one must economise.)

Once again, many thanks to all who have sent us ravelling material, also magazines, etc., for the wounded.

A. J. and C. C.

Valete.

Clarke, S. F., Form VI., Dugard's, Bugler C.C., Dramatic Society.
Halls, G. A., Form VI., Dugard's, K.P., House Football, Cricket, Hockey, Shooting (capt.), Captain School Shooting VIII., C.Q.S. Cadet Corps, joined L.R.B.
Layzell, O. W., Form VI., Schoolhouse, House Shooting, Pte. Cad. Corps, joined R.F.C.
Crighton, J. F. R., Form VI., Schoolhouse, K.P., Captain House Football, Cricket, Shooting, 1st XI. Cricket, School Shooting VIII., Band Sergt. C.C., joined R.F.C.
Felgate, F. W., Form Va., Parr's, House Football, Cricket, Hockey, Shooting, Lce.-Cpl. C.C.
Hunneyball, H. H. T., Form Va., Parr's, House Football and Shooting, Pte. C.C.
Prescott, E. C., Form Va., Schoolhouse, 1st XI. Football, House Football, Cricket, Shooting, Pte. C.C.
Procter, H. W., Form Va., Harsnett's, Pte. C.C.
Wilson VII., G. R., Form Vb., Dugard's, House Football, Pte. C.C.
Murphy, W. T. P. D., Form IIIa., Schoolhouse, Scout, J.H. Football.
Wilson VIII., H., Form IIIa., Dugard's, J.H. Football, Scout.
Wombwell, L. A. R., Form IIIb., Harsnett's, Scout.

PRE.

D. Weeks } Upper School.
R. Wicks }

Salvete.

VA.		Curd, F. H. S.	.. Harsnett's
Griffith, R. H.	.. Parr's	Elliott, F. A.	.. Parr's
IVB.		Pine, F. ..	.. Harsnett's
Offord, W. A.	.. Schoolhouse	Ram, W. F. W.	.. Schoolhouse
Tovell, J. ..	.. Schoolhouse	Weeks, D. F.	.. Parr's
Nichols, J.	.. Schoolhouse	Wicks, A. R.	.. Dugard's
IIIA.			
Brunton, P. D.	.. Schoolhouse	PRE.	
Jackson II., L. J. ..	.. Schoolhouse	Woodman, K.	
Mathams, A. L. G...	Dugard's	Secker, T.	
Nocton, R. H.	.. Schoolhouse	Uff, F.	
IIIB.		Rudsdale, E.	
Nocton, C. E.	.. Schoolhouse	Hucklesby, E.	
II. & I.		Dennis, E.	
Canham, L. J. D.	.. Schoolhouse	Benham, H.	

Cadet Corps.

(*Attached 5th Essex.*)

Our hearty congratulations are due to Capt. E. B. Deakin, a former O.C., on his well-earned decoration.

* * * *

We cordially welcome the return of Mr. Barker to the staff, from every point of view. He has kindly undertaken the arduous duties of Treasurer of the Corps, as well as the Editorial duties connected with the school section of the Magazine. Gilberd House is young again with his presence, and we of the Corps know how valuable his advice and help will prove.

* * * *

A most acceptable gift of a buzzer set has been received from our good friend, Second-Lieut. P. Henstock, and we hope it will spur on the Signallers to greater effort.

* * * *

We have had visits from Eves, " Skimmy " Hudson, Fisher, Butler mi., Bugg, Ward, Nicholson mi., Crighton, Fisher and " Archie," among the old Cadets in khaki : they report " All's well."

* * * *

Discharged : Sergts. Halls and Crighton, Lance-Corpl. Felgate, Cadets Hunneyball, Proctor, Clarke, Blandford, Layzell, Wallis, Wright I. and Prescott. Joined : Mathams, Beatty I., Nocton I., Nocton II., Offord, Sayer, Nicholls.

* * * *

A good half-term's work has been done on the drill ground, and an improvement in steadiness is to be noted. The route march early in the term showed the need for more march discipline.

* * * *

By kind permission of the Warwickshire Yeomanry, their ground at Stanway was the scene of a well-organised and useful exercise on " The Platoon in Attack." On the whole the results were good, and valuable lessons were taught. We hope for more of this kind of work.

* * * *

Before setting our for the Field Day the Headmaster presented Lance-Corpl. White with the Best Recruit's medal, awarded on an unanimous vote of the N.C.O.'s. The Head kindly gave an extension of time for the Stanway scheme.

J. A. P.

Scouting Motes.

In the examination for the Pathfinder badge, held at the end of last term by the Borough Surveyor, the following boys passed :—P. L.'s. Burleigh, H. Osborne, J. W. Weeks and Scout Beckett. Eight other boys are reported as having done very good papers, but that they failed to answer one particular question essential to any " Pathfinder " test. I hope that these will all qualify for the badge next time. By obtaining this badge P. L. Burleigh has now qualified as an " All-round " Scout.

In future there will be held, twice a term, a patrol competition, after which the patrols will be arranged in order of efficiency. A great help towards this is the gift of a large number of patrol forms giving a weekly return of all work done by each patrol. It is one more thing that we owe to the kindness of Mr. Cape, and we are very grateful to him, not only for the gift, but also for the idea, which has done much to quicken the right sort of patrol rivalry.

* * * *

One pleasing feature of the term's work is the large number of boys who have qualified for the Second Class Scout Badge. In the past there has always been a certain number of Scouts who have taken far too long over this test. In future the Court of Honour will exclude from parades, until they have won their badge, all boys who fail to complete this test within a reasonable time.

Other badges recently awarded are :—

Public Service Badge, 100 *Days* : Weeks ma. and Weeks mi.

Public Service Badge, 28 *Days* : P. L. Loyd, Scouts Turner, C. Smith and H. Smith.

1st Class Scout Badge : P. L.'s. Burleigh and Weeks ma.

* * *

This term's recruits are : Brunton and Walkden III., who has come up from the Cub Pack ; Prescott, who took charge of the Pack last term, and Murphy have gone to Bedford Grammar School ; and Clarke and Bailey have left to join the Cadet Corps.

* * * *

The Wolf Cub Pack is flourishing, and several of the senior boys show promise of becoming first-class Scouts later on. This term we welcome as recruits : D. Weeks, Muirhead, Harper, Nunn, Ram, Canham, Elliott and D. Wilson.

G. E. P.

Gardening.

The weather during this term has been ideal for work on the plots, and though the amount of digging done has not been great, we can report considerable progress. A few of the plots already are partly sown, and we hope that before the end of term much more may have been done in this line. In a little more than a fortnight's time we shall be having a few days' holiday, owing to Easter falling in term time ; and much can then be done. About half the plots have changed owners since last season, and all are in the hands of day boys, who will no doubt be busy during the Easter holidays.

Owing to the pavilion having been commandeered by the

military, we have no place to store our tools on the field at present, but it should be remembered that in this respect we are in exactly the same position as the majority of allotment holders. At the same time it would be a very great convenience if we could have a tool shed put up near the plots, and should there be any budding carpenters, who could knock up even a rough shed during the holidays, they can be assured of the gratitude of other workers.

As seed time approaches we should like to repeat the statement that it is much better to sow on well prepared ground in April than on ill-prepared in March. Many boys are too anxious to get things sown, but, at the present time we would rather see zeal in digging than desire for sowing. Much can now be done in the way of tidying up, and we should like to see all edges trimmed and rubbish burnt as early as possible.

Potatoes, parsnips and beans were our best crops last year, and we hope to see still more of these useful vegetables produced during the coming season. The best advice we can give for the present is dig deeply.

Speech Day.

Speech day was held on Thursday, December 6, in the Moot Hall, when the prizes and certificates won during the school year were presented by Sir Arthur Duckham, K.C.B., a member of the Council of the Ministry of Munitions. The Mayor (Councillor A. M. Jarmin) took the chair, and was supported by the members of the Town Council, who attended in state, also by the Bishop of Colchester, the Rev. Dr. Rendall, Mr. C. E. Gooch, the Revs. E. Spurrier and K. L. Parry, Mr. G. C. Holland (secretary to the Higher Education Committee), the Town Clerk and Clerk to the Governors (Mr. H. C. Wanklyn), and the headmaster of the school (Mr. H. J. Cape, M.A.) and staff.

The spacious hall and gallery were both crowded with parents and supporters of the town school, who were greatly impressed by the success of the new " head's " first year of office.

The Mayor, in welcoming Sir Arthur Duckham, said they all regretted that he was not accompanied by Sir L. Worthington Evans, M.P., who was a good friend to the school. (Applause.) He had sent a telegram in which he much regretted that his work prevented his attendance, but he sent his hearty greetings to the boys. (Applause.) Having referred to the regretted decease during the year of Mr. Douglass Round, one of the senior governors of the school, and Mr. W. W. Hewitt, of Dedham (another governor), the Mayor said the school was facing the future under happier auspices than ever before. He reminded them that the school was founded nearly 400 years ago by Henry the Eighth. It did not meet with any great success in its early days, but the then headmaster did his best for the school on a salary of £6..13..4 a year. (Laughter.) The pupils of the school included the famous Archbishop Harsnett, and also Samuel Parr and a number of other distinguished men. The numbers on the books at present far exceeded the numbers of the past, and never was the school so much appreciated by Colchester people as it was to-day. (Applause.) The Mayor added that they appreciated the fact that Sir Arthur Duckham came to them direct from a visit to the French battle field. (Hear, hear.)

The Headmaster, who received a very hearty reception, then presented his first report, which he introduced with a happy vein of humour, which pleased the large audience immensely. Mr. Cape went on to say that the number of scholars at the present time was a record in the history of the school. Their previous record was 205, whereas the number this term was 240. (Applause.) During the year the school had increased by 62 boys—35 per cent. of the total number. (Applause.) The numbers had increased in every department, and that in spite of the fact that like every other school in the country they had hardly any older boys. Like every other school also they had not many successes of older scholars, for the satisfactory reason that they had not the older boys to get them. Of the younger boys, whom they had got, he ventured to think they would find the results very satisfactory. (Applause.)

Having referred to the excellent results (as given in the prize list), the Headmaster went on to allude to the success achieved in sports and added that both the Cadet Corps and the Scouts Troop were larger than they had ever been, and were in a flourishing condition. The cadets, through the courtesy and kindness of Mr. Gurney Benham, were fully equipped with weapons of warfare, and they had colours presented to them by their O.C., Lieut. Peart. The gymnastic classes had been re-started, and other innovations during the year were instruction in scientific gardening, the formation of a school library, and the introduction of the Spanish language into the curriculum, a language of the utmost value commercially. Hardly any language was so valuable for commercial purposes, and with the conflict for the world's markets after the war the importance of a knowledge of the language spoken throughout South America could hardly be over-rated. (Hear, hear.) Mr. Cape went on to say it was 22 years since he first became a schoolmaster, and this year, the 23rd, was the happiest he had known. (Applause.) That was due to the perfect co-operation of the governors, masters, parents and the boys. When he came to the school for the first time a year ago, one feature struck him more than anything else—more even than the beautiful school buildings—and that was the wonderful list of those young Colcestrians who had given their services and lives to the country. The list of Colcestrians serving and the list of distinctions gained amazed him by their length and diversity—the numbers ran into many hundreds. There were Old Colcestrians in France, in Flanders, in Egypt, in the Balkans, and in every scene of the war. There were many in the R.F.C. and the R.N.A.S., and there were many at sea. The list of those who had made the great sacrifice included the names of W. Bareham (East Yorks Regt.), Claud Barnes, R.N., Lieut. Bennett, Capt. Brooke, D.S.O. (whose C.O. said he deserved the V.C.), F. S. Bultitude, Reginald Bultitude, Sec.-Lieut. Cheshire, L. Clark, Sec.-Lieut. Deane, Sec.-Lieut. Everett, Sec.-Lieut. Flanagan, Sec.-Lieut. Horwood, C. H. Jarrard, M.M., Lieut. Keeble, M.C., R. P. Malyn, H.A.C., Conrad Mason, Sec.-Lieut. Roland Minor, Flight Lieut. Orfeur, Arnold Pocock, W. H. Salisbury (lost in the sinking of the Hampshire), Harry Sanger, Sec.-Lieut. Secker, Capt. A. G. M. Slade, Douglas Wagstaff, Capt. Dudley Wallace, M.C., Sec.-Lieut. A.H. Webb and Capt. A. White. What honours were there in this world that could compare with the honours gained by those whose names he had just read? (Hear, hear.) In conclusion the headmaster said it was proposed to raise a suitable memorial to the old boys of the school who had served their country at this time. (Loud applause.)

Sir Arthur Duckham then distributed the prizes, after which he gave an address in which he referred to the wonderful work of the Ministry of Munitions, one department of which was responsible for the famous tanks. He had twice lately been to the front. It was marvellous what our troops had done, but he was certain that the next six or eight months would be an important period of the war. Having added that he was the first man seen on the battle field with a bowler hat and umbrella —(laughter)—the speaker went on to refer to the wonderful spirit of the men at the front, and said the spirit of the Flying Corps was the finest spirit he had ever seen. (Applause.) To-day we were living in a period of utter waste—waste of lives, resources and everything else. He hoped good would come of it, and he thought it would, because the lessons of heroism and unselfishness that we had seen in this war must abide. But we were losing tremendously that class of man whom we relied upon to maintain the country, and the boys of to-day had got to take this weight on their shoulders much sooner than they would in normal times. At school they were learning to be loyal—a loyalty which would be invaluable to them in later life, to the nation, the empire and the world, because it was only by loyalty that the world could be made better. At school they learned to realise the importance of pulling together. Then with regard to learning. He had never made a greater mistake in his life than in not liking Latin, because the greatest thing to success in life was the power of being able to express oneself, he did not mean in talking, but in writing, in which Latin was a great help. It was essential also that a boy should have a good knowledge of geography and history—they were of the greatest importance—and also of mathematics and science. The great thing about science was to know the simple things—such a thing as "you can't get anything for nothing," which was a scientific fact. It was the simple things that mattered. The other great thing they learned at school was sport—to play the game—which was one of the most important things to be cultivated to its utmost extent. When they had finished their life and looked back and saw they had played the game he was sure they would all be satisfied. (Loud applause.)

Alderman W. Gurney Benham proposed, and Alderman Blaxill seconded, a vote of thanks to the speaker.

Sir Arthur Duckham and the Mayor were each presented with a silver matchbox engraved with the school crest by Masters Peter Robinson and Jack Girling, two of the youngest scholars. Sir Arthur presented the school with an interesting photograph of a Tank.

Carol Service.

The sixth annual carol service took place in Big School on Sunday afternoon, December 16, before a large and appreciative assembly. A string quartette, conducted by Miss South Adams, opened the service with an exquisite rendering of " Come, ye lofty," and after prayers had been read by the Headmaster (Mr. H. J. Cape, M.A., B.Sc.), the following carols were tastefully sung :—" A Virgin Unspotted," " Lullay," " God rest ye merry, Gentlemen," " Sleep, Holy Babe," " On the Birthday of the Lord," " The snow lay deep," " Joyfully, joyfully," " We Three Kings " and " Holy Night."

The hymn, " In Memoriam, D.W.," was also sung. This—written by Mr. Peart and set to music by Band-Sergt. Abdy, Mus.Doc.—was in memory of Douglas Wagstaff, who lost his life in a gallant deed in action in France. The hymn breathed the Christmas spirit, and one verse reads :—

" O Prince of Peace, on this Thy natal day
Our hardened hearts with love renew, restore ;
Give peace on Earth, and on our madness lay
Thy wounded hands, and make us whole once more."

The Rev. K. L. Parry, B.Sc., minister of Lion Walk Congregational Church, delivered an eloquent address.

During a collection for the Mayor's Fund for Wounded Soldiers—amounting to £10 7s. 2d.—the " Adeste Fideles " was sung. The carols were interspersed by lessons read by boys of the School. Harwood ma., was at the piano, and the singing was conducted throughout by Mr. Peart.

ffootball.

The First Eleven have not yet completed their season, and with three or four matches still to be played, they may finally have a fair season. Much of the old enthusiasm for football has returned, with a consequent rise in the standard. We were unfortunate at Christmas in losing two of our best members, Prescott and Felgate. Prescott's absence from the left wing has especially been felt this term.

The impossibility of travelling still forbids proper school matches, which we look forward to with great longing and high hopes. In nearly all our matches we have had to concede a very considerable advantage in weight to our opponents; a fact which has visibly handicapped the defence as well as the attack.

Wilson led the attack in the early part of the season with considerable skill, but latterly he has been rather below form. Osborne on the right wing has been the best forward of the season, and his dashes down the wing, followed by excellent centres, have led to many of the school's goals. The forwards on the whole have been good in mid-field, but very weak in front of goal. The combination between the halves and forwards has mostly been of the poorest. Gilbert in the earlier part of the season was excellent at half, and lately has led the attack with success. Burleigh, at left half, was excellent last term, but has only been able to turn out once this term, owing to illness. Lilley, at back, although new to the team this term, has been consistently good, and has cleared in excellent style. Lastly Harwood mi., in goal, has given us several splendid displays, and when he has gained a little more height and strength, he should develop into a really good goalkeeper.

Considering that we have rarely been able to turn out a full strength team, and that our opponents have mostly been much heavier, the results are not so bad. The season's results to date are : Played 12, won 2, drawn 4, lost 6. Goals 30—51.

First XI. colours have been awarded to Burleigh, French, Gilbert, Harwood mi., Lilley, Osborne ma., and Wilson.

The following have also played, and have been given 2nd XI. colours : Cox, Harwood ma., Warden and White.

C.R.G.S. v. 50TH STATIONARY HOSPITAL, R.A.M.C.—The school were opposed by a much stronger and heavier team, and did well to keep the score down. Combination between the forwards and the halves was again poor. Result, lost 7—1.

C.R.G.S. v. MUMFORD'S 3RD XI.—The school had a very weak team, but even so the play was disappointing. The game was lost 6—2.

C.R.G.S. v. ST. GILES.—Playing with the wind in the first half, the school gave a poor display. Play was mostly in our opponents' half, but the forwards did everything but score. At half-time the score was 1—0 in our favour. Resuming against a strong wind, the school played better, but the opportunities lost in the first half were not repeated, and we lost 4—2.

C.R.G.S. v. DENTAL MECHANICAL CENTRE.—The school were up against a really good team. We felt throughout that we were being played with. Harwood, in goal, gave an excellent display. Result, lost 11—0.

C.R.G.S. v. 50TH STATIONARY HOSPITAL.—Our opponents were much heavier, but rather slow. The school played up well and finally drew 2—2.

C.R.G.S. v. MARKS TEY.—For once we met a team of our own weight. The school played well throughout, although the shooting of the forwards was rather poor. Result, won 5—0.

The 2nd XI. have so far had only one match, which they won easily· 9—1. There are in the school plenty of good juniors, and the prospect for the future is of the brightest.

SENIOR HOUSE MATCHES.

It is always the improbable that happens in football as well as in sterner walks of life. No one at the beginning of the term would have arranged the Houses as they finally stand. Dugard's are deservedly placed first. Parr's, while still mostly juniors, are runners up. The spirit and zeal that they have shown this term are thoroughly commendable, and they fully deserve their place. Schoolhouse, with the strongest paper team, are only placed third. They owe their two defeats to their constant bickerings on the field—one might indeed think they were females from their seeming jealousy of each other. Harsnett's have sunk to the bottom, although they have played their best. In the Juniors they are also placed bottom,· and their prospects' for' the future are not of the brightest. The average ages of the four house teams are very instructive : they are :— Dugard's 15.10 ; Schoolhouse 15.10, Harsnett's 15.8, Parr's 13.3.

1st R und, Thursday, 31st Jan., 1918.

PARR'S v. HARSNETT'S.

This game was excellently contested. Both teams played well throughout. Parr's 'featherweight line of forwards combined well together, and although opposed by a couple of very weighty backs, they tackled excellently. The Parrite defence was also very good, and all showed excellent dash. Of Harsnett's the defence were the best.· Their forwards failed to combine, and paid the penalty of their folly. Most of the play was in mid-field with rushes down the wing. Parr's gradually gained the upper hand, and after several attempts Tricker at last opened the scoring with a good shot from the left. Half-time came with no further score. On resuming Harsnett's started off well, and after about 20 minutes they drew level, from a run through by Cox. Parr's then went all out, and were soon rewarded by a second goal. Play then became very fast, but there was no further scoring, and so Parr's won 2—1.

DUGARD'S v. SCHOOLHOUSE.

This, although a first round match, was regarded by all as the one which would decide the fate of the cup for the term. Dugard's were all out to win, and throughout were the better team. Schoolhouse started off badly, and as the game progressed they developed tempers, and became worse and worse. The first half, although much in Dugard's favour, saw but little scoring, the whistle blowing with the score 1—0. On resuming Schoolhouse were better, but they soon fell away, and Dugard's, scoring three more goals, finally won 4—0. Dugard's thoroughly deserved their · win, but the thoughts of Schoolhouse must be left unrecorded.

2nd Round, Thursday, 14th February, 1918.

SCHOOLHOUSE v. HARSNETT'S.

This was the only match in which Schoolhouse really found their form. Harsnett's did their best, but were hopelessly outclassed by their opponents, who for once showed what they could do. The game was very one-sided from the start, Harsnett's only reaching the Schoolhouse goal in occa-sional rushes. At half-time the score stood 4—1 in favour of Schoolhouse. The second half was still more uneven, and finally Schoolhouse won 9—2. Harsnett's were not to blame for the heavy score, they did their best against a better team. Schoolhouse forwards for once combined well, and it is a wonder they learnt nothing from this game.

PARR'S v. DUGARD'S.

The football in this match was of quite a high standard. Both teams played well, both individually and as teams. The start was fairly even, but Dugard's opened the scoring, and secured a second goal before half-time. In the second half the game was very fast, and Dugard's finally won 5—0. Parr's on many occasions had the hardest of luck. Although Dugard's deservedly won, the score is very flattering to them, 5—3 would better represent the run of the game.

3rd Round, Thursday, 28th February, 1918.

DUGARD'S v. HARSNETT'S.

Harsnett's, who were without Burleigh, put up a very good fight through-out. Dugard's with practically all the play in their favour, could not score, while Harsnett's, from a break-a-way, scored the only goal of the first half. Dugard's had been thoroughly scared, and on resuming they at once started out for goals, to such a purpose that they finally won 6—1. Harsnett's are to be congratulated on their excellent stand, while the shooting of Dugard's can only evoke our pity.

SCHOOLHOUSE v. PARR'S.

Writing before the match, one would naturally have predicted a win for Schoolhouse. Comparing strength on paper, it seemed silly to place the two teams in the field. However, Parr's made up for their terrible lack of weight by their excellent dash and spirit. From the first they played in excellent style. The combination of the small forwards was of the first order, and the football of the whole team left nothing to be desired. In the first half Griffith scored twice for Parr's, with excellent shots from the left wing. On resuming Schoolhouse slightly re-organised their team, and for a time more than held their own. After scoring their only goal, however, they again relapsed to their putrid state of the first half. Parr's, however, fully kept up the pace, and were rewarded with a third goal, thus winning 3—1.

Below are the House teams :—

Dugard's.	Parr's.	Schoolhouse.	Harsnett's.
Harwood mi.	Wilson III.	Nash	Ingle
Gilbert (capt.)	French (capt.)	Lilley	Burleigh I.
Clough	Jones II.	Nocton I.	Hill
Twyman	Wyncoll	Linfoot	Burleigh II.
Hollaway I.	Osborne I.	White	Sier
Tracey	Wagstaff	Warden	Beattie I.
Jones I.	Hayes	Tricker I.	Charlton I.
Hollaway II.	Ebsworth I.	Wilson II.	Everett
Harwood I.	Osborne II.	Wilson I. (capt.)	Cox (capt.)
Nicholls	Hunneyball	Downing	Pleasants
Powell	Griffith	Joel	Thomas

JUNIOR HOUSE MATCHES.

The Juniors are not nearly so even as their seniors. Parr's and School-house, who are respectively first and second, are fairly well matched, but both Dugard's and Harsnett's stand far below.

1st Round,..

Parr's 20 v. Harsnett's 0 ; Schoolhouse 5 v. Dugard's 0.

2nd Round.

Parr's 20 v. Dugard's 0 ; Schoolhouse 19 v. Harsnett's 0.

3rd Round.

Parr's 2 v. Schoolhouse 1 ; Dugard's 3 v. Harsnett's 1.

The first two rounds were very uneven games, all four matches being practically walk-overs. The third round saw the best two games. Dugard's and Harsnett's had a hard tussle, but the former finally proved superior, and won 3—1. Parr's were rather below form; but Schoolhouse gave an excellent display, scoring the only goal of the first half. Parr's played better in the second half, and finally won 2—1.

Appended are the House Teams.

Parr's.	Schoolhouse.	Dugard's.	Harsnett's.
Hearsum	Harrington	Crowther	Denman (capt.)
Payne	Tyson	Moore II. (capt.)	Robinson I.
Baker	Sayer (capt.)	Palmer	Smith V.
Walkden I.	Mackay	Adams	Ryder.
Osborne II. (capt.)	Church I.	Beckett	Brown I.
Walkden II.	Gosling II.	Dowsett I.	Harper
Tait	Church II.	Dowsett II.	Heasman
Ebsworth II.	Barnes	Bullough	Clark
Tricker II.	Nocton II.	Gascoigne	Griffin
Weeks II.	Robinson II.	Mustard	Oakley
Wilson IV.	Ram	Worsp	Denman

Acknowledgments.

Our thanks are due to Editors of the following :—The Viking, Stortfordian, Framlinghamian, Wyggestonian, O.H.S., Chelmsfordian, Williamsonian, Ipswich G.S. Magazine, Chigwellian.

Old Colcestrian Section.

OFFICERS.

President: C. T. WRIGHT, Crouch Street, Colchester.
Hon. Treasurer: B. MASON, Crouch Street, Colchester.
Hon. Secretaries: A. T. DALDY, Head Street, Colchester (O.A.S.)
B. MASON, Crouch Street, Colchester.

Old Colcestrians are requested to notify any change of address and to forward contributions to the O.C. Section to Mr. B. Mason, Hon. Sec., Crouch Street, Colchester.

Our Annual Meeting.

The Annual Meeting of the Old Colcestrian Society was held on February 12th at the Headmaster's House. The President, Mr. C. T. Wright, occupied the chair. Among others present were the Headmaster (Mr. H. J. Cape), Messrs. C. E. Benham, C. Griffin, H. H. Hollaway, A. O. Farmer, J. H. Nunn. E. Reeve, J. A. Peart, P. Matthews, F. D. Barker, A. Burleigh, O. W. Layzell and B. Mason (Hon. Secretary).

The Secretary read the report of the last Annual Meeting and presented a statement of accounts showing a decided improvement in the financial position of the Society.

On the proposition of Mr. C. E. Benham, seconded by Mr. J. H. Nunn, Mr. C. T. Wright was unanimously re-elected President, making the fourth year in succession.

It was proposed by Mr. J. H. Nunn, seconded by Mr. H. H. Hollaway, that the old Committee be re-elected with the exception of Mr. J. G. Salmon, who has left the neighbourhood. Mr. B. H. Kent was elected in his place.

Mr. J. A. Peart tendered his resignation as sub-editor of the Magazine, owing to pressure of work, and proposed that Mr. F. D. Barker should be elected. This was seconded by Mr. Wright and carried unanimously.

Mr. J. H. Nunn, in proposing a vote of thanks to Mr. Peart, expressed the appreciation of the committee for his valuable services in connection with the Editorial work of the Magazine. This was seconded by Mr. C. E. Benham and carried unanimously.

It was proposed by Mr. Reeve and seconded by Mr. Benham, that a vote of thanks be passed to the Secretary for his work during the past year. This was put to the meeting and carried.

On the proposition of Mr. C. E. Benham it was decided that Mr. A. O. Farmer and Mr. Bernard Mason should select from the School Registers a small representative committee to cover the last thirty years, the work of this committee to be the compilation of as complete a Roll of Honour as possible.

At the close of the business for the evening Mr. Nunn proposed a vote of thanks to Mr. Cape for kindly placing his rooms at the disposal of the Society for the meeting.

This was seconded by Mr. C. T. Wright and carried unanimously.

SIDNEY ARTHUR BACON.

Sidney A. Bacon died at sea from pneumonia on December 7, 1917, at the age of 28 years. He was second officer on the P. and O. R.M.S.S. Khiva, and the eldest son of the late Mr. A. J. Bacon, of Brewood Hall, Great Horkesley, and Mrs. Bacon, of Beaconsfield Avenue, Colchester. He was educated at the Colchester Grammar School and on leaving there served his apprenticeship with Messrs. Herron and Co., of Liverpool, joining the P. and O. Line when his time was completed. Although so young, he has taken an active and responsible part during the war, and has had many narrow escapes from death—at one time saving the lives of the ship's company by his foresight and promptness. He had a very promising career in front of him and held splendid testimonials from all captains under whom he served. He married in January, 1915, Miss Ada V. Bancroft, youngest daughter of the late Capt. Bancroft, 17th Lancers, and Mrs. Bancroft, Sanderstead, and leaves one son. The funeral service took place at Sanderstead, Surrey.

LEONARD A. FROST.

Leonard A. Frost, of the Queen's Westminster Rifles, elder son of the late Arthur T. Frost and of Helen Frost, of 14, St. Barnabas' Road, Cambridge, was killed in action in Palestine on February 20th. He was at the C.R.G.S. about 15 years ago, and his father was also an Old Colcestrian.

The many friends of Mr. L. C. Brook, R.N.V.R., formerly of Colchester, and now stationed at Halifax in Nova Scotia, where the great disaster took place, will be glad to hear that his parents have received a cablegram from him that he is quite safe.

CAPT. C. COLLINS REPORTED PRISONER.

Capt. Charles Collins, eldest son of Mr. and Mrs. A. G. Collins, 207, Maldon Road, Colchester, reported missing since November 30, is now a prisoner of war at Carlsruhe, Germany. Capt. Collins was educated at Clacton and Colchester Royal Grammar School, proceeding later to the College of St. Vincent and St. Paul, Ypres. After twelve months in Belgium he entered the service of Messrs. Barclays Bank, Ltd., and was stationed at their Southend Branch. Upon the outbreak of war, Capt.

Collins enlisted as a private in the 20th Hussars, being gazetted a few months later to the Essex Regiment. At the time of his capture he was in command of the 35th Trench Mortar Battery attached to the Essex Regiment. He was wounded in the early part of 1917.

LIEUT. A. T. DALDY WOUNDED.

Just as we go to press we learn with regret that Lieut. A. T. Daldy, the esteemed Hon. Sec. of the Old Colcestrian Society, has been admitted to a hospital in France, suffering from a gunshot wound in the head. The injury is happily a slight one. Lieut. Daldy, before joining the army, did yeoman service to our Society and spared no effort to gather together the disjointed threads which had somehow become unravelled in its financial affairs. In this work he was eminently successful, and the committee rendered him very special thanks for his able services. The work during his absence is being admirably carried out by his coadjutor, Mr. Bernard Mason.

Sapper Hudson writes from " a top-hole dug-out, somewhere in France," stating that he is still in the pink, and in May will have seen three years of army life and just over one of active service in France. He went out as a telegraphist, but is now a " wireless man," and has done some excellent and most useful work.

W. M. Town is at Cairo training for a commission and reports that Watsham is in hospital in England, minus two fingers of his left hand and a bad wound in the left thigh. Town met Clover in Cairo, on leave from his battalion, and he also reports that Wheeler is out there and that they hope to be well represented by C.R.G.S. men soon. Town adds :—" We formed the Guard of Honour the other day when the Duke of Connaught, the High Commissioner and Gen. Allenby paid their visit to the Sultan. We presented arms 'umpteen' times and finally were inspected by the Duke, making a triumphal return in coal trucks."

Rainbird is back, invalided, and Mitchell is home on leave.

ROLL OF HONOUR.
ADDITIONS.

Green, M. H. C., Artists Rifles O.T.C.
Head, A., Motor Transport.
Barnes, C. H., Royal Flying Corps.

434

No. 51.]
New Series.

JULY, 1918.

The Colcestrian

PRICE SIXPENCE.

BENHAM & COMPANY, LIMITED COLCHESTER.

The Colcestrian.

VITÆ CORONA FIDES.

No 51].   JULY, 1918.   [NEW SERIES.

Grammaria.

More Honours.

It gives us very great pleasure to add to the announcement in our last issue, that Major Deakin has also won the D.S.O. He was recently home on leave and was then married. We wish him all luck. W. M. Town, who was closely associated with Major Deakin in the School Corps, has been awarded the Military Medal.

Held Up.

Whatever other considerations have affected cricket this term, the grass round our "square" has been so long that runs have been very difficult to get. What looked like an easy "two" has often proved a hard-run "one." Still, there have been compensations for batting sides, as many runs have been obtained, with the ball eluding all the efforts of the fielding side to find it.

Mr. Reeve and Mr. Seamer.

We learn that Mr. Reeve is going to be married in the holidays. Remembering his long and intimate association with every aspect of School life, there will be many who, with us, will congratulate him very heartily and wish him every joy. In getting married, Mr. Reeve is only following the example of an old member of the staff, who was for many years Editor of this magazine. Mr. Seamer was married in 1914, and we are now able to congratulate him on the birth of a daughter, as well as on his marriage. His old friends will be glad to know that he is likely soon to be resident in Colchester.

Our Leagues

The league system of "footer" introduced by Mr. Cape has proved a great success. For the first time, probably, even the smallest boys have had the opportunity of feeling that they were playing for a definite side and with a definite object, viz., to head the league. Mr. Cape also very kindly presented medals to the winning teams. The names appear elsewhere.

Alma Mater.

We are able, once more, to report an all-round increase in our numbers, and Mr. Cape is to be congratulated most heartily. In such a school as this there can never be too many to work and play in happiness and good-comradeship.

The Pre.

On Thursday, April 4th, quite a number of parents and friends assembled in the Art Room to see some of the first term's work of the " Pre Patrol." Mrs. Craske very kindly presented the badges, and Richer carried off the knife promised by Mrs. Cross to the boy who gained the greatest number of badges. We are indebted to Mr. Pepper, who gave up the whole afternoon, and spoke very nicely to the little boys, whose great ambition is to join his Wolf Cubs. After a few exercises given by each of the two Patrols, under their respective leaders, the audience voted, and " Pawsey's men " won the picture by eleven votes.

Five years ago we began the summer term with thirteen pupils. This term we number thirty-eight, and our Scouts are now sub-divided into four Patrols. The work is going on with little inspections from time to time, and we hope to give some invitations for the final one next month.

A great deal of trouble was taken early in the season to sow seeds in the gardens. We are pleased to note that good steady work has since been done by Uff, Jarred, Crowther, Benham, Durrant, Jennens, Richer, Saunders and Weeks. All stand a good chance of getting the gardener's badge in the near future.

Since our last report four more pillows have been sent to the Essex County Hospital, and the ravelling is going on well at the present moment.

Sincere thanks to J. and F. Horwood for their pillow, also to Harwood and Dennis for parcels of material, and to all who have brought cigarettes, flowers and magazines for the wounded. With bad cases time hangs heavily; and the men are especially glad of books and papers. Should any reader have either that are quite finished with, may we beg them ?

NEW BOYS, SUMMER TERM.—J. Jones, E. Durrant, A. Hirst, F. Potter, J. Potter, E. Eastwood, G. Weeks, J. Argent, J. Hewitt, J. Gulley, A. Jennens, R. Pettitt, A. Saunders, D. Crossley, H. Jarred.

BOYS FOR LOWER SCHOOL.—E. Secker, C. Richer, C. Pawsey, F. Horwood, M. Wicks.

Cadet Corps.

(Attached 5th Essex.)

Major E. B. Deakin was recently home on leave, receiving the D.S.O. from H.M. the King at the Palace. We had kindly messages from him, and we hope on his next leave he will have time to visit us.

* * * *

It is pleasing to record that old Cadets looking us up in

parade hours consider that there is an improvement in bearing
and steadiness in the ranks ; if this is so, it is but another tribute
to the help Mr. Barker has lent us. Among the old faces seen
this term were :—Ward, Halls, Felgate, Oliver, White, Green
and Layzell. We have a record number—five, training for
commissions with the Artists O.T.C. Second-Lieut. J. Pertwee
(Queen's R.) writes happily from Dalhousie, India; Burton,
who has put in three years' service in the Navy, is awaiting commission in the R.N.V.R. ; Clark ("Snotty") is accepted for
R.A.F.

* * * *

We are fortunate in securing the services of Sergt. Potts,
R.A.M.C., kindly lent by the Military Hospital, in Ambulance
instruction ; of Band Sergt. Clarke, D.L.I., attached by the
courtesy of the Band President, for drum and bugle instruction.
Both sections keenly appreciate their advantages.

* * * *

Discharged : Sergt. Burleigh (A.R., O.T.C.), Sergt. French
(Queen's), Cadets Woodward ma., Charlton ma., Wilson, G.,
Parsons, Wright ma., Wilson (Lance-Corpl). Enlisted : Badcock,
Grove ma., Downing, Hickinbotham, Cheshire, Wenden, Alder-
ton, Bailey, Johnstone.

* * * *

Twenty-one boys are going to Marlborough Camp this year
to keep up the reputation, it is hoped, won by our contingent
in the past two years. Many Cadets, we trust, will spend at
least three weeks on the land in farm work—a pleasant and
practical way of helping on to victory.

* * * *

Our Whit Monday operations were successful, if only in revealing the difficulties of path-finding : Sergts. Cox and
Lilley brought their parties to the rendezvous within three minutes
of each other—a good piece of work. We are indebted to Mr.
Wicks, of North Station, for the arrangements made for en-
training.

* * * *

Time flies apace, and it behoves the P.C.'s to get their platoons
in training for the Wagstaff Competition, which will be held
before the Locals begin.

* * * *

An excellent field day was held on June 13th, when the
Headmaster kindly allowed us to leave early. The schemes
of defence and attack at Copford were well prepared by Sergts.
Chase and Lilley, and each small party had a definite place
and definite work allotted. Praise was meted out by the two
umpires to Tricker, White, Ritchie and Lilley for good individual efforts. Altogether it was one of the most useful and enjoyable of our days out.

Major Gurney Benham, E.V.R., was kind enough to pay us a visit on Saturday, June 22nd, and to present the Best Recruit's medal to Beatty ma. We very much appreciate a visit from one who is so keen on Cadet work and who is, in addition to his position as a Governor, an old boy of the School ; we must strive to deserve the praise he bestowed.

* * * *

R. E. Doubleday, whose interesting letter is quoted in another place, won Mention in Despatches for good work done in the East. His brother, we are glad to know, is better and we hope will continue to improve.

* * * *

Jimmy Clover writes us from Palestine, where he has been sharing the perils and achievements of our Mother Regiment, the 5th Essex. He says " the fighting up the line now has become rather difficult, as we encounter mighty hills covered with rocks. There are no roads, very little water and a good many mosquitoes of the dangerous kind."

J. A. P.

Scouting Notes.

The patrol competition held at the end of last term resulted in the Wolf Patrol taking first place for general efficiency and smartness While each member of the patrol shares the credit for good work, P.L. Burleigh and his Second, Horwood, deserve mention for their keenness as leaders.

Our numbers this term still show an upward tendency, which is very pleasing. The recruits are :—Garvie (already a 2nd Class Scout), Griffith, Royce, Hearsum, Haigh, Webb, Neale, Spooner, Grubb, Wells, Ward, Jackson and C. Jeffrey, who comes up from the Wolf Cub Pack. Alderton, Downing, Pawsey and Howard ma. have left the troop.

We have had two field days this term to date, the first being held on Whit Monday at Abberton and Layer, with the other troops of the local Association. The weather was ideal and the day most enjoyable as an outing, but the scouting work left very much to be desired.

The work on the occasion of the second field day on June 13 was of a much higher order. We marched out at 11 o'clock to Mr. Royce's farm, where a scheme of attack and defence was carried out. The attacking party was composed of the Wolf, Peewit and Curlew Patrols, and the Beavers, Woodpigeons and otters defended. A good game ended in a victory for the defenders by 20 points to 17.

The Wolf Cubs also had a day out on June 13th, at Fordham, under Cub Leaders W. Wilson and Mirrington, who are to be complimented on the smartness of the Pack.

The Club recruits this term are :—F. Horwood, Richer, M. Hirst, D. Hirst, Pawsey, Secker, Thurston, Harris and M. Wicks. G. E. P.

Valete.

H. Burleigh, Harsnett's, Captain of School, School Football, House Football, Cricket and Shooting, Band Sergt. Cadet Corps.

S. C. H. French, Parr's, Captain of School, Captain of School Football and Cricket, Captain of House Football, Cricket and Shooting, Sergt. Cadet Corps.

R. S. Gilbert, Dugard's, Captain of School Football, School Cricket and Shooting, Captain of House Football, Cricket and House Shooting, Pte. Cadet Corps.

A. M. Wilson, Schoolhouse, School Football and Cricket, Captain of House Football, House Cricket and Shooting, Lce.-Cpl. Cadet Corps.

R. W. Woodward, Harsnett's, House Cricket, Pte. in Cadet Corps.

J. M. Wright, Harsnett's, Pte. Cadet Corps.

D. R. Charlton, Harsnett's, House Football and Cricket, Pte. Cadet Corps.

C. A. Parsons, Harsnett's.

J. D. Hick, Parr's.

R. S. Roberts, Schoolhouse.

A. D. Dunn, Dugard's, Scout.

Salvete.

VI.
Johnstone, R. D.

Upper V.
Bell, R. H.

Lower V.
Cheshire, O. J.
Garvie, H. G.

Upper IV.
Badcock, N. C. F.

Lower IV. B.
Riches, L. A.
Garrett, H. A.

Upper III.
Ward, F. W.
Neale, C. T. K.
Wenden, G. C.
Grubb, G. B.
Haigh, N. C.
Grove, G. E.
Spooner, E. D.
Wells, V. J.
Hirst, M. B.
Webb, L. N.

Royce, H. L.
Salisbury, C. H.

Lower III.
Wright, C. M.
Ray, G. H.

II and I.
Horwood, F. W. (from Pre.)
Wicks, M. R. (from Pre.)
Pawsey, C. (from Pre.)
Richer, C. T. (from Pre).
Secker, G. E. M. (from Pre.)
Grove, W. L.
Mathams, R. W.
Hirst, D. G.
Lambert. G. L.
Cousins, G. G.
Day, C. R.
Riches, K.
Hood, C. J. G.
Harris, E. W.
Boden, P. T.
Horlock, A. E.
Horden, M.
Horden, P.

Cricket.

1st XI.

Up to the present three school matches have been played, all of which have been won. The fielding of the eleven is better than it was last year, but there is still room for improvement. Griffith and Warden, both new members of the team, are safe catches. Nicholls has fielded well at mid-off.

The bowling is steadier ; Cox and Harwood have both bowled well. Harwood has a very good average. Osborne and Johnstone are useful change bowlers.

The batting of the team is fairly sound. Harwood and Cox have made the highest individual scores, but several other members have made quite useful scores.

Lilley has captained the team well. He has shown considerable judgment in placing his field and in making the best use of his bowlers.

Congratulations to Osborne ma. and Tricker mi. on winning bats for " fifties " in House Matches, and to Harwood ma., who also received one for his bowling against the Queen's.

Mr. Cape very kindly presented the bats.

1ST XI. v. WEST BERGHOLT.

May 25th. The School batted first and made 80. Cox and Warden batted well, making 24 and 13 respectively. The visitors were dismissed for 10, Harwood taking 7 wickets for 6 runs. West Bergholt followed on and made 31. Harwood again bowled well and took five wickets.

SCHOOL v. R.A.M.C.

June 15th. The R.A.M.C. won the toss and batted first, making 38. The School made a total of 98, Harwood making 21, White 14 and Joel 13.

SCHOOL v. "B" COY. QUEEN'S.

June 19th. The School won the toss and batted first. The scoring was fairly even ; Harwood ma. and Harwood mi. were the chief scorers, making 16 each. A total of 11 was reached. The Queen's only made 19, owing to the very good bowling of Harwood ma., who took 9 wickets for 13 runs, the last 5 wickets being taken with 5 successive balls.

SENIOR HOUSE MATCHES.

PARR'S v. DUGARD'S.

This match was played in weather ideal for cricket. Parr's won the toss and decided to let Dugard's bat first. Dugard's went in and determined to stay in, and scored 65 in the first innings. Parr's opened their innings well, but soon a rot set in, which continued all the rest of the innings. Parr's score for the first innings was 19.

Dugard's were not yet confident of victory, and played up just as well in the second innings as in the first. The side obtained 64 runs in the second innings, thus making a total of 129. Parr's tried all they knew to stay in, but only succeeded in adding 17 runs to their first score, their total being 36.

Thus Dugard's won the match by 93 runs.

It is interesting to note that the supporters on both sides were very few and very far between.

SCHOOLHOUSE v. HARSNETT'S.

On winning the toss Schoolhouse batted first. A total of 52 was reached, the chief individual scorers being White 12 and Joel 14. Harsnett's reached a total of 46, of which Cox scored 25. Schoolhouse opened their second innings badly, one wicket falling before any runs had been scored. The situation was saved by Johnstone, who made 40, and a total of 54 was obtained.

Harsnett's made a great effort to get the required number of runs. Cox again batted well, making 17. The last wickets did not put on many runs and a total of 15 was reached, Schoolhouse winning by 16 runs.

DUGARD'S v. HARSNETT'S.

Played on June 6th, 1918. Dugard's, on winning the toss, decided to bat first. The first five of the Dugard's batsmen were dismissed very cheaply by Harsnett's. Then, however, a stand was made by Ritchie and Loyd, making 46 between them, of which Ritchie contributed 36. Dugard's were dismissed for a total of 76. Harsnett's batted very badly indeed the whole side only making 11. Harsnett's, on being put in again, batted worse than ever, this time only making a total of 7. Thus Dugard's won by an innings and 58 runs. For Dugard's Harwood I. and Ritchie bowled excellently.

SCHOOLHOUSE v. PARR'S.

June 8th. Parr's won the toss and decided to bat first. There was no very high scoring and they were dismissed for 41.

Schoolhouse batted badly with the exception of Joel and Johnstone. Joel played a good innings and made 35 without giving a chance. Schoolhouse made a total of 62, thus gaining a lead of 21. In the second innings Parr's made 45. Schoolhouse wanted 25 to win, and only made 31. The quick dismissal of the team was due to the good fielding of Griffith and Morton, who brought off some good catches in long field.

PARR'S v. HARSNETT'S.

Played on June 20th, 1918. Harsnett's, on winning the toss, batted first, but were all dismissed for a total of 14 runs. In the Parr's innings, Osborne ma. got well set, making 55 not out, bringing Parr's total up to 98. Harsnett's followed on, but only succeeded in making 29. Thus Parr's won by an innings and 55 runs.

JUNIOR HOUSE MATCHES.

Five matches have been played so far. Parr's have still to play Harsnett's. The first match was between Schoolhouse and Harsnett's, which Schoolhouse won easily. Schoolhouse also beat Dugard's, but were badly beaten by Parr's, in which match Tricker mi. made 51 for Parr's.

Parr's easily beat Dugard's and are almost certain to be top again this year.

In the Harsnett's and Dugard's match Harsnett's defeated Dugard's, thus taking the third place, Dugard's being fourth.

Football.

LEAGUES.

1st round : Pinks v. Blues, Reds v. Blacks, Greens v. Browns.
2nd round : Blues v. Greens, Reds v. Pinks, Blacks v. Browns.
3rd round : Blues v. Browns, Reds v. Greens, Blacks v. Pinks.
4th round : Blues v. Blacks, Reds v. Browns, Pinks v. Greens.
5th round : Blues v. Reds, Greens v. Blacks, Pinks v. Browns.

PINKS v. BLUES (1st Round).

This produced a hard and keenly contested game resulting in a draw 2—2, which, on the whole, fairly represented the play.

GREENS v. BROWNS.

The Greens were considerably the stronger team and won 8—0. Nicholl scored five times for the Greens.

BLUES v. GREENS (2nd Round).

The Blues were considerably below full strength and it is to be wondered that the Greens did not manage to effect an easy win, but the finish of the match saw a score of 3—3.

PINKS v. GREENS (4th Round).

This match was played in bad weather, with the Pinks below full strength, so the Greens obtained an easy victory, the score being 8—2 in their favour.

BLUES v. BLACKS.

This match was played under trying weather conditions, which, however, proved a material advantage to the losers, in that the winners were unable to score as frequently as might otherwise have been the case. The game resulted in a win of 4—3 for the Blues.

BLUES V. BROWNS (3rd Round).

As was expected, this game was very one-sided. The Browns' forwards were utterly outclassed, although their only goal was the result of good play. The Blues' defence was very sound, but their forwards did not combine. Result—Blues 9, Browns 1.

REDS V. BROWNS (4th Round).

Played on the first pitch. Rain spoilt the first part of the game, but later on the sun came out and a good game resulted. Final score 12—2.

PINKS V. BROWNS (5th Round).

This game was played in heavy rain. The ground was slippery and it was almost impossible to "hold" the ball. Neither team was complete, and the game lasted only for one hour. Result—Pinks 5, Browns 2.

REDS V. BLACKS (1st Round).

This was a very one-sided game. The Blacks made several ineffectual rushes, while the Reds' forwards had a busy time. Charlton ma. scored 4 goals for the Reds. Result 11—0 for Reds.

REDS V. PINKS (2nd Round).

This was a very good game, as the teams were pretty equal. The Pinks had bad luck in their shooting, and the game finished with the score 4—2 for the Reds.

REDS V. GREENS (3rd Round).

The result 7—0 for the Reds is not a good indication of the game. The Reds were only slightly superior to the Greens, whose forwards were well held.

REDS V. BLUE (5th Round).

Played in pouring rain. Osborne ma. was the chief support of the Reds, and the score 5—1 for the Reds was chiefly due to his good play.

Second Round played on March 7th.

BLACKS V. BROWN.

At the very beginning there was no doubt as to the result of this match. The play was practically all in the Browns' half, goals coming fairly freely for the Blacks. The Browns managed to score twice from two dashes through by Wagstaff. Final score was 8—2 in favour of the Blacks.

Third Round played on March 21.

BLACKS V. PINKS.

Unfortunately the Pinks were rather short of men, including their Captain (Gilbert). Nevertheless the Pinks played a very plucky game, the Blacks only just managing to win by 3—1. Much must be said for the play of Thomas and Seer, who repeatedly kept out the Blacks.

Fifth Round played on April 6th.

BLACKS V. GREENS.

This match was played in the pouring rain, and on a very slippery pitch. The Greens were four men short, but nevertheless managed to win by 3—0.

FOOTBALL LEAGUE COMPETITIONS—EASTER TERM, 1918.

SENIOR.	JUNIOR.
White (Captain)	Church ma (Captain).
Charlton ma.	Nocton i.
Charlton mi.	Ebsworth ii.
Pleasants	Church ii.
Everett	Worsp
Hunneyball	Walkden ii.
Osborne ma.	Smith v.
Goodway	Smith vi.
Twyman	Ram
Jones	Canham
Ritchie	Rolfe ii.

The above were recipients of "League" Medals presented by Mr. Cape.

Gardening.

Compared with last year at this time, the state of the plots shows a marked improvement, and it is pleasing to note that attempts are being made to produce greater variety. As is only to be expected, the chief crop will be potatoes, which are looking very well indeed, while some of the earlies have already been lifted.

Much improvement might be made in the appearance of the plots by a more liberal use of the hoe, while it should be remembered that its use is not only in keeping down the weeds, but during a dry season a well loosened surface tends to conserve moisture and therefore becomes almost a necessity if good results are to be obtained.

The pathways are rather an eyesore, and there is not enough attention being given to the removal of rubbish, which when left about forms a happy breeding ground for many of the garden pests. At the same time it should not be deposited in the ditch, for the cleaner this is kept the better is the drainage of the plots.

Opinion seems to be about evenly divided between plot-holders as to the merit of inter-cropping, and a much larger quantity of green crop is being grown this year, while one or two plucky holders are risking a few rows of peas. It is to be hoped that these will not suffer the fate of the carrots last year. Broad beans were attacked by mice, but this was noticed in good time, and the culprits were caught and suspended on a sort of keeper's gallows on the fence. Last year the onions in most of the plots were disappointing, and it is pleasing to see such good results this season in growing this difficult crop. We hope boys will not be in too great a hurry to lift their main crop potatoes, as they are better left in the ground till ripe, and should not be taken up for storage purposes until the haulm can be easily pulled out of the ground.

Special commendation should be given to Sier, whose plot is well worthy of examination by the other holders. He has attended to his work regularly, and the results of this are obvious in the excellence of his crops.

Acknowledgments.

Our thanks are due to the Editors of the following :—The Viking, Stortfordian, Framlinghamian, Wyggestonian, O.H.S., Chelmsfordian, Williamsonian, Ipswich G.S. Magazine, Chig-wellian, The Arrow, The Maltonian.

Old Colcestrian Section.

OFFICERS.

President: C. T. WRIGHT, Crouch Street, Colchester.

Hon. Treasurer: B. MASON, Crouch Street, Colchester.

Hon. Secretaries: A. T. DALDY, Head Street, Colchester (O.A.S.); B. MASON, Crouch Street, Colchester.

Old Colcestrians are requested to notify any change of address and to forward contributions to the O.C. Section to Mr. B. Mason, Hon. Sec., Crouch Street, Colchester.

HENRY GILBERT TOWN.

It is with deep regret that we have to record the death of Henry Gilbert Town, who was one of the ten missing in a gallant attack on the enemy at Monchy, on May 3, and who has since been officially assumed to have been killed on that date. His father, Mr. W. H. Town, has written to the Headmaster as follows :—

46, Cambridge Street,
Norwich,
1st May, 1918.

DEAR SIR,—

I am sending a photograph (for the school collection) of my dear son, Henry Gilbert Town, a former C.R.G.S. boy and an O.C., who has given his life for his country. On May 3rd, 1917, his regiment (the L.R.B.) made an attack on the German trenches at Monchy, and he was one of the ten missing. The War Office have now officially informed me that, no news having been received of him, they are regretfully constrained to assume that he was killed on that date.

His brother, W. M. Town, has been awarded the Military Medal.

Yours sincerely,
WM. H. TOWN.

Cyril L. L. Cole's Experiences with the 24th Division.

Writing to Mr. P. Shaw Jeffrey from "somewhere in France," Cyril L. L. Cole gives the following graphic account of his experiences during the recent German advance :—

France,
29th April, 1918.

DEAR SIR.—

. . . . . I have made it a rule to abstain from military matters always—even when on leave—but I don't think I shall offend Mr. Censor when I say it was one of the most thrilling, exciting experiences a fellow could ever wish to go through, although personally I was in a somewhat menial position as a Mounted Despatch Rider. You possibly read of my Division —the 24th—doing so well, and I am indeed proud to be a small cog in the machinery of it.

Apart from the wretched sordidness of seeing the civilians troop broken-hearted back kilometre after kilometre, with all their worldly possessions strapped to their backs, or pushing an old wheelbarrow arrangement, I think what pleased me most was the assistance on divers occasions given them by the Tommy en route, and also when lorries came back filled up with aged people, beds, furniture, etc., and their farming implements pulled by army horseflesh. I couldn't help thinking "Well, to be British is something after all," because I can't imagine the Germans doing likewise.

Believe me,
Your sincere pupil,
CYRIL L. L. COLE.

On Patrol in the Mediterranean.

(The writer of the following is second in command of the first Australian Torpedo Boat commissioned for service with the British Navy.)

Two days ago we had a rather exciting experience, and one I am thankful is over. When it was blowing a gale and we were plodding along not too comfortably on our patrol, we and another T.B. were ordered by wireless to the rescue of a ship which was sinking some forty miles to the south-westward of us. We with the " R " (the other T.B.) started off at nineteen knots. Up till then we had been doing a comfortable twelve and not shipping anything beyond a light spray now and then. At 19, and steaming into a high head sea, it was a different matter. "Despatch is necessary" came through at 5.30; we "despatched" at 21 knots and things began to hum. At 6.30 "Despatch is necessary" again came through, so we chanced 23 knots, and then things began to break up. The first big sea enveloped the bridge, smashing it and knocking the quartermaster and myself flat, broke up the quarter deck awning, flattened down a gun shelter, tore up several shot racks, bent double a lot of steel stanchions, broke the anchors adrift from their moorings and swept a boy over the side. The latter, poor little beggar, we never saw again. We eased down and repaired what damage we could, and then crashed on again. At times I could just catch sight of the " R " looking for all the world like a black pebble in a setting of cotton wool, so

immersed was she in the foam from the breaking waves. We
ourselves seemed like a travelling Niagara, and I thanked God,
for the good workmanship that is put into these small craft.
By 7.30 a.m. we reached the scene of the disaster and found
a French T.B. and the " R," who had preceded us by half an
hour, searching for survivors. The spot was marked by a lane
of oil two or three miles long by half a mile broad. Wreckage
and dead bodies everywhere. Horrible !

Up and down this lane we steamed, the oil-covered sea
now and then flopping on board, and making it impossible
to stand without support. At 7.20 we sighted a raft containing
one man, who was feebly waving a hand, and two more, who
were lying prone face downwards and taking no interest in life
at all. Manœuvring the ship—it was impossible to lower a
boat, the sea being too rough—we brought her close to the raft
and flung them a line, but they were too far gone to make it fast.
The ship was then stopped and Mr. S. (who was my right hand
man in the New Guinea scrap and is now our gunner) jumped
overboard with a line round his body and another to make
fast to the raft. Just as he did so, however, a huge sea came
along and swept the three men off the raft, but the sea, fortunately for them, threw them alongside the ship, where dozens
of hands waited to pull them out. This was no easy task, as,
their clothes and limbs being covered with oil, as fast as we
could get a grip of them the ship would give a frightful lurch
and they slid through our fingers. The poor devils were moaning
horribly all the time ; it was very pitiful. By means of clamber-
ing over the rail and getting ropes under them—the gunner
doing most of this difficult work—all three were eventually
landed like so many breathless trout gasping for breath on our
decks. We took them down to the engine room, pumped the
salt water and oil out of them, and brandy and hot cocoa into
them. One poor beggar had his teeth so tightly clenched that
a chisel had to be used to prise them apart in order to pour
some brandy down his throat. Well, to end a long story, we
cruised around for another hour, but found no living souls, so
proceeded to the nearest port with our survivors, convoying
at the same time a ship which had her bows blown off, but
could still float and steam. We arrived about noon and sent
our survivors ashore. They had very much recovered by then
and were profuse in their thanks. " Inglesi, molto, molto bono,
molto grazie, Signori " (they were Italian), they kept on re-
peating

Poor devils, they were lucky to see land again.

The " R " also picked up three, including the captain, and
the Frenchman, who was on the spot at the time of the disaster,
picked up 39. About 30 were drowned, a bad show ! .

Just as we got to our Patrol a large ship was reported right ahead. Looking through the glasses, she was seen to be a transport, escorted by four T.B.'s. Suddenly a vast tower of foam shot up and over her. "Torpedoed! By the Lord Harry," shouted the officer of the watch, and immediately rang down for full speed and pressed the alarm gongs, which sent us all rushing to our action stations. There were six of us in the Division which was out, and we all went hell for leather toward the now sinking ship. As we closed we could see the boats being lowered into the water crammed with troops, while rafts were being thrown over the side as fast as they could get them adrift from their securings. The T.B.'s were rushing round, like so many terriers in search of a rat which had run to earth, looking for the gentleman responsible for the disaster. By the time we had closed within half a mile the after deck of the transport was awash and the surrounding water one mass of boats, rafts and struggling people, for whom there was no room on the floats. Luckily for everyone it was a perfect day, the sea almost flat calm, and as all were provided with lifebelts or had support of one sort or another, there did not appear much chance of any of them drowning. We picked up some 200 of them, while the Division searched the vicinity for Fritz. Within half an hour of her having been struck the waters had reached the transport's funnel, her bows then rose up in the air until quite perpendicular, and instantly disappeared into the four hundred odd fathoms which covered the ocean bed. A puff of steam and much wreckage was all that marked the spot where but a few minutes before had floated a very fine vessel.

P. S. J.

LIEUT. W. H. KING.

Lieut. William Hugh King, born in 1894, killed on April 11th, 1918, through an accident when returning from a bombing raid on the German lines, was the eldest son of Mr. and Mrs. William Hedley King, of Inglis Road, Colchester. We sincerely regret to announce the death of this promising young officer, and much sympathy is felt for his parents and family in their sad bereavement. He was educated at Colchester Grammar School, and on. leaving went to Germany, where he acquired a thorough knowledge of both the French and German languages. Lieut. King adopted engineering as his profession, and was articled to Messrs. Davey, Paxman and Co., Ltd., of Colchester. The firm held an extremely high opinion of his abilities, and it was quite anticipated that he had a bright and successful career before him in his profession. He was extremely popular with all with whom he came in contact, and made many friends. He joined up in the ranks immediately after the war broke out, and soon afterwards obtained a commission and was appointed Sec.-Lieut. in the 2/8th Essex (Cyclist) Battalion, being promoted to lieutenant in July, 1917. He went to France in March, 1917,and was for some time attached to the 2/5th North Staffordshires, and later was engaged for some months at the headquarters of the XV. Corps, on account of his fluent knowledge of both the French and German languages. In November, 1917, he obtained a transfer as observer in the Royal Air Force, returning to England for a course of training. He passed all examinations with distinction and was highly commended. He left for France again early last month. The following is an extract from a letter from the squadron to which he was attached :—" He had made an astonishingly quick progress as an observer, and was very popular in the squadron. His loss will be greatly felt here. It was a tragic accident which robbed you of your boy and us of a very gallant comrade and observer. His death is a real loss to the squadron, for everybody had the very highest opinion of his work, and the sincerest admiration of his character. He wasn't with us very long, but long enough to prove that he was good all through—brave, conscientious and thorough in all he undertook, and a very loyal and charming comrade."

PRVT. J. HEDLEY KING.

We regret to learn that Private John Hedley King, second son of Mr. and Mrs. William Hedley King, of 16, Inglis Road, Colchester, died in France on April 28, in his 21st year. His parents received news on Monday, April 29, that he had been seriously wounded, and on May 1 heard that he had succumbed to his injuries. He enlisted in the 1/8th (Cyclist Battalion) Essex Regiment in September, 1916, and went to France in August, 1917, attached to the 2nd Battalion Northamptonshire Regiment. He was home on leave in March, returning to France on Good Friday.

Private King was educated at the Colchester Royal Grammar School, and on leaving was apprenticed to a firm of seed growers at Colne Engaine. He was quiet and of unassuming manners, a general favourite with all. A good all-round athlete, his chief hobby was boating. Much sympathy is felt with the family in their double bereavement.

SEC.-LIEUT. F. J. COLLINGE A PRISONER.

Second-Lieut. F. J. COLLINGE, Oxford and Bucks Light Infantry, second son of Mr. F. S. Collinge, solicitor, Colchester, who was officially reported missing since March 21, has, we are glad to learn, been heard of as a prisoner of war in Germany.

In a letter received, one of his brother officers says :—" Your son did splendid work on that morning (March 21) and earned the admiration of all. He was last seen with a few of his men disappearing into the mist in the direction of the enemy." Second-Lieut. Collinge joined the Artists Rifles O.T.C. on September 25, 1916, receiving his commission in May of last year, and proceeding to France in January last. Mr. Collinge was at one time a member of the choir at St. Mary-at-the-Walls, and his high gifts as a vocalist are well known in Colchester. .

SEC.-LIEUT. CLAUDE LINDSAY HARVEY.

Great sympathy will be felt for the mother, sister and relatives of the above young officer, who is reported "wounded and missing" on March 23. He was just entering upon his 28th year. He joined as a private in the London Scottish (1st Battalion) and saw four months' active service in France, returning home wounded in Nov., 1916. He obtained a commission in the Queen's Royal West Surrey Regt., in June, 1917, and proceeded to France again on Sept. 10 of that year, where he has been ever since. He is the only son of Mrs. Harvey, late of Holmesdale, Ardleigh, and grandson of the Rev. Anthony Cox Fenn, a former rector of Wrabness.

SERGT. H. WATCHAM, D.C.M.

Sergt. H. Watcham has been awarded the D.C.M. for bravery during the action in which he was severely wounded in Palestine. He has now recovered and having been discharged from the army is back at his old job at Wickam.

W. M. Town has been awarded the Military Medal (see note under Cadet Corps). .

Alec Head, who is driving in the Motor Transport in France, writes that he is having an exciting time. A few weeks back his lorry, together with several others, was surrounded, but we are glad to say he was able to break through.

H. Burleigh, who joined the Artists' Rifles a short time back, is proceeding to an Artillery Training School to train for his commission.

M. R. Salew has obtained his commission in the R.A.F., and is proceeding to France to complete his training. He hopes to transfer to the Indian Army.

It is with deep regret that we announce the death, from pneumonia, of Leonard B. Fitch. He joined the Essex Yeomanry early in the war, and saw considerable service in France. He was invalided home during 1915. and subsequently discharged from the army. He then returned to Messrs. Ernest S. Beard and Daniell, to whom he was articled before the war. He had recently passed his auctioneer's and surveyor's examinations and obtained a good appointment at Chelmsford.

He was a great favourite at school and took a keen interest in all sports. At the time of leaving he was a member of the 2nd XI. Football and Cricket and House Football, Cricket and Shooting elevens. He will be greatly missed by all who knew him.

Our congratulations to Capt. and Mrs. A. S. Mason on the birth of a daughter. They are still stationed at Dalhousie, India, where centres Capt. Mason's work as D.A.Q.M.G.

NOTE.—We should welcome any letters from Old Colcestrians giving accounts of their experiences.—PLEASE WRITE.

Roll of Honour.

ADDITIONS.

Bayliss, R. V. J., 2/Lt. County of London Regt.
Burleigh, H., Artist Rifles.
Fletcher, L. B., Royal Navy.
Beard, E. E., Royal Air Force.
Creighton, J. F. R., Artist Rifles.
Baskett, T., Royal Air Force.
Salew, N. R., Royal Air Force.
Deane, R. P., Royal Marines.

Casualties.

KILLED.

King, Lieut. W. H., Royal Air Force.
King, John H., Northants Regt.
Harvey, 2/Lt. C. L., London Scottish, wounded and missing.

PRISONERS OF WAR.

Collinge, 2/Lt. F. J., Oxford and Bucks L.I.
Barrell, G., Gunner R.F.A.
Plummer, N. A.

453

No. 52.]
NEW SERIES.

DECEMBER, 1918.

The Colcestrian

PRICE SIXPENCE.

BENHAM & COMPANY, LIMITED, COLCHESTER.

The Colcestrian.

VITÆ CORONA FIDES.

No. 52].   DECEMBER, 1918.   [NEW SERIES

Grammaria.

THE SCHOOL EDITORSHIP OF THE COLCESTRIAN.

The departure of Mr. Barker to Clifton, so serious a loss in many ways to the School, involves, *inter alia*, a change in the School Editorship of the Colcestrian. The Headmaster wishes to express the thanks of us all to Mr. Barker for the care and trouble that he has taken in the past for our magazine, and to Mr. Paul Mathews, M.A., who has most kindly undertaken the School Editorship for the future. Mr. Mathews comes to the task equipped with the advantage of some previous experience, for he was at one time the Joint Editor of the Rochester Dickens Fellowship Magazine.

Where (as we are credibly informed) there was once nothing but peaceful calm and monastic stillness, there is now the free laughter and chatter of irresponsible youth. In other words, Gilberd House, once the secluded home of a celibate staff, now shelters some two dozen of the junior boarders. The management of Gilberd House, as well as of the School House, is in the very capable hands of Miss Pretty, so that the youngsters are well cared for and happy. Of the masters who were resident at Gilberd House last term, Mr. Reeve (as elsewhere stated) has earned our congratulations and our envy, Mr. Barker has gone to Clifton, Mr. Mathews has joined Mr. Cape at the School House and Mr. Pepper and Mr. Peart remain in Gilberd House to look after the welfare of the boys and help them in their difficulties. Much has been done to improve the accommodation and arrangement of the house, and it is rumoured that further improvements are planned. The junior boarders wish to express their thanks to Mr. Peart for his kindness in giving up his former large ground-floor room in order that it might be made into a play-room.   H. J. C.

THE PROPOSED WAR MEMORIAL.

We print a copy of a letter which is being sent by the Headmaster to the parents of Old Colcestrians of recent date. Some of these, though not very many, it has been impossible to trace. Some were omitted because their sacrifices were known to us. and such a letter would be merely a painful reminder. A Committee of the Old Colcestrian Society has been appointed to trace what has been done by those who were at the

School at an earlier time. We are asked to state that the Headmaster would be grateful for information as to the services which Old Colcestrians have rendered to their country on la nd at sea or in the air. He is most anxious that the list should be as complete and accurate as possible. The following is a copy of the letter :—

SCHOOL HOUSE,

THE ROYAL GRAMMAR SCHOOL,

COLCESTER.

20th November, 1918.

DEAR SIR OR MADAM,

It is hoped that it will be possible, for the honour of Colcestrians of the past and as an example and incentive to Colcestrians of the future, to set up in some permanent shape a Memorial of all those Old Boys of the School who have given their services, and in many cases their lives, for their country during the war.

As a preliminary measure it is necessary that we should have a record as complete as it is possible to make it. Of the work of many Old Colcestrians we have details, but our record is far from complete.

For this reason I venture to ask you to send to me as early as possible a note as to your son, giving us the fullest information that you can as to his rank, regiment or ship, military or naval history, decorations, honours, mentions, etc.

In asking this I realise very fully that in many cases I am running the risk of reviving sorrows and of re-opening old wounds, but rather even this than that there should be the danger that such sacrifices should be unrecorded and unhonoured.

I write on behalf of the Committee of the Old Colcestrian Society, specially appointed for this purpose.

Please let me have a reply, even if you are of opinion that we have the particulars that you would send. In such a case duplication of information is far better than omission.

Yours very faithfully,

H. J. CAPE,

Headmaster.

THANKSGIVING SERVICE.

A joint service of thanksgiving was held on Nov. 15th, by our boys and the girls of the County High School. The Mayor kindly gave permission for the use of the Moot Hall and attended the service in person. The prayers (some of which were composed for the occasion)were read by the Rev. Stanley Wilson, A.K.C., Chaplain to His Worship the Mayor, and the lessons by Mr. P. Mathews, M.A. An impressive address was given by the Rev. K. Lloyd Parry, B.Sc. The Borough organist

(Mr. W. Christian Everett, A.R.C.O., A.R.C.M.) officiated at the organ. The Moot Hall was completely filled by the boys and girls. The singing was thoroughly good and the service bright and inspiring. It should make a lasting impression on those who attended it.

CONGRATULATIONS.

Mr. Reeve returned to us after the summer holiday as a married man. We would extend to Mrs. Reeve our heartiest welcome on coming into our circle, and wish both her and her husband all happiness and prosperity.

* * * *

Congratulations to Mr. Peart, O.C. the Cadet Corps on attaining the rank of Captain. His commission, though only just received, is dated February 1st, 1916. It is a well-earned recognition of the great pains he has taken with, and the interest he has shown in, the Corps for so long a time.

* * * *

Staff Changes.

It is with genuine regret that we chronicle the passing from us of Mr. F. D. Barker, B.A. An old boy of the school, Mr. Barker gained a scholarship at Oxford and was distinguished in colloquial French in the Degree-Examination at the University. He returned to his old school as Foreign Language Master in September, 1913. His skill in music was also found valuable. Joining the army in 1916, he was, after being severely wounded, invalided out of the service and returned hither in February, 1918. In September of this year Mr. Barker took up an appointment at Clifton College.

While at Colchester Mr. Barker took a great interest in the Cadet Corps, and during his second term of service acted as School Editor of the "Colcestrian." His colleagues on the staff miss him much. They heard with extreme sorrow that he had fallen a victim to the all-prevalent 'flu, and consequent pneumonia; at the time of writing, however, we believe that he is well on the way to recovery.

* * * *

New members of the staff this term are Mr. P. P. Ferry, M.A. (Harvard Univ., U.S.A.) and the Rev. H. Hughes, M.A. (Oxon.), who also acts as Curate of St. Peter's, Colchester.

* * * *

Alma Mater.

Our numbers now stand at 317 (49 boarders), an increase of some 30 on last term.

In accordance with the Headmaster's promise early in the term a holiday was granted to mark the addition of a hundred to the roll since the last celebration of the same kind, not so very long ago. The addition took place far sooner than was expected. * * *

The 'flu played havoc with our attendance, and the School was closed from October 14th to October 26th (both dates inclusive). The greatest depletion took place on October 12th. In Form u. 3 only 11 turned up out of 30, and in l.4b, 13 out of 31. Fortunately, the staff did not all succumb at once, though several had a touch of the epidemic. The worst sufferers were Messrs. Reeve, Peart and Bisson. In fact, for some little time, Mr. Bisson's work has been done by Sergt.-Maj. Spooner (R.W.K.). * * * *

The new Studies are now occupied, and greatly appreciated by the School House Boarders. The Studies have been presented to the School, fully furnished, by the Head Master.

Acknowledgments. * * *

Maltonian, O.H.S. Magazine, Viking, Wyggestonian. Chelmsfordian.

The Pre.

It is a Scout's duty " to smile and whistle under all difficulties," we learn. and when it poured incessantly on the first day fixed for the July Inspection. the members of the " Pre Patrol " certainly accepted their disappointment in the right spirit. They turned up with all their badges in keen anticipation, and then patiently ravelled till School was over.

On the following Tuesday the rain again prevented any outdoor display, and they did better still, obeyed orders quite smartly, and carried out the programme in Big Hall as if they had been used to drilling there all through the term. We are indebted to Mr. Cape, who kindly explained to the large number of parents and friends present the disadvantages under which we were working, and to Mrs. Cecil Cant, who presented the badges. F. Uff carried off the prize offered by Mrs. Craske for the boy who gained most points.

With our increased numbers the prospective Wolf Cubs are doing quite good work, and hope to show some of it on December 19th, though the term has, of necessity, been so seriously interrupted.

On Friday, November 15th. we attended the Thanksgiving Service at the Moot Hall, and, in order that this unparalleled occasion may be ever remembered in " The Pre," a frame containing the names of all present pupils is to be hung in the School. The older boys have painted Union Jacks. Each hopes his will be chosen to decorate the inscription.

Our War Collection last term. which amounted to 14s., was again given to the Needlework Depot.

Though the object to which we mean to contribute this term is still a profound secret, we may say that it is connected with our wounded friends in Ward VI. at the Essex County Hospital.

In response to the appeal for literature on behalf of our troops, many books and magazines have been collected and forwarded by the Pre boys.

Although the fighting is over, there are still many who appreciate an extra pillow. Eighty-five have been sent out from the Pre during the four years of war. By Christmas we hope five more will be ready. In years to come it will mean a great deal to these boys, who are now under nine, to be able to say, " I was too young to fight in the Great European War, but I did what I could for those who did fight."

Cadet Corps.

(Attached 5th Essex.)

Very reluctantly we parted last term with Lieut. F. D. Barker, whose help and sympathy, no less than his practical experience, proved so valuable to us. As an old boy and as a master, he had endeared himself to all, and his going is a grave loss. We wish him every success at Clifton, where, we regret to record, a serious illness prevented him taking a House tutorship. He is, we are glad to know, now on the road to health.

* * * *

The outstanding event of an otherwise dull term was the cessation of hostilities on November 11th, a date of such moment that a serious suggestion has been made that the years should be calculated in future with this amazing year as the starting point. Certainly we shall never live through another week so wonderful. As a corps we marked the Armistice by joining the Scouts in a simplified ceremony of trooping the colours. The only sad thought was that many of the boys— some of ours among them—would never share in the great welcome which awaits our returning heroes.

* * * *

We are pleased to hear from our fellow townsmen that the bearing of the Scouts and Cadets on their way to the Mayoral inauguration, and the Thanksgiving Service, was to be commended. The credit of the School, as well as that of the Corps, is carried under the cap of each cadet.

* * * *

The Wagstaff Trophy, competed for at the end of last term, was won by Platoon 1—Harwood, Sergeant. Points:—I., 74; II., 58; III., 52; IV., 70. The platoons were all keen, most of them getting top place in one or more of the divisions of the test. * * * *

Marlborough camp was an unqualified success in every way— weather, food, work, sport, organization and good-feeling.

Colchester won the warm commendation of the O.C. " A " Co., and won seventh place in contingent sports. Your O.C., whose place on Headquarters Staff was a distinct compliment to the Corps, wishes to congratulate them on the smart and efficient work of the camp representatives, on the excellence of their lines, on the able command of the N.C.O.'s, on the good work of C.-S.-M. Hill, and on the irreproachable conduct throughout. He was proud to command them, although his duties kept him from seeing them often on parade.

* * * *

With our splendidly growing numbers, can we not next year beat the record of Brentwood, who sent 126 cadets to camp from a school of 400 ?

* * * *

It is gratifying to note that many of our boys arranged to spend part of their holidays on the land, despite the M.N.S. muddle.

* * * *

We wish to thank Lieut. E. A. Andrews for his useful gift of bandages and splints for the Ambulance section ; also Mrs. Ebsworth, who has kindly presented the corps with a Sam Browne belt, as a remembrance of Lieut.-Colonel Ebsworth, the heroic father of one of our members. The story of his hard work, self-sacrifice and noble end will always, we are sure, remain an inspiration to all of us. She has also given us two German bayonets. * * * *

At the beginning of the term we re-organized on the principles laid down by Colonel Gallagher, with the section as the unit. We hope to present the recruit's medal in the first term, have a Section trophy to be won in the second, and compete for the Wagstaff Trophy in the third, annually.

* * * *

Plague and pestilence have interrupted the work of this term, but steady practice in section command has proceeded, and, with the kind help of Sergt.-Instructor Clark, musketry positions have been learned.

* * * *

General Sir Malcolm Grover has kindly postponed his visit of inspection whilst illness ravaged our attendance, but we must now be prepared for short notice.

* * * *

: Major Deakin, D.S.O., M.C., writing from Palestine, congratulates the Corps on its old members, Town, Watsham, Clover and Doubleday, whose record in the victorious Palestine offensive is, he says, something for which the corps may be very proud.

* * * *

Discharged :—Sergt.-Drummer Chase, Corpl. White, Lance-

Corpl. Harvey, Lance.-Corpl. Wilson, Cadets Last, Powell, Church, Ritchie, Wyncoll mi., Tyson, Hayes, and Taylor.

Enlisted :—Holloway ma., Riches, Fowler, Miller, Reynolds, Bailey mi., Webber, Thompson, Farmer, Osborne, Harwood mi., Dowsett, MacIntyre, Clarkson and Clubb..

* * * *

We are now members of the Secondary Schools Cadet Association, a powerful body with representatives at the War Office, and on Territorial Associations.

J. A. P.

Scouting Motes.

The wet weather and the influenza epidemic have prevented us from doing as much outdoor work as usual this term. However, much good patrol work has been done, though our chief drawback is a lack of patrol leaders. The troop now contains over seventy members, to say nothing of the large Pack of Cubs ; and to run the troop really well we need quite a dozen P.L.'s. It is up to the keen senior scouts to try to qualify as patrol leaders as soon as possible, if we are to maintain our efficiency. This is the more important as we have lost three of our number this term, P.-L.'s Weeks, Hollaway and Osborne. The two last-named, together with Scouts Harwood, Dowsett and Farmer, have joined the Cadet Corps, and Weeks has left the School. To Weeks we are especially sorry to say goodbye, as he has always been one of the keenest boys in the Troop, of which he has been a member since its foundation in January, 1912.

On November 9th the Troop attended the installation of Councillor George Wright, O.C., as Mayor of Colchester for the ensuing year. On the following day we were again at the Moot Hall for a service in commemoration of all those former Scouts of the Colchester district who have fallen in the war. Amongst that number, we especially mourn the death of Sec.-Lieut. Alan Barnes, R.A.F., formerly P.-L. of the Curlews, and one of the best Scouts the Troop has ever had.

On Thursday, Nov. 14th, in celebration of the signing of the Armistice, the Scouts took part with the Cadet Corps in the ceremony of trooping the colours, and on the following day they attended a thanksgiving service at the Moot Hall.

For the Allied Scout Relief Fund, the Troop subscribed £5..10.

Promotions :—Scouts Butler, C. Smith and H. Smith have been promoted to be Patrol Leaders.

The following have qualified for proficiency badges :— Interpreter's badge, P.-L.'s Butler, W. Wilson and Griffiths. Boatman's badge, P.-L. Butler. Electrician's badge, P.-L. J. W. Weeks.

This term's recruits are :—Coulsell, J. W. Smith, Pursey,

G. Robinson, Hickford, Starling, Downing ii., Newson. Church i., Brooke and Ram. J. Smith and Nunn have come up from the Wolf Cub Pack.   .E. E. P.

Valete.

White, G. H., Form VI., Schoolhouse, School and House Cricket, School and House Football, Corpl. Cadet Corps.

Chase, J. E., Form Va., Prefect, Dugard's, House Cricket and Shooting, Band Sergt. Cadet Corps.

Harvey, C. P., Form Va., Prefect, Schoolhouse, House Shooting, L.-Cpl. Cadet Corps.

Hayes, F. J., Form Va., Parr's, House Cricket and Football, Pte. Cadet Corps.

Last, F. A., Form Va. Dugard's, Pte. Cadet Corps.

Wilson, H. S., Form Va., Schoolhouse, School and House Cricket, School and House Football, L.-Cpl. Bugler Cadet Corps

Taylor, L. C., Form Vb., Harsnett's, Pte. Cadet Corps.

Wyncoll, F. P., Form Vb., Dugard's, Pte. Cadet Corps.

Jones, C. W., Form U IV., Parr's, House Football,

Powell, B. E., U IV., Dugard's, House Cricket and Football, Pte. Cadet Corps.

Browne, F. G., L IV.b., Harsnett's.

Hordern, A. C., U III., Harsnett's.

Jennens, J., Pre.

Salvete.

Lower V.
MacIntyre, J. F., Harsnett's.

Upper IV. A.
Fox, G. N., Parr's.
Fowler, D. C., Schoolhouse.

Upper IV. B.
Miller, J. E. C., Schoolhouse.
Clarkson, K., Schoolhouse.

Lower IV. A.
Clubb, N. A. C., Harsnett's.
King, E. W., Harsnett's.
Bailey, D. S., Dugard's.
Reynolds, C. J., Harsnett's.
Gunton, H. E., Dugard's.
Thompson, F. J., Dugard's.
Wilson, W. T., Dugard's.
Wilson, F. W., Dugard's.
Bishop, C. E., Dugard's.
Willson, A. E., Harsnett's.
Ford, S. W., Parr's.

Lower IV. B.
Phillips, C. F., Harsnett's.
Brooke, N. C. D., Harsnett's.
Barnes, H. M., Schoolhouse.
Lee, P. H., Parr's.
Robinson, G. S., Schoolhouse.
Gale, H. C., Harsnett's.
Carter, J. M., Dugard's.
Cracknell, P. G., Schoolhouse.
Laws, S. R., Parr's.

Upper III.
Pursey, H. O., Harsnett's.

Longworth, A. E., Parr's.
Newson, P. E., Schoolhouse.
Bacon, G. C., Dugard's.
Hickford, R. E., Dugard's.
Smith, J. W., Parr's.
Hayward, J. A., Parr's.
Downing, A. W., Parr's.
Winder, R. W. C., Parr's.

Lower III.
Starling, L. S. J., Schoolhouse.

II. & I.
Lister, F. J., Harsnett's.
Robinson, M. S., Schoolhouse.
Jackson, R. H., Schoolhouse.
Hayward, S. T., Parr's.
Gwyn, J. N., Parr's.
Moore, H. E., Parr's.
Scarff, K. C., Dugard's.
Croyden, A. G. H., Parr's.
Mitchenall (from Pre), Schoolhouse.

Pre.
Bacon, P.
Culverwell, B.
Eldridge, L.
Howard, R.
Townsend, J.
Page, R.
Walford, K.
Willis, B.
Welton, W.
Wicks, E.

Examination Results.

LONDON MATRIC.
C. W. Thomas, 1st Division.
R. G. Harwood, 2nd Division.

FIRST SCHOLARSHIP, FINSBURY TECHNICAL COLLEGE.
Geoffrey H. White was bracketed equal with another student,
with whom he divides the Scholarship.

CAMBRIDGE LOCAL EXAMINATIONS.
Senior : Pass, T. M. Clough.
Junior : 1st Class, T. W. Y. Alderton.
2nd Class (Div. 2), H. C. Sier.
3rd Class (Div. 2), C. G. Lufkin.
Pass (Div. 1), H. N. Butler, R. N. Griffith, R Hum, T. H.
Jackson, H. L. Pattle, R. M. Pleasants, T. R. Smith,
J. W. Weeks. (Div. 2), H. J. Ingle, E. R. Keeble. W. E.
Pryor, F. P. Wyncoll.
The mark of distinction in individual papers was obtained by Alderton
in Shakespeare, Geometry and Practical Chemistry ; by Pattle in English
Composition and Shakespeare ; by Smith in Shakespeare and Practical
Chemistry ; and by Jones, Sier and Weeks in Shakespeare.

Cricket.

SCHOOL v. MECHANICAL DENTAL CENTRE.
The School lost the toss and the visitors batted first, making 57. For
the School Cox bowled well, taking 8 wickets for 16 runs. The School
were only able to make 30 runs, thus losing the match by 17.

SCHOOL v. 2/7TH DURHAM LIGHT INFANTRY.
The School batted first and obtained 41, of which Johnstone made
16. The visitors made a total of 80.

SCHOOL v. WEST BERGHOLT.
This match was played at West Bergholt and resulted in an easy win
for the School by an innings and six runs.
West Bergholt batted first and obtained 35. The School then went
in and of the 57 which were scored Johnstone made the top score of
30. In the second innings West Bergholt only made 16, owing to the
good bowling of Cox and Harwood ma.

LEADING AVERAGES IN 1st XI. MATCHES.

BATTING.

	No. of Innings.	Runs.	Average.
Johnstone	6	67	11.17
Harwood mi.	6 (2 not out)	42	10.5
Cox	6	43	7.17
Harwood ma.	6	42	7.0

BOWLING.

	Overs.	Maidens.	Runs.	Wkts.	Av.
Harwood ma.	53	12	106	44	2.41
Osborne ma.	10	1	22	7	3.14
Cox	46	7	86	21	4.1
Johnstone	17	1	55	4	13.75

HOUSE MATCHES.
SCHOOLHOUSE v. DUGARD'S.

Dugard's won the toss and decided to bat first. Dugard's batted well and the individual scores were fairly even, a total of 68 being obtained. Schoolhouse only managed to make 41 in their first innings. Dugard's went in a second time with a useful lead of 27. The first two wickets fell quickly, but the third did not fall until 31 had been reached. Of the final total of 77 Chase made 26.

Schoolhouse now went in with 105 to get to win. In this they failed miserably, owing to Dugard's good bowling. A total of 25 was obtained, of which Nocton made 19. Dugard's thus won the match by 79 runs, thereby gaining the cup.

The last of the Junior House matches was played between Parr's and Harsnett's in July, and resulted in a win for Parr's, who thus became holders of the Cup.

The following have been awarded First Eleven Cricket Colours :—
Cox, Harwood ma., Harwood mi., Johnstone, Lilley, Osborne ma.

Football.

SCHOOL v. CHELMSFORD SCHOOL.

November 9th.

This match was played at Chelmsford. In the first half the School played against the wind and up hill. The scoring was opened by Chelmsford, but Cox soon equalised from a good centre by Osborne ma. Before half time Chelmsford scored twice more.

On resuming, Cox soon added another goal, and a few minutes later Griffith scored for the School. The play was now of an even nature until about a quarter of an hour before the end, when the weight of the Chelmsford team began to tell and three more goals were scored in quick succession. The School thus lost the match by 6 goals to 3. Harwood mi. played an excellent game in goal, and it was owing to him that further goals were not scored. His play was frequently noticed by the Chelmsford spectators.

SCHOOL v. IPSWICH MUNICIPAL SCHOOL.

This match was played at Ipswich on Saturday, November 16th. The School team failed to combine and did not win by so big a margin as it might have. The School opened the scoring soon after play commenced, but Ipswich equalised with a good shot, which gave School goal keeper no chance. Both teams scored twice more before half-time, making the score 3—3.

In the second half, the School had much the better of the game, scoring five more goals, while Ipswich scored two. The result was, therefore, 8—5 for the School. The scorers for the School were Griffith, Osborne ma., Cox and Joel.

SCHOOL v. CHELMSFORD SCHOOL.

The return match was played at Colchester on Saturday, November 23rd, and resulted in a win for the School by 4—0.

The first goal was scored by Cox from a good pass of Garvie's. Soon after this Griffith scored again with a good shot from the left. Play was now fairly even and once or twice Chelmsford looked like scoring. Before half-time, however, Joel scored after a good run down the line by Garvie.

On recommencing Osborne ma. received a pass and scored neatly. After this the School continued to have most of the play. A ground shot near the upright was put in by the Chelmsford centre forward, but Harwood mi. brought off a good save. Garvie must be congratulated for his good work on the right wing.

CHARACTERS OF FIRST ELEVEN.

Cox (Vice-Capt.) (inside right).—A hard worker ; does not use his weight sufficiently. Should remember he has two feet.

Garvie (outside right).—A very fast forward ; centres well ; could save time by not always working to corner.

Griffith (outside left).—Has a good turn of speed. Apt to wait for the ball to come to him. CAN centre well.

Harwood ma. (centre half).—A dogged player ; uses his head well ; does not always pass to the right man.

Harwood mi. (goal).—His one fault is size ; otherwise he is clean and safe.

Holloway ma. (left half).—A very robust player, but wastes energy through eagerness.

Joel (inside left).—Has good control, but is light and easily knocked off the ball.

Lilley (Capt.) (left back).—A clean kick with a good idea of tackling, but somewhat slow. Plays the game in the right spirit.

Linfoot (right half).—Has a good idea of half-back play and works hard; apt to tie himself up in knots.

Osborne ma. (centre forward).—A sound player, with splendid control over the ball, but does not hold his forwards together.

Twyman (right back).—Not a strong kick. Useful in a scrimmage in front of goal ; goes straight.

Johnstone.—A very sound player and a good shot. Unfortunately had to stand down through lameness.

SECOND ELEVEN.

SCHOOL v. IPSWICH MUNICIPAL SCHOOL.

The match was played on the School ground under favourable weather conditions. As this was the first time the team had played together, they did not combine as well as they might have done, and the shooting was also weak.

In the first half the game was slow and ended with a score of 2—2. The second half the game livened up a bit and, although we were in their halfmost of the time, we only managed to score one more goal. They, on the other hand, broke away several times and scored two more goals, the game thus ending with a score of 4—3 for the visitors.

HOUSE MATCHES.

1st Round.

PARR'S v. DUGARD'S.

This match resulted in a much better game than one would have expected after glancing at the teams as they appeared on paper. Dugard's, of course, were much heavier, but the team as a whole failed to combine. Parr's, on the other hand, got together rather well, and their forwards gave a plucky display against a defence about twice their weight.

For some time after the start the game was fairly even. At last Dugard's scored. Parr's, however, quickly equalised with a really fine shot from Osborne ma. Before half-time Dugard's, encouraged by the shouts of their House-master, put on two more goals, the score at half-time being 3—1 in favour of Dugard's.

On resuming, Parr's speedily went to pieces, and the second half of the game was very one-sided. They scored two more goals, whilst Dugard's scored seven more. The final score therefore was 10—3. For Parr's Osborne ma., in the defence, and Garvie in the forward line deserve special mention. For Dugard's Nicholls, who scored five goals, and Harwood mi., who brought off some fine saves, may be congratulated upon their performances.

1st Round.

HARSNETT'S v. SCHOOLHOUSE.

Schoolhouse were without Johnstone and Warden and a close game was expected. At first Harsnett's made several rushes and, at times, looked like scoring. The Schoolhouse forwards soon got together and before half-time the score was 3—0 in their favour. In the second half Schoolhouse continued to have most of the play. Downing scored the fourth goal with a good shot; after this three others were added. In the last ten minutes Harsnett's again pressed and Thomas, the Harsnett centre half, scored with a well-placed shot. The scorers for Schoolhouse were Tricker, Joel and Downing, two each, and Church ma. one. For Harsnett's Cox worked hard and played a good game. Final score: 7—1 in favour of Schoolhouse.

DUGARD'S v. HARSNETT'S.

Played on November 21.

This match was played in ideal football weather. Dugard's won the toss and started Harsnett's kicking against the sun. For the first few minutes after the kick-off, Dugard's pressed very hotly, but failed to score. The Harsnett forwards had, by that time, found their positions, and play was fairly equal, in both halves of the field. Dugard's scored twice before half-time and Harsnett's once. In the second half the Harsnett forwards made many efforts to break through the Dugard defence, and combined quite creditably, but Holloway I. at centre half and Harwood mi. in goal repeatedly saved the situation for their side. Dugard's however, succeeded in scoring three more goals, although Harsnett's seemed to have more of the play. This made the final result 5—1 in favour of Dugard's. For Dugard's Harwood ma. scored 3, Jones 1 and Holloway II. 1. Thomas scored the only Harsnett's goal.

2nd Round.

SCHOOLHOUSE v. PARR'S.

For the first twenty minutes of the game Parr's pressed hard and Lilley put the ball through his own goal. Soon after this, however, Schoolhouse scored two in quick succession, both being obtained by Tricker ma.

On recommencing Schoolhouse pressed, but were unable to score, several open goals being missed. Towards the end of the game Parr's had most of the play and Osborne mi. scored the eqalising goal from a good centre by Griffith.

JUNIOR HOUSE MATCHES.

Only one round of Junior House Matches has been played so far. In the match between Dugard's and Schoolhouse, Schoolhouse pressed in the first half, but were unable to score. After half-time, however, the team combined better and got five goals.

In the match between Parr's and Harsnett's, Parr's were the stronger team and won easily by 7—1.

Old Colcestrian Section.

OFFICERS.

President : C. T. WRIGHT, Crouch Street, Colchester.

Hon. Treasurer : BERNARD MASON, Crouch Street, Colchester.

Hon. Secretaries : A. T. DALDY, Head Street, Colchester (O.A.S.) ; BERNARD MASON, Crouch Street, Colchester.

Old Colcestrians are requested to notify any change of address and to forward contributions to the O.C. Section to Mr. Bernard Mason, Hon. Sec., Crouch Street, Colchester.

Rosemary.

"My beloved is gone down into his garden
To gather lilies."

I have no wreath of asphodel
For those dear souls we mourn,
The words that should their praises tell
Find me, alas, forlorn.
So with the laurel and the bay—
The guerdon of the brave—
Some rosemary and rue I lay
Upon each lonely grave.

With open hands they gave their all
That we their all might share ;
With death they held high festival,
Gallant and debonair,
And so the ordered seasons passed
With shriek of shot and shell
Until the challenge came at last,
Who goes ? Pass, friend ! All's well !

A splendid sorrow ours to hold
Whose courage falters never.
Nor fails sad hearts, but makes them bold
For new and high endeavour.
The souls we loved unflinching made
Their sacrament of pain,
So we may speed them, unafraid,
GOD will assess their gain.　　　　J.

The New Mayor.

In Councillor George F. Wright, O.C., Colchester has a most popular and respected Mayor. To mark their appreciation of the many services which he has rendered to his School, the boys attended on November 9th the very interesting ceremony of "Mayor-making" at the Moot Hall. As an old boy of the School, as a former President of the Old Colcestrian Society (of which his brother is President now), and as one of the most enthusiastic and hard-working of the Governors of the School, there are few who have so great a claim upon our gratitude. It was a real pleasure to us all that he should have been elected as Chief Citizen of the Borough.

3 Weary of it, Living in the Twilight.

(Reprinted from " The New Age," May 23rd, 1918.

I weary of it, living in the twilight—
　Do you not weary of it sometimes too ?
Weary of shadows and of dim illusions,
　Weary of watching the far distant blue
Fair all in vain, sweet as a mocking echo,
　Spread with a flush unreal and sighing sad,
Sad with its falseness, wistful and elusive,
　Like the strange visions of a soul gone mad.
Where all things haunt, but none are true or earnest,
　And all the fairest whispers are but sounds
Caught in the boughs by autumn winds a-moaning,
　Or from the distant bay of fretting hounds,
Or in the whirlpool stirring in a fury,
　Or by the footsteps through the scattered leaves,
Trampling the red souls in the dust all weary.
　Or by the raindrops in among the sheaves ?
All sounds that sob and sigh in bitter meaning.
　All that would speak, but cannot, and in vain
Clutch at the fragments of a passing shadow
　To chase each other through my weary brain :
I weary of it, weary of the stillness.
　I sometimes think that one day I may be
A shadow haunting through the faint-lit chambers,
　Groping for something that I cannot see.

COLCHESTER MASON, O.C., *age* 16.

The Fire at Colchester Theatre.

Sympathy will be extended to Mr. Albert J. Clamp, O.C., in the serious loss he has sustained by the destruction by fire of Colchester Theatre, of which he was proprietor. Mr. Clamp has since been able to arrange for the resumption of his theatrical productions, which now attract good audiences at the Corn Exchange. His son, Pte. G. J. V. Clamp, O.C., who left the School, April, 1907, has been severely wounded in France.

Notes from the East.

INTERESTING LETTER FROM R. E. DOUBLEDAY.

Mr. J. A. Peart has received a good letter from R. E. Double-day, O.C., detailing some of his experiences and incidentally giving news of other O.C.'s serving with the Forces. Doubleday, who writes from somewhere in Palestine, says :—

I have had the School Magazine sent to me fairly regularly, and have been delighted to read something about my old friends, with whom I have practically lost touch. I would like to hear a little more about them, and as you seem to gather in quite a lot of news concerning them, I hope you will be able to spare a little time to let me know how they are progressing.

I have been fortunate enough to run across one or two O.C.'s. First of all I struck Brand in France, being stopped by him to ask the way to some place, which, like many others out there, had disappeared off the face of the earth. We managed to meet occasionally after that, as he was in the same division as I, until he left Salonica to take up a commission. When we came to Egypt I knew that Watsham and Town were somewhere around, but could never manage to get near them, until I was on leave in Cairo, when I met Town, who was at that time training at the Cadet School. That led to a meeting with Capt. Deakin, who was getting over the effects of his wound at Kantara. The latter has since been lucky enough to secure leave to England, so perhaps you have seen him.

Taken all the way round, I have had rather a good time since leaving England, for, cutting out the warlike parts, it has been one big continuous tour for us. (Only one drawback to that—a pack big enough for a camel has to be lumped about at the same time.) After four months in the trenches in France, we wandered about for a month, ending up with a three-day railway journey to Marseilles. Then we slipped over to Salonica, calling at Malta. From Salonique we went to a little place called Katrina, near Mount Olympus, as at that time, December, 1916, it was feared that the Greek Royalist army would attempt to break through our rear and connect up with Von Falkenhayn. It did not come off, and beyond plenty of digging and rain, we had a most jolly time for a couple of months. Then suddenly we were rushed off to the Doiran-Vardar front, covering 100 miles in just under a week, having to put up with tropical heat, pouring rain, and a blizzard on successive days—the worst conditions we have ever had. We had a few side shows on that front, in connection with which I managed to get mentioned in despatches, and then we switched off back to Salonica and from there to Egypt. From August to the end of October, our division did nothing but train for the stunt which captured Beersheba, and set the ball rolling out here, but before that came off I distinguished myself by getting myself landed in hospital with malaria and dysentery, which kept me away about five months. During that time a good deal of scrapping was done by my battalion, but although I was sorry to miss it, I was probably very lucky to be out of it.

However, I managed to get back in time for one little " do," the raid on the Turkish railway leading to Amman. It was quite a big affair, although it was only a raid. To carry it out we had to cross the Jordan, drive back the Turks, capture Es Salt—a fairly big town with a Turkish garrison in it—and Amman, and then destroy as much of the railway as possible, especially a certain big bridge spanning a wide and deep ravine. Es Salt lies some 15 miles East of Jordan, and to reach it one has to climb the mountains of Moab, a rise of 5,000 including the depression in the Jordan valley, and of course, as you know, out here roads are few and far between. Our battalion had to push on from the Jordan to Es Salt, which we did without any trouble, beyond the usual soaking and the difficult paths we had to follow. It appears that any clouds which visit Palestine invariably burst on the Blue Mountains of Moab, and they were no exception to the rule while we were there, nearly a week. We arrived in a cloud and left in one. Es Salt (Ramoth Gilead of old) and its people were most interesting. The inhabitants were chiefly Arabs of rather a fierce nature—a point which is somewhat accentuated as they go about armed with all sorts of weapons from a hefty club to a Mark vii. pattern and W. L. E., pinched or bought from Johnny Turk. We expected to find them hostile, especially when next morning we heard continual rifle fire. However, the natives were delighted to see us, as the Turks had been treating them very harshly, and the rifle volleys were merely a means of showing their pleasure. The Turkish garrison had "impshied" about two hours before we reached the town, but a couple of days later a division came back with the intention of re-capturing the place, but beyond one or two half hearted attempts he failed entirely. When we had completed our plans we left that district at a hell-for-leather rate. We marched continuously for some 20 hours, coming back by the same break neck paths at night, and finishing up at Jericho. Th inhabitants of Es Salt, who had reason to fear the Turks, on learning of our departure left the town, and on our way back we passed some hundreds of them. While near the town we saw one or two curious sights. The funniest was when we saw a highly decorated Arab drive some four camels into a small one-roomed building (the Arab's home), capable of holding about four small people. In addition, a few donkeys found their way in, and so altogether it must have been a sweet scent. It quite put the Irishman and his pig into the shade.

Since arriving back at Jericho we have been "resting" by means of marching from place to place. We found our way to close by Jerusalem, and I was fortunate to be able to spend an afternoon wandering about the old city. But Jerusalem is a very disappointing place, as there is very little of interest there which can be called authentic. The church of the Holy Sepulchre is probably the first place in the eyes of Christians, but as Jerusalem has been destroyed so many times, and the present church is only 100 years old, it is more than probable that the many tombs, etc., pointed out are either imitation or surmises. I found the Mosque of Omar the most interesting and the most beautiful sight in Jerusalem. This is built on the site of the Jews' temple, and I was very surprised on entering the mosque to see a huge slab of rock carefully partitioned off by iron railings. This rock, I was told, was the top of Mount Moriah, on which the Jews used to make their sacrifices. In connection with the latter there is a hole at one end of the rock which was once used to act as a drain for the blood and water ; this hole leads down to a cave where one is religiously shown a huge dent in the roof made by Mahomet hitting his head against the rock !

The present district of Palestine is rather nice. We are near the central portion of the line, where it is somewhat hilly. The ground has been comparatively well cultivated and all around us is well treed with olives and figs. The hills themselves are all carefully terraced off with stones (it is a terrible stony country), a job which must have taken some hundreds of years if the people of old worked as hard as the present generation. Must now ring off to catch our doubtful post.

Roll of Honour.

ADDITIONS.

Burleigh, A., R.F.A. Cadet School, Exeter.
White, H. C. P., R.A.F. (discharged).
Mumford, Lieut. R. H. Bond, R.A.F. (killed by accidental collision in the air in Egypt, Sept. 26).

PROMOTIONS.

Nunn, J. H., 2/Lt. 6th Vol. Batt. Essex Regiment.
Wright, G. T., Capt., R.G.A.
Lines, E., 2/Lt., S.L.I.

WOUNDED.

Benham, Capt. G. C., Essex Regiment.
Richards, Lieut. R. F. (gassed).
Campling, Lieut. A. H., Essex Regiment.
Bugg, 2/Lt. E. P., Essex Regiment.
Watsham, C., R.F.
Clamp, G. J. V.

KILLED.

Barnes, 2/Lt. A., R.A.F.
Brand, 2/Lt. E. J., Essex Regiment.
Hussey, 2/Lt. F., Leicester Regiment.
Orfeur, Lieut. H. W., Essex Regiment.
Shenton, Capt. A. K., M.C., R.E.
Harsum, G. F. (lost at sea).
Lawrence, Albert Dudley (killed in France on 27 Sept., 1918).

RAYMOND VICTOR JARMIN.

Raymond Victor Jarmin, O.C. (son of the Deputy-Mayor, Councillor A. M. Jarmin), died under sad circumstances from influenza on November 2. He entered the Grammar School in January, 1908, and left July, 1909. His illness was contracted during a period of debility, in which he was suffering from the after effects of gas in the Loos advance. His age

.was 24. Only two days before his wife succumbed to the prevailing epidemic. Both resided at Highbury, where Mr. Jarmin was in business. He was discharged from the army invalided, after 12 months' service in France. The funeral with military honours took place at Colchester Cemetery on November 7. On arrival at Colchester station the coffin, covered with the Union Jack, was placed on a gun-carriage. Men of the R.A.M.C., deceased's old regiment, acted as bearers, and Sergt. the Rev. Dan Hughes, R.A.M.C., officiated. At the Cemetery gates a small detachment of Boy Scouts, of which deceased was formerly a member, under Troop Leader Twyman, met the cortege. The principal mourners were the Mayor and Mayoress, Mr. A. F. Jarmin (brother), Mrs. A. F. Jarmin, Miss Jarmin and Mrs. Ward. Among those present at the graveside were Alderman E. A. Blaxill (Scout Commissioner for N.E. Essex), Mr. H. Geoffrey Elwes, Crs. W. Littlebury, W. Chopping and F. W. Richards, Mr. Doe (representing the special police), and Messrs. Hopwood and Alderton. Among the many beautiful floral tributes were those from the staff at Headgate, the staff at George Street and from the Scouts.

CAPT. AUSTIN KIRK SHENTON, M.C., R.E.

Captain Austin Kirk Shenton, M.C., R.E., whose death as the result of a riding accident took place on Friday, July 26, on the Amiens front, was the eldest living son of the Rev. G. D. Shenton, Rector of St. Anthony's, Stepney, E., and for some time Vicar of Elmstead, near Colchester. Born in 1895 at Moseley, Birmingham, he was at school successively at Wychwood, Bournemouth, St. John's, Leatherhead, and Colchester, until joining the London University (City and Guilds Engineering College) in 1913. He was at the Colchester Grammar School from January, 1911, to December, 1912. His previous training in School O.T.C.'s obtained him a commission in the R.E. at the outbreak of the war, and as O.C. of a cable section he did excellent work successively in several corps and divisions. He gained his M.C. for exceptionally good work in command of a cable section during the battle of Arras and in all subsequent operations and was gazetted Captain after gallantly establishing and maintaining a forward telephone post across the Cambrai Canal during the attack on Nov. 23-30, 1917. His last post was on the Headquarters Staff. His fellow-soldiers describe him, in the many sympathetic letters they have written, as " one of the coolest men under fire, and one of those who don't know what fear is. He has done good work for us in many unpleasant places, and his services were invaluable, but we valued him most for his cheery good nature. One of the finest characters we have ever known. His command was in splendid order. He has played the game all through and was one of the very few who was fit to die. If you could see how upset everyone at Divisional H.Q. and Artillery H.Q. is, it would, I think, help you all to bear your terrible loss."

GEO. FREDERICK HARSUM.

George Frederick Harsum, O.C., who entered the School May, 1906, leaving in December, 1910, was, unhappily, lost at sea on Aug. 10, on board the ill-fated s.s. Yatarrax (H.M. transport service), on which he served as Eng.-Lieut. He was the only son of Mr. and Mrs. G. A. Harsum, 88, Bourne Road, Colchester, and his age was 23.

SEC.-LIEUT. ALAN BARNES.

On September 26, Sec.-Lieut. Alan Barnes, O.C., R.A.F., was killed in action in France. He entered the School in April, 1913, and was there just a year. He was the eldest son of Mr. and Mrs. C. Barnes, of 171, Maldon Road, Colchester, and was winner of the Paxman scholarship. He joined the R.A.F. on November 28th, 1917, and passed through Blackdown, Hastings, Uxbridge, Oxford, Harlaxton, and Winchester, being gazetted August, 1918. After a few days only at Winchester he was sent to France, where he remained two or three weeks at the Pool Pilots Range on the coast. On September 26 he was posted to No. 5 Squadron, No. 1 Wing, and on that day wrote home to his parents, whose only further information so far is that he was killed that same day by some accident of which no particulars have been supplied.

SEC.-LIEUT. BRAND.

Sec.-Lieut. Eric Jermyn Brand, O.C., Essex Regiment, aged 22, only son of Mr. and Mrs. J. E. Brand, 34, High Street, Colchester, was killed in action in France while gallantly leading a successful attack on August 25. We was one of the many Colchester Grammar School boys who joined the colours, enlisting as a private in the Rifle Brigade, in May, 1915. In August he was sent to France, and was invalided home the following February. In July he returned to France, was sent to Salonika in December, 1916, and in April, 1917, was sent home for training as an officer. He received a commission in November, 1917, and was attached to the Essex Regiment at Felixstowe, whence he was sent to Egypt, and returned to France with another battalion. He was a great favourite with school chums, and was captain of cricket and football teams. Brand joined the School in December, 1907, and left March, 1915.

LIEUT. FRANK W. HUSSEY.

Lieut. Frank W. Hussey, O.C.; of the Leicester Regiment, was killed in action on September 24, 1918. He entered the School in 1902 and was the only son of Mrs. Hussey, of 15, Audley Road.

Writing from France, a brother officer says :—

" He volunteered to go with his men into an enterprise which was entirely successful, and, having gained all objectives, he was observing fire on the enemy, when a piece of bomb or shell hit him in the neck and he died immediately."

Lieut.-Colonel Foster also writes :—" You will understand how much we feel his loss in the Battalion. Without doubt he was one of the best, and it will be a long time before his men forget his splendid example."

He was killed at Pontruet, a village a few miles N. of St. Quentin. The enterprise was one of exceptional danger and he asked specially to be allowed to go and carried it out with success, but unfortunately paid the price of his own life. Previous to joining the army he was manager for Messrs. W. R. Ponting and Co., Incorporated Insurance Brokers, Oxford Street, London, and in 1915 he married Miss Dorothy Worth, of Bournemouth.

LIEUT. H. W. ORFEUR.

Lieut. H. W. Orfeur, eldest son of Mr. and Mrs. Orfeur, of Colchester, was killed in action on August 23. His Commanding Officer writes :—" He died a very gallant death in attempting to rush a machine gun post, which was holding up the advance of his company, and from the nature of his wounds death must have been instantaneous and quite painless. He was buried in the English cemetery at Albert."

Lieut. Orfeur, an Old Colcestrian and Territorial, a few days after the declaration of war rejoined his old regiment, 8th Essex (Cyclists), serving successively as private, Sec.-Lieut. and Lieutenant on the East Coast and in Kent. He also served six months in France in 1917, as musketry officer, returning home to hospital on account of a small accidental injury. On recovery he was last April again drafted to France, attached to the Essex Regiment, and went through the engagement at

Morlancourt on August 8 unhurt. Lieut. Orfeur entered the School in May, 1900, and left December, 1906.

Mr. Orfeur's second son died of wounds in June, 1917, and his third son, Lieut. R. F. Orfeur, R.M.L.I., was dangerously wounded by a shell on October 23 last at Passchendaele, involving the loss of a leg and eye, besides sustaining other injuries, but he is slowly making recovery in hospital.

LIEUT. R. F. RICHARDS GASSED.

Councillor Richards, of Colchester, has received official notification that his only son, Lieut. R. F. Richards, attached Essex Regiment, has been admitted to hospital in France, severely gassed. He is now in a West End London Hospital and progressing favourably. O.C., entered Midsummer 1901; left July, 1904.

PTE. CLAUDE WATSHAM WOUNDED.

Pte. Claude Watsham, R.F., Vine Farm, Wivenhoe, has been severely wounded in the chest. His brother, Sergt. Harold Watsham, has been awarded the D.C.M. for bravery, having been severely wounded in Palestine. Sergt. Watsham has since been discharged. Claude entered the School in January, 1911, and left July, 1915.

CAPT. G. C. BENHAM, M.C.

Captain Gerald C. Benham, Essex Regt., of Colchester, who was wounded on Sept. 17, sustained severe injuries, being wounded in four or five places by a shell, which burst close to him. He is now resting at Eastbourne.

Capt. Benham has been awarded the Military Cross. He was at the Grammar School, January, 1893—December, 1894.

SEC.-LIEUT. E. P. BUGG WOUNDED.

Second-Lieut. E. P. Bugg, Essex Regiment, only son of Mr. F. C. Bugg, chief clerk at Colchester Post Office, was wounded in the thigh by gunshot during the heavy fighting in France. Having recovered from his injuries, he joined a battalion at Felixstowe. He entered the Grammar School in January, 1914, and left in July, 1916.

LIEUT. A. H. CAMPLING WOUNDED.

Lieut. A. H. Campling, Essex Regiment, son of Capt. F. Campling, of Winsley House, Colchester, has been severely wounded in the thigh and has now recovered. He joined the School in January, 1907, and left December, 1908.

COMMISSION FOR EDGAR LINES.

Edgar Lines, O.C., only son of Mr. and Mrs. Lines, of Great Bentley, has, after passing through the 20th Officers Cadet Batt., obtained a commission in the Somerset Light Infantry. As soon as he became of military age he joined the ranks of the Grenadier Guards. He was promoted to Corporal and fought with this gallant brigade during his two and a half years' service in France, both at Ypres and Cambrai, and was recommended for a commission. He joined the School in April, 1910, and left December, 1913.

CAPT. G. T. WRIGHT.

Lieut. G. T. Wright, son of Mr. and Mrs. C. Wright, of Crouch Street, Colchester, and nephew of the Mayor of Colchester, has been gazetted captain in the R.G.A. He left School April, 1908.

ARTHUR BURLEIGH, O.C.

Arthur Burleigh, O.C., son of Councillor Burleigh, of Colchester who came home from the Malay States last February on purpose to join up, is now in the R.F.A. Cadet School at Exeter.

Mr. J. H. Nunn, O.C., has been granted a commission in the 6th Volunteer Battalion Essex Regiment.

POST-WAR

THE WAR MEMORIALS
1918 - 1924

APRIL 1919

WAR MEMORIAL.

After this matter had been discussed by the meeting, Mr. W. G. Benham proposed that the Hon. Treas. be empowered to open a subscription list and submit for the approval of the Committee a scheme for the proposed war memorial and roll of Honour in the Big School. This was seconded by Mr. C. F. Midgley and carried unanimously.

After a long discussion, it was proposed by Mr. E. G. Pepper, seconded by Mr. H. Burleigh, that the future colours of the O.C.S. should be purple, white and gold. This was carried.

JULY 1920

War Memorial.

The Hon. Secretary will be pleased to receive suggestions for a suitable War Memorial, to place before a special meeting of the Committee to be called early in September to discuss this matter.

JULY 1922

An appeal has been sent out to parents and old boys for subscriptions to the war memorial, which it has been decided should take the form of a swimming bath in the school grounds. It is early yet to make any definite statement as to finance, but the scheme has met with warm approval and enthusiasm and the promises already made are very hopeful indeed.

Editorial.

No apology is needed for giving so much space in this issue to the appeal for funds for a School Swimming Bath. We have a chance now which may never come again; and it would be foolish to throw it away for want of a little more effort. Probably no one needs convincing of the desirability of every one learning to swim. In our School, only thirty per cent. can swim twenty-five yards. We certainly cannot feel that this is satisfactory. The only remedy is to have our own Bath where swimming instruction can form part of the regular time table in the same way that physical training does.

Societies have been formed for the suppression of most human activities, but no one has yet been mad enough to found a Society for the Abolition of Swimming Baths, or the S.A.S.B. This general acceptance of the idea is really a danger, for we imagine that if every one supports the scheme, the Bath is bound to materialise. It is necessary to convince you that, unless you do all you can *now* to get the necessary funds, the scheme will have to be dropped. We feel certain that when you have read the appeals which follow you will realize the critical position, and you will forthwith go out into the Highways and Hedges and compel the subscribers to come in.

The War Memorial.

The amount of the subscriptions received and promised up to date is £385, including £25 given by Viscount Cowdray, through Alderman Benham, O.C. A large number of O.C.'s have not yet responded to the appeal for subscriptions, but the secretary hopes they are considering the matter and will communicate their decision shortly.

October, 1922.

Dear Sir,

At a meeting of the O.C. Committee in June it was agreed to associate the War Memorial with the larger project for an Open-Air Swimming Bath, to which many of the Society were eager to give effect, and for which generous promises of support were forthcoming. Plans and tenders were prepared accordingly, and we are now able to submit illustrations of the Model Bath designed. The Bath (90ft. by 36) will occupy the corner of ground adjoining the west side of the School Close, between it and Gilberd House. As will be seen from the plan, the one decorative feature will be the Memorial Shrine and Tablet, which will be placed at the end nearest the School Buildings, and made as rich and ornamental as the funds subscribed for that prupose will admit.

Independently of the Memorial, the cost will be £1,040. The first appeal, launched in the holiday season, resulted in promises amounting to £300. The realisation of our aims will depend upon the generous and united response of Old Colcestrians and friends of the Royal Grammar School. A Swimming Bath does much for efficiency, health, happiness and good fellowship in School life : and in this case will become also a monument and an incentive to courage and to patriotism.

May we ask you to assist our endeavours to the best of your power, and to favour us with an early reply in the envelope enclosed. If you have already promised a donation, we take this opportunity of expressing our grateful thanks.

Donations may, if so desired, be appropriated specifically to the Bath, or to the Memorial Tablet and Shrine.

We are, Dear Sir,
Yours very truly,

F. PERTWEE,
President Old Colcestrian Society.

H. J. CAPE,
Headmaster, Colchester Royal Grammar School.

Subscriptions may be sent to Bernard Mason, Esq., 10 Crouch Street, Colchester.

Schoolhouse, Colchester.
November 25th, 1922.

Dear Mr. Editor,

May I, through your help, make urgent appeals to all Colcestrians, past and present, to do everything in their power to help forward our War Memorial Fund ?

As our greatest asset—which one could hardly overstate—we have the very generous help of Mr. John Stuart, F.R.I.B.A., the County Architect for Essex, who has given us fully and freely his labour, his time and all the advantage of his wide practical experience. We have a strong committee, consisting of representatives of the Governing Body, and of the Old Colcestrian Society. We have—I may be permitted to say this—an extremely good Chairman in Mr. Frank Pertwee, President of the O.C.S.

All that we want now is sufficient funds to carry the scheme through. Many have subscribed already—both of O.C.'s and parents of present boys—and we are very grateful to them. But many have not. Some of these would, to my personal knowledge, wish to subscribe and would regret our decision if we were forced to give up the whole scheme for a War Memorial. But they have not subscribed yet and this is the critical time. Within the next few weeks the Committee will have to decide whether they are going on with the scheme or not.

The boys are doing their share. Many of them are subscribing regularly every week from their pocket-money. Such a spirit forms the strongest appeal, and if we all made similar sacrifice, there would soon be the necessary funds.

I have heard the view expressed that a Swimming Bath is not the best form of Memorial, in that we should not show our reverence for the dead by providing what is of use to the living. I do not agree with the opinion, but I can respect those who hold it and I do not propose to combat it, except so far as to mention that we have always stipulated that subscriptions can, if the donors so desire, be assigned solely to the cost of the Memorial Tablet.

I would put the matter from another point of view, not of the past, but of the future, not of those who have given their lives, but of those whose lives might possibly be saved. This appeals to me because I knew intimately one little lad of ten years who was drowned and *who could have saved himself if he could have swum two yards*. The point, then, is this: Our Swimming Bath, if built, will be the means of teaching generation after generation of C.R.G.S. boys to swim ; hundreds now, accumulating to thousands in the course of years. Is it too much to assume that one of these may, through the knowledge which he acquired in our Bath, be able at some time to save the life of himself or some other person ?

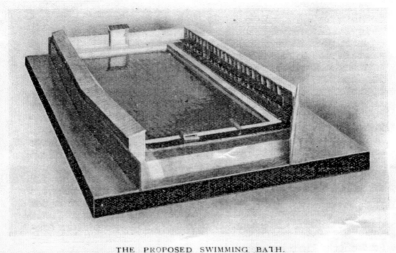

THE PROPOSED SWIMMING BATH.

APRIL 1923

An Octogenarian O.C.

JOHN STANTON.

That interest in the old school is retained throughout life is exemplified in a letter from Mr. John Stanton, O.C., Chorley, who, on writing to express regret at not being able to attend the annual dinner, states that he is over eighty years of age. " I have subscribed to so many war memorials," he adds, " that I have little left for Colchester, but if a guinea will be of any use I will send it." It will, and Mr. B. Mason has duly received the kind cheque.

Mr. Stanton, who is an enthusiastic historical student, celebrated his 80th birthday last October by reading a very interesting paper to the Chorley Historical Society on the antiquities, history, and ancient customs of Chorley, a paper so full of interest that the *Chorley Guardian* devoted over three columns to a report of it. We regret that lack of space prevents us from reproducing it in full in *The Colcestrian*.

"Can you tell me," asks Mr. Stanton, " in what year St. Peter's Church was closed owing to a plague of acari ? " It was, of course, in the year 1859.

Mr. Stanton likes to be remembered as the member who first suggested an Old Colcestrian Society.

The Annual Dinner.

After a reference to the successes of Old Boys, Mr. Cape described the School cricket team last year as the best school team he had ever known. He declared that the School owed its success more than anything else to the extraordinary devotion of the governors, of whom he especially mentioned Mr. Gurney Benham and Dr. Rendall. In conclusion he repeated his statement at Speech Day regarding the proposed swimming-bath as a war memorial, and spoke strongly in favour of the scheme.

The President, who was given a warm welcome, briefly replied. He said he was very glad to state that the swimming-bath had now become an accomplished fact as far as they could see, and the scheme only awaited the approval of the Governors in order to set it in motion. It should be possible to start building during the coming summer, and complete it by next March. Between £500 and £600 had already been collected, and he did not think there would be any trouble in finding the remainder of the money. The President also warmly acknowledged the work done by Mr. Bernard Mason in connection with the memorial.

Old English Fair: Expectation.

MAY 31ST, JUNE 1ST AND 2ND.

Within a short time now the Fair will be upon us. For months the good friends of the School—and their name is legion —have been hard at work devising and arranging all kinds of attractions and getting complicated schemes and plans into order. If careful preparation and consideration of the smallest details count for anything, then the Fair will be a tremendous success. Three things are, however, absolutely necessary to make this success certain. The first is heaps and heaps of contributions to the various stalls ; the second is crowds and crowds of people ; and lastly, decent weather. The first two are *your* concern. Go through the list of stalls, and if you can help anyone of them by sending along suitable articles, please let us know. As far as crowds are concerned, you can get them by making sure that every one you know comes to the Fair.

We mentioned above the good friends of the School. It would take up more than our available space to detail the many kind offers of help that have been received from the minute that the Fair was first suggested. The programme will reveal many of the names of these good friends and we hope that in the next issue of *The Colcestrian* it will be possible to acknowledge all the help that has been given—this will, however, be no light undertaking.

The arrangements are under the control of a General Purposes Committee. Of this Mrs. W. Gurney Benham is Chairman, and the members are, Mrs. H. A. Saunders, Miss Sparling, and Messrs. F. R. Prime, I. Lott, H. Ray, S. T. Payne and the Rev. T. J. L. Davies. The heavy duties of Secretary have been most kindly undertaken by the Headmaster.

Other Committees have been formed to carry out various sections of the work involved. The Entertainments Com-

SITE OF THE NEW SWIMMING BATHS.

mittee is in charge of arranging Programmes of Displays, Plays, Concerts, etc., for each day. The Tennis Tournament Committee is arranging the details of Tournaments which will be played off on the School Courts. To the Ground Committee is allotted the delicate task of deciding where various stalls, shows, etc., shall be. The Mayoress's Committee is organising a Flower Stall which promises to be a great attraction.

A number of stalls have been arranged for, and offers of contributions in kind are urgently needed. The Home-made Cake and Produce Stall has an inviting sound! There will be a Work Stall, a Pound Stall, a stall of Toys, one for Tobacco, another for Foreign Stamps, a Stall for articles made by the Boys (what is your contribution ?), a White Elephant Stall (for articles you no longer want, e.g. those numerous carpet slippers, Maiden Aunts *will* send at Christmas), a Book Stall, a Sweet Stall, and, of course, most important, a Tea Stall. There will probably be others on the days, but this list is sufficient to convince anyone that there will be no lack of interest or variety.

Provisional Programmes for each of the three days have been drawn up by the Entertainments Committee. Thursday and Friday will open with selections by Military Bands, from 2.30—3.40 p.m. From 3—3.40 the Scouts will give displays of open-air Scoutcraft, camping, cooking, bridge building, etc. The Colchester and District Musical Society is contributing generously to each day's programme. On the first two days there will be folk dancing by the Pre, and performances of scenes from " A Midsummer Night's Dream " ; on these days there will also be gym displays. Saturday will be made specially attractive by roundabouts, sports (entries on the ground), and a fancy dress parade (for which you should immediately think out some wonderful and weird costume.) There will be dancing each evening at 8.

In addition to all these delights, there will be various sideshows— ccooanut shies, lucky dips, fishponds, bran pies, etc., etc., in short, all the fun of the Fair ! All sorts of other pleasant surprises for you are being arranged in secret—so they musn't be mentioned here !

One feels rather breathless after reading all this, and it is difficult to visualise the whole thing, but enough has been said to conv nce you that if you come, or rather *when* you come, you will have the time of your life, and incidentally you will be helping to provide the School with the Swimming Bath it so badly needs.

" *So save up your pennies, and book up the days,*
And bring all the friends and the funds you can raise."

COME TO THE FAIR !

JULY 1923

On July 5th the long-wished for swimming bath was opened, and all the boarders welcomed it. Several members of the House were in the swimming team that dived in at the opening. Since the 5th all those who could swim 50 yards have enjoyed early morning bathing. There has been a marked decrease in the number of " lates " for breakfast owing to this early rising ! All members of School House are very grateful to Mr. Cape for the trouble he has taken to get the swimming bath.

Editorial.

The sudden arrival of a heat wave possibly accounts for the small number of original contributions to this issue of the Magazine. The Summer Term is usually a very busy one, and does not leave much spare time for literary efforts, but this term must have beaten all records. The first month was full of preparations of all kinds for the Fair, which happily was a great success, in spite of a low temperature and a lack of sunshine. The complicated accounts of such a big undertaking are not yet cleared up, and there is still the Entertainments Tax fiend to placate. It can, however, be said that the balance will, with previous subscriptions, cover the cost of the bath.

The fact that we have a swimming bath is due entirely to the Headmaster. To him the School will always be grateful for having started the idea, for having planned for many months ways and means for getting the necessary funds—plans which culminated in the enormous amount of work which the organisation and running of the Fair entailed. We can best show our gratitude by doing all we can to realise the ideal that no boy who is physically fit shall leave the C.R.G.S. without being able to swim.

It will be of interest year by year to put on record the number of swimmers in the School. When the bath was opened the number of boys who could swim 50 yards was 70.

The bath could not have been opened at a more favourable time. The heat has made swimming the most popular of pastimes, and even the compulsory ordeal of the shower bath is welcomed by all. It has been possible to arrange a scheme of extra times, so that every boy can get three voluntary periods in addition to the two provided in the time table. This means that the bath is in use practically every minute of the day. Next year it will be possible to arrange for water polo with House matches, for relay races with other schools, and for life-saving classes. A modest beginning will be made this season in swimming sports, and it is hoped that these will prove an annual event of great popularity in the Summer Term.

The C.R.G.S. "Old English Fair."

The "Old English Fair" in aid of the Colchester Royal Grammar School Swimming Bath, was formally opened at 2 p.m. on the 31st May by Lady Worthington-Evans, who delivered a speech from the bandstand, in which afterwards the band of the 1st Batt. the Norfolk Regiment played throughout the afternoon. There were some twenty stalls, gaily decked out with articles which had been presented, or made to be sold ; there were stalls for practically every want.

Just after the opening the American Lawn Tennis Championship (mixed doubles) commenced and continued till past teatime. The prizes for this fell to :—1st, Mr. L. Fookes and Mrs. Cork, and the 2nd to Capt. Rogers and Miss O'Sullivan. On Saturday there was another mixed doubles, and this time the winners were :—1st, Mr. and Mrs. G. C. Benham, and 2nd, Mr. and Mrs. J. A. Parish. There were also men's doubles and boys' singles. In the men's the first prize went to N. R. M. Tait and J. A. Parish, while the 2nd went to B. Hindes and H. C. Hilton. C. A. Heasman won the 1st prize in the boys' singles, and I. L. D. Davies came second.

At 3 o'clock on Thursday, Friday, and Saturday, the C.R.G.S. troop of Boy Scouts gave a display of tent pitching, bridge-building, camp cooking, and games, such as they do at troop meetings at camp, or on trek. Patrol Leader Thackery gave a display with the lariat and spinning rope, and with Scout M. Jacobs made fire by friction in the American Indian style.

After the Scouts' display the Colchester and District Musical Society gave a concert, which consisted of glees and madrigals. By this time people were looking towards the tea tents and buying tickets for tea.

The next item was a folk-dancing display by the boys of the Preparatory School, accompanied by S. J. Freestone on the violin. The dancers were :—J. Argent, A. Locke, E. Uff, R. Potter, P. Pawsey, G. Gower, H. Turner, J. Geernaert, P. Wilson, D. Beaumont, A. Everett, J. Forsdike, D. Argent, A. Amos.

About this time the wireless concert had commenced, and at intervals one could hear a deep voice booming across the field, telling one to " Roll up for the wireless." These concerts went on each night from 5 o'clock till about ten.

All during the days of the Fair people were sending up their balloons for the " Grand Balloon Race," the object of which was to see whose would go the farthest. The one that did go the farthest was unsigned, and therefore did not get a prize. It was found in a field $11\frac{1}{2}$ miles from Llanelly in Carnarvonshire. The first prize went to Lance-Corpl. A. Barker, whose balloon was found in Monmouthshire. The second was won by M. O. Tooley, whose balloon went to Herefordshire. The third, which was found in Herefordshire, was sent up by Mr. W. G. Benham. C. Sanger got the 4th prize ; his balloon was found near Cheltenham. The next was the Headmaster's, which was found in Gloucestershire, but he resigned his claim to a prize. The 5th and 6th prizes went to Miss South Adams and Miss Roe, whose balloons came down in Oxfordshire.

There was a gym. display each night after tea, which consisted of horse work, Swedish drill, and club exercises. The members of the team were : R. G. Baily, L. F. Brinkman, K. S. Cheshire, E. L. W. Davies, I. L. D. Davies, H. W. Francis, W. E. Gredley, P. W. Godfrey, C. G. Godfrey, F. W. Horwood, R. L. Leach, G. E. Morris, K. E. Morris, C. Pawsey, R. H. Ranson, J. Smith, G. O. Wilson, S. E. Wilson, M. R. Wicks, G. B. Walkden. They were instructed by Sergt.-Major Collier.

The next item of any special interest was another theatrical effort, representing scenes from Shakespeare's " A Midsummer Night's Dream." The characters were :—

Theseus, Duke of Athens	R. V. Howell
Hippolyta, Queen of the Amazons	T. C. Richer
Philostrate, Master of Revels to Theseus	J. Stuart
Lysander ⎫ Young Noblemen	F. W. Barber
Demetrius ⎭	H. E. Nicholls
Quince, a carpenter (Prologue)	C. A. Heasman
Snug, a joiner (Lion)	G. O. S. Reid
Bottom, a weaver (Pyramus)	T. W. Hawkes
Flute, The Bellows mender (Thisbe)	M. R. Wicks
Snout, a tinker (Wall)	W. F. Dowsett
Starveling, a tailor (Moonshine)	R. H. Crush
THE FAIRIES.	
Oberon, King of the Fairies	T. R. McGeorge
Puck, his attendant	A. F. Palmer
Titania, Queen of the Fairies	A. G. Edwards
Peaseblossom ⎫	K. D. Bruce
Cobweb ⎬ her attendant Fairies	M. Cape
Mustardseed ⎭	D. Neave

In the evenings there was open-air dancing, which was very popular. The Georgians gave concerts at 8 and 8.45 p.m. on both the Thursday and Friday evenings.

Each evening finished up with a grand firework display by Messrs. J. Wells and Sons. The rockets, etc., could be seen for miles around.

There were numerous competitions and games of skill on the field, such as darts and cocoanut shies, etc. One of the most popular ones was the " Staking the claim," in which a £1 treasury note was buried in a plot of ground, and one bought a stake and drove it in where you thought the " treasure " was likely to be.

On Saturday the roundabouts and swing boats arrived, and the sports and gymkhana took place, in which there were about twenty races of a different nature. There were sack races, bicycle races, races for ladies, gentlemen, girls, and boys of all ages.

One of the prettiest places on the field was the Mayoress's of Colchester's flower marquee, in which there were hundreds of flowers of all colours. Mr. Pat Rooney kindly lent his services and was busy all the time making " lightning sketches." He had previously made a sketch of each of the masters. Some of these sketches fetched high prices at the auction sale of all unsold articles on Saturday. We reproduce his sketch of the Head-master.

On the whole the Fair was a tremendous success, and we are sure that none went away without having enjoyed themselves to the best of their ability. Certainly we were not disappointed in realizing the rest of the money necessary to complete our swimming bath.

P. E. LONGREN.

Schoolhouse,

17th July, 1923.

To the Editor of THE COLCESTRIAN,

Dear Sir,

Can you spare me a little space in your columns to express my most grateful thanks to the many friends and supporters of the School who gave so much invaluable help in connection with the Fair ? To me it was a most delightful experience. All who took part in it worked very hard, and with the utmost enthusiasm, and good feeling. There was not a hitch, nor a difficulty, nor to the best of my knowledge even a single com-plaint about even a trifle. I feel that this is but a lame attempt to express the thanks that I feel, but, after all, those who worked so hard for us will, I know, feel amply rewarded by the happiness which the boys enjoy in the Swimming Bath, which the success of the Fair ensured.

Yours very faithfully,

H. J. CAPE.

Opening of the Swimming Bath.

At 2.30 on July 5th, the bath was lined with people who were all eager to see the bath. The Scouts formed a line round the edge, and held their staves to prevent people from falling in.

On one side there were about fifteen boys clad in swimming costumes eagerly waiting their dip, after Mr. Leonard Brook had taken the first plunge.

The mace-bearer entered, followed by the Mayor and Council, the Headmaster, and members of the governing body.

Mr. Cape said that he was very happy that at last the boys had got a swimming bath. He made it clear that it was only the bath that was being opened, and not the memorial. He thought that the latter should be a religious ceremony. Mr. Cape said that the smallest gift received was two glass (not clay) marbles, from one of the smallest boys. These were embedded in the concrete, and he hoped that they would stop as long as the bath. He then asked the Mayor to declare the bath open.

The Mayor said that he was very pleased to see such a good bath in Colchester. He said that if he had known it was so good he would have taken the first plunge himself.

The bath was then declared open.

Mr. Leonard Brook (President of O.C.'s Club) took the first plunge, and was followed by several of the boys.

At the conclusion of the ceremony the visitors adjourned to the cricket ground to watch the annual match, O.C.'s v. Present.

J. Ratcliff.

" The Pre."

The subjects which must be at the tip of every pen, as we write our Magazine notes this term, are the Old English Fair and the Swimming Bath, to some extent the outcome of its great success. We are very glad to take this opportunity of thanking all our friends (and there were many) who helped us to make the Pre. contribution to the funds a very gratifying one. Our sweet stall, bran pie, and folk dancing display were so well patronised that we handed over to the Secretary the substantial sum of £30, after our expenses were paid. Since probably many of our present pupils will enjoy using the bath for several years to come, this is as it should be. Whether they should use it at the moment has not been an easy matter to decide. Owing to the depth of water it is unsafe for some of the smaller boys, and it is difficult to draw the line at any form. A boy need not necessarily stand over 3ft. to be a member of IVa., for instance, if he can tackle compound addition, and so on ! However, it has been arranged for about 30 of our boys to share this great advantage, and Miss Stanyon hopes to have a few swimmers by the end of the season.

During the intense heat we have indeed reaped the benefit of our enlarged class-room. The alteration was made at the beginning of June, just after the Fair.

We made the usual appeal for Pound Day on Saturday, July 14, but owing to the fact that we had to spend so much at the Fair we could not do as well as we hoped for the Essex County Hospital.

"ONE OF THE STALLS."

From left to right : Mr. T. C. Richer (who held the stall) ; Lady Worthington-Evans (who opened the Fair) ; Mr. H. A. Saunders (as a Pirate Bold) ; Mrs. W. Gurney Benham (Chairman of the Committee).

The Swimming Bath.

The day was hot, and work did not go well,
Exams were on ; of work we all felt sick,
And everyone declared his head was thick :
When all at once we heard the welcome bell.
Oh, what a great relief is this short spell !
Off to the Swimming Bath we rushed so quick,
Our clothes were off our backs in half a tick,
And quickly in the Bath we splashed pell-mell,
Now everyone enjoys the water cool,
And swimmers are on diving stunts intent.
Of course the Masters must be there to rule,
Or many boys would be on mischief bent.
The Bath is such a joy to all the school,
It's worth the labour, time and money spent.

W. J. Scott.

OPENING OF THE SWIMMING BATH.   "THE FIRST PLUNGE."

THE OPENING OF THE SWIMMING BATH.   "THE FIRST BOYS TO USE IT."

THE FIRST DAY'S SWIMMING.

The War Memorial Tablet.

The memorial tablet which is being presented by Mr. and Mrs. P. Shaw-Jeffrey, is now nearing completion, and awaits only the list of Old Boys who were killed during the war.

The following list has been compiled and is believed to be accurate, and as far as possible complete. As, however, the names are being cast in bronze we are particularly anxious that no error or omission should be made. We shall be glad, therefore, if all members will not only read through the list carefully themselves, but also bring it to the notice of anyone who might add or correct the information given :—

T. Allen	W. Cheshire	L. A. Frost
S. A. Bacon	S. C. Chignell	O. E. Gladwell
C. W. Barber	L. W. Clark	F. G. Gregg
W. Bareham	L. Clarke	G. F. Harsum
A. Barnes	H. Craske	C. L. Harvey
C. H. Barnes	G. F. F. Deane	F. B. Helps
G. J. Barnes	A. Denton	J. T. Higginson
V. Barrell	A. E. Dunningham	R. B. Horwood
E. J. Brand	F. G. Dunningham	F. W. Hussey
J. Barker	P. C. Essex	R. V. Jarmin
E. C. Beard	W. R. Everett	C. H. Jarrard
C. H. Becker	S. C. Fairhead	J. H. Keeble
—. Bennett	R. L. Fieldgate	J. King
G. F. Bennett	L. B. Fitch	W. H. King
C. B. Brook	—. Flannagon	A. D. Lawrence
F. S. Bultitude	J. Flux	R. P. Malyn

E. C. Miller	Capt. Ram	H. G. Town
R. Minor	H. Sanger	D. Wagstaff
R. H. B. Mumford	W. H. Salisbury	D. W. Wallace
A. E. Norfolk	J. D. Secker	C. Waring
C. B. Orfeur	A. K. Shenton	J. L. Watson
W. H. Orfeur	C. G. M. Slade	A. H. Webb
A. Peacock	A. E. Sparling	S. A. White
E. J. Prime	A. Thompson	J. H. V. Willmott
A. L. Pulford		

The work will be put in hand on January 15, so that any corrections or additions should be sent to Mr. Bernard Mason before that date.

Old Colcestrian War Memorial.

MEMORIAL TABLETS UNVEILED AT THE SCHOOL.

Impressive ceremonies attended the unveiling by Brig.-Gen. F. W. Towsey, C.M.G., C.B.E., D.S.O., of the Stone of Remembrance (presented by the Headmaster, Mr. H. J. Cape, M.A.), and the Memorial Tablet (presented by Mr. P. Shaw Jeffrey, former Headmaster of the School, and Mrs. Jeffrey) at the Grammar School on Thursday afternoon, May 1. The dedication was performed by the Bishop of Colchester.

Among the large company were the Mayor of Colchester (Mrs. Cr. C. B. Alderton) and many others.

The first ceremony was performed at the Swimming Bath, and the Mayor, Chairman of the Governors of the School, in asking Gen. Towsey to unveil the Stone of Remembrance, said that once again they remembered with pride, thankfulness and gratitude how the flower of their youth went to their country's call with sublime forgetfulness, and suffered hardships and faced death with a fortitude and heroism which amazed the whole world, and referring to Brig.-Gen. Towsey said there was no more fitting man than he, who went through the hardships of the war showing such bravery, heroism and ability, that he received decorations of a kind which any soldier might envy (Applause.)

Gen. Towsey said he thought the credit was due to those who had no idea of soldiering, but who gave everything for their country, to come back and find their places filled by others.

He then unveiled the Stone of Remembrance, revealing the inscriptions, after which the company proceeded to the Central Hall of the School, where a service was held.

Gen. Towsey gave a short address before unveiling the tablet, and a two minutes' silence of remembrance followed the falling of the flag. The Last Post was sounded by buglers of the Norfolk Regiment, and the Bishop of Colchester then pronounced the dedication.

After prayers, led by Canon Rendall, the Bishop of Colchester gave an address. Those fallen men, he said, were true to the traditions of their country; they came forward joyfully and showed their readiness to serve, and willingness to die. Their names would live for evermore, to be a noble example of self-sacrifice to others.

At the conclusion of the service Mr. Cape tendered Mr. and Mrs. P. Shaw Jeffrey an expression of thanks on behalf of the Governors, and past and present scholars, for the gift of the Memorial Tablet.

Mr. L. C. Brook, as President of the Old Colcestrian Society, and Mr. H. J. Cape, then placed wreaths at the foot of the memorial.

PACEM·BELLO·ADEPTI VITA CORONA FIDEI IN·PACE·REQUIESCANT

Photo by Oscar Way, Colchester.]

OLD COLCESTRIAN WAR MEMORIAL TABLET.

The names inscribed on the tablet are :—T. Allen, S. A. Bacon, C. W. Barber, W. C. Bareham, J. Barker, C. H. Barnes, A. Barnes, G. G. Barnes, V. Barrell, D. E. Bawtree, E. C. Beard, C. H. Becker, G. F. Bennett, E. J. Brand, C. B. Brooke, F. S. Bultitude, W. R. Cheshire, S. C. Chignell, L. W. Clark, E. G. Davies, H. Davis, G. F. F. Deane, A. Denton, T. G. Dunningham, P. C. Essex, W. R. Everett, S. C. Fairhead, R. L. Fieldgate, L. V. Fitch, L. C. Flanagan, J. Flux, H. French, L. A. Frost, O. E. Gladwell, F. G. Gregg, G. F. Harsum, C. L. Harvey, F. B. Helps, J. T. G. Higginson, R. B. Horwood, F. W. Hussey, R. V. Jarmin, C. H. Jarrard, J. R. Keeble, W. H. King, J. H. King, A. D. Lawrence, R. P. Malyn, C. Mason, E. C. Miller, R. Minor, R. H. B. Mumford, A. E. Norfolk, H. W. Orfeur, C. B. Orfeur, A. Peacock, E. J. Prime, A. L. Pulford, W. H. Salisbury, H. Sanger, J. D. Secker, A. K. Shenton, C. G. M. Slade, A. G. Smith, H. G. Town, D. T. Wagstaff, D. W. Wallace, C. Waring, J. L. Watson, A. E. Webb, A. H. Webb, S. A. White, J. H. V. Willmott, A. C. B. Wilson.

J. E. Statter, Colchester, photo.]

WAR MEMORIAL STONE OF REMEMBRANCE.

This stone, unveiled by Brigadier-General Towsey, was dedicated by the Bishop of Colchester (Dr. Chapman). The photograph shows the Bishop after the dedication, with the Mayor of Colchester (Mrs. Alderton), and behind Alderman Asher Prior (one of the Governors of the School), and the headmaster (Mr. H. J. Cape, M.A.). In the foreground is Canon Rendall, Litt.D., Chairman of the Management Committee of the School.

JULY 1924

Swimming.

As this is the first year in which the Bath has been in use for a full term, it will be interesting to see what can be done. Last season 133 passed the 50 yds. test : of these 31 left before this season began ; up to July 15, 210 have passed the test, so that we can say that 102 new swimmers are to our credit this year. Many others can do a width or more ; these only need steady practice during the holidays for them to pass the test at the beginning of next term.

Life Saving classes have been practicing for the various awards of the Royal Life Saving Society, and an examination will be held at the end of the Term. We still have a large number of strong swimmers who could take these tests, but every new season should see that number increase.

A Higher Swimming Certificate has been arranged as award for the following tests :—

1. Distance Swim. 10 lengths (300 yds).
2. Swimming on the back without use of arms. 60 yds.
3. Clothes, coat, shirt, trousers. 60 yds.
4. Dive from surface to pick up a brick in 5' of water. Twice out of three attempts.
5. Speed test, 60 yds. in 52 secs.
6. Running dives, two good dives in three attempts.
7. Platform dives, two good dives in three attempts.

G. MORRIS DIVING.

Only one attempt in the season is allowed for these tests. The standard is kept purposely high so that the winning of the certificate may be considered a real achievement.

The Headmaster has very kindly presented a shield for the Inter-House Swimming Championship The method of awarding this is as follows :—

1 point for each 50 yards certificate.
5 points for Higher Certificate.
8 points for Proficiency Certificate of the Royal Life Saving Society.
10 points for Bronze Medallion of R.L.S.S. (only the highest R.L.S.S. award counts).
Sports, events other than comic, 3, 2, 1. Relay Races, 5, 3, 1.

It will be noticed that in this scheme, the emphasis is put on ability to swim and willingness to make that swimming of service, rather than on racing achievements. It is consequently possible for any fit boy to get at least 1 point for his House. The shield will not be awarded until the Bath is closed for the winter, so that every certificate gained this year will count.

SPORTS, FRIDAY, JULY 11TH.
RESULTS :—

Beginners' Race.—1 Cunningham, 2 Goodwin, 3 D. Baker.
One width under 12.—1 J. May, 2 Fogg, 3 Rampling.
20 Yards (under 15).—1 Culverwell, 2 J. Leach, and Sari.
One Length (open).—1 Banks (19 secs.), 2 G. O. Wilson, 3 Leach ma.
One Length (breast).—1 Banks (24 4-5th secs.), 2 Ratcliff, 3 Thorn.
Two Lengths (open).—1 Banks (41 2-5th) secs. 2 G. O. Wilson, 3 Thorn.
300 Yards (open).—1 Banks (5' 24"), 2 Thorn (6' 19"), 3 Leach ma.
Diving.—1 G. Morris, 2, R. Leach, 3 K. Morris.
One Length (clothes).—1 Banks (25 2-5th secs.), 2 G. O. Wilson, 3 Ratcliff.
One width Life Saving Race.—1 Ratcliff, 2 Scarff, 3 Sugg.
Tub Race.—1 Kasem, 2 Kasarn, 3 Nash.
One Length (back).—1 Ratcliff (30), 2 G. Morris, 3 Thorn.
Junior House Relay.—1 School House, 2 Dugard's, 3 Parr's.
Senior House Relay.—1 Parr's, 2 School House, 3 Harsnett's.
Mop Tournament.—Parr's.
House Points.—Parr's 38, School House 36, Harsnett's 7, Dugard's 4.

We must express our thanks to the judges, Messrs. L. Brook, Tweed, and Lamb.

The O.C. Swimming Section.

It seems to be almost an impossibilty to run any sub-sections of the Society with any measure of success. There seems to be one good reason why this is so, and that being that most of the boys of the school, as soon as they leave, leave the town also.

Each section must be self supporting, but because there are so few who can join, this is impossible, and it is equally impossible for the Society to bear any of the expenses.

The swimming section is a good example of this. There are perhaps a dozen members. With twelve subscriptions what can possibly be done? The instructor's fees alone come to a great deal more than this. Then, if the bath is to be used during the holidays, the cost of filling it at least once has to be borne. This item alone runs into £6 or £7.

Therefore, it is impossible to continue the section unless some financial support is forthcoming. If anybody could suggest some way out of this difficulty it would be a great help to those who try, but usually fail, to make their sections active.

What, however, would be better still, would be for some of the more or less wealthy O.C.s to subscribe towards this fund and so help in a very practical way to keep things from going backwards instead of forwards.

Vitae Corona Fides.

COLCHESTER
ROYAL GRAMMAR SCHOOL,

—◻◻—

THURSDAY, MAY 1st, 1924, at 3 p.m.

—◻◻—

UNVEILING

BY

Brig. Gen. F. W. TOWSEY, C.M.G., C.B.E., D.S.O.

OF THE

STONE OF REMEMBRANCE,

(Presented by the Headmaster, H. J. CAPE, Esq., M.A).

IN THE

MEMORIAL SWIMMING BATH,

AND THE

MEMORIAL TABLET,

(Presented by MR. & MRS. P. SHAW JEFFREY).

IN THE

SCHOOL HALL.

———:O:———

DEDICATION

BY THE

Right Rev. The BISHOP of COLCHESTER. D.D.

THE MAYOR (COUNCILLOR CATHARINE B. ALDERTON, J.P.,

CHAIRMAN OF THE GOVERNORS,)

WILL ASK

BRIG. GEN. F. W. TOWSEY, C.M.G., C.B.E., D.S.O.,

TO UNVEIL THE

STONE OF REMEMBRANCE,

(Presented by H. J. CAPE, Esq. M.A).

———:o:———

AFTER THE UNVEILING, THOSE PRESENT ARE ASKED
TO PROCEED, BY WAY OF PROCESSION, TO THE

CENTRAL HALL OF THE SCHOOL.

———:o:———

Order of Service.

THE MAYOR WILL THEN CALL UPON

BRIG. GEN. F. W. TOWSEY, C.M.G., C.B.E., D.S.O.,

TO UNVEIL THE

MEMORIAL TABLET,

(Presented by MR. & MRS. P. SHAW JEFFREY).

———:o:———

Unveiling OF THE TABLET.

———:o:———

Two Minutes Silence of Remembrance.

———:o:———

The Last Post.

———:o:———

Dedication BY THE RIGHT REV.
THE BISHOP OF COLCHESTER, D.D.

𝔓rayer BY THE REV. DR. RENDALL, D.D.

We will lift up our eyes unto the hills :
R. From whence cometh our help.
Our help cometh from the Lord :
R. Who hath made heaven and earth.
The Lord shall preserve us from all evil :
R. Yea even he shall keep our soul.
The Lord shall preserve our going out, and
our coming in ;
R. From this time forth for evermore.

OUR Father, which art in heaven, hallowed be Thy Name. Thy Kingdom come. Thy will be done, in earth as it is in heaven. Give us this day our daily bread. And forgive us our trespasses, as we forgive them that trespass against us, and lead us not into temptation ; but deliver us from evil. For Thine is the Kingdom, the power and the glory. For ever and ever. AMEN.

ALMIGHTY GOD, from whom all thoughts of truth and peace proceed ; Kindle, we pray thee, in the hearts of all men the true love of peace, and guide with Thy pure and peaceable wisdom those who take counsel for the nations of the earth ; that in tranquillity Thy Kingdom may go forward, till the earth is filled with the knowledge of Thy love ; through Jesus Christ our Lord. AMEN.

O Eternal God, our heavenly Father, who alone makest men to be of one mind in a house, give us grace so to order our desires and lives according to Thy will, that we may dwell together in unity of spirit, and in the bond of peace, through Jesus Christ our Lord.
AMEN.

ALMIGHTY God with whom do live the spirits of them that depart hence in the Lord, we praise and magnify Thy holy name for all Thy servants, who having fought the good fight have finished their course in Thy faith and fear ; and we beseech Thee that encouraged by their examples and strengthened by their fellowship we with them may be found meet to be partakers of the inheritance of the Saints in light ; through the merits of Thy Son, Jesus Christ our Lord·
AMEN.

———:o:———

𝔄ddress by The Right Rev. The Bishop of Colchester, D.D.

———:o:———

NOW unto the King Eternal, Immortal, Invisible, the only wise God, be honour and glory for ever and ever. AMEN.

Hymn.

NOW thank we all our God,
 With hearts and hands and voices,
Who wondrous things hath done,
 In whom His world rejoices :
Who from our mothers arms
 Hath blessed us on our way
With countless gifts of love,
 And still is ours today.

O may this bounteous God
 Through all our life be near us,
With ever joyful hearts
 And blessèd peace to cheer us :
And keep us in His grace,
 And guide us when perplex'd
And free us from all ills
 In this world and the next.

All praise and thanks to God
 The Father now be given,
The Son, and Him who reigns
 With Them in Highest Heaven,
The One Eternal God,
 Whom earth and Heav'n adore,
For thus it was, is now,
 And shall be evermore.   AMEN.

School Prayer.

GIVE us grace, we beseech Thee, O Lord, to use aright and to Thy
 glory the gifts bequeathed to our use by King Henry, Queen
Elizabeth and all other our benefactors. Help us to gain and hold
fast those principles of true religion and sound learning which they
desired for us and so to follow their pious example as to remember
always that the trust we acquired from them we must strive to pass on
unimpaired to those who follow after.   We ask this most humbly for
the sake of Thy Son, our Saviour Jesus Christ. AMEN.

GRANT, O Lord we beseech Thee, that the course of this world
 may be so peaceably ordered by Thy governance that Thy
Church may joyfully serve Thee in all godly quietness ; through Jesus
Christ our Lord. AMEN.

———:o:———

At the conclusion of the Service, the Headmaster will
tender to Mr. & MRS. P. SHAW JEFFREY an expression of
thanks of the Governors, and of Past and Present Scholars,
for their gift of the Memorial Tablet, recording the names of
the Old Colcestrians who gave their lives in the Great War.

Mr. P. SHAW JEFFREY *to Respond.*

———:o:———

National Anthem.

507

At the conclusion of the Ceremony the President of the Old Colcestrian Society will place a wreath at the foot of the Memorial Tablet.

———:o:———

NAMES OF THOSE TO WHOM THE MEMORIAL HAS BEEN ERECTED.

T. Allen
S. A. Bacon
C. W. Barber
W. C. Bareham
J. Barker
C. H. Barnes
A. Barnes
G. G. Barnes
V. Barrell
D. E. Bawtree
E. C. Beard
C H. Becker
G. F. Bennett
E. J. Brand
C. B. Brooke
F. S. Bultitude
W. R. Cheshire
S. C. Chignell
L. W. Clark
E. G. Davies
H. Davis
G. F. F Deane
A. Denton
T. G. Dunningham
P. C. Essex

W. R. Everett
S. C. Fairhead
R. L. Fieldgate
L. B. Fitch
L. C. Flanegan
J. Flux
H. French
L. A. Frost
O. E. Gladwell
F. G. Gregg
G. F. Harsum
C. L. Harvey
F. B. Helps
J. T. G. Higginson
R. B. Horwood
F. W. Hussey
R. V. Jarmin
C. H. Jarrard
J. R. Keeble
W. H. King
J. H. King
A. D. Lawrence
R. P. Malyn
C. Mason
E. C. Miller

R. Minor
R. H. B. Mumford
A. E. Norfolk
H. W. Orfeur
C. B. Orfeur
A. Peacock
E. J. Prime
A. L. Pulford
W. H. Salisbury
H. Sanger
J. D. Secker
A. K. Shenton
C. G. M. Slade
A. G. Smith
H. G. Town
D. T. Wagstaff
D. W. Wallace
C. Waring
J. L. Watson
A. E. Webb
A. H. Webb
S. A. White
J. H. V. Willmott
A. C. B. Wilson

AFTERWORD

FIVE YEARS AFTER the Armistice of November 1918, a provisional list of names was published in the Colcestrian of those old boys killed in the 1914-1918 war, with the request for any errors or omissions to be reported before the War Memorial was unveiled in 1924.

What few would have imagined was that ten of the names on the list were not subsequently engraved on the memorial hanging high above the heads of future generations assembled in the Hall. Nor would many have understood why an additional seven names appeared on the Memorial, having not been confirmed as qualifying at least five years, and up to nine years, after they had fallen!

It seems strange that anyone from such a tight knit and relatively small community as the Grammar School should either have been reported as having died when they were alive, or not be reported as killed in the five years following the end of the war. The 'fog of war' had long since lifted, and gossip and anecdote surely would have been verified, or not, by the end of 1923, yet two of the ten were alive and well!

However, like statistics which are capable of misinterpretation and variation, depending on the source, so names on memorials are capable of being subject to uncertainty, even dispute. Vagaries of spelling of surnames, the use of a middle initial as the preferred forename and the problem that the style of the time meant that boys at school were often only referred to by their surname, and in the case of brothers as 'major' and 'minor' means that it is often very difficult if not impossible to be absolutely accurate in present day identifications of names on the boards. Two of several examples are L W Clark and L C Clarke both named on the provisional list; of the two only L W is recorded on the memorial. Similarly, G J Barnes on the provisional list appears as G G Barnes on the memorial and is, we believe, the same man! No confirmatory evidence can be found in the Commonwealth War Graves Register about three others on the Memorial!

Of the ten names appearing in the provisional list in 1923 but not on the War memorial, I included them in my book Every One a Hero on the grounds that unless information had come in to the contrary they should be assumed to have been killed but just not identified beyond doubt. They may have been reported missing, believed killed in action or taken prisoner and may well have been 'heroes' who did actually live. When the name appears on the CWGC database the justification for including them seems to be made, yet the problem with initials and the frequent absence of any 'confirming' address makes for residual doubt.

The discovery in 2013 of an additional name, definitely an OC, of a soldier killed in 1916 but never reported, highlights an ongoing problem in absolute identification for war memorial names. After leaving the school H D Keigwin had largely lived in Rhodesia until, aged 36, he had volunteered in 1916 only to be killed within days in France. Who would necessarily have notified the school? (In the Second World War, the absence of the name of OC Admiral Bertram Ramsay, CIC of both the Dunkirk and D day naval operations from the memorial in the Library, was only rectified in 2013 and further illustrates the problem of names on memorials or not on them!)

British military deaths in at least seventeen conflicts since 1945 are rarely named on war memorials; at the Grammar School that omission has largely been put right as far as is possible by five names being inscribed on the new 'third' memorial board, in the Library. The list is unlikely to be complete and information is urgently required to put right any anomalies on that or either of the World War memorials. Please contact the headmaster with any information you may have.

A final thought in this centenary year, what might those killed in the 1914-1918 war, often in their teens, have looked forward to in the rest of their lives had they returned from war. Most could have looked forward to family life and good jobs and everyone expected world peace, ensured by the League of Nations, to be some compensation for four years of utter horror and depredation and nearly a million British deaths.

Few could have envisaged being young enough to serve again when another war broke out in 1939, or the lack of houses and jobs which bedevilled the Twenties or the Depression of the Thirties which ground down theirs and other generations before world order collapsed again in 1939.

Hopefully they would have felt they had done their bit to thwart the overweening ambition of autocratic aggressors at the time who threatened the British way of free speech, freedom of trade, and an Empire which gave her and the members of it untold and enduring strengths despite any of the criticisms levelled against it. They felt that the war had had to be fought because the alternative was worse, however, the accumulated wealth of Victorian Britain was spent and debt incurred by the gigantic cost of the war and by Britain subsidising some of its Allies would have consequences for the rest of their lives. The world and life in Britain in particular had changed for ever.

Godfrey Thomas,
Honorary OC

'requiescat in pace'

POSTFACE

IT MAY BE argued that one of the key elements that contribute to success in a battle or a campaign in war is communication. Indeed, Napoleon's maxim was that "the whole secret of the art of war lies in making oneself master of the communications." Clear lines of communication are essential in war: between the generals and the divisional commanders, between the forward scouts and the artillery and between soldiers themselves in the line of duty. Aside from the logistics of communication on the battlefield, there is the more personal communication between soldiers on the front line and families back home. Often, letters from home are the only way for serving soldiers to receive news of their loved ones and provide a comfort in the incessant noise of battle. Likewise, letters received by families from soldiers abroad allay the fears that arise in the horrors of war.

In September 2014 Old Colcestrian Tom Cullen (1927 – 1934) was interviewed at home about his experiences as a prisoner of war during the Second World War and the comfort that letters from home brought in those dark days. After being held prisoner for three and a half years, Tom escaped and made it safely back to England but had to leave in his cell the collection of letters he had received from his mother during his incarceration. Fortunately, his mother had kept all the letters that Tom had sent her from prison and these are lovingly retained today. In spite of the importance of these letters between families and soldiers, there was a marked reluctance from those who served to talk about their experiences upon their return. Tom mentioned that when he joined Colchester Royal Grammar School in 1927, a mere nine years after the end of the war, not one of the staff who had served their country spoke about the conflict or their individual roles.

There were many former pupils and members of staff who went off to fight in the First World War, leaving families and friends behind as they pursued the cause of freedom. A fascinating collection of letters and reports was received by the school from serving soldiers of news from the front or from devastated families on the loss of loved ones. These letters and reports were published in the school magazine, *The Colcestrian*, from 1914 to 1918 and they are reproduced here in this book in their entirety, as they were published in the magazines at the time. They are intensely personal views of the war from people who experienced the raw emotions derived from the battlefields in Europe and beyond. They are emotional, heart-rending, funny and tear-inducing but they are all honest accounts from a very bleak time. They are a precious account from a time which we hope will never be repeated and they will remain a precious record of the sacrifices made by staff and pupils from our school for which we will forever be grateful.

Trevor J Hearn
(Old Colcestrian 1971 –1978)
Author of *The Gardens at Colchester Royal Grammar School*, Paragon Pubishing 2014

APPENDIX

TOM CULLEN

Tom Cullen, attending the Armistice Day service held in the CRGS Library 2012

Thomas Henry CULLEN MBE

I WAS RECENTLY privileged to meet Tom Cullen, a celebrated Old Colcestrian, now 97 years of age, who finished his studies at Colchester Royal Grammar School in 1934. Tom was a popular student throughout his time at CRGS, amongst students and staff alike. Headmaster Cape described him as 'a brilliant boy'. Tom was the winner of the medal presented by the Mayor of Colchester in 1934 and was also a talented sportsman, resulting in his appointment as the school cricket Vice-Captain.

Following his time at CRGS Tom went on to study medicine at Middlesex Hospital Medical School. By the time he had qualified, war had been declared so he decided to join the Royal Air Force as a doctor. During the 'phoney war' he was posted to various locations in the UK but in 1940 everything changed for him.

Off to the Middle East he went, traveling the length of Africa by ship, and finally spending time in Egypt. He was posted to Crete, after the invasion of Greece by Germany, and one of the fiercest battles commenced over this island. The German attack was overwhelming and the men had to relocate to Maleme airfield in Western Crete, abandoning precious equipment. Maleme and 'Hill 107', as it became known,

514

soon became a focal point of German bombs and gunfire. Tom Cullen and his comrades were hopelessly outnumbered and underequipped and knew it was just a matter of time before they, too, were attacked.

Formation after formation of German bombers attacked Crete, starting the 20th of May. Tom, weak from dysentery, supported by only one orderly, set up a makeshift first aid tent in the centre of this maelstrom. For three days and nights he worked, focusing on the wounded. The German parachutists landed, and it wasn't long, in spite of a valiant effort, before Tom and the survivors were captured.

They were taken to a house in Malerme where Tom, now joined by three New Zealand medical officers, treated countless wounded servicemen who passed through his surgery, with only the most basic of equipment, in a room in the house in Malerme. For his service in Crete, Tom was awarded the MBE (Military).

After several internments in Greece, under deplorable conditions, Tom was transferred to Poland, a prisoner of war camp, Stalag XXA, near Thorun. Tom made friendships and learned through a British Sergeant that some of the Poles who delivered the Red Cross parcels to the camp were willing to help when he decided to escape. When we spoke, he gave me his personal account of his escape. It really is truly unbelievable. The POW camp was surrounded by a moat which at most times of the year would be impassable. However, it was January 1943 and the moat happened to be frozen over. Tom explained how he and another Doctor carefully navigated the route across the ice before climbing a barbed wire fence, through a guard room - where an accomplice distracted the guards - through a gap in another barbed wire and then, dressed in civilian clothing, they were picked up as planned by a Pole (the first of many to assist them) awaited a ship in a farmhouse for a week then smuggled to a port and stowed away on a ship to neutral Sweden. When he arrived in Sweden, he visited the consulate and asked to be returned home. Three days later he was flown back to England. it was not long before he resumed work in the UK.

During our conversation we spoke about how he communicated with his loved ones back at home whilst imprisoned. Tom produced a ream of letters sent home to his mother (unfortunately those that he had received were left in Poland). Tom allowed me to read one of these letters. It struck me as incredibly upbeat considering the unimaginable situation that he found himself in. One line is particularly memorable - Tom light-heartedly advises his mother that his brother should at least 'attend a school that plays good rugby'. Taking care not to be censored, Tom carefully wrote as often as he could, although there was not really much pleasure to be had in the boring circumstances and not too much to write home about. Tom was always careful to keep a supply of his favourite pipe tobacco 'Three Nuns' asking for it to be sent when he was running low.

In the centenary year of the outbreak of World War One, I imagine that communications between military personnel and their families and loved ones at home in the UK were much the same. The servicemen who wrote home remained hopeful and encouraging, as I am sure the letters returned did too. Both parties would have tried to be optimistic as they strived to make the best of a difficult situation. The 'Great War' is sometimes referred to as the bloodiest war in history. I cannot imagine the heartache and pain felt by the many relatives of those who fell in the violent bloodshed, the ones who never received a reply.

Celeyn Evans
Year 13, Senior Student Archivist

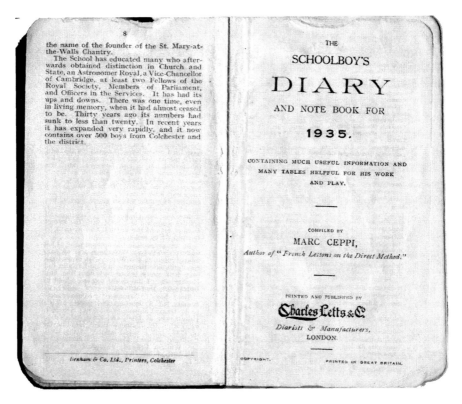

8

the name of the founder of the St. Mary-at-the-Walls Chantry.
The School has educated many who afterwards obtained distinction in Church and State, an Astronomer Royal, a Vice-Chancellor of Cambridge, at least two Fellows of the Royal Society, Members of Parliament, and Officers in the Services. It has had its ups and downs. There was one time, even in living memory, when it had almost ceased to be. Thirty years ago its numbers had sunk to less than twenty. In recent years it has expanded very rapidly, and it now contains over 500 boys from Colchester and the district.

Benham & Co. Ltd., Printers, Colchester

THE

SCHOOLBOY'S

DIARY

AND NOTE BOOK FOR

1935.

CONTAINING MUCH USEFUL INFORMATION AND
MANY TABLES HELPFUL FOR HIS WORK
AND PLAY.

COMPILED BY
MARC CEPPI,
Author of "French Lessons on the Direct Method."

PRINTED AND PUBLISHED BY
Charles Letts & Co
Diarists & Manufacturers,
LONDON.

COPYRIGHT.   PRINTED IN GREAT BRITAIN.

Schoolboy's Diary from Tom Cullen's days at CRGS

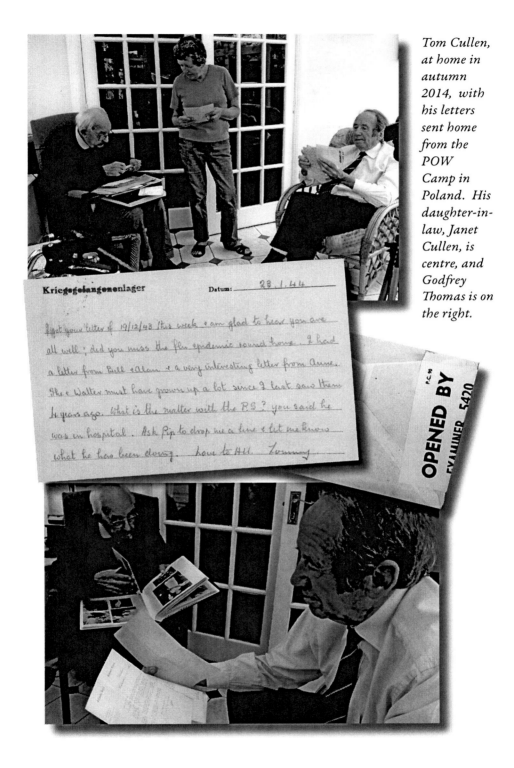

Tom Cullen, at home in autumn 2014, with his letters sent home from the POW Camp in Poland. His daughter-in-law, Janet Cullen, is centre, and Godfrey Thomas is on the right.

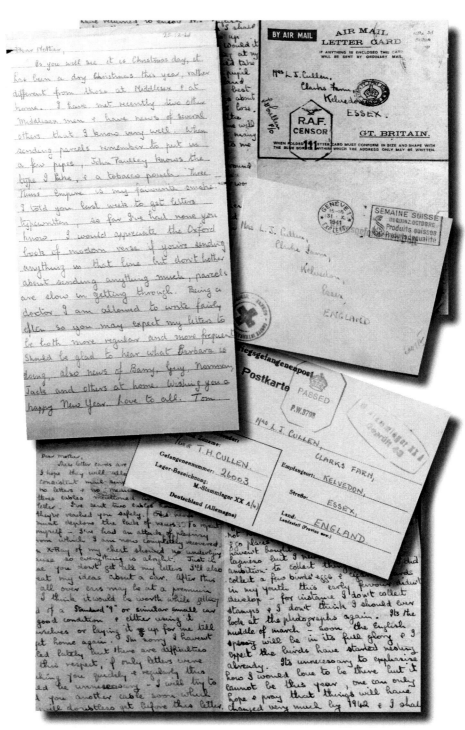

Various POW letters sent from Tom Cullen, in Stalag XXA in Poland, to his parents in Essex. Note the RAF censor stamp.

A MASTER REMEMBERS, THE GREAT WAR, 'J's' CHARACTER

The most vivid and unforgettable figure was Percy Shaw Jeffrey with whom I was lucky enough to work from 1912 until he retired, when "Ichabod" might well have been inscribed over the C.R.G.S. entry, fortunately only for a brief spell. To 'J' I owed much in learning teacher-pupil, Head-staff, employers-staff relations, before Juvenile Employment Officers and Careers Masters were invented.

His vitality, originality and humour, combined with a discipline which was just, firm and consistent, endeared him to pupil and assistant master alike.

The complete freedom that he gave us to experiment and to initiate encouraged us to do our best for the School. When we faltered his "Courage, mes enfants" kept us going. With 'J' there was no attempt to belittle the successes of his colleagues; as he frequently quoted, "My **rod** and my staff they comfort me", though corporal punishment was always a last resort.

Shaw Jeffrey had the gift of spotting your favourite 'line' and giving you every opportunity of developing it, if to the School's advantage. Hence, a free hand to 'Daddy' Reeve on Sports and Games; to Pepper to produce excellent Scouts, year after year; to Freddy Barker to mould a Cadet Corps that was a most valuable asset to Colchester during the war, when its band was almost the only one operating in that garrison town.

To me he gave time and encouragement in initiating the annual carol service in the candle-lit Big School—the only relic of my seven years at the School still surviving. The "House Singing", which 'J' also allowed me to orgainse gradually, became too competitive and although much enjoyed by pupils and parents, was not popular with masters who expected much week-end "prep". I never found 'J' unreasonable when I submitted proofs of the "Colcestrian" for his censorship; his lively contributions were always welcome, as were some of his delightful carols—which he allowed me to use.

The "House Singings" (later deplored and stopped) not only prepared the way for the fine dramatic work since established, but led to the formation of a Concert Party that visited the crowded hospitals and performed in village halls for funds for aid and comfort to the wounded.

For every Grammar School the years 1914–19 were a testing time; one by one junior members of their staffs went off to the Front. Retired teachers and women came in to fill the vacancies; transport difficulties played havoc with the attendance of day boys, and the feeding of boarders was a nightmare. It is a tribute to the calm efficiency of 'J's' regime that the school suffered academically so little.

appointments: it was, we later learned, whilst similarly waiting on his wife, that his end came.

Now, the picturesque old town possesses the ancient dwelling, replete with treasures collected by the Shaw Jeffreys and generously given to its citizens: it should be a place to visit for those whose gratitude to 'J' remains.

the late J. A. Peart (School staff 1912–19)

THE SCHOOL SWIMMING POOL

In 1923, under the Headmastership of Harry J. Cape (when the School was an independent fee-paying school), it was decided to have the bath built. To raise sufficient money to cover this venture, boys, Old Colcestrians, masters, parents, Governors of the School, and some prominent townsfolk contributed towards the cost.

An Old English Fayre was organised and held on the Playing Fields (I believe for three days) and I remember it was a great success. It is recalled that a small boy from Lower IIIA, meeting the Headmaster in one of the Corridors, said, "Please Sir, I have no money for the School Bath, but would you accept these?" In his hand were two glass ally marbles! The Head, affectionately known as 'Harry J' was very amazed, and readily accepted this gift, and when the Bath was being built he had these two marbles embedded in the concrete side by the step on the right side of the deep end. I wonder if they are still there today.

G. W. Roberts (1916–27)
President, Old Colcestrian Society, 1951–52

THE RUSSIANS ARRIVE

During the First World War rumour had it that Russian troops passed through the county with snow on their boots! It is, however, a fact that in the spring of 1915 I was one of the long line of boys who were positioned on the pavement in front of the School at

9.30 a.m. to cheer a party of Russian officers who were expected to arrive. Sure enough, after an interminable wait, a cavalcade of cars containing Russian officers drove slowly past at 1.30 p.m.— and were duly cheered to the echo.

J. V. Ramage (1913–16)

520

During the latter part of the War, the School stopped giving book prizes at the annual Speech Day and awarded Certificates of Honour instead, as a mark of respect to the former pupils who were serving in the Armed Forces.

The School magazine "The Colcestrian" continued to be issued each term, giving news of former pupils who were serving in the Armed Forces.

B A B "Dick" Barton, OC

PSJ AT CRGS

INTRODUCTION

Between 1900 and 1916 Percy Shaw Jeffrey (PSJ, or "J' as he was known to the boys) was headmaster of Colchester Royal Grammar School (CRGS). He revived the school, established it as the leading secondary school in North East Essex and struck a relationship with Essex County Council, as the education authority established under the 1902 (Balfour) Education Act, which enabled the school to survive and flourish. He was a pioneer in developing day grammar schools, and the identity and "brand" he established for CRGS survive in large measure to this day.

This study was originally conducted in 1965-66 by a group of sixth formers at the school, namely: Robert Alford, David Belfall, Robert Davis, Maurice Garnharn, Godfrey Gypps, Clive Holder, Alan Johnson, Russell Jones, Mervyn King, Barry Langston, Mark Lowe, Julian Mlynarski, Robert Niblett, David Robinson, and Ian Woodward, under the supervision of Maurice Isaac and William Shreeves, both history masters at the school. The manuscript report of the study was stored in David Belfall's loft for 40 years. This typed version was prepared and revised by him in 2010-11.

CHAPTER 8
THE WAR

By August 1914, Shaw Jeffrey had accomplished most of his objectives for the school. It was established as the leading secondary school in North East Essex, the relationship with the county council as education authority was settled, the building work had been (for the time) completed and numbers were approaching 200.

The final 2 years of his headmastership were however overshadowed by the First World War, first the euphoria and the expectations of being home by Christmas and then during 1915 and 1916 the emerging horrors of the trenches.

To men like Shaw Jeffrey, who had studied at Marburg University and was an admirer of many aspects of German education, the war must have come as a profound shock. However he was in no doubt about where right and wrong lay. The editorial in the November 1914 edition of The Colcestrian proclaimed the necessity of removing the "hideous menace of militarism and savagery set up by the wild ambitions of unspeakable caste and Kaiser" and, in the same edition, a mild suggestion from an Old Colcestrian that "England and the Allies seem to be getting rather the worst of it" received firm rebuttal from the editor that "German facts (?) and German points of view are better presented and distributed than our own."

At the 1914 Speech Day, picking up the jingoistic tone of the time, Shaw Jeffrey went so far as to claim that:-

"It is a fight not between nations, but between the powers of good and evil."

and:-

"British methods of colonization have been vindicated, the idle rich have fought like Paladins, the British soldier has shown his quality, and in Colchester we might well say we have been living for years among heroes and never knew it." (The Colcestrian, March 1915)

The school itself sought to make a contribution. The Cadet Corps and the Scout Troop set to work guarding telegraph poles, running messages and acting as observers for the Colchester garrison. Even the little boys of the "Pre" were employed in making pillows for wounded soldiers.

But the main burden fell of course on the Old Colcestrians who joined the armed forces. Although conscription was not introduced until 1916 when Shaw Jeffrey left the school, many OCs joined up voluntarily. Almost all of these were boys who had been at the school under Shaw Jeffrey's headmastership. Under the strain of war the bond between the school and OCs serving in the trenches became ever stronger. The Old Colcestrian Society turned its pages in The Colcestrian over to recording the war activities of old boys, remarking that "at least they should inspire us each to do his little bit for old England in her hour of need" (The Colcestrian November 1914). The lists of serving soldiers, and of casualties, as well as the poignant letters from the trenches, could not fail to bring home the realities of war. The Old Colcestrian Society found a new reason for existence, and the whole community of boys, masters and OCs drew closer together. Fifty years later, one of the assistant masters, Jack Peart, wrote to us, not unemotionally, that:-

"As the years 1912-14 had been the happiest of my teaching life, the last years at CRGS became my saddest. Daily one read of the loss of an OC; there was the too-swift jump from the Corps (for which the fates had left me responsible) to a commission in the trenches – average life there for a second lieutenant, was it 6 months? And what is forgotten, even by those who recall the loss of a generation, there were the appalling after-effects among survivors. Apart from the wounded there were those whose health – moral or physical or both – had been ruined. Return to civil life was too often a failure to cope with life; every teacher was bitterly conscious of the waste of young promising lives."

523

Revealing too of the attitude of OCs serving in the trenches are their letters back to Shaw Jeffrey as reprinted in The Colcestrian. Many of them compared their current situation with their earlier happiness at school and would end with sentiments such as: "Good luck to our glorious Alma Mater". Many, faced with the emotional watersheds of their lives found new depths of literary flair and devotion to the school. One letter ended with: "I hope that CRGs flourishes like a green bay tree" and another "every one of us will individually see to it that Alma Mater Colcestriensis will have cause to be proud of her sons in this shambles of mortality, which sets ten million bayonets gleaming merely at the atavistic snarl of super armed twentieth century cavemen." Such sentiments could scarcely fail to make Shaw Jeffrey proud that even in the trenches Old Colcestrians remembered his training.

From Shaw Jeffrey's point of view the War took forward the emphasis on loyalty to house and school which he had always stressed, and which was closely linked by him with "faith in our country, faith in our King, faith in our God" (The Colcestrian, July 1911). He made this link clearly in his speech at the 1914 Speech Day:-

> "...never has the system of education in our British public schools [among which he clearly included CRGS] shown itself in brighter colours than under the stress of our common necessity. They have answered their country's call with a unanimity and self-sacrifice that is beyond rubies" (Essex County Standard December 1914).

The theme was developed even further in The Colcestrian editorial of March 1915:-

> "Contrast the typical English gentleman – the gentle man, be it understood – and the equally typical Prussian Junker, a bully to all his subordinates, cringing and servile to all above him.
>
> Nor is the reason for this divergence far to seek. In the whole of Germany there exists nothing that corresponds to the English Public School, nor the discipline for which it stands...
>
> In an English school the boy is led, not driven. Any boy developing bullying, meanness, swagger or any other German vice is promptly set in his place by public opinion – and probably a prefect. For the rest he learns on the Playing Field self-control, fairness, chivalry, unselfishness and respect for law, even when opposed to his own immediate interest, and with no brute force behind it."

This idealised picture of an English education – and the belief that bullying did not exist in English schools – is hard to justify, but Shaw Jeffrey may perhaps be forgiven for wanting at this crucial point to give as much moral support as possible, and the conviction that they were in the right, to those serving in the trenches. And it is entirely consistent with the man and his approach to the education he had sought to provide at Colchester Royal Grammar School that he should draw a causal link between the education that the school had provided and the bravery of the men in the trenches.

In October 1915, after just over one full year of war, Shaw Jeffrey submitted his resignation as headmaster, with effect from the following summer. The main reason, he explained, was his wife's ill-health but:-

> "a subsidiary reason is to be found in the large increase in numbers of the Junior Technical College [formerly the Albert School on North Hill] which has doubled itself in the past year and might conceivably reach 100 by the end of the present school year. If the Grammar School is to hold its own in the face of this new situation there must be drastic changes financial and otherwise and these can be more easily carried out under a new Headmaster"
> (Governors minutes for 12 October 1915).

Shaw Jeffrey's fears about the Technical College were overstated but his wife's health was certainly a concern. Perhaps, having raised CRGS, as he described it "from a fantastic failure to a reputable institution", after 15 years he had simply had enough and decided to call it a day.

After retiring from CRGS at the age of 53 in 1916, he never again held a full-time appointment but found occupation in writing, inspecting, examining, assessing and giving lectures on cruises. The Shaw Jeffreys initially moved to South Africa and then to Whitby, North Yorkshire, though frequently spending the winters in the Southern hemisphere. He died in 1952 just before his ninetieth birthday – his wife outlived him.

On 21st August, 1916, at a public meeting in the Town Hall, Colchester, the Mayor of Colchester presented the retiring Headmaster, on behalf of the Governors and the Old Colcestrian Society, with his framed portrait in oils by Mr. Frank Daniells.

The inscription on the portrait reads as follows:

Presented to
PERCY SHAW JEFFREY, M.A.,
Queen's College, Oxford,
Headmaster of Colchester School, 1900-1916
By Public Subscription, 1916

Garden of Remembrance
(behind the George Young Building)
Bench and Plaque donated by the Old Colcestrian Society
Rowan Tree (not pictured) donated by Trevor Hearn OC

Lightning Source UK Ltd.
Milton Keynes UK
UKOW04n1916291214

243740UK00002B/23/P